Published in 2003 by
Sweet & Maxwell Limited
100 Avenue Road,
London NW3 3PF
Computerset by
LBJ Typesetting Ltd of Kingsclere
Printed in Great Britain
by Ashford Colour Press Ltd, Gosport, Hants

No natural forests were destroyed to make this product;
only farmed timber was used and replanted.

A CIP catalogue record for this book is
available from the British Library

Main work ISBN: 0 421 661 402
Supplement ISBN: 0 421 849 207

DICEY AND MORRIS

ON

THE CONFLICT OF LAWS

*THIRD CUMULATIVE SUPPLEMENT
TO THE THIRTEENTH EDITION*

Up-to-date to March 1, 2003

UNDER THE GENERAL EDITORSHIP OF

SIR LAWRENCE COLLINS

LL.D., LL.M., F.B.A.

WITH

SPECIALIST EDITORS

LONDON
SWEET & MAXWELL
2003

CONTENTS

Contents

Contents

Contents

Contents

TABLE OF CASES

xi

Table of Cases

Table of Cases

xiii

Table of Cases

xiv

Table of Cases

Table of Cases

Table of Cases

Table of Cases

Table of Cases

Table of Cases

Table of Cases

Table of Cases

Table of Cases

Table of Cases

Table of Cases

Decisions of the European Court of Justice are listed below numerically. These decisions are also included in the preceding alphabetical table.

Table of Cases

liii

Table of Cases

Table of Cases

TABLE OF STATUTES

lix

TABLE OF STATUTORY INSTRUMENTS

TABLE OF CIVIL PROCEDURE RULES

TABLE OF COUNCIL REGULATION (E.C.) No. 44/2001 OF DECEMBER 22, 2000 ON JURISDICTION AND THE RECOGNITION AND ENFORCEMENT OF JUDGMENTS IN CIVIL AND COMMERCIAL MATTERS

[For text of Council Regulation (E.C.) No. 44/2001, see Appendix, Part I, post]

CHAPTER 1

NATURE AND SCOPE OF THE CONFLICT OF LAWS

See Collins, in *Reform and Development of Private International Law* **1–010**
(Fawcett ed., 2002), p. 89.

NOTE 42. See also North (2001) 50 I.C.L.Q. 477. **1–015**

NOTE 46. See also *Higgs v. Minister of National Security* [2000] 2 A.C. 228 **1–018**
(P.C.).

Section 196 of the Employment Rights Act 1996 has been repealed by **1–046**
section 32(3) of the Employment Relations Act 1999. The consequence is
that the territorial scope of the employment legislation will be left to the
general law, and it will apply, according to the Government, when there is
"some proper connection" with the United Kingdom: H.C. Deb. 1998–1999,
vol. 336, col. 31.

NOTE 74. S.I. 1997 No. 278 is amended by S.I. 2002 No. 250. **1–069**

See Vischer, *International Encyclopedia of Comparative Law*, Vol. III, Chap. **1–074**
4 (1999).

1

CHAPTER 2

CHARACTERISATION AND THE INCIDENTAL QUESTION

2–001 Note 1. Add: Lipstein, *International Encyclopedia of Comparative Law*, Vol. III, Chap. 5 (1999); Mistelis, *Charakteriserungen und Qualifikation im internationalen Privatrecht* (1999). Lipstein, in *Private Law in the International Arena—Liber Amicorum Kurt Siehr* (Basedow *et al.* (eds), 2000) pp. 405–412.

2–013 Under Spanish law it is provided that civil proceedings, if brought separately during the currency of criminal proceedings about the same matter, have to be stayed pending the conclusion of the criminal proceedings; there is also a general rule (albeit one which is subject to exceptions) that, where conduct gives rise to both criminal and civil liability, if criminal proceedings are not brought, the civil proceedings cannot be brought *ex delicto* under Article 1092 of the Spanish Civil Code, but must be brought under Article 1902. One of the many issues raised in *Grupo Torras S.A. v. Al-Sabah* [1999] C.L.C. 1469 (reversed in part on other grounds [2001] Lloyd's Rep. Banking 36 (C.A.)) was whether these rules are to be regarded as substantive or procedural. Mance J. decided that they are procedural and, in reaching this conclusion, noted (at p. 1662): "Although this is not conclusive, the basic principles are to be found in the Spanish Procedural Code . . . "

2–034 *Macmillan Inc. v. Bishopsgate Investment Trust Plc* [1996] 1 W.L.R. 387 (C.A.) was discussed and applied by the Court of Appeal in *Raiffeisen Zentralbank Osterreich A.G. v. Five Star General Trading L.L.C.* [2001] Q.B. 825 (C.A.). See also *Grupo Torras S.A. v. Al-Sabah* [2001] Lloyd's Rep. Banking 36, 62 (C.A.).

CHAPTER 4

RENVOI

NOTE 1. Add: Lipstein in Basedow *et al.* (eds), *Private Law in the* **4R–001**
International Arena—Liber Amicorum Kurt Siehr (2000) pp. 405–412; Kassir,
Réflexions sur le renvoi en droit international privé comparé (2002).

The question whether the doctrine of renvoi applies in cases concerning **4–023**
title to movables was left open by Moore-Bick J. in *Glencore International*
A.G. v. Metro Trading International Inc. [2001] 1 Lloyd's Rep. 284 at p. 297.

3

CHAPTER 5

THE EXCLUSION OF FOREIGN LAW

5–003 See *Kuwait Airways Corp. v. Iraqi Airways Co. (Nos. 4 and 5)* [2002] UKHL 19, [2002] 2 A.C. 883, 1078, *per* Lord Nicholls of Birkenhead.

5–005 See *Kuwait Airways Corp. v. Iraqi Airways Co. (Nos. 4 and 5)* [2002] UKHL 19, [2002] 2 A.C. 883, 1102, *per* Lord Steyn.

5–010 NOTE 45. Order 11, r. 1(1) has been replaced by CPR, r. 6.20.

5–013 Text at note 58. In *Kuwait Airways Corp. v. Iraqi Airways Co. (Nos. 4 and 5)* [2002] UKHL 19, [2002] 2 A.C. 883 it was held that the public policy exception extends to breaches of public international law, and was not limited to grave breaches of human rights. See also *R. (on the Application of Abassi) v. Secretary of State for Foreign and Commonwealth Affairs* [2002] EWCA Civ. 1598; *The Times*, November 8, 2002 (C.A.).

5R–018 Add: Briggs [2001] Sing. J.L.S. 280.

5R–018 NOTE, 83. See also *Gersten v. Law Society of New South Wales* [2002] NSWCA 344.

5–023 NOTE 7. See *QRS 1 ApS v. Frandsen* [1999] 1 W.L.R. 2169 (C.A.), noted Briggs (1999) 70 B.Y.I.L. 341, Smart (2000) 116 L.Q.R. 360: a claim by the liquidator of a Danish company against the shareholder of a company in respect of the stripping of its assets was held to be an unenforceable revenue claim; the only creditors were the Danish tax authorities, and the claim was for the indirect enforcement of revenue laws; the claim was a revenue matter within the meaning of the 1968 Convention and so excluded from its scope (as to which see main work, para. 11–015) and the rule that English courts would not directly or indirectly enforce the revenue laws of another country was not overridden by the 1968 Convention. See also *Air India Ltd v. Caribjet Inc* [2002] 2 All E.R. (Comm.) 76.

5–025 NOTE 25. In *Old North State Brewing Co. v. Newlands Services Inc.* [1999] 4 W.W.R. 573 (B.C.C.A.) a North Carolina judgment for treble damages was enforced.

5–028 NOTE 40. See also Case C–271/00 *Gemeente Steenbergen v. Baten* [2003] I.L.Pr. 176.

5–035 In two decisions in British Columbia, United States judgments in civil actions for disgorgement of the proceeds of fraud in favour of the United States Securities and Exchange Commission have been enforced: *United States of America (Securities and Exchange Commission) v. Shull* and *United States Securities and Exchange Commission v. Cosby*, unreported.

NOTE 60. In *United States v. Levy* (1999) 45 O.R. (3d) 129, the United States Government was granted a *Mareva* injunction in aid of United States proceedings in connection with the illegal resale of Canadian lottery tickets in the United States.

The decision in *Kuwait Airways Corp. v. Iraqi Airways Co. (No. 2)* [1999] **5–038—** C.L.C. 31 has been affirmed by the Court of Appeal and by the House of **041** Lords: *Kuwait Airways Corp. v. Iraqi Airways Co. (Nos. 4 and 5)* [2002] UKHL 19; [2002] 2 A.C. 883 (C.A. and H.L.). Iraq decrees confiscating Kuwaiti planes in the aftermath of the Iraqi invasion of Kuwait were refused recognition.

It was held that it was legitimate for an English court to have regard to public international law in deciding whether to refuse to recognise a foreign law on the ground that it was contrary to public policy. Lord Nicholls of Birkenhead said (at 1081) that the non-justiciability principle in *Buttes Gas and Oil Co. v. Hammer (Nos. 2 and 3)* [1982] A.C. 888 did not require the court to shut its eyes to a breach of an established principle of international law committed by one State against another. Enforcement or recognition of the Iraqi legislation would be manifestly contrary to public policy, and also contrary to the United Kingdom's obligations under the UN Charter. Lord Hope of Craighead said (at 1110–1) that there was no need for judicial restraint on grounds of public policy where a clearly established norm of international law had been violated. Security Council Resolution 662 called upon all States to refrain from any action which might be interpreted as an indirect recognition of the annexation of Kuwait by Iraq. The responsibility for compliance lay in the first instance with the executive arm of government, but, in seeking which direction to take in such matters where decisions must be taken on grounds of public policy, the judges should try to work in harmony with the executive. There was nothing precarious or delicate, or subject to diplomacy, which judicial adjudication might threaten in this case. There could be no embarrassment to diplomatic relations. Accordingly a legislative act by a foreign state which was in flagrant breach of clearly established rules of international law ought not be recognised.

On non-justiciability see also *R. (on the Application of Abassi) v. Secretary of State for Foreign and Commonwealth Affairs* [2002] EWCA Civ. 1598, *The Times*, November 8, 2002 (C.A.); *R. (on the Application of Campaign for Nuclear Disarmament) v. Prime Minister of the United Kingdom* [2002] EWHC 2759 (Div. Ct.); *Petrotimor v. Commonwealth of Australia* [2003] FCFCA 3 (Full Court of the Federal Court of Australia); *Attorney-General for England and Wales v. R.* [2002] 2 N.Z.L.R. 91, 97 (C.A.); Collins (2002) 51 I.C.L.Q. 485.

NOTE 85. See also *R. v. Home Secretary, ex p. Johnson* [1999] Q.B. 1174; *R. v.* **5–039** *Home Secretary, ex p. Launder (No. 2)* [1998] Q.B. 994; *Azov Shipping Co. v. Baltic Shipping Co.* [1999] 2 Lloyd's Rep. 159; *Re Banco Nacional de Cuba* [2001] 1 W.L.R. 2039, 2053–2054.

NOTE 97. The decision in *Nuova Safim SpA v. Sakura Bank Ltd.* [1998] **5–041** C.L.C. 306 has been affirmed by the Court of Appeal: [1999] C.L.C. 1830 (C.A.).

CHAPTER 6

DOMICILE AND RESIDENCE

1. GENERAL PRINCIPLES

6–019 In *Irvin v. Irvin* [2001] 1 F.L.R. 178, Cazalet J., citing this paragraph, held that cogent and convincing evidence was needed to show that the balance of probabilities had been tipped. This applied both to the acquisition and loss of a domicile of choice. In *North v. Skipton Building Society* (Ch.D., June 7, 2002, unreported) it was said that while the domicile of origin has a tenacious quality, the standard of proof for the acqusion of a domicile of choice was the normal civil standard: statements that the criminal standard applied could not be taken literally.

2. ASCERTAINMENT OF DOMICILE

B. *Domicile of choice*

(1) ACQUISITION

6–035 An Australian court has held that a decision on "residence" as such is not an essential prerequisite for a finding of domicile. Residence was the best, or very good, evidence of the *animus manendi*, but it was not the only means of proving the required intention: *In the Marriage of Ferrier-Watson and McElrath* (2000) 26 Fam. L.R. 169.

6–041 In *Bheekhun v. Williams* [1999] 2 F.L.R. 229 (C.A.), a decision to take British rather than Mauritius nationality when the latter country became independent was treated as a "clear pointer" to the acquisition of a domicile of choice in England.

6–047 NOTE 56. Add: *In the Marriage of Ferrier-Watson and McElrath* (2000) 26 Fam. L.R. 169.

6–049 NOTE 69. Add: *Cf. Irvin v. Irvin* [2001] 1 F.L.R. 178 (repeated applications for jobs in England, and regular contributions to English technical journals evidence of retention of English domicile of choice). *Cf. North v. Skipton Building Society* (Ch.D., June 7, 2002, unreported) where the fact that the propositus had held four different jobs over a ten-year period, all in the same country and without returning to the country of his domicile of origin between those jobs was a factor in holding that he had acquired a domicile of choice.

NOTE 70. Add *D.T. v. F.L.* (Irish High Ct., 2001) (temporary tax advantages in living abroad).

NOTE 71. Add: *Reddington v. Riach's Executor*, 2002 S.L.T. 537.

NOTE 74. Add: *North v. Skipton Building Society* (Ch.D., June 7, 2002, unreported) (ceasing to pay U.K. national insurance contributions).

NOTE 76. Add: *Irvin v. Irvin* [2001] 1 F.L.R. 178.

NOTE 80. Add: *Marsh v. Marsh*, 2002 S.L.T. (Sh.Ct.) 87.

NOTE 82. Add: *D.T. v. F.L.* (Irish High Ct., 2001) (sailor to Olympic standards resigned from Irish sailing clubs on taking up residence in Holland).

NOTE 88. Add: *Irvin v. Irvin* [2001] 1 F.L.R. 178 (living in expatriate context, without learning language of country of residence). *Cf. Marsh v. Marsh*, 2002 S.L.T. (Sh. Ct.) 87 (woman of Thai origin taking course in English while resident in Scotland).

NOTE 6. Add: *Reddington v. Riach's Executor*, 2002 S.L.T. 537.   **6–051**

NOTE 48. Add: *Reddington v. Riach's Executor*, 2002 S.L.T. 537.   **6–062**

(2) LOSS

NOTE 86. Add: *Breuning v. Breuning* [2002] EWHC 236 (Fam); [2002] 1 **6–075** F.L.R. 888.

C. *Domicile of dependency*

NOTE 32. Add: *Breuning v. Breuning* [2002] EWHC 236 (Fam); [2002] 1 **6–087** F.L.R. 888.

(3) RESIDENCE

Section 50(5) of the British Nationality Act 1981 is amended by the British **6–121** Overseas Territories Act 2002, s. 1(2).

NOTE 21. See also *Leyvand v. Barasch*, *The Times*, March 23, 2000 (court willing to find ordinary residence in two countries; security for costs context).

NOTE 26. Add: *R. v. Kent County Council, ex p. S.* [2000] 1 F.L.R. 155.   **6–122**

See Beaumont and McEleavy, *The Hague Convention on International Child* **6–123** *Abduction* (1999), Chap. 7; Rogerson (2000) 49 I.C.L.Q. 86.

The European Court has held (in the context of Council Regulation **6–124** 1408/71 of June 14, 1971 dealing with social security schemes) that in considering habitual residence, account must be taken of the family situation of the propositus, his reasons for moving, the length and continuity of residence, the possession of stable employment (if that be the case) and his intentions: Case C–90/97 *Swaddling v. Administration Officer* [1999] E.C.R. I–1075.

The House of Lords held, in the context of entitlement to social security benefits, that a person newly arrived from Bangladesh and intending to

7

remain in England did not, without more, acquire an immediate habitual residence in England: to acquire an habitual residence, a person must take up residence in the relevant country and live there for a period which shows that the residence has become habitual: *Nessa v. Chief Adjudication Officer* [1999] 1 W.L.R. 1937 (H.L.). The length of that period is not fixed; it must depend on the circumstances: *ibid.*, citing the dictum of Butler-Sloss L.J. in *Re A.F. (A Minor) (Child Abduction)* [1992] 1 F.C.R. 269, 277 that "a month can be an appreciable period of time".

In *Breuning v. Breuning* [2002] EWHC 236 (Fam), [2002] 1 F.L.R. 888, it was held that residence in England for medical treatment, the patient having no choice but to remain in England, could not amount to habitual residence. As a general proposition this seems incorrect, requiring a degree of intention more appropriate to domicile; but as the period of residence was short the decision can be supported on other grounds.

NOTE 36: Add: *D. v. D.,* 2002 S.C. 33 (residence too brief and its circumstances too unsettled and uncertain to be habitual).

NOTE 37. Add: *Re V. (Jurisdiction: Habitual Residence)* [2001] 1 F.L.R. 253.

NOTE 38: Add: *Dombrowicz v. Gray* (Court of Session, O.H., May 2, 2001).

NOTE 43. Add: *Al Habtoor v. Fotheringham* [2001] EWCA Civ. 186 (C.A.).

6–125 The habitual residence of a newborn child was held in *B. v. H. (Habitual Residence: Wardship)* [2002] 1 F.L.R. 388 to be determined by the position of the parent or parents with parental responsibility, and not by its place of birth. In that case, a child was born in Bangladesh during what had been intended to be a short visit, extended by the husband's unilateral decision that the family should remain in that country. The mother returned to England, where the family had previously been habitually resident, but the child remained in Bangladesh. Although the child had never been in England, it was held, taking a broad view of the facts, to be habitually resident there. However, in *W. and B. v. H. (Child Abduction: Surrogacy)* [2002] 1 F.L.R. 1008, the proposition that a newborn child's habitual residence is that of its parents and not its place of birth was repudiated. There, children were born in England to an Englishwoman acting as a surrogate mother, the ovum from an anonymous donor having been fertilised by the sperm of a man habitually resident in California. It was held that the children had no habitual residence, and that they had no such link with California as would justify a finding that they were habitually resident there.

Text and note 45. Adoption Act 1976, s. 17(2) is repealed by Adoption and Children Act 2002 (not yet in force).

NOTE 46. Add *Chan v. Chow* [2002] 8 W.W.R. 63 (B.C.C.A.) (where custody shared).

NOTE 49. Add *B. v. H. (Habitual Residence: Wardship)* [2002] 1 F.L.R. 388. However in *Re S. (A Child)* [2002] EWCA Civ. 1771 it was emphasised that section 41 had no relevance where one of the relevant countries is outside the United Kingdom.

It has been said that the two concepts of habitual residence and ordinary **6–126** residence share "a common core of meaning" but Lord Slynn reserved the question whether the terms were always synonymous; each might take a shade of meaning from the context in which it was used: *Nessa v. Chief Adjudication Officer* [1999] 1 W.L.R. 1937, 1941 (H.L.). But in *Ikimi v. Ikimi* [2001] EWCA Civ. 873; [2002] Fam. 72 (C.A.), the Court of Appeal held that the two terms must be synonymous in the context of family law legislation. No clear test could be adopted to answer the question as to how much absence from one country would make it impossible to find habitual residence there, but the person concerned would have to have spent "an appreciable part" of the year there; there must, citing *Oundjian v. Oundjian* [1980] 1 F.L.R. 198 in the context of divorce jurisdiction, be a proper and sufficient connection between the propositus and the courts of this country.

NOTE 52. Add: *W. and B. v. H. (Child Abduction: Surrogacy)* [2002] 1 F.L.R. 1008.

NOTE 53. Add: *Ikimi v. Ikimi* [2001] EWCA Civ. 873; [2002] Fam. 72.

CHAPTER 7

SUBSTANCE AND PROCEDURE

7R–001–   NOTE 1 and text thereto. Rule 17 was applied and the text was cited with
    002   approval in *De Gartori v. Smithwick* [2000] 1 I.L.R.M. 463 (Sup. Ct.).

7–014   In the context of English proceedings, whether or not a document is
privileged is to be determined by English law; the fact that under a foreign
law the document is not privileged or that the privilege that existed is
deemed to have been waived is irrelevant: *Bourns Inc. v. Raychem Corp.*
[1999] C.L.C. 1029 (C.A.).

7–014   Final sentence. See *Loutchansky v. Times Newspapers Ltd. (Nos. 2–5)* [2001]
EWCA Civ. 1805; [2002] Q.B. 783, 820 (C.A.).

7–032   NOTE 16. The principle that priorities are governed by the *lex fori* is equally
applicable in cases where all the competing claims are governed by the
same (foreign) *lex causae*: *Fournier v. The Ship "Margaret Z"* [1999] 3
N.Z.L.R. 111.

7–034   NOTE 27. See also *Edmunds v. Simmonds* [2001] 1 W.L.R. 1003, a case
decided under Part III of the Private International Law (Miscellaneous
Provisions) Act 1995 in which Garland J. held that heads of damage are
matters of substantive law and how damages are quantified under those
heads is a procedural matter; *Hulse v. Chambers* [2001] 1 W.L.R. 2386. See,
however, *King v. T. Tunnock Ltd.*, 2000 S.L.T. 744, in which the Court of
Session (Inner House) decided that, in the context of a claim for compensation under the Commercial Agents (Council Directive) Regulations (S.I.
1993 No. 3053), which implement Council Directive (E.C.) 653/86, the
principles of French law on which the Directive's compensation system is
based, rather than the common law rules governing the quantification of
damages, are relevant for determining the level of compensation to which
the claimant might be entitled.

7–038   In *John Pfeiffer Pty Ltd. v. Rogerson* (2000) 172 A.L.R. 625 the plaintiff sued
his employer in the Australian Capital Territory (A.C.T.) in relation to
injury suffered in an accident at work in New South Wales. In the A.C.T.
damages were assessed at A$30,000 plus out of pocket expenses; under the
Workers' Compensation Act 1987 (N.S.W.) damages would have been
limited to a considerably lesser sum. The Supreme Court of the A.C.T. and
the Federal Court of Australia, applying *Stevens v. Head* (1993) 176 C.L.R.
433, held that the N.S.W. provision imposing a limit on the damages
recoverable was procedural and, therefore, not applicable in A.C.T. proceedings. The employer appealed to the High Court of Australia. The High
Court reconsidered the rule laid down in *Stevens v. Head* (that a statutory
rule laying down a limit on damages is procedural in nature) and decided
that the N.S.W. provision, which places a cap on damages, is a substantive

rule. A majority of the High Court (comprising Gleeson C.J. Gaudron, McHugh, Gummow and Hayne JJ.) went further and indicated (at p. 651) that *all* questions about the amount of damages that may be recovered ought to be treated as substantive issues. See further entry at para. 35–005, n. 38 and text, *infra*.

The rule of Ontario law which bars an action for precuniary losses in road **7–036** accident cases (under section 267.1 of the Insurance Act, R.S.O. 1990) is a substantive rule, not a procedural one: *Wong v. Lee* (2001) 211 D.L.R. (4th) 69 (Ont. C.A.).

In *Roerig v. Valiant Trawlers Ltd* [2002] EWCA Civ. 21; [2002] 1 W.L.R. **7–039** 2304 (C.A.) the claimant, a Dutch woman, brought a claim under the Fatal Accidents Act 1976 as a dependant of a Dutchaman who was killed in an accident on board a trawler owned by the defendants. At the time of the accident, the trawler was in English waters. One of the questions facing the court was whether section 4 of the Fatal Accidents Act 1976 (which provides that "benefits which have accrued or will or may accrue to any person from his estate or otherwise as a result of his death shall be disregarded") applied to the claim. The defendants argued that the law applicable to the tort was Dutch law and that section 4 was not applicable. The Court of Appeal held, however, that the applicable law was English law. Even if Dutch law had been the law applicable to the tort, the Court of Appeal considered that section 4 would nevertheless have been relevant— on the basis that it is a procedural rule rather than a substantive one. In the words of Waller L.J.: "The question whether deductions should be made for benefits is not a question which goes to liability: it is a question going to assessment" (at p. 2315).

See also *John Pfeiffer Pty Ltd. v. Rogerson* (2000) 172 A.L.R. 625 in which **7–041** the High Court of Australia indicated (*obiter*) that, at common law, statutes of limitation are substantive, rather than procedural.

NOTE 56. For the analogous position in Scotland under s. 23A(1) of the **7–043** Prescription and Limitation (Scotland) Act 1973 see *Kleinwort Benson Ltd. v. Glasgow City Council (No. 3)*, 2002 S.L.T. 1190.

NOTE 73. Add: Briggs (1998) 69 B.Y.I.L. 352, 355. **7–044**

NOTE 76. *Connelly v. RTZ Corp. (No. 2)* is now reported at [1999] C.L.C. 533.

In *Somers v. Fournier* (2002) 214 D.L.R. (4th) 611 the Ontario Court of **7–049** Appeal held, in the context of a tort action, that (i) the issue of litigation costs was a procedural matter; (ii) Ontario's "cap" on non-pecuniary general damages was also a procedural matter; but (iii) the availability of pre-judgment interest was akin to a head of damage and, therefore, substantive.

CHAPTER 8

INTERNATIONAL LITIGATION: PROTECTIVE MEASURES AND JUDICIAL ASSISTANCE

8–002 In *Grupo Mexicano de Desarrollo, S.A. v. Alliance Bond Fund, Inc.*, 527 U.S. 308 (1999) the United States Supreme Court decided, by a majority of five to four, that United States federal courts had no power to grant an interlocutory injunction to restrain a defendant from disposing of its assets pending the determination of an action. The decision turned on the scope of the jurisdiction conferred by the Judiciary Act of 1789 on federal courts over "all suits in equity," which in previous decisions had been interpreted as jurisdiction to administer in equity suits the principles of judicial remedies which were administered by the Court of Chancery in England at the time of American independence. The basis of the majority decision was that in 1789 (and until 1975, when the *Mareva* practice was developed) there was a well-established general rule that judgment establishing a debt was necessary before a court of equity would interfere with a debtor's use of his property. The minority considered that such an injunction was consistent with the principles which had been devised and which were being administered by the Chancery Court in 1789: the development of the *Mareva* jurisdiction was based on the traditional power of equity to remedy the abuse of legal process by defendants and the injustice which would result from defendants making themselves judgment-proof. See Collins (1999) 115 L.Q.R. 601. It should be noted that generally under State law the plaintiff will be able to obtain an attachment of assets within the State pending trial. In this case the plaintiff was seeking to enjoin the disposal of assets in Mexico, where the defendant was incorporated and had its principal place of business. The connection of the case with the United States was that the plaintiffs were suing on bonds issued by the defendant which were governed by New York law and provided for the jurisdiction of the New York courts. See also *Credit Agricole Indosuez v. Rossiyskiy Kredit Bank*, 94 N.Y. 2d 541 (N.Y. Ct. App. 2000), where the New York Court of Appeals applied the decision of the Supreme Court to hold that the New York courts did not have jurisdiction to grant what in effect would have been equivalent to an extra-territorial *Mareva* injunction.

NOTE 1. See also Maher and Rodger (1999) 48 I.C.L.Q. 302; Gerhard, 1999 Rev. suisse de dr. int. et de dr. eur. 97. On Scottish arrestment see Aird (2002) 51 I.C.L.Q. 155.

8–005 NOTE 10. See also *Walsh v. Deloitte & Touche Inc.* [2001] UKPC 58 (P.C.).

8–008 NOTE 24. Add: *Re Q's Estate* [1999] 1 Lloyd's Rep. 931.

8–009 For the importance of disclosure orders see *Motorola Credit Corp. v. Uzan* [2002] EWCA Civ. 989, [2002] 2 All E.R. (Comm.) 945 (C.A.).

8–010 See the United States practice referred to at para. 8–002, *supra*. For the Republic of Ireland see *Bennett Entreprises Inc. v. Lipton* [1999] 1 I.L.R.M. 81.

In *Bank of China v. NBM LLC* [2001] 4 All E.R. 954 the claimant brought **8–017**
proceedings in New York seeking damages for alleged misappropriation of
its funds. None of the defendants was domiciled in England. The claimant
obtained from the English court a worldwide freezing injunction in aid of
the New York proceedings. Notice of the order was served on the London
branch of Union Bank of Switzerland, whose Zurich head office and
Cayman Islands branch had had relationships with some of the defendants.
David Steel J. acceded to the bank's application for a variation of the order
providing that, in respect of assets outside the jurisdiction, nothing in the
order prevented the bank or its subsidiaries from complying with what it
reasonably believed to be its obligations, contractual or otherwise, under
the laws and obligations of the country or state in which those assets were
situated or under the applicable law of any account in question. The
decision has been affirmed by the Court of Appeal ([2001] EWCA Civ.
1933; [2002] 1 All E.R. 717), which recommended that the Supreme Court
Rules Committee and the Commercial Court should re-consider the
prescribed standard form in the light of its judgment.

Text at note 61. Order 11, r. 1(1)(*b*) is replaced by CPR, r. 6.20(2).   **8–019**

NOTE 60. *Cf. Rowland v. Gulfpac (No. 1)* [1999] Lloyd's Rep. Bank. 86; *Re
Q's Estate* [1999] 1 Lloyd's Rep. 931. See also *Meespierson (Bahamas) Ltd.
v. Grupo Torras S.A.* [2000] 1 L.R.C. 627 (Bahamas C.A.).

NOTE 62. See also *Amoco (U.K.) Exploration Co. v. British American
Offshore Ltd.* [1999] 2 Lloyd's Rep. 772.

In *Ryan v. Friction Dynamics Ltd.*, *The Times*, June 14, 2000, Neuberger J. **8–021**
said that where the foreign court with primary jurisdiction has made an
order equivalent to a world-wide freezing injunction, that does not prevent
the English court granting a freezing order under section 25 of the Civil
Jurisdiction and Judgments Act 1982, at least in relation to English assets
and/or against defendants resident and domiciled in England. But cogent
reasons must be given to justify overlapping freezing orders, because they
lead to substantial increased costs, and also to a risk of double jeopardy for
defendants and the opportunity for forum-shopping by claimants. Where
the English order overlaps with a freezing order of the foreign court, it
would be sensible to have some indication as to which is to be the court
with the primary role for enforcing the overlapping injunctions, and that
court should normally be the foreign court. Where a overlapping order is
made under section 25 it should normally track the terms of the order made
by the foreign court. See also *State of Brunei Darussalam v. Bolkiah*, *The
Times*, September 5, 2000.

See also *Wermuth v. Wermuth* [2003] EWCA Civ. 50; [2003] 1 W.L.R. 942 **8–024**
(C.A.).

NOTE 80. See also *Indosuez International Finance BV v. National Reserve* **8–026**
Bank [2002] EWHC 744 (Comm). In *Lewis v. Eliades* [2003] EWHC 368
(QB), *The Times*, February 28, 2003, it was said that overseas lawyers
seeking international asset-freezing orders in the English courts in aid of
foreign proceedings should be aware of the heavy responsibilities which
solicitors and counsel had towards the court with regard to disclosure of
material matters.

8–029 *Cf. Walsh v. Deloitte & Touche Inc.* [2001] UKPC 58 (P.C.).

8–036 NOTE 10. See now McClean, *International Co-operation in Civil and Criminal Matters* (2002).

8–039 NOTE 13. See now CPR, r. 6.25(2).

8–040 NOTE 15. See now McClean, *op. cit.* (para. 8–036 above), pp. 12–75.

NOTE 16. See also *Knauf UK GmbH v. British Gypsum Ltd.* [2001] EWCA Civ. 1570; [2002] 1 W.L.R. 907 (C.A.).

8–041 The procedure for alternative service in CPR, r. 6.8 cannot be used to outflank the service provisions in the Hague Conventions and in the bilateral Convention with Germany: *Knauf UK GmbH v. British Gypsum Ltd.* [2001] EWCA Civ. 1570; [2002] 1 W.L.R. 907 (C.A.).

NOTE 21. See now McClean, *op. cit.* (para. 8–036 above), pp. 47–55.

8–043 The European Community Convention on the service in the Member States of judicial and extrajudicial documents in civil or commercial matters never came into force, and was overtaken by the extension of the competence of the European institutions by the Treaty of Amsterdam's establishment of an "area of freedom, security and justice". The draft Convention was converted, with very minor modifications, into Council Regulation 1348/2000 (for text see [2000] O.J. L160) binding on Member States and coming into force on May 31, 2001. Statements in the text about, and references to Articles of the Convention, apply to the Regulation and its Articles. For service abroad under the Regulation, see CPR, r. 6.26A.

8–049 Order 11, rr. 5 and 6 have have been replaced by CPR, rr. 6.24 to 6.26.

8–052 Service of foreign process is governed either by Council Regulation 1348/2000, [2000] O.J. L160/37 (see above at para. 8–043) or by CPR, rr. 6.32–6.35.

8–053 In 2001 the European Union adopted Council Regulation (E.C.) 1206/2001, May 28, 2001 on co-operation between the courts of the Member States in the taking of evidence in civil or commercial matters ([2001] O.J. L174, June 27, 2001). The Regulation will come fully into effect on January 1, 2004 (Art. 24(2); certain formal articles are already in force). The Regulation builds on the Hague Convention of 1970, a major difference being that the Regulation provides for the direct transmission of requests from court to court, dispensing with the device of Central Authorities, though preserving a limited role for what are termed "central bodies". The Regulation prevails over other provisions contained in bilateral or multilateral agreements or arrangements concluded by the Member States and in particular the Hague Convention (Art. 21(1)).

The Regulation applies in civil or commercial where the court of a Member State ("Member State" does not include Denmark), in accordance with the provisions of the law of that State, requests (a) the competent court of another Member State to take evidence; or (b) to take evidence directly in another Member State (Art. 1(1)). A request may not be made to obtain evidence which is not intended for use in judicial proceedings, commenced or contemplated (Art. 1(2)). Requests are to be transmitted by the court before which the proceedings are commenced or contemplated, "the requesting court", directly to the competent court of another Member State, "the requested court", for the performance of taking of evidence (Art. 2(1)). Member States must by July 1, 2003 (Art. 22) draw up a list of the courts competent for the performance of taking of evidence under the Regulation, indicating the territorial and, where appropriate, the special jurisdiction of those courts (Art. 2(2)).

The Regulation contains an Annex of Forms which specify the detailed information to be provided. Requests and other communications sent under the Regulation must be in the official language of the requested State or, if there are several official languages in that State, in the official language or one of the official languages of the place where the requested taking of evidence is to be performed, or in another language which the requested State has indicated it can accept (Art. 5). Requests and other communications are to be transmitted by the swiftest possible means which the requested State has indicated it can accept: in many cases this will included electronic means. The only essential is that the document received accurately reflects the content of the document forwarded and that all information in it is legible (Art. 6).

A request for the taking of evidence by the requested court must be executed without delay and, at the latest, within 90 days of receipt of the request (Art. 10(1); charges are payable only in special circumstances, *e.g.* involving a special procedure, expert evidence, or the use of communications technology (Art. 18)). Where necessary, in executing a request the requested court is to apply the appropriate coercive measures in the instances and to the extent as are provided for by the law of the requested State for the execution of a request made for the same purpose by its national authorities or one of the parties (Art. 13). If the requested court is not in a position to execute the request within 90 days of receipt, it must inform the requesting court, giving reasons (Art. 15).

Where the request involves testimony by a witness, it is not to be executed when the person concerned claims the right to refuse to give evidence or to be prohibited from giving evidence (a) under the law of the requested State; or (b) under the law of the requesting State, where that right has been specified in the request, or, if need be, at the instance of the requested court, has been confirmed by the requesting court (Art. 14(1)). The only other grounds on which the execution of a request may be refused are that (a) the request does not fall within the scope of the Regulation; or (b) the execution of the request under the law of the requested State does not fall within the functions of the judiciary; or (c) the requesting court fails to repair the omissions in an incomplete request within 30 days of being asked to do so; or (d) a deposit or advance is not made within 60 days after the requested court requested one (Art. 14(2)). Execution may not be refused by the requested court solely on the ground that under the law of the requested State a court of that State has exclusive jurisdiction over the subject matter of the action or that the law of that State would not admit the right of action on it (Art. 14(4)).

The Regulation includes (Art. 17) novel provisions as to the taking by the requesting court itself of evidence on the territory of another Member State. In this type of case, the request is submitted to the designated central body of the requested State. The direct taking of evidence may only take place if it can be performed on a voluntary basis without the need for coercive measures.

8–056 NOTE 64. See now McClean, *op. cit.* (para. 8–036 above), pp. 92–100.

8–058 Orders may be made for disclosure and inspection of documents, even if obedience to such an order might constitute an offence under the country in which the documents are to be found. This was held in *Morris v. Banque Arabe et Internationale d'Investissement S.A.* [2001] I.L.Pr. 37 (C.A.) citing two cases decided under earlier rules of court (*The Heidberg* [1993] 2 Lloyd's Rep. 324 and *Canada Trust Ltd. v. Stolzenberg* [1998] I.L.Pr. 290) and the related issues examined in *Brannigan v. Davison* [1997] A.C. 238 (P.C.). In exercising its discretion, the English court will consider the degree of risk to which the foreign party would be exposed: in *Morris v. Banque Arabe et Internationale d'Investissement S.A.* a French "blocking statue" (Art. 1 *bis* of Loi 80-583 of July 16, 1980) was regarded as virtually a dead letter, any risk being purely hypothetical.

8–061 NOTE 84. See now McClean, *op. cit.* (para. 8–036 above), pp. 133–143.

8–064 In *South Carolina Insurance Co. v. Assurantie Maatshappij "De Zeven Provincien"* [1987] A.C. 24 the injunction sought was limited to the discovery of documents, the proposed pre-trial deposition of witnesses under United States procedures being abandoned. In *Omega Group Holdings Ltd v. Kozeny* [2002] C.L.C. 132 it was held that the *South Carolina* case did not prevent the making of an injunction restraining such pre-trial depositions where they would be unconscionable, as where it was proposed to take pre-trial depositions from persons whom it was proposed to call (and who were willing to act) as witnesses in the English trial: exposure to double cross-examination would be unconscionable, vexatious and an abuse of the due process of the English court. A U.S. Court of Appeals has held that assistance can only be given where the evidence is to be used in actual or pending proceedings in the foreign court: in the instant case, the foreign proceedings involved an appeal to the French Cour de Cassation where no new evidence could be tendered, and so assistance was refused: *Euromepa S.A. v. R. Esmerian Inc.*, 154 F. 3d 24 (2d Cir. 1998).

NOTE 93. The reference should be to 28 U.S.C. s. 1782.

8–068 R.S.C. Order 70 has been replaced by CPR, rr. 34.16–34.21.

8–071 An approach similar to that taken in the *Golden Eagle Refinery* case was adopted in *Securities and Exchange Commission v. Credit Bancorp Ltd.* (Q.B.D., unreported, February 20, 2001).

8–074 NOTE 43. Add: *Genira Trade and Finance Inc v. Refco Capital Markets Ltd* [2001] EWCA Civ. 1733, [2002] C.L.C. 301.

8–075 NOTE 46. Discovery may be ordered against third parties in some circumstances in which no such order would be made in the country of the requested court: *Fecht v. Deloitte & Touche* [2000] I.L.Pr. 398 (Ont.).

8–078 NOTE 67. See now McClean, op. cit. (para. 8–036 above), pp. 335–339.

8–080 Security for costs is now governed by CPR Part 25, and in particular rr. 25.12–25.15. Under r. 25.13 as amended by S.I. 2002 No. 3219, the court may make an order for security for costs if (a) it is satisfied, having regard to all the circumstances of the case, that it is just to make such an order; and (b) either an enactment permits the court to require security for costs or one of the following conditions applies. These are (a) the claimant is resident out of the jurisdiction; but not resident in a Brussels Contracting State, a Lugano Contracting State or a Regulation State; or (b) the claimant is a company or other body (whether incorporated inside or outside Great Britain) and there is reason to believe that it will be unable to pay the defendant's costs if ordered to do so; or (c) the claimant has changed his address since the claim was commenced with a view to evading the consequences of the litigation; or (d) the claimant failed to give his address in the claim form, or gave an incorrect address in that form; or (e) the claimant is acting as a nominal claimant, other than as a representative claimant under CPR Part 19, and there is reason to believe that he will be unable to pay the defendant's costs if ordered to do so; or (f) the claimant has taken steps in relation to his assets that would make it difficult to enforce an order for costs against him. Rule 25.15 imposes the same conditions where security for costs is sought from an appellant in respect of the costs of the appeal.

In *White Sea & Onega Shipping Co. v. International Transport Workers Federation* [2001] EWCA Civ. 377 (C.A.), it was held that a shipping line whose ships frequently entered ports in Member States was a body against whom a claim could be enforced under the 1968 Convention or the Lugano Convention.

The effect of the condition in the then text of CPR r. 25.13(2)(a) ("the claimant is an individual—(i) who is ordinarily resident out of the jurisdiction; and (ii) is not a person against whom a claim can be enforced under [the Brussels or Lugano Conventions]") was considered by the Court of Appeal in *De Beer v. Kanaar & Co* [2001] EWCA Civ. 1318, [2003] 1 W.L.R. 38. At first instance it had been held that the presence of assets in a Convention country meant that the condition could not be satisfied. The Court of Appeal, lamenting the unsatisfactory drafting of the rule, held that the effect of the provision was to confine the jurisdiction to order security for costs to cases where the claimant is an individual who is not ordinarily resident either in the jurisdiction or in a Convention country. The mere presence of assets in a Convention country did not exclude the jurisdiction. The text of CPR r. 25.13 was subsequently amended to reflect this judgment: see above.

In *Aoun v. Bahri* [2002] EWHC 29 (Comm), [2002] 3 All E.R. 182, the court held that CPR r. 25.13(2)(d) on change of address was not limited to cases in which the relevant change of address was from that given in the claim form; later changes of address could be relied upon where they were with a view to avoiding any of the ordinary consequences of litigating in England. In the instant case, the claimant had become resident in England, but the court was satisfied that this was for family and business reasons unconnected with the effects of litigation. The court declined to rule on the effect of possibly unlawful residence in terms of immigration law. In the same case, the court held that in the context of CPR r. 25.13(2)(g) (taking steps in relation to assets that would make it difficult to enforce an order for costs) the claimant's motives were irrelevant: the sale of a house in Australia could attract the rule.

The Civil Procedure Rules contain not only a revised set of rules dealing directly with security for costs but also other new provisions which enable orders to similar effect being made under other Parts of the CPR. An order that a party pay a sum of money into court can be ordered on an application under Part 24 for summary judgment or under r. 3.1 when a party has failed to comply with a rule, practice direction or protocol; the order can be made against any party, not just the claimant. The existence of these powers was confirmed by the Court of Appeal in *Olatawura v. Abiloye* [2002] EWCA Civ. 998; [2002] 4 All E.R. 903. In exercising its discretion the court must have regard not only to the ability of the party concerned to pay (bearing in mind Art. 6 of the European Convention on Human Rights) but also the party's conduct in the proceedings, and the apparent strength of that party's case: *ibid.* Under CPR r. 3.1 there is power to order payment into court in respect of past costs orders which have remained unpaid, but this should not be done when the effect would be to prevent the party making a further application to the court (or would in practice require third parties to make the payment for the party concerned): *CIBC Mellon Trust Co v. Mora Hotel Corp NV* [2002] EWCA Civ. 1688; [2003] 1 All E.R. 564.

NOTE 77. Add: *Leyvand v. Barasch, The Times*, March 23, 2000 (no presumption that security will be ordered unless foreign claimant can discharge onus of proving property here); *Cripps v. Heritage Distribution Corp., The Times*, November 10, 1999 (C.A.) (existence of related but distinct proceedings can properly be taken into account).

8–084 NOTE 2. Add: *Bunzl v. Martin Bunzl International Ltd., The Times*, September 19, 2000.

8–085 The Treaty of Rome does not require a Member State to treat all its nationals equally, and so does not prevent security for costs being ordered against a party ordinarily resident in the Isle of Man in circumstances in which a similar order would not have been made against an English party: *Greenwich Ltd. v. National Westminster Bank plc* [1999] 2 Lloyd's Rep. 308.

In *Pordéa v. Times Newspapers Ltd.* [2000] I.L.Pr. 763 (French Cour de Cassation, March 16, 1999) it was held that an order for costs made by an English court against a French party (before the decision in *Fitzgerald v. Williams* [1996] Q.B. 657) on dismissing a claim when the claimant failed to give the required security for costs was a matter which objectively presented an obstacle to the claimant's free access to justice and was thus contrary to Article 6(1) of the European Convention on Human Rights.

The Court of Appeal considered the relevance of Article 6 to the practice of ordering security for costs generally (and especially in relation to appeals) in *Nasser v. United Bank of Kuwait* [2001] EWCA Civ. 556; [2002] 1 All E.R. 401 (C.A.). It noted that in *Tolstoy Miloslavsky v. United Kingdom* (1995) 20 E.H.R.R. 442 the European Court of Human Rights had held that an order that an appellant furnish security for costs made under the then text of the Civil Procedure Rules did not offend against Article 6. Under the new form of CPR, r. 25.13(2)(a), a clear distinction is drawn between claimants against whom a claim can be enforced under the 1968 or Lugano Conventions and other claimants. The Court of Appeal in *Nasser v. United Bank of Kuwait* considered the relevance of the anti-discrimination provisions of Article 14 of the E.C.H.R. (as given effect by the Human Rights Act 1998), which had to be given a similar effect to that given in *Fitzgerald v. Williams* to what is now Article 12 of the Treaty of Rome. For this purpose all personal claimants (or appellants) before the English courts form the relevant class within which there must be no unjustified discrimination. It would be such discrimination were the mere fact of residence outside the geographical scope of the 1968/Lugano texts to be a basis for an order for security for costs. Other countries, such as Commonwealth countries and (despite the absence of any treaty) the United States, were countries in which the enforcement of judgments presented little difficulty. Where substantial difficulties or extra costs were likely, an order for security for costs could be objectively justifiable.

Evidence cannot be obtained under the 1975 Act in aid of a private arbitral **8–086** tribunal in another country: *Commerce and Industry Insurance Co., Canada v. Lloyd's Underwriters* (Q.B.D., August 1, 2001).

For the practice in Scotland, see *Rossmeier v. Mounthooly Transport*, 2000 S.L.T. 200.

NOTE 13. See *Fallimento La Pantofola D'Oro S.p.A. v. Blane Leisure Ltd.* **8–087** *(No. 2)*, 2000 S.L.T. 1264 (where on the facts an order against an insolvent Italian company refused).

CHAPTER 9

PROOF OF FOREIGN LAW

9–002 NOTE 4. Add: *Glencore International A.G. v. Metro Trading International Inc.* [2001] 1 Lloyd's Rep. 284.

9–003 Text to note 6. But for the view the exceptions to this proposition are much wider than this would suggest, see *Damberg v. Damberg* [2001] NSWCA 87, (2001) 52 N.S.W.L.R. 492 discussed in detail at para. 9–025, below.

9–010 Add after end of paragraph: But a finding upon foreign law made by arbitrators is a finding of fact and cannot form the basis for an appeal on a point of law to an English court pursuant to Arbitration Act 1996, s. 69: *Egmatra v. Marco* [1999] 1 Lloyd's Rep. 862. To similar effect, see also *Reliance Industries Ltd. v. Enron Oil and Gas (India) Ltd.* [2002] 1 All E.R. (Comm.) 59 (where arbitrators have found Indian law to be applicable but Indian law has not been proved to differ from English law with the result that English law has been applied by default, any appeal would not be on a "question of law" for the purposes of s. 82 of the Arbitration Act 1996, and an appeal under s. 69 of the Act does not lie).

9–012 But if the content of the foreign law which is sought to be proved is contrary to English public policy, Rule 3 will prevent the party seeking to rely on that foreign law from proving it, and as a result it will not be proved and cannot be applied. And *cf. Kuwait Airways Corp. v. Iraq Airways Co. (Nos. 4 and 5)* [2002] UKHL 19; [2002] 2 A.C. 883. See also Briggs (2002) 6 Sing. J. Int. & Comp. L. 953.

9–013 For the need for expert witnesses to assist the court in the evaluation of evidence of foreign law, see *Dymocks Franchise Systems (NSW) Pty. Ltd. v. Todd* [2002] UKPC 50, P.C.

NOTE 44. Add: *Glencore International A.G. v. Metro Trading International Inc., supra.*

9–014 Second paragraph. For an illustration of the relative status of various expert witnesses, see *Glencore International A.G. v. Metro Trading International Inc., supra*, at pp. 299–300. A general employee of a foreign company which was the victim of an alleged crime is not competent to give expert evidence on foreign criminal law: see *R. v. Okolie, The Times,* June 16, 2000 (C.A.).

9–016 Second paragraph. The court is not inhibited from "using its own intelligence as on any other question of evidence": *Glencore International A.G. v. Metro Trading International Inc., supra* at p. 300, quoting *A/S Tallinna Laevauhisus v. Estonian State Steamship Line* (1947) 80 Ll. L. R. 99, 107 (C.A.).

The proposition that the content of foreign law will be taken to be the same **9–025** as that of the *lex fori* was heavily qualified by the New South Wales Court of Appeal in *Damberg v. Damberg* [2001] NSWCA 87; (2001) 52 N.S.W.L.R. 492. In the context of the law on tax and the consequences of its evasion, the court refused to accept that German law, the *lex causae* on the particular point in issue, was the same as the law of Australia, criticising the presumption of identity of foreign and local law as requiring the court "to embrace an entirely artificial and almost certainly misleading fiction". The judgment contains an exhaustive survey of cases from many jurisdictions in which variously-worded exceptions to the general rule have been essayed, but rested its conclusion on the impossibility of accepting that fiscal legislation was "assumed to be a field resting on great and broad principles likely to be part of any legal system". So while the court was prepared to accept that the principles of Australian law on trusts resulting from incomplete transfers of property were similar to those found in German law, it was not prepared to make the same assumption in relation to fiscal laws. In those cases where the court will not accept the identity of foreign and local law, the fact that the parties have agreed to proceed on the basis of identity of foreign and local law will not bind the court, nor oblige the judge to reach a decision which he believes to be contrary to fact. It follows from this analysis that the party whose case depends on the application of German law will have failed to discharge the burden of proof if no evidence of the foreign law is presented by him, even though that party would succeed if (as the court will not accept) the foreign law was indeed the same as the Australian.

To broadly similar effect, though not referring to *Damberg v. Damberg* is *Shaker v. Al-Bedrawi* [2002] EWCA Civ. 1452, [2003] 2 W.L.R. 922 (C.A.), where the court considered the potential artificiality of applying provisions of the Companies Act 1985, applicable only to registered companies, to a case governed by foreign law and concerning an unregistered company, and accepted that, in such cases, a provision of English law may be inapplicable even though foreign law had not been proved to be different.

CHAPTER 10

JURISDICTIONAL IMMUNITIES

10R–001 See Fox, *Law of State Immunity* (2002).

10–002 **State immunity and human rights.** In November 2001 the European Court of Human Rights decided three cases in which the application of the principles of state immunity under international law was held to be compatible with the right of access to court under Article 6(1) of the European Convention on Human Rights: *McElhinney v. Ireland* (2002) 34 E.H.R.R. 322 (arising out of *McElhinney v. Williams* [1996] 1 I.L.R.M. 276); *Al-Adsani v. United Kingdom* (2002) 34 E.H.R.R. 273 (arising out of *Al-Adsani v. Government of Kuwait, The Times*, March 29, 1996; 107 Int.L.R. 536 (C.A.)) and *Fogarty v. United Kingdom* (2002) 34 E.H.R.R. 302. The European Court of Human Rights held that, whilst a limitation on the right of access must pursue a legitimate aim and must be proportionate, the grant of state immunity in civil proceedings pursued the legitimate aim of complying with international law to promote comity and good relations between States through respect for another State's sovereignty; and measures taken which reflected generally recognised rules of public international law could not in principle be regarded as imposing a disproportionate restriction on the right of access to a court. Just as the right of access to a court was an inherent part of the fair trial guarantee, so some restrictions on access were inherent, such as those limitations generally accepted by the community of nations as part of the doctrine of state immunity. In the *McElhinney* case the Court noted the trend towards limiting state immunity in respect of personal injury caused within the forum State, but that Ireland was not alone in holding that immunity attached to such suits in respect of torts committed by *acta jure imperii*. It was not possible, in the present state of the development of international law, to conclude that Irish law conflicted with its general principles. In the *Fogarty* case the Court noted that there appeared to be a trend limiting state immunity in employment related disputes; but international practice was divided on the question whether immunity applies to employment in a mission or embassy, and the level of employees to which it applies. The case related to discrimination in the employment process, and such questions might involve sensitive and confidential issues relating to the diplomatic and organisational policy of a foreign State. The Court was not aware of any trend towards relaxation of state immunity as regards issues of recruitment. In the *Al-Adsani* case (a 9–8 decision) the Court noted the growing recognition of the overriding importance of the prohibition of torture, but did not find that it established that there was yet acceptance in international law of the proposition that States were not entitled to immunity in respect of civil claims for damages for alleged torture committed outside the forum State. For a similar approach see *Holland v. Lampen-Wolfe* [2001] 1 W.L.R. 157 (H.L.). See also *Waite and Kennedy v. Germany* (1999) 6 B.H.R.R. 499 (immunity of international organisation); *Waite and Kennedy v. Germany*

(1999) 6 B.H.R.R. 499 (immunity granted by German courts to the European Space Agency); *N.C.F. and A.G. v. Italy* (1995) 111 Int.L.R. 153 (European Commission on Human Rights). See also Garnett (2002) 118 L.Q.R. 367; Voyiakis (2003) 52 I.C.L.Q. 297; Lloyd Jones (2003) 52 I.C.L.Q. 463.

NOTE 1. For recent developments in public international law, see International Law Commission, *Report of Working Group on Jurisdictional Immunities of States and their Property*, 1999; United Nations, *Draft Report of the Ad Hoc Committee on Jurisdictional Immunities of States and their Property*, February 2003 (UN General Assembly, A/AC.262/L.4).

NOTE 14. See also *Adams v. DPP* [2001] 2 I.L.R.M. 401 (Sup. Ct.).   **10–004**

NOTE 25. *Schmidt v. Home Secretary* [1995] 1 I.L.R.M. 301 was affirmed   **10–007** [1997] 2 I.R. 121 (Sup. Ct.).

See *Sabah Shipyard (Pakistan) Ltd v. Islamic Republic of Pakistan* [2002]   **10–012** EWCA Civ. 1643, *The Times*, November 27, 2002 (C.A.) (waiver of immunity held to extend to anti-suit injunction restraining proceedings in Pakistan).

Order 11, r. 1(1) is replaced by CPR, r. 6.20.   **10–016**

NOTE 60. Ord. 11, r. 7 is replaced by CPR, r. 6.27.

NOTE 66. Ord. 11, r. 1(1)(*d*)(iv) is replaced by CPR, r. 6.20(5)(d).

NOTE 68. See CPR 6BPD, para. 5.3.   **10–017**

See also *United States v. Friedland* (1999) 182 D.L.R. (4th) 614 (Ont. C.A.).   **10–027**

In *Holland v. Lampen-Wolfe* [2000] 1 W.L.R. 1573 (H.L.) (on which see   **10–030** Tomonori (2001) 64 M.L.R. 472) the plaintiff was an American citizen and a professor at an American university which provided courses at a number of United States military bases in Europe. She taught at a military base in England which was operated and maintained by the United States government as part of its functions as a member of NATO. The defendant, who was also a United States citizen, was employed by the United States government as education services officer at the base, and in that capacity sent a memorandum to the programme director listing complaints about the plaintiff's conduct as an instructor. The plaintiff commenced libel proceedings in England against the education services officer. The question of immunity fell to be decided at common law because, by section 16(2) of the State Immunity Act 1978, section 1(1) did not apply to proceedings relating to "anything done by or in relation to the armed forces of a state." It was held that since the provision within a military base of education and training for military personnel was part of a state's sovereign function of maintaining its armed forces, the publication of the memorandum in the course of the defendant's supervision of such provision was an act within the sovereign authority of the United States so as to attract immunity.

In *Kuwait Airways Corp. v. Iraqi Airways Co. (No. 2)* [2001] 1 W.L.R. 428 (H.L.) Kuwait Airways petitioned the House of Lords for a variation of the order made following its judgment on the ground that the decision giving Iraqi Airways the benefit of state immunity had been procured by false and perjured evidence. The House of Lords held that the allegations should be pursued by a separate claim alleging fraud. In January 2003 David Steel J. held that the result in the earlier decision had been procured by perjured evidence: *Kuwait Airways Corp. v. Iraqi Airways Co.* [2003] 1 Lloyd's Rep. 448.

10–032 Order 11, r. 1(1) is replaced by CPR, r. 6.20.

10E–037 NOTE 25. See *Schreiber v. Canada (Att. Gen.)* (2002) 216 D.L.R. (4th) 513 (Sup. Ct. Can.) on the origin of the exception for death and personal injury.

10–063 Accordingly, members of the administrative and technical staff are not immune from the making of interim care orders in respect of their children, even if the order cannot be enforced effectively: *Re B (A Child) (Care proceedings: Diplomatic Immunity)* [2003] 2 W.L.R. 168 (embassy driver: allegation of abuse of daughter).

10–086 The Commonwealth Secretariat Arbitration Tribunal is not immune from review under the Arbitration Act 1996: *Mohsin v. Commonwealth Secretariat* [2002] EWHC 377 (Comm).

CHAPTER 11

JURISDICTION IN CLAIMS *IN PERSONAM*

1. GENERAL PRINCIPLE

Delete clause (2) of Rule 22 and substitute: **11R–001**

(2) Where a claim relates to a civil or commercial matter within the meaning of (a) Council Regulation (E.C.) 44/2001 on jurisdiction and the recognition and enforcement of judgments in civil and commercial matters ("the Judgments Regulation" or "the Regulation") or (b) the Brussels and the Lugano Conventions on jurisdiction and the enforcement of judgments in civil and commercial matters (respectively "the 1968 Convention" and "the Lugano Convention," and together "the Conventions") the High Court has jurisdiction to entertain a claim *in personam* solely in accordance with the provisions of the Regulation and the Conventions.

The text of the 1968 Convention is in the Civil Jurisdiction and Judgments **11–004**
Act 1982, Sched. 1, as substituted by S.I. 2000 No. 1824.

Generally the rules of the Judgments Regulation and the 1968 and Lugano Conventions apply where the defendant is domiciled in a Regulation State or in a Contracting State, even if the plaintiff is not domiciled in a Regulation State or a Contracting State (as the case may be); and as a general rule the place where the plaintiff is domiciled is not relevant for the purpose of applying the rules on jurisdiction of the Regulation or the Conventions: Case C-412/98 *Universal General Insurance Co. (UGIC) v. Group Josi Reinsurance Co. S.A.* [2000] E.C.R. I–5925; [2001] 1 Q.B. 68.

The 1996 Accession Convention to the 1968 Convention is now in force for **11–006—**
the United Kingdom, and Poland has acceded to the Lugano Convention: **007**
S.I. 2000 No. 1824. But as from March 1, 2002 the practical importance of the 1968 Convention and the Lugano Convention will be much reduced. The Council Regulation on jurisdiction and the recognition and enforcement of judgments in civil and commercial matters (E.C.) 44/2001, *post*, para. 11–011 ("the Judgments Regulation") applies to all the Member States of the European Union, apart from Denmark. The 1968 Convention will be effective only as regards Denmark, which alone among the European Union States did not participate in the Judgments Regulation. The Lugano Convention will be effective only as regards Iceland, Norway, and Switzerland (three EFTA countries) and Poland, which acceded in 2000. Likely future developments include the negotiation of a new Convention with Denmark to bring its situation into line with the Judgments Regulation, and the renegotiation of the Lugano Convention to bring it also into line with the Judgments Regulation. There are pending negotiations for the accession of the Czech Republic and Hungary to the Lugano Convention.

There are also proposals for the conclusion of a new convention with non-Member States to replace the Lugano Convention. The European

Commission has expressed the view that such a Convention would fall within the exclusive competence of the Community.

The negotiations at the Hague Conference for a worldwide jurisdiction and judgments Convention have not met with success, and what is now under consideration is a more limited Convention dealing only with jurisdiction agreements. See generally McClean, in *Reform and Development of Private International Law* (Fawcett ed., 2002), p. 255.

11–011 **Council Regulation on jurisdiction and the recognition and enforcement of judgments in civil and commercial matters (E.C.) 44/2001.** The Regulation, which will be referred to in this Chapter as the "Judgments Regulation" or as "the Regulation," applies to all Member States of the European Union other than Denmark. It will therefore supersede (except as regards Denmark) the 1968 Convention, and also, except as regards Iceland, Norway, Switzerland, and Poland, the Lugano Convention. The Regulation came into force on March 1, 2002. The text is at [2001] O.J. L12, January 16, 2001, and is reproduced in Part I of the appendix to this Supplement. See Beaumont, in *Reform and Development of Private International Law* (Fawcett ed., 2002), p. 9; North (2002) 55 Curr. Legal Prob. 395.

Because the Regulation is directly applicable in the United Kingdom by virtue of section 2(1) of the European Communities Act 1972, there is no implementing United Kingdom legislation, except for matters left to national law, and these are the subject of the Civil Jurisdiction and Judgments Order 2001 (S.I. 2001 No. 3929). S.I. 2001 No. 3929 contains provisions for the purposes of the Regulation which are equivalent to those in the Civil Jurisdiction and Judgments Act 1982 (sections 4 to 8, 10 to 11, 41 and 43 to 45) for the purposes of the 1968 and Lugano Conventions, in particular the provisions for the ascertainment of domicile where it is left to national law: Sched. 1, paras. 9 to 12. Schedule 2 amends Schedule 4 of the 1982 Act by introducing provisions for the allocation of intra-United Kingdom jurisdiction which are modelled on the Regulation, except for Rule 3(a) of Schedule 4, which continues to be based on Article 5(1) of the 1968 Convention, and not on Article 5(1) of the Regulation: below, entry at para. S11–226. The new Schedule 4 is reproduced in Part II of the appendix to this Supplement. S.I. 2001 No. 3929 also makes similar amendments to Schedule 8 to the 1982 Act containing the provisions on jurisdiction in Scotland.

Background. Revision of the 1968 Convention and the Lugano Convention. In December 1997 the Council of the European Union instructed an ad hoc working party comprised of representatives of all Member States and the EFTA State parties to the Lugano Convention, with observers, to work on parallel revision of the 1968 and Lugano Conventions.

The revised E.C. Treaty. The new Article 65 of the E.C. Treaty (introduced by the Treaty of Amsterdam) provides that measures in the field of judicial co-operation in civil matters having cross-border implications, to be taken in accordance with Article 69 and insofar as necessary for the proper functioning of the internal market, shall include (among other things) improving and simplifying the recognition and enforcement of decisions in civil and commercial cases, and promoting the compatibility of the rules applicable in the Member States concerning the conflict of laws and of jurisdiction. By Article 67, during the transitional period of five years following the entry into force of the Treaty of Amsterdam, the Council is to act unanimously on a proposal from the Commission or on the initiative of a Member State and after consulting the European Parliament.

Position of the United Kingdom and Ireland, and of Denmark. By Article 69 the application of Title IV is to be subject to the provisions of the protocol on the position of the United Kingdom and Ireland and to the protocol on the position of Denmark. By Article 3 of the protocol on the position of the United Kingdom and Ireland, the United Kingdom or Ireland have the power to notify the President of the Council in writing, within three months after a proposal or initiative had been presented to the Council pursuant to what became Title IV of the E.C. Treaty, that it wishes to take part in the adoption and application of any such proposed measure. Title IV was not applicable in Denmark.

Commission proposal for Council Regulation. The Treaty of Amsterdam came into effect on May 1, 1999. On July 14, 1999 a proposal was made (COM [1999] 348 final, [1999] O.J. C376) in which the Commission converted its previous proposals for reform of the 1968 Convention into a proposal for a Council regulation on jurisdiction and enforcement of judgments in civil and commercial matters. In March 1999 the United Kingdom and Ireland indicated their intention to adopt Community instruments in relation to judicial co-operation in civil matters. Denmark has not waived its opt-out, and it did not participate in the adoption of the Regulation. Denmark will therefore not be bound by or subject to it. The Regulation was adopted on December 22, 2000.

References to the European Court. By Article 68 of the revised E.C. Treaty, Article 234 (which provides for references to the European Court under the same circumstances as Article 177) is to apply to Title IV of the E.C. Treaty under the following circumstances and conditions: where a question on the interpretation of Title IV or on the validity or interpretation of acts of the institutions of the Community based on that title is raised in a case pending before a court or a tribunal of a Member State against whose decisions there is no judicial remedy under national law, that court or tribunal shall, if it considers that a decision on the question is necessary to enable it to give judgment, request the European Court to give a ruling thereon. The Council, the Commission or a Member State may request the European Court to give a ruling on a question of interpretation of Title IV or of acts of the institutions of the Community based on the Title, but the ruling given by the European Court in response to such a request is not to apply to judgments of courts or tribunals of the Member States which have become *res judicata*. See further, entry at paras. 11–043—11–054.

Summary of the jurisdictional provisions of the Judgments Regulation. The following paragraphs summarise the main provisions of the Judgments Regulation, with particular reference to differences between the Regulation and the 1968 Convention. The Regulation uses the expression "Member State" (which is, however, defined to mean Member States of the European Union with the exception of Denmark) to refer to the States which are subject to it. This Chapter will (like S.I. 2001 No. 3929) use the expression "Regulation State" to reflect the fact that Denmark is not subject to the Regulation.

Scope. The Regulation applies to the same matters as the 1968 Convention, and with the same exceptions. By Article 1(3) the term "Member State" means Member States of the European Union with the exception of Denmark. The basic rules of jurisdiction in Articles 2 to 4 are the same as those in the 1968 Convention. Subject to the provisions of the Regulation, persons domiciled in a Regulation State shall, whatever their nationality, be sued in the courts of that Regulation State: Article 2(1). Persons who are not nationals of the Regulation State in which they are domiciled shall be governed by the rules of jurisdiction applicable to nationals of that State: Article 2(2). Persons domiciled in a Regulation State may be sued in the courts of another Regulation State only by virtue of the rules set out in sections 2 to 7 of Chapter II of the Regulation: Article 3(1). Section 2 deals with special jurisdiction; section 3 relates to jurisdiction in matters relating to insurance; section 4 relates to jurisdiction over consumer contracts; section 5 relates to jurisdiction over individual contracts of employment; section 6 relates to the heads of exclusive jurisdiction; and section 7 relates to prorogation of jurisdiction, namely jurisdiction agreements and submission by conduct.

Basic rules of jurisdiction. The rules of national jurisdiction set out in Annex I (which include the English and Irish rules giving jurisdiction in the case of the temporary presence of the defendant) are not applicable as against persons domiciled in a Regulation State: Article 3(2). If the defendant is not domiciled in a Regulation State, the jurisdiction of the courts of each Regulation State shall, subject to Articles 22 and 23 (exclusive jurisdiction and prorogation of jurisdiction) be determined by the law of that Regulation State: Article 4(1). As against such a defendant, any person domiciled in a Regulation State may, whatever his nationality, avail himself in that State of the rules of jurisdiction there in force, and in particular those specified in Annex I, in the same way as the nationals of that State: Article 4(2).

Domicile of individuals. Article 59 of the Regulation, like Article 52 of the 1968 Convention, provides that, in order to determine whether a party is domiciled in the Regulation State whose courts are seised of a matter, the court shall apply its internal law: Article 59(1). If a party is not domiciled in the Regulation State whose courts are seised of the matter, then, in order to determine whether the party is domiciled in another Regulation State, the court shall apply the law of that other Regulation State: Article 59(2). S.I. 2001 No. 3929, Sched. 1, para. 9, contains provisions for determining the domicile of individuals, which are the same as those in section 41 of the 1982 Act.

Domicile of companies etc. The 1968 Convention provided in Article 53 that for the purposes of the Convention the seat of a company or other legal person or association of natural or legal persons was to be treated as its domicile, and that, in order to determine the seat, the court was to apply its rules of private international law. Article 60 of the Regulation contains new autonomous rules for the domicile of companies, other legal persons or associations of natural or legal persons. Such an entity is domiciled at the place where it has its (a) statutory seat, or (b) central administration or (c) principal place of business. Article 60(2) provides that for the purposes of the United Kingdom and Ireland "statutory seat" means the registered office or, where there is no such office anywhere, the place of incorporation or, where there is no such place anywhere, the place under the law of which the formation took place. But for the purpose of determining the seat of a company etc. for the purposes of the exclusive jurisdiction provision of Article 22(2) (formerly Article 16(2) of the 1968 Convention) the court is to apply its rules of private international law. The relevant rules are in S.I. 2001 No. 3929, Sched. 1, para. 10.

Special jurisdiction. Articles 5 to 7 deal with the matters which were previously in Articles 5 to 6A of the 1968 Convention.

Contract. Article 5(1) is the basic rule for contract claims, although special provision is made in Articles 8 to 21 for insurance, consumer contracts and employment contracts. Article 5(1) of the Regulation is substantially different from Article 5(1) of the 1968 Convention, although the starting point is the same. A person domiciled in a Regulation State may, in another Regulation State, be sued, in matters relating to a contract, in the courts for the place of performance of the obligation in question: Article 5(1)(a). But the special provisions for employment contracts are removed from Article 5(1) and new provision is made for them in section 5 (Articles 18 to 21), and an autonomous definition of the place of performance of the obligation is provided for sale of goods and the provision of services. Article 5(1)(b) provides that for the purposes of Article 5(1), unless otherwise agreed, the place of performance of the obligation in question shall be, in the case of the sale of goods, the place in a Regulation State where, under the contract, the goods were delivered or should have been delivered; and in the case of the provision of services, the place in a Regulation State where, under the contract, the services were provided or should have been provided. In other cases the basic rule in Article 5(1)(a) applies: Article 5(1)(c).

Maintenance. Article 5(2) is the same as the equivalent provision in the 1968 Convention.

Tort. Article 5(3) of the Regulation provides for jurisdiction, not only in the courts for the place where the harmful event occurred, as in the 1968 Convention and the Lugano Convention, but also in the place where the harmful event "may occur". This resolves a doubt in relation to the interpretation of the existing provision, which had never been the subject of a decision by the European Court. In Case C–167/00 *Verein für Konsumenteninformation v. Henkel* [2003] I.L.Pr. 16 the European Court relied on this amendment to decide that this was the proper interpretation of Article 5(3) under the 1968 Convention.

Damages or restitution in criminal proceedings. Article 5(4) is the same as the 1968 Convention.

Branch, agency or other establishment. Article 5(5) is in the same terms as the 1968 Convention and confers jurisdiction, as regards a dispute arising out of the operations of a branch, agency or other establishment, in the courts for the place in which the branch, agency or other establishment is situated.

Trusts. Article 5(6) of the Regulation is the same as the corresponding provision in the 1968 Convention, as is Article 60(3) on the domicile of trusts.

Salvage remuneration. Article 5(7) is the same as the 1968 Convention.

Additional parties. Article 6(1) of the Regulation provides, as did the 1968 Convention, that a person domiciled in a Regulation State may also be sued where he is one of a number of defendants, in the courts for the place where any one of them is domiciled. Article 6(1) of the Regulation adds the words "provided the claims are so closely connected that it is expedient to hear and determine them together to avoid the risk of irreconcilable judgments resulting from separate proceedings". This codifies the effect of the decision in Case 189/87 *Kalfelis v. Schröder* [1988] E.C.R. 5565. The other provisions of Article 6 of the Regulation are the same as in the 1968 Convention.

Limitation of liability from the use or operation of a ship. Article 7 of the Regulation is the same as Article 6A of the 1968 Convention.

Insurance. The changes in this section are these. First, an insurer domiciled in a Regulation State may be sued in another Regulation State, not only (as in the 1968 Convention) where the policyholder is domiciled, but also, in the case of actions brought by the policyholder, the insured or a beneficiary, in the courts where the plaintiff is domiciled: Article 9(1)(b). Secondly, Article 13(5) and Article 14 of the Regulation allow the jurisdiction provisions to be excluded by agreement in the case, not only of the particular risks referred to in Article 12a of the 1968 Convention, but also in respect of all "large risks" as defined in Council Directive 73/239 as amended by Council Directives 88/357 and 90/618, and as they may be amended in the future.

Consumer contracts. There are two main changes to the consumer contract provisions. First, a new Article 15(1)(c) provides that the consumer contracts jurisdiction provisions apply where "the contract has been concluded with a person who pursues commercial or professional activities in the Regulation State of the consumer's domicile or, by any means, directs such activities to that State or to several States including that Regulation State, and the contract falls within the scope of such activities". Article 15(1)(c) is intended to apply to contracts concluded as a result of marketing through e-commerce, via an interactive website accessible in the domicile of the consumer. The condition in the former Article 13 that the consumer must have taken the necessary steps in his State has been removed, with the consequence that Article 15 applies to contracts concluded in a State other than the domicile of the consumer. Secondly, Article 15(3) provides that the section on jurisdiction over consumer contracts is not to apply "to a contract of transport other than a contract which, for an inclusive price, provides for a combination of travel and accommodation". The reference to travel packages is new.

Employment contracts. A new section 5 of Chapter II of the Regulation (Articles 18 to 21) deals with jurisdiction over individual contracts of employment. Where an employee enters into an individual contract of employment with an employer who is not domiciled in a Regulation State but has a branch, agency or other establishment in one of the Regulation States, the employer shall, in disputes arising out of the operations of the branch, agency or other establishment, be deemed to be domiciled in that Regulation State: Article 18(2).

The bases of jurisdiction differ depending on whether the employer is the defendant or the plaintiff. Where the employer is a potential defendant, and is domiciled in a Regulation State, he may be sued in the courts of the Regulation State where he is domiciled, or in another Regulation State (a) in the courts for the place where the employee habitually carries out his work or in the courts for the last place where he did so; or (b) if the employee does not or did not habitually carry out his work in any one country, in the courts for the place where the business which engaged the employee is or was situated: Article 19.

Where the employer is the plaintiff, he may bring proceedings only in the courts of the Regulation State in which the employee is domiciled, except that the provisions of section 5 do not affect the rights of the employer to bring a counterclaim in the court in which, in accordance with this section, the original claim is pending: Article 20.

Jurisdiction agreements may depart from the jurisdictional rules of section 5 but only if the agreement on jurisdiction (a) is entered into after the dispute has arisen or (b) allows the employee to bring proceedings in courts other than those indicated in the section: Article 21.

Exclusive jurisdiction. The provisions formerly in Article 16 of the 1968 Convention are, with some minor modifications, now in Article 22 of the Regulation.

Immovable property. The effect of Article 22(1) is that the courts of the Regulation State in which the property is situated have exclusive jurisdiction in proceedings which have as their object rights *in rem* in immovable property or tenancies of immovable property. The exception relating to short tenancies is an amalgam of the differing provisions in the 1968 Convention and the Lugano Convention. Article 22(1) provides that in proceedings which have as their object tenancies of immovable property concluded for temporary private use for a maximum period of six consecutive months, the courts of the Regulation State in which the defendant is domiciled shall also have jurisdiction, provided that the tenant is a natural person and that the landlord and the tenant are domiciled in the same Regulation State. The proviso to Article 16(1) of the 1968 Convention is that both the landlord and the tenant are natural persons and are domiciled in the same Contracting State. The proviso in the Lugano Convention is that the tenant is a natural person and that neither party is domiciled in the Contracting State in which the property is situated.

Companies, etc. The exclusive jurisdiction provision in Article 22(2) relating to the validity of the constitution, etc. of companies has been amended to make it clear that where decisions of organs of companies, etc. are concerned in proceedings, the exclusive jurisdiction provisions apply only if their validity is in issue. This confirms the view which was taken in *Newtherapeutics Limited v. Katz* [1991] Ch. 226. Article 22(2) also provides (as did Article 16(2) of the 1968 Convention) that in order to determine the seat of the company, etc. for the purposes of the exclusive jurisdiction rules the court shall employ its rules of private international law. Accordingly the general rule for determining the domicile of a legal person in Article 60 does not apply in this context. The relevant rules are in S.I. 2001 No. 3929, Sched. 1, para. 10 and, for allocation within the United Kingdom, 1982 Act, s. 43, as amended by S.I. 2001 No. 3929, Sched. 2, para. 16(a).

Prorogation of jurisdiction. Article 23 deals with jurisdiction agreements, and is substantially the same as Article 17 of the 1968 Convention, except that (a) the new version recognises in Article 23(1) the effectiveness of "non-exclusive" jurisdiction agreements: see entry at para. 12–106; (b) it confirms in Article 23(2) that any communication by electronic means which provides a durable record of the agreement shall be equivalent to "writing". Article 24, dealing with non-contractual submission, is the same as Article 18 of the 1968 Convention.

Examination of jurisdiction and service. Article 25 of the Regulation is the same as Article 19 of the 1968 Convention: a court of a Regulation State which is seised of a claim which is principally concerned with a matter over which the courts of another Regulation State have exclusive jurisdiction by virtue of Article 22, shall declare of its own motion that it has no jurisdiction. On service, Article 20(3) of the 1968 Convention is replaced by Article 26(3) and (4) of the Regulation. Article 19 of Council Regulation 1348/2000 is to apply or, where it is not applicable, Article 15 of the Hague Convention of November 15, 1965 on the service abroad of judicial and extra-judicial documents in civil or commercial matters.

Lis pendens. The *lis pendens* provisions have been altered in two ways. Article 28(1) provides that where related actions are pending in the courts of different Regulation States, any court other than the court first seised may stay its proceedings. The 1968 Convention had provided that where related actions were "brought" in the courts of different Contracting States, any court other than the court first seised might (while the actions were pending at first instance) stay its proceedings. Article 28(2) has been redrafted, as compared with Article 22(2) of the 1968 Convention, so as to clarify that the law relevant to consolidation is the law of the court first seised. The most significant change to the *lis pendens* provisions is the new Article 30, which contains a definition of seisin. It provides that a court is deemed to be seised: (1) at the time when the document instituting the proceedings or an equivalent document is lodged with the court, provided that the plaintiff has not subsequently failed to take the steps he was required to take to have service effected on the defendant; or (2) if the document has to be served before being lodged with the court, at the time when it is received by the authority responsible for service, provided that the plaintiff has not subsequently failed to take the steps he was required to take to have the document lodged with the court. See, *infra*, entry at para. 12–050.

Provisional and protective measures. Article 31 (like Article 24 of the 1968 Convention) provides that application may be made to the courts of a Regulation State for such provisional, including protective, measures as may be available under the law of that State even if, under the Regulation, the courts of another Regulation State have jurisdiction as to the substance of the matter.

Transitional provisions. The Regulation applies only to legal proceedings instituted after its entry into force on March 1, 2002: Article 66(1). But a judgment of a Regulation State in proceedings commenced before that date is to be recognised and enforced in accordance with Chapter III of the Regulation if (a) the proceedings in that State were instituted after the entry into force of the 1968 Convention or the Lugano Convention in that State and the Regulation State in which it is to be recognised or enforced; or (b) in all other cases, if jurisdiction was founded upon rules which accorded with those in the Regulation or in a Convention in force between those States when the proceedings were commenced: Article 66(2).

Relationship between the Regulation and the 1968 and Lugano Conventions. The Regulation applies to defendants domiciled in the territory of a Member State (other than Denmark) or where Articles 22 or 23 confer jurisdiction on the courts of such a State. The 1968 Convention applies to defendants domiciled in Denmark or where Articles 16 or 17 of the 1968 Convention confer jurisdiction on the courts of Denmark. The Lugano Convention applies to defendants domiciled in the Lugano Convention countries, or where Articles 16 or 17 of the Lugano Convention confer jurisdiction on their courts. See Article 68 of the Regulation, Article 54B of the Lugano Convention, and 1982 Act, section 1(4), inserted by S.I. 2001 No. 3929, Sched. 2, para. 1.

Text at note 22. A reference on this question has been made in *Owusu v. Jackson* [2002] EWCA Civ. 877; [2002] I.L.Pr.813: Case C–281/02 (pending). A reference has also been made in *American Motorists Insurance Co. v. Cellstar Corp.* [2003] EWCA Civ. 206, [2003] I.L.Pr. 370 with the intention that both references be heard together. In a case on the Lugano Convention, the Court of Appeal has given permission to appeal to the House of Lords on the same point: *Anton Durbeck GmbH v. Den Norske Bank ASA* [2003] EWCA Civ. 147; [2003] 2 W.L.R. 1296 (C.A.). **11–012**

Article 1 of the Judgments Regulation is in the same terms as Article 1 of the Conventions. **11–013– 30**

In *R. v. Harrow Crown Court, ex p. UNIC Centre S.A.R.L.* [2000] 1 W.L.R. 2112 it was held that proceedings against a French company under the Trade Marks Act 1994 by the trading standards service for forfeiture of imported clothes falsely labelled as Levi's jeans were in a civil matter and were not criminal or administrative. The local authority did not have a duty to bring forfeiture proceedings, nor did it have any exclusive status in bringing such proceedings. The relief it obtained enured to the benefit of the private interests of individuals. Accordingly, the proceedings were predominantly concerned with private interests. Consequently the 1968 Convention applied. **11–014**

NOTE 27. See also Case C–167/00 *Verein für Konsumenteninformation v. Henkel* [2003] I.L.Pr. 16; Case C–334/00 *Fonderie Officine Meccaniche SpA v. HWS GmbH*, September 17, 2002.

NOTE 28. See also Case C–167/00 *Verein für Konsumenteninformation v. Henkel* [2003] I.L.Pr. 16; Case C–271/00 *Gemeente Steenbergen v. Baten* [2003] I.L.Pr. 176 (action by public authority against ex-husband for recovery of sums paid as social assistance to divorced wife and child a civil matter if basis of action is governed by rules of ordinary law with regard to maintenance obligation).

11–015 See *QRS 1 ApS v. Frandsen* [1999] 1 W.L.R. 2169 (C.A.), *supra*, para. 5–023: the rule that English courts will not directly or indirectly enforce the revenue laws of another country is not overridden by the 1968 Convention.

11–021 NOTE 41. See also *UBS A.G. v. Omni Holding A.G.* [2000] 1 W.L.R. 916.

11–022 The concept of social security is to be determined by Community law, and encompasses the matters covered by Council Regulation 1408/71: Case C–271/00 *Gemeente Steenbergen v. Baten* [2003] I.L.Pr. 176, adopting the Jenard Report, pp. 1, 12 and 13, and the Schlosser Report, para. 60, according to which the exclusion of social security concerns only disputes arising out of the relationship between the administration and employers and employees, and not cases where the administration exercises a direct right of action against a third party liable for injury or is subrogated to the rights of a victim insured by it, because it is then acting under the rules of the ordinary law.

11–027 Add: van Haersolte-van Hof (2001) J. Int. Arb. 27; Beraudo, *ibid.* 13.

11–028 NOTE 55. See also *Vale do Rio Doce Navegaçao SA v. Shanghai Bao Steel Ocean Shipping Co. Ltd.* [2000] C.L.C. 1200 (claim for declaration against brokers that their principals are bound by arbitration agreement not within arbitration exception).

11–029 NOTE 58. See also *The Ivan Zagubanski* [2002] 1 Lloyd's Rep. 106, entry at para. 12–131, *infra*.

11–031 The Judgments Regulation applies to defendants domiciled in the territory of a Member State (other than Denmark) or where Articles 22 or 23 confer jurisdiction on the courts of such a State. The 1968 Convention applies to defendants domiciled in Denmark or where Articles 16 or 17 of the 1968 Convention confer jurisdiction on the courts of Denmark. The Lugano Convention applies to defendants domiciled in the Lugano Convention countries, or where Articles 16 or 17 of the Lugano Convention confer jurisdiction on their courts. See Article 68 of the Regulation, Article 54B of the Lugano Convention, and 1982 Act, section 1(4), inserted by S.I. 2001 No. 3929, Sched. 2, para. 1.

11–033 See Articles 69 and 70 of the Judgments Regulation for the equivalent provisions.

11–034 See Article 71 of the Judgments Regulation for the equivalent provision.

11–036 Line 5. See also Article 71(2) of the Judgments Regulation.

11–037 The same considerations apply to the Judgments Regulation.

NOTE 76. See also *Andrea Merzario Ltd. v. Internationale Spedition Leitner Gesellschaft GmbH* [2001] EWCA Civ. 61; [2001] 1 Lloyd's Rep. 490. (C.A.), disapproving *Frans Maas Logistics (U.K.) Ltd. v. CDR Trucking B.V.* [1999] 2 Lloyd's Rep. 179.

11–038 The Civil Jurisdiction and Judgments Act 1982 is amended by S.I. 2001 No. 3929, Sched. 2.

Note 84. On the courts which might have made references under the 1968   **11–041**
Convention see Case C–69/02 *Reichling v. Wampach* [2002] I.L.Pr. 805.

All language versions of the Judgments Regulation are equally authentic.   **11–042**

References to the European Court on the interpretation of the Judgments   **11–043—**
Regulation. By Article 68 of the revised E.C. Treaty, Article 234 (which **054**
provides for references to the European Court under the same circumstances as Article 177) is to apply to Title IV of the E.C. Treaty under the
following circumstances and conditions: where a question on the interpretation of Title IV or on the validity or interpretation of acts of the institutions
of the Community based on that title is raised in a case pending before a
court or a tribunal of a Member State against whose decisions there is no
judicial remedy under national law, that court or tribunal shall, if it
considers that a decision on the question is necessary to enable it to give
judgment, request the Court of Justice to give a ruling thereon. This is more
restrictive than the 1971 Protocol to the 1968 Convention, which allows a
court exercising an appellate function to make a reference even if it is not a
court from whose decisions there is no remedy under national law. The
practical effect in the United Kingdom will be that only the House of Lords
will be able to make a reference: *cf. Chiron Corp. v. Murex Diagnostics*
[1995] All E.R. (E.C.) 88. The Council, the Commission or a Member State
may request the European Court to give a ruling on a question of
interpretation of Title IV or of acts of the institutions of the Community
based on the title, but the ruling given by the European Court in response
to such a request shall not apply to judgments of courts or tribunals of the
Member States which have become *res judicata*.

On the practice see Case C–420/97 *Leathertex Divisione Sintetici SpA v.*   **11–045**
Bodetex BVBA [1999] E.C.R. I–6747.

The equivalents of Articles 16, 17, 24, 30 and 38 of the Conventions are   **11–050**
Articles 22, 23, 31, 37 and 46 of the Judgments Regulation.

Note 95. Add: Case–167/00 *Verein für Konsumenteninformation v. Henkel*
[2003] I.L.Pr. 16; Case C–271/00 *Gemeente Steenbergen v. Baten* [2003]
I.L.Pr. 176.

Notes 96 and 97. Add: Case C–334/00 *Fonderie Officine Meccaniche SpA v.*
HWS GmbH, September 17, 2002; Case C–167/00 *Verein für Konsumen-*
teninformation v. Henkel [2003] I.L.Pr.16.

Note 99. Add: Case C–96/00 *Gabriel v. Schlank & Schick GmbH* [2002]
I.L.Pr. 642.

The equivalents of Articles 16 and 17 of the Conventions are Articles 22   **11–051**
and 23 of the Judgments Regulation.

Note 14. Add: Case C–8/98 *Dansommer A/S v. Götz* [2000] E.C.R. I–393.

See generally Tebbens (2001) 3 Yb. Private Int. L. 1.   **11–052**

Note 16. *Agnew v. Länsförsäkringsbolagens A.B.* [1997] 4 All E.R. 937
(C.A.) was affirmed on other aspects [2001] 1 A.C. 223.

11–055 NOTE 19. As from March 28, 2002 the period is 14 days (28 days in the Commercial Court) after filing an acknowledgment of service: CPR, rr. 11(4) and 58.7. After first sentence, add: See *USF Ltd. v. Aqua Technology Hanson NV/SA* [2001] 1 All E.R. (Comm.) 856. See also *Bank of Credit and Commerce International S.A. v. Al-Kaylani* [1999] I.L.Pr. 278 for disclosure orders on applications to challenge jurisdiction.

11–057 Order 11, r. 1(1) is replaced by CPR, r. 6.20.

Text at note 25, and note 26. The equivalents of Articles 19 and 20 of the Conventions are Articles 25 and 26 of the Judgments Regulation.

NOTE 24. See now CPR, r. 6.21(2A).

NOTE 28. CPR, r. 12.10(b) is amended by S.I. 2001 No. 4015 to take account of the Judgments Regulation.

2. DOMICILE

11R–059 Rule 23(1). For the purposes of the Judgments Regulation, there are identical provisions for determining the domicile of an individual: S.I. 2001 No. 3929, Sched. 1, para. 9. See Judgments Regulation, Art. 59.

As from March 1, 2002, clause (2) of Rule 23 applies only to jurisdiction under the 1968 and Lugano Conventions. From that date add a new clause (3):

(3) For the purposes of (a) jurisdiction under Rule 27 (CPR, r. 6.20) (b) jurisdiction under Schedule 4 to the Civil Jurisdiction and Judgments Act 1982 and (c) jurisdiction under the Judgments Regulation, a company or other legal person or association of natural or legal persons is domiciled at the place where it has its (a) statutory seat, or (b) central administration, or (c) principal place of business: Judgments Regulation, Article 60(1).
(4) In this Rule "statutory seat" means the registered office or, where there is no such office anywhere, the place under the law of which the formation took place: Article 60(2).

NOTE 29. For Judgments Regulation, see S.I. 2001 No. 3929, Sched. 1, para. 9(2), (3).

NOTE 30. See *ibid.* para. 9(4).

NOTE 32. Judgments Regulation, Art. 59(2).

NOTE 33. For Judgments Regulation, see S.I. 2001 No. 3929, Sched. 1, para. 9(7).

NOTE 34. See *ibid.* para. 11.

NOTE 36. See *ibid.* para. 10.

11–060 The 1968 Convention provides in Article 53 that for the purposes of the 1968 Convention the seat of a company or other legal person or association of natural or legal persons is to be treated as its domicile, and that, in order to determine the seat, the court is to apply its rules of private international law. Article 60 of the Judgments Regulation contains the new autonomous rules for the domicile of companies, other legal persons or associations of natural or legal persons. Such an entity is domiciled at the place where it has its (a) statutory seat, or (b) central administration or (c) principal place of business. Article 60(2) provides that for the purposes of the United Kingdom and Ireland "statutory seat" means the registered office or, where there is no such office anywhere, the place of incorporation or, where there is no such place anywhere, the place under the law of which the formation took place.

The new definition of domicile of companies, etc. applies to CPR, r. 6.20(1) and to 1982 Act, Sched. 4, Rule 1 (substituted by S.I. 2001 No. 3929, Sched. 2): see CPR, r. 6.18(g), as amended by S.I. 2001 No. 4015; S.I. 2001 No. 3929, Sched. 1, paras. 9 to 12.

But in order to determine the seat of a company, etc. for the purposes of the exclusive jurisdiction provision of Article 22(2) (formerly Article 16(2) of the 1968 Convention) the court is to apply its rules of private international law. For the seat of a company, legal person or association for the purposes of Article 22(2), S.I. 2001 No. 3929, para. 10, provides that it has its seat in the United Kingdom if it was incorporated or formed under the law of a part of the United Kingdom, or its central management and control is exercised in the United Kingdom; it has its seat in a Regulation State other than the United Kingdom if it was incorporated or formed under the law of that State; it is not to be regarded as having its seat in a Regulation State other than the United Kingdom if it has its seat in the United Kingdom, or if it is shown that the courts of that other State would not regard it for the purposes of Article 22(2) as having its seat there.

NOTE 40. For Judgments Regulation see Arts. 2(1), 3, 4(2), 5, 6, 9(1), 12, 13(3), 15(1), 16(1), 17, 23(1), 26(1), 43(5).

NOTE 42. For Judgments Regulation, see Arts. 4(1), 9(2), 13(4), 23(3).

NOTE 43. For Judgments Regulation, see Art. 51.

NOTE 44. For Judgments Regulation, see Arts. 5(2), 6(1), 39(2).

NOTE 47. See now CPR, r. 6.18(g), as amended by S.I. 2001 No. 4015, which applies to domicile under the Judgments Regulation and the 1968 and Lugano Conventions.

Article 59 of the Judgments Regulation is the same as Article 52 of the **11–061** 1968 and Lugano Conventions.

The definition of the domicile of an individual where the Judgments **11–062** Regulation applies is the same: S.I. 2001 No. 3929, Sched. 1, para. 9.

NOTE 49. Judgments Regulation, Art. 59(1). **11–063**

NOTE 50. S.I. 2001 No. 3929, Sched. 1, para. 9(2).

NOTE 51. *ibid.* para. 9(6). In *Canada Trust Co. v. Stolzenberg (No. 2)* [2002] A.C. 1 the House of Lords confirmed that the critical date for the determination of domicile is the date of the issue of proceedings. Consequently, where proceedings were issued against a defendant domiciled in England at the date of their issue, other defendants outside the jurisdiction could be added under Article 6 of the Conventions even if by the time the process was served on the additional defendants that person was no longer domiciled in England.

11–064 Note 53. Judgments Regulation, Art. 59(2).

11–065 Note 55. SI. 2001 No. 3929, Sched. 1, para. 9(4).

Note 56. *ibid.* para. 9(3).

Note 57. *ibid.* para. 9(5).

11–066 The same considerations apply where the Judgments Regulation is applicable. Article 59(2) is the same as Article 52(2) of the 1968 and Lugano Conventions. Order 11, r. 1(1)(d) has been replaced by CPR, r. 6.20(5).

11–067— For the position under the Judgments Regulation see Article 60 and the
072 new clause (3) of the Rule, *supra*.

11–067 On central management and control see *Latchin v. General Mediterranean Holdings SA* [2002] C.L.C. 330.

Note 63. See *Domansa v. Derrin Shipping and Trading Co. Inc.* [2001] 2 Lloyd's Rep. 362.

11–072 In *Phillips v. Symes* [2002] 1 W.L.R. 853 it was held that the expression "associations of natural or legal persons" in Article 16(2) included English partnerships.

11–073 The equivalent provisions for the purposes of the Judgments Regulation are Articles 9(2) and 15(2) and S.I. 2001 No. 3929, Sched. 1, para. 11, which also applies to Article 18(2) (employers).

11–074 See Judgments Regulation, Article 60(3): S.I. 2001 No. 3929, Sched. 1, para. 12.

11–075 Illustrations 6, 7 and 8. The position is the same under the Judgements Regulation, except that the reference is now to central administration rather than central management and control: see Article 60(1).

Note 82. See Judgments Regulation, Art. 60(1).

Note 83. *ibid.*

Note 84. *ibid.*

Note 85. S.I. 2001 No. 3929, Sched. 1, para. 11(2)(a).

3. RULES RELATING TO JURISDICTION

A. Where the Judgments Regulation, the 1968 Convention and the Lugano Convention do not apply or where the defendant is not domiciled in the United Kingdom or any part thereof or in any other State to which the Judgments Regulation applies or which is party to the 1968 Convention or the Lugano Convention

11R–076 For Rule 24 substitute:

Rule 24—The High Court has jurisdiction, subject to Rules 29 and 30 (exclusive jurisdiction under the Judgments Regulation and the 1968 and

Lugano Conventions) and Rules 53 and 54 (international conventions), to entertain a claim *in personam* against a defendant (other than a person domiciled or deemed to be domiciled in another Judgments Regulation State or in another State party to the 1968 and Lugano Conventions or in Scotland or Northern Ireland) who is present in England and duly served there with process.

NOTE 87. Order 11, r. 1(1) is replaced by CPR, r. 6.20.

This Rule applies to Regulation States in the same way as the 1968 and **11–077** Lugano Conventions. Article 3(2) and Annex 1 of the Regulation are to the same effect as Article 3(2) of the Conventions.

It has been held that it remains a fundamental principle of English procedure and jurisdiction that a defendant may be served with originating process within the jurisdiction only if he is present in the jurisdiction at the time of service, or deemed service: *Chellaram v. Chellaram (No. 2)* [2002] EWHC 632 (Ch); [2002] 3 All E.R. 17.

Article 4 of the Judgments Regulation is in material respects the same as **11–078** Article 4 of the 1968 and Lugano Conventions.

Article 4 of the Judgments Regulation is subject not only to Article 22 **11–079** (which, subject to some minor modifications, is the same as Article 16 of the 1968 and Lugano Conventions), but also to Article 23, the modified equivalent of Article 17 on jurisdiction agreements.

NOTE 93. See now Article 24 of the Judgments Regulation.

For Judgments Regulation see Article 23, which contains a modified **11–080** version of Article 17 of the 1968 Convention. Article 23 provides in particular for the effectiveness of non-exclusive jurisdiction agreements. See entry at para. 12–106.

See entry at para. 11R–076. **11–083**

NOTE 6. The deemed day of service is not rebuttable by evidence of prior **11–084** receipt: *Godwin v. Swindon B.C.* [2001] EWCA Civ. 1478; [2002] 1 W.L.R. 997 (C.A.); *Anderton v. Clwyd C.C.* [2002] EWCA Civ. 933; [2002] 1 W.L.R. 3174 (C.A.).

See entry at para. 11R–076. See generally on service by an alternative **11–086** method in international cases *Knauf UK GmbH v. British Gypsum Ltd.* [2001] EWCA Civ. 1570; [2002] 1 W.L.R. 907 (C.A.).

See entry at para. 11R–076. **11–090**

Order 11, r. 1(1)(*c*) is replaced by CPR, r. 6.20(3). On the method of service **11–092** see CPR, r. 6.4(5).

See entry at para. 11R–076. **11–093**

NOTE 28. A modified version of the Judgments Regulation has been **11–095** substituted by S.I. 2001 No. 3929, Sched. 2, para. 4.

11–096 See now *Saab v. Saudi American Bank* [1999] 1 W.L.R. 1861 (C.A.): for process to be validly served under Companies Act 1985, s. 694A(2), on an oversea company at its London branch it was not necessary that the action should be wholly or even substantially in respect of the business of the London branch, unless the connection between the process and the carrying on of the business of the branch was of so little significance that it should be disregarded.

11–098 See *Sea Assets Ltd. v. PT Garuda Indonesia* [2000] 4 All E.R. 371: the method of service under Companies Act 1985, s. 694A is not exclusive and the provision of an alternative method under CPR Part 6 was not *ultra vires*.

11–099 In line 2, after "domiciled" add: "in a Regulation State or". In line 4, after "outside" add: "the Judgments Regulation or".

11–101 NOTE 51. See also *Rakusens Ltd. v. Baser Ambalaj Plastik Sanayi Ticaret AS* [2001] EWCA Civ. 1820; [2002] 1 B.C.L.C. 104 (C.A.) (not a place of business because agent had no authority to conclude contracts).

11–105 Illustration 11. Poland is now a party to the Lugano Convention.

11–108 See entry at para. 11R–076.

NOTE 67. Add: *Glencore International AG v. Exter Shipping Ltd.* [2002] EWCA Civ. 528; [2002] 2 All E.R. (Comm.) 1 (C.A.)

11–109 NOTE 69. See also Judgments Regulation, Art. 6(3).

11–110 Text at note 74. As from March 28, 2002 the period is 14 days after filing an acknowledgment of service: CPR, r. 11(4), as amended by S.I. 2001 No. 4015. On the effect of the time limit *cf. Midland Resources Ltd v. Gonvarri Industrial SA* [2002] I.L.Pr. 74 and *Monrose Investments Ltd. v. Orion Nominees Frichmond Corporate Service Ltd* [2002] I.L.Pr. 267 (decided under the previous version of the rule).

NOTE 75. The reference to *ISC Technologies Inc. v. Guerin*, 1990, unreported, should be to *ISC Technologies Inc. v. Radcliffe*, December 7, 1990, unreported.

11–114 The position is the same under the Judgments Regulation, Article 22 of which is equivalent to Article 16 of the 1968 and Lugano Conventions.

NOTE 96. See entry at para. 11–114.

11–117—
118 Order 11, r. 1(2)(*b*) is replaced by CPR, r. 6.19(2). Rule 26 applies where an enactment indicates that it contemplates proceedings against persons who are not within the jurisdiction or where the wrongful act, neglect or default giving rise to the claim did not take place within the jurisdiction: *Re Harrods (Buenos Aires) Ltd. (No. 2)* [1992] Ch. 72, 116 (C.A.); *Re Banco Nacional de Cuba* [2001] 1 W.L.R. 2039 (not following *Jyske Bank (Gibraltar) Ltd. v. Spjeldnaes* [1999] 2 B.C.L.C. 101).

11–117 NOTE 9. See now Judgments Regulation, Art. 71.

Substitute the following for Rules 27 to 30:

RULE 27—The High Court has jurisdiction to entertain a claim *in personam* **S11R–120** **against a defendant (other than a person domiciled or deemed to be domiciled in another State to which the Judgments Regulation applies or in another State party to the 1968 Convention or the Lugano Convention[1] or in Scotland or Northern Ireland) who is not in England at the time for the service of process whenever it assumes jurisdiction in any of the cases mentioned in this Rule.[2]**

COMMENT

If the defendant is not in England and served there with process and does **S11–121** not submit to the jurisdiction, the court has no jurisdiction at common law to entertain a claim *in personam* against him. But this common law principle was modified, first by sections 18 and 19 of the Common Law Procedure Act 1852, and later by the Rules of the Supreme Court, Order 11. Rule 6.20, which was added to the new Civil Procedure Rules in 2000, replaces R.S.C. Order 11, r. 1. Under CPR, r. 6.20 the court has jurisdiction in a number of cases, corresponding to the 20 clauses of this Rule, a discretionary power to permit service of process[3] on a defendant irrespective of nationality who is out of England. Before these various cases are stated and discussed, the following general points should be noted.

(1) There is an essential difference between the jurisdiction exercised by **S11–122** the court when the defendant is in England (Rule 24) or when he submits to the jurisdiction (Rule 25) and its jurisdiction when the action comes under any of the clauses of Rule 27. Under Rules 24 and 25, the jurisdiction

---

[1] For the relevant States see *ante* entry at paras. 11–006 *et seq*. Rule 27 has no application also, even as respects persons not domiciled in a Regulation State or in a Contracting State, if Rules 28(15) and 29(1) (immovable property) or Rules 28(20) and 30 (jurisdiction agreements) apply.

[2] CPR, r. 6.20; Collins, *Essays*, p. 226. On service of orders made in proceedings see CPR, r. 6.30(2) and *Union Bank of Finland v. Lelakis* [1997] 1 W.L.R. 590 (C.A.).

[3] Substituted service (now called service by an alternative method) may be allowed at the discretion of the court either within or without England: CPR, r. 6.8; Practice Direction – Service, para. 9; see *Ford v. Shepherd* (1885) 34 W.R. 63; *Western, etc., Building Society v. Rucklidge* [1905] 2 Ch. 472. If the defendant is outside England, an order for substituted service in England cannot be obtained unless permission to serve proceedings out of the jurisdiction has been obtained: *Cadogan Properties Ltd. v. Mount Eden Land Ltd.* [2000] I.L.Pr. 722 (C.A.). In *The Vrontados* [1982] 2 Lloyd's Rep. 241 (C.A.) it was held by a majority (Lord Denning M.R. dissenting) that service could be effected on directors of a company who were present in England, without an order for substituted service, of a writ for service out of the jurisdiction if the law of the foreign country provided that service on a company was effective if its directors were served: *sed quaere*. See also *The Handgate* [1987] 1 Lloyd's Rep. 142 (C.A.); *The Sky One* [1988] 1 Lloyd's Rep. 238. The mode of service is regulated by CPR, rr. 6.24–6.26; there are numerous conventions, of which the most important is the Hague Convention of 1964, Cmnd. 2613. See *Civil Procedure*, 2003, notes to CPR, r. 6.24. For the European Union Convention see paras. 8–043 *et seq*. Service must be effected exactly where authorised; thus service in Hong Kong in lieu of Japan is a nullity; *Bonnell v. Preston* (1908) 24 T.L.R. 756 (C.A.). Process may not be served abroad in a manner which is contrary to the law of the foreign country: CPR, r. 6.24(2), but the court retains a discretion under CPR, r. 3.10 to waive the irregularity: *The Sky One* [1988] 1 Lloyd's Rep. 238; *The Anna* [1994] 2 Lloyd's Rep. 379; *National Commercial Bank v. Hague* [1994] C.L.C. 230 (C.A.); contrast *The Goldean Mariner* [1989] 2 Lloyd's Rep. 390, 398, affd. [1990] 2 Lloyd's Rep. 215 (C.A.): *The Oinoussin Pride* [1991] 1 Lloyd's Rep. 126. On the effect of failure to obtain permission in an appropriate case see *Leal v. Dunlop Bio-Processes Ltd* [1984] 1 W.L.R. 874 (C.A.); *Atco Industries (Aust.) Pty. Ltd. v. Ancla Maruima S.A.* (1984) 35 S.A.S.R. 408.

of the court is not discretionary[4]; the claimant has a right to demand that it shall be exercised, though the court has a discretion to stay the action to prevent injustice.[5] But under Rule 27, the jurisdiction of the court is essentially discretionary, for the court may, if it sees fit, decline to allow the service of process, and thus decline to exercise its jurisdiction.

S11–123   (2) Four cardinal points have been emphasised in the decided cases.[6] First, the court ought to be cautious in allowing process to be served on a foreigner out of England. This has frequently been said to be because service out of the jurisdiction is an interference with the sovereignty of other countries,[7] although today all countries exercise a degree of jurisdiction over persons abroad. Secondly, if there is any doubt in the construction of any of the heads of CPR, r. 6.20, that doubt ought to be resolved in favour of the defendant. Thirdly, since the application for permission is made without notice to the defendant, a full and fair disclosure of all relevant facts ought to be made.[8] Fourthly, the court will refuse permission if the case is within the letter but outside the spirit of the Rule.[9]

S11–124   (3) In exercising its jurisdiction under Rule 27 the court will consider, *inter alia*, whether England is the *forum conveniens*. This principle has been established since the nineteenth century,[10] and finds its modern expression in the speeches of Lord Wilberforce in *Amin Rasheed Shipping Corp. v. Kuwait Insurance Co.*[11] and of Lord Goff of Chieveley in *Spiliada Maritime*

---

[4] But it is discretionary in cases to which CPR, r. 15, applies: see para. 11–112.

[5] See Rule 31. Although a stay of proceedings is the normal remedy, the court has power to strike out or dismiss the action in appropriate circumstances: *Haji-Ioannou v. Frangos* [1999] 2 Lloyd's Rep. 337 (C.A.).

[6] See, especially for the first three points, *Société Générale de Paris v. Dreyfus Bros.* (1885) 29 Ch.D. 239, 242–243; (1887) 37 Ch.D. 215, 224, 225 (C.A.); *The Hagen* [1908] P. 189, 201 (C.A.); *Re Schintz* [1926] Ch. 710, 716–717 (C.A.).

[7] See, *e.g. George Monro Ltd. v. American Cyanamid Corporation* [1944] K.B. 432, 437 (C.A.); *The Brabo* [1949] A.C. 326, 357; *Mackender v. Feldia* [1967] 2 Q.B. 590, 599 (C.A.); *Derby & Co. Ltd. v. Larsson* [1976] 1 W.L.R. 202, 204 (H.L.); *The Sky One* [1988] 1 Lloyd's Rep. 238, 241 (C.A.). Lord Diplock expressed the view that the jurisdiction under Ord. 11 (now CPR, r. 6.20) was an exorbitant one, which ran counter to comity since it was a wider jurisdiction than was recognised in English law as being possessed by courts of foreign countries: *The Siskina v. Distos Compania Naviera S.A.* [1979] A.C. 210, 254; *Amin Rasheed Shipping Corp. v. Kuwait Insurance Co. Ltd.* [1984] A.C. 50, 65; and see also *The Alexandros P.* [1986] Q.B. 464, 478; *Insurance Co. of Ireland v. Strombus International Insurance* [1985] 2 Lloyd's Rep. 138, 146 (C.A.); *Spiliada Maritime Corp. v. Cansulex Ltd* [1987] A.C. 460, 481; *Agar v. Hyde* (2000) 201 C.L.R. 552, 570. But it is suggested that the jurisdiction exercised under CPR, r. 6.20 is not exorbitant, since it is similar to the jurisdiction exercised by many countries, and is also in many respects similar to the rules in the Judgments Regulation and the 1968 and Lugano Conventions: see Collins (1991) 107 L.Q.R. 10, 13–14.

[8] See also *Ellinger v. Guinness Mahon & Co.* [1939] 4 All E.R. 16; *Macaulay (Tweeds) Ltd. v. Independent Harris Tweed Producers Ltd.* [1961] R.P.C. 184, 193–196; *The Nimrod* [1973] 2 Lloyd's Rep. 91, 95; *G.A.F. Corporation v. Amchem Products Inc.* [1975] 1 Lloyd's Rep. 601, 607–608; *The Hida Maru* [1981] 2 Lloyd's Rep. 510 (C.A.); *Electric Furnace Co. v. Selas Corp. of America* [1987] R.P.C. 23 (C.A.); *The Volvox Hollandia* [1988] 2 Lloyd's Rep. 361, 372 (C.A.); *Trafalgar Tours Ltd. v. Henry* [1990] 2 Lloyd's Rep. 298 (C.A.); *Newtherapeutics Ltd. v. Katz* [1991] Ch. 226; *The Olib* [1991] 2 Lloyd's Rep. 108; *ABCI v. Banque Franco-Tunisienne* [1996] 1 Lloyd's Rep. 485, affd. [1997] 1 Lloyd's Rep. 531 (C.A.); *ANCAP v. Ridgley Shipping Inc.* [1996] 1 Lloyd's Rep. 570; *Konamaneni v. Rolls-Royce Industrial Power (India) Ltd.* [2002] 1 W.L.R. 1269; *Marubeni Hong Kong and South China Ltd. v. Mongolian Government* [2002] 2 All E.R. (Comm.) 873.

[9] *Johnson v. Taylor Bros.* [1920] A.C. 144, 153; *Rosler v. Hilbery* [1925] Ch. 250, 259–260 (C.A.); *George Monro Ltd. v. American Cyanamid Corporation* [1944] K.B. 432, 437, 442 (C.A.); *Beck v. Value Capital Ltd. (No. 2)* [1975] 1 W.L.R. 6; affd. [1976] 1 W.L.R. 572n. (C.A.).

[10] See Rule 31(3).

[11] [1984] A.C. 50.

Corp. v. Cansulex Ltd.[12] The claimant must show good reasons why service on a foreign defendant should be permitted, and in considering this question the court must take into account the nature of the dispute, the legal and practical issues involved, such questions as local knowledge, availability of witnesses and their evidence, and expense. The fundamental question (as it is in cases of staying of actions on *forum non conveniens* grounds[13]) is to identify the forum in which the case can suitably be tried for the interests of all the parties and for the ends of justice. To justify the exercise of the discretion, the claimant has to show that England is clearly the appropriate forum for the trial of the action.[14]

Where the defendant is present in a country which has the civil law **S11–125** system it is wrong for the English court to compare the relative efficiency of the civil law and common law procedures for the determination of disputed facts, or to compare the reputation and standing of the foreign court with the English court.[15] But the court may take into account that the claimant will be deprived of a fair trial in the foreign country, especially for political or racial reasons.[16] Where the claimant has acted reasonably in commencing proceedings in England, and has not acted unreasonably in failing to commence proceedings in the foreign jurisdiction, and would be met by a time bar in the foreign jurisdiction if permission to serve outside the jurisdiction were to be set aside, the court may make it a condition of setting aside permission that the defendant should waive the time bar in the foreign proceedings.[17] If the parties have agreed that the dispute between them shall be referred to the exclusive jurisdiction of a foreign court[18] or to arbitration,[19] permission will normally be refused.

(4) CPR, r. 6.21(2A) provides that the court will not give permission **S11–126** unless satisfied that England is the proper place in which to bring the claim. This provision imposes on the claimant the burden of showing good reason why service should in the circumstances be permitted on a foreign defendant.[20]

---

[12] [1987] A.C. 460.
[13] See Rule 31(1), (2).
[14] [1987] A.C. at 480–482. See also *The Handgate* [1987] 1 Lloyd's Rep. 142 (C.A.); *Islamic Arab Insurance Co. v. Saudi Egyptian American Reinsurance Co.* [1987] 1 Lloyd's Rep. 315 (C.A.); *E.I. du Pont de Nemours v. Agnew* [1987] 2 Lloyd's Rep. 585, 588–589 (C.A.); *Roneleigh Ltd. v. MII Exports Inc* [1989] 1 W.L.R. 619 (C.A.); *Metall und Rohstoff A.G. v. Donaldson Lufkin & Jenrette Inc.* [1990] 1 Q.B. 391, 482–489 (C.A.); *The Goldean Mariner* [1989] 2 Lloyd's Rep. 390; affd. [1990] 2 Lloyd's Rep. 25 (C.A.); *The Oinoussian Pride* [1991] 1 Lloyd's Rep. 126; *Bank of Baroda v. Vysya Bank Ltd.* [1994] 2 Lloyd's Rep. 87; *McConnell Dowell Constructors Ltd. v. Lloyd's Syndicate 396* [1988] 2 N.Z.L.R. 257. In jurisdictions, such as New Zealand and Canada, where service outside the jurisdiction is allowed without leave in specified circumstances, the court retains its discretion to set aside service on the application of the defendant: see *Kuwait Asia Bank E.C. v. National Mutual Life Nominees Ltd.* [1991] 1 A.C. 187, 217 (P.C.); and other cases cited para. 12–038, n. 58.
[15] *Amin Rasheed Shipping Corp. v. Kuwait Insurance Co.* [1984] A.C. 50, 65.
[16] *Oppenheimer v. Louis Rosenthal & Co.* [1937] 1 All E.R. 23 (C.A.); *Ellinger v. Guinness Mahon & Co.* [1939] 4 All E.R. 16. Contrast *Jeyaretnam v. Mahmood, The Times,* May 21, 1992.
[17] *Spiliada Maritime Corp. v. Cansulex Ltd.* [1987] A.C. at 483–484.
[18] *Re Schintz* [1926] Ch. 710 (C.A.); *Mackender v. Feldia* [1967] 2 Q.B. 590 (C.A.). Contrast *Ellinger v. Guinness Mahon & Co.* [1939] 4 All E.R. 16; *Evans Marshall & Co. Ltd. v. Bertola S.A.* [1973] 1 W.L.R. 349 (C.A.); *Re Jogia (A Bankrupt)* [1988] 1 W.L.R. 484. See Rule 32(2).
[19] *A. & B. v. C. & D.* [1982] 1 Lloyd's Rep. 166, affd. *sub nom. Qatar Petroleum v. Shell International Petroleum* [1983] 2 Lloyd's Rep. 35 (C.A.).
[20] *Amin Rasheed Shipping Corp. v. Kuwait Insurance Co.* [1984] A.C. 50, 72; see also *G.A.F. Corporation v. Amchem Products Inc.* [1975] 1 Lloyd's Rep. 601, 609 (C.A.).

S11–127   The claimant must show that he has a cause of action against the defendant and that the case falls within one of the heads of jurisdiction in CPR, r. 6.20. In *Seaconsar Far East Ltd. v. Bank Markazi Iran*[21] the House of Lords, resolving earlier inconsistent authorities, considered the question of the standard of proof which the claimant had to discharge on these questions, and the relationship of the strength of the claimant's case to the issue of *forum conveniens*. It was held that the standard of proof in respect of the cause of action was whether, on the affidavit evidence, there was a serious question to be tried, *i.e.* a substantial question of fact or law, or both, which the claimant *bona fide* desired to have tried. The standard to be applied in considering whether the jurisdiction of the court had been sufficiently established under one or more of the heads of what is now CPR, r. 6.20 was that of the good arguable case, *i.e.* a strong case for argument.[22] But if the applicability of CPR, r. 6.20 depends on a question of law or construction, there is no room for the application of the test of good arguable case: the court must decide the question on the application to set aside.[23]

S11–128   In *Seaconsar Far East Ltd. v. Bank Markazi Iran* the House of Lords also considered the relationship between the standard of proof on the existence of the cause of action and the principle of *forum conveniens*. It disapproved the view that they were inter-related in the sense that the more conspicuous the presence of one element the less consistent with the demands of justice that the other should also be conspicuous.[24] A case particularly strong on the merits could not compensate for a weak case on *forum conveniens*; and a very strong connection with the English forum could not justify a weak case on the merits, if a stronger case on the merits would otherwise be required. The two elements are separate and distinct. The invocation of the principle of *forum conveniens* springs from the often expressed anxiety that great care should be taken in bringing before the English court a foreigner who owes no allegiance here. But if jurisdiction is established under CPR, r. 6.20, and it is also established that England is the *forum conveniens*, there is no good reason why any particular degree of cogency should be required in relation to the merits of the claimant's case.[25]

---

[21] [1994] 1 A.C. 438. In the light of this decision, it is submitted that little assistance can now be derived from the many earlier authorities mentioned in the 12th edition of this work, p. 319. CPR, r. 6.21(1)(b) now requires the claimant to adduce evidence stating that he believes his claim has a "reasonable prospect of success." It is suggested that this does not differ in any material respect from the "serious issue to be tried" test hitherto applied.

[22] See *Vitkovice Horni a Hutni Tezirstvo v. Korner* [1951] A.C. 869. In *Attock Cement Co. Ltd. v. Romanian Bank for Foreign Trade* [1989] 1 W.L.R. 1147 (C.A.) it was held that, where there is a disputed question of fact which is essential to the applicability of Ord. 11, r. 1(1), the court had to reach a provisional or tentative conclusion that the plaintiff was probably right. It has been held that this test cannot stand with the decision in the *Seaconsar* case: *Agrafax Public Relations Ltd. v. United Scottish Society Inc.* [1995] I.L.Pr. 753 (C.A.); *Canada Trust Co. v. Stolzenberg (No. 2)* [1998] 1 W.L.R. 547 (C.A.); affd. [2002] 1 A.C. 1. As regards the relevant date for the existence of the factual circumstances to be taken into account see *I.S.C. Technologies Inc. v. Guerin* [1992] 2 Lloyd's Rep. 430 and *B.M.G. Trading Ltd. v. McKay* [1998] I.L.Pr. 691 (C.A.).

[23] *E. F. Hutton & Co. (London) Ltd. v. Mofarrij* [1989] 1 W.L.R. 488 (C.A.); *cf. The Brabo* [1949] A.C. 326; *B.P. Exploration Co. (Libya) Ltd. v. Hunt* [1976] 1 W.L.R. 786; *The Delfini* [1990] 1 Lloyd's Rep. 252 (C.A.); *Kuwait Asia Bank E.C. v. National Mutual Life Nominees Ltd.* [1991] 1 A.C. 187 (P.C.). Contrast *Unilever plc v. Gillette (U.K.) Ltd* [1989] R.P.C. 583, 602 (C.A.). See also *Chellaram v. Chellaram (No. 2)* [2002] EWHC 632 (Ch), [2002] 3 All E.R. 17, and *cf. Marubeni Hong Kong and South China Ltd. v. Mongolian Government* [2002] 2 All E.R. (Comm.) 873.

[24] *Soc. Commerciale de Réassurance v. Eras International Ltd.* [1992] 1 Lloyd's Rep. 570, 588 (C.A.), *per* Mustill L.J.

[25] [1994] 1 A.C. at 456.

(5) Proceedings may fall at the same time within more than one of the **S11–129**
clauses of Rule 27.[26] Thus a claim for the breach of a contract made in
England falls within clause (6), but if the contract be a contract concerning
land in England, the action falls also within clause (11). But if proceedings
fall within one or more of the clauses it is not permissible to litigate any
other cause of action which does not fall within one of the clauses.[27] Where
permission to serve out of the jurisdiction is based on one cause of action it
cannot be treated as permission based on some other cause of action.[28] Nor,
if a claim has been put forward on one legal basis, can the claimant
subsequently justify permission on another legal basis, unless, perhaps, that
other legal basis has been referred to in the evidence in support of the
application.[29]

(6) A defendant who wishes to contest the jurisdiction of the court, either **S11–130**
on the ground that the case is not within CPR, r. 6.20, or that the case is
not a proper one for the exercise of the discretion, should acknowledge
service of the proceedings, and, within 14 days (28 days in the Commercial
Court) after filing an acknowledgment of service, apply to the court for an
order declaring that it has no jurisdiction.[30]

Judgments Regulation, 1968 and Lugano Conventions and intra-United **S11–131**
Kingdom jurisdiction. As has been seen,[31] there are a number of cases in
which exclusive jurisdiction may be vested in the courts of other Regulation
States or Contracting States even though the defendant is not domiciled in
a Regulation State, or in a 1968 Convention or Lugano Convention State.
In such a case the English court would not be able to exercise jurisdiction
under CPR, r. 6.20. This will be a rare case since it is not easy to envisage
any but the most unlikely circumstances which would both give exclusive
jurisdiction to the courts of another Regulation State under Article 22 of
the Judgments Regulation or the courts of another Contracting State under
Article 16 of the 1968 and Lugano Conventions, and also found jurisdiction
in England under CPR, r. 6.20. Cases in which exclusive jurisdiction is given
to the courts of a Regulation State under Article 23 of the Judgments
Regulation or the courts of another Contracting State under Article 17 of
the Conventions and which also come within CPR, r. 6.20 are easier to
imagine. In such cases the English court would not be entitled to assume
jurisdiction under, for example, CPR, r. 6.20(5)(c), clause (6), on the basis
that the contract is governed by English law. But even apart from the
Regulation and the Conventions the English court would be reluctant to
assume jurisdiction in such a case.[32] Similar considerations apply where the

---

[26] *Tassell v. Hallen* [1892] 1 Q.B. 321, 323–325.
[27] *Holland v. Leslie* [1894] 2 Q.B. 450 (C.A.); *Waterhouse v. Reid* [1938] 1 K.B. 743 (C.A.); *The Siskina v. Distos Compania Naviera S.A.* [1979] A.C. 210, 255; *Donohue v. Armco Inc.* [2002] 1 Lloyd's Rep. 425, 432 (H.L.). *Cf. Beck v. Value Capital Ltd. (No. 2)* [1975] 1 W.L.R. 6; affd. [1976] 1 W.L.R. 572a. (C.A.); *Tricon Industries Pty, Ltd. v. Abel Lemon & Co. Pty. Ltd.* [1988] 2 Qd.R. 464; *Australian Iron & Steel Pty. v. Jumbo (Curacao) N.V.* (1988) 14 N.S.W.L.R. 507; *David Syme & Co. Ltd. v. Grey* (1992) 38 F.C.R. 303.
[28] *Parker v. Schuller* (1901) 17 T.L.R. 299 (C.A.); *Soc. Commerciale Réassurance v. Eras International Ltd.* [1992] 1 Lloyd's Rep. 570, 613 (C.A.).
[29] *Metall und Rohstoff A.G. v. Donaldson Lufkin & Jenrette Inc.* [1990] 1 Q.B. 391, 436 (C.A.). See also *Excess Insurance Co. Ltd. v. Astra S.A. Insurance and Reinsurance Co.* [1997] C.L.C. 160 (C.A.)
[30] CPR, r. 11(1), (2), (4) (as amended by S.I. 2001 No. 4015, para. 12); r. 58.7. See para. 11–055.
[31] para. 11–079.
[32] para. 11–125, n. 29.

defendant is domiciled in Scotland or Northern Ireland. But the cases of overlap are likely to be even rarer because Rule 12 in Schedule 4 to the 1982 Act does not attribute conclusive effect to jurisdiction clauses.[33]

S11–132   Conversely there will be a number of rare cases in which a defendant domiciled in another Regulation State or in another Contracting State or in Scotland or Northern Ireland may be sued under CPR, r. 6.20. These will include cases outside the scope of the Regulation and the Conventions because they are not civil or commercial matters or are otherwise excluded by Article 1 of the Regulation or the Conventions. Examples would be claims to enforce arbitral awards and revenue claims. Both are excluded by Article 1 of the Regulation and the Conventions from their scope, and both may found jurisdiction under CPR, r. 6.20[34] over persons not present in England and who are domiciled in another Regulation State or in another Contracting State or in Scotland or Northern Ireland.

S11–133   In the rare cases in which CPR, r. 6.20 will apply to defendants domiciled in Scotland or Northern Ireland, r. 6.21(3) provides that if it appears to the court that the claimant may also be entitled to a remedy in Scotland or Northern Ireland the court, in deciding whether to grant permission, shall compare the cost and convenience of proceeding there or in England, and (where that is relevant) to the powers and jurisdiction of the Sheriff Court in Scotland or the county court or courts of summary jurisdiction in Northern Ireland. The object of this rule is to protect persons living in Scotland or Northern Ireland from the inconvenience of an action which, though it might be brought in England, would cause them unnecessary cost. It is not an additional ground for giving permission to serve out of the jurisdiction, but an additional obstacle that the claimant has to surmount.[35]

S11R–134   (1) The court may assume jurisdiction if a claim is made for a remedy against a person domiciled in England.[36]

COMMENT

S11R–135   In this clause, which before an amendment to R.S.C. Order 11, r. 1(1) in 1983 applied to persons domiciled or ordinarily resident in England, the expression "domiciled" is to be interpreted[37] in accordance with the provisions of sections 41 to 46 of the 1982 Act or paragraphs 9 and 10 of the Civil Jurisdiction and Judgments Order 2001.[38] The clause applies not only to individuals but also to partnerships and bodies corporate.[39] The term "remedy" in this clause includes the recovery of a debt, or of damages in an action for breach of contract or tort,[40] or an injunction requiring an act abroad.[41] Hence domicile in England is of itself a ground of jurisdiction

---

[33] para. 12–109.
[34] Clauses (10) and (17).
[35] See *Tottenham v. Barry* (1879) 12 Ch.D. 797; *Kinahan v. Kinahan* (1890) 45 Ch.D. 78; *Washburn, etc., Co. v. Cunard Co.* (1889) 5 T.L.R. 592; *Re De Penny* [1891] 2 Ch. 63; *Williams v. Cartwright* [1895] 1 Q.B. 142 (C.A.); *Macaulay (Tweeds) Ltd. v. Independent Harris Tweed Producers Ltd*, [1961] R.P.C. 184, 192–193.
[36] CPR, r. 6.20(1).
[37] CPR, r. 6.18(g), as amended by S.I. 2001 No. 4015. See Rule 23.
[38] S.I. 2001 No. 3929. See CPR, r. 6.18(g), as substituted by S.I. 2001 No. 4015.
[39] See Interpretation Act 1978, Sched. 1.
[40] See *Hadad v. Bruce* (1892) 8 T.L.R. 409.
[41] *Re Liddell's Settlement* [1936] Ch. 365 (C.A.).

against a defendant who might otherwise, on account of his absence from England, be exempt from the jurisdiction of the court. If he is domiciled in England he would be put in the same position as a person who is in this country.[42]

This head of CPR, r. 6.20 is likely to be of little practical significance, **S11–136** since permission to serve process outside the jurisdiction on a defendant domiciled in England is required only in cases falling outside the scope of the Judgments Regulation and the 1968 and Lugano Conventions. If the case falls within the Regulation or either of those Conventions (or within the intra-United Kingdom provisions of Schedule 4 to the 1982 Act) permission to serve out of the jurisdiction is not required.[43]

(2) The court may assume jurisdiction if a claim is made for an injunction **S11R–137** **ordering the defendant to do or refrain from doing an act in England.**[44]

COMMENT

The injunction need not be the only relief sought, but it must be the **S11–138** substantial relief sought: permission will be refused if the claim for an injunction is not made bona fide, but merely to bring the case within the clause.[45] Permission will also be refused if a foreign court can more conveniently deal with the question,[46] or if there is no real ground to anticipate repetition of the action complained of,[47] or if the injunction cannot be made effective in England.[48] To come within this clause the injunction sought in the action has to be part of the substantive relief to which the claimant's cause of action entitles him, *e.g.* an injunction to restrain a threatened breach of contract.[49]

ILLUSTRATIONS

1. X, who is resident in New York, sends cards to A in London, through the post-office and otherwise, containing libellous and defamatory matter. A brings proceedings claiming an injunction to restrain X from sending such post-cards, and also claiming damages. The court may assume jurisdiction.[50]

2. X & Co. carry on business in South Africa. X & Co. at Manchester infringe A's trade mark. A brings proceedings to restrain infringement. The court may assume jurisdiction.[51]

---

[42] *ibid.* at p. 374.

[43] See Rule 28, clause (1).

[44] CPR, r. 6.20(2).

[45] Compare *Watson v. Daily Record* [1907] 1 K.B. 853 (C.A.); *De Bernales v. New York Herald* (1893) 68 L.T. 658; [1893] 2 Q.B. 97n. (C.A.); *Alexander & Co. v. Valentine & Sons* (1908) 25 T.L.R. 29 (C.A.); *G.A.F. Corporation v. Amchem Products Inc.* [1975] 1 Lloyd's Rep. 601, 605–606; *Joynt v. McCrum* [1899] 1 I.R. 217.

[46] *Société Générale de Paris v. Dreyfus* (1885) 29 Ch.D. 239; (1887) 37 Ch.D. 215 (C.A.); *Kinahan v. Kinahan* (1890) 45 Ch.D. 78; *Re De Penny* [1891] 2 Ch 63; *Rosler v. Hilbery* [1925] Ch. 250 (C.A.).

[47] *De Bernales v. New York Herald* (1893) 68 L.T. 658; [1893] 2 Q.B. 97n. (C.A.). Compare *Watson v. Daily Record Ltd.* [1907] 1 K.B. 853 (C.A.), and contrast *Alexander & Co. v. Valentine & Sons* (1908) 25 T.L.R. 29.

[48] See *Marshall v. Marshall* (1888) 38 Ch.D. 330 (C.A.).

[49] *James North & Sons Ltd. v. North Cape Textiles Ltd.* [1984] 1 W.L.R. 1428 (C.A.).

[50] *Cf. Tozier v. Hawkins* (1885) 15 Q.B.D. 650, 680 (C.A.); *Dunlop Rubber Co. v. Dunlop* [1921] 1 A.C. 367. See also *Alexander & Co. v. Valentine & Sons* (1908) 25 T.L.R. 29.

[51] *Cf. Re Burland's Trade Mark* (1889) 41 Ch.D. 542. Contrast *Marshall v. Marshall* (1888) 38 Ch.D. 330 (C.A.).

    3. X resides in New York, and there contracts with A & Co., an English company, to perform certain services in South Africa at a salary. He goes to South Africa, but returns thence before he has fully performed his contract. A & Co. refuse to pay X part of the salary which he claims. X threatens a petition for the winding-up of A & Co. A & Co. bring proceedings against X, claiming (1) rescission of contract, (2) return of moneys paid, (3) injunction to restrain X from presenting the petition. The court may assume jurisdiction.[52]

    4. N, a trader in England, orders goods from X, a manufacturer in Illinois. X addresses the goods to N in England and delivers them to the Chicago post office by which they are forwarded to England. The goods are manufactured by X according to an invention protected by an English patent. Proceedings are brought by A, the patentee, against X, claiming an injunction against infringement of patent. The court has no jurisdiction, because the sale and delivery of the goods by X was complete when he delivered them to the post office in Chicago.[53]

S11R–139   **(3) The court may assume jurisdiction if a claim is made against someone on whom the claim form has been or will be served and (a) there is between the claimant and that person a real issue which it is reasonable for the court to try and (b) the claimant wishes to serve the claim form on another person who is a necessary or proper party to that claim.[54]**

(4) The court may assume jurisdiction if the claim is a Part 20 claim and the person to be served is a necessary and proper party to the claim against the Part 20 claimant.[55]

COMMENT

S11–140   It may be necessary or proper that a claimant, A, should make not only one person, X, but also some other person, Y, defendant in the proceedings. This is so, for example, where X and Y are joint debtors,[56] or where A has a claim, alternatively, either against X or Y, or where otherwise the claims can be conveniently disposed of in the same proceedings.[57] This clause originally required X to be served within the jurisdiction but is not now so limited. It allows Y to be joined in the proceedings even though Y could not be served under any of the other clauses of this Rule if he had been sued alone, *e.g.* proceedings for a tort committed abroad.[58] But because the cause of action may have no connection with England, especial care is required before permission to serve out of the jurisdiction will be allowed.[59] In particular, the court should not grant permission under this clause as a matter of course merely because not to do so would mean that more than one set of proceedings would be required.[60]

---

[52] *Cf. Lisbon Berlyn Gold Fields v. Heddle* (1885) 52 L.T. 796.

[53] *Cf. Badische Anilin und Soda Fabrik v. Basle Chemical Works, Bindschedler* [1898] A.C. 200.

[54] CPR, r. 6.20(3). See *United Film Distribution Ltd. v. Chhabria* [2001] EWCA Civ. 416; [2001] 2 All E.R. (Comm.) 865 (C.A.); *The Baltic Flame* [2001] EWCA Civ. 418; [2001] 2 Lloyd's Rep. 203 (C.A.). See also *Analog Devices BV v. Zurich Insurance Co.* [2002] 2 I.L.R.M. 366 (Sup. Ct.).

[55] CPR, r. 6.20(3A). See Takahashi (2002) 51 I.C.L.Q. 127.

[56] If one joint debtor is outside the jurisdiction he need not be joined in proceedings against the other or others: *Wilson, Sons & Co. v. Balcarres Brook S.S. Co.* [1893] 1 Q.B. 422 (C.A.).

[57] CPR, r. 7.3.

[58] *Williams v. Cartwright* [1895] 1 Q.B. 142, 145, 148 (C.A.); *The Duc d'Aumale* [1903] P. 18 (C.A.).

[59] *The Brabo* [1949] A.C. 326, 328; *Multinational Gas Co. v. Multinational Gas Services Ltd.* [1983] Ch. 258, 271 (C.A.); *Arab Monetary Fund v. Hashim (No. 4)* [1992] 1 W.L.R. 553, 557, affd. [1992] 1 W.L.R. 1176 (C.A.).

[60] *The Goldean Mariner* [1990] 2 Lloyd's Rep. 215 (C.A.).

In order that the court may have jurisdiction within clause (3) the **S11–141** following conditions must be fulfilled:

(1) X has been or will be served. Service may be in England as of right, or **S11–142** abroad with permission under CPR, r. 6.20 or abroad as of right under CPR, r. 6.19(2). Where X is outside the jurisdiction and instructs solicitors to accept service on his behalf within the jurisdiction, A may join Y under this clause.[61]

(2) A must satisfy the court by written evidence that there is between A **S11–143** and X a real issue which it is reasonable for the court to try.[62] In cases decided under the former version of this clause (which required also that the action be "properly brought" against X) it was said that Y could not be served under this clause if the sole purpose of the action against X was to found jurisdiction against Y,[63] and this was reaffirmed by a majority of the Court of Appeal.[64] There is much to be said, however, for the minority view of May L.J. that these cases establish no more than that the claim against X must be a plausible one and not brought mala fide. This is probably also the position under the present version of the clause. Thus permission will not be granted if X has a complete answer to the claim by A,[65] or if Y has a complete answer.[66] But permission may be granted if the causes of action are alternative, so that the claim against one of them will ultimately fail.[67]

(3) Y, who is out of England, must be either a necessary or proper party **S11–144** to the proceedings. If Y is a proper party it is not also a requirement that he be a necessary party; but if adding Y is likely in practice to achieve no potential advantage for the claimant, it would not ordinarily be a proper case for service out of the jurisdiction.[68] The question whether Y is a proper party to proceedings against X depends on this: supposing both X and Y had been in England, would they both have been proper parties to the proceedings? If they would, and only one of them, X, is in this country, then

---

[61] *The Benarty (No. 1)* [1983] 1 Lloyd's Rep. 361 (C.A.), distinguishing *John Russell & Co. Ltd. v. Cayzer, Irvine & Co. Ltd.* [1916] 2 A.C. 298; followed, with some misgivings, in *Amanuel v. Alexandros Shipping Co.* [1986] Q.B. 464. A mere submission by X, without service of process on him then or thereafter, may not be sufficient to allow service on Y.

[62] CPR, r. 6.20(3)(a), derived from *Ellinger v. Guinness, Mahon & Co.* [1939] 4 All E.R. 16, 22. See also *Soc. Commerciale Réassurance v. Eras International Ltd.* [1992] 1 Lloyd's Rep. 570 (C.A.); *The Ines* [1993] 2 Lloyd's Rep. 492; *The Xing Su Hai* [1995] 2 Lloyd's Rep. 15; *The Flecha* [1999] 1 Lloyd's Rep. 612.

[63] See, *e.g. Witted v. Galbraith* [1893] 1 Q.B. 577; *Flower v. Rose & Co.* (1891) 7 T.L.R. 280; *Bloomfield v. Serenyi* [1945] 2 All E.R. 646 (C.A.); *Sharples v. Eason & Son* [1911] 2 I.R. 436 (C.A.); *Ross v. Eason & Son* [1911] 2 I.R. 459 (C.A.), distinguished in *Cooney v. Wilson and Henderson* [1913] 2 I.R. 402 (C.A.). That this is the purpose may be inferred from the fact that X is a subordinate or secondary defendant: *Yorkshire Tannery v. Eglington Co.* (1884) 54 L.J.Ch. 81; *Rosler v. Hilbery* [1925] Ch. 250.

[64] *Multinational Gas Co. v. Multinational Gas Services Ltd.* [1983] Ch. 258 (C.A.). See also *Goldenglow Nut Food Co. Ltd. v. Commodin (Produce) Ltd.* [1987] 2 Lloyd's Rep. 569, 578 (C.A.).

[65] *The Brabo* [1949] A.C. 326; *Witted v. Galbraith* [1893] 1 Q.B. 577 (C.A.); *Flower v. Rose & Co.* (1891) 7 T.L.R. 280.

[66] *Multinational Gas Co. v. Multinational Gas Services Ltd.* [1983] Ch. 258 (C.A.); *Kuwait Asia Bank E.C. v. National Mutual Life Nominees Ltd.* [1991] 1 A.C. 187 (P.C.); *DSQ Property Co. Ltd. v. Lotus Cars Ltd., The Times*, June 28, 1990 (C.A.) (in which both X and Y had a complete answer); *Barings plc v. Coopers & Lybrand* [1997] I.L.Pr. 12 (C.A.). But the fact that Y would have a complete answer if sued in the courts for the place where he is domiciled is not of itself a sufficient reason to refuse joinder: *The Baltic Flame* [2001] EWCA 418; [2001] 1 Lloyd's Rep. 203 (C.A.).

[67] *Massey v. Heynes* (1888) 21 Q.B.D. 330 (C.A.).

[68] *Electric Furnace Co. v. Selas Corp. of America* [1987] R.P.C. 23, 32–33 (C.A.).

Y is a proper party and permission may be given to serve him out of the jurisdiction.[69] It is not necessary that the alleged liability of Y be joint or several with that of X.[70]

S11–145 In the rare cases falling outside the intra-United Kingdom provisions of the 1982 Act, clause (3) applies to a defendant domiciled or ordinarily resident in Scotland or Northern Ireland[71]; and CPR, r. 6.21(3), which requires the court to have regard to the comparative cost and convenience of proceeding there or in England, applies to such a case.[72]

S11–146 Part 20 claims are counterclaims and what used to be known as third party claims. A Part 20 claim is defined by the Civil Procedure Rules[73] to mean any claim other than a claim by a claimant against a defendant, and includes (a) a counterclaim by a defendant against the claimant or against the claimant and some other person; (b) a claim by a defendant against any person (whether or not already a party) for contribution or indemnity or some other remedy; and (c) where a Part 20 claim has been made against a person who is not already a party, any claim made against any other person (whether or not already a party). A Part 20 claimant is a person who makes a Part 20 claim.[74]

S11–147 CPR, r. 6.20(3A) is somewhat obscurely drafted. It would appear that the requirement that the foreign defendant should be a necessary *and* proper party is a slip for necessary *or* proper party, and that the position is the same as under clause (3).[75] It seems that it would apply not only where the defendant seeks a direct remedy against a foreign third party, but also (as under the former version of clause (3)) where the defendant adds a new foreign defendant to a counterclaim against the claimant.[76]

ILLUSTRATIONS

S11–148 1. X, on instructions from Y, enters, as agent for Y, into a contract with A. Y repudiates the contract. A brings proceedings against X, who is in England, for breach of warranty that X was authorised to contract for Y, who is in New York, and has an alternative claim against Y if X was authorised to contract for him. The court may assume jurisdiction to entertain an action against Y as co-defendant with X.[77]

2. A & Co., an American company, own a patent for barbed wire. Y, carrying on business in Japan, buys from N, in America, wire which is an infringement of A & Co.'s

---

[69] *Massey v. Heynes* (1888) 21 Q.B.D. 330, 338 (C.A.); *Lightowler v. Lightowler* [1884] W.N. 8; *The Elton* [1891] P. 265; *The Duc d'Aumale* [1903] P. 18 (C.A.); *Oesterreichische Export, etc. Co. v. British Indemnity Co. Ltd.* [1914] 2 K.B. 747 (C.A.); *Macaulay (Tweeds) Ltd. v. Independent Harris Tweed Producers Ltd.* [1961] R.P.C. 184; *Qatar Petroleum v. Shell International Petroleum* [1983] 2 Lloyd's Rep. 35 (C.A.); *The Goldean Mariner* [1989] 2 Lloyd's Rep. 390, 395 (approving the statement in the text); affd. [1990] 2 Lloyd's Rep. 215 (C.A.). See also *Aiglon Ltd. v. Gau Shan & Co. Ltd.* [1993] 1 Lloyd's Rep. 164; *C Inc. v. L* [2001] 2 Lloyd's Rep. 459.

[70] See, *e.g. Oesterreichische Export, etc., Co. v. British Indemnity Co. Ltd.* [1914] 2 K.B. 747 (C.A.); *Bank of N.S.W. v. Commonwealth Steel Co. Ltd.* [1983] 1 N.S.W.L.R. 69.

[71] See *Washburn, etc., Co. v. Cunard Co. & Parkes* (1889) 5 T.L.R. 592; *Croft v. King* [1893] 1 Q.B. 419; *Williams v. Cartwright* [1895] 1 Q.B. 142 (C.A.); *Oesterreichische Export, etc., Co. v. British Indemnity Co. Ltd.* [1914] 2 K.B. 747 (C.A.).

[72] *Washburn, etc., Co. v. Cunard Co. & Parkes* (1889) 5 T.L.R. 592; *Williams v. Cartwright* [1895] 1 Q.B. 142 (C.A.); *Macaulay (Tweeds) Ltd. v. Independent Harris Tweed Producers Ltd.* [1961] R.P.C. 184, 192–193.

[73] CPR, r. 20.2(1).

[74] CPR, r. 20.2(2).

[75] See *Civil Procedure*, 2003, para. 6.21.31.

[76] *Derby & Co. Ltd. v. Larsson* [1976] 1 W.L.R. 202 (H.L.).

[77] *Massey v. Heynes* (1888) 21 Q.B.D. 330 (C.A.).

patent. X & Co., an English shipping company, carry the wire for Y and land it at Liverpool for transhipment to Y in Japan. A & Co. bring proceedings against X & Co. to obtain an injunction against their dealing with the wire. A & Co. apply for permission to add Y and serve Y in Japan. The court may assume jurisdiction.[78]

3. A brings proceedings for deceit against X and Y in respect of a fraud jointly committed by them in London. X is in England. Y is domiciled in New York. X has been served with process, and Y is a necessary and proper party to the proceedings. The court may assume jurisdiction.[79]

4. A brings proceedings against X, residing in England, who supplied him with defective goods, and applies for permission to serve Y, residing in the United States, who designed the goods. The court may assume jurisdiction.[80]

5. A & Co., a Liberian corporation, through its liquidator sues, alleging negligence and   **S11–149**
breach of duty, X & Co., an English company, Y and others (directors of A & Co.), all resident abroad, and Z & Co. and others, foreign companies who own the shares in A & Co. X & Co. and Y and the other directors are not in a position to satisfy the substantial claim, and the predominant (but not the sole) purpose of suing X & Co. is to enable A & Co. to join the parties outside the jurisdiction. But as a matter of English company law Y and the other directors and Z & Co. and the other shareholders are not liable to A & Co. Although the proceedings are "properly brought" against X & Co., notwithstanding the predominant purpose of joining the foreign defendants, Y and the other directors and Z & Co. and the other shareholders are not "proper parties" because the proceedings against them are bound to fail.[81]

6. A brings proceedings against X, residing in the United States, who supplied him with defective goods, and obtains permission to serve him abroad. X is served and defends the proceedings. X applies for permission to serve a Part 20 claim (previously called third party proceedings) against Y, who supplied him with the goods. The court may assume jurisdiction.

(5) The court may assume jurisdiction if a claim is made for an interim   **S11R–150**
remedy under section 25 of the Civil Jurisdiction and Judgments Act
1982.[82]

COMMENT

In *The Siskina*[83] the House of Lords held that clause (2) of Rule 27 could   **S11–151**
not be used to found an action, or obtain interim relief, when the only claimed basis of jurisdiction was an interlocutory injunction to restrain a defendant from removing his assets out of the jurisdiction.[84] The same result was reached by the Privy Council in *Mercedes Benz A.G. v. Leiduck*,[85] on the basis that clause (2) applied only to claims advanced in an action and for relief founded on a right asserted by the claimant in that action, to be enforced ultimately through the medium of a judgment given by the court in that action. A *Mareva* injunction in support of proceedings in a foreign

---

[78] *Cf. Washburn, etc., Co. v. Cunard Co. & Parkes* (1889) 5 T.L.R. 592.

[79] *Cf. Williams v. Cartwright* [1895] 1 Q.B. 142 (C.A.).

[80] *The Manchester Courage* [1973] 1 Lloyd's Rep. 386; see also *Adastra Aviation Ltd. v. Airparts (N.Z.) Ltd.* [1964] N.Z.L.R. 393; *Pratt v. Rural Aviation Ltd.* [1969] N.Z.L.R. 46.

[81] *Multinational Gas Co. v. Multinational Gas Services Ltd.* [1983] Ch. 258 (C.A.).

[82] CPR, r. 6.20(4).

[83] *The Siskina v. Distos Compania Naviera* [1979] A.C. 210; followed in *Caudron v. Air Zaire* [1986] I.L.R.M. 10; *Suncorp Realty Inc. v. PLN Investments, Inc.* (1985) 23 D.L.R. (4th) 83 (Man.); *cf. Perry v. Zissis* [1977] 1 Lloyd's Rep. 607 (C.A.). See para. 8–019; and Collins, *Essays*, pp. 30–34.

[84] A *Mareva* injunction (after *Mareva Naviera S.A. v. International Bulkcarriers S.A.* [1975] 2 Lloyd's Rep. 509 (C.A.)), as to which see paras. 8–004 *et seq.* The Civil Procedure Rules now call it a freezing order.

[85] [1996] A.C. 284 (P.C.).

court was not such a claim, and therefore service of process claiming a *Mareva* injunction only did not fall within clause (2).

S11–152   Under the Judgments Regulation and the 1968 and Lugano Conventions the courts of a relevant State may exercise jurisdiction to grant interim relief of this kind even though the courts of another relevant State have jurisdiction over the substance of the matter,[86] and section 25(1) of the 1982 Act gives the English court power to grant interim relief in such cases within the scope of the Judgments Regulation and the Conventions and in intra-United Kingdom cases. This power has been extended under section 25(3) to give the court power to grant interim relief so as to make it exercisable in relation (*inter alia*) to proceedings commenced or to be commenced in States to which the Judgments Regulation and the Conventions do not apply or to proceedings outside the scope of the Regulation and the Conventions. Consequently, the effect of the decisions in *The Siskina* and *Mercedes Benz A.G. v. Leiduck* was reversed.

S11–153   A claim form for an interim remedy under section 25 may be served out of the jurisdiction with the permission of the court under CPR, r. 6.20(4). An application for the grant of permission must be supported (*inter alia*) by evidence of a belief that the applicant has a good claim to an interim remedy. On an application for interim relief under section 25 of the 1982 Act, the court may refuse to grant the relief if, in the opinion of the court, the fact that the court has no independent jurisdiction in relation to the subject-matter of the proceedings makes it inexpedient for the court to grant it.[87]

ILLUSTRATION

S11–154   X & Co., a Panamanian company, own a vessel, which they let on charter. On the failure of the charterers to pay the freight in full, X & Co. cause the vessel to be arrested in Cyprus by order of the courts of Cyprus and the cargo is unloaded. Subsequently the vessel sinks and becomes a total loss. X & Co. claim against their insurers, London underwriters. The cargo-owners commence proceedings in the High Court against X & Co., alleging breach of duty or of contract. The court may issue an injunction restraining X & Co. from removing the insurance moneys from the jurisdiction.[88]

S11R–155   **(6) The court may assume jurisdiction if the claim is made in respect of a contract where the contract**
       (i) was made in England, or
       (ii) was made by or through an agent trading or residing in England, or
       (iii) is governed by English law, or
       (iv) contains a term to the effect that the court shall have jurisdiction to determine any claim in respect of the contract.[89]

COMMENT

S11–156   This clause applies to four cases: (i) where a contract is made in England; (ii) where a contract is made by or through an agent trading or residing in England; (iii) where a contract is governed by English law; (iv) where a

---

[86] Judgments Regulation, Art. 31; 1968 and Lugano Conventions, Art. 24; Rule 28, clause (22).
[87] s.25(2) on which see *Crédit Suisse Fides Trust S.A. v. Cuoghi* [1998] Q.B. 818 (C.A.), and para. 8–025.
[88] CPR, r. 6.20(4) reversing the effect of *The Siskina v. Distos Compania Naviera S.A.* [1979] A.C. 210.
[89] CPR, r. 6.20(5).

contract contains a submission to the jurisdiction of the English court. These cases are, of course, to be read disjunctively, *i.e.* it is sufficient if the claimant can bring his case within any one of them.[90] The claimant must have a good arguable case that the conditions of clause (6) are fulfilled, namely that there was a contract and that, *e.g.* it was made in England, and must also show that there is a serious issue to be tried on the merits of the claim.[91] It includes an alleged contract, provided the claimant shows an arguable case that one existed.[92]

A "contract" in the previous versions of this clause has been held to **S11–157** include a quasi-contract,[93] and a covenant in a declaration of trust,[94] but not the mere holding of an office of director without a contract of employment.[95]

Under the version of this clause in R.S.C. Order 11, r. 1(1)(1)(*d*) the **S11–158** power to grant permission under this clause referred to a claim brought "to enforce, rescind, dissolve, annul or otherwise affect" a contract. It is now necessary only that the claim be made "in respect of a contract," and it is not likely that the authorities[96] on the application of the version of R.S.C. Order 11 will be of much assistance in interpreting the new version. Clause (6) applies to a claim that a contract is valid[97]; or to a claim that a contract has been frustrated[98]; to a claim for an injunction to restrain foreign proceedings in breach of an arbitration agreement governed by English law.[99] But it does not apply to a claim for inducement of breach of contract.[1] It has been held that it does not apply to interpleader proceedings brought by charterers to determine whether charterparty hire should be paid to owners or owners' assignees: CPR, r. 6.20 was concerned with a claim which the claimant wished to bring, not with a claim which might be brought against a claimant, and with claims asserted by claimants, and not with claims asserted against claimants.[2]

---

[90] *Wansborough Paper Co. Ltd. v. Laughland* [1920] W.N. 344 (C.A.).

[91] *Seaconsar Far East Ltd. v. Bank Markazi Iran* [1994] 1 A.C. 438, 454–455. See, *e.g. Maritrop Trading Corp. v. Guangzhou Ocean Shipping Co.* [1998] C.L.C. 224.

[92] *Hemelryck v. William Lyall Shipbuilding Co. Ltd.* [1921] 1 A.C. 698 (P.C.); *Cromie v. Moore* [1936] 2 All E.R. 177 (C.A.); *Vitkovice Horni A Hutni Tezirstvo v. Korner* [1951] A.C. 869: *Britannia Steamship Insurance Assn. v. Ausonia Assicurazioni SpA* [1984] 2 Lloyd's Rep. 98 (C.A.); *The Parouth* [1982] 2 Lloyd's Rep. 351 (C.A.); *Egon Oldendorff v. Libera Corp.* [1995] 2 Lloyd's Rep. 64; see *ante*, para. S11–127.

[93] *Bowling v. Cox* [1926] A.C. 751 (P.C.); *Rousou's Trustee v. Rousou* [1955] 1 W.L.R. 545; *Re Jogia (A Bankrupt)* [1988] 1 W.L.R. 484; *The Kurnia Dewi* [1997] 1 Lloyd's Rep. 552; *Durra v. Bank of N.S.W.* [1940] V.L.R. 170; *Earthworks Ltd. v. F.T. Eastment & Sons Ltd.* [1966] V.R. 24. A claim under statute for harbour dues is not a contractual or quasi-contractual claim for the purposes of clause (6): *Carlingford Harbour Commissioners v. Everard & Sons Ltd.* [1985] I.R. 50, following *Shipsey v. British and South American Steam Navigation Co. Ltd.* [1936] I.R. 65.

[94] *Official Solicitor v. Stype Investments Ltd.* [1983] 1 W.L.R. 214.

[95] *Newtherapeutics Ltd. v. Katz* [1991] Ch. 226.

[96] See cases cited para. 11–154. See also *ABCI v. Banque Franco-Tunisienne* [2003] EWCA Civ. 205 (C.A.).

[97] Cf. *Gulf Bank K.S.C. v. Mitsubishi Heavy Industries Ltd.* [1994] 1 Lloyd's Rep. 323.

[98] Cf. *B.P. Exploration Co. (Libya) Ltd. v. Hunt* [1976] 1 W.L.R. 788; *Gulf Bank K.S.C. v. Mitsubishi Heavy Industries Ltd.* [1994] 1 Lloyd's Rep. 323.

[99] Cf. *Schiffahrtgesellschaft Detlev von Appen GmbH v. Voest Alpine Intertrading GmbH* [1997] 2 Lloyd's Rep. 279 (C.A.).

[1] Cf. *E.F. Hutton & Co. (London) Ltd. v. Mofarrij* [1989] 1 W.L.R. 488, 494 (C.A.). Contrast *South Adelaide Football Club v. Fitzroy Football Club* (1988) 92 F.L.R. 117.

[2] *Cool Carriers AB v. HSBC Bank U.S.A.* [2001] 2 Lloyd's Rep. 22.

S11–159   It has been held[3] that if, on the claimant's own showing, no such contract as he alleges was made with the defendant, permission will not be granted under this clause, but specific provision has been introduced to allow permission to be given in proceedings for such a declaration.[4]

S11–160   **(i) Where a contract is made in England.** If the parties enter into negotiations by correspondence from different countries, the contract is made where the letter of acceptance is posted.[5] But in commercial transactions today communication by telephone, telex, fax and electronic mail is much more common than by post. It is now well established, following the decision of the Court of Appeal in *Entores v. Miles Far East Corporation*[6] (which has been approved by the House of Lords[7]) that if the parties use "instantaneous" means of communication such as telephone, fax or electronic mail,[8] the contract is made where the acceptance is communicated to the offeror.

It has been held that if a contract made in England contains a submission to arbitration in a foreign country, an action in England at common law to enforce the foreign arbitration award is within this part of the clause.[9]

The contract must actually be made in England as that phrase is understood in English law. It is not sufficient if it merely says that it shall be deemed to be so made, though this may be sufficient to make it one which is governed by English law.[10] A contract may be made in England within the meaning of this clause although it was preceded by a less formal agreement made abroad.[11]

S11–161   **(ii) Where a contract is made by or through an agent trading or residing in England.** It will be observed that the clause says "by or through" an agent, not "by" an agent. Hence the case is within the clause, although the agent has no authority to make contracts on behalf of his foreign principal, but only has authority to obtain orders and transmit them to his principal for acceptance or rejection.[12] This part of the clause is designed to bring within Rule 27 foreigners who transact business in England by or through agents,

---

[3] *Finnish Marine Insurance Co. Ltd. v. Protective National Insurance Co.* [1990] 1 Q.B. 1078.

[4] CPR, r. 6.20(7), clause (8) of this Rule.

[5] *Wansborough Paper Co. Ltd. v. Laughland* [1920] W.N. 344 (C.A.); *Benaim v. Debono* [1924] A.C. 514, 520 (P.C.); *Clarke v. Harper and Robinson* [1938] N.Ir. 162: *Williams v. Society of Lloyd's* [1994] 1 V.R. 274. See also *Cowan v. O'Connor* (1888) 20 Q.B.D. 640; *Lewis Construction Co. Ltd. v. M. Tichauer S.A.* [1966] V.R. 341.

[6] [1955] 2 Q.B. 327 (C.A.); *Gill & Duffus Landauer v. London Export Corp.* [1982] 2 Lloyd's Rep. 627; *Kelly v. Cruise Catering Ltd.* [1994] 2 I.L.R.M. 394; *Hampstead Meats Pty. Ltd. v. Emerson and Yates Pty. Ltd.* [1967] S.A.S.R. 109; *Express Airways v. Port Augusta Air Services* [1980] Qd. 543; *Mendelson-Zeller Co. Inc. v. T. & C. Providores Pty. Ltd.* [1981] 1 N.S.W.L.R. 366; *Re Modern Fashions Ltd.* (1969) 8 D.L.R. (3d) 590 (Man.); *McDonald & Sons Ltd. v. Export Packers Co. Ltd.* (1979) 95 D.L.R. (3d) 174 (B.C.); *Eastern Power Ltd. v. Azienda Communale Energia e Ambiente* [2001] I.L. Pr. 55 (Ont. C.A.).

[7] *Brinkibon Ltd. v. Stahag Stahl* [1983] 2 A.C. 34. *Cf. Bank of Baroda v. Vysya Bank Ltd.* [1994] 2 Lloyd's Rep. 87.

[8] But the place of receipt of electronic mail is a concept by no means free from difficulty. See *Dow Jones & Co. Inc. v. Gutnick* [2002] HCA 56, (2003) 194 A.L.R. 433.

[9] *Bremer Oeltransport v. Drewry* [1933] 1 K.B. 753 (C.A.). See para. 16–064. But see now CPR, r. 6.20 (9), clause (10), *infra*.

[10] See Rule 174 and *cf. British Controlled Oilfields Ltd. v. Stagg* [1921] W.N. 319.

[11] *Gibbon v. Commerz und Creditbank A.G.* [1958] 2 Lloyd's Rep. 113.

[12] *National Mortgage and Agency Co. of N.Z. Ltd. v. Gosselin* (1922) 38 T.L.R. 832 (C.A.); *cf. BHP Petroleum Pty. Ltd. v. Oil Basins Ltd.* [1985] V.R. 725; affd. [1985] V.R. 756.

and consequently it does not apply where the agent's principal is the claimant. Hence a claimant cannot invoke clause (6)(ii) where the contract was made by or through his agent.[13]

If proceedings are brought by consignees of a cargo against foreign shipowners under the bills of lading, the case is not within this part of the clause if the charterparty (but not the bills of lading) was made by or through agents of the shipowners in England, even though it refers to the bills of lading and was made by charterers acting on behalf of the consignees.[14] It may be otherwise, however, if the charterers are identical with the consignees.   **S11–162**

Rule 6.16 of the Civil Procedure Rules provides an alternative method of service if the conditions laid down in clause (6)(ii) of Rule 27 are satisfied together with two other conditions, namely, that the contract was made in England, and that the agent's authority has not been terminated or he is still in business relations with his principal. This method is to issue proceedings against the principal, and serve process with permission of the court on the agent in England.   **S11–163**

When an order under CPR, r. 6.16 has been obtained, a copy of the order and of the claim form must be sent to the defendant. The procedure is essentially discretionary, not normally to be resorted to when there is no difficulty in proceeding under CPR, r. 6.20, *i.e.* Rule 27. It is more appropriate in a case where the foreign principal has a general agent doing large business for him in England than where the foreign principal makes a single contract through a broker.[15]   **S11–164**

(iii) Where a contract is governed by English law. The rules for ascertaining the governing law of a contract are considered in Rules 172 to 174.[16] The Rome Convention on the Law Applicable to Contractual Obligations, to which effect is given by the Contracts (Applicable Law) Act 1990 applies its rules to "any situation involving a choice between the laws of different countries" (Article 1). The rules of the Convention, as incorporated by the 1990 Act, have been applied[17] to determine whether a contract by its terms or by implication is governed by English law for the purposes of this clause.   **S11–165**

Although the fact that a contract is governed by English law is an important factor in the exercise of the discretion under this head in favour of the English forum,[18] it is not conclusive. This head of jurisdiction was described as exorbitant in *Amin Rasheed Shipping Corp. v. Kuwait Insurance Co.*,[19] where the House of Lords held that in the circumstances it was not appropriate for the English court to determine a dispute involving a marine insurance policy governed by English law when the Kuwaiti courts were the *forum conveniens*. Until that decision it was generally thought that the fact   **S11–166**

---

[13] *Union International Insurance Co. Ltd. v. Jubilee Insurance Co. Ltd.* [1991] 1 W.L.R. 415.

[14] *The Metamorphosis* [1953] 1 W.L.R. 543.

[15] See the Practice Memorandum quoted in *The Supreme Court Practice 1999*, 10/2/3. This has not yet been reproduced in the CPR Practice Directions.

[16] Several important cases on the common law rules as to the ascertainment of the governing law were decided under clause (6) of Rule 27, the most important modern example of which was *Amin Rasheed Shipping Corp. v. Kuwait Insurance Co.* [1984] A.C. 50.

[17] *Bank of Baroda v. Vysya Bank Ltd.* [1994] 2 Lloyd's Rep. 87; *Egon Oldendorff v. Libera Corp.* [1995] 2 Lloyd's Rep. 64, stated *post*, Illustration 10.

[18] *B.P. Exploration Co. (Libya) v. Hunt* [1976] 3 All E.R. 879, 893, as explained in *The Elli 2* [1985] 1 Lloyd's Rep. 107, 118 (C.A.).

[19] [1984] A.C. 50, 65, Illustration 7, *infra*. It is regarded as exorbitant in civil law countries; see Schlosser, para. 87.

that a contract was governed by English law was in itself sufficient to justify leave. But now the claimant has a heavier burden. In *Amin Rasheed* Lord Diplock suggested[20] that, in order to justify leave under this head, the plaintiff had to show that justice could not be obtained by him in the foreign court, or could only be obtained at excessive cost, delay or inconvenience. But it was subsequently held that Lord Diplock was merely giving examples, and was not providing an exhaustive list, of the relevant factors.[21] The court has to consider all factors, and the fact that English law is the applicable law may be of great importance, or it may be of little consequence as seen in the context of the whole case.[22] Thus if there is likely to be no dispute on matters of law or construction, or if the law of the foreign forum is substantially the same as English law, the fact that English law is the applicable law will be of little weight. But where an issue of English public policy arises in relation to a contract which is (or may be) governed by English law, it is desirable that it should be decided by the English court[23]; conversely, where the foreign court may apply its own public policy to defeat a claim based on a contract governed by English law, that too is a reason for the English court taking jurisdiction.[24] If the claimant has alternative remedies in contract and tort upon the same facts, he can choose his remedy.[25]

S11–167   Although the Judgments Regulation and the 1968 and Lugano Conventions supersede this clause as regards defendants domiciled in other Regulation States or Contracting States, it should be noted that there are transitional provisions in the Conventions (but not in the Judgments Regulation) which deal with cases where the parties to a dispute concerning a contract had agreed in writing that the contract was to be governed by English law. In such cases the English court may retain the right to exercise jurisdiction in the dispute over a domiciliary of another Contracting State. In the case of the 1968 Convention, the exception applies if the parties to the dispute had agreed in writing before January 1, 1987, that the contract was to be governed by the law of a part of the United Kingdom.[26] In the case of the Lugano Convention, the critical date is the date of "the entry into force of this Convention."[27] It would seem that this means May 1, 1992, when the Lugano Convention first entered into force generally and also for the United Kingdom, and not any later date on which it came into force as between the United Kingdom and the Contracting State of which the proposed defendant is a domiciliary. The exceptions only apply if there is an express choice of English law in writing, and do not apply if the contract is governed by English law merely because a choice of English law can be implied or because the contract is most closely connected with England.[28]

---

[20] [1984] A.C. at 68.

[21] *Spiliada Maritime Corp. v. Cansulex Ltd.* [1987] A.C. 460, 480, approving *The Elli 2* [1985] 1 Lloyd's Rep. 107 (C.A.).

[22] [1987] A.C. at 481, 486. *Cf. New Hampshire Insurance Co. v. Strabag Bau AG* [1992] 1 Lloyd's Rep. 361, 370 (C.A.); *Trade Indemnity plc v. Forsakringsaktiebolaget Njord* [1995] 1 All E.R. 796; *Macsteel Commercial Holdings (Pty) Ltd. v. Thermasteel* [1996] C.L.C. 1403.

[23] *E. I. du Pont de Nemours v. Agnew* [1987] 2 Lloyd's Rep. 585 (C.A.); *Mitsubishi Corp. v. Alafouzos* [1988] 1 Lloyd's Rep. 191.

[24] *The Magnum* [1989] 1 Lloyd's Rep. 47 (C.A.).

[25] *Matthews v. Kuwait Bechtel Corporation* [1959] 2 Q.B. 57 (C.A.), stated *infra*, Illustration 6.

[26] 1968 Convention, Art. 54(3) (formerly 1978 Accession Convention, Art. 35).

[27] Lugano Convention, Art. 54(3).

[28] See *New Hampshire Insurance Co. v. Strabag Bau AG* [1992] 1 Lloyd's Rep. 361 (C.A.).

(iv) Where a contract contains a term to the effect that the court shall have S11–168
jurisdiction to determine any claim in respect of the contract. This clause
had its origin in 1920,[29] when it was introduced to allow service out of the
jurisdiction in cases where there was a contractual submission but where no
other head of Order 11, r. 1(1) was applicable. It is dealt with more fully in
connection with Rule 32(1) on jurisdiction clauses which confer jurisdiction
on English courts.[30]

ILLUSTRATIONS

(1) CONTRACT MADE IN ENGLAND

1. X, by letter posted in New York, orders goods from A in England. A accepts the S11–169
order by letter posted in England. The contract is made in England and the court may
assume jurisdiction.[31]

2. A in London sends an offer by telex to buy goods to X in Tokyo. X accepts the offer
in a similar manner. The contract is made in England and the court may assume
jurisdiction.[32]

3. X in Delhi sends by telex an offer to sell goods to A is London. A accepts the offer by
sending a telex to Delhi. The contract is made in Delhi and the court has no jurisdiction.[33]

4. A charterparty made in London between A, a Swedish firm of shipowners, and X,
who resides in Spain, contains a clause providing for the submission of disputes to
arbitration in Stockholm. Under an arbitration conducted in Stockholm in pursuance of
this clause, an award is made against X of £20,000, payable in English currency. A brings
proceedings against X to enforce the award. The court may assume jurisdiction because
the contract containing the submission to arbitration was made in England.[34]

(2) CONTRACT MADE BY OR THROUGH AN AGENT TRADING OR RESIDING IN ENGLAND

5. X, who resides and carries on business in Canada, employs N, who resides and carries S11–170
on business in England, as his agent to obtain orders for goods and submit them to X in
Canada for acceptance or rejection. N has no authority to make contracts on X's behalf. N
obtains an order from A and submits it to X, who accepts it. A brings proceedings against
X for breach of warranty. The court may assume jurisdiction.[35]

(3) CONTRACT GOVERNED BY ENGLISH LAW

6. A is employed by X & Co. in Kuwait under a contract governed by English law. He S11–171
sustains personal injuries in Kuwait in the course of his employment there. He brings
proceedings against X & Co. in England for breach of an implied term in the contract of
service. The court may assume jurisdiction.[36]

7. X & Co., a Kuwaiti insurance company, issues a policy insuring a vessel owned by A
& Co., a Liberian corporation. The policy is based on the form scheduled to the Marine
Insurance Act 1906. The vessel is seized by the Saudi Arabian authorities and A & Co.
claims under the policy for constructive total loss. X & Co. claims that the vessel was
engaged in smuggling and that accordingly the exclusion in the policy relating to
infringement of customs regulations applies. The court has jurisdiction because the policy
is governed by English law. But the court will not exercise its jurisdiction because the
Kuwaiti courts are the *forum conveniens* in the circumstances of the case.[37]

8. A & Co., Liberian shipowners, chartered a ship to Y & Co., an Indian company, for
the carriage of a cargo of sulphur from Vancouver, Canada, to Indian ports. X & Co., a

---

[29] To reverse the decision in *British Wagon Co. v. Gray* [1896] 1 Q.B. 35 (C.A.).
[30] See paras. 12–111 *et seq.*
[31] *Cf. Wansborough Paper Co. Ltd. v. Laughland* [1920] W.N. 344 (C.A.).
[32] *Cf. Entores Ltd. v. Miles Far East Corporation* [1955] 2 Q.B. 327 (C.A.).
[33] *Cf. Brinkibon Ltd. v. Stahag Stahl* [1983] 2 A.C. 34.
[34] *Cf. Bremer Oeltransport GmbH v. Drewry* [1933] 1 K.B. 753 (C.A.). The Judgments Regulation
and the Conventions do not apply to the enforcement of arbitral awards: paras. 11–024 *et. seq.*
See now clause (10), *infra.*
[35] *Cf. National Mortgage and Agency Co. of N.Z. Ltd. v. Gosselin* (1922) 38 T.L.R. 832 (C.A.).
[36] *Matthews v. Kuwait Bechtel Corporation* [1959] 2 Q.B. 57 (C.A.).
[37] *Amin Rasheed Shipping Corp. v. Kuwait Insurance Co.* [1984] A.C. 50.

Canadian company, sold the sulphur to Y & Co., and bills of lading, expressed to be governed by English law, were issued to and accepted by X & Co. A & Co. allege that the cargo of sulphur was wet and caused severe corrosion of the ship, and claim under the contract of carriage contained in, or evidenced by, the bills of lading. The court assumes jurisdiction (even though much of the factual dispute relates to events in British Columbia), particularly because there has been extensive litigation in England arising out of a similar shipment on another ship owned by different shipowners, which had been settled, but in the course of which an enormous amount of factual and scientific evidence had been collected; the owners' insurers and solicitors are the same in both sets of litigation; and there is a dispute as to the effect under English law of the bill of lading contract and as to the nature of the obligations under the contract in respect of dangerous cargo.[38]

9. A & Co., a Japanese company, agrees to build a bulk carrier for Y & Co., a Greek company, which is owned by X, a Greek shipowner. The shipbuilding contract is governed by English law, and provides for arbitration in London. X signs a performance guarantee, which contains no express choice of law. X alleges that the guarantee is illegal and contrary to English public policy because it was drafted in such a way as to mislead the Japanese authorities about the price in order to obtain an export licence. The guarantee is governed by English law, and the court will exercise its jurisdiction against X because it is highly desirable that the issue of English public policy should be decided by the English court.[39]

10. A & Co., a German partnership, agrees with X & Co., a Japanese company, that X & Co. will charter to A & Co. two bulk carriers to be built for X & Co. in Japan. The charter contains a London arbitration clause. The court has jurisdiction because the charter is governed by English law under Rule 174.[40]

(4) CONTRACT CONTAINS A TERM TO THE EFFECT THAT THE COURT SHALL HAVE JURISDICTION

S11–172   11. A contract is made abroad (and governed by foreign law) between A & Co., a Japanese company, and X & Co., an American company, whereby A & Co. agree to tow X & Co.'s oil rig from Venice, Louisiana, to Ravenna, Italy. The contract provides that "any dispute arising must be treated before the London court of justice." The tug and tow are forced to take refuge in Tampa, Florida, each alleging that this was the other's fault. X & Co. bring proceedings against A & Co. in Florida, and A & Co. bring an action against X & Co. in England. The court may assume jurisdiction.[41]

S11R–173   **(7) The court may assume jurisdiction if the claim is made in respect of a breach of contract committed in England.[42]**

COMMENT

S11–174   A contract may be broken in one of three ways, namely, by express repudiation, implied repudiation or failure to perform.

Breach by express repudiation occurs when one party informs the other that he no longer intends to perform the contract. If X who is abroad writes a letter of repudiation to A in England, the breach is not committed in England.[43] On the other hand, if X who is abroad sends his agent to

---

[38] *Spiliada Maritime Corp. v. Cansulex Ltd.* [1987] A.C. 460.

[39] *Mitsubishi Corp. v. Alafouzos* [1988] 1 Lloyd's Rep. 191 (a pre-1968 Convention case).

[40] *Egon Oldendorff v. Libera Corp.* [1995] 2 Lloyd's Rep. 64.

[41] *Cf. The Chaparral* [1968] 2 Lloyd's Rep. 158 (C.A.). For the sequel in the American courts, see *M/S Bremen v. Zapata Offshore Co.*, 407 U.S. 1 (1972); [1972] 2 Lloyd's Rep. 315; Collins, *Essays*, p. 253; Kahn-Freund (1977) 26 I.C.L.Q. 825, 845–848.

[42] CPR, r. 6.20(6). It has been held that for the purposes of a predecessor of this clause, contract includes quasi-contract: *McFee Engineering Pty. Ltd. v. C.B.S. Construction Pty. Ltd.* (1980) 28 A.L.R. 339. For restitutionary claims, see clause (16), *infra*.

[43] *Cherry v. Thompson* (1872) L.R. 7 Q.B. 573, 579; *Holland v. Bennett* [1902] 1 K.B. 867 (C.A.). both approved in *Martin v. Stout* [1925] A.C. 359, 368–369 (P.C.); *Atlantic Underwriting Agencies Ltd. v. Compagnia di Assicurazione di Milano* [1979] 2 Lloyd's Rep. 240; *Safran v. Chani* [1970] 1 N.S.W.L.R. 70; *Stanley Kerr Holdings Pty. Ltd. v. Gibor Textile Enterprises Ltd.* [1978] 2 N.S.W.L.R. 372.

England, or writes to his agent who is in England, instructing him to repudiate the contract, and the agent does so, *e.g.* by letter posted in England to A in England, then the breach is committed in England.[44]

Breach by implied repudiation occurs when one party does an act which **S11–175** is inconsistent with his performance of the contract, for instance, when X promises to sell a house to A but sells it to B instead. Although there is no authority on the point, the breach in such a case presumably occurs where the inconsistent act is done. This principle would appear to apply wherever the contractual obligation consists in an omission rather than an act, *e.g.* an obligation not to sell certain goods in England. The clause would apply if the goods were sold there.

If a contract is broken in England by express or implied repudiation, it **S11–176** would seem to be immaterial, for the purposes of CPR, r. 6.20(6) whether or not the contract was to be performed in England. Formerly the rule referred to a contract which "according to the terms thereof ought to be performed in England"; but there are no such words in the operative part of the present rule.

The normal form of breach is the failure of one party to perform one or **S11–177** more of his obligations under the contract. In such a case it is not necessary that the whole contract was to be performed in England by both the parties thereto, but it is necessary that some part of it was to be performed in England and that there has been a breach of that part.[45] It is not sufficient if the contract or part of it might be performed either in England or abroad; it is necessary that the contract or part of it was to be performed in England and not elsewhere.[46] The contract need not contain an express term providing for performance in England.[47] It is enough if the court can gather that this was the intention of the parties by construing the contract in the light of the surrounding circumstances, including the course of dealing between the parties.[48] In most of the reported cases, the breach complained of was the failure to pay money, a matter in which it is especially difficult to determine the place of performance in the absence of an express term in the contract.[49] "The general rule is that where no place of payment is specified, either expressly or by implication, the debtor must seek out his creditor."[50] But this is only a general rule[51] and, as stated, it only applies

---

[44] *Mutzenbecher v. La Aseguradora Espanola* [1906] 1 K.B. 254 (C.A.); *Oppenheimer v. Louis Rosenthal & Co. A.G.* [1937] 1 All E.R. 23 (C.A.).

[45] *Rein v. Stein* [1892] 1 Q.B. 753 (C.A.).

[46] *Bell & Co. v. Antwerp London and Brazil Line* [1891] 1 Q.B. 103 (C.A.); *The Eider* [1893] P. 119 (C.A.); *Comber v. Leyland* [1898] A.C. 524; *Cuban Atlantic Sugar Sales Corporation v. Compania de Vapores San Elefterio Lda.* [1960] 1 Q.B. 187. *Cf. BHP Petroleum Pty. Ltd. v. Oil Basins Ltd.* [1985] V.R. 725; affd. [1985] V.R. 756.

[47] *Reynolds v. Coleman* (1887) 36 Ch.D. 453 (C.A.), decided at a time when the clause referred to a contract which "according to the terms thereof" ought to be performed in England.

[48] The course of dealing was stressed in the following cases: *Rein v. Stein* [1892] 1 Q.B. 753 (C.A.); *Fry & Co. v. Raggio* (1891) 40 W.R. 120; *Charles Duval & Co. Ltd. v. Gans* [1904] 2 K.B. 685 (C.A.); *O'Mara Ltd. v. Dodd* [1912] 2 I.R. 55; *Shallay Holdings Pty. Ltd. v. Griffith Co-operative Society Ltd.* [1983] 1 V.R. 760.

[49] See also Law Commission, *Report on Council of Europe Convention on Place of Payment of Money Liabilities* (1972), Law Com. No. 109 (1981), p. 28.

[50] *The Eider* [1893] P. 119, 136–137 (C.A.). See also *Bank of Scotland v. Seitz*, 1990 S.L.T. 584 (a case on the 1968 Convention).

[51] *Deutsche Ruckversicherung AG v. La Fondaria Assicurazioni SpA* [2001] 2 Lloyd's Rep. 621; *Earthworks Ltd. v. F.T. Eastment & Sons Ltd.* [1966] V.R. 24; *B.P. Australia Ltd. v. Wales* [1982] Qd.R. 386.

where no place of payment is expressed *or implied* in the contract. It certainly does not mean that a creditor can confer jurisdiction on the English court merely by taking up his residence in England after the making of the contract.[52]

S11–178   If the contract is for the sale of goods by a seller in England to a buyer abroad, it will, in the absence of a contractual term to the contrary, be easy to infer that the buyer's obligation was to pay for the goods in England.[53] The same is the case if a principal in England sends goods to an agent abroad to be sold by him on commission.[54] But it is otherwise if, on the true construction of the contract, the only duty of the foreign agent is to sell the goods and remit the proceeds to England from abroad in a specified manner, because it will be inferred that his duty is at an end when he makes the remittance.[55] If a foreign principal appoints an agent in England to sell his goods on commission, it is usually inferred that the commission is payable in England.[56] In such a case, the fact that the agent claims an account of sales does not take the case out of the clause.[57]

S11–179   The duties of the seller of goods under a c.i.f. contract are to ship the goods and deliver the shipping documents to the buyer. It is not his duty to deliver the goods to the buyer.[58] Consequently, if the foreign seller ships goods which are found to be defective upon their arrival in England,[59] or if he fails to ship them at all, the breach is not committed in England within the meaning of the clause.

S11–180   In a contract of service, wages or salary would normally be payable where the service is to be performed, in the absence of an express or implied term in the contract.[60] But if the servant is employed in only a nominal or consultative capacity, and is free to reside where he likes, his salary may be payable in England, if that is where he decides to live.[61] In a contract for services, it may be possible to infer that the fee or commission is payable at the contractor's usual place of business, even if the work is to be performed abroad.[62]

S11–181   The fact that the contract provides for payment to be made in English currency has sometimes been held to yield the inference that payment was to be made in England,[63] but this is by no means a decisive consideration.[64]

---

[52] *Malik v. Narodni Banka Ceskoslovenska* [1946] 2 All E.R. 663 (C.A.); *cf. Fessard v. Mugnier* (1865) 18 C.B. (N.S.) 286.

[53] *Robey & Co. v. Snaefell Mining Co. Ltd.* (1887) 20 Q.B.D. 152; *Hassall v. Lawrence* (1887) 4 T.L.R. 23; *Fry & Co. v. Raggio* (1891) 40 W.R. 120; *O'Mara Ltd. v. Dodd* [1912] 2 I.R. 55.

[54] *Rein v. Stein* [1892] 1 Q.B. 753 (C.A.); *Charles Duval & Co. Ltd. v. Gans* [1904] 2 K.B. 685 (C.A.).

[55] *Comber v. Leyland* [1898] A.C. 524, a case "of a somewhat special character", *per* Stirling L.J. in *Charles Duval & Co. Ltd. v. Gans* [1904] 2 K.B. 685, 691 (C.A.).

[56] *Hoerter v. Hanover, etc., Works* (1893) 10 T.L.R. 103 (C.A.); *International Corporation Ltd. v. Besser Manufacturing Co.* [1950] 1 K.B. 488 (C.A.).

[57] *ibid.*

[58] See *Clemens Horst Co. v. Biddell* [1912] A.C. 18, approving the dissenting judgment of Kennedy L.J. in the C.A. [1911] 1 K.B. 214.

[59] *Crozier Stephens & Co. v. Auerbach* [1908] 2 K.B. 161 (C.A.); *Cordova Land Co. Ltd. v. Victor Bros. Inc.* [1966] 1 W.L.R. 793.

[60] See *Malik v. Narodni Banka Ceskoslovenska* [1946] 2 All E.R. 663 (C.A.).

[61] *Vitkovice Horni A Hutni Tezirstvo v. Korner* [1951] A.C. 869.

[62] *Thompson v. Palmer* [1893] 2 Q.B. 80 (C.A.); *International Power and Engineering Consultants Ltd. v. Clark* (1964) 43 D.L.R. (2d) 394 (B.C.C.A.). Contrast *Auckland Receivers Ltd. v. Diners Club* [1985] 2 N.S.W.L.R. 652.

[63] *Fry & Co. v. Raggio* (1891) 40 W.R. 120.

[64] *Bremer Oeltransport GmbH v. Drewry* [1933] 1 K.B. 753 (C.A.).

Conversely, the fact that payment is to be made in foreign currency does not necessarily mean that England was not to be the place of payment.[65] No inference as to the place of payment can properly be drawn from the fact that the contract contains a gold clause.[66]

If money is due under a compromise of a disputed claim, it is usually **S11–182** inferred that the money is payable where litigation is pending or would probably have taken place.[67]

An implied warranty of authority has been held to have been broken where the warranty was relied on.[68]

If the contract is governed by a foreign applicable law, the applicable law of the contract will determine where money due thereunder is payable.[69]

ILLUSTRATIONS

1. X, who resides in Toronto, is the owner of a New York newspaper. He employs A to **S11–183** act as London correspondent for the newspaper's European edition. He writes a letter from Naples to A in England, wrongfully dismissing him. The court has no jurisdiction by reason of the letter of repudiation.[70] But it would have jurisdiction if the letter was followed by non-payment of salary, because of the concluding words of the clause.

2. By a contract made in the Canary Islands X & Co., a Brazilian insurance company, appoint A, a London insurance agent, to act as their exclusive agent for five years for insurance business in the United Kingdom, and her overseas Colonies and Dominions, in continental Europe (except Spain, Portugal and Turkey) and in the United States. After one year X & Co. send their agent-general to England with instructions to terminate A's appointment. The agent-general does so by letter posted in London to A in England. A brings proceedings against X & Co. for breach of contract. The court may assume jurisdiction.[71]

3. A, an American citizen resident in England, and X, an American citizen resident in the United States, agree that if A will transfer certain patents to X, X will transfer to A 500 shares in an English company. A transfers the patents but X refuses to transfer the shares. The court may assume jurisdiction.[72]

4. X & Co., a Panamanian company, charter a ship from A & Co., English shipowners, **S11–184** to load a cargo in London and proceed therewith to Rio de Janeiro and Santos. The charterparty provides that the freight shall be paid as to part at the ports of discharge and as to the balance in London, and that all lighterage at ports of discharge shall be at charterers' risk and expense. A & Co., having paid the lighterage at the ports of discharge, bring proceedings against X & Co. for reimbursement. The court has no jurisdiction.[73]

5. A ship belonging to X & Co., Liberian shipowners, while on passage from New York to Bremen is stranded on the Wolf Rock, *i.e.* outside English territorial waters. A contract is made between the master and the agents of A & Co. and B & Co., Swedish and German

---

[65] *Rein v. Stein* [1892] 1 Q.B. 753 (C.A.); *Drexel v. Drexel* [1916] 1 Ch. 251; *Vitkovice Horni A Huni Tezirstvo v. Korner* [1951] A.C. 869.

[66] *Vitkovice Horni A Hutni Tezirstvo v. Korner, supra.*

[67] *Golden v. Darlow* (1891) 8 T.L.R. 57 (C.A.); *Anger v. Vasnier* (1902) 18 T.L.R. 596 (C.A.).

[68] *The Piraeus* [1974] 2 Lloyd's Rep. 266 (C.A.).

[69] *Cf. Malik v. Narodni Banka Ceskoslovenska* [1946] 2 All E.R. 663 (C.A.); *Vitkovice Horni A Hutni Tezirstvo v. Korner* [1951] A.C. 869; and see *ibid. sub nom. Korner v. Witkowitzer* [1950] 2 K.B. 128, esp. at pp. 159–161. See now Contracts (Applicable Law) Act 1990, Sched. 1, Art. 10(1)(*b*).

[70] *Cf. Holland v. Bennett* [1902] 1 K.B. 867 (C.A.), following *Cherry v. Thompson* (1872) L.R. 7 Q.E. 573, 579 (promise in Germany to marry in Germany, repudiated by letter sent from Germany to England: held, broken in Germany). Contrast *Cooper v. Knight* (1901) 17 T.L.R. 299 (C.A.) (promise in England to marry in England, repudiated by letter sent from Belgium to England: held, broken in England).

[71] *Cf. Mutzenbecher v. La Aseguradora Espanola* [1906] 1 K.B. 254 (C.A.); *cf. Oppenheimer v. Louis Rosenthal & Co. A.G.* [1937] 1 All B.R. 23 (C.A.).

[72] *Reynolds v. Coleman* (1887) 36 Ch.D. 453 (C.A.).

[73] *Cf. Bell & Co. v. Antwerp London and Brazil Line* [1891] 1 Q.B. 103 (C.A.).

salvage companies, whereby the salvage companies agree to salve the ship and tow it to Falmouth for repairs in return for 50 per cent, of its value when salved. The contract provides for payment of the salvage money to B & Co., the German company, no place of payment being specified. It is orally agreed between the agents of the two salvage companies that A & Co. will receive half the salvage money. Disputes arise as to the value of the ship when salved, and A & Co. bring proceedings against X & Co. for their share. The court has no jurisdiction.[74]

6. X & Co., a Manx company, order a boiler and machinery to be supplied by A & Co. in England and delivered to X & Co.'s mine in the Isle of Man for £585. A & Co. accept and execute the order. In proceedings by A & Co. for non-payment of the price, the court may assume jurisdiction.[75]

S11–185   7. A sends goods from England to X, his agent in Brazil, X contracts with A to sell the goods and remit the proceeds to England by first-class bank bills. X sells the goods but keeps the proceeds. The court has no jurisdiction, because X can perform his part of the contract by posting the bills from Brazil.[76]

8. By a contract made in New York, A & Co., wine shippers in London, appoint X, a firm of New York wine merchants, their sole agents for the sale of champagne in the United States, Canada and Cuba. The contract does not state where the champagne is to be paid for, but the course of dealing between the parties is for X to pay by drafts on a London bank. The court may assume jurisdiction.[77]

9. By a contract made in the United States X & Co., an American company, appoint A & Co., an English company, their sole agents for the sale of X & Co.'s products in England and the countries of continental Europe, and agree to pay A & Co. a commission of 15 per cent on all products sold. A & Co. bring proceedings against X & Co. claiming an account of all sales effected by them and payment of commission on such sales. The court may assume jurisdiction.[78]

S11–186   10. A, a Czech, is employed by X & Co., a Czech bank, as manager of the bank's foreign exchange department. His contract of employment provides for salary to be paid in Czech crowns. In August 1939 A goes to Switzerland, partly on leave and partly to safeguard the bank's deposit of gold there in the event of war. A then proceeds to England. In proceedings by A for nonpayment of salary, the court has no jurisdiction.[79]

11. By a contract made in Czechoslovakia in 1929 X & Co., a Czech company, agrees to pay a pension to A, a Czech, one of the directors of X & Co., on his retirement. The contract provides for payment in Czech crowns. It is agreed between the parties that A shall be entitled to live where he likes and to be paid his pension in the place where he resides. A retires in 1938, and by another contract X & Co. agrees to retain his services in a consultative capacity in Switzerland, France or England at A's option, and to pay him a salary of £2,000 a year in addition to his pension. A retires to England. In proceedings by A for non-payment of his pension and salary, the court may assume jurisdiction.[80]

12. A, a Newcastle mining engineer, is engaged by X to design and superintend the construction of docks which X is to build in Hungary for the Hungarian Government. A brings proceedings against X for non-payment of his commission and travelling expenses to Hungary. The court may assume jurisdiction.[81]

13. A bill of exchange is drawn by A in London on X and accepted by X in London, "payable at the C.M. Bank, Kandy." In proceedings by A for non-payment the court may assume jurisdiction, because under section 19 of the Bills of Exchange Act 1882 an acceptance payable at a particular place is a general acceptance unless it expressly states that the bill is to be paid there only and not elsewhere.[82]

---

[74] *Cf. The Eider* [1893] P. 119 (C.A.), where the stranding occurred and the contract was made in English territorial waters. At that date the fact that a contract was made in England did not bring a case within clause (6), *supra*, para. S11–160.

[75] *Robey & Co. v. Snaefell Mining Co. Ltd.* (1887) 20 Q.B.D. 152.

[76] *Comber v. Leyland* [1898] A.C. 254.

[77] *Charles Duval & Co. Ltd. v. Gans* [1904] 2 K.B. 685 (C.A.).

[78] *International Corporation Ltd. v. Besser Manufacturing Co.* [1950] 1 K.B. 488 (C.A.).

[79] *Malik v. Narodni Banka Ceskoslovenska* [1946] 2 All E.R. 663 (C.A.).

[80] *Vitkovice Horni A Hutni Tezirstyo v. Korner* [1951] A.C. 869.

[81] *Cf. Thompson v. Palmer* [1893] 2 Q.B. 80 (C.A.). *Cf. International Power and Engineering Consultants Ltd. v. Clark* (1964) 43 D.L.R. (2d) 394 (B.C.C.A.).

[82] *Ex. p. Hayward* (1887) 3 T.L.R. 687.

(8) The court may assume jurisdiction if the claim is made for a   S11R–187
declaration that no contract exists where, if the contract were found to
exist, it would comply with the conditions in clause (6).[83]

COMMENT

It had been held, in relation to the predecessor of clause (6), that if, on the   S11–188
claimant's own showing, no contract was made with the defendant, then
permission could not be granted under clause (6).[84] Accordingly if the
claimant was seeking a declaration that there was no contract, then the
court would have no jurisdiction, whereas if the other party had brought the
converse claim for a declaration that there was a contract, the court would
have jurisdiction. Clause (8) now allows what would be an essentially
contractual dispute to be determined in England if the requisite English
connections exist, and jurisdiction does not depend on which party seeks
the declaration.

ILLUSTRATION

A, a Hungarian insurance company, seeks a declaration that it is not bound by reinsurance   S11–189
contracts to indemnify X, a United States insurance company, because the brokers who
purportedly placed the reinsurance on behalf of X had no authority from A. If the
reinsurance contracts had been validly placed they would be governed by English law. The
court has jurisdiction.[85]

(9) The court may assume jurisdiction if the claim is made in tort where   S11R–190
the damage was sustained in England, or the damage sustained resulted
from an act committed within England.[86]

COMMENT

The question where a tort is committed for the purposes of choice of law is   S11–191
fully considered elsewhere.[87] Until the amendment of R.S.C., Order 11, r.
1(1) in 1987 jurisdiction could be assumed under this clause only if the
action was "founded on a tort committed within the jurisdiction." As both
the Privy Council[88] and the Supreme Court of Canada[89] have pointed out,
the competing theories for the determination of the place of a tort have
been that (i) all ingredients of the cause of action must have occurred

---

[83] CPR, r. 6.20(7).
[84] *Finnish Marine Insurance Co. Ltd. v. Protective National Insurance Co.* [1990] Q.B. 1078.
[85] CPR, r. 6.20 (7), reversing the effect of *Finnish Marine Insurance Co. Ltd. v. Protective National Insurance Co.* [1990] Q.B. 1078.
[86] CPR, r. 6.20(8). See generally *Transnational Tort Litigation: Jurisdictional Principles*, ed. McLachlan and Nygh (1996).
[87] paras. 35–081 *et seq.*
[88] *Distillers Co. Ltd. v. Thompson* [1971] A.C. 458.
[89] *Moran v. Pyle National (Canada) Ltd.* (1973) 43 D.L.R. (3d) 239. In this case, discussed by Collins (1975) 24 I.C.L.Q. 325, the court held, in a product liability case where the plaintiff had suffered injury in one province from a product negligently made in another province, that the province where the harm had occurred could exercise jurisdiction. It was extended to purely economic loss in *Skyrotors v. Carrière Technical Industries* (1979) 102 D.L.R. (3d) 323 (Ont.); see also *Ichi Canada Ltd. v. Yamauchi Rubber Industry Co.* (1983) 144 D.L.R. (3d) 533 (B.C.C.A.).

within the jurisdiction, or (ii) the last ingredient, the event which completes a cause of action, must have occurred within the jurisdiction, or (iii) the act which the defendant committed must have occurred within the jurisdiction.

S11–192   In *Distillers Co. Ltd. v. Thompson*[90] the Privy Council adopted the test of the place where in substance the act or omission occurred which gave the plaintiff his cause of action. So that where the essence of the complaint was failure to warn the consumer of the dangers of a product (rather than the faulty manufacture of the product) the cause of action was held to have arisen at the place where the failure to warn occurred[91]; and the torts of negligent and fraudulent misrepresentation, where the negligent or fraudulent statement was communicated from one country to another, were held to have been committed where the statement was received and acted upon.[92] Prior to the adoption of that test, but consistently with it, it had been held that the tort of defamation was committed where the defamatory statements were published and not where they were posted or uttered.[93]

S11–193   The current version of this clause was adopted originally in order to bring the tort provision of R.S.C., Order 11, r. 1(1) into line with the 1968 Convention and intra-United Kingdom provisions.[94] These provisions (and those of the Judgments Regulation and the Lugano Convention) grant jurisdiction to the courts of "the place where the harmful event occurred" and this expression was interpreted by the European Court in 1976[95] to grant alternative jurisdiction to the courts of the places, if different, (a) where the damage occurred, and (b) where the event which gave rise to the damage occurred. Clause (9) accordingly applies where the claim is founded on a tort, and (a) the damage was sustained within the jurisdiction, or (b) the damage sustained resulted from an act committed within the jurisdiction.

S11–194   In *Metall und Rohstoff A.G. v. Donaldson Lufkin & Jenrette Inc.*[96] the Court of Appeal posed the question of what law is to be applied in

---

[90] [1971] A.C. 458 (P.C.). This decision related to a differently formulated rule in N.S.W., but it was applied to the former English rule in *Diamond v. Bank of London and Montreal Ltd.* [1979] Q.B. 333 (C.A.); *Castree v. Squibb & Sons Ltd.* [1980] 1 W.L.R. 1248 (C.A.); *Multinational Gas Co. v. Multinational Gas Services Ltd.* [1983] Ch. 258 (C.A.); *cf. Russell v. Woolworth & Co.*, 1982 S.C. 20; *Kirkcaldy D.C. v. Household Manufacturing Ltd.*, 1987 S.L.T. 617; *Scott Lithgow Ltd. v. GEC Electrical Projects Ltd.*, 1992 S.L.T. 244 (cases on Scots law prior to the 1982 Act). The Supreme Court of Ireland held that there is jurisdiction (for the purposes of the unamended clause (9) if "*any* significant element" has occurred within the jurisdiction: *Grehan v. Medical Inc.* [1986] I.R. 528, 541–542.

[91] *Distillers Co. Ltd. v. Thompson, supra*, discussed by Bissett-Johnson (1970) 48 Can. Bar Rev. 548; Collins, *Essays*, pp. 234–237; *Castree v. Squibb & Sons Ltd., supra*; *Buttigeig v. Universal Terminal and Stevedoring Corp.* [1972] V.R. 626; *My v. Toyota Motor Co. Ltd.* [1977] 2 N.Z.L.R. 113.

[92] *Multinational Gas Co. v. Multinational Gas Services Ltd.* [1983] Ch. 258 (C.A.); *The Albaforth* [1984] 2 Lloyd's Rep. 91 (C.A.); *Original Blouse Co. Ltd. v. Bruck Mills Ltd.* (1963) 42 D.L.R. (2d) 174 (B.C.); *Petersen v. A/B Bahco* (1980) 107 D.L.R. (3d) 49 (B.C.); *Canadian Commercial Bank v. Carpenter* (1990) 62 D.L.R. (4th) 734 (B.C.C.A.); *National Bank of Canada v. Clifford Chance* (1996) 30 O.R. (3d) 746; *Pei v. Bank Bumiputra Malaysia Berhad* (1998) 41 O.R. (3d) 39. Contrast *Cordova Land Co. Ltd. v. Victor Bros Inc.* [1966] 1 W.L.R. 793 (C.A.). *Cf. Minster Investments Ltd. v. Hyundai Precision and Industry Co. Ltd.* [1988] 2 Lloyd's Rep. 621; but see *Domicrest Ltd. v. Swiss Bank Corp.* [1999] Q.B. 547, para. S11–264.

[93] *Bata v. Bata* [1948] W.N. 366 (C.A.); *Jenner v. Sun Oil Co.* [1952] 2 D.L.R. 526 (Ont.); *Pindling v. N.B.C.* (1984) 14 D.L.R. (4th) 391 (Ont.); *cf. Bree v. Marescaux* (1881) 7 Q.B.D. 434. For libel on the internet see *Dow Jones & Co. Inc. v. Gutnick* [2002] HCA 56, [2003] 194 A.L.R. 433.

[94] See paras. S11–261 *et seq.*

[95] Case 21/76 *Bier v. Mines de Potasse d'Alsace S.A.* [1976] E.C.R. 1735; [1978] Q.B. 708. For later developments see Rule 28(3).

[96] [1990] 1 Q.B. 391 (C.A.), overruled in *Lonrho plc v. Fayed* [1992] 1 A.C. 448 on other aspects.

resolving whether the claim is "founded on a tort" (the then expression: now "made in tort"), and answered it in part by citing a statement in the eleventh edition of this work that the question concerned the interpretation of a connecting factor, which would always be answered in accordance with the English rules of the conflict of laws.[97] Accordingly, relying exclusively on principles of English law, the Court of Appeal decided that claims based on constructive trust, or procuring a breach of trust, were not claims based on tort.[98]

Damage sustained within the jurisdiction must refer to recoverable damage, including recoverable economic loss. In Canada and Australia, similar wording has been held to apply to consequential pecuniary damage sustained in the forum flowing from physical injury caused outside the forum.[99] The fact that the centre of the claimant's business is within the jurisdiction does not necessarily mean that the economic damage is sustained there.[1] In the second part of the formula, "an act committed within the jurisdiction" also extends to negligent omissions such as a failure to give adequate warning about the dangers of a product. In the *Metall und Rohstoff* case it was held that, for the purposes of each part of the formula, it is not necessary that all of the damage be sustained within the jurisdiction, or that all of the acts be committed within the jurisdiction. Some significant damage must have occurred in England; or the damage (wherever sustained) must result from substantial and efficacious acts committed within the jurisdiction, irrespective of whether or not other substantial and efficacious acts have been committed elsewhere.[2]

By contrast, however, with Article 5(3) of the Judgments Regulation and **S11–195** the Conventions, the exercise of jurisdiction under clause (9) is discretionary, and the court must consider what is the *forum conveniens*. In principle the jurisdiction where the tort is committed is prima facie the natural forum for the determination of the dispute: "If the substance of an alleged tort is committed within a certain jurisdiction, it is not easy to imagine what other facts could displace the conclusion that the courts of that jurisdiction are the natural forum."[3] But where the acts or omissions occur, and the damage is sustained, in different countries, the *forum conveniens* may depend on the extent to which the issues are likely to relate to liability or to damage, and the relative importance of the place of acting and the place of damage from the point of view of the convenience of the parties and of witnesses and the other factors which the court takes into account in the exercise of the

---

[97] At pp. 437, 441.

[98] At pp. 473–474, 480–481. *Cf. Suncorp Realty Inc. v. PLN Investments Inc.* (1985) 23 D.L.R. (4th) 83 (Man.) (action to set aside fraudulent conveyance not an action in tort).

[99] *Skyrotors Ltd. v. Carrière Technical Industries* (1979) 102 D.L.R. (3d) 323 (Ont.); *Vile v. von Wendt* (1979) 103 D.L.R. (3d) 356 (Ont. C.A.); *Poirier v. Williston* (1980) 113 D.L.R. (3d) 252; app. dismissed (1981) 118 D.L.R. (3d) 576 (Ont. C.A.); *Challenor v. Douglas* [1983] 2 N.S.W.L.R. 405; *Girgis v. Flaherty* [1984] 1 N.S.W.L.R. 56; affd. *sub nom Flaherty v. Girgis* (1985) 4 N.S.W.L.R. 248.

[1] *Soc. Commerciale Réassurance v. Eras International Ltd.* [1992] 1 Lloyd's Rep. 570 (C.A.); *Bastone & Firminger Ltd. v. Nasima Enterprises (Nigeria) Ltd.* [1996] C.L.C. 1902. Contrast *Skyrotors Ltd. v. Carrière Technical Industries Ltd.* (1979) 102 D.L.R. (3d) 323 (Ont.).

[2] [1990] 1 Q.B. 391, 437 (C.A.).

[3] *The Albaforth* [1984] 2 Lloyd's Rep. 91, 96 (C.A.), *per* Robert Goff L.J., applied in *Metall und Rohstoff A.G. v. Donaldson Lufkin & Jenrette Inc.* [1990] 1 Q.B. 391, 484 (C.A.). See also *Electric Furnace Co. v. Selas Corp. of America* [1987] R.P.C. 23, 35 (C.A.); *ISC Technologies Ltd. v. Guerin* [1992] 2 Lloyd's Rep. 430; *Schapira v. Ahronson* [1998] I.L.Pr. 587 (C.A.).

discretion under CPR, r. 6.20.[4] *In Berezovsky v. Michaels*[5] an influential American business magazine called "Forbes" published an article alleging that the first plaintiff, a Russian businessman, was a leader of organised crime and corruption in Russia, and that the second plaintiff, another Russian businessman, was his criminal associate. Sales of the issue of the magazine were 785,000 in the United States and Canada, 1,900 in England, and 13 in Russia. Each of the plaintiffs was a frequent visitor to England, and each sought leave to serve English proceedings, which claimed relief only in respect of publication in England, against the editors and publishers in the United States. It was held that the publication in England of an internationally disseminated libel was a separate tort so as to permit the bringing of an action in England. The burden was on the plaintiffs to prove that England was clearly the appropriate forum, but regard was to be had to the principle that the jurisdiction in which a tort was committed was prima facie the natural forum for the dispute.

If the claimant has a cause of action in both contract and tort he can elect to sue in either (or both) and may apply for permission under clause (6), (7) or (9), at his option.[6]

ILLUSTRATIONS

S11–196   1. A brings proceedings against X & Co., an American company, for a libel contained in X & Co.'s French and Belgian newspapers, of which only a few copies have been sold in England. A has no connection whatsoever with England, and has only taken up residence here for the purposes of the libel claim. His real complaint is the publication of the libel in France and Belgium. The court will not exercise jurisdiction.[7]

2. Under a contract made in New York and governed by its law, X & Co., an American company, sell rat poison to A & Co., an English company. It is agreed that the property shall pass in New York. X & Co. omit to warn A & Co. that the poison is dangerous unless certain precautions are taken. An English farmer who purchases the rat poison from A & Co. in England suffers losses to his livestock in consequence of using it, and A & Co. are compelled to compensate him. A & Co. bring proceedings in tort for negligence against X & Co. The court has jurisdiction because the damage was sustained in England.[8]

3. X & Co., a Canadian company, manufactures and sells in Canada to Y & Co., its English wholly owned subsidiary, a drug the principal ingredient of which is obtained in bulk from German manufacturers. The drug is intended for resale in England. X & Co. does not warn either Y & Co. or potential purchasers, in the printed matter supplied with the drug, of the harmful effect on a foetus if the drug is taken by a pregnant mother. A, whose mother has purchased the drug in England, is born with defective eyesight and without arms. A brings proceedings for negligence against X & Co. for failure to warn his mother of the dangers of taking the drug while pregnant. The court may assume jurisdiction under this clause because the damage was sustained in England and it resulted from an act (negligent failure to warn) within the jurisdiction.[9]

---

[4] See *ante*, para. S11–124.

[5] [2000] 1 W.L.R. 1004 (H.L.) (noted Harris (2000) 116 L.Q.R. 562). See also *Chadha v. Dow Jones & Co.* [1999] I.L.Pr. 829 (C.A.). For defamation on the internet see *Dow Jones & Co. Inc. v. Gutnick, supra,* n. 93.

[6] *Matthews v. Kuwait Bechtel Corporation* [1959] 2 Q.B. 57 (C.A.).

[7] *Cf. Kroch v. Rossell et Cie* [1937] 1 All E.R. 725 (C.A.); contrast *Buttes Gas and Oil Co. v. Hammer* [1971] 3 All E.R. 1025 (C.A.). See also *Pillai v. Sarkar, The Times,* July 21, 1994. For the different position under the Judgments Regulation and the 1968 and Lugano Conventions, see paras. S11–263 *et seq.*

[8] *Cf. George Monro Ltd. v. American Cyanamid and Chemical Corporation* [1944] K.B. 432 (C.A.), decided under the previous version of clause (9), where it was held that even if the tort had been committed in England, the discretion would be exercised against the plaintiff.

[9] *Cf. Distillers Co. Ltd. v. Thompson* [1971] A.C. 458 (P.C.). The court would also have jurisdiction over X Ltd. under clause (3) in an action against Y Ltd.

4. Circular letters containing a libel on A are posted by X in New York to addresses in **S11–197**
England. The court may assume jurisdiction.[10]

5. A brings an action for libel in England against X & Co., the owner of an American broadcasting station. The alleged libel was contained in a broadcast transmitted by satellite from the station and heard in England. *Semble* the court may assume jurisdiction.[11]

6. A, a London commodity broker, wishes to purchase a consignment of sugar from U.S. brokers acting for undisclosed principals. In fact the sugar does not exist and the transaction is not completed. A alleges that an employee of X Ltd., a Nassau bank, had confirmed to him in London by telephone and telex that the sugar was available and the U.S. brokers were able to undertake the sale. In A's proceedings for negligent and fraudulent misrepresentation, the court has jurisdiction but will not exercise it because A does not have a good arguable case on the merits.[12]

7. A & Co., a Swiss company, trades on the London Metal Exchange with X & Co., an English company carrying on business as metal brokers, whose immediate parent company is Y & Co., an American company, and whose ultimate holding company is Z & Co., another American company. A & Co.'s chief aluminium trader, with the assistance of X & Co.'s employees, trades fraudulently. The fraud is discovered by X & Co., Y & Co., and Z & Co. and X & Co. (in breach of its contract with A & Co., and on the instruction of Y & Co. and Z & Co.) closes out A & Co.'s accounts and seizes metal warrants belonging to A & Co. which X & Co. had held as security for advances. A & Co. are awarded substantial damages against X & Co., but recover only a small proportion because X & Co. is insolvent. The court has jurisdiction in proceedings against Y & Co. and Z & Co. for inducement of breach of contract. Although the acts alleged against Y & Co. and Z & Co. of inducing or procuring a breach of contract had in the main taken place in New York, it was the breaches of contract by X & Co. which had caused A & Co. substantial damage in England and in substance the tort was committed in England.[13]

**(10) The court may assume jurisdiction if the claim is brought to enforce S11R–198
any judgment or arbitral award.**[14]

COMMENT

This clause was introduced in 1983 to fill a gap which had been revealed in **S11–199**
cases where judgment creditors sought to enforce at common law judgments emanating from countries whose judgments were not capable of registration in England. Where enforcement by registration is possible,[15] the *in personam* jurisdiction of the English court over the defendant is irrelevant.[16] But where it was not possible (*e.g.* in the case of a judgment of a United States court) the remedy open to a judgment creditor who wished to proceed against assets in England was an action *in personam* at common law against the judgment debtor. Where the judgment debtor was in England at the date of service of the writ, the English court had jurisdiction.[17] But where the judgment debtor was outside England, and was not domiciled there, he could not be served with the writ and there was no basis for service out of the jurisdiction even though he had assets in

---

[10] *Cf. Bata v. Bata* [1948] W.N. 366 (C.A.).
[11] *Cf. Jenner v. Sun Oil Co.* [1952] 2 D.L.R. 526 (Ont.).
[12] *Cf. Diamond v. Bank of London & Montreal Ltd.* [1979] Q.B. 333 (C.A.).
[13] *Metall und Rohstoff A.G. v. Donaldson Lufkin and Jenrette Inc.* [1990] 1 Q.B. 391 (C.A.). The decision was overruled in *Lonrho plc v. Fayed* [1992] 1 A.C. 448 on other aspects.
[14] CPR, r. 6.20(9).
[15] Under the Administration of Justice Act 1920, Foreign Judgments (Reciprocal Enforcement) Act 1933, and the Civil Jurisdiction and Judgments Act 1982, Pts I and II. See CPR, r. 74.6(2).
[16] *Cf. Hunt v. B.P. Exploration Co. (Libya) Ltd.* (1980) 144 C.L.R. 565; *Hunt v. B.P. Exploration Co. (Libya) Ltd.* [1980] 1 N.Z.L.R. 104.
[17] As in *Colt Industries Inc. v. Sarlie (No. 1)* [1966] 1 W.L.R. 440 (C.A.).

England which could be attached to satisfy the judgment.[18] Clause (10) remedies this defect and allows service abroad on the judgment debtor in proceedings at common law to enforce a foreign judgment or award.[19] But it does not justify service out of the jurisdiction of process designed to enforce a judgment which has not yet been obtained but which may be obtained in the future.[20]

ILLUSTRATION

S11–200   A, an Englishman, obtains a judgment in California against X, a resident of California, who never comes to England, but who owns property in England. The court may assume jurisdiction by A in proceedings against X to enforce the judgment at common law.[21]

S11R–201   **(11) The court may assume jurisdiction if the whole subject-matter of the claim relates to property located within England.[22]**

COMMENT

S11–202   Clause (11) reproduces CPR, r. 6.20(10), which is a considerably simplified and much wider version of its predecessors, which dealt separately with proceedings relating to land situate in England, and the perpetuation of testimony relating to land; to claims for rectification of instruments relating to land in England; to claims relating to debts secured on immovable property in England; and claims relating to rights in movable property in England.[23]

S11–203   In *Re Banco Nacional de Cuba*[24] it was held that the new rule was not to be construed as confined to claims relating to the ownership or possession of property. It extended to any claim for relief, whether for damages or otherwise, so long as it was related to property located within the jurisdiction. Since the exercise of the jurisdiction was discretionary, the court would consider in each case whether the character and closeness of the relationship with England was such that the jurisdiction against foreigners abroad should be exercised.

ILLUSTRATIONS

S11–204   1. X, as beneficial owner, conveyed to A by way of mortgage his interest in movables under an English marriage settlement, in order to secure a loan and the interest payable on it. Both X and A were then resident in England, but X is now residing in Australia. A issues proceedings against X claiming an account of the sum due under the mortgage deed

---

[18] *Perry v. Zissis* [1977] 1 Lloyd's Rep. 607 (C.A.). In *Nominal Defendant v. Motor Vehicle Insurance Trust of W. Australia* (1983) 81 F.L.R. 29 it was held that a foreign judgment could be enforced under clause (6); *sed quaere*. The court followed, but doubted the correctness of, the dictum in *Grant v. Easton* (1883) 13 Q.B.D. 302, 303 that liability on a foreign judgment arises upon an implied contract to pay the amount of the judgment. But *Grant v. Easton* was not a case on service out of the jurisdiction.
[19] See, *e.g. Midland International Trade Services Ltd. v. Sudairy, Financial Times*, May 2, 1990.
[20] *Mercedes Benz A.G. v. Leiduck* [1996] A.C. 284 (P.C.).
[21] Contrast *Perry v. Zissis, supra*, decided before clause (10) was introduced.
[22] CPR, r. 6.20(10).
[23] R.S.C. Ord. 11, r. 1(1) (*g*), (*h*), (*i*). See paras. 11R–193—11R–197.
[24] [2001] 1 W.L.R. 2039.

and enforcement of payment of that sum by foreclosure or sale, and applies to the court for leave to serve the summons on X in Australia. The court may allow service.[25]

2. A & Co., bankers, carrying on business in England, claim as against X, residing in Panama, a declaration that they are entitled to a charge on certain policies of life insurance deposited with them, and that the charge may be enforced by foreclosure. The court may assume jurisdiction.[26]

3. A, having obtained judgment against X for £2,000, obtains an order charging the judgment debt with interest on X's shares in a public company in England. X is resident in America. In order to enforce the charge A institutes proceedings asking for the sale of the shares. The court may assume jurisdiction.[27]

(12) The court may assume jurisdiction if the claim is made for any remedy which might be obtained in proceedings to execute the trusts of a written instrument, where the trusts ought to be executed according to English law, and the person on whom the claim form is to be served is a trustee of the trusts.[28]   S11R–205

COMMENT

This clause confers jurisdiction in proceedings against trustees to execute a written trust governed by English law. Before its amendment in 1983 this clause related to the execution of trusts "as to property situate within the jurisdiction" and it had been held[29] that the clause did not apply when a trustee of stock sold it in breach of trust before leaving England, so that where at the time of leave being given to serve him there was no property in England subject to the trust, service was set aside. This decision was criticised on the ground that the relevant date for determining the situation of the property was the date of accrual of the cause of action,[30] but the decision is now obsolete. In *Chellaram v. Chellaram (No. 2)*[31] it was held that the critical date for determining the law applicable to the trust was the date when permission to serve out of the jurisdiction was sought, and not the date when the cause of action arose.   S11–206

ILLUSTRATION

X is sole trustee of an English settlement. Under the trusts of the settlement, A is beneficially entitled to stock. X sells the stock and leaves England, and has not returned there. There is no other property in England which is subject to the trusts of the settlement. The court has jurisdiction to entertain proceedings by A for execution of the trusts of the settlement.[32]   S11–207

(13) The court may assume jurisdiction if the claim is made for any remedy which might be obtained in proceedings for the administration of the estate of a person who died domiciled[33] in England.[34]   S11R–208

---

[25] Contrast *Hughes v. Oxenham* [1913] 1 Ch. 254 (C.A.), which was decided before the rules were amended to cover proceedings to enforce charges.

[26] Contrast *Deutsche National Bank v. Paul* [1898] 1 Ch. 283, decided under the old rules.

[27] Contrast *Kolchmann v. Meurice* [1903] 1 K.B. 534.

[28] CPR, r. 6.20(11).

[29] *Winter v. Winter* [1894] 1 Ch. 421.

[30] *Official Solicitor v. Stype Investments Ltd.* [1983] 1 W.L.R. 214.

[31] [2002] EWHC 632 (Ch), [2002] 3 All E.R. 17.

[32] Contrast *Winter v. Winter* [1894] 1 Ch. 421, decided under the former version of this clause.

[33] Within the meaning of the 1982 Act, s.41; CPR, r. 6.18(g).

[34] CPR, r. 6.20(12).

S11R–209 **(14) The court may assume jurisdiction if the claim is made in probate proceedings, including a claim for the rectification of a will.**[35]

COMMENT

S11–210 Probate proceedings are claims for the grant of probate or letters of administration, or the revocation of such a grant, or for a decree pronouncing for or against the validity of an alleged will.[36]

S11R–211 **(15) The court may assume jurisdiction if the claim is made against the defendant as constructive trustee where the defendant's alleged liability arises out of acts committed within England.**[37]

S11R–212 **(16) The court may assume jurisdiction if a claim is made for restitution where the defendant's alleged liability arises out of acts committed within England.**[38]

COMMENT

S11–213 A claim against a defendant as constructive trustee normally arises in one of three situations. The first is where a person receives for his benefit trust property transferred to him in breach of trust; he is liable as a constructive trustee if he received it with notice, actual or constructive, that it was trust property and that the transfer to him was a breach of trust, or subsequently discovered the facts. The second is where a person receives trust property lawfully and then misappropriates it or otherwise deals with it in a manner inconsistent with the trust. The third is where a person dishonestly assists in the furtherance of a fraudulent and dishonest breach of trust.[39] The first and second categories were often referred to as "knowing receipt" cases, and the third as "knowing assistance", and are referred to today as "recipient liability" and "accessory liability".[40] Clause (15) was added in 1990 after it had been held that a claim based on constructive trust (in each of the three categories) was not founded on a tort for the purposes of clause (9).[41]

S11–214 There has been a division of judicial opinion as to the extent to which the relevant acts necessary to establish liability must occur in England in order to bring the case within clause (15). In a case on a previous version of clause (16), when it provided that the acts done in England could be those of the defendant or another person, Millett J. held that the clause only applied if all the acts necessary to impose liability were committed in England; and that clause (15) therefore applied to knowing participation by acts in a fraudulent breach of trust committed in England, but not knowing receipt abroad of the proceeds of such fraud.[42] In subsequent proceedings in

---

[35] CPR, r. 6.20(13).
[36] CPR, r. 57.1(2). For rectification of wills, see CPR, r. 57.12.
[37] CPR, r. 6.20(14).
[38] CPR, r. 6.20(15).
[39] See, *e.g. Agip (Africa) Ltd. v. Jackson* [1990] Ch. 265, 291–293; affd. [1991] Ch. 547 (C.A.). See also *Ghana Commercial Bank v. C, The Times*, March 3, 1997.
[40] See *Royal Brunei Airlines Sdn. Bhd. v. Tan* [1995] 2 A.C. 378 (P.C.).
[41] *Metall und Rohstoff A.G. v. Donaldson Lufkin & Jenrette Inc.* [1990] 1 Q.B. 391, 473–474 (C.A.). See also *DSQ Property Co. Ltd. v. Lotus Car Sales Ltd., The Times*, June 28, 1990 (C.A.).
[42] *ISC Technologies Ltd. v. Radcliffe*, December 7, 1990, unreported (Millett J.).

the same litigation, Hoffmann J. suggested, *obiter*, that this was too narrow a view and that clause (15) was primarily designed for a foreign entity which had not participated in the fraud but had been used as a receptacle for the proceeds.[43] The latter view was followed by Knox J. in *Polly Peck International plc v. Nadir.*[44] He held that a construction of clause (15) which required all the acts constituting the alleged constructive trust to have been committed in England would empty it of nearly all its practical utility. It was sufficient if some, at least, of the acts which gave rise to the claim (but not necessarily the acquisition of knowledge) had occurred in England. The decision was reversed by the Court of Appeal on other grounds, but Hoffmann L.J. said that he adhered to the view which he had expressed in *ISC Technologies Ltd. v. Guerin.*

It is probably not necessary for the purposes of clause (16) that the acts done within the jurisdiction be those of the defendant to be served under this clause, but if they are, then it would be a stronger case for permission to serve out of the jurisdiction.[45] **S11–215**

(17) The court may assume jurisdiction if the claim is made by the Commissioners of Inland Revenue relating to duties or taxes against a defendant not domiciled in Scotland or Northern Ireland.[46] **S11R–216**

(18) The court may assume jurisdiction if the claim is made by a party to proceedings for an order that the court exercise its powers under section 51 of the Supreme Court Act 1981 to make a costs order in favour of or against a person who is not a party to those proceedings.[47] **S11R–217**

COMMENT

Section 51 of the Supreme Court Act 1981 provides that the award of costs is in the discretion of the court. It was held by the House of Lords that the power includes a power to award costs against a person who is not a party to the proceedings.[48] There was some doubt as to how this power could be exercised against a person outside the jurisdiction. It was held that permission could be sought under the former Rules of the Supreme Court[49] to serve the non-party with the application to make him liable for the costs, but the Court of Appeal drew attention to a possible gap in the new Civil Procedure Rules, Rule 48.2 of which contains a procedure for making the non-party a party to the proceedings for the purposes of the costs application, but which contained no provision for service out of the jurisdiction of the application.[50] Consequently, CPR, r. 6.20(17) was added. **S11–218**

ILLUSTRATION

A, an English bank, brings proceedings for possession of a house in Chelsea occupied by X, who is domiciled in England. She defends the proceedings on the ground that she has an equitable interest in the house because of promises made to her by her second husband. **S11–219**

---

[43] *ISC Technologies Ltd. v. Guerin* [1992] 2 Lloyd's Rep. 430.
[44] *The Independent*, September 2; 1992; revd. on other grounds, *The Times*, March 22, 1993 (C.A.). See also *Nycal (U.K.) Ltd. v. Lacey* [1994] C.L.C. 12. *Cf. Cronos Containers NV v. Palatin* [2002] EWHC 2819 (Comm); [2003] I.L.Pr. 283 (a case under Art. 5(3) of the 1968 Convention).
[45] *Cf. Dexter Ltd. v. Harley, The Times*, April 2, 2001 (a case on Art. 5(3) of the 1968 Convention).
[46] CPR, r. 6.20(16).
[47] CPR, r. 6.20(17).
[48] *Aiden Shipping Co, Ltd. v. Interbulk Ltd.* [1986] A.C. 965.
[49] R.S.C. Ord. 11, r. 9(4), (5) (summons within existing proceedings).
[50] *National Justice Co. Naviera S.A. v. Prudential Assurance Co. Ltd. (No. 2)* [2000] 1 W.L.R. 603 (C.A.).

After a trial her defence is rejected. The bank seeks an order for costs from her first husband, who is in the United States, and who has funded her defence. The court has jurisdiction under clause (18).[51]

S11R–220 **(19) A claim is (a) in the nature of salvage and any part of the services took place within England; or (b) to enforce a claim under section 153, 154 or 175 of the Merchant Shipping Act 1995.**[52]

COMMENT

S11–221 A salvage claim is a non-contractual claim arising under maritime law. The sections of the Merchant Shipping Act 1995 deal with claims in connection with oil pollution.

S11R–222 **(20) The court may assume jurisdiction if a claim is made under the following enactments**[53]**:**
   (1) The Nuclear Installations Act 1965;
   (2) The Social Security Contributions and Benefits Act 1992;
   (3) The Directive of the Council of the European Communities dated March 15, 1976, 76/308/EEC, where service is to be effected in a Member State of the European Union;
   (4) The Drug Trafficking Offences Act 1994;
   (5) Part VI of the Criminal Justice Act 1988;
   (6) The Immigration (Carriers' Liability) Act 1987;
   (7) Part II of the Immigration and Asylum Act 1999;
   (8) Schedule 2 to the Immigration Act 1971; and
   (9) The Financial Services and Markets Act 2000.

COMMENT

S11–223 CPR, r. 6.20(18) provides for service out of the jurisdiction in the case of enactments specified in the practice direction to Part 6 of the Civil Procedure Rules, and clause (20) lists those which have been specified to date.

S11–224 **Nuclear Installations Act 1965.** The Act gives effect to various international conventions on civil liability for nuclear occurrences to which the United Kingdom is a party. The jurisdiction of the United Kingdom courts under this Act is discussed in Chapter 15. There are circumstances under the conventions in which the jurisdiction of the court depends on international agreement at ministerial level, and this is why the rules of the conventions as to jurisdiction are not set out in a Schedule to the Act.

Social Security Contributions and Benefits Act 1992. This deals with claims for the recovery by the Secretary of State of contributions by earners and employers.

Council Directive 76/308/EEC. This relates to claims by H.M. Customs and Excise for sums due under the European Agricultural Guidance and Guarantee Fund and for agricultural levies and customers duties.

---

[51] Based on the facts of *Locabail (U.K.) Ltd. v. Bayfield Properties Ltd. (No. 3), The Times,* February 29, 2000.
[52] CPR, r. 6.20(17A), added by S.I. 2001 No. 4015.
[53] CPR, r. 6.20(18) and Part 6 Practice Direction, para. 5.2.

Drug Trafficking Offences Act 1994. This relates to claims in connection with the proceeds of drug trafficking.

Criminal Justice Act 1988, Part VI. This relates to claims in connection with the confiscation of the proceeds of crime.

Immigration (Carriers' Liability) Act 1987. Immigration and Asylum Act 1999. The 1987 Act imposes liability (in a prescribed amount in relation to each passenger) on the owners or agents of a ship or aircraft in which a person has arrived in the United Kingdom and where that person has failed to produce a valid passport and (if applicable) a valid visa.
Part II of the Immigration and Asylum Act 1999 imposes penalties on those responsible for clandestine entrants, and imposes charges on carriers in respect of passengers without proper documents. The latter provisions will supersede the Immigration (Carriers' Liability) Act 1987 when they are brought fully into force.

Immigration Act 1971. Under Schedule 2 to the Immigration Act 1971[54] the owners or agents of a ship or aircraft in which a person refused leave to enter may be liable to the Secretary of State for expenses incurred in respect of custody, accommodation or maintenance after his arrival while he was detained or liable to be detained.

Financial Services and Markets Act 2000. This Act provides actions for damages for such matters as unlawful regulated activities, false or misleading particulars, and unlawful investment schemes, and restitutionary remedies for market abuse (such as insider trading).

B. Where the Defendant is domiciled in a Regulation State, in a 1968 Convention or Lugano Convention Contracting State, or in Scotland or Northern Ireland

Substitute for Rule 28:   11R–223—
                                                                352

**RULE 28—Subject to Rules 29 and 30 (exclusive jurisdiction under the   S11R–225
Judgments Regulation and under the 1968 and Lugano Conventions), 53
and 54 (international conventions) and 31(3) (*lis alibi pendens*) the High
Court has jurisdiction to entertain a claim *in personam* in a civil or
commercial matter falling within the scope of the Regulation or the
Conventions in the cases mentioned in this Rule.**

COMMENT

This Rule deals with the heads of *in personam* jurisdiction under the   S11–226
Judgments Regulation and the 1968 Convention and the Lugano Convention, and the similar, but not identical, counterpart in Schedule 4 to the
1982 Act,[55] which allocates jurisdiction within the United Kingdom in

---

[54] para. 19.
[55] The new Schedule 4 is inserted by S.I. 2001 No. 3929, Sched. 2.

relation to matters within the scope of the Judgments Regulation. Although the heading of this section refers to the domicile of the defendant, several qualifications have to be made to it. First, even if the defendant is domiciled in a State to which the Judgment Regulation applies ("a Regulation State"), or a State to which the Conventions apply ("a Contracting State"), the jurisdictional rules discussed here do not apply if the case is outside the scope of the Regulation or the Conventions.[56] Matters which are outside their scope or excluded from Schedule 4 will be governed by Rules 24 to 27. Secondly, the provisions relating to exclusive jurisdiction[57] (and the corresponding provisions of Schedule 4) are not confined to cases where the defendant is domiciled in a Regulation State or Contracting State (or in a particular part of the United Kingdom). Thirdly, Article 23 of the Regulation and Article 17[58] of the Conventions confer jurisdiction on the court chosen by a jurisdiction agreement where one of the parties is domiciled in a Regulation State or a Contracting State, and that party may not necessarily be the defendant. Fourthly, powers[59] under the Regulation and the Conventions (given effect by section 25 of the 1982 Act) to grant interim remedies may be exercised where proceedings on the substance of the matter are in another Regulation State or Contracting State, irrespective of the domicile of the defendant.

S11–227   It is important to note that the jurisdiction under this Rule is not subject to the discretion of the court even as regards defendants to be served outside England. By CPR, r. 6.19 service of process out of the jurisdiction is permissible without the permission of the court if the claim is one to which the Regulation or the Conventions or the intra-United Kingdom rules apply.[60] There is no room for the application of discretionary *forum conveniens* principles as between Regulation States or Contracting States.[61] A defendant who wishes to dispute the jurisdiction of the court may apply for an order declaring that it has no jurisdiction, and also for an order setting aside service.[62] The European Court has held that it is for the national court to determine the standard of proof required to establish that the conditions for the establishment of jurisdiction under the 1968 Convention are satisfied, provided that they do not impair the effectiveness of the Convention.[63] In England it has been held that the standard to be applied in considering whether the jurisdiction of the court has been established for the purposes of the Conventions is the same as that under Rule 27, *i.e.* a

---

[56] See paras. 11–013 *et seq.*

[57] See Rule 29.

[58] See Rule 32(3).

[59] Judgments Regulation Art. 31; 1968 and Lugano Conventions, Art. 24.

[60] The only exception is CPR, r. 6.20(4), which requires permission for the service of a claim form for an interim remedy under section 25(1) of the 1982 Act: see para. 8–022.

[61] See para. 11–012, and paras. 12–015 *et seq.*

[62] CPR 11(1), (6). If the defendant is to be served out of the jurisdiction the claim form (and the particulars of claim, if contained in a separate document) must be endorsed with a statement that the court has power under the 1982 Act to deal with the claim and that no proceedings based on the same claim are pending between the parties in another part of the United Kingdom or another Convention territory: CPR PD7, para. 3.5. On the effect of non-compliance with the requirement in CPR, r. 6.19(3) to state the grounds for entitlement to serve the claim form out of the jurisdiction, see *Trustor AB v. Barclays Bank plc, The Times*, November 22, 2000. See also CPR 6BPD, para. 1.

[63] Case C–68/93 *Shevill v. Presse Alliance* [1995] E.C.R. I–415, [1995] 2 A.C. 18.

good arguable case.[64] The more stringent test of balance of probabilities might require the trial of an issue and involve great expense and delay. Although jurisdictional issues are very important, they ought generally to be decided with due despatch without hearing oral evidence.[65]

Allocation of jurisdiction within the United Kingdom. The primary rule of **S11–228** jurisdiction in the Regulation and the Conventions is that a defendant domiciled in a Regulation State or in a Contracting State is to be sued in the courts of that State. Because the United Kingdom is not a unitary State for the purposes of civil jurisdiction it was necessary to allocate jurisdiction as between its constituent parts. But instead of confining itself to determining in which part of the United Kingdom a party is domiciled, the 1982 Act goes much further in laying down rules for determining jurisdiction in cases where the parties are domiciled in different parts of the United Kingdom. These rules are set out in Schedule 4 to the Act: they were originally modelled closely on those in the 1968 Convention, and are now modelled on the Judgments Regulation, but they are not identical with the rules in the Regulation.[66] They apply where (a) the subject-matter of the proceedings is within the scope of the Regulation as determined by Article 1 (whether or not it has effect in relation to the proceedings) and (b) the defendant is domiciled in the United Kingdom or the proceedings are of a kind mentioned in Article 22 (exclusive jurisdiction).[67] Where, in a case to which the Regulation applies, the courts of the United Kingdom have jurisdiction as the Regulation State in which the defendant is domiciled, Schedule 4 determines in which part of the United Kingdom the defendant must be sued. Similarly, the reference in Article 22 is to the courts of "the Regulation State" in which the property is situate, the company has its seat, the register is kept, etc. In these cases too it is necessary to allocate the resulting jurisdiction. Where the defendant is not domiciled in the United Kingdom and Article 22 does not apply, the problem of intra-United Kingdom jurisdiction will rarely arise in relation to the Regulation. Allocation is irrelevant in relation to those provisions[68] which give jurisdiction to a "place" and it will be that part of the United Kingdom in which that place is situated which will be the relevant part of the United Kingdom for the purposes of jurisdiction. Where the Regulation refers to a "court"[69] in which proceedings are pending it will be the law district in which the relevant court is situated which will be the court with jurisdiction.

There are two further cases which require allocation. First, Article 5(6) **S11–229** gives jurisdiction in actions against settlors, trustees or beneficiaries to the courts of the Regulation State in which the trust is domiciled. Any proceedings which by virtue of Article 5(6) are brought in the United Kingdom shall be brought in the courts of the part of the United Kingdom

---

[64] See *Canada Trust Co. v. Stolzenberg (No. 2)* [1998] 1 W.L.R. 547 (C.A.) (affd. [2002] 1 A.C. 1, 13, applying *Tesam Distribution Ltd. v. Schuh Mode Team GmbH* [1990] I.L.Pr. 149 (C.A.) and *Mölnlycke AB v. Procter & Gamble Ltd*, [1992] 1 W.L.R. 1112 (C.A.), in the light of *Seaconsar Far East Ltd v. Bank Markazi Iran* [1994] 1 A.C. 438.
[65] *Canada Trust Co. v. Stolzenberg (No. 2)* [2002] 1 A.C. 1, 13, *per* Lord Steyn.
[66] The European Court has no jurisdiction to give preliminary rulings on the interpretation of Sched. 4 to the 1982 Act: Case C–346/93 *Kleinwort Benson Ltd. v. City of Glasgow District Council* [1995] E.C.R. I–615; [1996] Q.B. 57.
[67] 1982 Act, s. 16(1) (as amended by S.I. 2001 No. 3929, Sched. 2, para. 3).
[68] Arts. 5(1), (2), (3), (5) and 6(1).
[69] Arts. 5(4), (7), 6(2), (3) and 7.

in which the trust is domiciled.[70] Secondly, Article 16(1) allows a consumer to bring proceedings in the courts of the State in which he is domiciled. Any proceedings which, by virtue of Article 16(1) are brought in the United Kingdom by a consumer on the ground that he is himself domiciled there, shall be brought in the court for the part of the United Kingdom in which he is domiciled.[71]

S11–230 The primary rule of jurisdiction in Schedule 4 is, like that in the Regulation and the Conventions, the domicile of the defendant, but there are differences between Schedule 4 and the Judgments Regulation equivalent in the other heads of jurisdiction. Certain types of proceeding are excluded from the operation of Schedule 4.[72] Most of these are cases which would fall outside the Regulation scheme, but there are others, such as (a) winding-up of solvent companies or (b) proceedings concerned with registration of patents, etc., which are within the Regulation and the Conventions but outside Schedule 4. The former is excluded because it was not appropriate to apply the standard tests for seats of companies in the intra-United Kingdom context, where place of incorporation is the only appropriate test for the winding-up of domestic companies. Proceedings relating to registration of patents, etc., are excluded because the principle of Article 22(4) cannot be applied to allocate jurisdiction between courts in the United Kingdom since the registers of patents, trade marks and designs are all situated in London. The main differences between the Judgments Regulation and the new Schedule 4 are as follows. Rule 3(a) reproduces Article 5(1) of the 1968 Convention on jurisdiction in matters relating to a contract, and not the new version in Article 5(1) of the Regulation. Rule 3(h) of Schedule 4 confers jurisdiction on the courts of the part of the United Kingdom in which property is situated in proceedings (a) concerning a debt secured on immovable property or (b) which are brought in connection with proprietary or possessory rights, or security rights in relation to movable property.[73] The provisions of Articles 8 to 14 relating to jurisdiction in matters relating to insurance are entirely deleted. It would follow from this that, in proceedings between an insurer and an insured, they must be brought in the court which has jurisdiction under the general Regulation scheme. A number of other differences of detail are noted at the appropriate points when the corresponding provisions of the Regulation are discussed.[74]

ILLUSTRATIONS

S11–231 1. A resides in London. While on a visit to France he is injured as a result of the negligence of X, who is domiciled in France. The court has no jurisdiction in proceedings by A against X.

2. A resides in London. While X, who is domiciled in France, is on a visit to England he negligently injures A. The court has jurisdiction in proceedings by A against X.[75]

---

[70] S.I. 2001 No. 3929, Sched. 1, para. 7(2), *post*, para. S11–278.

[71] *ibid.*, para. 7(3), *post*, clause (14). See also para. 11(2) for the allocation of domicile in the case of insurers domiciled outside the Regulation States, but with a branch in a Regulation State, and in the equivalent case for consumer contracts and employment contracts. See 1982 Act, ss. 10(2), (3) and 44(2) for the position under the Conventions.

[72] See Sched. 5.

[73] *post*, clause (7).

[74] See especially Rule 4 (decisions of organs of companies), *post*, para. S11–334; Rule 12 (removal of formal requirement; subject to mandatory legislation) *post*, Chap. 12, para. 12–109.

[75] Judgments Regulation, Art. 5(3).

3. A resides in London. While A and X, who is domiciled in England, are on a trip to France, A is injured as a result of the negligence of X. The court has jurisdiction in proceedings by A against X.[76]

4. The facts are as in Illustration 3, except that X is domiciled in Scotland. The court has no jurisdiction.[77]

5. A resides in London. While A and X, who is domiciled in Scotland, are driving in England A is injured as a result of the negligence of X. The court has jurisdiction.[78]

(1) The court has jurisdiction if the claim is made against a person domiciled in England.[79]   **S11R–232**

COMMENT

The basic principle of the Regulation and Convention schemes (which is also reflected in the intra-United Kingdom provisions of Schedule 4) is that persons domiciled in a Regulation State or a Contracting State may be sued there, and may be sued in another Regulation State or Contracting State only by virtue of the special rules of jurisdiction in the Regulation and the Conventions. The primary rule of domicile as the basis of jurisdiction is set out in Article 2 which provides that persons domiciled in a Regulation State or Contracting State (as the case may be) shall, whatever their nationality, be sued in the courts of that State. In *Canada Trust Co. v. Stolzenberg (No. 2)*[80] it was held that the critical date for testing whether the defendant was domiciled in England for the purposes of Article 2 (in that case, of the Lugano Convention) was the date of the *issue* of proceedings rather than the date of service.[81]   **S11–233**

Article 2 is expressly subject to the other provisions of the Regulation and the Conventions; but the overriding importance of the principal rule of domicile has been the starting point of the European Court's interpretation of the scope of the special jurisdictions under the 1968 Convention, because the basis of the system of jurisdiction under Title II of the Convention "is the general conferment of jurisdiction on the court of the defendant's domicile"[82] and "it is in accord with the objective of the Convention to avoid a wide and multifarious interpretation of the exceptions to the general rule of jurisdiction contained in Article 2."[83]   **S11–234**

It is the domicile of the defendant which is crucial for the purposes of jurisdiction. Only rarely is the domicile of the claimant relevant.[84] If the defendant is not domiciled in a Regulation State or Contracting State,   **S11–235**

---

[76] *ibid.*, Art. 2.

[77] Sched. 4, Rule 2.

[78] *ibid.*, Rule 3(c).

[79] Judgments Regulation, Art. 2, 1968 Convention, Art. 2, and Lugano Convention, Art. 2, in 1982 Act, Scheds. 1 and 3C; 1982 Act, Sched. 4, Rule 2 (as substituted by S.I. 2001 No. 3929, Sched. 2).

[80] [2002] 1 A.C. 1.

[81] *Cf.* Judgments Regulation, Art. 30 (for purpose of *lis pendens* principles court is seised on issue of proceedings).

[82] Case 12/76 *Industrie Tessili Italiana Como v. Dunlop A.G.* [1976] E.C.R. 1473, 1485. Generally, the Regulation and Convention schemes are hostile to jurisdiction being vested in the claimant's domicile: see Case C–220/88 *Dumez France v. Hessische Landesbank* [1990] E.C.R. I–49, 79.

[83] Case 33/78 *Somafer S.A. v. Saar-Ferngas A.G.* [1978] E.C.R. 2183, 2191.

[84] See Judgments Regulation and Conventions, Art. 5(2) (domicile of maintenance creditor); Judgments Regulation, Art. 9(1)(b); Conventions, Art. 8(1)(2) (domicile of policyholder); Judgments Regulation, Art. 16(1) and Conventions, Art. 13(1) (domicile of consumer).

normally[85] Rules 24 to 27 apply. Article 3(1) provides that persons domiciled in a Regulation State or Contracting State may be sued in the courts of another Regulation State or Contracting State only by virtue of the rules set out in Articles 5 to 24 of the Regulation (5 to 18 of the Conventions). Annex I to the Regulation (and Article 3(2) of the Conventions) contains a (non-exhaustive) catalogue of jurisdictional rules which may not be invoked against domiciliaries of Regulation (and Contracting) States. Strictly, this provision is not necessary and is merely declaratory, because Article 3(1) makes it clear that domiciliaries may only be sued in the circumstances set out in the Regulation and the Conventions. The rule in English law which is in effect branded as exorbitant is the rule allowing the exercise of jurisdiction over an individual by virtue of his mere presence at the time of the service of process.[86] But in practice the operation of this much-criticised rule does not today work inconvenience or injustice, since, in the case of a genuinely contested claim, the courts have come to accept that a stay of the proceedings will be granted if they have no real connection with England.[87]

S11–236 Even if the defendant is domiciled in England, the court will not be able to assume jurisdiction in the following cases: (a) where the courts of another Regulation State or Contracting State have exclusive jurisdiction pursuant to Article 22 of the Regulation or Article 16 of the Conventions[88]; (b) where the courts of Scotland or Northern Ireland have exclusive jurisdiction pursuant to Rule 11 of Schedule 4[89]; (c) where the parties have agreed that the courts of another Regulation State or Contracting State or of Scotland or Northern Ireland shall have jurisdiction pursuant to the terms of Article 23 of the Regulation or Article 17 of the Conventions or Rule 12 of Schedule 4[90]; (d) where proceedings involving the same cause of action have already been commenced in the courts of another Regulation State or Contracting State. In the latter case the court has no discretion (as it has if the proceedings are pending in Scotland or Northern Ireland) to assume jurisdiction.[91]

ILLUSTRATIONS

S11–237 1. X, who resides in and is domiciled in France, is an art dealer. A is an Indian princess. X in France sells and delivers a picture to A for cash and represents that it was painted by the French artist Boucher. A is later advised that the picture was not painted by Boucher and issues a writ claiming rescission and damages. X is served at Ascot races during his temporary visit to England. Service will be set aside.[92]

2. A & Co., an American company, brings an action against X, who is domiciled in Switzerland, in respect of a debt incurred in New York, and serves X while X is staying for a few days at a London hotel. Service will be set aside.[93]

---

[85] For exceptions see Judgments Regulation, Arts. 9(2), 15(2), 22, and 23. The corresponding provisions of the Conventions are Arts. 8(2), 13(2), 16 and 17.

[86] Rule 24.

[87] Rule 31.

[88] Rules 29 and 114.

[89] *ibid.*

[90] Rule 32(3).

[91] Rule 31.

[92] Judgments Regulation, Art. 3. Contrast *Maharanee of Baroda v. Wildenstein* [1972] 2 Q.B. 283 (C.A.).

[93] Lugano Convention, Art. 3. Contrast *Colt Industries v. Sarlie* [1966] 1 W.L.R. 440 (C.A.).

3. The facts are as in Illustration 2, except that X is domiciled in New York. The court has jurisdiction.[94]

4. The facts are as in Illustration 2, except that X is domiciled in Scotland. Service will be set aside.[95]

(2) (a) Where the Judgments Regulation applies, the court has jurisdiction, subject to clauses (13), (14) and (14A) of this Rule, in matters relating to a contract, if England is the place of performance of the obligation in question.[96] — S11R–238

(b) For the purpose of sub-clause (a), and unless otherwise agreed, the place of performance of the obligation in question shall be England if, in the case of the sale of goods, England was the place where, under the contract, the goods were delivered or should have been delivered; and in the case of the provision of services, England was the place where, under the contract, the services were provided or should have been provided.[97]

(c) Where the 1968 and Lugano Conventions apply, the court has jurisdiction, subject to clauses (13), (14) and (14A) of this Rule, in matters relating to a contract, if England is the place of performance of the obligation in question.[98]

(d) Where the defendant is domiciled in Scotland or Northern Ireland, the court has jurisdiction, subject to clauses (13), and (14A) of this Rule, in matters relating to a contract, if England is the place of performance of the obligation in question.[99]

COMMENT

Introduction. Article 5(1) of the Judgments Regulation is the basic rule for contract claims against a defendant domiciled in another Regulation State, although special provision is made in Articles 8 to 21 for insurance contracts, consumer contracts and employment contracts, which are the subject of clauses (13), (14) and (14A) of this Rule. Article 5(1) of the Regulation is substantially different from Article 5(1) of the 1968 Convention and the Lugano Convention (and from Rule 3(a) of the 1982 Act, Sched. 4), although the starting point is the same. — S11–239

Under the 1968 Convention (and the Lugano Convention) "the obligation in question" whose place of performance must be in England is the obligation which is the basis of the action. The European Court held consistently that it was for the court before which the matter was brought to establish whether the place of performance was situate within its territorial jurisdiction, and that it must for that purpose determine in accordance with its own rules of the conflict of laws what was the law applicable to the relationship, and define, in accordance with that law, the place of performance of the contractual obligation in question.[1] The Judgments Regu- — S11–240

---

[94] Judgments Regulation, Art. 4.
[95] 1982 Act, Sched. 4, Rule 2.
[96] Judgments Regulation, Art. 5(1)(a). See generally Hertz, *Jurisdiction in Contract and Tort under the Brussels Convention* (1998); Hill (1995) 44 I.C.L.Q. 591; Kennett (1995) 15 Yb. Eur. L. 193; Takahashi (2002) 27 Eur. L.R. 530.
[97] Art. 5(1)(b).
[98] 1968 and Lugano Conventions, Art. 5(1).
[99] 1982 Act, Sched. 4, Rule 3(a).
[1] See *infra*, paras. S11–253 *et seq.*

lation makes provision for an autonomous definition of the place of performance of the obligation in the case of the sale of goods and the provision of services. Article 5(1)(b) provides that for the purposes of Article 5(1), unless otherwise agreed, the place of performance of the obligation in question shall be, in the case of the sale of goods, the place in a Regulation State where, under the contract, the goods were delivered or should have been delivered; and in the case of the provision of services, the place in a Regulation State where, under the contract, the services were provided or should have been provided. In other types of contract the basic rule in Article 5(1)(a) applies.[2] The reason for the change is to prevent an unpaid seller routinely being able to sue in its own courts on the footing that the law governing the contract of sale requires payment to be made at the seller's place of residence.

S11–241 Article 5(1) of the 1968 Convention (and Article 5(1) of the Lugano Convention, but in slightly different terms) makes special provision for individual contracts of employment. The Judgments Regulation has no special provisions for employment contracts in Article 5(1), but contains new and more extensive provisions in section 5 (Articles 18 to 21), which are dealt with in connection with clause (14A) below.

S11–242 **Intra-United Kingdom jurisdiction.** The changes made by the Judgments Regulation to the basic rule in contract jurisdiction have not been adopted for the purposes of intra-United Kingdom jurisdiction. Rule 3(a) in Schedule 4 to the 1982 Act[3] contains the same rule as the 1968 and Lugano Conventions, and simply gives jurisdiction to the courts for the place of performance of the obligation in question.

S11–243 Article 5(1) confers jurisdiction "in matters relating to a contract, in the courts for the place of performance of the obligation in question". This provision relates to contractual claims (*"en matière contractuelle"*). In England, jurisdiction over persons not present, domiciled or resident within England may be exercised in non-Regulation and non-Convention cases in contractual matters (a) where the contract was made within the jurisdiction, or (b) where the contract was made by or through an agent trading or residing within the jurisdiction, or (c) where the contract is by its terms, or by implication, governed by English law or (d) for a breach of contract committed within the jurisdiction; and (e) where there is a contractual choice of English jurisdiction.[4] The Regulation and Convention rules are significantly different. There is no provision corresponding to (a), (b) or (c). Although (d) has some superficial similarity to the Regulation/Convention rule, it differs from it in at least one important respect. Under the English rule it is possible to envisage a breach in England of a contractual obligation to be performed elsewhere, *e.g.* by express or implied repudiation.[5] Under the Regulation and the Conventions, however, jurisdiction is conferred on the place of performance of the obligation in question and not on the place of the breach.

---

[2] Art. 5(1)(c). See generally Briggs, *International Litigation News* (International Bar Association), October 2001, pp. 25–26; Rodger, 2001 Jur. Rev. 59 and 69.

[3] As substituted by S.I. 2001 No. 3929, Sched. 2. Sched. 4 to the 1982 Act (which is reproduced in Part II of the appendix to this Supplement), unlike the Judgments Regulation, contains no special provision for insurance contracts: see Rule 28(14A).

[4] *supra*, Rule 27(4), (5).

[5] para. S11–176.

Article 5(1) must be read subject to three other matters. The first matter **S11–244** is that the Judgments Regulation makes special provision for Luxembourg domiciliaries, as do the 1968 and Lugano Conventions. A person domiciled in Luxembourg and sued in the court of another Regulation State pursuant to Article 5(1) may refuse to submit to the jurisdiction of that court if the final place of delivery of the goods or provision of the services is in Luxembourg.[6] Where the final place of delivery of the goods or provision of the services is in Luxembourg, any agreement conferring jurisdiction must, in order to be valid, be accepted in writing or evidenced in writing within the meaning of Article 23(1)(a).[7] The special provisions will expire on February 29, 2008 and do not apply to contracts for the provision of financial services.[8] The second matter is that there are special provisions for contractual claims (especially debts secured on immovable property) connected with actions in matters relating to rights *in rem* in immovable property, and for claims connected with tenancies.[9]

The third matter (which will now be only very rarely applicable) is **S11–245** relevant only where the 1968 Convention or the Lugano Convention applies. Article 54(3) provides that if the parties to a dispute concerning a contract had agreed in writing before January 1, 1987[10] (in the case of the 1968 Convention) or before (in the case of the Lugano Convention) its entry into force,[11] that it was to be governed by the law of a part of the United Kingdom, the courts of the United Kingdom are to retain the right to exercise jurisdiction in the dispute. This means that, in addition to the place of performance jurisdiction under Article 5(1), the English court will retain the right to exercise jurisdiction under clause (4) of Rule 27. It should be noted that: (a) this jurisdiction will remain discretionary; (b) it will apply only if there is an express choice of law in writing[12]; and (c) it will apply only if the choice of law is made before the relevant date. This jurisdiction will also apply (for agreements made before January 1, 1987) in relation to defendants domiciled in Scotland and Northern Ireland,[13] even though what is now CPR, r. 6.20(5)(c), Rule 27, clause (6), did not formerly apply to defendants resident in Scotland.

Contract. Whether a matter relates to a contract will not usually give rise **S11–246** to difficulty. There is a sufficiently common core on the meaning of contract to result in the term being given an autonomous interpretation. In four decisions on the 1968 Convention[14] the European Court has confirmed that

---

[6] Art. 63(1).
[7] Art. 63(2).
[8] Art. 63(3), (4). The special provisions for Luxembourg domiciliaries in the 1968 and Lugano Conventions are in Art. I of the 1968 Protocol and of Protocol No. 1 to the Lugano Convention.
[9] Judgments Regulation, Arts. 6(4) and 22(1); 1968 and Lugano Convention, Arts. 6(4) and 16(1); 1982 Act, Sched. 4, Rules 5(d) and 11(a).
[10] The relevant date in relation to the Republic of Ireland is June 1, 1988.
[11] May 1, 1992.
[12] *New Hampshire Insurance Co. v. Strabag Bau AG* [1992] 1 Lloyd's Rep. 361 (C.A.).
[13] 1982 Act, Sched. 13, Pt II, para. 1(2).
[14] Case 34/82 *Peters v. ZNAV* [1983] E.C.R. 987; Case 9/87 *Arcado Sprl v. Haviland S.A.* [1988] E.C.R. 1539; Case C–26/91 *Soc. Jacob Handte et Cie GmbH v. TMCS* [1992] E.C.R. I–3967; Case C–51/97 *Réunion européenne S.A. v. Spliethoff's Bevrachtingskantoor B.V.* [1998] E.C.R. I–6511. See also, in relation to 1982 Act, Sched. 4, Art. 5(1), *Bank of Scotland v. IMRO*, 1989 S.L.T. 432, criticised by Mennie, 1990 S.L.T. (News) 1 (doubted whether obligations arising under bank's membership of self-regulating scheme were contractual in nature); *Engdiv Ltd. v. G. Percy Trentham Ltd.*, 1990 S.L.T. 617 (claim for contribution by architects against main contractors held a matter relating to a contract between main contractors and owners).

the concept of "matters relating to a contract" is to be regarded as an independent concept, and is not to be tested simply by reference to national law. In *Arcado Sprl v. Haviland*[15] a Belgian court asked the European Court whether proceedings relating to the repudiation of a commercial agency agreement and the payment of commission under it were proceedings in matters relating to a contract within Article 5(1). Under Belgian law (as under English law) it was clear that such proceedings were for breach of contract and for sums due under contract, but a doubt appears to have arisen because in France there have been suggestions that a claim for breach of contract in bad faith may be delictual in nature.[16] The European Court answered that there is no doubt that a claim for commission is contractual because it finds its basis in the agreement; and similarly a claim for compensation is contractual in nature because its basis is the failure to comply with a contractual obligation. The latter conclusion was supported by the fact that the EEC directives on commercial agents recognised the contractual nature of compensation in lieu of notice; and by the fact that the Rome Convention on the Law Applicable to Contractual Obligations[17] provided that the law applicable to a contract governed the consequences of failure to comply.

S11–247   In *Soc. Handte et Cie GmbH v. TMCS*,[18] the plaintiffs were a French company which had bought metal-polishing machines from a Swiss company. It fitted to the machines a suction system sold and installed by a French company. That system had been manufactured by a German company. Under French law the plaintiffs' claim against the German manufacturer that the equipment was unfit for its purpose was contractual in nature, even though there was no contract directly between the plaintiffs and the German company. The then prevailing[19] theory in French law was that the intermediate buyer transmitted to the sub-buyer his contractual rights against the manufacturer. The European Court held that such a claim was not contractual for the purpose of Article 5(1). Article 5(1) only applies to cases in which there is an agreement freely entered into between the parties, and in most of the Contracting States such a claim would not be regarded as contractual. Similarly, it was held that although a claim by a consignee (or its insurer) against the carrier who has issued a bill of lading may be contractual, a claim against a carrier who is not in a contractual relationship with the consignee is not within Article 5(1).[20]

S11–248   In *Kleinwort Benson Ltd. v. Glasgow City Council*[21] the House of Lords held by a majority (Lords Nicholls and Mustill dissenting) that a claim for restitution of money paid under a purported contract which was void did not fall within Article 5(1),[22] as it was not a matter "relating to a contract."[23]

---

[15] *supra.*

[16] See Allwood (1988) 16 Eur. L. Rev. 366.

[17] Contracts (Applicable Law) Act 1990, Sched. 1, Art. 10, Rule 178.

[18] *supra.*

[19] But see now *Donovan Data Systems Europe v. Soc. Dragon Rouge Holding*, in 2000 Rev. Crit. 67 (Cr de cass. 1999).

[20] Case C–51/97 *Réunion européenne S.A. v. Spliethoff's Bevrachtingskantoor B.V.* [1998] E.C.R. I–6511.

[21] [1999] 1 A.C. 153. See also *Ferguson v. Shipbuilders Ltd. v. Voith Hydro GmbH & Co. AG*, 2000 S.L.T. 229

[22] Sched. 4, in the same terms as the 1968 and Lugano Conventions. The European Court refused to give a ruling in the proceedings: see *supra*, para. S11–228.

[23] Nor was it a matter "relating to a tort or delict" within Article 5(3): see *infra*, para. S11–260.

A claim fell within Article 5(1) if it could properly be said to be based upon a particular contractual obligation, the place of performance of which was within the jurisdiction of the court. Where the claim was for the recovery of money paid under a supposed contract which in law never existed, it was impossible to say that the claim for the recovery of the money was based upon a particular contractual obligation. A claim to restitution based upon the principle of unjust enrichment did not *per se* fall within Article 5(1). It was not necessary to hold that a claim to restitution could never fall within Article 5(1). Very exceptionally, there might be particular circumstances in which it could properly be said that the claim in question, although a claim to restitution, was nevertheless based on a contractual obligation and fell within Article 5(1). Lord Goff left open the question whether Article 5(1) applied to a claim for the recovery of money paid under a valid contract on the ground of failure of consideration following the defendant's breach.

The question has arisen in England whether an action to avoid an **S11–249** insurance or re-insurance contract on the ground of misrepresentation or non-disclosure is a matter "relating to a contract" for the purposes of Article 5(1), and whether the duty of good faith can be the "obligation in question". These questions arise because the proceedings are based on breach of the duty of good faith owed to the insurer or re-insurer, and it is controversial as a matter of English law whether the duty of good faith is properly to be regarded as a contractual obligation or as an equitable obligation under the general law. It was held by the House of Lords in *Agnew v. Länsförsäkringsbolagens AB*[24] that a claim to set aside a contract for non-disclosure was a matter relating to a contract. It was also held (by a majority, with Lords Hope of Craighead and Millett dissenting) that pre-contractual obligations fell within Article 5(1); that the "obligation in question" was apt to comprise the defendant's obligations to make a fair presentation of the risk, not to misrepresent it and to disclose material facts; that those obligations were to be performed in London, and the English court had jurisdiction under Article 5(1). It is by no means clear on what basis the majority distinguished the *Kleinwort Benson* case, except perhaps that the *Kleinwort Benson* concerned a void contract.[25]

But in *Fonderie Officine Meccaniche SpA v. HWS GmbH*,[26] the European Court held that an action in Italy based on the breach of the obligation to act in good faith in negotiations was a matter relating to tort, delict or quasi-delict and not contract. Article 5(1) did not require a contract to have been concluded, but it was essential, for Article 5(3) to apply, to identify an obligation, since the jurisdiction of the national court was determined by the place of performance of the obligation in question. Article 5(1) did not apply where there was no obligation freely assumed by one party to the other. The obligation to make good damage allegedly caused by the unjustified breaking off of negotiations could derive only from breach of rules of law, in particular the rule which required the parties to act in good faith in negotiations with a view to the formation of a contract.

---

[24] [2001] 1 A.C. 223. See also *Alfred Dunhill Ltd. v. Diffusion Internationale de Maroquinerie de Prestige SARL* [2001] C.L.C. 949 a claim for damages for misrepresentation alleged to have induced a contract is not a matter "relating to a contract," applying [2001] 1 A.C. at 252–253, *per* Lord Hope of Craighead (a dissenting speech, but not on this point).
[25] See Lord Woolf MR at p. 242.
[26] Case C–334/00, September 17, 2002.

S11–250   The jurisdiction under Article 5(1) may be invoked even if the existence of the contract is denied by the defendant. In *Effer SpA v. Kantner*[27] the dispositive holding was that the plaintiff may invoke this jurisdiction "even when the existence of the contract on which the claim is based is in dispute between the parties." It has been held that this is so even where it is the claimant who denies the existence of the contractual relationship and seeks a negative declaration that he is not bound by any obligation, and it is the defendant who asserts there is a contractual obligation,[28] but this must be regarded as doubtful.[29] The mere allegation of a contract is not enough to found jurisdiction: service may be set aside if there is no basis for the existence of a contract, *i.e.* no serious question which calls for a trial.[30]

S11–251   **The obligation in question.** Subject to the special provision for contracts for the sale of goods and supply of services in the Judgments Regulation,[31] "the obligation in question" whose place of performance must be in England is the obligation which is the basis of the action. In *De Bloos Sprl v. Bouyer S.A.*[32] the European Court held that the "obligation" in Article 5(1) of the 1968 Convention was the contractual obligation which formed the basis of the legal proceedings[33]; where the plaintiff seeks damages for faulty performance or non-performance of a contractual obligation, it is the latter obligation which is the relevant obligation for the purposes of Article 5(1). But as regards compensation for termination, it was for the national court to decide whether the obligation to pay it was a separate independent contractual obligation or whether it merely replaced the unperformed contractual obligation.[34] This decision gave rise to considerable practical problems in cases of exclusive agency or distribution contracts where the defendant had repudiated a contract containing obligations to be performed in more than one country. In *Ivenel v. Schwab*[35] (a case concerned with a

---

[27] Case 38/81 [1982] E.C.R. 825. See also Case 73/77 *Sanders v. Van der Putte* [1977] E.C.R. 2383 (jurisdiction under 1968 Convention, Art. 16(1), in dispute over existence of lease). *Cf.* Case C–269/95 *Benincasa v. Dentalkit Srl* [1997] E.C.R. I–3767 (jurisdiction clause effective under 1968 Convention, Art. 17 where party resisting its application claims contract is void).

[28] *Boss Group Ltd. v. Boss France S.A.* [1997] 1 W.L.R. 351 (C.A.). *Cf. Fisher v. Unione Italiana de Riassicurazione SpA* [1998] C.L.C. 682; also Batiffol and Lagarde, Vol. 2, pp. 475–476; *Soc. I.S.I. v. Soc. C.P.A.V.*, Cour de cassation, France, in 1983 *Rev. Crit.* 516, note Gaudemet-Tallon. See also the position under CPR, r. 6.20(5), *supra*, para. S11–157.

[29] The decision was, however, mentioned with apparent approval by Lord Clyde in *Kleinwort Benson Ltd. v. Glasgow City Council* [1999] 1 A.C. 153, 182. In *Agnew v. Länsförsäkringbolagens AB* [2001] 1 A.C. 223, 258, Lord Hope approved the decision, but Lord Millett (at 264) said it was doubtful. See also *USF Ltd. v. Aquatechnology Hanson NV/SA* [2001] 1 All E.R. (Comm.) 856. See Briggs (1997) 58 B.Y.I.L. 331, 335.

[30] *Tesam Distribution Ltd. v. Schuh Mode Team GmbH* [1990] I.L.Pr. 149 (C.A.), applied in *Rank Film Distributors Ltd. v. Lanterna Editrice Srl* [1992] I.L.Pr. 58; *New England Reinsurance Corp. v. Messoghios Insurance Co. S.A.* [1992] 2 Lloyd's Rep. 251 (C.A.).

[31] Many of the cases establishing the general principles on the operation of Art. 5(1) relate to contracts for the sale of goods or the supply of services and might be decided differently under the Judgments Regulation.

[32] Case 14/76 [1976] E.C.R. 1497.

[33] This is so even if it leads to a claim being subject to the jurisdiction of a court which does not have the closest connection with the dispute: Case C–282/92 *Custom Made Commercial Ltd. v. Stawa Metallbau GmbH* [1994] E.C.R. I–2913; *Boss Group Ltd. v. Boss France S.A.* [1997] I W.L.R. 351 (C.A.).

[34] In England it is the latter: *cf. Photo Production Ltd. v. Securicor Transport Ltd.* [1980] A.C. 827, 849, *per* Lord Diplock, whose dicta, it is suggested, do not affect this conclusion. See *Medway Packaging Ltd. v. Meurer Maschinen GmbH* [1990] 1 Lloyd's Rep. 383, 389, affd. [1990] 2 Lloyd's Rep. 112 (C.A.).

[35] Case 133/81 [1982] E.C.R. 1891.

claim by a commission agent employed under a contract of employment) the European Court modified its approach to deal with a case involving mutual obligations to be performed in different countries. It held that in such a case the relevant obligation was the obligation which was characteristic of the contract. This is a concept borrowed from the Rome Convention on the Law Applicable to Contractual Obligations.[36]

But in *Shenavai v. Kreischer*[37] the Court held that the decision in *Ivenel v. Schwab* was limited to contracts of employment.[38] In other cases it is not necessary or appropriate to identify the obligation which characterises the contract. Accordingly, in such cases regard should be had solely to the contractual obligations whose performance was sought. The court said that where a dispute is concerned with a number of obligations arising under the contract, the court before which the matter is brought will be guided by the maxim *accessorium sequitur principale, i.e.* where various obligations are at issue, it will be the principal obligation which will determine jurisdiction. Thus in *Medway Packaging Ltd. v. Meurer Maschinen GmbH*[39] the English distributor of German machinery could sue in England for the German manufacturer's repudiation because the principal obligation which was the basis of the proceedings was the obligation to give reasonable notice of termination, which was performable in England at the distributor's place of business. Similarly, in *Union Transport plc v. Continental Lines S.A.*[40] English charterers could sue Belgian shipowners in London in a claim arising out of the shipowners' failure to ship a cargo of telegraph poles from Florida to Bangladesh. The relevant obligation was the obligation to nominate a vessel for the voyage charter, and the place of performance of that obligation was in London. In *Source Ltd. v. T.U.V. Rheinland Holding A.G.*[41] the plaintiffs, an English company, engaged a German company to conduct quality control inspections in the Far East of goods which the plaintiffs were proposing to import into England from suppliers in Hong Kong and Taiwan. When the plaintiffs received complaints about the quality of the goods, they instituted proceedings in England against the German company. It was held that the principal obligation of the contract was the inspection of the goods in the Far East and not the delivery of reports in England, and accordingly the English court did not have jurisdiction under Article 5(1).

This approach, however, is inapplicable in cases where no single obligation can be regarded as principal. In *Leathertex Divisione Sintetici SpA v. Bodetex BVBA*[42] proceedings were brought in Belgium against an Italian

S11–252

---

[36] See Rule 174.

[37] Case 266/85 [1987] E.C.R. 239.

[38] For which special provision is now made: see, *infra*, paras. S11–334 *et seq.* See also *Mercury Publicity Ltd. v. Wolfgang Loerke GmbH* [1993] I.L.Pr 142 (C.A.).

[39] [1990] 2 Lloyd's Rep. 112 (C.A.). See also *Carl Stuart Ltd. v. Biotrace* [1993] I.L.R.M. 633; *Bio-Medical Research Ltd. v. Delatex S.A.* [2000] I.L.Pr. 23 (Irish High Ct). On distribution agreements in the context of Art. 5(1) see Hertz, *Jurisdiction in Contract and Tort under the Brussels Convention* (1998), pp. 132–138.

[40] [1992] 1 W.L.R. 15 (H.L.).

[41] [1998] Q.B. 54 (C.A.), stated *infra*, Illustration 4. See also *A.I.G. Group (U.K.) Ltd. v. The Ethniki* [2000] 2 All E.R. 566 (C.A.); *W.H. Martin Ltd. v. Feldbinder GmbH* [1998] I.L.Pr. 794. The principal obligation may be an implied term: *Raiffeisen Zentralbank Oesterreich A.G. v. National Bank of Greece S.A.* [1999] 1 Lloyd's Rep. 408.

[42] Case C–420/97 [1999] E.C.R. I–6747. See also *A.I.G. Group (U.K.) Ltd. v. The Ethniki* [2000] 2 All E.R. 566 (C.A.); *Ferguson v. Shipbuilders Ltd. v. Voith Hydro GmbH & Co. AG*, 2000 S.L.T. 229

company for arrears of commission and compensation in lieu of notice of termination of an agency contract. The Belgian court held that the obligation to give notice and, in the event of failure to give notice, to pay compensation was to be performed in Belgium, but that the obligation to pay commission was to be performed in Italy under the principle that debts are payable at the residence of the creditor. Accordingly it asked the European Court whether both claims under the two separate obligations (neither of which was accessory to the other) could be brought in Belgium as the place of performance of one of them. The European Court held that a court does not have jurisdiction to hear the whole of an action founded on two obligations of equal rank arising from the same contract when, acording to the conflict rules of the State where that court is situated, one of those obligations is to be performed in that State and the other in another Contracting State.

S11–253 **Place of performance.** Once the relevant contractual obligation has been determined, the next problem is what law determines where it is to be performed.[43] Article 5(1) of the Regulation and the Conventions is silent on this question. In *Industrie Tessili Italiana Como v. Dunlop A.G.*[44] the European Court held that it is for the court before which the matter is brought to establish whether the place of performance is situated within its territorial jurisdiction, and that it must for that purpose determine in accordance with its own rules of the conflict of laws what is the law applicable to the legal relationship in question, and define, in accordance with that law, the place of performance of the contractual obligation in question. This ruling was reaffirmed in 1994 in *Custom Made Commercial Ltd. v. Stawa Metallbau GmbH*,[45] where the European Court also held that the same principle applied where the conflict of laws rules of the court seised referred to a uniform law, such as Article 59(1) of the Uniform Law on the International Sale of Goods Act 1964, which provides that the buyer must pay the price to the seller at the seller's place of business, or, if he does not have a place of business, at his habitual residence (subject to agreement to the contrary).[46] Consequently, the German court had jurisdic-

---

[43] On place of performance see also *Ocarina Marine Ltd. v. Marcard Stein & Co.* [1994] 2 Lloyd's Rep. 524; *Sameon Co. S.A. v. N.V. Petrofina S.A., The Times*, April 18, 1996; *The Sea Maas* [1999] 2 Lloyd's Rep. 281; *Barry v. Bradshaw* [2000] I.L.Pr. 706 (C.A.); *Chailease Finance Corp. v. Credit Agricole Indosuez* [2000] 1 Lloyd's Rep. 348 (C.A.); *cf. Montagu Evans v. Young*, 2000 S.L.T. 1083; *Olympia Products Ltd. v. Mackintosh* [1992] I.L.R.M. 204; *Handbridge Services Ltd. v. Aerospace Communications Ltd.* [1993] 3 I.R. 342 (Sup.Ct.); *Ferndale Films Ltd. v. Granada Television Ltd.* [1993] 3 I.R. 363 (Sup.Ct.). Where the place of performance is in dispute, the claimant must show a good arguable case that England is the place of performance: *Mercury Publicity Ltd. v. Wolfgang Loerke GmbH* [1993] I.L.Pr. 142 (C.A.).

[44] Case 12/76 [1976] E.C.R. 1473, applied in *Domicrest Ltd. v. Swiss Bank Corp.* [1999] Q.B. 548. See also Case 133/81 *Ivenel v. Schwab, supra*. The obligation may be a negative one, and it will then be necessary to identify the country in which the defendant was obliged not to act: *cf. USF Ltd. v. Aquatechnology Hanson NV/SA* [2001] 1 All E.R. (Comm.) 856; *Kenburn Waste Management Ltd. v. Bergmann* [2002] EWCA Civ. 98; [2002] F.S.R. 711 (C.A.). But in Case C–265/00 *Besix SA v. WABAG* [2002] E.C.R. I–1699; [2003] 1 W.L.R. 1113, the European Court held that where the negative obligation had no geographical limitation, the place of performance could not be regarded as being in every Contracting State, and consequently Art. 5(1) did not apply. In those circumstances only the court of the domicile would have jurisdiction.

[45] Case C–288/92 [1994] E.C.R. I–2913.

[46] Contrast *San Carlo Gruppo Alimentare SpA v. Vico* [1996] I.L.Pr. 493 (French Cour de Cassation, 1996) (Hague Convention on International Sale of Goods 1955, jurisdiction at domicile of buyer).

tion in an action for the price payable by an English buyer for goods supplied by a German seller. The reference had been made by the German Federal Supreme Court because the apparent effect of the combination of Article 5(1) of the 1968 Convention and Article 59(1) of the Uniform Law was to confer jurisdiction on the courts of the plaintiff's domicile, which was contrary to the general scheme of the 1968 Convention.

In *GIE Groupe Concorde v. The Master of the Vessel "Suhadiwarno*   **S11–254**
Panjan"[47] the European Court, not following the opinion of Ruiz-Jarabo Colomer A.-G., has reaffirmed that the place of performance of the obligation is to be determined in accordance with the law governing the obligation in question according to the conflict of laws rules of the court seised. The Court recognised that it had adopted a different approach in the case of contracts of employment, where it had ruled that the place of performance should be determined by reference to uniform criteria, which led to the choice of the place where the employee actually performed the work covered by the contract: *Mulox IBC v. Geels.*[48] But that depended on the peculiar characteristics of the contract of employment, which had been reflected in the 1989 Accession Convention. The principle of legal certainty was one of the objectives of the 1968 Convention, and that principle required that the jurisdictional rules which derogated from the basic principle of domicile should be interpreted in such a way as to enable a normally well-informed defendant reasonably to foresee before which courts, other than those of the State in which he was domiciled, he may be sued. The Rome Convention had standardised the relevant conflict rules. Accordingly it was not appropriate to adopt the formula suggested by the French Cour de Cassation that the place of performance of the obligation should be determined by seeking to establish, in the light of the relationship creating the obligation and the circumstances of the case, the place where performance actually took place or should have taken place, without reference to the law governing the obligation.

Thus, the position under the Conventions (but not the Regulation) is that   **S11–255**
in sale of goods cases (subject to the special provisions relating to consumer contracts)[49] English courts will have jurisdiction over a seller domiciled in a Contracting State for damages for breach of warranty of quality if under the law applicable to the contract delivery was to be made in England.[50] Where the claim is for payment of the price it will be necessary to determine the due place of payment, a matter of some difficulty in the absence of agreement. Where there is no agreement, the normal English rule is that, in the absence of contrary indications, the debtor must seek out his creditor.[51] In practice, therefore, English courts will normally have jurisdiction in claims by the seller where the seller is English, and will normally have

---

[47] Case C–440/97 [1999] E.C.R. I–6307.
[48] Case C–125/92 [1993] E.C.R. I–4075. See also Case C–37/00 *Weber v. Universal Ogden Services Ltd.* [2002] E.C.R. I–2013; [2002] Q.B. 1189.
[49] As to which see *post*, clause (14).
[50] See generally Hertz, *op. cit., supra,* n. 39, pp. 114–124. See also *Viskase Ltd. v. Paul Kiefel GmbH* [1999] 1 W.L.R. 1305 (C.A.); *MBM Fabri-Clad Ltd. v. Eisen und Huttenwerke Thale AG* [2000] I.L.Pr. 505 (C.A.); *Eddie v. Alpa Srl,* 2000 S.L.T. 1062. Contrast *Ferguson v. Shipbuilders Ltd. v. Voith Hydro GmbH & Co. AG,* 2000 S.L.T. 229.
[51] *Ante,* para. S11–177. See *Gamlestaden plc. v. Casa de Suecia S.A.* [1994] 1 Lloyd's Rep. 433; *Definitely Maybe Ltd. v. Lieberberg GmbH* [2001] 1 W.L.R. 1745; *Bank of Scotland v. Seitz,* 1990 S.L.T. 584; *Unidare plc v. James Scott Ltd.* [1991] 2 I.R. 88. Contrast *Royal Bank of Scotland v. Cassa di Risparmio delle Provincie Lombardi* [1992] I.L.Pr. 411 (C.A.).

jurisdiction in claims by the buyer where the goods were to be delivered in England. The result will be different if the applicable law is foreign, and if the foreign law has a different rule.

S11–256   The European Court has considered in two cases the question (in relation to the 1968 Convention) whether the parties may confer jurisdiction on the courts of a Contracting State by specifying that the performance of the obligation is deemed to be due there. The result of the cases is that a choice of the place of performance is effective for the purposes of Article 5(1), but it must be a place where the obligation is capable of being performed. In *Zelger v. Salinitri (No. 1)*[52] the European Court held that if the parties to the contract are permitted by the law applicable to the contract, subject to any conditions imposed by that law, to specify the place of performance of an obligation without satisfying any special condition of form, an agreement (even an oral agreement) on the place of performance of the obligation is sufficient to found jurisdiction in that place under Article 5(1). In the *MSG* case[53] the European Court acknowledged that the parties are free to agree on a place of performance for contractual obligations which differs from that which would be determined under the law applicable to the contract. But it held that they are nevertheless not entitled, with the sole aim of specifying the courts having jurisdiction, to designate a place of performance having no real connection with the reality of the contract at which the obligations arising under the contract could not be performed in accordance with the terms of the contract. Article 5(1)(b) of the Judgments Regulation provides that the new rules on place of performance of contracts for the sale of goods and provision of services are subject to agreement to the contrary.

S11–257   **Judgments Regulation: sale of goods and contracts for services.** The operation of Article 5(1) of the 1968 Convention (and of the Lugano Convention), as interpreted by the European Court, gave rise to criticism,[54] in particular because (especially where the obligation sued on was a payment obligation) it tended to give jurisdiction to the courts of the claimant's domicile, and did not fulfil the original expectation that it would give jurisdiction to the courts of the country which had the closest connection with the dispute. Article 5(1)(b) of the Judgments Regulation provides that, for the purposes of Article 5(1), and unless otherwise agreed, the place of performance of the obligation in question shall be: in the case of the sale of goods, the place in a Regulation State where, under the contract, the goods were delivered or should have been delivered; and, in the case of the provision of services, the place in a Regulation State where, under the contract, the services were provided or should have been provided. The following points should be noted. First, Article 5(1)(b) recognises that the parties can agree that a different place shall be regarded as the place of performance of the obligation in question. Secondly, it will in international sale of goods cases tend to remove jurisdiction from England as the domicile of the seller. Thirdly, the classification of the

---

[52] Case 56/79 [1980] E.C.R. 89.
[53] Case C–106/95 *Mainschiffahrts-Genossenschaft v. Les Gravières Rhénanes Sarl* [1997] E.C.R. I–911, [1997] Q.B. 731. See para. 12–104, on the relationship between the decisions in these cases and the requirements of Art. 17 of the 1968 and Lugano Conventions and Art. 23 of the Judgments Regulation.
[54] See *e.g.* Hill (1995) 44 I.C.L.Q. 591; Ancel (2001) 3 Yb. Private Int. L. 101, 108–110.

contract will almost certainly be given an autonomous Community definition. Fourthly, there will be contracts, such as those distribution contracts where the distributor acquires title to the goods, which may fall into both categories.[55]

ILLUSTRATIONS

1. A in England sells goods to X for delivery in France. By English law the due place of **S11–258** payment of the price is England, and (in the circumstances of the case) by French law the due place of payment is France. The contract of sale is governed by English law. In proceedings by A against X for the price, the court has no jurisdiction.[56]

2. X & Co., a German company, appoints A to be the exclusive distributor of its machines in England. X & Co. repudiates the agreement and, in breach of the agreement, sells its machinery to Y & Co. The court has jurisdiction in proceedings by A against X & Co. for damages.[57]

3. A & Co., an English company, buys the business of L Ltd. from its receiver. L Ltd. had previously appointed X & Co., a French company, as the distributor of L Ltd.'s products in France. After A & Co. buys the business of L Ltd., A & Co., appoints a new French distributor. X & Co. complains that this is a breach of its distribution agreement. A & Co. brings proceedings in England for a declaration that it was not in a contractual relationship with X & Co. The court had jurisdiction, even though A & Co. claimed there is no contract, because if there had been a contract, it was to be performed in England by delivery of the products to X & Co. in England, and the negative obligations not to supply others extended to England as well as France.[58]

4. A & Co. agrees to buy promotional goods from suppliers in Hong Kong and Taiwan for importation and resale in England. A & Co. engages X & Co., a German company, to conduct quality control inspections of the goods in the Far East prior to payment by A & Co. for the goods. X & Co. sends reports on the goods to A & Co. in England, and supplies certificates of quality to the sellers to enable them to obtain payment from A & Co. When A & Co. receives complaints about the quality of the goods, it brings proceedings in England against X & Co. The court has no jurisdiction because the principal contractual obligation of X & Co. was the inspection of goods in the Far East rather than the supply of reports to A & Co. in England.[59]

5. A & Co., an English company, concludes with X & Co., a Belgian company, a voyage charter of a vessel to be nominated by X & Co. for the carriage of a cargo of telegraph poles from Florida to Bangladesh. A dispute arises, as a result of which X & Co. informs A & Co. that it is no longer interested in lifting the cargo. A & Co. sues for breach of charterparty. The court has jurisdiction, because the obligation in question is the obligation to nominate a vessel, and the place of performance of that obligation is England.[60]

(3) The court has jurisdiction, in matters relating to tort, if England is the **S11R–259** **place where the harmful event occurred,[61] *i.e.* if England is the place where the damage occurred or where the event which gave rise to the damage occurred.[62]**

---

[55] *Cf. Print Concept GmbH v. GEW (EC) Ltd.* [2002] C.L.C. 382 (C.A.), entry at para. 33–401, post: distributorship contract treated as contract of sale for choice of law purposes.

[56] Judgments Regulation, Art. 5(1)(b). Contrast Case 12/76 *Industrie Tessili Italiana Como v. Dunlop A.G.* [1976] E.C.R. 1473.

[57] *ibid. Cf. Medway Packaging Ltd. v. Meurer Maschinen GmbH* [1990] 2 Lloyd's Rep. 112 (C.A.).

[58] *Boss Group Ltd. v. Boss France S.A.* [1997] 1 W.L.R. 351 (C.A.).

[59] Judgments Regulation, Art. 5(1)(b). *Cf. Source Ltd. v. T.U.V. Rheinland Holding A.G.* [1998] Q.B. 54 (C.A.).

[60] *Union Transport plc v. Continental Lines S.A.* [1992] 1 W.L.R. 15 (H.L.).

[61] Judgments Regulation, Art. 5(3); 1968 Convention, Art. 5(3) and Lugano Convention, Art. 5(3), in 1982 Act, Scheds. 1 and 3C; 1982 Act, Sched. 4, Rule 3(c).

[62] Case 21/76 *Bier v. Mines de Potasse d'Alsace S.A.* [1976] E.C.R. 1735, [1978] Q.B. 708. See generally *Transnational Tort Litigation: Jurisdictional Principles*, eds. McLachlan and Nygh (1996).

COMMENT

S11–260　By Article 5(3) of the Regulation and the Conventions jurisdiction is conferred in matters "relating to tort, delict or quasi-delict on the courts of the place where "the harmful event occurred."[63] In *Kalfelis v. Schröder*[64] the European Court held that the expression "matters relating to tort, delict or quasi-delict" should not be interpreted solely by reference to national law, but should be regarded as an autonomous concept which "covers all actions which seek to establish the liability of a defendant and which are not related to a 'contract' within the meaning of Article 5(1)."[65] It was also held that where a national court had jurisdiction over an action in so far as it was based on tort or delict it did not for that reason alone have jurisdiction in relation to other types of claim. It has been decided that in those cases in English law where a claim may be based alternatively in contract and in tort,[66] the claim will be regarded for the purposes of the Conventions as being contractual in nature, and that Clause (3) will not be available as a head of jurisdiction.[67]

S11–261　Most of the original parties to the 1968 Convention had a form of jurisdiction in tort matters equivalent to Article 5(3); the draftsmen of the 1968 Convention deliberately left open the question whether the relevant "place" was the place of the wrongful act or the place where the damage occurred if they were different places. The tendency of the English case law on the equivalent provision in R.S.C. Order 11 had been to look to the place where in substance the act or omission occurred which gave rise to the cause of action.[68] The point arose for decision under Article 5(3) of the 1968 Convention in the European Court in *Bier v. Mines de Potasse d'Alsace.*[69] The European Court held that the "place" was to be determined,

---

[63] Art. 5(3) of the Judgments Regulation and Rule 3(c) in the new Sched. 4 to the 1982 Act also apply where the harmful event "may occur."

[64] Case 189/87 [1988] E.C.R. 5565. See also Case C–51/97 *Réunion européenne S.A. v. Spliethoff's Bevrachtingskantoor B.V.* [1998] E.C.R. I–6511; Case C–96/00 *Gabriel v. Schlank & Schick GmbH* [2002] I.L.Pr. 642; Case C–334/00 *Fonderie Officine Meccaniche SpA v. HWS GmbH*, September 17, 2002 (action for breach of obligation to act in good faith in negotiations); Case C–167/00 *Verein für Konsumenteninformation v. Henkel* [2003] I.L.Pr. 16 (action by consumer protection organisation to prevent trader from imposing unfair terms within Art. 5(3)).

[65] At p. 5585. This must be read in context, and does not include a claim for restitution: *Kleinwort Benson Ltd. v. Glasgow City Council* [1999] 1 A.C. 153, 167. See also Case C–261/90 *Reichert v. Dresdner Bank (No. 2)* [1992] E.C.R. I–2149 (action to set aside transaction in fraud of creditor not within Art. 5(3)); Case 814/79 *Netherlands State v. Rüffer* [1980] E.C.R. 3807, 3832–3835, *per* Warner A.G.; *Mölnlycke AB v. Procter & Gamble Ltd. (No. 4)* [1992] R.P.C. 21 (C.A.) (patent infringement). In *Davenport v. Corinthian Motor Policies at Lloyd's*, 1991 S.L.T. 774, it was held that for the purposes of what is now 1982 Act, Sched. 4, Rule 3(c), a statutory claim against an insurer for payment of a judgment by the insured is not based on tort or delict. *Cf. Kitechnology B.V. v. Unicor GmbH Plastmaschinen* [1995] F.S.R. 765 (C.A.) (breach of confidence: not decided whether within Art. 5(3)). Art 5(3) applies to a claim in constructive trust based on wrongdoing: *Casio Computer Co. Ltd. v. Sayo* [2001] I.L.Pr. 694 (C.A.); *Dexter v. Harley*, The Times, April 2, 2001 (on which see also Briggs (2001) 72 B.Y.I.L. 470). See also *Compagnie Commercial André SA v. Artibell Shipping Co. Ltd.*, 1999 S.L.T. 1051.

[66] See, *e.g. Matthews v. Kuwait Bechtel* [1959] 2 Q.B. 57 (C.A.).

[67] See *Source Ltd. v. T.U.V. Rheinland Holding A.G.* [1998] Q.B. 54 (C.A.). Contrast *Domicrest Ltd. v. Swiss Bank Corp.* [1999] Q.B. 548; *William Grant & Sons International Ltd. v. Marie-Brizard & Roger International S.A.*, 1998 S.C. 536. This will not normally make much practical difference, as the place of the tort will usually be the same as the place of performance of the obligation.

[68] *ante*, para. S11–192. CPR, r. 6.20 (8), Rule 27, clause (6), adopts the same solution as the Regulation and the Conventions.

[69] Case 21/76 [1976] E.C.R. 1735; [1978] Q.B. 708.

not by the diverging solutions of national law, but by an autonomous interpretation and that the meaning of the expression "place where the harmful event occurred" in Article 5(3) must be interpreted so that the plaintiff has an option to commence proceedings either at the place where the damage occurred or at the place of the event giving rise to it.

The place of damage connotes the place where the physical damage is **S11–262** done or the recoverable economic loss is actually suffered. Even though in one sense a claimant may suffer economic loss at the place of its business, that is not of itself sufficient to confer jurisdiction on that place, for otherwise the place of business of the claimant would almost automatically become another basis of jurisdiction.[70] In particular, a claimant cannot confer jurisdiction on the court of his domicile by alleging that, by suffering economic loss there, he was the victim of a harmful act committed abroad. Thus French companies, whose German subsidiaries had been made insolvent as a result of the alleged negligence of German banks in relation to a property development in Germany, could not sue the German banks in France. The fact that the French companies had experienced financial repercussions in France and had ascertained their loss there did not give the the French court jurisdiction.[71] So also an Italian who claimed that the wrongful conduct of employees of Lloyds Bank in England had led to his arrest in England and seizure of promissory notes could not sue in Italy for the exchange value of the promissory notes and for damage to his reputation. The jurisdiction could not be interpreted so extensively as to encompass any place where the adverse consequences of an event which had already caused actual damage elsewhere could be felt.[72] A consignee of goods who complains that the goods were delivered in a damaged state may sue in the country where the damage occurred or where the event occurred which gave rise to the damage. But the place of damage is not the place of final delivery or the place where the damage was ascertained. To allow the consignee to sue in those places would in effect attribute jurisdiction to the place of the plaintiff's domicile. The place where the damage arose is the place where the carrier was to deliver the goods.[73]

The concept of "the place of the event giving rise" to the damage has **S11–263** received little elucidation from the European Court. In *Shevill v. Press Alliance*[74] the Court considered the question of the appropriate jurisdiction in the case of an action in England by plaintiffs established respectively in England, France and Belgium in respect of an alleged libel published in a French newspaper with a small circulation in England. The European Court held that the victim of a libel by a newspaper article distributed in several Contracting States may bring an action for damages against the publisher

---

[70] *Cf.* Warner A.-G. in Case 814/79 *Netherlands State v. Rüffer* [1980] E.C.R. 3807, 3836.

[71] Case C–220/88 *Dumez France v. Hessische Landesbank* [1990] E.C.R. I–49.

[72] Case C–364/93 *Marinari v. Lloyds Bank plc* [1995] E.C.R. I–2719; [1996] Q.B. 217. *Cf. Kitechnology B.V. v. Unicor GmbH Plastmaschinen* [1995] F.S.R. 765 (C.A.); *Modus Vivendi Ltd. v. British Products Sanmex Co. Ltd.* [1996] F.S.R. 790.

[73] Case C–51/97 *Réunion européenne S.A. v. Spliethoff's Bevrachingskantoor B.V.* [1998] E.C.R. I–6511. *Cf. Henderson v. Jaouen* [2002] EWCA Civ. 75; [2002] 1 W.L.R. 2971 (C.A.) (deterioration in England of injury suffered in France does not make England the place where damage occurred).

[74] Case C–68/93 [1995] E.C.R. I–415; [1995] 2 A.C. 18. See also *Mecklermedia Corp. v. D.C. Congress GmbH* [1998] Ch. 40; *Murray v. Times Newspapers Ltd.* [1997] 3 I.R. 97 (Sup. Ct.); *Ewins v. Carlton U.K. Television Ltd.* [1997] 2 I.L.R.M. 223; *Hunter v. Gerald Duckworth & Co.* [2000] I.L. Pr. 229 (Irish High Ct.).

either before the courts of the Contracting State of the place where the publisher of the defamatory publication is established, which will have jurisdiction to award damages for all the harm caused by the defamation; or before the courts of each Contracting State in which the publication was distributed and where the victim claims to have suffered injury to his reputation, which will have jurisdiction to rule solely in respect of the harm caused in the State of the court seised. It also held that the criteria for assessing whether the event in question is harmful and the evidence required of the existence and extent of the harm alleged by the victim of the defamation are not governed by the 1968 Convention but by the substantive law determined by the national conflict of laws rules of the court seised, provided that the effectiveness of the 1968 Convention is not thereby impaired. Subsequently the House of Lords, applying this ruling, held that, where English law presumes that the publication of a defamatory statement is harmful to the person defamed without specific proof of damage, that is sufficient for the application of Article 5(3).[75]

S11–264 In that case the place of the event giving rise to the damage was said to be the place where the publisher was established, since that was the place where the harmful event originated and from which the libel was issued and put into circulation. In *Domicrest Ltd. v. Swiss Bank Corp.*[76] it was held that, for the purposes of Article 5(3), in an action for negligent misstatement the place where the harmful event giving rise to the damage occurs is, by analogy with defamation, the place where the misstatement originated and that the place where the misstatement is received and relied upon is likely to be the place where the damage occurs.

S11–265 Threatened wrongs. Article 5(3) of the Judgments Regulation confers jurisdiction on the courts of the place where the harmful event occurred "or may occur," and Rule 3(c) of Schedule 4 to the 1982 Act also confers jurisdiction for threatened wrongs. Article 5(3) of the 1968 and Lugano Conventions is silent on the point. Schlosser[77] gave hesitant support to the view that Article 5(3) would also provide a basis of jurisdiction in proceedings where the main object was to prevent the imminent commission of a tort. But in *Verein für Konsumenteninformation v. Henkel*[78] the European Court (relying on the Schlosser Report, and on the clarification of Article 5(3) by the Judgments Regulation) held that Article 5(3) of the 1968 Convention applied to an action to prevent the occurrence of damage.

---

[75] [1996] A.C. 959.

[76] [1999] Q.B. 548, not following *Minister Investment Ltd. v. Hyundai Precision and Industry Ltd.* [1988] 2 Lloyd's Rep. 621. See also *Source Ltd. v. T.U.V. Rheinland Holding Ltd.* [1998] Q.B. 54; *Waterford Wedgwood Ltd. v. David Nagll Ltd.* [1999] 3 All E.R. 185; *Raiffeisen Zentral Bank Osterreich AG v. Tranos* [2001] I.L.Pr. 85; *ABCI v. Banque Franco-Tunisienne* [2003] EWCA Civ. 205 (C.A.); *Casey v. Ingersoll-Rand Sales Co. Ltd.* [1997] 2 I.R. 115. In *Cronos Containers NV v. Palatin* [2002] EWHC 2819 (Comm), [2003] I.L.Pr. 283 it was held that where a defendant procures the payment of money by a third party from a foreign bank account into his account in England, rather than the claimant's account, and used the money, the English court had jurisdiction under Art. 5(3) on the basis that knowing assistance of a fraud took place in England, or the defendants converted the property to their own use in England.

[77] para. 134. This view has been followed in German courts: see Kaye (ed.), *European Case Law on the Judgments Convention* (1998), p. 483.

[78] Case C–167/00 [2003] I.L.Pr. 16. For a similar view see *Bonnier Media Ltd v. Greg Lloyd Smith,* 2002 S.C.L.R. 977, *The Times*, July 10, 2002 (O.H.).

ILLUSTRATIONS

1. A brings proceedings against X & Co., a French company with its seat in France, for **S11–266** libel contained in X & Co.'s French newspaper, of which only a few copies have been sold in England. The court has jurisdiction, but only in respect of damage to A's reputation resulting from publication of the copies in England.[79]

2. X & Co., a German company, manufacture in Germany a motor car with faulty brakes. The motor car fails in England, injuring A, the driver, who cannot work at his business in London for several months. A brings proceedings for negligence against X & Co. The court has jurisdiction.

3. The facts are as in Illustration 2, except that the accident occurs in Germany. The fact that A suffers economic loss to his business in England does not give the court jurisdiction.

4. X & Co., an English company, manufacture in England a motor car with faulty brakes. A, a Frenchman, buys it in France and is injured in an accident when the brakes fail. A brings proceedings against X & Co. The court has jurisdiction.[80]

5. A & Co. is an English company which supplies electronic goods. In a telephone conversation, an officer of X & Co., a Swiss bank, assures the agent of A & Co. in England that it would be safe to release goods to a buyer on receipt of payment orders from the bank. In reliance on the assurance, A & Co. releases goods to the buyer, who is unable to pay, and X & Co. refuses to honour the payment orders because it does not have funds from the buyer. In proceedings by A & Co. against X & Co. for negligent misrepresentation, it is held that the court has no jurisdiction because the place where the harmful event giving rise to damage occurred was the place where the misstatement occurred, in Switzerland, and not the place (England) where it was received and acted upon.[81]

6. A & Co. carry on business in England under the name "Harrods." X & Co., a French company, threaten to open a shop in London called "Harrods." (*Semble*) the court has jurisdiction under this clause in an action by A & Co. to restrain the passing-off and trade-mark infringement.

(4) A criminal court has jurisdiction to make an order for damages or **S11R–267** **restitution in criminal proceedings against a defendant domiciled in another Regulation State or Contracting State or in Scotland or Northern Ireland.**

COMMENT

This clause, which is based on Article 5(4) of the Regulation and the **S11–268** Conventions, is included here for the sake of completeness since claims for restitution in criminal proceedings are outside the scope of this work.[82]

(5) The court has jurisdiction to determine a dispute arising out of the **S11R–269** **operations of a branch, agency or other establishment, if the branch, agency or other establishment is situated in England.**[83]

---

[79] Case C–68/93 *Shevill v. Presse Alliance S.A.* [1995] E.C.R. 1–415; [1995] 2 A.C. 18. *Cf. Kroch v. Rossell et Cie* [1937] 1 All E.R. 725 (C.A.), where the court did not exercise jurisdiction because A's real complaint related to the damage to his reputation in France and Belgium.

[80] Judgments Regulation, Art. 2.

[81] *Domicrest Ltd. v. Swiss Bank Corporation* [1999] Q.B. 548.

[82] Art. 5(4) (which is reproduced in 1982 Act. Sched. 4, Rule 3(d)) is based on the idea, reflected in the legal systems of the original Contracting States, that the right to obtain compensation for damage suffered following behaviour contrary to criminal law is generally recognised as being civil in nature: Case C–172/91 *Sonntag v. Waidmann* [1993] E.C.R. 1–1963. See also *Haji-Ioannou v. Frangos* [1999] 2 Lloyd's Rep. 337 (C.A.). See also Case C–7/98 *Krombach v. Bamberski* [1999] E.C.R. I–1935 (jurisdictional basis of criminal proceedings irrelevant).

[83] Judgments Regulation, Art. 5(5); 1968 Convention, Art. 5(5) and Lugano Convention, Art. 5(5), in 1982 Act, Scheds. 1 and 3C; 1982 Act, Sched. 4, Rule 3(e). See Fawcett (1984) 9 Eur.L.Rev. 326.

COMMENT

S11–270 Article 5(5) of each of the Regulation and the Conventions confers jurisdiction in relation to a "dispute arising out of the operations of a branch, agency or other establishment" on the courts of the place where the branch, agency or other establishment is situated.[84] It relates only to defendants domiciled in a Regulation State or Contracting State, *i.e.* companies or firms with their seat in another Regulation State or Contracting State or in Scotland or Northern Ireland and a branch in England. Companies with their seats outside the Regulation States or Contracting States but with a branch in England fall within Rule 24.[85] But an insurer not domiciled in a Regulation State or a Contracting State but which has a branch, agency or other establishment there is, in disputes arising out of the operations of the branch, agency or establishment, deemed to be domiciled in that State.[86] Similar provision is made in relation to suppliers of goods and services in consumer contracts,[87] and in relation to employers.[88]

S11–271 Two main questions arise. First, what is a "branch, agency or other establishment"? Secondly, what disputes arise out of its operations? On the first question, it is clear that the concept must be interpreted by autonomous Community or Convention standards and not by purely national notions.[89] The obvious case of a branch bearing the same business name and staffed by the employees of the main undertaking needs no comment. In two cases the European Court has declined to extend the concept of a branch to distributors or sales agents for goods of foreign companies. In *De Bloos Sprl v. Bouyer S.A.*[90] the Court held that one of the essential characteristics of the concept of branch or agency was the fact of being subject to the direction and control of the parent body; that the concept of "establishment" should be interpreted in a similar way, and that an exclusive distributor was therefore not a "branch," etc., of the manufacturer. In *Blanckaert and Willems P.V.B.A. v. Trost*[91] the Court held that an independent commercial agent who merely negotiates business, who is free to arrange his own work and decide what proportion of his time to devote to the interests of the undertaking which he agrees to represent, who may represent at the same time several firms competing in the same manufacturing marketing sector, and who merely transmits orders to the parent undertaking without being involved in either their terms or their execution does not have the character of a branch, agency, or other establishment within the meaning of Article 5(5).

---

[84] Art. 5(5) concerns the branch, etc., operations of the defendant. A claimant cannot confer jurisdiction on the court by relying on the presence of the *claimant's* branch: *New Hampshire Insurance Co. v. Strabag Bau* [1990] 2 Lloyd's Rep. 61, 68; affd. on other grounds [1992] 1 Lloyd's Rep. 361 (C.A.).

[85] paras. 11–096 *et seq.*

[86] Judgments Regulation, Art. 9(2); 1968 and Lugano Convention, Art. 8(2).

[87] Judgments Regulation, Art. 15(2); 1968 and Lugano Convention, Art. 13(2). See *infra*, paras. S11–308 and S11–330.

[88] Judgments Regulation, Art. 18(2). There is no corresponding provision in the 1968 and Lugano Conventions.

[89] See Case 33/78 *Somafer S.A. v. Saar-Ferngas A.G.* [1978] E.C.R. 2183, 2190.

[90] Case 14/76 [1976] E.C.R. 1497.

[91] Case 139/80 [1981] E.C.R. 819, applied in *New Hampshire Insurance Co. v. Strabag Bau* [1990] 2 Lloyd's Rep. 61, 69; affd. on other grounds [1992] 1 Lloyd's Rep. 361 (C.A.). Contrast *Latchin v. General Mediterranean Holdings SA* [2002] C.L.C. 330.

In addition to the element of direction and control the Court has **S11–272**
required the element of the "appearance of permanency." In *Somafer S.A.*
v. Saar-Ferngas A.G.[92] the European Court held that the concept of branch,
agency or other establishment implies a place of business which has the
appearance of permanency, such as the extension of a parent body, so that
third parties do not have to deal directly with such parent body but may
transact business at the place of business constituting the extension. An
important point which was raised but not decided in the *Somafer* case was
whether the defendants were estopped from denying that they had an
establishment in Germany by virtue of their letterhead which indicated that
they had an office there. Advocate General Mayras thought that, having
regard to the special nature of the jurisdiction under Article 5(5),
appearances should be disregarded and the realities considered; it was for
third parties who wished to rely on Article 5(5) to adduce evidence that the
entity which they wished to bring before the national court was in fact
subject to the control and direction of the parent company. But in *SAR*
Schotte GmbH v. Parfums Rothschild SARL[93] the European Court held that,
where the letterhead of a German company appeared to indicate that it was
acting as a place of business of a French company, a third party which did
business with it was entitled to rely on the appearance thus created.
Accordingly the German court had jurisdiction over the French company
because the dispute arose out of the operations of the establishment in
Germany. This was so even though the French company maintained no
dependent branch, agency or other establishment. What established jurisdiction in Germany was that the French company pursued its activities
there through a German company (which, in the unusual circumstances of
the case, was its parent company) with the same name and identical
management which negotiated and conducted business in the name of the
French subsidiary and which was used by the French subsidiary as an
extension of itself.

The second question will be whether the claim arises out of the **S11–273**
operations of the branch, agency or other establishment. In *Somafer S.A. v.*
Saar-Ferngas A.G. the European Court explained that the concept of
operations included matters relating to the rights and contractual and non-
contractual obligations concerning the actual management of the branch,
agency, or other establishment itself, such as those relating to the situation
of its building or the local engagement of staff to work there. It also
included those relating to undertakings which had been entered into at the
place of business in the name of the parent body and which had to be
performed in the State where the place of business was established and also
actions concerning torts arising from the activities in which it had engaged.

The wording of Article 5(5) suggests that it grants jurisdiction to the **S11–274**
courts of the place of the branch in relation to any contract entered into by
it. In *Somafer S.A. v. Saar-Ferngas A.G.* the European Court seemed to
limit the jurisdiction to cases where performance is to take place in the
same Contracting State as the branch. That would have meant that Article
5(5) adds little to Article 5(1) in matters relating to contract. But in *Lloyd's*
Register of Shipping v. Soc. Campenon Bernard[94] the Court held that it is not

---

[92] Case 33/78 [1978] E.C.R. 2183.
[93] Case 218/86 [1987] E.C.R. 4905.
[94] Case C–439/93 [1995] E.C.R. I–961. See also *Re A Counterclaim under Italian law* [1995] I.L.Pr.
133 (German Fed.Sup.Ct., 1993).

a pre-condition of jurisdiction under Article 5(5) that the obligations entered into by the branch in the name of its parent body were to be performed in the Contracting State in which the branch is situated. Accordingly, in *Anton Durbeck GmbH v. Den Norske Bank ASA*[95] it was held that in claims in tort as well as in contract all that was necessary to establish jurisdiction under Article 5(5) was such nexus between the operations of the branch and the dispute as rendered it natural to describe the dispute as one which had arisen out of the operations of the branch. It was not necessary to establish in addition that the activities of the branch had produced the harmful event within the jurisdiction of the court.

It may be that an essential element of this jurisdiction is that it is designed for the benefit of third parties, and not for intra-company or intra-firm disputes.[96]

ILLUSTRATIONS

S11–275   1. X & Co. is a French bank with a branch in London. Through the London branch it employs A to act as its manager in London. X & Co. repudiates the contract, and A brings proceedings in London against X & Co. The court has jurisdiction.

2. X & Co. is a German manufacturing company. It appoints Y, who is domiciled in England and has an office in London, as its non-exclusive agent for England. Y does not have authority to bind X & Co. Y agrees with A, who is domiciled in England, that X & Co. will sell a quantity of its products to A for delivery in France. X & Co. repudiates the agreement purportedly made by Y. The court does not have jurisdiction, since Y's office is not a branch of X & Co.[97]

S11R–276   **(6) The court has jurisdiction if the claim is made against a settlor, trustee or beneficiary of a trust created by the operation of a statute, or by a written instrument, or created orally and evidenced in writing, if the trust is domiciled in England,[98] or, in the case of a trust instrument and where relations between settlor, trustee or beneficiary or their rights under the trust are involved, if the trust instrument confers jurisdiction on the English court.[99]**

COMMENT

S11–277   Article 5(6) was first introduced by the 1978 Accession Convention to provide for jurisdiction over a settlor, trustee or beneficiary of a trust created by the operation of a statute, or by a written instrument, or created orally and evidenced in writing, in the courts of the Contracting State in which the trust is domiciled.[1] The phrase "created by the operation of a statute, or by a written instrument, or created orally and evidenced in writing" is intended to indicate that the rules apply only to cases in which a trust has been expressly constituted or for which provision is made by

---

[95] [2003] EWCA Civ. 147, [2003] 2 W.L.R. 1296 (C.A.).

[96] *Cf.* Reischl A.-G. in Case 14/76 *De Bloos Sprl v. Bouyer S.A.* [1976] E.C.R. 1497, 1519 and in Case 139/80 *Blanckaert and Willems P.V.B.A. v. Trost* [1981] E.C.R. 819, 838.

[97] Cases at para. S11–271, *supra.*

[98] Judgments Regulation, Art. 5(6); 1968 Convention, Art. 5(6) and Lugano Convention, Art. 5(6), in 1982 Act, Scheds. 1 and 3C; 1982 Act. Sched. 4, Rule 3(f).

[99] Judgments Regulation, Art. 23(4); 1968 and Lugano Conventions, Art. 17(2).

[1] It is wider than clause (12) of Rule 27, *i.e.* CPR, r. 6.20(11), *supra.*

statute—it does not include "constructive" or implied trusts.[2] Nor will it apply to testamentary trusts or to trustees in bankruptcy.[3] Article 5(6) is intended only to deal with disputes relating to the internal relationships of the trust, *e.g.* disputes between beneficiaries and trustees, and not to its external relations, *e.g.* the enforcement by third parties of contracts made by a trustee.[4] In *Chellaram v. Chellaram (No. 2)*[5] it was held that the critical date for determining the law applicable to the trust was the date when the proceedings were commenced, and not the date when the cause of action arose.

Whether a trust is domiciled in the Regulation State or Contracting State **S11–278** whose courts are seised, depends on its rules of private international law.[6] A trust is domiciled in the United Kingdom if the trust has its closest and most real connection with a system of law of one of the constituent parts of the United Kingdom and any proceedings which are brought in the United Kingdom by virtue of Article 5(6) are to be brought in the part of the United Kingdom in which the trust is domiciled.[7]

Subject to other provisions of the Regulation and the Conventions for **S11–279** exclusive jurisdiction,[8] the English court will have exclusive jurisdiction in an action concerning relations between settlor, trustee or beneficiary or their rights or obligations under a trust instrument if the trust instrument confers jurisdiction on the English courts.[9]

ILLUSTRATIONS

1. A, who is domiciled in England, is a beneficiary under a trust expressed to be **S11–280** governed by English law. X, who is domiciled in France, is a trustee. A brings proceedings against X. The court has jurisdiction.[10]

2. The facts are as Illustration 1, except that the trust is governed by Bermuda law. The court has no jurisdiction.

3. A trust deed governed by Bermuda law provides that all disputes arising out of it shall be submitted to the jurisdiction of the English court. A dispute arises concerning the right of X, a trustee domiciled in France, to charge for his professional services. The court has jurisdiction.[11]

(7) The court has jurisdiction over a defendant domiciled in Scotland or S11R–281 Northern Ireland in proceedings (a) concerning a debt secured on immovable property, or (b) which are brought to assert, declare or determine proprietary or possessory rights, or rights of security, in or over movable property, or to obtain authority to dispose of movable property, if the property is situated in England.[12]

---

[2] Schlosser, para. 117.

[3] Art. 1, exclusion of wills and succession, bankruptcy. On trust deeds for creditors and marriage contract trusts see Maxwell Report, para. 5.63.

[4] Schlosser, para. 120.

[5] [2002] EWHC 632 (Ch); [2002] 3 All E.R. 17.

[6] Judgments Regulation, Art. 60(3); 1968 and Lugano Conventions, Art. 53(2).

[7] 1982 Act, ss. 10(2) and 45; S.I. 2001 No. 3929, Sched. 1, paras. 7(2) and 12.

[8] This may arise especially if settled land is involved.

[9] Judgments Regulation, Art. 23(4); 1968 and Lugano Conventions, Art. 17; *cf.* 1982 Act, Sched. 4, Rule 12(2).

[10] Judgments Regulation, Art. 5(6).

[11] Art. 23(4).

[12] 1982 Act, Sched. 4, Rule 3(h).

COMMENT

S11–282 This is a head of jurisdiction conferred by Rule 3(h) of Schedule 4 to the 1982 Act and has no directly corresponding provision in the jurisdictional rules of the Regulation or the Conventions.[13]

ILLUSTRATION

S11–283 X, who is domiciled in Scotland, borrows money from A, who is domiciled in Scotland, under an agreement which charges (*inter alia*) shares in a public company in England. A institutes proceedings in England to enforce the charge. The court has jurisdiction.

S11–284 **(8) The court, in cases where it has jurisdiction in an action relating to liability from the use or operation of a ship, has jurisdiction over claims for limitation of such liability.**[14]

COMMENT

S11–285 A claim for limitation of liability allows a shipowner and others who incur liability in connection with a ship to limit their liability to a specific amount based on the tonnage of the ship. In England a claim for limitation of liability is brought against a potential claimant, or by way of counterclaim. The purpose of this clause which originally was added by the 1978 Accession Convention, and applies also in intra-United Kingdom cases, is to allow limitation claims to be brought in the court of the domicile of the shipowner, or, *e.g.* in the court of the place where the harmful event occurred[15] or where the ship (or sister ship) has been arrested. But if the claimants have already brought proceedings in another Regulation State or Contracting State, the claim for limitation would have to be made by way of counterclaim abroad.[16]

S11R–286 **(9) The court has jurisdiction, where a defendant is domiciled in England, over a co-defendant who is domiciled in another Regulation State or Contracting State or in another part of the United Kingdom.**[17]

COMMENT

S11–287 Article 6(1) provides that a person domiciled in a Regulation State or Contracting State may also be sued, where he is one of a number of defendants, in the courts for the place where one of them is domiciled. Article 6(1) refers to the "courts for the place" of the local defendant's domicile, and not to the court of the State of the domicile. The High Court's jurisdiction[18] is not local and it will have jurisdiction under this

---

[13] But *cf.* Art. 6(4).

[14] Judgments Regulation, Art. 7; 1968 Convention, Art. 6A and Lugano Convention, Art. 6A, in 1982 Act, Scheds. 1 and 3C; 1982 Act, Sched. 4, Rule 6.

[15] See *The Falstria* [1988] 1 Lloyd's Rep. 495. *Cf. The Volvox Hollandia* [1988] 2 Lloyd's Rep. 361 (C.A.).

[16] See also CPR, r. 6.11 and Practice Direction, para. 10.18.

[17] Judgments Regulation, Art. 6(1); 1968 Convention, Art. 6(1), and Lugano Convention, Art. 6(1), in 1982 Act, Scheds. 1 and 3C; 1982 Act, Sched. 4, Rule 5(a).

[18] The jurisdiction of county courts is local.

clause whenever the defendant is domiciled in England. Although this head of jurisdiction fulfils a function similar to the "necessary or proper party" provisions of CPR, r. 6.20(3), *i.e.* Rule 27, clause (3),[19] it is narrower in scope than the latter. It was adopted in order to prevent the handing down in the Contracting States of judgments which are irreconcilable with one another.[20] In *Canada Trust Co. v Stolzenberg (No. 2)*[21] it was held that the critical date for the determination of the domicile of the defendant domiciled in England is the date of the issue of proceedings against him, and other defendants can be added under this clause even if he subsequently becomes domiciled outside England. It is not necessary for there to be prior service on the defendant domiciled in England.

In *Kalfelis v. Schröder*[22] the European Court confirmed the view of the **S11–288** Jenard Report that Article 6(1) must be interpreted so as to avoid it being abused to oust the jurisdiction of the courts of the Contracting State in which a defendant is domiciled. There must therefore be a connection between the claims made against each of the defendants, and the nature of that connection is to be given a uniform interpretation: Article 6(1) applies where the proceedings brought against the various defendants are related when the proceedings are instituted, *i.e.* where it is expedient to hear and determine them together in order to avoid the risk of irreconcilable judgments resulting from separate proceedings. The most obvious case of such a risk is where there are joint debtors, but it is not limited to such a case.[23]

The effect of the decision in *Kalfelis v. Schröder* has been codified in the **S11–289** Judgments Regulation, which (like Rule 5(a) in Schedule 4 to the 1982 Act) adds the words "provided the claims are so closely connected that it is expedient to hear and determine them together to avoid the risk of irreconcilable judgments resulting from separate proceedings".

In *Watson v. First Choice Holidays and Flights Ltd.*[24] the claimant was **S11–290** injured during a package holiday in Spain as a result of being chased by a security guard at the resort complex next to the one at which he was staying. He sued the English tour operator, and also sued in negligence the Spanish operator of the resort block for whom the security guard worked. The claim against the tour operator was in contract for the purposes of the 1968 Convention and was in tort against the Spanish company, but there was a substantial connection between the two claims in fact and in law. But in *Réunion européenne S.A. v. Spliethoff's Bevrachtingskantoor B.V.*[25] the European Court indicated that for the purposes of Article 6(1) claims in contract and in tort could not be regarded as connected. The Court of Appeal doubted the underlying basis for the ruling, and said that, but for that decision, it would have held that the fact that one claim was based on

---

[19] *supra*, para. S11R–139.
[20] Jenard, p. 26.
[21] [2002] 1 A.C. 1.
[22] Case 189/87 [1988] E.C.R. 5565. See *Aiglon Ltd. v. Gau Shan Co. Ltd.* [1993] 1 Lloyd's Rep. 164; *Gascoine v. Pyrah* [1994] I.L.Pr. 82 (C.A.); *Fort Dodge Animal Health Ltd. v. Akzo Nobel N.V.* [1998] F.S.R. 222 (C.A.); *Société Commerciale de Réassurance v. Eras International Ltd. (No.2)* [1995] 2 All E.R. 278; *Latchin v. General Mediterranean Holdings SA* [2002] C.L.C.330; *Gannon v. B & I Steampacket Co.* [1993] 2 I.R. 359 (Sup.Ct.). See also *Compagnie Commercial André SA v. Artibell Shipping Co. Ltd.*, 1999 S.L.T. 1051.
[23] *Cf.* Darmon A.-G. [1988] E.C.R. at 5575.
[24] [2001] 2 Lloyd's Rep. 339 (C.A.).
[25] Case C–51/97 [1998] E.C.R. I–6511.

contract and the other on tort was, at most, only one factor to be considered in deciding whether the connection shown between different claims by one claimant against two or more defendants was sufficient, on the basis of whether it was expedient to allow the claims to be joined in order to avoid irreconcilable judgments. A reference to the European Court by the Court of Appeal was withdrawn when the case was settled.

S11–291　　Under English law the claimant has to show that there is a real issue that the court may reasonably be asked to try as to the liability of the additional defendant domiciled in England.[26] The court of the domicile must be validly seised of the claim. Thus if X is domiciled in England, but has agreed with A that the courts of France are to have exclusive jurisdiction over disputes between them, A cannot use Article 6(1) to justify bringing an action in England against X and adding Y and Z, domiciled in Germany, as additional defendants. If the additional defendant has a contract with the claimant providing for the exclusive jurisdiction of another court, then the provisions of Article 23 of the Judgments Regulation would supersede those of Article 6(1) and the chosen court would continue to have exclusive jurisdiction.[27]

ILLUSTRATIONS

S11–292　　1. A enters into a contract with X, who is domiciled in England and Y, who is domiciled in France, whereby A is to perform services for X and Y in the Republic of Ireland. X and Y repudiate the contract. A brings proceedings against X in England, and seeks to join Y. The court has jurisdiction over Y.

2. A & Co. sues X & Co., domiciled in England, and Y & Co., its U.S. parent company, alleging that X & Co. and Y & Co. have infringed A & Co.'s patent for disposable nappies. A & Co. seek to join Z GmbH, a German subsidiary of Y & Co. Its primary purpose in joining Z GmbH is to obtain discovery of documents in its possession. Jurisdiction may be taken under Article 5(3), *i.e.* clause (3), but not (*semble*) under Article 6(1) where the predominant purpose is to obtain discovery.[28]

S11R–293　　**(10) The court has jurisdiction, where a defendant is sued in proceedings in England, to determine a third party claim[29] by the defendant against a person domiciled in another Regulation State or Contracting State or in another part of the United Kingdom, unless the proceedings were instituted in order to deprive the third party of the jurisdiction of the courts of the country which would otherwise be competent to determine the claim against him.[30]**

---

[26] *The Rewia* [1991] 2 Lloyd's Rep. 325, 329 (C.A.); *The Xing Su Hai* [1995] 2 Lloyd's Rep. 15; *Gannon v. B & I Steampacket Co. Ltd.* [1993] 2 I.R. 359 (Sup.Ct.).

[27] See *Hough v. P & O Containers Ltd.* [1999] Q.B. 834 (a case on Art. 6(2) of the 1968 Convention, *infra*). See also Droz, para. 92. *Cf. Soc. Berlit Staudt v. Cie d'assurances l'Alsacienne*, Cour de Cassation, France, 1989, in 1991 *Clunet* 155.

[28] *Mölnlycke AB v. Procter & Gamble Ltd.* [1992] 1 W.L.R. 1112 (C.A.), *per* Dillon L.J. (Woolf and Leggatt L.JJ. expressed no view).

[29] A third party claim is now described as a "Part 20" claim (CPR, r. 20.2) and a third party is now described as a Part 20 defendant (CPR PD20, para. 7). In *National Justice Compania Naviera S.A. v. Prudential Assurance Co. Ltd. (No. 2)* [2000] 1 W.L.R. 603 (C.A.) it was held that a non-party to litigation domiciled in a Convention country could be made liable for costs under the Supreme Court Act 1981, s. 51, either on the basis that the application did not involve "suing" him within Art. 2, or if it did, that he was being sued as a third party under Art. 6(2).

[30] Judgments Regulation, Art. 6(2); 1968 Convention, Art. 6(2), and Lugano Convention, Art. 6(2), in 1982 Act, Scheds. 1 and 3C; 1982 Act, Sched. 4, Rule 5(b). Art. 65 of the Judgments Regulation makes special provision for proceedings in Germany and Austria, and for recognition and enforcement in those countries of judgments given in other Regulation States by virtue of Art. 6(2).

COMMENT

The English text of Article 6(2) provides for jurisdiction in proceedings on **S11–294** a warranty or guarantee or other third party proceedings[31] in the court seised of the original proceedings unless they were instituted solely with the object of removing the third party from the jurisdiction of the court which would otherwise be competent. The *"demande en garantie"* is equivalent to a claim for indemnity, and this provision deals with what in England is regulated by what was previously known as third party procedure and are now called Part 20 claims.[32] A third party may be sued in England, even if England has little connection with the claim against the third party, *e.g.* if the jurisdiction of the court over the original action is derived from a contract between the claimant and defendant. An attempt is made to prevent abuse of this head of jurisdiction by providing that it is not to apply if the original proceedings were brought solely with the object of removing the third party from the jurisdiction which would otherwise have been competent. If the third party has an agreement with the defendant providing for the jurisdiction of the courts of another Regulation State (or Contracting State), the agreement will be given effect under Article 23 of the Regulation (or Article 17 of the Conventions)[33] in priority to Article 6(2).[34]

In *Kongress Agentur Hagen GmbH v. Zeehaghe B.V.*[35] the European Court **S11–295** confirmed that Article 6(2) applied if the national court had jurisdiction under the 1968 Convention over the defendant in the plaintiff's original claim, irrespective of the domicile of the original defendant. In that case jurisdiction over the defendant had been taken on the basis of Article 5(1). It was also held that Article 6(2) does not *require* the national court to exercise jurisdiction against the third party, and it may apply its own procedural rules in order to determine whether the action is admissible, provided that the effectiveness of the Convention is not impaired, and, in particular, that leave to bring the claim on the guarantee is not refused on the ground that the third party resides or is domiciled in a Contracting State other than that of the court seised of the original proceedings.

In England the court has a wide discretion under the Civil Procedure **S11–296** Rules 1998 to dismiss or strike out third party (Part 20) claims. But the effect of the decision of the European Court is that the third party proceedings cannot be set aside solely on the ground of the delay which would be caused by the fact that the third party is domiciled in another Regulation State or Contracting State.[36]

---

[31] *"une demande en garantie ou . . . une demande en intervention."*
[32] CPR, Pt. 20. See *e.g. Kinnear v. Falcon Films N.V.* [1996] 1 W.L.R. 920; *Waterford Wedgwood plc v. David Nagli Ltd.* [1999] 3 All E.R. 185; *Caltex Trading Pte Ltd. v. Metro Trading International plc* [1999] 2 Lloyd's Rep. 724; *Knauf UK GmbH v. British Gypsum Ltd. (No. 2)* [2002] EWHC 739 (Comm), [2002] 2 Lloyd's Rep. 416. Foreign third parties may now be joined as necessary or proper parties to an English proceeding under CPR, r. 6.20(3), Rule 27, clause (3), *supra*.
[33] *infra*, Rule 32(3).
[34] *Hough v. P & O Containers Ltd.* [1999] Q.B. 834. *Cf. Soc. de Groot Nijkerk v. Soc. Rhenania*, 1993 *Clunet* 151 (French Cour de Cassation, 1992).
[35] Case C–365/88 [1990] E.C.R. I–1845. It would seem to follow that jurisdiction under Art. 6(2) is available even if the defendant in the original claim is domiciled outside the Regulation States or Contracting States and is sued on an "exorbitant" ground (such as mere presence) under Art. 4: *cf.* Kaye, p. 648; *Veenbrink v. Banque Internationale pour l'Afrique Occidentale*, French Cour de Cassation, 1992, in 1993 *Clunet* 151, note Huet.
[36] See Lenz A.-G. [1990] E.C.R. I–1845, 1858.

ILLUSTRATIONS

S11–297   1. A buys a French machine for delivery in England from X, who is domiciled in France and who bought it from Y, who is also domiciled in France. The machine is faulty and A brings proceedings in England against X, X may join Y.[37]

2. The facts are as in Illustration 1, except that the machinery was bought and delivered in France. When A brings proceedings in England against X, X (who would not otherwise be subject to the jurisdiction) submits to the jurisdiction. *Semble*, X may join Y.

3. The facts are as Illustration 2, except that X submits to the jurisdiction as part of a collusive plan between A and X to procure that X may join Y in the English proceedings. The court has no jurisdiction.

4. The facts are as in Illustration 1, except that X's claim against Y is time-barred under French law. The court may set aside the claim against Y.

5. A film actor was injured in an accident while making a film in Spain, and subsequently died in hospital in Madrid. His administrators sued the film company, and the producer and director of the film. The defendants were able to join the Spanish orthopaedic surgeon and the Spanish hospital as third parties claiming contribution under the Civil Liability (Contribution) Act 1978 and damages for breach of contract allegedly concluded between the defendants and the hospital for treatment of the actor.[38]

6. A was injured while working for X & Co., an English company, as an electrician on board one of its ships while it was undergoing repairs in a German shipyard. A sued X & Co. in England for negligence and breach of statutory duty. The repairs were being done by Y & Co. pursuant to a contract which was governed by German law and provided for the jurisdiction of the Hamburg courts. The English court had no jurisdiction over X & Co.'s third party claim against Y & Co. because the jurisdiction agreement provisions of Article 17 of the 1968 Convention[39] took priority over the third party jurisdiction under Article 6(2).[40]

S11R–298   **(11) The court has jurisdiction, where a claimant domiciled in another Regulation State or Contracting State or in Scotland or Northern Ireland sues in England, to determine a counterclaim arising from the same contract or facts on which the original claim was based.**[41]

COMMENT

S11–299   Article 6(3) provides that a person domiciled in a Regulation State (or, as the case may be, in a Contracting State) may be sued on a counterclaim,[42] arising from the same contract or facts on which the original claim was based, in the court in which the original claim is pending. This is similar to the English rule of jurisdiction that a claimant submits to counterclaims.[43]

---

[37] Case C–365/88 *Kongress Agentur Hagen GmbH v. Zeehaghe B.V.* [1990] E.C.R. I–1845.

[38] *Kinnear v. Falcon Films N.V.* [1996] 1 W.L.R. 920.

[39] para. 12–108.

[40] *Hough v. P & O Containers Ltd.* [1999] Q.B. 834.

[41] Judgments Regulation, Art. 6(3); 1968 Convention, Art. 6(3), and Lugano Convention, Art. 6(3), in 1982 Act, Scheds. 1 and 3C; 1982 Act, Sched. 4, Rule 5(c).

[42] *"une demande reconventionnelle"*—which is not quite the same as a counterclaim since it does not have to be brought in the same action: see Anton, *Civil Jurisdiction*, p. 88 on the Scots procedure of reconvention. Art. 6(3) does not regulate the circumstances when a set-off (as distinct from a counterclaim) may be raised. That is a matter for national law: Case C–341/93 *Danvaern Productions A/S v. Schuhfabriken Otterbeck GmbH & Co.* [1995] E.C.R. I–2053. Nor does it allow an additional party to be joined by counterclaim: *cf. Jordan Grand Prix Ltd. v. Baltic Insurance Group* [1999] 2 A.C. 127 (a case on Art. 11 of the Conventions, now Art. 12(2) of the Regulation).

[43] para. 11–108. On the special problems raised by set-off or counterclaim when the parties have entered into an agreement providing for the exclusive jurisdiction of the courts of Regulation States or Contracting States see Case 23/78 *Meeth v. Glacetal Sàri* [1978] E.C.R. 2133; Case 48/84 *Spitzley v. Sommer Exploitation S.A.* [1985] E.C.R. 787. See also *Hough v. P & O Containers Ltd.* [1999] Q.B. 834 (on Art. 6(2), *supra*). *Cf. Aectra Refining & Marketing Inc. v. Exmar N.V.* [1994] 1 W.L.R. 1634, 1649–1651 (C.A.) (arbitration).

In Article 6(3) the requirement that the claims be related is expressed in the following way: the counterclaim must (a) "arise" (b) from the same contract or (c) from the same facts (d) on which the original claim was "based." These requirements are stricter than a requirement that the matters merely be "related."

ILLUSTRATION

A & Co., a German company, buys a paper-making machine from X, who is domiciled in England, the price to be payable in Germany. When the machine fails, A & Co. refuses to pay and sues X in England for damages. X counterclaims for the unpaid price. The court has jurisdiction. **S11–300**

(12) The court has jurisdiction in matters relating to a contract, if the action may be combined with an action against the same defendant in matters relating to rights *in rem* in immovable property situated in England. **S11–301**

COMMENT

This clause is based on Article 6(4) of the Judgments Regulation, of the 1968 Convention (which was added by the 1989 Accession Convention), and of the Lugano Convention. It is primarily concerned with actions to recover secured debts and to enforce the security, and is considered below in connection with clause (15).[44] There is an equivalent provision in Schedule 4, Rule 5(d), to the 1982 Act. **S11–302**

(13) In matters relating to insurance (but not as regards defendants domiciled in Scotland or Northern Ireland[45]) **S11–303**

> **(1) the court has jurisdiction in an action against an insurer:**
>> **(i) if the insurer is domiciled in England[46]; or**
>> **(ii) in disputes arising out of the operations of its branch, agency or other establishment, if the branch, agency or other establishment is in England[47]; or**
>> **(iii) (a) where the Judgments Regulation applies, if the policyholder, the insured or a beneficiary is domiciled in England[48];**
>> **(b) where the 1968 and Lugano Conventions apply, if the policyholder is domiciled in England.[49]**
>> **(iv) if the insurer is a co-insurer, and proceedings are brought in England against the leading insurer[50]; or**

---

[44] *Cf.* clause (7), *supra*.
[45] There is no equivalent in Sched. 4 of the provisions relating to insurance in the 1968 Convention. Proceedings relating to insurance contracts will therefore fall within the other provisions of Sched. 4, especially Rule 3(a). See *infra*, para. S11–321.
[46] Judgments Regulation, Art. 9(1)(a); 1968 Convention, Art. 8(1)(1), Lugano Convention, Art. 8(1)(1), in 1982 Act, Scheds. 1 and 3C.
[47] Judgments Regulation, Arts. 8, 5(5); 1968 and Lugano Conventions, Arts. 7, 5(5).
[48] Judgments Regulation, Art. 9(1)(b).
[49] 1968 and Lugano Conventions, Art. 8(1)(2).
[50] Judgments Regulation, Art. 9(1)(c); 1968 and Lugano Conventions, Art. 8(1)(3).

     (v) **in the case of liability insurance or insurance of immovable property, if the harmful event occurred in England[51]; or**

    (vi) **in a third party claim by the insured in the case of liability insurance, where the insured has been sued in England[52]; or**

  (vii) **in the case of a counterclaim against the insurer, if the insurer has commenced proceedings in England arising from the same contract or facts[53]; or**

 (viii) **if the insurer has entered into an agreement conferring jurisdiction on the English court[54];**

(2) the court has jurisdiction over a policyholder, insured or beneficiary:

     (i) **if he is domiciled in England[55]; or**

    (ii) **in the case of a counterclaim, if he has commenced proceedings in England arising from the same contract or facts[56]; or**

   (iii) **in the case of the policyholder or insured, where a direct action has been brought against the insurer in England and the law governing direct actions permits the policyholder or insured to be joined[57]; or**

   (iv) **if the parties have conferred jurisdiction on the English court by agreement,**

        (a) **where the agreement was entered into after the dispute arose[58]; or**

        (b) **where the policyholder and insurer were both domiciled or habitually resident in England when the agreement was entered into[59]; or**

        (c) **where the agreement relates to insurance relating to loss of or damage to ships, aircraft or cargoes,[60] and (where the Judgments Regulation applies) to all large risks as defined in Council Directive 73/239/EEC as amended.[61]**

COMMENT

S11–304 The draftsmen of the 1968 Convention made special provision for insurance in order to protect policyholders.[62] In the negotiations for accession, the United Kingdom sought to adapt the Convention to meet the needs of the London insurance market; in particular, the United Kingdom stressed that the nature of the London market was such that a large proportion of its business was with policyholders outside the Community; and that a large proportion was insurance of "large risks" with substantial industrial and

---

[51] Judgments Regulation, Art. 10; 1968 and Lugano Conventions, Art. 9.

[52] Judgments Regulation, Art. 11(1); 1968 and Lugano Conventions, Art. 10(1).

[53] Judgments Regulation, Arts. 12(2), 6(3); 1968 and Lugano Conventions, Arts. 11(2), 6(3).

[54] Judgments Regulation, Art. 13(2); 1968 and Lugano Conventions, Art. 12(2).

[55] Judgments Regulation, Art. 12(1); 1968 and Lugano Conventions, Art. 11(1).

[56] Judgments Regulation, Art. 12(2); 1968 and Lugano Conventions, Art. 11(2).

[57] Judgments Regulation, Art. 11(3); 1968 and Lugano Conventions, Art. 10(3).

[58] Judgments Regulation, Art. 13(1); 1968 and Lugano Conventions, Art. 12(1).

[59] Judgments Regulation, Art. 13(3); 1968 and Lugano Conventions, Art. 12(3).

[60] 1968 and Lugano Convention, Arts. 12(5) and 12A.

[61] Judgments Regulation, Arts. 13(5), 14.

[62] See Case 201/82 *Gerling v. Treasury Administration* [1983] E.C.R. 2503, 2516.

commercial concerns; neither of these groups needed the special protection of the Convention rules. The special position of the United Kingdom did result in some changes to the Convention, but these were not of a very far-reaching character, and did not much mitigate the problems of forum-shopping to which the insurance provisions give rise.[63]

The main changes made by the Judgments Regulation to the insurance **S11–305** provisions are these. First, an insurer domiciled in a Regulation State may be sued in another Regulation State, not only (as in the 1968 Convention) where the policyholder is domiciled, but also, in the case of actions brought by the policyholder, the insured or a beneficiary, in the courts where the claimant is domiciled: Article 9(1)(b). Secondly, Article 13(5) and Article 14 of the Regulation allow the jurisdiction provisions to be excluded by agreement in the case, not only of the particular risks referred to in Article 12a of the 1968 Convention, but also in respect of all "large risks" as defined in Council Directive 73/239 as amended by 88/357 and 90/618, and as they may be amended in the future.

The provisions discussed here apply "in matters relating to insurance." **S11–306** The expression is not defined, but the 1978 Accession Convention was negotiated on the basis that it did not apply to reinsurance, and the Schlosser Report said that reinsurance contracts could not be equated with insurance contracts, and that accordingly these provisions did not apply to reinsurance contracts.[64] In *Universal General Insurance Co. (UGIC) v. Group Josi Reinsurance Co. S.A.*[65] the European Court confirmed that reinsurance contracts were not covered by Articles 7 to 12a of the 1968 Convention. The object of those provisions was to protect the weaker party to a contract of insurance. The rules protecting a party deemed to be economically weaker and less experienced in legal matters should not be extended to persons for whom that protection was not justified. No particular protection was justified in the relationship between a reinsured and reinsurer, since both parties were professionals in the insurance sector. The House of Lords had come to the same conclusion in *Agnew v. Länsförsäkringsbolagens A.B.*[66]

Where there is doubt whether a contract is one of insurance, the national **S11–307** court (and ultimately the European Court) will have to apply a Community or Convention, rather than a national, interpretation. In *New Hampshire Insurance Co. v. Strabag Bau AG*[67] the Court of Appeal rejected an argument[68] that what was on its face an insurance contract should not be so regarded for the purposes of these provisions because it was made between commercial concerns. It was held that the expression "matters relating to insurance" meant what it said and was not restricted to insurance for domestic or private purposes.

---

[63] See Kerr (1978) Law Soc. Gaz. 1190; Collins, p. 68.
[64] Schlosser, para. 151; *Citadel Insurance Co. v. Atlantic Union Insurance Co. S.A.* [1982] 2 Lloyd's Rep. 543, 549 (C.A.). Whether it applied to reinsurance was raised, but not decided, in Case C–351/89 *Overseas Union Insurance Ltd. v. New Hampshire Insurance Co.* [1991] E.C.R. I–3317; [1992] Q.B. 434. See also Rule 187.
[65] Case C–412/98 [2000] E.C.R. I–5925; [2001] 1 Q.B. 68.
[66] [2001] 1 A.C. 223.
[67] [1992] 1 Lloyd's Rep. 361 (C.A.).
[68] Based by analogy on Case 150/77 *Société Bertrand v. Paul Ott K.G.* [1978] E.C.R. 1431, *post*, para. S11–326.

S11–308 The complex effect of these provisions is summarised in clause (13). In addition to the heads of jurisdiction set out there, the defendant can also confer jurisdiction on the English court by submission under Article 24 of the Judgments Regulation or Article 18 of the Conventions. The provisions apply only where the defendant is domiciled in a Regulation State or in a Contracting State, and where the defendant is not so domiciled Rules 24 to 25 and 27 will apply. This is subject to one important qualification. An insurer who is not domiciled in a Regulation State or Contracting State but has a branch, agency or other establishment in one of the Regulation States or Contracting States shall, in disputes arising out of the operations of the branch, etc., be deemed to be domiciled in that State.[69] A person who is deemed to be domiciled in the United Kingdom as a result is to be treated as domiciled in the part of the United Kingdom in which the branch, etc., is situate.[70] Thus for the purposes of the provisions on insurance a United States insurance company with branches in London, Paris and Geneva will be deemed to be domiciled in England, France and Switzerland.

S11–309 **Policyholder, insured and beneficiary.** The insurance provisions of the Regulation and the Conventions distinguish between policyholder, insured and beneficiary. The purpose of these expressions is to distinguish between the original party to the contract of insurance (*"preneur d'assurance"*) who may not necessarily be the same person as the insured or beneficiary. The practical effect of these distinctions is considerable, particularly when the benefit of the policy is assigned or transmitted with goods, or when the beneficiary is different from the person who takes out the policy.

S11–310 **General scope.** An insurer domiciled in a Regulation State or Contracting State may be sued: (1) in the courts of the State where he is domiciled, or (2) in the Regulation State or Contracting State in which the policyholder is domiciled (and, in the case of the Judgments Regulation, where the insured or beneficiary is domiciled), or (3) if he is a co-insurer, in the courts of the State in which proceedings are brought against the leading insurer.[71]

S11–311 In the case of the 1968 and Lugano Conventions (by contrast with the position under the Judgments Regulation) the jurisdiction in favour of the policy-holder's domicile will allow proceedings in that place by the policy-holder but not also by the insured and the beneficiary if they are different from the policyholder. Leading insurer is not defined, and it does not impose an obligation for proceedings to be concentrated in one court. There is nothing in theory to prevent a policyholder from suing the various co-insurers in different courts.[72] An insurer may normally be sued at any place where it has a branch if the dispute arises from an insurance contract entered into at that branch, whether or not the insurer is domiciled in a Regulation State or Contracting State.[73]

S11–312 Articles 10 and 11 of the Judgments Regulation (corresponding to Articles 9 and 10 of the Conventions) create additional bases of jurisdiction

---

[69] Judgments Regulation, Art. 9(2); 1968 and Lugano Conventions, Art. 8(2).

[70] S.I. 2001 No. 3929, Sched. 1, para. 11; 1982 Act, s. 44.

[71] Judgments Regulation, Art. 9(1); 1968 and Lugano Conventions, Art. 8(1).

[72] Schlosser, para. 149. But they may be regarded as related actions, and relief granted in respect of the proceedings other than those brought first: see Judgments Regulation, Art. 28; 1968 and Lugano Conventions, Art. 22: Rule 31(4)(b).

[73] Judgments Regulation, Arts. 8 and 9(2); 1968 and Lugano Conventions, Arts. 7 and 8(2).

against insurers. In the case of liability insurance (*i.e.* insurance against legal liability to third parties), jurisdiction is conferred on the courts of the State where the harmful event occurred.[74] The relevant harmful event is the event which gives rise to the cause of action against the insured party, and the English court will have jurisdiction if the damage occurred in England or the event which gave rise to the damage occurred in England.[75]

The court may also exercise jurisdiction in a third party claim by the **S11–313** insured against an insurer domiciled in another Regulation State or Contracting State if it is seised of an action by the injured party against the insured.[76] This would be so even if the parties to the original proceedings were both domiciled in England, but not if the insurer and insured are bound by a jurisdiction clause validly conferring jurisdiction on the courts of another Regulation State or Contracting State.

In the case of insurance of immovable property, the court may exercise **S11–314** jurisdiction if England is the place where the harmful event occurred,[77] which will in practice be the place where the immovable property is situated.

Article 11(2)–(3) of the Judgments Regulation (corresponding to Article **S11–315** 10(2)(3) of the Conventions) deals with direct proceedings against insurers, which are found, at least to a limited extent, in most of the Regulation States and Contracting States.[78] The effect of these provisions is that such proceedings may only be brought in those places where the policyholder could have brought proceedings pursuant to Articles 8 to 10 of the Judgments Regulation, and Articles 7, 8 and 9 of the Conventions. Jurisdiction is not therefore extended to the places where the injured party is domiciled unless, for example, that is also the place where the policy-holder (or insured or beneficiary, in the case of the Judgments Regulation) is domiciled.[79] These provisions apply only "where such direct actions are permitted" under the *lex fori*, including its rules of private international law. The policyholder or insured may be joined "if the law governing such direct actions" provides for such joinder.[80] The governing law in this context means, it seems, the law to which the private international law rules of the *lex fori* point. In England there is no clear answer as to the applicable law. Although the question of direct liability depends on the law governing the contract of insurance rather than on the rules applicable to torts,[81] the question what law governs the joinder of the policyholder or insured to such proceedings may be a question purely of procedure for the *lex fori*.[82] Where there is a jurisdiction agreement valid under the restrictive provisions for such agreements in insurance contracts[83] Article 11 of the Regulation and

---

[74] Judgments Regulation, Art. 10; 1968 and Lugano Convention, Art. 9.
[75] Case 21/76 *Bier v. Mines de Potasse d'Alsace S.A.* [1976] E.C.R. 1735; [1978] Q.B. 708.
[76] Art. 10(1); Jenard, p. 32.
[77] Judgments Regulation, Art. 10; 1968 and Lugano Convention, Art. 9.
[78] See, *e.g.* Third Parties (Rights Against Insurers) Act 1930.
[79] Jenard, p. 32.
[80] Judgments Regulation, Art. 11(2); 1968 and Lugano Conventions, Art. 10(2).
[81] paras. 35–042 *et seq.*
[82] It is not easy to envisage circumstances in which the policyholder or insured would be joined in proceedings under the Third Parties (Rights Against Insurers) Act 1930 and ss. 151–152 of the Road Traffic Act 1988. The former transfers the rights of a bankrupt insured against his insurer to the third party. The latter makes an insurer of compulsory third party risk liable to the third party on an unsatisfied judgment against the insured.
[83] *infra*, para. S11–317.

Article 10 of the Conventions (as between the parties to the agreement) are superseded by the agreement.[84]

S11–316 The Regulation and the Conventions[85] provide that, without prejudice to the right granted by Article 10(3) to join the policyholder or insured in a direct action, an insurer may bring proceedings only in the courts of the Regulation State or Contracting State in which the defendant is domiciled, irrespective of whether the defendant is the policyholder, the insured or a beneficiary, without prejudice to the right to bring a counterclaim in the court in which the original claim against the insurer is pending. This provision does not apply where the defendant is domiciled outside the Regulation States and the Contracting States. In *Jordan Grand Prix Ltd. v. Baltic Insurance Group*[86] the House of Lords held that it applies to any insurer, whether or not domiciled in a Contracting State; and that the reference to a counterclaim in the court in which the original claim against the insurer is pending meant a counterclaim against the original plaintiff. Consequently an insurer who was sued in England by an English insured could not add Irish domiciliaries as defendants to counterclaim.

S11–317 **Jurisdiction clauses.** Clauses attributing jurisdiction to courts receive special treatment in the Regulation and the Conventions in the case of insurance contracts, and the general provisions relating to jurisdiction agreements do not apply, although the formal requirements are applicable.[87] The position with regard to insurance contracts may be summarised as follows: (1) if there is an arbitration agreement between the parties the case will be outside the scope of the Regulation and the Conventions[88]; (2) if there is a jurisdiction clause conferring jurisdiction on the courts of a particular State (perhaps even a non-Regulation State or non-Contracting State) then it will be given effect (a) in favour of a policyholder, insured or beneficiary generally[89] (b) in favour of the insurer only if (i) it is entered into after the dispute has arisen,[90] or (ii) the agreement is between a policyholder and an insurer both domiciled[91] or habitually resident in the same Regulation State or Contracting State and confers jurisdiction on the courts of that State,[92] or (iii) the agreement was concluded with a policyholder not domiciled in a Regulation State or Contracting State, unless the insurance is compulsory or relates to immovable property in a Regulation State Contracting State,[93] or (iv) it relates to one of the risks specified in Article 14 of the Judgments Regulation or in Article 12A of the Conventions.[94] In *Charman v. WOC Offshore B.V.*[95] Staughton L.J.

---

[84] Schlosser, para. 148.

[85] Judgments Regulation, Art. 12; 1968 and Lugano Conventions, Art. 11. See *New Hampshire Insurance Co. v. Strabag Bau AG* [1992] 1 Lloyd's Rep. 361 (C.A.).

[86] [1999] 2 A.C. 127.

[87] Judgments Regulation, Arts. 13, 14, 23; 1968 and Lugano Conventions, Arts. 12, 12A and 17. *Cf.* Case 201/82 *Gerling v. Treasury Administration* [1983] E.C.R. 2503.

[88] Judgments Regulation, Art 1(2)(d); 1968 and Lugano Conventions, Art. 1(2)(4).

[89] Judgments Regulation, Art. 13(2); 1968 and Lugano Conventions, Art. 12(2).

[90] Judgments Regulation, Art. 13(1); 1968 and Lugano Conventions, Art. 12(1).

[91] This may include an insurer not domiciled in a Regulation State or Contracting State but with a branch in a Contracting State in relation to a policy issued through that branch: Judgments Regulation, Art. 9(2); 1968 and Lugano Conventions, Art. 8(2).

[92] Judgments Regulation, Art. 13(3); 1968 and Lugano Conventions, Art. 12(3).

[93] Judgments Regulation, Art. 13(4); 1968 and Lugano Conventions, Art. 12(4).

[94] Judgments Regulation, Art. 13(5); 1968 and Lugano Conventions, Art. 12(5).

[95] [1993] 2 Lloyd's Rep. 551, 557–558 (C.A.).

expressed the view (*obiter*, and differing from Hirst J. at first instance) that for a jurisdiction agreement to be effective under Article 12(5) of the 1968 Convention it was necessary for it to relate to one of the specified risks and no other: if it related to other risks, it was wholly ineffective and not merely to the extent it related to other risks.

The following points are worthy of note: first, it is not likely that express **S11–318** agreements on choice of court after a dispute has arisen will in practice be common; secondly, an exclusive jurisdiction clause will always be effective for the benefit of a policyholder, insured or beneficiary; thirdly, the relevant time for testing the domicile or habitual residence of the insurer and the policyholder for the purposes of these provisions is the date of the contract, and not (as under the previous version) the date of commencement of the proceedings; fourthly, they apply where the policyholder is not domiciled in a Regulation State or a Contracting State, but there are proceedings by or against an insured or beneficiary in a Regulation State or a Contracting State on a policy containing a jurisdiction clause. The conferment of jurisdiction is to be effective unless one of two exceptions is applicable: the first is where the insurance is compulsory, in which case no departure from the basic jurisdictional provisions is permitted, even if the policyholder is domiciled outside the Regulation States and the Contracting States.[96] The second exception is for insurance relating to immovable property, where the other applicable provisions will continue to apply even if the national law of the State in which the immovable property is situated allows jurisdiction agreements.[97]

The specified risks in Article 12A of the Conventions are (1) any loss of **S11–319** damage to (a) ships, offshore installations or aircraft, arising from perils relating to their use for commercial purposes or (b) goods in transit, other than passengers' baggage, where the transit consists of or includes carriage by ships or aircraft; (2) any liability, other than for bodily injury to passengers or loss of or damage to their baggage (a) arising out of the use or operation of ships, etc., (b) for loss or damage caused by goods in transit as above; (3) any financial loss connected[98] with the use or operation of ships, etc., in particular loss of freight or charter hire; (4) any risk or interest connected with any of those referred to in (1) to (3) above.[99] The corresponding provisions of the Judgments Regulation are the same, except that Articles 13(5) and 14 of the Regulation allow the jurisdiction provisions to be excluded by agreement in the case, not only of the particular risks referred to in Article 12A of the Conventions, but also in respect of all "large risks" as defined in Council Directive 73/239 as amended by 88/357 and 90/618, and as they may be amended in the future.

The practical effect is that an insurer in London can effectively confer **S11–320** exclusive jurisdiction on the English court by the original insurance contract only in the following cases: (1) where the policyholder is domiciled in the United Kingdom at the time the insurance contract is entered into, or (2) where the policyholder is not domiciled in any of the Regulation States or Contracting States at the time the insurance contract is entered into; or (3) the insurance relates to one of the relevant major risks.

---

[96] See Schlosser, para. 138; *e.g.* aviation and motor vehicle insurance.

[97] Schlosser, para. 139; *sed quaere*.

[98] See *Charman v. WOC Offshore B.V.* [1993] 2 Lloyd's Rep. 551 (C.A.) (jurisdiction agreement valid even if insurance covered land-based equipment, such as crawling crane, because sufficiently connected with sea-going vessels covered by insurance).

[99] See *Tradigrain SA v. SIAT SpA* [2002] EWHC 106 (Comm), [2002] 2 Lloyd's Rep. 553.

S11–321   These provisions find no counterpart in the intra-United Kingdom scheme in Schedule 4 to the 1982 Act. This means that where the Regulation or the Conventions confer jurisdiction on the courts of the United Kingdom, a Scottish defendant will only be subject to the English jurisdiction in insurance matters where one of the general provisions in Schedule 4 applies. In practice the most likely cases are where the Scottish defendant is domiciled in England or where he is sued on an obligation in an insurance contract to be performed in England.

ILLUSTRATIONS

S11–322   1. X & Co. and Y & Co. are German companies and are participants in a joint venture for the construction of an airport in Iraq. They take out a policy of insurance through London brokers in the London market indemnifying them against certain risks in connection with the project. The leading underwriter is A & Co., an American company, but the bulk of the risk is placed with English insurers, and the contract of insurance is impliedly governed by English law. The members of the joint venture claim on the policy for corrosion damage amounting to up to £60 million. A & Co. and the other insurers seek to avoid the policy for non-disclosure and commence proceedings in England against (*inter alios*) X & Co. and Y & Co. for a declaration that they have validly avoided the policy and are under no liability. The court has no jurisdiction.[1]

2. A, domiciled in England, takes out a policy of insurance covering his stamp collection with X & Co., a German insurance company. When the stamp collection is stolen X & Co. dispute liability under the policy. A sues X & Co. in England. The court has jurisdiction.[2]

3. The facts are as in Illustration 2, except that the insurance policy contains a clause providing that the German courts are to have exclusive jurisdiction over any disputes. The court has jurisdiction because the clause is ineffective.[3]

4. X, a resident of Palermo and domiciled in Italy, insures his valuable collection of antiques through a Lloyd's broker with A, a Lloyd's syndicate in London. The insurance policy provides for the exclusive jurisdiction of the English court. The antiques are stolen and A pays a substantial sum under the policy. A subsequently alleges that as a result of material non-disclosure it is entitled to avoid the policy and to have the compensation returned. A brings proceedings against X in London. The court has no jurisdiction.[4]

5. X, a Greek shipowner, insures his fleet with A, a Lloyd's syndicate. The policy provides for the exclusive jurisdiction of the English courts. A brings proceedings for rescission of the contract. The court has jurisdiction.[5]

S11R–323   **(14) In proceedings concerning consumer contracts,**

> **(1) the court has jurisdiction in an action against a supplier of goods, or lender, or supplier of services:**
>> **(i) if the defendant is domiciled in England[6];**
>> **(ii) if the consumer is domiciled in England[7];**
>> **(iii) if the defendant has a branch, agency or establishment in England and the dispute arises out of its operations[8];**

---

[1] Judgments Regulation, Art. 12; *New Hampshire Insurance Co. v. Strabag Bau A.G.* [1992] 1 Lloyd's Rep. 361 (C.A.).

[2] Judgments Regulation, Art. 9(1)(b).

[3] Judgments Regulation, Art. 13.

[4] But a London arbitration clause in the policy would have been effective.

[5] Judgments Regulation, Arts. 13(5), 14.

[6] Judgments Regulation, Art. 16(1); 1968 Convention, Art. 14(1), and Lugano Convention, Art. 14(1), in 1982 Act, Scheds. 1 and 3C; 1982 Act, Sched. 4, Rule 8(1) (as substituted by S.I. 2001 No. 3929, Sched. 2).

[7] Judgments Regulation, Art. 16(1) (and S.I. 2001 No. 3929, Sched. 1, para. 7(3)); 1968 and Lugano Conventions, Art. 14(1) (and 1982 Act, s. 10(3); 1982 Act, Sched. 4, Rule 8(1)).

[8] Judgments Regulation, Arts. 15(2), 5(5) (and S.I. 2001 No. 3929, Sched. 1, para. 11); 1968 and Lugano Conventions, Arts. 13(1), 5(5) (and 1982 Act, s. 44(2)).

    (iv) **in the case of a counterclaim against the supplier, etc., where he has commenced proceedings in England arising from the same contract or facts[9];**

    (v) **if the supplier, etc. has entered into an agreement conferring jurisdiction on the English court[10];**

(2) **the court has jurisdiction in an action against the consumer:**

    (i) **if the consumer is domiciled in England[11];**

    (ii) **in the case of a counterclaim against the consumer, where the consumer has commenced proceedings in England arising from the same contract or facts[12];**

    (iii) **if the parties conferred jurisdiction on the English court by agreement and either (a) the agreement was entered into after the dispute arose[13]; or (b) the supplier, etc., and the consumer were both domiciled or habitually resident in England.[14]**

In this clause a consumer contract means a contract concluded by a person for a purpose outside his trade or profession and which is

(1) **a contract for the sale of goods on instalment credit terms; or**

(2) **a contract for a loan repayable by instalments, or for any other form of credit, made to finance the sale of goods; or**

(3) **(i) where the 1968 Convention or the Lugano Convention applies, any other contract for the supply of goods or a contract for the supplies of services, where in the State of the consumer's domicile (a) the conclusion of the contract was preceded by a specific invitation addressed to him or by advertising, and (b) the consumer took the steps necessary for the conclusion of the contract;**

(ii) where the Judgments Regulation applies, the contract has been concluded with a person who pursues commercial or professional activities in the State of the consumer's domicile or, by any means, directs such activities to that State or to several States including that State, and the contract falls within the scope of such activities.[15]

This clause does not apply, where the 1968 Convention or the Lugano Convention is applicable, to contracts of transport, or, where the Judgments Regulation is applicable, to a contract of transport other than a contract which, for an inclusive price, provides for a combination of travel and accommodation.[16]

---

[9] Judgments Regulation, Art. 16(3); 1968 and Lugano Conventions, Art. 14(3); 1982 Act, Sched. 4, Rule 8(3).

[10] Judgments Regulation, Art. 17(2); 1968 and Lugano Conventions, Art. 15; 1982 Act, Sched. 4, Rule 9(b).

[11] Judgments Regulation, Art. 16(2); 1968 and Lugano Conventions, Art. 14(2); 1982 Act, Sched. 4, Rule 8(1).

[12] Judgments Regulation, Art. 16(3); 1968 and Lugano Conventions, Art. 14(3); 1982 Act, Sched. 4, Rule 8(3).

[13] Judgments Regulation, Art. 17(1); 1968 and Lugano Conventions, Art. 15(1); 1982 Act, Sched. 4, Rule 9(a).

[14] Judgments Regulation, Art. 17(3); 1968 and Lugano Conventions, Art. 15(3); 1982 Act, Sched. 4, Rule 9(c).

[15] Judgments Regulation, Art. 15(1); 1968 and Lugano Conventions, Art. 13(1); 1982 Act, Sched. 4, Rule 7(1)

[16] 1968 and Lugano Conventions, Art. 13(3); Judgments Regulation, Art. 15(3); *cf.* 1982 Act, Sched. 4, Rule 7(2)

COMMENT

S11–324   The objectives of the consumer contract provisions of the 1968 Convention (reproduced in the Lugano Convention) were inspired by a desire to protect consumers; national laws, by contrast, were designed partly to protect the "weaker" party, but also to serve economic, monetary and savings policy.[17] The main change introduced by the 1978 Accession Convention was to make it clear that the provisions applied only to consumer contracts, and not to all instalment sales and financing contracts irrespective of whether the buyer was a businessman or a private consumer. In *Société Bertrand v. Paul Ott K.G.*[18] the European Court held, on the original wording of these provisions, that they applied only to private final consumers and not to those who were engaged, while buying the product, in trade or professional activities. This was confirmed in amendments to the 1968 Convention, which were influenced by the drafts of the Rome Convention on the Law Applicable to Contractual Obligations, which makes special provision for choice of law in consumer contracts.[19] Further changes were introduced by the Judgments Regulation to take account of the growth in e-commerce, and the fact that consumers might be induced to contract abroad as a result of accessing the websites of foreign sellers directed at the country of the consumer's domicile. The other change introduced by the Judgments Regulation is the provision that the exclusion of contracts of transport from these provisions does not extend to "a contract which, for an inclusive price, provides for a combination of travel and accommodation."[20] The reference to travel packages is new.

S11–325   The consumer contract provisions in clause (14) apply only where the defendant is domiciled, or deemed to be domiciled, in a Regulation State or Contracting State. Where the defendant is not so domiciled, then jurisdiction depends, under Article 4 of the Regulation and the Conventions (to which the consumer contract provisions are expressly subject[21]), on the law of the Regulation State or Contracting State where the action is brought.[22] These provisions relate to proceedings concerning a contract concluded by a person for a purpose which can be regarded as being outside his trade or profession, "the consumer."[23] They apply to contracts for the sale of goods on instalment credit terms; or contracts for a loan repayable by instalments, or for any other form of credit, made to finance the sale of goods.

S11–326   The meaning of sale of goods on "instalment credit terms" was considered in *Société Bertrand v. Paul Ott K.G.*[24] where the European Court held

---

[17] Case 150/77 *Société Bertrand v. Paul Ott K.G.* [1978] E.C.R. 1431. See generally Mennie, 1987 S.L.T. (News) 181.

[18] *supra.* See also Case C–269/95 *Benincasa v. Dentalkit Srl* [1997] E.C.R. I–3767.

[19] See Contracts (Applicable Law) Act 1990, Sched. 1, and Rule 181.

[20] Judgments Regulation, Art. 15(3); 1982 Act, Sched. 4, Rule 7(2).

[21] Judgments Regulation, Art. 15(1); 1968 and Lugano Conventions, Art. 13(1).

[22] Case C–318/93 *Brenner v. Dean Witter Reynolds Inc.* [1994] E.C.R. I–4275.

[23] They do not apply to a contract which an individual has concluded with a view to pursuing a trade in the future: Case C–269/95 *Benincasa v. Dentalkit Srl* [1997] E.C.R. I–3767 (franchise agreements to sell dental hygiene products not within Art. 13 of the 1968 Convention). Nor do they apply to a claim by an assignee of a consumer, where the assignee is acting in pursuance of its trade or professional activity: Case C–89/91 *Shearson Lehman Hutton Inc. v. TVB* [1993] E.C.R. I–139. See also Case C–96/000 *Gabriel v. Schlank & Schick GmbH* [2002] I.L.Pr. 642; Case C–167/00 *Verein für Konsumenteninformation v. Henkel* [2003] I.L.Pr. 16; *Standard Bank London Ltd. v. Apostolakis* [2000] I.L.Pr. 766; *Standard Bank London Ltd. v. Apostolakis (No. 2)* [2001] Lloyd's Rep. Banking 240.

[24] *supra.*

that it was necessary to give the expression a Convention interpretation, and that it meant a transaction in which the price is discharged by way of several payments or which is linked to a financing contract. In *Mietz v. Intership Yachting Sneek B.V.*[25] the European Court held that taking payment by instalments from the purchaser, but where the purchase price is paid in full by the time the purchaser takes possession, is not a sale on instalment credit terms.

The consumer contract provisions are not limited to instalment sales and **S11–327** loans to finance them. They also apply to certain contracts for the supply of goods or services. Where the 1968 Convention or the Lugano Convention is applicable, the consumer contract provisions extend to contracts for the supply of goods or services where there has been an invitation to purchase (either specific[26] or by advertising) and the consumer has taken the steps necessary to conclude the contract in the State of his domicile. The steps necessary to conclude the contract would seem to include buying by mail order (although in English law it is probable that it is the consumer who makes the offer and the seller who accepts) since Article 13(1)(3) was intended to cover mail order and door-step selling, but may have much wider effects, *e.g.* where a French company places an advertisement in a United States publication which circulates in the United Kingdom. The concepts of "advertising" and "specific invitation addressed" cover all forms of advertising carried out in the Contracting State in which the consumer is domiciled, whether disseminated generally by the press, radio, television, cinema or any other medium, or addressed directly, for example, by means of catalogues sent specifically to that State, as well as commercial offers made to the consumer in person, in particular by an agent or door-to-door salesman. The expression "steps necessary for the conclusion" of the contract refers to any document written or any other step whatever taken by the consumer in the State in which he is domiciled and which expresses his wish to take up the invitation made by the professional.[27]

Where the Judgments Regulation is applicable, Article 15(1)(c) provides **S11–328** that the consumer contract provisions extend to contracts for the supply of goods or services where "the contract has been concluded with a person who pursues commercial or professional activities in the [Regulation] State of the consumer's domicile or, by any means, directs such activities to that [Regulation] State or to several States including that [Regulation] State, and the contract falls within the scope of such activities." This provision is intended to apply to contracts concluded as a result of marketing through e-commerce, via an interactive website accessible in the domicile of the consumer. The Commission explanatory memorandum[28] says that the criteria in the 1968 Convention were being reframed to take account of developments in marketing techniques; the condition in Article 13 of the 1968 Convention that the consumer must have taken the necessary steps in

---

[25] Case C–99/96 [1999] I.L.Pr. 541.
[26] In *Standard Bank London Ltd. v. Apostolakis (No. 2)* [2001] Lloyd's Rep. Banking it was held that the words "specific invitation" in Article 13 should not be accorded anything other than a natural and common-sense meaning.
[27] Case C–96/00 *Gabriel v. Schlank & Schick GmbH* [2002] I.L.Pr. 642. In that case a claim by a consumer for a prize which the supplier had promised was held to be contractual in nature, and therefore a claim under a consumer contract. See also *Rayner v. Davies* [2002] EWCA Civ. 1880, [2003] I.L.Pr. 258 (C.A.)
[28] COM (99) 348.

his State had been removed, with the consequence that Article 15 applied to contracts concluded in a State other than the domicile of the consumer; under the 1968 Convention the consumer could not rely on the protective jurisdiction when he had been induced, at the instigation of the other party, to leave his home State to conclude the contract; and the mere fact that the consumer had knowledge of a service or possibility of buying goods via a passive website accessible in his country of domicile would not trigger the protective jurisdiction. The provisions were much criticised by the e-commerce industry on the ground that they will impose unnecessary restraints on the development of this new form of economic activity.[29]

S11–329 Where the provisions of the Regulation or the Conventions apply they supersede national law, *e.g.* the Consumer Credit Act 1974, section 141.[30]

The effect of these provisions is that a consumer may bring proceedings in England if the supplier is domiciled in England or if the consumer is domiciled in England. The consumer may only be sued in England if he is domiciled in England; but a foreign consumer may be subject to a counterclaim if he sues in England, and, it seems, he may submit to the jurisdiction by voluntary appearance.[31]

S11–330 Where a consumer enters into a contract with a party who is not domiciled in a Regulation State or a Contracting State but has a branch, agency or other establishment in one of those States, that party shall, in disputes arising out of the operations of the branch, etc., be deemed to be domiciled in that State; and the defendant is deemed to be domiciled for this purpose in the part of the United Kingdom in which the branch is situate.[32]

S11–331 *Jurisdiction agreements.* The consumer contract provisions of the Regulation and the Conventions may be departed from only by an agreement (1) which is entered into after the dispute has arisen or (2) which allows the consumer to bring proceedings in courts other than those indicated in the provisions, or (3) which is entered into when the consumer and the other party are both domiciled or habitually resident in the same Regulation State or Contracting State and which confers jurisdiction on the courts of that State, provided that such an agreement is not contrary to the law of that State.[33] The relevant date for testing domicile is that of the commencement of proceedings, subject to two points: first, if the provisions apply because of Article 15(1)(c) of the Regulation or Article 13(1)(3) of the Conventions (advertising in the State of the consumer's domicile) then it will also be necessary to determine the consumer's domicile at the time of the conclusion of the contract; secondly, if there is a jurisdiction agreement involved it may be necessary to consider the party's domicile at the date of the conclusion of the contract. In practice, therefore, standard form

---

[29] See Kennett (2001) 50 I.C.L.Q.725, 728–729, and Report by the Committee on Legal Affairs and the Internal Market (Rapporteur: Diana Wallis) of the European Parliament, September 18, 2000 (a5–0253/2000).

[30] *Cf.* Case 25/79 *Sanicentral v. Collin* [1979] E.C.R. 3423.

[31] To this effect, see *Re Jurisdiction in a Consumer Contract* [2002] I.L.Pr. 157 (Koblenz Regional Court of Appeal, 2000).

[32] Judgments Regulation, Art. 15(2), and S.I. 2001 No. 3929, Sched. 1, para. 11(2); 1968 and Lugano Conventions, Art. 13(2) and 1982 Act, s. 44(2).

[33] Judgments Regulation, Art. 17; 1968 and Lugano Conventions, Art. 15; 1982 Act, Sched. 4, Rule 9.

consumer contracts will only be effective to confer exclusive jurisdiction on the English court if both the consumer and the supplier are domiciled, or deemed to be domiciled, in England.

These provisions apply as between the constituent parts of the United Kingdom[34] but their application is without prejudice to the jurisdiction of the court under Rule 3(h)(ii) of Schedule 4 in proceedings to enforce possessory or security rights in movable property. Thus a supplier may claim possession in the English court of goods held in England to the order of a consumer domiciled in Scotland.

ILLUSTRATIONS

1. A & Co., an English company, sells an expensive piece of household equipment to X, **S11–332** an individual domiciled in France. Delivery is in England, and the price is payable in England by instalments. When X defaults A & Co. commences proceedings in England. The court has no jurisdiction.

2. A, an individual domiciled in England, buys a washing machine from X & Co., a French company, while he is on a visit to France. The price is payable in France by instalments. A alleges that the machine is faulty and commences proceedings in England for the return of the instalments already paid. The court has jurisdiction.

3. The facts are as in Illustration 2, except that the contract provides for the exclusive jurisdiction of the French courts. The court has jurisdiction, because the clause is ineffective.

4. A, an individual domiciled in France, buys a washing machine on instalment credit terms from X & Co., a French company. The contract provides for the exclusive jurisdiction of the French courts. A moves to England and becomes domiciled there. When the machine proves to be faulty. A commences proceedings in England against X & Co. The court has no jurisdiction.

(14A) In matters relating to individual contracts of employment[35]   S11R–333

    (1) the court has jurisdiction in proceedings against an employer

        (i) if the employer is domiciled (or deemed to be domiciled) in England[36];

        (ii) if England is the place where the employee habitually carries out his work or (where the Judgments Regulation or the intra United Kingdom provisions apply) England was the last place where he did so[37];

      (iii) where the 1968 Convention or the Lugano Convention applies and the employee does not habitually carry out his work in one country, if England was the place of business through which he was engaged[38];

      (iv) where the Judgments Regulation applies and the employee does not or did not habitually carry out his work in any one

---

[34] See *Waverley Asset Management Ltd. v. Saha*, 1989 S.L.T. (Sh.Ct.) 87 (provisions do not apply to sale of unit trusts).

[35] For the purposes of this clause, work carried out on installations on or above the continental shelf of a State are to be regarded as work carried out in that State: Case C–37/00 *Weber v. Universal Ogden Services Ltd.* [2002] E.C.R. I–2013, [2002] Q.B. 1189. For claims against employees see *Swinthenbank Foods Ltd. v. Bowers* [2002] 2 All E.R. (Comm.) 974.

[36] Judgments Regulation, Art. 19(2); 1968 and Lugano Conventions, Art. 2; 1982 Act, Sched. 4, Rule 10(2)(a).

[37] 1968 and Lugano Conventions, Art. 5(1); Judgments Regulation, Art.19(2)(a); 1982 Act, Sched. 4, Rule 10(2)(b);

[38] 1968 and Lugano Conventions, Art. 5(1) (with slightly differing language).

country, if England was the place where the business which engaged the employee is or was situated.[39]

(2) Where the Judgments Regulation applies, an employee may only be sued in England if he is domiciled there.[40]

(3) These provisions are without prejudice to the power of either party to bring a counterclaim.[41]

(4) Jurisdiction agreements are, in principle, effective only if they are entered into after the dispute has arisen, or if they allow the employer to be sued in a State which would not otherwise have jurisdiction.[42]

COMMENT

S11–334   In all countries certain aspects of labour or employment law claims are regulated by public law, but in *Sanicentral v. Collin*[43] the European Court confirmed that employment law came within the field of application of the 1968 Convention, and that litigation arising out of contracts of employment was subject to the Convention. It has already been seen that in *Ivenel v. Schwab*[44] the European Court held that, where claims were based on different obligations arising under a contract of employment, the obligation to be taken into account for the purposes of the application of Article 5(1) of the 1968 Convention was the obligation which characterised the contract, which was normally the obligation to carry out the work.

Special provisions relating to contracts of employment were introduced into Article 5(1) of the Lugano Convention, and then into Article 5(1) of the 1968 Convention by the 1989 Accession Convention. These provisions, in slightly different terms, defined the place of performance of the obligation for the purposes of matters relating to individual contracts of employment. Article 17 of each of the Conventions was amended to restrict the power of employers to rely on jurisdiction agreements in contracts of employment. Schedule 4 to the 1982 Act was also amended to bring it into line with the 1968 Convention in relation to contracts of employment. There are similar, but not identical, provisions in the new section 5 of Chapter II of the Judgments Regulation.[45]

S11–335   Article 5(1) of the Lugano Convention, and Article 5(1) of the 1968 Convention, as amended by the 1989 Accession Convention, contain special provision for employment contracts, but not in quite the same terms. Each

---

[39] Judgments Regulation, Art. 19(2)(b); 1982 Act, Sched. 4, Rule 10(2)(c).

[40] Judgments Regulation, Art. 20(1); 1982 Act, Sched. 4, Rule 10(3).

[41] Judgments Regulation, Art. 20(2); 1968 and Lugano Conventions, Art. 6(3); 1982 Act, Sched. 4, Rule 10(4).

[42] Judgments Regulation, Art. 21; 1968 Convention, Art. 17(6); Lugano Convention, Art. 17(5); 1982 Act, Sched. 4, Rule 10(5).

[43] Case 25/79 [1979] E.C.R. 3423; Jenard, p. 24.

[44] Case 133/81 [1982] E.C.R. 1891. See also Case 266/85 *Shenavai v. Kreischer* [1987] E.C.R. 239, 255–256, for the special characteristics of employment contracts.

[45] There are special provisions relating to disputes relating to terms of service of crews of ships registered in Greece and Portugal (for the purposes of the Judgments Regulation), in Denmark (for the purposes of the 1968 Convention) and in Norway (for the purposes of the Lugano Convention): 1968 Protocol, Art. VB; Protocol No. 1 to the Lugano Convention, Art. VB; Judgments Regulation, Art. 64(1),(2).

of them confirms the decision in *Ivenel v. Schwab* by providing that in individual contracts of employment[46] the place of performance of the obligation is that where the employee habitually carries out his work. If the employee does not carry out his work in any one country, the Lugano Convention provides that "this place shall be the place of business through which he was engaged"; whereas the 1968 Convention, as amended, provides that in such a case "the employer may also be sued in the courts for the place where the business which engaged the employee was or is now situated."[47] In *Rutten v. Cross Medical Ltd.*[48] it was held that where an employee carried out his work in several Contracting States, the place where he habitually carried out his work was the place where he had established the effective centre of his working activities. The European Court emphasised that the purpose of these provisions is to afford protection to the employee, as the weaker party to the contract; that protection is best assured if disputes relating to a contract of employment fall within the jurisdiction of the courts of the place where the employee discharged his obligations towards his employer; that is the place where it is least expensive for the employee to engage in court proceedings.

There is an important distinction between the versions of Article 5(1) in **S11–336** the Lugano Convention and in the amended 1968 Convention. Each gives jurisdiction to the courts of the place of business through which the employee was engaged in cases in which the employee does not habitually carry out his work in any one country. But the Lugano Convention does not expressly limit this jurisdiction to actions by the employee against the employer, whereas the amended 1968 Convention limits the basis of jurisdiction to cases in which the employer is being sued.[49] It is likely (but not certain) that the Lugano Convention would be interpreted in the same sense.[50] The expression "place of business" is to be understood in a broad sense, and includes a branch or agency.[51]

Judgments Regulation. The new section 5 of Chapter II of the Judgments **S11–337** Regulation contains similar provisions.[52] Save in one respect, it does not affect jurisdiction over defendants domiciled outside the Regulation States and the Contracting States, nor the rule that a defendant domiciled in another Regulation State which has a branch in England may be sued in

---

[46] It does not apply to collective agreements between employers and workers' representatives: Jenard-Möller, p. 73.

[47] In relation to the unamended version of Art. 5(1), the European Court had held that where a French employee of a Belgian company worked in a number of non-Contracting States, Art. 5(1) was not applicable (Case 32/88 *Six Constructions Ltd. v. Humbert* [1989] E.C.R. 341), but that where the employee carried out his activities in more than one Contracting State, the place where the obligation characterising the contract had been or had to be performed was the place where or from which the employee mainly performed his obligations *vis-à-vis* his employer (Case C–125/92 *Mulox IBC Ltd. v. Geels* [1993] E.C.R. I–4075). See also Case C–37/00 *Weber v. Universal Ogden Services Ltd.* [2002] E.C.R. I–2013; [2002] Q.B. 1189 (court should take account of whole of duration of relationship to determine the place where the employee has worked the longest, unless the claim is more closely connected with a different place of work, which would, in that case, be the relevant place for the purposes of Art. 5(1)). For special provision in relation to jurisdiction clauses in employment contracts, see below, para. S11–339.

[48] Case C–383/95 [1997] E.C.R. I–57, [1997] I.C.R. 715.

[49] Almeida Cruz-Desantes Real-Jenard, p. 45.

[50] *Cf.* Jenard-Möller, p. 73, para. 44.

[51] de Almeida Cruz-Desantes Real-Jenard, p. 45.

[52] The new 1982 Act, Sched. 4, Rule 10 is modelled on the Judgments Regulation.

England if the dispute arises out of its operations.[53] If the employer is domiciled outside the Regulation States and has a branch in a Regulation State, the employer is deemed to be domiciled in that Regulation State in disputes arising out of the operations of the branch.[54] An employer domiciled in a Regulation State may be sued in the courts of the Regulation State in which he is domiciled; and may also be sued in another Regulation State (a) in the courts for the place where the employee habitually carries out his work or in the courts for the last place where he did so, or (b) if the employee does not or did not habitually carry out his work in any one country, in the courts for the place where the business which engaged the employee is or was situated.[55] The employer may bring proceedings only in the courts of the Regulation State in which the employee is domiciled.[56] But counterclaims may be brought in the court in which an original claim has been brought in accordance with section 5 of Chapter II.[57]

S11–338   The Rome Convention on the Law Applicable to Contractual Obligations[58] provides that, in the absence of express choice of law or unless it appears from the circumstances as a whole that the contract is more closely connected with another country, a contract of employment is governed by the law of the country in which the employee habitually carries out his work in performance of the contract, even if he is temporarily employed in another country; or if the employee does not habitually carry out his work in any one place, by the law of the country in which the place of business through which he was engaged is situated. The effect of the employment contract provisions in the Judgments Regulation and the Conventions is that in many countries the State which has jurisdiction will also be the State whose law governs.[59]

S11–339   Jurisdiction Agreements. The 1968 Convention, the Lugano Convention, and the Judgments Regulation each contain provisions limiting the right of employers to rely on jurisidction agreements.[60] Each provides that such an agreement is effective only if entered into after the dispute has arisen, or (in the case of the 1968 Convention[61]) if the employee invokes it to seise courts other than those of the defendant's domicile or those specified in Article 5(1) or (in the case of the Judgments Regulation) if the jurisdiction agreement allows the employee to bring proceedings in courts other than those specified in section 5 (Articles 18 to 21) of Chapter II of the Regulation.

ILLUSTRATIONS

S11–340   1. A, who is domiciled in France, is employed by X & Co., a German company, to work for a year in England. After six months A is wrongfully dismissed. A sues X & Co. in England. The court has jurisdiction.[62]

---

[53] Art. 18(1).
[54] Art. 18(2). See also S.I. 2001 No. 3929, Sched. 1, para. 11(2).
[55] Art. 19.
[56] Art. 20(1).
[57] Art. 20(2).
[58] Contracts (Applicable Law) Act 1990, Sched. 1, Art. 6(2), Rule 182(2).
[59] Jenard-Möller, p. 73.
[60] 1968 Convention, Art. 17(6); Lugano Convention, Art. 17(5); Judgments Regulation, Art. 21.
[61] The Lugano Convention does not have an equivalent provision in Art. 17.
[62] Judgments Regulation, Art. 19(2)(a).

2. A, who is domiciled in England, is employed through a recruitment office in London of X & Co., a French company, to work as a sales agent in Germany, France and Italy. A is wrongfully dismissed, and sues X & Co. in England. The court has jurisdiction.[63]

(15) The court has jurisdiction in proceedings which have as their object rights *in rem* in, or tenancies of, immovable property, if the property is situated in England.[64]   S11R–341

COMMENT

This clause is based on Article 22(1) of the Judgments Regulation and 16(1)(a) of the Conventions, which provide that in proceedings which have as their object rights *in rem* in, or tenancies of, immovable property, the courts of the Regulation State or Contracting State in which the property is situated have exclusive[65] jurisdiction. The basic principle is found in the law of most countries.[66] The *lex situs* is paramount both from the point of view of convenience of evidence and because its law will apply.[67] Where the court has jurisdiction under this clause, it will also be able to deal with contractual claims connected with rights *in rem*, particularly debts secured on immovable property.[68] This clause is dealt with more fully in connection with the Rule relating to jurisdiction over immovable property.[69]   S11–342

(16) The court has jurisdiction in proceedings which have as their object the validity of the constitution, the nullity or the dissolution of companies or other legal persons or associations of natural or legal persons, or the validity of the decisions of their organs, if the company, legal person or association has its seat in England.[70]   S11R–343

COMMENT

This clause is based on Art. 22(2) of the Judgments Regulation and Article 16(2) of the Conventions, which applies also in intra-United Kingdom cases in a modified form. Article 22(2) provides that in proceedings which have as their object the validity of the constitution, the nullity or the dissolution of   S11–344

---

[63] *ibid.* Art. 19(2)(b).

[64] Judgments Regulation, Art. 22(1); 1968 Convention, Art. 16(1)(a), and Lugano Convention Art. 16(1)(a), in 1982 Act, Scheds. 1 and 3C; 1982 Act, Sched. 4, Rule 11(a).

[65] The courts of the domicile of the defendant also have jurisdiction if the proceedings have as their object tenancies of immovable property included for temporary private use for a maximum period of six consecutive months, and (under the 1968 Convention, Art. 16(1)(b), added by the 1989 Accession Convention) the landlord and tenant are natural persons and are domiciled in the same Contracting State, or (under the Lugano Convention, Art. 16(1)(b)) the tenant is a natural person and neither party is domiciled in the United Kingdom or (under the Judgments Regulation, Art. 22(1) the tenant is a natural person and the landlord and tenant are domiciled in the same Regulation State. See also 1982 Act, Sched. 4, Rule 11(a)(ii).

[66] See para. 23–003.

[67] Case 73/77 *Sanders v. Van Der Putte* [1977] E.C.R. 2383, 2390–2391. See White [1983] Conv. 180, 306.

[68] See clause (12), and para. 23–016.

[69] Rule 114.

[70] Judgments Regulation, Art. 22(2); 1968 Convention, Art. 16(2), and Lugano Convention, Art. 16(2), in 1982 Act, Scheds. 1 and 3C; 1982 Act. Sched. 4, Rules 4 and 11(b). These provisions do not apply to the winding-up of insolvent companies: Judgments Regulation, Art. 1(2)(b); 1968 and Lugano Conventions, Art. 1(2)(b).

companies or other legal persons or associations of natural or legal persons, or the validity of the decisions of their organs, the courts of the Regulation State in which the company, legal person or association has its seat shall have exclusive jurisdiction. The purpose is to avoid conflicting judgments being given as regards the existence of a company or with regard to the validity of the decisions of its organs, by providing that all proceedings should take place in the courts of the State in which the company has its seat, where information about the company will have been notified and made public.[71] The expression "associations of natural or legal persons" includes English partnerships.[72] Art. 22(2) of the Judgments Regulation makes it clear (as the 1968 and Lugano Conventions did not) that this clause is concerned with the validity of decisions of organs. It had been held in England, by reference to the French and German texts of the 1968 Convention, that the phrase "the validity of" governed not only the constitution of the company, but also the decisions of its organs.[73]

S11–345 The scope of the operation of this clause has been considered in two decisions in England. In *Newtherapeutics Ltd. v. Katz*[74] an English company sued two of its directors, one of whom was domiciled in the United States, and the other of whom was domiciled in France, claiming that they had acted in breach of duty, and without board authority, in signing contracts which reduced amounts payable to a French company for which the English company was performing pharmaceutical trials. Knox J. held that the English court had exclusive jurisdiction under Article 16(2) of the 1968 Convention in relation to the claim that the directors had acted without the authority of the board; but not in relation to the claim that the directors were in breach of duty because they had committed the company to a transaction which was so detrimental to the interests of the company that no reasonable board could properly have assented to it. The Court of Appeal, in *Grupo Torras S.A. v. Sheikh Fahad Mohammed Al-Sabah*,[75] agreed with Knox J. on the first aspect, but left open the question whether he was right on the second aspect. In the *Grupo Torras* case the allegations against the directors were of a fraudulent conspiracy to misappropriate a Spanish company's funds. It was held that Article 16(2) did not apply so as to deprive the English court of jurisdiction: the subject matter of the action was the fraud which it was alleged that the defendants had practised on the company.

S11–346 In order to determine the seat of a company for the purposes of this clause the court seised shall apply its rules of private international law.[76] In the United Kingdom this is effected by the Civil Jurisdiction and Judgments Order 2001,[77] and Section 43 of the 1982 Act, which provide for the purposes of this clause that a corporation (or company) or association has its seat in the United Kingdom if, and only if, (a) it was incorporated or

---

[71] Jenard, p. 35.

[72] *Phillips v. Symes* [2002] 1 W.L.R. 853; Schlosser, para. 162.

[73] See *Newtherapeutics Ltd. v. Katz* [1991] Ch. 226. See also *Grupo Torras S.A. v. Sheikh Fahad Mohammed Al-Sabah* [1996] 1 Lloyd's Rep. 7 (C.A.).

[74] [1991] Ch. 226; stated, *post*, Illustration 2. See Kaye (1991) 10 C.J.Q. 220.

[75] [1996] 1 Lloyd's Rep. 7 (C.A.). See also *Papanicolaou v. Thielen* [1998] 2 I.R. 42; *Grupo Torras S.A. v. Al-Sabah* [1999] C.L.C. 1473, 1532; rvsd. in part on other grounds [2001] C.L.C. 221 (C.A.).

[76] Judgments Regulation, Art. 22(2); 1968 and Lugano Conventions, Art. 53.

[77] S.I. 2001 No. 3929, Sched. 1, para. 10.

formed under the law of a part of the United Kingdom or (b) its central management and control is exercised in the United Kingdom.[78] Thus a company incorporated under the Companies Act 1985 with its registered office in England, but with its central management and control in France, will be regarded in the United Kingdom as having its seat exclusively in England[79]; a company incorporated in the Netherlands with its central management and control in England will be regarded as having its seat in England, and also in the Netherlands if by Netherlands law its seat is in the Netherlands.[80]

Under the Regulation and the Conventions jurisdiction is vested **S11–347** *exclusively* in the courts of the Regulation State or Contracting State of the seat of the entity concerned, but the combined effect of Rules 4 and 11(b) of Schedule 4 is that although the English court will always have jurisdiction where the seat of the entity is in England, the jurisdiction will be non-exclusive as regards domiciliaries of Scotland and Northern Ireland where the proceedings have as their object a decision of an organ of the entity concerned.

ILLUSTRATIONS

1. Z Ltd. is a Netherlands company with its place of central management and control in **S11–348** England and most of its assets in England. X, Y and Z are directors and each of them is domiciled in the Netherlands. At a board meeting they resolve to transfer the assets of the company to Bermuda. A Ltd., which owns the share capital of Z Ltd., brings proceedings seeking a declaration that the board resolution is void and outside the powers of X, Y and Z. The court has jurisdiction.

2. A & Co., an English company, has a contract with a French company for the development of medicines for the treatment of AIDS. X, who is domiciled in France, is a director of A & Co. Shortly before he resigns as a director he executes (together with Y, another director, domiciled in the United States) a document varying the terms of A & Co.'s contract with the French company in a manner which A & Co. claims is substantially to its disadvantage. A & Co. claims (*inter alia*) that X and Y were in breach of duty by executing the variation documents in the absence of a board meeting and that it was beyond their powers as directors to sign them. The court has jurisdiction over X, but the writ is set aside since the action is bound to fail because A & Co. had waived all its claims against X.[81]

3. A & Co., a Spanish company, and its English subsidiary, B & Co., sue X, Y and Z, former directors of A & Co., claiming damages for breaches of directors' duties relating to a number of transactions entered into by them on behalf of A & Co. The English court has jurisdiction because the subject matter of the action is not the decision of the organs of A & Co., but the misappropriation of A & Co.'s money.[82]

(17) The court has jurisdiction in proceedings which have as their object **S11R–349** **the validity of entries in public registers, if the register is kept in England.**[83]

---

[78] s.43(2); S.I. 2001 No. 3929, Sched. 1, para. 10(2). Provision is made for allocation within the United Kingdom of jurisdiction in s.43(3)–(5). Association means an unincorporated body of persons, and corporation means a body corporate, and includes a partnership subsisting under Scots law: s. 50. s. 43(6)–(7) and S.I. 2001 No. 3929, Sched. 1, para. 10(3)–(4) contain the rules for determining whether the corporation or association has its seat in another Regulation State or Contracting State, in which case the English court will have no jurisdiction unless (as is possible) the corporation or association also has its seat in England. See also *supra*, entry at para. 11–060.

[79] S.I. 2001 No. 3929, Sched. 1, para. 10(2), (4).

[80] *ibid.*, para. 10(2), (3). *Cf. The Deichland* [1990] 1 Q.B. 361 (C.A.).

[81] *Newtherapeutics Ltd. v. Katz* [1991] Ch. 226.

[82] *Grupo Torras S.A. v. Sheikh Fahad Mohammed Al-Sabah* [1996] 1 Lloyd's Rep. 7 (C.A.).

[83] Judgments Regulation, Art. 22(3); 1968 Convention, Art. 16(3), and Lugano Convention, Art. 16(3), in 1982 Act, Scheds. 1 and 3C; 1982 Act, Sched. 4, Rule 11(c).

COMMENT

S11–352 Article 22(3) of the Judgments Regulation and Article 16(3) of the Conventions deal with proceedings which have as their object the validity of entries in public[84] registers, and assigns exclusive jurisdiction to the courts of the Regulation State or the Contracting State in which the register is kept.[85] It corresponds to the provisions which appear in the internal laws of the original parties to the 1968 Convention and covers entries in land registers, land charges registers and commercial registers. In England it is not likely to be of practical significance except in connection with problems relating to registered land, which would in any event come within the provisions of clause (15).[86]

S11R–351 **(18) The court has jurisdiction in proceedings concerned with the registration or validity of patents, trade marks, designs or other similar rights required to be deposited or registered, if the deposit or registration has been applied for or has taken place (or is deemed to have taken place) in England.[87]**

COMMENT

S11–352 Clause (18) assigns exclusive jurisdiction in proceedings concerned with registration or validity of patents, trademarks, designs or other similar rights required to be deposited or registered, to the courts of the Regulation State or Contracting State in which the deposit or registration has been applied for, has taken place or is under the terms of an international convention deemed to have taken place. Article Vd of Protocol to the 1968 Convention (which was added by the Accession Convention) and of the Protocol No. 1 to the Lugano Convention provide, broadly, that the courts of each Contracting State are to have jurisdiction in proceedings concerned with the registration or validity of any European patent granted for that State, provided it is not a "Community patent" which, if instituted, will be valid for the whole Community.[88] Article 22(4) of the Judgments Regulation provides that, without prejudice to the jurisdiction of the European Patent Office under the Convention of 1973 on the Grant of European Patents, the courts of each Regulation State shall have exclusive jurisdiction, regardless of domicile, in proceedings concerned with the registration or validity of any European patent granted for that State.

---

[84] See *Re Fagin's Bookshop plc* [1992] B.C.L.C. 188 (register of members of company held to be public register: *sed quaere*).
[85] Or in the particular part of the United Kingdom in which the register is kept: Sched. 4, Rule 11(c).
[86] *Cf. Re Hayward* [1997] Ch. 45; *Ashurst v. Pollard* [2001] Ch. 595 (C.A.).
[87] Judgments Regulation, Art. 22(4); 1968 Convention, Art. 16(4) and Lugano Convention, Art. 16(4), in 1982 Act, Scheds. 1 and 3C.
[88] For the system of European Patents and Community Patents see Paterson, *The European Patent System* (1992); *Kakkar v. Szelke* [1989] F.S.R. 225 (C.A.). There is no equivalent of Art. 16(4) in the intra-United Kingdom provisions of Sched. 4 to the 1982 Act. Actions for infringement could be brought at the domicile of the defendant or the place of infringement or threatened infringement in accordance with the normal rules. See also the jurisdiction provisions in the Protocol on Litigation to the Agreement Relating to Community Patents of December 15, 1989 which will, when it comes into force, take precedence over the 1968 Convention: [1989] O.J. L401/1.

The term "proceedings concerned with the registration or validity of **S11–353**
patents" must be interpreted by reference to a uniform Community or
Convention concept, and not by national law.[89] It includes proceedings
connected with the place of the grant of the right, such as proceedings[90]
relating to the validity, existence or lapse of the right, or an alleged right of
priority by reason of an earlier registration.[91] It does not apply to disputes
relating to ownership.[92] Nor does clause (18) apply in principle to proceedings for infringement.[93] But in England an action for infringement of a
patent may be defended on the basis that the patent is invalid. In *Coin
Controls Ltd. v. Suzo-International (U.K.) Ltd.*[94] it was held by Laddie J. that
an action for infringement could be within this clause if the infringement
proceedings were "principally concerned"[95] in a broad sense with validity,
i.e. validity was a major feature of the litigation. This view was approved by
the Court of Appeal in *Fort Dodge Animal Health Ltd. v. Akzo Nobel N.V.*,[96]
but because it did not regard the question as free from doubt, the Court of
Appeal made a reference to the European Court, which was withdrawn
when the case was settled.

ILLUSTRATIONS

1. A petitions the High Court for revocation of a patent granted to X, the respondent, **S11–354**
who is domiciled in Italy. The court has jurisdiction.[97]
2. A is the owner of a trade mark registered in the United Kingdom. X, domiciled in the
Republic of Ireland (where the mark is not registered), uses the same mark in connection
with his business in Dublin. A commences proceedings in England for an account of the
profits X has made as a result of the passing-off and trade mark infringement. The court
has no jurisdiction.[98]
3. A & Co., an English company, brings proceedings against X & Co., an English
company, Y & Co., a Dutch company, and Z & Co., a German company, for infringement
of UK, German and Spanish patents for a coin-dispensing machine. The defendants
challenge the validity of the patents. The court has no jurisdiction over the claims for
infringement of the German and Spanish patents because the proceedings became
principally concerned with the validity of the patents.[99]

(19) The court has jurisdiction in proceedings concerned with the enforce- **S11R–355**
ment of judgments, if the judgment has been or is to be enforced in
England.[1]

---

[89] Case 288/82 *Duijnstee v. Goderbauer* [1983] E.C.R. 3663.
[90] See, *e.g. Napp Laboratories v. Pfizer Inc.* [1993] F.S.R. 150 (revocation petition).
[91] *ibid.*
[92] *ibid.*
[93] *Mölnlycke AB v. Procter & Gamble Ltd.* [1992] 1 W.L.R. 1112 (C.A.)
[94] [1999] Chap. 33; *infra*, Illustration 3. These decisions are criticised by Fawcett and Torremans,
Intellectual Property and Private International Law (1998), pp. 204–207, who prefer the contrary
view expressed in the twelfth edition of this work, p. 386.
[95] See para. 11–057.
[96] [1998] F.S.R. 222 (C.A.). See also *GAT v. LUK* [2003] I.L.Pr. 60 (LGD Düsseldorf); Fawcett, in
Reform and Development of Private International Law (Fawcet, ed., 2002), p. 137; Pertegas
Sender, *Cross-border Enforcement of Patent Rights* (2002).
[97] See Patents Act 1977, s. 72; *Encyclopedia of United Kingdom and European Patent Law* (ed.
Vitoria & others), paras. 10–201—203.
[98] This Illustration was approved in *L.A. Gear Inc. v. Gerald Whelan & Sons Inc. Ltd.* [1991]
F.S.R. 670.
[99] *Coin Controls Ltd. v. Suzo International (U.K.) Ltd.* [1999] Ch. 33.
[1] Judgments Regulation, Art. 22(5); 1968 Convention, Art. 16(5), and Lugano Convention, Art.
16(5), in 1982 Act, Scheds. 1 and 3C; 1982 Act, Sched. 4, Rule 11(d).

COMMENT

S11–356 This clause is based on Article 22(5) of the Judgments Regulation and Article 16(5) of the Conventions, and is included here only for the sake of completeness.[2]

S11R–357 **(20) The court has jurisdiction over a dispute which the parties have agreed to submit to the English court if the agreement is in writing, or evidenced in writing, or, in a form which accords with practices which the parties have established between themselves, or in international trade or commerce, in a form which accords with a usage of which the parties are or ought to have been aware and which in such trade or commerce is widely known to, and regularly observed by, parties to contracts of that type involved in the particular trade or commerce concerned.[3]**

COMMENT

S11R–358 This clause is based on Article 23 of the Judgments Regulation, Article 17 of the 1968 Convention (as amended by the 1978 and 1989 Accession Conventions)[4] and of the Lugano Convention. Similar provisions (with some modifications) apply in the intra-United Kingdom cases under Rule 12 of Schedule 4 to the 1982 Act. These Articles are dealt with in connection with Rule 32.[5]

S11R–359 **(21) The court has jurisdiction over a defendant who submits to its jurisdiction by appearance, except (a) where appearance was entered[6] to contest the jurisdiction, or (b) the courts of another Regulation State or Contracting State have exclusive jurisdiction pursuant to the terms of the Judgments Regulation or the 1968 Convention or the Lugano Convention.[7]**

COMMENT

S11–360 Article 24 of the Judgments Regulation and Article 18 of each of the Conventions provide that, in addition to jurisdiction derived from other provisions, a court of a Regulation State or Contracting State before whom

---

[2] See Collins, p. 83, for a fuller discussion. See also Case 220/84 *AS-Autoteile Service GmbH v. Malhé* [1985] E.C.R. 2267, where it was held that a court in which enforcement is sought cannot take jurisdiction (by dealing with an alleged set-off against the judgment debt) over a dispute which falls within the jurisdiction of another Contracting State. In Case C–261/90 *Reichert v. Dresdner Bank (No. 2)* [1992] E.C.R. 1–2149 it was held that Art. 16(5) of the 1968 Convention relates to measures taken to ensure the practical implementation of judgments, and did not apply to an action to set aside a transaction in fraud of creditors. *Cf. The Filiatra Legacy* [1994] 1 Lloyd's Rep. 513n. In *Kuwait Oil Tanker Co. S.A.K. v. Qabazard* [2003] UKHL 31, [2003] 3 W.L.R. 14 (H.L.) it was held that the effect of Art. 16(5) of the Lugano Convention was that the English court had no jurisdiction to make a garnishee order in respect of a debt situate in Switzerland.

[3] Judgments Regulation, Art. 23; 1968 Convention, Art. 17, and Lugano Convention, Art. 17, in 1982 Act, Scheds. 1 and 3C; 1982 Act, Sched. 4, Rule 12.

[4] For parties see paras. 11–006 *et seq.*

[5] On jurisdiction provisions in trust instruments, see *supra*, clause (6).

[6] The English language versions of the 1968 and Lugano Convention, but not the Judgments Regulation, say "solely to contest the jurisdiction."

[7] Judgments Regulation, Art. 24; 1968 Convention, Art. 18, and Lugano Convention, Art. 18, in 1982 Act, Scheds. 1 and 3C; 1982 Act, Sched. 4, Rule 13.

a defendant enters an appearance shall have jurisdiction. It applies only to cases within the scope of the Regulation or Conventions, but if the case is within their scope appearance will confer jurisdiction even though without appearance jurisdiction could not have been taken. Clause (21) does not apply in a case which is covered by the exclusive jurisdiction provisions of Article 22 of the Judgments Regulation or Article 16 of the Conventions.[8] But it does apply where the parties have agreed to submit their disputes to the jurisdiction of the courts of a Regulation State or Contracting State under Article 23 of the Regulation or Article 17 of the Convention. In such a case appearance by the defendant (including a defendant to a counterclaim[9]) in the courts of another State will confer jurisdiction on the courts of the latter.[10]

In *Elefanten Schuh GmbH v. Jacqmain*[11] the European Court drew **S11–361** attention to the fact that the French text of the 1968 Convention (unlike the English, German, Italian and Dutch texts) did not have any requirement that *solely* jurisdiction must be contested[12] and held that a defendant did not submit by pleading to the merits as well as contesting the jurisdiction, but "only if the plaintiff and the court seised of the matter are able to ascertain from the time of the defendant's first defence that it is intended to contest the jurisdiction."[13] If the challenge to jurisdiction was not a preliminary matter[14] then, to avoid pleading to the merits being regarded as a submission, the challenge must not occur after the making of submissions which under national procedural law are considered to be the first defence put to the court. Article 24 of the Judgments Regulation omits the word "solely".

In England, since 1979 (when conditional appearances were abolished) a **S11–362** defendant who wishes to contest the jurisdiction of the English court can do so without risk of submitting. Under the Civil Procedure Rules 1998 a defendant who wishes to dispute the jurisdiction of the court, or argue that the court should not exercise its jurisdiction, must file an acknowledgment of service and apply for an order declaring that it has no jurisdiction, or should not exercise any jurisdiction which it may have. A defendant who follows this course is not treated as having submitted to the jurisdiction, and does not thereby lose any right he may have to dispute the jurisdiction of the court. If the challenge to the jurisdiction or its exercise fails, the acknowledgment of service ceases to have effect. The defendant may then file a further acknowledgment of service, in which case he is treated as having accepted that the court has jurisdiction to try the claim.[15]

---

[8] It does however apply, it seems, in insurance and consumer contract cases.

[9] Case 48/84 *Spitzley v. Sommer Exploitation S.A.* [1985] E.C.R. 787.

[10] Case 150/80 *Elefanten Schuh GmbH v. Jacqmain* [1981] E.C.R. 1671; Case 48/84 *Spitzley v. Sommer Exploitation S.A.* [1985] E.C.R. 787.

[11] *supra*; see also Case 27/81 *Rohr v. Ossberger* [1981] E.C.R. 2431; Case 25/81 *CHW v. GJH* [1982] E.C.R. 1189; Case 201/82 *Gerling v. Treasury Administration* [1983] E.C.R. 2503; *Kurz v. Stella Musical GmbH* [1992] Ch. 196. See also *The Xing Su Hai* [1995] 2 Lloyd's Rep. 15; *Caltex Trading Pte Ltd. v. Metro Trading International Inc.* [1999] 2 Lloyd's Rep. 724; *Clydesdale Bank plc v. Ions*, 1993 S.C.L.R. 964; *Campbell International Trading House Ltd. v. Van Aart* [1992] 2 I.R. 305; *Devrajan v. District Judge Ballagh* [1993] 3 I.R. 377. *Cf. The Atlantic Emperor (No. 2)* [1992] 1 Lloyd's Rep. 624 (C.A.); *Toepfer International GmbH v. Molino Boschi Srl* [1996] 1 Lloyd's Rep. 510 (cases on submission to jurisdiction of foreign court).

[12] "*si la comparution a pour objet de contester la competence.*"

[13] At p. 1685.

[14] As it is under English law.

[15] CPR, rr. 11(1), (2), (3), (5), (7). An application for security for costs up to and including the hearing of the application to challenge jurisdiction is not an appearance for the purposes of clause (21): *Hewden Stuart Heavy Cranes Ltd. v. Leo Gottwald*, unrep., 1992 (C.A.).

ILLUSTRATIONS

S11–363   1. A, who is domiciled in England, enters into a contract with X, who is domiciled in France. The contract is to be performed wholly in France. In proceedings by A against X, X instructs English solicitors to accept service and serve a defence. The court has jurisdiction by virtue of X's submission.

2. A, who is domiciled in England, commences proceedings against X, who is domiciled in France, in connection with a tort committed in France, and seeks a *Mareva* injunction restraining X from removing his English assets. X files evidence resisting the injunction, in which (*inter alia*) he denies that he has committed any tort and indicates that he does not accept that the English court has jurisdiction. X's conduct does not amount to a submission.[16]

S11R–364   **(22) The court has jurisdiction to grant interim relief where proceedings have been or are to be commenced in another Regulation State or Contracting State or in another part of the United Kingdom.**[17]

COMMENT

S11–365   Article 31 of the Judgments Regulation and Article 24 of each of the Conventions provide that application may be made to the courts of a Contracting State for such provisional measures, including protective measures, as may be available under the law of that State, even if, the courts of another Regulation State or Contracting State have jurisdiction as to the substance of the matter. The Regulation and the Conventions apply to provisional measures.[18] Section 25 of the 1982 Act gives the English court the powers necessary to give effect to these provisions. In this case, by contrast with the other bases of jurisdiction under the Convention, permission is required to serve process claiming interim relief under section 25 abroad.[19] The jurisdiction to grant interim measures is discussed in Chapter 8.

S11R–366   RULE 29—**The court has no jurisdiction when the courts of another Regulation State or Contracting State or of Scotland or Northern Ireland have exclusive jurisdiction in the cases mentioned in this Rule.**

COMMENT

S11–367   The cases in this Rule are based on Article 22 of the Judgments Regulation and Article 16 of the Conventions, and their counterparts in Schedule 4 for the purposes of intra-United Kingdom jurisdiction. These provisions have been discussed in connection with the jurisdiction of the English court, *i.e.* where England is the place of exclusive jurisdiction for these purposes. Detailed comment is not therefore necessary in connection with this Rule. It is important to note that the exclusive jurisdiction provisions are not

---

[16] *Cf. Obikoga v. Silvernorth Ltd., The Times*, July 6, 1983, distinguished in *Esal Ltd. v. Pujara* [1989] 2 Lloyd's Rep. 479 (C.A.), para. 11–111.

[17] 1982 Act, s.25; Judgments Regulation, Art. 31; 1968 Convention, Art. 24, and Lugano Convention, Art. 24, in 1982 Act, Scheds. 1 and 3C; 1982 Act, Sched. 4, Rule 16.

[18] Case 143/78 *De Cavel v. De Cavel. (No. 1)* [1979] E.C.R. 1055; Case 120/79 *De Cavel v. De Cavel (No. 2)* [1980] E.C.R. 731.

[19] CPR, r. 6.20(4).

subject to submission or contrary agreement and apply irrespective of the domicile of the defendant.

(1) The court has no jurisdiction in proceedings which have as their object S11R–368
rights *in rem* in, or tenancies of, immovable property situated in another Regulation State or Contracting State or in Scotland or Northern Ireland, unless in the case of tenancies concluded for temporary private use for a maximum period of six consecutive months (i) the defendant is domiciled in England, and (ii) in the case of the 1968 Convention, the landlord and the tenant are natural persons and are both domiciled in the United Kingdom, or, in the case of the Lugano Convention, the tenant is a natural person and neither party is domiciled in the Contracting State in which the property is situate or, in the case of the Judgments Regulation the tenant is a natural person and the landlord and tenant are both domiciled in England.[20]

COMMENT

This case is dealt with in connection with the Rule relating to jurisdiction S11–369
over foreign land.[21]

(2) The court has no jurisdiction in proceedings which have as their object S11R–370
the validity of the constitution, the nullity or the dissolution of companies or other legal persons or associations of natural or legal persons or the validity of the decisions of their organs if the company in question (or other legal person or association) (a) does not have its seat in England and (b) has its seat in another Regulation State or Contracting State or (except as regards proceedings relating to the validity of the decisions of organs) in Scotland or Northern Ireland.[22]

COMMENT

This clause has been discussed above.[23] Three points should be noted. First, S11–371
the version in Schedule 4 differs from that in the Regulation and the Conventions. Under the Schedule 4 scheme the head of jurisdiction relating to decisions or organs of companies is not exclusive.[24] Secondly, Schedule 4 does not apply to winding up.[25] Thirdly, it is possible for more than one court to have exclusive jurisdiction.[26] This arises because Article 22 of the Regulation and Article 53 of the Conventions leave it to the law of each Regulation State or Contracting State to determine the seat of a company in accordance with its rules of private international law. The United

---

[20] Judgments Regulation, Art. 22(1); 1968 and Lugano Conventions, Art. 16(1); *cf.* 1982 Act, Sched. 4, Rule 11 (a).
[21] Rule 114.
[22] Judgments Regulation, Art. 22(2); 1968 and Lugano Conventions, Art. 16(2), 1982 Act, Scheds. 1 and 3C; 1982 Act, Sched. 4, Rules 4 and 11(b).
[23] Rule 28(16), *supra*.
[24] See Sched. 4, Rule 4.
[25] Sched. 5, para. 1.
[26] Where actions come within the exclusive jurisdiction of more than one court, any court other than the court first seised must decline jurisdiction in favour of the court first seised: Judgments Regulation, Art. 23; 1968 and Lugano Conventions, Art. 23; *infra*, Rule 31(4).

Kingdom rules use the alternative tests of place of incorporation and place of central management and control. Thus, as has been seen,[27] by United Kingdom law a Dutch company with its place of central management and control in England may have its seat in both England and the Netherlands. This problem will not arise frequently in intra-United Kingdom cases because the effect of section 43(5) of the 1982 Act is that companies incorporated under the Companies Act 1985 and its predecessors will be regarded as having their seat in the part of Great Britain (England or Scotland) in which they have their registered office even if their place of central management and control is in another part.

S11R–372   **(3) The court has no jurisdiction in proceedings which have as their object the validity of entries in public registers if the register is kept in another Regulation State or Contracting State or in Scotland or Northern Ireland.**[28]

S11R–373   **(4) The court has no jurisdiction in proceedings concerned with the registration or validity of patents, trade marks, designs, or other similar rights required to be deposited or registered, if the deposit or registration in question has been applied for, has taken place or is under the terms of an international convention deemed to have taken place in another Regulation State or Contracting State.**[29]

COMMENT

S11R–374   This provision has been discussed above.[30]

S11R–375   **(5) The court has no jurisdiction in proceedings concerned with the enforcement of judgments if the judgment has been or is to be enforced in another Regulation State or Contracting State.**[31]

COMMENT

S11–376   This clause is based on Article 22(5) of the Judgments Regulation and Article 16(5) of the 1968 Convention and the Lugano Convention. It does not prevent the English court from making a disclosure order relating to foreign assets situate in a Regulation State or Contracting State where the judgment is to be enforced[32]: the reason is that the use of CPR Part 71 (which allows examination of a judgment debtor) in order to discover the *existence* of foreign assets, does not confer jurisdiction on the English court in relation to enforcement proceedings in any other country in which those assets may be situate.[33] Nor does it prevent the grant of a *Mareva* injunction

---

[27] *supra*, para. S11–346.
[28] Judgments Regulation, Art. 22(3); 1968 and Lugano Conventions, Art. 16(3), 1982 Act, Scheds. 1 and 3C; 1982 Act, Sched. 4, Rule 11(c).
[29] Judgments Regulation, Art. 22(4); 1968 and Lugano Conventions, Art. 16(4).
[30] *ante*, paras. S11–351 *et seq.*
[31] Judgments Regulation, Art. 22(5); Art. 1968 and Lugano Conventions, Art. 16(5), 1982 Act, Scheds. 1 and 3C; 1982 Act, Sched. 4, Rule 11(d) See Case 220/84 *AS-Autoteile Service GmbH v. Malhé* [1985] E.C.R. 2267; *The Filiatra Legacy* [1994] 1 Lloyd's Rep. 513n.
[32] Collins, p. 83.
[33] *Interpool Ltd. v. Galani* [1988] Q.B. 738 (C.A.).

relating to assets situate in another Regulation State or Contracting State where the claimant intends to enforce a judgment.[34] But it does prevent the making of a garnishee order in respect of a debt situate in a Regulation State or in a Contracting State.[35]

RULE 30—Unless the defendant submits to the jurisdiction, the court has no jurisdiction to determine a dispute which has arisen or may arise in connection with a particular legal relationship in the following circumstances: S11R–377

    (1) if one or more of the parties is domiciled in a Regulation State or Contracting State and the parties have agreed in accordance with Article 23 of the Judgments Regulation or Article 17 of the 1968 Convention or the Lugano Convention that the courts of another Contracting State are to have jurisdiction to settle any such dispute;

    (2) if none of the parties is domiciled in a Regulation State or a Contracting State and the parties have agreed in accordance with Article 23 of the Judgments Regulation or Article 17 of the 1968 Convention or the Lugano Convention that the courts of another Regulation State or Contracting State are to have jurisdiction to settle any such dispute and the courts chosen have not declined jurisdiction;

    (3) if proceedings are brought against a settlor, trustee or beneficiary, which involve relations between them or their rights or obligations under a trust, and the trust instrument confers jurisdiction on the courts of another Regulation State or Contracting State.[36]

COMMENT

This rule is based on Article 23 of the Judgments Regulation and Article 17 of the Conventions, which is discussed below in connection with Rule 32.[37] They apply in two situations where the defendant is not domiciled in a Regulation State or a Contracting State. First, they apply where either of the parties is domiciled in a Regulation State or a Contracting State, so that where the claimant is so domiciled the chosen court will have jurisdiction irrespective of the domicile of the defendant. Secondly, if neither of the parties is domiciled in a Regulation State or a Contracting State, no court other than the chosen court has jurisdiction unless the chosen court declines jurisdiction. These provisions are subject to the principle of submission, so that a defendant may waive the jurisdiction agreement.[38] S11–378

---

[34] *Babanaft International Co. S.A. v. Bassatne* [1990] Ch. 13, 34–35 (C.A.) (where it was said that in such a case the English court would have jurisdiction under Art. 24 of the 1968 Convention to grant the injunction).

[35] *Kuwait Oil Tanker Co. S.A.K. v. Qabazard* [2003] UKHL 30, [2003] 3 W.L.R. 21 (H.L.).

[36] Judgments Regulation, Art. 23; 1968 and Lugano Conventions, Art. 17, 1982 Act. Scheds. 1 and 3C. The corresponding provisions of Sched. 4 do not provide for *exclusive* jurisdiction. Their effect is that a court which would have jurisdiction but for the jurisdiction clause will have a discretion not to give the clause effect: see Rule 34(3), *infra*.

[37] para. 12R–074.

[38] Case 150/80 *Elefanten Schuh GmbH v. Jacqmain* [1981] E.C.R. 1671.

ILLUSTRATIONS

S11–379 1. A, who is domiciled in New York, enters into a contract with X, who is domiciled in England. The contract provides that the courts of France are to have exclusive jurisdiction. When a dispute arises A commences proceedings against X in England. The court has no jurisdiction.

2. The facts are as in Illustration 1, except that X instructs a solicitor to give notice of intention to defend and put in a defence on his behalf. The court has jurisdiction.

CHAPTER 12

FORUM NON CONVENIENS, LIS ALIBI PENDENS, ANTI-SUIT INJUNCTIONS AND JURISDICTION AGREEMENTS

Sub-rule (2) is also subject to the provisions of Council Regulation (E.C.) **12R–001** 44/2001 ([2001] O.J. L12, January 16, 2001) ("the Judgments Regulation"), which substantially supersedes the 1968 Convention; and sub-rule (4) must be read as including cases in which the jurisdiction of the English court is derived from the provisions of the Judgments Regulation. References in this Rule to "Contracting State" must be read as also applying, *mutatis mutandis*, to Member States bound by the provisions of the Regulation ("Regulation States"), unless the contrary is made clear. The Judgments Regulation is reproduced in Part I of the appendix to this Supplement.

NOTE 1. Add, as a leading authority, *Lubbe v. Cape plc* [2000] 1 W.L.R. 1545 (H.L.) (on which see Peel (2001) 117 L.Q.R. 187). See also Bell, *Forum Shopping and Venue in International Litigation* (2003).

NOTE 4. Or, as the case may be, Art. 27 of the Judgments Regulation. For the States to which the Judgments Regulation and the 1968 and Lugano Conventions are subject, see entry at paras. 11–006—11–007.

NOTE 5. Or, as the case may be, Art. 28 of the Judgments Regulation.

NOTE 6. Or, as the case may be, Art. 29 of the Judgments Regulation.

Last sentence: the "very different mechanism" is also applicable to cases **12–002** where the Judgments Regulation applies to establish or to deny the jurisdiction of the court.

NOTE 2. Add: *Lubbe v. Cape plc* [2000] 1 W.L.R. 1545 (H.L.).

NOTE 18. With effect from March 25, 2002, CPR, rr. 11.4 and 11.5 are **12–006** amended, so that the period within which the defendant must make his application is 14 days (but in the Commercial Court, 28 days: CPR, r. 58.7) after filing an acknowledgment of service. Prior to this, it was held in *Monrose Investments Ltd. v. Orion Nominees* [2002] I.L.Pr. 267 (not following *Lawson v. Midland Travellers Ltd.* [1993] 1 W.L.R. 735 (C.A.)); a decision in relation to the earlier procedure in R.S.C. Ord. 12, r. 8) that the application must be brought within this period, and that any extension under CPR, r. 15 of time for the service of a defence, by order or consent, did not affect the date on which the jurisdictional challenge was required to be made.

NOTE 19. Add: *Sepracor v. Hoechst Marion Roussel Ltd.*, *The Times*, March 1, 1999 (no stay of proceedings where action brought in a court which had jurisdiction under the European Patent Convention and in which the claimant was therefore entitled to proceed).

NOTE 19. Add new paragraph at end: The court has power to grant a stay of proceedings to allow a case to await the outcome of the arbitration of a related claim in a case, which will be exceptional, where such an order is required for the purposes of proper case management: *Reichhold Norway A.S.A. v. Goldman Sachs International* [2000] 1 W.L.R. 173 (C.A.).

12–007   Order 11, r. 1(1) has been replaced by CPR, r. 6.20.

NOTE 38. The Supreme Court of Canada has reconfirmed that the doctrine of *forum non conveniens* applies to govern the court's discretion whether to exercise jurisdiction, but (at least in cases decided under the Quebec Civil Code) the discretion to stay is to be treated as exceptional: *Spar Aerospace Ltd. v. American Mobile Satellite Corp.* (2002) 220 D.L.R. (4th) 57 (Sup. Ct. Can.).

12–011   NOTE 43. But in *Régie National des Usines Renault SA v. Zhang* [2002] HCA 10, (2002) 187 A.L.R. 1, the High Court of Australia reaffirmed that even where proceedings had been commenced by service out of Australia, they would be allowed to continue unless it was oppressive or vexatious for the plaintiff to sue the defendant in an Australian court. In *Reinsurance Australia Corporation Ltd. v. HIH Casualty and General Insurance Ltd. (in liquidation)* [2003] FCA 56, it was held [at 293] that where a cause of action pleaded in Australia (*in casu*, under various provisions of the Trade Practices Act 1974) could not be "fully and properly entertained" before a foreign court, the Australian court cannot be regarded as a clearly inappropriate forum, and a stay cannot be granted even though, apart from this cause of action, it would be have been clearly inappropriate to proceed on the remainder of the claim in Australia. See also *Eastern Power Ltd. v. Azienda Communale Energia e Ambiente* [2001] I.L.Pr. 55 (Ont. C.A.).

12–012   NOTE 45. *Cf. Lough Neagh Exploration Co. v. Morrice* [1999] N.I. 258.

12–013   What is said in this section on the impact of the 1968 Convention and the Lugano Convention applies with equal force to the Judgments Regulation (though this does not depend on the 1982 Act for its effect in England), where Articles 27–30 deal with the problems of pending actions in two or more Regulation States. Section 49 of the 1982 Act has not been amended to make similar provision for the Judgments Regulation, but this fact will not prevent the court granting a stay of proceedings when to do so is consistent with the scheme of the Regulation.

12–014   Schedule 4 to the 1982 Act is amended by S.I. 2001 No. 3929, Sched. 2, para. 4 but the amended version does not contain provision corresponding to what now appears as Articles 27–30 of the Judgments Regulation.

NOTE 49. However, in cases where the Judgments Regulation (or the 1968 Convention or the Lugano Convention) confers jurisdiction on the courts for the *place* where the harmful event occurred, as would be the case under Art. 5(3) of the Regulation or the Conventions, it would be inconsistent with the Regulation or the Conventions for a stay of proceedings to be ordered in favour of the courts of another place (such as Scotland) within the United Kingdom.

12–015   See generally the entry at para. 12–013. The decision of the Court of Appeal in *Turner v. Grovit* is now reported at [2000] Q.B. 345. On further appeal to the House of Lords [2002] 1 W.L.R. 107, proceedings were stayed while there was referred to the European Court (Case C–159/02) the following question: "Is it inconsistent with the Convention . . . for the courts of the United Kingdom to grant restraining orders against defendants who are threatening to commence or continue legal proceedings in another Convention country when those defendants are acting in bad faith with the intent and purpose of frustrating or obstructing proceedings properly before the English courts?".

A reference to the European Court from a French court of first instance, purporting to seek a ruling on various aspects of an English anti-suit injunction, was dismissed as inadmissible: Case C–24/02 *Marseille Fret SA v. Seatrano Shipping Co Ltd.* [2002] E.C.R. I–3383.

See generally the entry at para. 12–013.   **12–016**

NOTES 54, 58. *Haji-Ioannou v. Frangos* [1999] 2 Lloyd's Rep. 337 (C.A.) is noted by Briggs (1999) 70 B.Y.I.L. 326.

See generally the entry at para. 12–013.   **12–017**

In C–412/98 *Universal Insurance Co. v. Group Josi Reinsurance Co. S.A.* [2000] E.C.R. I–5925; [2001] 1 Q.B. 68, it was held that the jurisdictional rules of the 1968 Convention were applicable even though the claimant was not domiciled in any Contracting State. For the suggestion that this may affect the decision in *Re Harrods (Buenos Aires) Ltd.* [1992] Ch. 72 (C.A.), see Fentiman [2000] C.L.J. 7, and (2003) 3 C.Y.B.E.Eur.L. 107. See *Owusu v. Jackson* [2002] EWCA Civ. 877; [2002] I.L.Pr. 813, (C.A.) (below, entry at para. 12–018).

NOTE 60. Insert, after *Re Polly Peck International plc (No. 2)* [1998] 3 All E.R. 812 (C.A.): *Mercury Telecommunications Ltd. v Communications Telesystems International* [1999] 2 All E.R. (Comm.) 33; *Eli Lilly & Co. v. Novo Nordisk A/S* [2000] I.L.Pr. 73 (C.A.); *Ace Insurance S.A.-N.V. v. Zurich Insurance Co.* [2001] EWCA Civ. 173; [2001] 1 Lloyd's Rep. 618 (C.A.) (right to obtain a stay is not limited to an English-domiciled defendant).

For the position in Ireland, see *Intermetal Group Ltd. v. Worslade Trading Ltd.* [1998] 2 I.R. 1.

Add at end of paragraph. In *Lubbe v. Cape plc* [2000] 1 W.L.R. 1545,   **12–018**
1561–62 (H.L.) Lord Bingham of Cornhill stated that had it otherwise been shown to be appropriate to stay the proceedings brought against Cape plc, which was domiciled in England, in favour of the courts of South Africa, he would have made a reference to the European Court for a ruling on the applicability of Article 2, as the answer to the question raised and decided in *Re Harrods (Buenos Aires) Ltd.* [1992] Ch. 72 (C.A.) was not clear. A reference has now been made to the European Court, which asks, in effect, whether *Re Harrods (Buenos Aires) Ltd* [1992] Ch. 72 (C.A.) was correctly decided. In *Owusu v. Jackson* [2002] EWCA Civ. 877; [2002] I.L.Pr. 813 an English claimant brought proceedings against six defendants, one of whom was English and the other five Jamaican, for damages arising from an accident sustained by him while on holiday in Jamaica. The first defendant had rented accommodation to the claimant, the other defendants were Jamaican entities alleged to be implicated in the accident. The Court of Appeal considered that the correctness of *Re Harrods* had been called into quesiton by Case C–412/98 *Universal General Insurance Co. v. Groupe Josi Reinsurance Co. S.A.* [2000] E.C.R. I–5925, and made the reference, which

is pending as Case–281/02. A reference has also been made in *American Motor Insurance Co. v. Cellstar Corp.* [2003] EWCA Civ. 206, [2003] I.L.Pr. 370 (C.A.), with the intention that both references be heard together. In a case on the Lugano Convention, the Court of Appeal has given permission to appeal to the House of Lords on the same point: *Anton Durbeck GmbH v. Den Norske Bank ASA* [2003] EWCA Civ. 147; [2003] 2 W.L.R. 1296 (C.A.)

12–019 The principle of "reflexive effect" was discussed by the Court of Appeal in *Ace Insurance S.A.–N.V. v. Zürich Insurance Co.* [2001] EWCA Civ. 173; [2001] 1 Lloyd's Rep. 618 (C.A.).

NOTE 68. In Case C–387/98 *Coreck Maritime GmbH v. Handelsveem B.V.*, [2000] E.C.R. I–9337 it was said that where a court was seised of a case in which there was an agreement conferring jurisdiction on the courts of a non-Contracting State, it should assess its validity by reference to its own conflict of laws.

12–020 Order 11, r. 1(1) is replaced by CPR, r. 6.20.

12–021 NOTE 75: The power of a court to stay proceedings in a matrimonial cause is now restricted by Council Regulation (E.C.) 1347/2000; and Domicile and Matrimonial Proceedings Act 1973, Sched. 1, para. 9 is correspondingly amended and restricted by S.I. 2001 No. 310, reg. 4: see the entry at para. 18–227, *infra*.

NOTE 76. Add *Merrill Lynch v. Raffa* [2001] I.L.Pr. 437.

12–023 Text to note 86. In *Lubbe v. Cape plc* [2000] 1 W.L.R. 1545 (H.L.) the House of Lords upheld the decision of the Court of Appeal at [1999] I.L.Pr. 113 (C.A.) and refused to stay the action. But it disapproved the proposition that because the South African court had jurisdiction only by reason of an undertaking by the defendant to submit to its jurisdiction, it was not an "available" forum in the sense of the first limb of the *Spiliada* test: see at pp. 1556 (Lord Bingham of Cornhill), 1562–66 (Lord Hope of Craighead). It is sufficient that the undertaking to submit has been given by the time of the hearing of the application for a stay.

NOTE 89. Add: *Lubbe v. Cape plc* [2000] 1 W.L.R. 1545 (H.L.).

12–024 For the issues as they arose in a complex action concerning derivative actions brought on behalf of a foreign corporation, see *Konamaneni v. Rolls-Royce Industrial Power (India) Ltd.* [2002] 1 W.L.R. 1269; and as they applied to a dispute substantially about the internal management of a Czech company, see *Ceskoslovenska Obchodni Banka AS v. Nomura International plc* [2003] I.L.Pr. 321.

Add after text to note 94: In the case of an international libel, the court should confine its attention to publication only in the country or countries pleaded in making its assessment of where the natural forum is: *Berezovsky v Michaels* [2000] 1 W.L.R. 1004 (H.L.) (noted Harris (2000) 116 L.Q.R. 562) (a case on service out of the jurisdiction). A similar principle was applied by the High Court of Australia in *Dow Jones & Co. Inc. v. Gutnick* [2002] H.C.A. 56, (2003) 194 A.L.R. 433, in relation to a defamation claim founded on the fact that readers in the state of Victoria had accessed a publication on the World Wide Web by internet. The court treated this as a tort committed in Victoria for the purpose of jurisdiction as well as choice of law, despite the fact that there were (but was no complaint made in relation to) a much larger number of readers outside the state. And see also *Chadha v. Dow Jones & Co. Inc.* [1999] I.L.Pr. 829 (C.A.).

On how the application for a stay of proceedings is affected by the issue of which country's law will be applied to the dispute and whether the foreign court will apply a foreign law, see *Nima SARL v. Deves Insurance Public Co. Ltd.* [2002] EWCA Civ. 1132.

Add at end: Even if the English court has been given jurisdiction by means of a valid and binding choice of court agreement, the proceedings may still be stayed on *forum non conveniens* grounds, though strong reason will be required for such an order to be granted, and the existence of the jurisdiction clause does not oust the power of the court to stay the proceedings: *U.B.S. A.G. v. Omni Holding A.G.* [2000] 1 W.L.R. 916; *Marubeni Hong Kong & South China Ltd v. Mongolian Government* [2002] 2 All E.R. (Comm.) 873.

NOTE 99. Order 11, r. 1(1) is replaced by CPR, r. 6.20.   **12–025**

NOTE 2. The English court may take account of the inexperience of the foreign judiciary in the handling of group litigation in assessing the overall argument that it would be unjust to order a stay: *Lubbe v. Cape plc* [2000] 1 W.L.R. 1545, 1560 (H.L.). And see also *X.N. Corp. Ltd. v. Point of Sale Ltd.* [2001] I.L.Pr. 525 (availability of expedited trial in England a significant reason against the staying of proceedings).

See also *Radhakrishna Hospitality Service Pte. Ltd. v. E.I.H. Ltd.* [1999] 2 Lloyd's Rep. 249 (delay and lower level of damages not indicative of a lack of substantial justice); *Mercury Telecommunications Ltd. v. Communications Telesystems International* [1999] 2 All E.R. (Comm.) 33 (if natural forum is contractually agreed, a very strong case will be needed to justify the court in not allowing the case to proceed in it).

Add after second sentence: In *Lubbe v. Cape plc* [2000] 1 W.L.R. 1545 **12–026** (H.L.) it was held that the practical impossibility of the claimant being able to obtain the funding to commission the requisite expert evidence, and to prosecute the claim before the South African courts, was of substantial weight in demonstrating that it would be unjust to impose a stay of proceedings. It followed that as a stay would not be ordered in any case where the claimant would lack adequate funding and legal representation which he needed in order to obtain justice in the foreign court, Article 6 of the European Convention on Human Rights will not support any conclusion which is not already reached on the application of *Spiliada* principles: *Lubbe*, at p. 1561. *Hewitson v. Hewitson* [1999] 2 F.L.R. 74 must be read in the light of the decision in *Lubbe* on this point.

Add at end: It was stated in *Lubbe v. Cape plc* [2000] 1 W.L.R. 1545, 1561, **12–027** 1566–67 (H.L.) that no account was to be taken of factors of public interest which were not related to the private interests of the parties and to the ends of justice. It appears to follow that a concern to remove cases from a crowded court list, in the broad interests of those litigants who have a better claim to a quick hearing, is irrelevant (see, for the view that this should be a relevant point, *James Hardie Industries Pty. Ltd. v. Grigor* (1998) 45 N.S.W.L.R. 20, 40, 43 (N.S.W. C.A.)).

NOTE 10. Add: *Tiernan v. Magen Insurance Co Ltd.* [2000] I.L.Pr. 517 (preference for the conflict rules of the forum—*in casu* those of the Rome Convention).

NOTE 11. Add: *Lubbe v. Cape plc* [2000] 1 W.L.R. 1545, 1560 (H.L.).

12–029 See generally entry at para. 12–013.

12–032 Second sentence: With effect from March 25, 2002, CPR, r. 11 is amended, so that the period within which the defendant must make an application to challenge jurisdiction or to seek a stay of proceedings is 14 days (but in the Commercial Court, 28 days: CPR, r. 58.7) after filing an acknowledgment of service.

After second sentence, add: If an application for a stay is dismissed, but the defendant proposes to appeal or to seek permission to appeal, he needs to obtain an extension of time for acknowledgment of service, because the original suspension of the time limited will have come to an end with the dismissal of the application for a stay: *Sithole v. Thor Chemicals Holdings Ltd., The Times,* February 5, 1999 (C.A.).

Final sentence. See the entry, *supra,* under para. 12–006.

The suggestion in the final sentence was accepted as correct by the court in *Monrose Investments Ltd. v. Orion Nominees* [2002] I.L.Pr. 267.

12–033 R.S.C. Ord. 15, r. 16, which governed the making of declarations, is reproduced in amended form as CPR, r. 40.20.

For the view that claims for negative declarations are common in the legal systems of the Contracting States, see *Andrea Merzario Ltd. v. International Spedition Leitner Gesellschaft GmbH* [2001] EWCA Civ. 61, [2001] 1 Lloyd's Rep. 49 (C.A.).

,5

NOTE 27. See also Widmer and Maurenbrecher, in *International Practice of Law: Liber Amicorum for Thomas Bär and Robert Karrer* (1997), p. 263; Von Mehren, in *Festschrift Drobnig* (ed. Basedow *et al.* 1999), p. 409.

12–034 Second sentence. The proposition that proceedings for a declaration of non-liability must be viewed with great caution was treated with reservation by the Court of Appeal in *Messier Dowty Ltd. v. Sabena S.A.* [2000] 1 W.L.R. 2040 (C.A.). The court should check that the procedure for obtaining such relief is not invoked abusively, but the declaration may serve a useful function, and it is wrong to circumscribe its utility by artificial limits wrongly related to jurisdiction. And where jurisdiction is conferred over the defendant to the action by the 1968 or Lugano Conventions, there is no basis for making allegations of forum shopping against the claimant.

Order 11, r. 1(1) is replaced by CPR, r. 6.20.

12–035 Add at end: In *Messier Dowty Ltd. v. Sabena S.A.* [2000] 1 W.L.R. 2040 (C.A.) (which was applied in *Chase v. Ram Technical Services Ltd.* [2000] 2 Lloyd's Rep. 418) the Court of Appeal held that the sole test to be applied was whether it would be useful in the circumstances to make the declaration, and "subject to the exercise of appropriate circumspection" there should in such cases be no reluctance to grant such relief.

NOTE 38: Add *Tiernan v. Magen Insurance Co. Ltd.* [2000] I.L.Pr. 517; *CGU International Insurance plc v. Szabo* [2002] 1 All E.R. (Comm.) 83.

NOTE 40. See also *American Motorists Insurance Co. v. Cellstar Corp.* [2002] 2 Lloyd's Rep 216 (service out set aside as not useful to make declaration of non-liability (affd. [2003] EWCA Civ. 206, [2003] I.L.Pr. 370 (C.A.); see also *Lincoln National Life Insurance Co. v. Employers' Reinsurance Corp.* [2002] EWHC 28 (Comm.) (declaration served useful purpose).

See entry at para. 12–013. The corresponding provisions of the Judgments **12–036** Regulation are Articles 27–30 (though Art. 30, which is discussed *infra*, has no predecessor in the Conventions).

Add at end: Moreover, the proposition that proceedings for a declaration of non-liability must be viewed with great caution was treated with reservation by the Court of Appeal in *Messier Dowty Ltd. v. Sabena S.A.* [2000] 1 W.L.R. 2040 (C.A.). Where jurisdiction is conferred over the defendant to the action by the 1968 or Lugano Conventions, there is no basis for making allegations of forum shopping against the claimant.

Order 11, r. 1(1) is replaced by CPR, r. 6.20. **12–037**

NOTE 51. Order 11, r. 4(3) is replaced by CPR, r. 6.21(3).

Text to note 58. In *Lubbe v. Cape plc* [2000] 1 W.L.R. 1545 (H.L.) it was **12–038** held that it would be unjust to stay proceedings under clause (2) of this Rule where to do so would deprive the claimant of the financial support or legal representation which he required for the bringing of the claim.

In cases to which the Judgments Regulation applies: that is, where there are **12–039** proceedings in the courts of another Regulation State and which were, like the English proceedings, instituted after the coming into effect of the Regulation on March 1, 2002, the provisions of the Regulation, and not those of the 1968 Convention, will apply to situations of *lis pendens* and related actions in the courts of another Regulation State. Article 27 of the Regulation is in all material respects identical to Article 21 of the 1968 Convention, as amended. Article 28 of the Regulation is, subject to two points (one of clarification and one of alteration) which are discussed in the note to para. 12–056, in all other respects materially identical to Article 22 of the 1968 Convention. Article 29 of the Regulation is in all material respects identical to Article 23 of the 1968 Convention. Article 30 of the Regulation, which has no predecessor in the 1968 Convention, makes provision for definition of the date on which a court in a Member State is seised: it is discussed in detail in the note to paras. 12–050 *et seq.*

NOTE 60. For judicial acceptance of the proposition that a potential claimant is therefore wise to start anticipated proceedings without delay, even though this contradicts the underlying policy of the Civil Procedure Rules, see *Messier Dowty Ltd. v. Sabena S.A.* [2000] 1 W.L.R. 2040 (C.A.).

NOTE 61: Art. 23 of the Judgments Regulation corresponds to Art. 16 of the Convention.

In cases which fall outside the temporal scope of the Judgments Regulation, **12–040** because at least one set of proceedings was instituted before the entry into force of the Regulation, it is probable that the provisions of Articles 21–23 of the 1968 Convention will apply in any event, though without the particular effect of Article 30 of the Regulation (which is discussed in detail in the note to paras. 12–050 *et seq.*).

NOTE 62. See also *Andrea Merzario Ltd. v. Internationale Spedition Leitner Gesellschaft GmbH* [2001] 1 Lloyd's Rep. 490 (C.A.), disapproving *Frans Maas Logistics (U.K.) Ltd. v. C.D.R. Trucking B.V.* [1999] 2 Lloyd's Rep. 179.

NOTE 63. Likewise if the essential subject matter of the dispute is arbitration: *The Ivan Zagubanski* [2002] 1 Lloyd's Rep. 106.

12–041 Article 21 of the 1968 Convention corresponds to Article 27 of the Judgments Regulation.

12–042 NOTE 74. *Cf. U.B.S. A.G. v. Omni Holding A.G.* [2000] 1 W.L.R. 916 (proceedings in another Contracting State, but in a matter falling outside the scope of the Convention).

12–043 First paragraph: Article 16 of the 1968 Convention corresponds to Article 23 of the Judgments Regulation.
   Final paragraph: Article 24 of the 1968 Convention corresponds to Article 31 of the Judgments Regulation.

NOTE 80. Sections 3 and 4 of Title II and Article 28 of the 1968 Convention correspond to Sections 3 and 4 of Chapter II and Article 35 of the Judgments Regulation.

NOTE 81. The question whether *Continental Bank N.A. v. Aeakos Compania Naviera S.A.* was correctly decided by the Court of Appeal forms the basis of a case now pending before the European Court on reference from the Austrian courts: Case C–116/02 *Erich Gasser GmbH v. MISAT srl.* (pending).

NOTE 82. Article 17 of the 1968 Convention corresponds to Article 23 (though some alterations of substance have been made) of the Judgments Regulation.

12–044 NOTE 86. Where jurisdiction is governed by the Judgments Regulation, the solution will be different: see the note to paras. 12–050 *et seq., infra.*

12–048 Add at end of first sentence: It was held in *Glencore International A.G. v. Shell International Trading and Shipping Co. Ltd.* [1999] 2 Lloyd's Rep. 692 that the court was required to identify the essential issue raised between the parties.

NOTE 98. Add after *The Happy Fellow* [1998] 1 Lloyd's Rep. 13 (C.A.): But it was observed in *Glencore International A.G. v. Shell International Trading and Shipping Co. Ltd.* [1999] 2 Lloyd's Rep. 692 that there was no reason to consider an action to enforce a claim of liability to have the same cause of action as a limitation action. The question whether proceedings to constitute a limitation fund have the same cause of action as substantive proceedings to establish liability is now pending before the European Court: Case C–39/02 *Maersk Olie & Gas A/S v. De Haan and De Boer.* Add at end: *Eli Lilly & Co. v. Novo Nordisk A/S* [2000] I.L.Pr. 73 (C.A.) (actions to rectify contract and to obtain a ruling on the interpretation of the contract not the same cause of action: a case decided at common law and not under Article 21); *Glencore International A.G. v. Metro Trading International* [1999] 2 Lloyd's Rep. 632; *Glencore International A.G. v. Shell International Trading and Shipping Co. Ltd.* [1999] 2 Lloyd's Rep. 692 (claim

for substantive relief in relation to property and proceedings for interpleader relief not the same cause of action); *The Winter* [2000] 2 Lloyd's
Rep. 298 (possibility of substantive issues being determined by foreign court
in interlocutory proceedings leads to application of Article 21); *Re Cover
Europe Ltd; Kvaerner-Masa Yards Inc v. Barrett* [2002] EWHC 861 (Ch),
[2002] 2 B.C.L.C. 61 (proceedings for declaration that guarantee was invalid
involved the same cause of action as contested claim to admit in insolvency
proceedings proof of the debt created by the guarantee).

Article 24 of the 1968 Convention corresponds with Article 31 of the **12–049**
Judgments Regulation.

Date of seisin for the purpose of the Judgments Regulation. Paragraphs **12–050**
12–050 to 12–054 in the main work deal with the rules by which the date on
which a court is seised is ascertained for the purposes of Articles 21 to 23 of
the 1968 Convention and the Lugano Convention. In essence the material
question is to ask, separately in relation to each court which is alleged to
have been seised, when the action was *definitively pending* before the
particular court. The question was and is answered by reference to the
procedural law of the particular court. Unless the two (or more) sets of
proceedings were instituted after March 1, 2002, in the courts of two (or
more) Regulation States, the account of the law in the main work will be
decisive.

But the practical shortcomings inherent in the interpretation of this part
of the 1968 and Lugano Conventions were many: it could be difficult to
obtain reliable advice as to when a court in another Contracting State
would regard itself as seised; and it was perceived by some that differences
from one law to another gave courts (or claimants) an unprincipled
advantage over other courts in the race to institute proceedings. In
recognition of this, Article 30 of the Judgments Regulation states a uniform
definition of the point in time at which a court in a Regulation State is
seised. It provides:

> "For the purposes of this Section, a court shall be deemed to be seised:
>
> 1. at the time when the document instituting the proceedings or an
>   equivalent document is lodged with the court, provided that the
>   plaintiff has not subsequently failed to take the steps he was required
>   to take to have service effected on the defendant, or
> 2. if the document has to be served before being lodged with the court, at
>   the time when it is received by the authority responsible for service,
>   provided that the plaintiff has not failed to take the steps he was
>   required to take to have the document lodged with the court."

So far as concerns the seisin of an English court, Article 30(1) states the
applicable rule, and the court will therefore be seised on the issue of the
claim form by the court registry or office and date-stamped by that office
(CPR, r. 7.2(2)), always provided that the claimant has not failed to effect
service of the claim form. It is unclear whether the defendant can invoke
the proviso in a case in which, for example, he succeeded in evading service
until the claim form was no longer good for service.

Where new parties or fresh claims are added by amendment, it seems
most likely that Article 30 will mean that the date of reissue (whether or
not this was required to be preceded and obtained by an application for
permission to amend) will be the date on which the court is seised of the

new claim. If the court dispenses with the need for reservice of the amended claim form and/or statement of case, the proviso to Article 30(1) will become irrelevant.

Add at end of paragraph: In *Molins p.l.c. v. G.D. SpA* [2000] 1 W.L.R. 1741 (C.A.) it was explained that this meant that the requirements for an action to be definitively pending had to be fulfilled. Accordingly in a case where Italian law required process to be served for the action to become definitively pending, but service had been irregular, the proceedings were not definitively pending unless and until this irregularity was cured by appearance or by order of the judge. In the interim period the court was not seised.

NOTE 2. For the position in Finland, see *Carnoustie v. I.T.W.F.* [2002] EWHC 1624 (Comm), [2002] 2 All E.R. 657.

12–051 In *Canada Trust Co. v. Stolzenberg (No. 2)* [2002] 1 A.C. 1, a case concerning the meaning of "sued" in Articles 2 and 6 of the Lugano Convention (see entry at para. 11–063, *supra*), the House of Lords declined to rule on the correctness of *Dresser U.K. Ltd. v. Falcongate Freight Management Ltd.* [1992] Q.B. 502 (C.A.). See also the elaborate discussion by Lord Hoffmann at pp. 1389–1394.

12–052 A claimant who applied for an order that service be permitted to be made by alternative means, and who does so for the principal purpose of attempting to seise the English court more quickly than would be the case if such an order were not made, will not usually be entitled to such an order: *Knauf U.K. GmbH v. British Gypsum Ltd.* [2001] EWCA Civ. 1570; [2002] 1 W.L.R. 907, distinguished in *Carnoustie v. I.T.W.F.* [2002] EWHC 1624 (Comm); [2002] All E.R. (Comm.) 657. A French court, which has been applied to and has appointed an expert to investigate possible causes of loss-causing events, is not to be regarded as seised of substantive proceedings: *Miles Platt Ltd v. Townroe Ltd.* [2003] EWCA Civ. 145, [2003] 1 All E.R. (Comm.) 561 (C.A.).

12–053 NOTE 11. Add *Glencore International A.G. v. Metro Trading International Inc.* [1999] 2 Lloyd's Rep. 632.

NOTE 13. Cf. *Molins plc v. G.D. SpA* [2000] 1 W.L.R. 1741 (C.A.), para. 12–050, *supra*.

12–055 In cases where the Judgments Regulation applies: that is, there are related actions in the courts of two Regulation States, each of which being instituted after the coming into force of the Regulation on March 1, 2002, Article 28 of the Regulation applies in place of Article 22 of the 1968 Convention. Article 28 differs in two respects from Article 22 of the 1968 Convention. First, the power to stay proceedings may be exercised if a related action is pending in the courts of another Regulation State: by contract, Article 22 permitted a stay only where the related action was pending at first instance. Secondly, a court may dismiss for consolidation of its proceedings with those pending at first instance in another Regulation State if the law of that Regulation State whose court was first seised allows the consolidation of the two actions. The uncertainty in the interpretation of Article 22 of the 1968 Convention, discussed in para. 12–056 at note 92, is not carried across into the Regulation.

First sentence. An action is not pending at first instance if all that remains alive is an appeal against the striking out of the action: *Lough Neagh Exploration Ltd. v. Morrice* [1999] N.I. 258 (C.A.).

Add at end: for further analysis of related actions, see *Watson v. First Choice Holidays and Flights Ltd.* [2001] EWCA Civ. 972; [2001] 2 Lloyd's Rep. 339 (C.A.) (in the context of Art. 6(1) of the 1968 Convention: a reference to the European Court as withdrawn after the action was settled); *Apple Computer International v. Digit S.r.l.*, October 5, 2001.

NOTE 94. For cases covered by Art. 28 of the Judgments Regulation, see the **12–056** entry for para. 12–055, *supra*.

See generally Briggs, in *Lex Mercatoria: Essays in Honour of Francis* **12–057** *Reynolds* (ed. Rose, 2000), p. 219.

Text to note 31. In *Turner v. Grovit* [2002] 1 W.L.R. 107, 117, Lord Hobhouse objected to the expression "anti-suit injunction" as being liable to misstate the nature of the order, on the basis that it tended to suggest that the order was directed at the foreign court, when it was not.

NOTE 26. See also *Turner v. Grovit* [2002] 1 W.L.R. 107 (H.L.). In line 24, delete the reference for *Allstate Life Insurance Co. v. A.N.Z. Banking Corporation* and substitute (1996) 64 F.C.R. 1, 44, 61 (Aust. Fed. Ct.).

NOTE 32. See also *National Westminster Bank p.l.c. v. Utrecht-America Finance Co.* [2001] EWCA Civ. 658; [2001] 2 All E.R. (Comm.) 7 (C.A.), accepting that for an interlocutory anti-suit injunction, the basis for the claim to relief must be more than just arguable. For an anti-anti-suit injunction, ordered to restrain a respondent from obtaining from the American court an anti-suit injunction which would have prevented the English court from ruling on its own jurisdiction, and which was in the circumstances oppressive or vexatious, see *General Star International Indemnity Ltd v. Stirling Cooke Browne Reinsurance Brokers Ltd* [2003] I.L.Pr. 314.

In relation to anti-anti-anti-suit injunctions, see also *National Australia Bank Ltd v. Idoport* [2002] NSWSC 623.

Text prior to note 34. *Cf. Amoco (U.K.) Exploration Co. v. British American* **12–058** *Offshore Ltd.* [1999] 2 Lloyd's Rep. 772.

Text to note 35. In cases where the jurisdiction of the court is governed by the Judgments Regulation, the references to the 1968 or Lugano Conventions must be understood as a reference to this Regulation. Art. 21 of the Conventions corresponds to Art. 27 of the Regulation.

NOTE 33. Discontinuance is now more straightforward and not dependent upon permission, so the analysis in *Castanho v. Brown & Root (U.K.) Ltd.* [1981] A.C. 557 must be read with this in mind: see CPR Part 38.

The grant of a anti-suit injuncton does not involve a breach of Article 6 of **12–059** the European Convention on Human Rights. Article 6 E.C.H.R. guarantees a right of access to a court, but does not constitute a guarantee of access to any and every court which the claimant might wish to seise: *O.T. Africa Line Ltd. v. Hijazy* [2001] 1 Lloyd's Rep. 76. See also entry at para. 12–026.

12–062 In *Turner v. Grovit* [2002] 1 W.L.R. 107, 119 (H.L.), it was stated that in the absence of the claimant having a legal right to be sued in the foreign court, an English court would only exercise its discretion to grant an injunction if the applicant were party to existing proceedings before the English court, and that in the absence of such pending proceedings, the applicant would not have a sufficient or legitimate interest in applying for the order. There is no trace of such a requirement in the earlier English cases. But in *Glencore International A.G. v. Exter Shipping Ltd.* [2002] EWCA Civ. 524, [2002] C.L.C. 1090, the injunction was justified because the respondent was party to proceedings before the English court (as defendant and as claimant), thereby establishing the jurisdiction of the court over the respondent *in personam*, and the existence of a legitimate or sufficient interest on the part of the applicant in applying for the injunction. In *Sabah Shipyard (Pakistan) Ltd v. Islamic Republic of Pakistan* [2002] EWCA Civ. 1643; *The Times*, November 27, 2002 (C.A.) a third position was identified: where there was a non-exclusive jurisdiction clause, it nevertheless provided the background against which the behaviour of the respondent was to be assessed. Such a clause did not justify an anti-suit injunction without more, but it would make it considerably easier to demonstrate vexatious or oppressive behaviour on the part of the respondent.

NOTE 57. In *Australian Broadcasting Corp. v. Lenah Game Meats Pty. Ltd.* [2001] H.C.A. 63, the High Court of Australia explained the distinction between the English and Australian rules which govern the grant of an anti-suit injunction. The decision was handed down prior to *Turner v. Grovit*.

12–063 NOTE 59. Add at end: *Allstate Life Insurance Co v. A.N.Z. Banking Corp. Ltd.* (1996) 64 F.C.R. 61 (Aust. Fed. Ct.) (application for discovery under U.S.C. s.1782 restrained). Such an injunction was also granted in *Omega Group Holdings Ltd. v. Kozeny*, [2002] C.L.C. 132.

NOTE 62. *Cf. Shell International Petroleum Co. Ltd. v. Coral Oil Co. Ltd.* [1999] 2 Lloyd's Rep. 606 (claim utterly absurd).

NOTE 65. An injunction was ordered in *Glencore International A.G. v. Exter Shipping Ltd.* [2002] EWCA Civ. 524; [2002] C.L.C. 1090, to restrain the bringing of American proceedings which encroached on a large piece of complex litigation being actively managed in the Commercial Court, and in respect of which it was enormously burdensome to have common issues investigated in two separate proceedings.

NOTE 66. *Cf. Turner v. Grovit* [2000] Q.B. 345 (C.A.) (claim advanced in foreign proceedings could have been brought in English action, even if only as counterclaim: injunction granted). On further appeal to the House of Lords: [2002] 1 W.L.R. 107, proceedings were stayed while a question was referred to the European Court (see the entry at para. 12–015).

12–065 But see the entry at para. 12–062, for the proposition that there must be pending proceedings before the English courts to which the applicant is party before the court may exercise its discretion to grant the injunction.

Add after third sentence: But *cf. Shell International Petroleum Co. Ltd. v. Coral Oil Co. Ltd.* [1999] 2 Lloyd's Rep. 606 (prior proceedings having been brought in England gave the English court sufficient interest to act, even if it was not *the* natural forum).

NOTE 71. See also *Amoco (U.K.) Exploration Co. v. British American Offshore Ltd.* [1999] 2 Lloyd's Rep. 772.

The second and fourth sentences of this paragraph were cited with approval **12–066** by Lord Hobhouse in *Turner v. Grovit* [2002] 1 W.L.R. 107, 122.

First sentence. Where the proceedings are brought in the courts of a Regulation State, the principles (whichever they are) which apply in relation to the 1968 and Lugano Conventions will be equally applicable.

Second sentence. In *Turner v. Grovit* [2000] Q.B. 345 (C.A.) (noted Briggs (1999) 70 B.Y.I.L. 332, Harris (1999) 115 L.Q.R. 576, Hartley (2000) 49 I.C.L.Q. 166), it was held that as proceedings had been brought in the courts of a Contracting State which should have concluded that they had no jurisdiction, an injunction would be granted. For further proceedings in the House of Lords, see [2002] 1 W.L.R. 107; and see the entry at para. 12–015. In the House of Lords, it was accepted at p. 116 that the question whether or not the Spanish court was in breach of Article 21 of the Convention in concluding that it had jurisdiction was a matter for it alone, and was not relevant to the grant of an injunction by an English court. At p. 123 it was stated that the injunction was not concerned with, and did not deny, the jurisdiction of the foreign court.

NOTE 73. Add: *First Security National Bank Association v. Air Gabon* [1999] I.L.Pr. 617 (usual to apply to second seised court for relief under what is now Article 27 of the Regulation rather than to apply to court first seised for an anti-suit injunction).

NOTE 75. But for a different appreciation of the issues, see *O.T. Africa Line Ltd. v. Hijazy* [2001] 1 Lloyd's Rep. 76.

NOTE 77. For further authorities on the manner in which an injunction will be granted in support of an agreement on arbitration or jurisdiction, see the entry for para. 12–123, *infra*.

But see *Turner v. Grovit* [2002] 1 W.L.R. 107, and the entry for para. **12–067** 12–062.

But for the possible impact of Article 6 of the European Convention on **12–068** Human Rights on "single forum" cases, see *O.T. Africa Line Ltd. v. Hijazy* [2001] 1 Lloyd's Rep. 76.

See also Briggs, in *Lex Mercatoria: Essays in Honour of Francis Reynolds* **12–069** (ed. Rose, 2000), p. 219.

NOTE 90. On the effect of delay in application, see the divergent views expressed in *Donohue v. Armco Inc.* [2000] 1 Lloyd's Rep. 579 (C.A.). But the point was not specifically dealt with on further appeal to the House of Lords: [2002] 1 Lloyd's Rep. 425 though the decision of the Court of Appeal was reversed on other grounds. And see the entry under para. 12–114.

NOTE 94. It was said in *Amoco (U.K.) Exploration Co. v. British American Offshore Ltd.* [1999] 2 Lloyd's Rep. 772 that whether an application could or should have been made to the foreign court was relevant to the exercise of the court's discretion.

12–070 Illustration 3. Ord. 11, r. 1(1) is replaced by CPR, r. 6.20.

12–071 Illustration 4. Ord. 11, r. 1(1) is replaced by CPR r. 6.20.

12–072 NOTE 8. If the proceedings in Italy and in England were both instituted after March 1, 2002 (but not otherwise) the applicable rule would be Art. 27 of the Judgments Regulation.

12–073 NOTE 9. See the entry at para. 12-072 *supra*.

Illustrations 11 and 12. But if the proceedings in England and in France were both instituted after March 1, 2002 (but not otherwise), the question which court was seised first would be answered by applying the rule in Article 30 of the Judgments Regulation. According to that, the English court is seised on the issue of process, always assuming that service of the claim form is effected in due course. If the corresponding French procedure involves the service of a writ prior to its being lodged with the court, the French court will be seised on the date on which process was served.

12–074 NOTE 11. Add Judgments Regulation, Art. 23. Art. 17 of Sched. 4 to the 1982 Act is replaced by Rule 12 of Sched. 2, para. 4 of S.I. 2001 No. 3929, which, like its predecessor, does not exactly reproduce the provision which now appears as Art. 23 of the Regulation.

Text of sub-rule (3). Add a reference to Judgments Regulation; and where the case falls within the scope of that Regulation, substitute "Regulation State" for "Contracting State", and "Article 23 of the Regulation" for "Article 17".

NOTE 15. Add: Judgments Regulation, Art. 23.

NOTE 17. Add at end *Assicurazioni Generali SpA. v. Ege Sigorta A/S*, [2002] Lloyd's Rep. I.R. 480; *A.I.G. Europe S.A. v. QBE International Insurance Ltd.* [2001] 2 Lloyd's Rep. 268.

12–075 The reference to the 1968 and Lugano Conventions must, if the proceedings are instituted after March 1, 2002, be understood as including a reference to the Judgments Regulation.

NOTE 17. The decision in *AIG Europe (U.K.) Ltd. v. The Ethniki* was affirmed by the Court of Appeal: [2000] 2 All E.R. 566 (C.A.). Accordingly the incorporation of a jurisdiction agreement into one contract from another is a matter of construing the intention of the parties by reference to the law which governs the contract alleged to have effected the incorporation.

In the context of insurance, the words "all terms . . . as original" will not suffice to incorporate a jurisdiction agreement from one contract to another, because they do not demonstrate a sufficiently clear and precise consensus on the issue of incorporation (*A.I.G. Europe S.A. v. Q.B.E. International Insurance Ltd.* [2001] 2 Lloyd's Rep. 268); and as an agreement on jurisdiction is ancillary to the risk, not germane to it, general words of incorporation will be insufficient to encompass it (*Assicurazioni Generali SpA v. Ege Sigorta A/S* [2002] Lloyd's Rep. I.R. 480).

12–078 NOTE 31. Add at end of first sentence: *Sinochem International Oil (London) Co. Ltd. v. Mobil Sales and Supply Corp.* [2000] 1 Lloyd's Rep. 670.

NOTE 32. But for scepticism whether any principle or presumption of construction was appropriate, see *McGowan v. Summit at Lloyd's*, 2002 S.L.T. 1258 (Inner House), where the court preferred to construe the words with close attention to their precise meaning.

On the particular issues raised by non-exclusive jurisdiction agreements, see Fawcett [2001] L.M.C.L.Q. 234. On whether a service of suit clause is to be seen as a non-exclusive jurisdiction agreement, see *Ace Insurance S.A.– N.V. v. Zürich Insurance Co.* [2001] EWCA Civ. 173; [2001] 1 Lloyd's Rep. 618 (C.A.).

The question whether an exclusive jurisdiction agreement also serves to make it a breach of contract to apply for provisional or protective relief from a court in another country is likewise a question to be answered by the construction of the words of the agreement. It was held that there was no breach of contract by so doing in *Bankgesellschaft Berlin A.G. v. First International Shipping Corp. Ltd.* [2001] C.L. (Jan.) 61.

But in *Sabah Shipyard (Pakistan) Ltd. v. Islamic Republic of Pakistan* [2002]   **12–079**
EWCA Civ. 1643; *The Times*, November 27, 2002 (C.A.) it was held that, though on its true construction the jurisdiction clause nominating the English courts was not exclusive, once proceedings had been instituted in England it was (in the absence of exceptional reasons) a clear breach of contract for parallel proceedings to be brought in the courts of Pakistan, and that an injunction should go to restrain such a breach. It was also suggested (at paras [37], [38]) that proceedings brought in Pakistan before any English action, which had the purpose of frustrating the jurisdiction agreement, would have been vexatious.

NOTE 34. Add: *Mercury Communications Ltd. v. Communications Telesystems International* [1999] 2 All E.R. (Comm.) 33, where it was suggested that the effect of a non-exclusive jurisdiction agreement was, if anything, stronger than the proposition in the text would suggest. See also *J.P. Morgan Securities Asia Pte. Ltd. v. Malaysian Newsprint Industries Sdn. Bhd.* [2001] 2 Lloyd's Rep. 41 (C.A.).

First two sentences. It was reiterated in *Donohue v. Armco Inc.* [2002] 1   **12–080**
Lloyd's Rep. 425 that when the issue arises as between the parties to an agreement on jurisdiction, the English practice is to give the words a generous interpretation. Though in that case it was suggested by Lord Scott of Foscote at 442 that where an agreement gave exclusive jurisdiction to the English courts, it cannot (unless worded very clearly) have been intended to apply in relation to causes of action arising under a foreign law which could not have been prosecuted before an English court, this view did not appear to be accepted by the other members of the House. Accordingly it may constitute a breach of an agreement giving exclusive jurisdiction to the English courts for a party to bring a claim in the courts of the United States alleging liability under the Racketeer Influenced and Corrupt Organisations Act (R.I.C.O.).

NOTE 36. Insert before *Sarabia v. The Ocean Mindoro* [1997] 2 W.W.R. 116: *Youell v. Kara Mara Shipping Co. Ltd.* [2000] 2 Lloyd's Rep. 102 (claim in form of direct action by victim against tortfeasor's insurer contractual in nature and therefore subject to jurisdiction agreement in contract of insurance); *Clare Taverns v. Gill* [2001] I.L.Pr. 260 (Irish High Ct.) (tort claim inextricably linked to contract within scope of agreement on jurisdiction). Contrast *Donohue v. Armco Inc.* [2002] 1 Lloyd's Rep. 425, 442 (H.L.) (conspiracy, fraud and Racketeer Influenced and Corrupt Organisations Act (R.I.C.O.) claims within ambit of jurisdiction agreement).

NOTE 38. But *cf. Domansa v. Derin Shipping and Trading Co. Inc.* [2001] 1 Lloyd's Rep. 362.

12–081 Article 17 of the Conventions is substantially reproduced, though with some changes, by Article 23 of the Judgments Regulation. For an illustration of the inability of a court to override such an agreement, see *Hough v. P. & O. Containers* [1999] Q.B. 834.

On the question whether a claim in damages may be made for losses caused by a party who sues in a court in breach of a contractual agreement to sue elsewhere, see *Union Discount Co. Ltd. v. Zoller* [2001] EWCA Civ. 1755; 1 W.L.R. 1517 (C.A.) (where the jurisdiction agreement was for the English courts and proceedings were brought in the courts of New York.)

12–082 The Judgments Regulation also contains restrictions on the effectiveness of jurisdiction agreements in the contexts of insurance, certain consumer, and employment, contracts.

Text to note 39. In *Donohue v. Armco Inc.* [2002] 1 Lloyd's Rep. 425 the House of Lords set aside the injunction which had been ordered by the Court of Appeal on the basis that as persons who were not party to and bound by the jurisdiction agreement could not be prevented from bringing claims before the American courts, this furnished a strong reason not to enforce the agreement by injunction as between those who were bound by it.

12–083 Add at end of first sentence: For the case of two contracts, each containing jurisdiction agreements but which are different or inconsistent, see *Sinochem International Oil (London) Co. Ltd. v. Mobil Sales and Supply Corp.* [2000] 1 Lloyd's Rep. 670.

An agreement on jurisdiction may be invalidated by the Unfair Terms in Consumer Contracts Regulations 1999 (S.I. 1999 No. 2083): Case C–240/90 *Océano Grupo Editorial S.A. v. Quintero* [2000] E.C.R. I–4941; *Standard Bank London Ltd. v. Apostolakis (No. 2)* [2001] Lloyd's Rep. Banking 240 (on which see Withers [2002] L.M.C.L.Q. 56; the Greek court subsequently ruled that it did not have jurisdiction: [2003] I.L.Pr. 342).

12–085 The principle that a jurisdiction clause is severable from the contract in which it is contained, so that it survives any argument that the contract may be impeached for duress or other vitiating factor, was accepted in *IFR Ltd v. Federal Trade SpA*, September 19, 2001.

Final sentence. The same conclusion will follow from Article 23 of the Judgments Regulation in cases to which it applies.

NOTE 48. Ord. 11 is replaced by CPR, r. 6.20.

NOTE 51. Add at end: *Morrison v. Society of Lloyd's* [2000] I.L.Pr. 92 (N.B.).

12–086 This analysis will be equally applicable in cases where the validity and effect of an agreement on jurisdiction is governed by Article 23 of the Judgments Regulation.

Article 23 of the Judgments Regulation. The account in the main work, **12–087** which explains the effect of Article 17 of the 1968 and Lugano Conventions, will apply equally to cases in which the validity and effect of an agreement to confer jurisdiction on the courts of a Regulation State is governed by Article 23 of the Regulation. There are three principal differences between Article 23 of the Regulation and Article 17 of the Conventions. (1) Article 23(1) of the Regulation provides that it confers exclusive jurisdiction on the nominated court "unless the parties have agreed otherwise". The uncertainty as to the compatibility of non-exclusive jurisdiction agreements with Article 17 of the Conventions, discussed at para. 12–107 of the main work, is not relevant to the Regulation. (2) Article 23(2) makes special provisions for contracts made by electronic means, and which might not otherwise comply with the requirements as to form, as discussed in para. 12–098 of the main work: it provides that "any communication by electronic means which provides a durable record of the agreement shall be equivalent to 'writing'". (3) The special provision made in Article 17 of the Conventions, validating jurisdiction agreements made for the benefit of one party, is omitted from the Regulation. As this provision was principally of use as a means of giving effect to a non-exclusive jurisdiction agreement, it is not needed in the light of Article 23(1) of the Regulation. Aside from these points of difference, there is no reason to suppose that the interpretation of Article 23 of the Regulation will differ from that stated in respect of Article 17 of the 1968 and Lugano Conventions, and the following paragraphs of the main work should be read with this in mind.

NOTE 55. Case C–158/97 *Soc. Trasporti Castelletti Spedizioni Internazionali SpA v. Hugo Trumpy SpA* is now reported at [1999] E.C.R. I–1597 (noted Hartley (2000) 25 Eur.L.R. 178). For further discussion of the position of assignees and other third parties, see *infra* at paras. 12–100 *et seq.*

NOTE 58. Add at end: It was suggested in *AIG Europe (U.K.) Ltd. v. The Ethniki* [2000] 2 All E.R. 566 (C.A.) that the formal requirements set out in Article 17 of the 1968 Convention may be applicable when it had to be decided whether a jurisdiction agreement in one contract had been incorporated by reference into another. See also *A.I.G. Europe S.A. v. Q.B.E. International Insurance Ltd.* [2001] 2 Lloyd's Rep. 268. And see the entry for note 55, *supra*.

It is unlikely that the application of the Judgments Regulation is restricted **12–089** to cases with an "international" character.

NOTE 66. Add Case C–387/98 *Coreck Maritime GmbH v. Handelsveem B.V.*, **12–090** [2000] E.C.R. I–9337, where at para. 19 of the judgment it was stated that a court seised of a case to which a jurisdiction agreement conferring jurisdiction on the courts of a non-Contracting State applies must assess the validity of the clause according to the applicable law, including conflicts rules, thereby confirming the view expressed in the text to this note.

Third sentence. *Cf. LAFI Office v. Meridien Animal Health* [2000] 2 Lloyd's **12–093** Rep. 51.

Text to note 70. But the particular provision dealing with agreements for the benefit of one party is not reproduced in Art. 23 of the Judgments Regulation: see the entry at para. 12–087, *supra*.

12–094 For the impact of the Unfair Terms in Consumer Contracts Regulations 1999 (S.I. 1999 No. 2083), see the entry at para. 12–083, *supra*.

12–095 For cases to which the Judgments Regulation applies, the validity of an agreement on jurisdiction as between parties to an individual contract of employment is governed by Article 21 of the Regulation. This provides that the jurisdictional provisions of section 6 of Chapter II of the Regulation may be departed from only by an agreement on jurisdicion which is entered into after the dispute has arisen, or which allows the employee to bring proceedings in courts other than those indicated in that Section.

12–096 On the question of how to assess a plea by a party that he did not consent to an alleged agreement on jurisdiction, the analysis in relation to Article 17 of the Conventions, set out in the main work, will apply equally to Article 23 of the Judgments Regulation.

NOTE 81. Case C–159/97 *Soc. Trasporti Castelletti Spedizioni Internazionali SpA v. Hugo Trumpy SpA* is now reported at [1999] E.C.R. I–1597 (noted Hartley (2000) 25 Eur.L.R. 178).

NOTE 83. Add: *LAFI Office v. Meridien Animal Health* [2000] 2 Lloyd's Rep. 51 (dispute as to incorporation matter for English law to determine); *AIG Europe (UK) Ltd. v. The Ethniki* [2000] 2 All E.R. 566 (C.A.) (incorporation of jurisdiction from another document a matter for the applicable law of the contract, but it may be proper to apply Article 17 instead); *Implants International v. Stratec Medical* [1999] 2 All E.R. (Comm.) 933 (agreement not intended to be legally binding is not within Article 17); *Tradigrain SA v. SIAT SpA* [2002] 2 Lloyd's Rep. 553 (incorporation in context of insurance).

12–097 The analysis of jurisdiction agreements in insurance contracts and certain consumer contracts is equally applicable to jurisdiction taken under the Judgments Regulation where the provisions are Articles 13 and 17.

12–098 The rules of the Judgments Regulation for the formal validity of jurisdiction agreements are, subject to one point, identical with those contained in the 1968 Convention (as amended) and the Lugano Convention. The one difference is that for the purposes of the Regulation, Article 23(2) provides that "any communication by electronic means which provides a durable record of the agreement shall be equivalent to writing".

12–099 NOTE 86. See also *Lafarge Plasterboard Ltd. v. Fritz Peters & Co. K.G.* [2000] 2 Lloyd's Rep. 689 (jurisdiction clause printed on reverse of order form not sufficient to amount to an agreement in writing, because no guarantee of agreement). But for a different view, holding that acceptance by conduct of a contractual offer containing a jurisdiction clause sufficed to satisfy Article 17 of the Convention (now Article 23 of the Judgments Regulation), see *Middle East Tankers and Freighters Ltd. v. Abu Dhabi Container Lines* [2002] 2 Lloyd's Rep. 643. On whether Art. 17 needs to be applied with strictness when there is no reason to doubt the presence of consent, see *Astilleros Zamakona SA v. MacKinnons*, 2002 S.L.T. 1206 (Outer House).

12–100 Add after first sentence: In Case C–387/98 *Coreck Maritime GmbH v. Handelsveem B.V.* [2000] E.C.R. I-9337 it was held, following Case 71/83 *The Tilly Russ* [1984] E.C.R. 2417 and Case C–159/97 *Trasporti Castelletti*

Spedizioni Internazionali SpA v. Hugo Trumpy SpA [1999] E.C.R. I–1597, that the formal validity of the jurisdiction clause in a bill of lading was to be assessed by reference to the relationship between the parties to the original contract, and not by reference to the written consent or otherwise of a third party said to be bound by the agreement. If under the national law applied by the court seised (in England, the law governing the contract containing the jurisdiction clause) a third party succeeds to rights and obligation of the bill of lading (or other contract), it is irrelevant that he has not separately "accepted" or otherwise indicated his consent to the jurisdiction clause. But if, by contrast, he did not, as a matter of national law, succeed to these rights and obligations, the court must determine by reference to Article 17 whether he did actually accept the jurisdiction clause before it may be relied on against him.

NOTE 91. Case 71/83 *The Tilly Russ* [1984] E.C.R. 2417 was applied in *Glencore International A.G. v. Metro Trading International Inc.* [1999] 2 Lloyd's Rep. 632.

NOTE 95. See also *Lafarge Plasterboard Ltd. v. Fritz Peters & Co. K.G.* [2000] **12–102** 2 Lloyd's Rep. 689 (jurisdiction clause printed on reverse of order form not sufficient to amount to an agreement in writing, because no guarantee of agreement; and if each party used its own form of jurisdiction clause in its documents, this could not be seen as evidencing a continued trading relationship on which an oral contract was based, as the agreement did contain a single basic term). On practices which the parties have established, see *O.T. Africa Line Ltd. v. Hijazy* [2001] 1 Lloyd's Rep. 76 (liner services).

NOTE 96. Case C–159/97 *Soc. Trasporti Castelletti Spedizioni Internazionali SpA v. Hugo Trumpy SpA* is now reported at [1999] E.C.R. I–1597.

See the entry at para. 12–102, *supra*. **12–103**

NOTE 98. See also Case C–387/98 *Coreck Maritime GmbH v. Handelsveem B.V.*, *supra*.

Article 63 of the Judgments Regulation makes provision to restrict the **12–105** effect of jurisdiction agreements in relation to defendants domiciled in Luxembourg: if under a contract for the delivery of goods or the provision of services, the final place of delivery or of provision is in Luxembourg, an agreement on jurisdiction will not be valid unless it is in writing or is evidenced in writing within the meaning of Article 23(1)(a); but this limitation is to remain in effect for only six years from March 1, 2002; and it has no effect where the contract is for the provision of financial services.

Apart from the fact that it expressly accepts that an agreement on **12–106** jurisdiction, which is intended not to confer exclusive jurisdiction on the nominated court, is to be given the effect the parties wished it to have, the analysis of the contents of the agreement is equally applicable to Article 23 of the Judgments Regulation.

Add after first sentence: In Case C–387/98 *Coreck Maritime GmbH v. Handelsveem B.V.*, *supra*, it was held that the nomination of the courts "in the country where the carrier has his principal place of business" was sufficient for the purposes of Article 17 as it stated objective factors which expressed the agreement of the parties and which were precise enough to enable the court to ascertain whether it had jurisdiction.

12–107 For non-exclusive jurisdiction agreements, see the entry at para. 12–106. In relation to non-exclusive jurisdiction agreements under the Lugano Convention, see also: *Insured Financial Structures Ltd v. Elektrocleplownia Tychy SA* [2002] EWCA Civ. 110; [2003] 2 W.L.R. 656.

Note 6. Add to the list of English authorities: *Mercury Communications Ltd. v. Communications Telesystems International* [1999] 2 All E.R. (Comm.) 33.

12–109 Schedule 4 to the 1982 Act is replaced, and new text is inserted, by S.I. 2001 No. 3929, Sched. 2, para. 4. Rule 12 of these new provisions makes provision for agreements on jurisdiction. It differs from Article 23 of the Judgments Regulation in two respects. First, there are no requirements of form, and secondly, there is no reason to suppose that it is not subject to other rules of English law which might override its effectiveness. Jurisdiction agreements in consumer contracts are also provided for by Rule 9, and in employment contracts by Rule 10(5) of the new text of Sched. 4. The new text of Schedule 4 to the 1982 Act is reproduced in Part II of the appendix to this Supplement.

12–111 Order 11, r. 1(1)(*iv*) is replaced by CPR, r. 6.20(5)(d) and, where jurisdiction is established by the Judgments Regulation, Sched. 4 to the 1982 Act is replaced by S.I. 2001 No. 3929, Sched. 2, para. 4.

Note 18: Ord. 11, r. 1(2) is replaced by CPR, r. 6.19.

12–112 Order 11, r. 1(1)(iv) is replaced by CPR, r. 6.20(5)(d).

12–113 S.I. 2001 No. 3929, Sched. 2, para. 4, replaces and inserts a new Sched. 4 to the 1982 Act; and the provision on agreement on choice of court is Rule 12.

It was reaffirmed in *Donohue v. Armco Inc.* [2002] 1 Lloyd's Rep. 425 (H.L.) that a court would enforce an agreement on jurisdiction, whether for the English or a foreign court, by stay or injunction, as the case may be; but that where a strong reason was shown for not doing so, such relief would not be granted. It was suggested at pp. 436, 439 in that case that where the court refrained from the specific enforcement of the agreement, and a party to the agreement proceeded to bring proceedings which constituted a breach of the agreement, an action for damages for breach would in principle lie. See also on this *Union Discount Co. Ltd. v. Zoller* [2001] EWCA Civ. 1755; [2002] 1 W.L.R. 1517 (C.A.).

12–114 Text to note 23. Similarly, even if the English court has been given jurisdiction by means of a valid and binding choice of court agreement, the proceedings may still be stayed on *forum non conveniens* grounds, though strong reason will be required for such an order to be granted, and the existence of the jurisdiction clause does not oust the power of the court to stay the proceedings: *U.B.S. A.G. v. Omni Holding A.G.* [2000] 1 W.L.R. 916; *Marubeni Hong Kong & South China Ltd. v. Mongolian Government* [2002] 2 All E.R. (Comm.) 873.

12–115 Clause (2) of Rule 32 is likewise subject to Article 23 of the Judgments Regulation. Where this applies to establish the jurisdiction of the court,

Article 17 of Sched. 4 to the 1982 Act is replaced by S.I. 2001 No. 3929, Sched. 2, para. 4, Rule 12.

NOTE 31. *Cf. Ingosstrakh Ltd. v. Latvian Shipping Co.* [2000] I.L.Pr. 164 **12–117** (C.A.) (stay in favour of courts of Latvia).

Add at end of paragraph: *Cf. Baghlaf Al Zafer Factory Co. Br. for Industry v.* **12–119** *Pakistan National Shipping Co. (No. 2)* [2000] 1 Lloyd's Rep. 1 (C.A.) (if it appears that the defendant may not be able to cause the court to overlook the time bar, it may be inappropriate to order a stay).

NOTE 38: Ord. 11, r. 1(1) is replaced by CPR, r. 6.20.   **12–120**

The analysis in the main work under paras. 12–121 and 12–122 is equally **12–121** applicable where jurisdiction is determined by the Judgments Regulation Articles 23, 27, and 22 of the Regulation are, in this respect, identical to Articles 17, 21, and 16 of the Conventions.

NOTE 41. Art. 24 of the 1968 and Lugano Conventions corresponds to Art. 31 of the Judgments Regulation; and 1982 Act, section 25(1) is applicable to proceedings to which the Regulation applies: S.I. 2001 No. 3929, Sched. 2, para. 10.

NOTE 45. Art. 28(1) of the 1968 and Lugano Conventions corresponds to Art. 35(1) of the Judgments Regulation.

Add at end of second sentence: *Youell v. Kara Mara Shipping Co. Ltd.* **12–123** [2000] 2 Lloyd's Rep. 102.
    Where jurisdiction is established by the Judgments Regulation, Article 23 of the Regulation corresponds to Article 17 of the Conventions. There is no reason to suppose that the extent of the power to grant an anti-suit injunction when the proceedings are in the courts of another Regulation State is any different from the corresponding principles as developed in relation to proceedings in the courts of another Contracting State to the Conventions.

The same principles apply when, *mutatis mutandis*, jurisdiction is deter- **12–124** mined by the Judgments Regulation.

Text to note 58. Moreover, in *Donohue v. Armco Inc.* [2000] 1 Lloyd's Rep. **12–126** 579 (C.A.) it was considered that the fact that the foreign court had been applied to and had refused jurisdictional relief was not a sufficient reason not to grant an injunction. The point was not specifically dealt with on further appeal to the House of Lords: [2002] 1 Lloyd's Rep. 425, but the decision of the Court of Appeal was reversed. And see the entry under para. 12–114.

NOTE 58. Add *Society of Lloyd's v. White* [2000] C.L.C. 961.

NOTE 61. Delete and replace with: *Cf. ante*, para. 12–069. If the decision whether to order the injunction depends upon whether a foreign statutory cause of action falls within the scope of the jurisdiction agreement, *Credit Suisse First Boston (Europe) Ltd. v. M.L.C. (Bermuda) Ltd.* [1999] 1 Lloyd's Rep. 767 may suggest that the issue should be left for determination by the foreign court. But in *Donohue v. Armco Inc.* [2000] 1 Lloyd's Rep. 579

(C.A.), revd. on other grounds [2002] 1 W.L.R. 425 (H.L.), the court construed the agreement in relation to American causes of action, and ordered an injunction, despite the fact that the American court had refused to grant corresponding jurisdictional relief. To the same effect is *National Westminster Bank p.l.c. v. Utrecht-America Finance Co.* [2001] EWCA Civ. 658; [2001] 2 All E.R. (Comm.) 7 (C.A.). The case appears to regard it as oppressive or vexatious to bring proceedings in breach of contract. See also *Apple Computer International v. Digit S.r.l.*, October 5, 2001.

For the possibility of an action for damages when proceedings have been brought in a foreign court in breach of contract, see *Union Discount Co. Ltd. v. Zoller* [2001] EWCA Civ. 1755; [2002] 1 W.L.R. 1517 (C.A.); *Donohue v. Armco Inc.* [2002] 1 Lloyd's Rep. 425, at 436 and 439 (H.L.).

12–127 See the entry at para. 12–123, *supra*.

12–128 The principles discussed in the main work under paras. 12–128 to 12–131 will apply, *mutatis mutandis*, with equal effect when the jurisdiction of the English court and the foreign court is determined by the Judgments Regulation. For general discussion, see Beraudo (2001) J.Int.Arb. 13; van Haersolte-van Hof, *ibid.* 27.

NOTE 65. And see also: *W.S.G. Nimbus Pte. Ltd. v. Board of Control for Cricket in Sri Lanka* [2002] 3 Sing. L.R. 603 (H.C.).

NOTE 68. Add: *XL Insurance Ltd. v. Owens Corning* [2000] 2 Lloyd's Rep. 500.

12–131 Add at end of paragraph: In *The Ivan Zagubanski* [2002] 1 Lloyd's Rep. 106, proceedings were brought in London for a declaration that the parties had agreed to arbitrate their dispute, and for an injunction to restrain proceedings, commenced prior to the English action, in the French courts. It was held that, as the essential subject matter of the claim was the validity of the arbitration agreement, the case fell within the arbitration exception to Article 1 of the Convention (not following *The Heidberg* [1994] 2 Lloyd's Rep. 287 on this point), with the result that Article 21 was ineffective to remove the jurisdiction of the English court; and the injunction was granted on the ground that the conflicting views of the French court on the matter furnished no good reason for withholding from a party who had a contractual right to the enforcement of the arbitration agreement. See also *Welex AG v. Rosa Maritime Ltd ("The Epsilon Rosa") (No. 2)* [2002] EWHC 2003 (Comm), [2002] 2 Lloyd's Rep. 80 (granting injunction).

12–132 NOTE 77. R.S.C. Ord. 11 r. 1 (1)(d)(iv) is replaced by CPR, r. 6.20(5)(d).

NOTE 78. If the proceedings are instituted on or after March 1, 2002, the governing provision is Art. 23 of the Judgments Regulation; and the absence of any need to obtain permission to serve out of the jurisdiction is established by CPR, r. 6.19(1A).

12–133 NOTE 82. If the proceedings are instituted on or after March 1, 2002, the governing provision is Art. 23 of the Judgments Regulation.

Illustration 8. If the proceedings are instituted on or after March 1, 2002, the provision governing jurisdiction, and supporting the claim for an injunction, would be Art. 23 of the Judgments Regulation.

CHAPTER 13

JURISDICTION IN ADMIRALTY CLAIMS IN REM

Delete clause (2) and substitute: **13R–001**

(2)(a) Where the defendant is not domiciled in the United Kingdom, but is domiciled in a State to which Council Regulation (E.C.) 44/2001[4] ("the Judgments Regulation") applies (a "Regulation State"), the High Court does not have jurisdiction to entertain an Admiralty claim *in rem* (even if the process is served on the *res* in England) unless it has jurisdiction under the Regulation or under a convention "on a particular matter" within the terms of Article 71 of the Judgments Regulation.

(b) Where the defendant is domiciled neither in the United Kingdom nor in another Regulation State, but is domiciled in a State party to the Brussels Convention on jurisdiction and the enforcement of judgments in civil and commercial matters ("the 1968 Convention"), the High Court does not have jurisdiction to entertain an Admiralty claim *in rem* (even if the process is served on the *res* in England) unless it has jurisdiction under the 1968 Convention or under a convention "on a particular matter" within the terms of Article 57 of the 1968 Convention.

(c) Where the defendant is not domiciled in the United Kingdom, but is domiciled in a State which is party to the Lugano Convention on jurisdiction and the enforcement of judgments in civil and commercial matters (but not the 1968 Convention), the High Court does not have jurisdiction to entertain an Admiralty claim *in rem* (even if the process is served on the *res* in England) unless it has jurisdiction under the Lugano Convention or under a convention "on a particular matter" within the terms of Article 57(1) of the Lugano Convention.

NOTE 12. Add: *The Oakwell* [1999] 1 Lloyd's Rep. 249.   **13–003**

NOTE 20. In *The Bumbesti* [2000] Q.B. 559, Aikens J. declined to follow *The* **13–004**
St. Anna [1983] 1 W.L.R. 895 and decided that he was bound by the
decision of the Court of Appeal in *The Beldis* [1936] P. 51 (C.A.). Where a
dispute arising out of a charterparty is referred to arbitration, a claim to
enforce the resulting arbitration award is not to be regarded as a "claim
arising out of any agreement relating to . . . the use or hire of a ship"
(Supreme Court Act 1981, s. 20(2)(*h*)).

NOTE 41. For consideration of the 1999 Arrest Convention see Gaskell and **13–009**
Shaw [1999] L.M.C.L.Q. 470.

---

[4] Council Regulation (E.C.) 44/2001 is at [2001] O.J. L12, January 16, 2001, and is reproduced in Part I of the appendix to this Supplement. For Member States bound by the Regulation ("Regulation States") and Contracting Parties to the 1968 Convention and the Lugano Convention, see entry at paras. 11–006—11–007.

13–016 Second sentence. Section 21(4) of the Supreme Court Act 1981 refers to two points in time: when the cause of action arises and when the claim is brought. In a case where proceedings are brought in respect of the ship in connection with which the claim arises, the relevant person must be either the beneficial owner or a charterer by demise when the claim is brought (s. 21(4)(i)). However, when the cause of action arises the relevant person may be either "the owner or charterer of, or in possession or in control of, the ship" (s. 21(4)(b)). In *The Tychy* [1999] 2 Lloyd's Rep. 11 (C.A.) (noted by Baughen [2000] L.M.C.L.Q. 129; Davenport (2000) 116 L.Q.R. 36) the question arose as to what exactly "charterer" means in the context of section 21(4)(b). Although it had been established in *The Span Terza* [1982] 1 Lloyd's Rep. 225 that the term "charterer" includes a "time charterer", the defendant argued that it did not extend to a "voyage charterer" or a "slot charterer". The Court of Appeal rejected the defendant's argument; once it is established that a charterer under a time charter is covered by the term "charterer", it would be illogical if a charterer under a voyage charter or a slot charter (which is simply an example of a voyage charter of part of a ship) were not also covered.

NOTE 64. See also *Vostok Shipping Co. Ltd. v. Confederation Ltd.* [2000] 1 N.Z.L.R. 37 (N.Z.C.A.).

13–019 NOTE 71. Add: *"Iran Amanat" v. KMP Coastal Oil Pte Limited* (1999) 196 C.L.R. 130 (High Ct. Australia).

S13–022 **Effect of the Judgments Regulation, the 1968 Convention and the Lugano Convention.** Admiralty claims *in rem* fall within the scope of the Judgments Regulation (which is reproduced in Part I of the appendix to this Supplement), the 1968 Convention and the Lugano Convention[77]; it follows, therefore, that an English court cannot take jurisdiction in such a claim if this is precluded by the provisions of the Regulation or the Conventions. If the defendant is domiciled (for the purposes of the Regulation) in the United Kingdom, the court will have jurisdiction under Article 2 of the Regulation. If the defendant is not domiciled in the United Kingdom, a Regulation State or a Contracting State to either Convention, Article 4 of either the Regulation or the applicable Convention allows the English court to take jurisdiction under the provisions of English law. Where, however, the defendant is not domiciled in the United Kingdom, but is domiciled in a Regulation State or a Contracting State to either Convention, the provisions of the Regulation or the applicable Convention must be satisfied. Which instrument applies depends on the domicile of the defendant: if he is domiciled in a Regulation State, the Regulation applies; if the defendant is not domiciled in another Regulation State, but is domiciled in a State party to the 1968 Convention (*i.e.* Denmark), that Convention is to be applied; if he is domiciled in a State which is a party to the Lugano Convention but not the 1968 Convention (*i.e.* Iceland, Norway, Poland or Switzerland), the Lugano Convention is to be applied.[78]

---

[77] *The Deichland* [1990] 1 Q.B. 361 (C.A.). The scope of the Regulation and the Conventions as regards subject matter is defined by Art. 1, by which they apply in civil and commercial matters, whatever the nature of the court or tribunal. This is subject to certain exceptions, none of which concerns proceedings *in rem*.

[78] Lugano Convention, Art. 54B.

Where the defendant is not domiciled in the United Kingdom, but is **S13–023** domiciled in another Regulation State or Contracting State, Article 3 provides that the English court may take jurisdiction only by virtue of the rules set out in sections 2 to 7 of Chapter II of the Regulation (Articles 5 to 24) or sections 2 to 6 of Title II of the relevant Convention (Articles 5 to 18). However, Article 71 of the Judgments Regulation (and Article 57 of each Convention) provides that it does not prevent the court of a Regulation State (or Contracting State) from assuming jurisdiction in accordance with a convention "on a particular matter" to which the Regulation State (or Contracting State) is a party, even where the defendant is domiciled in another Regulation State (or Contracting State). Consequently, where the Judgments Regulation (or either Convention) applies, the English court must have jurisdiction under the provisions of the Regulation (or the relevant Convention) or under the provisions of a convention on a particular matter.

Meaning of "defendant". It has not yet been definitively determined who **S13–024** would be regarded as a defendant in a claim *in rem* for the purposes of the Judgments Regulation and the 1968 and Lugano Conventions, but the owner of the *res* or anyone with an interest in it whose interest would be affected by the claim would probably be so regarded. In *The Deichland*,[79] which was approved by the House of Lords in *Republic of India v. India Steamship Co. Ltd. (No. 2)*,[80] a company which was the demise charterer of the ship at the time when the process was issued (though the charter had ended by the time it was served) was regarded as the defendant for the purposes of the 1968 Convention.

Sections 2 to 7 of Chapter II of the Judgments Regulation; Sections 2 to 6 **S13–025** **of Title II of the Conventions.** With two exceptions, none of these provisions is specifically concerned with Admiralty claims. The first exception is Article 7 of the Regulation (which corresponds to Article 6A of the Conventions), which deals with limitation claims. This has already been discussed.[81] The second exception is Article 5(7), which deals with claims for remuneration for the salvage of cargo or freight, but not ships. It provides that such claims may be brought in the court under whose authority the cargo or freight (a) has been arrested or (b) could have been arrested, but bail or other security has been given. The reason why this very narrow head of jurisdiction is included in the Regulation is explained below.

Conventions on particular matters. The question of Admiralty jurisdiction **S13–026** *in rem* was discussed in the negotiations preceding the United Kingdom's accession to the 1968 Convention. The solution adopted was to rely on Article 57 of the 1968 Convention, as interpreted and expanded by Article 25(2) of the 1978 Accession Convention. Following the 1989 Accession Convention, Article 57 was amended and consolidated; the equivalent provision of the Judgments Regulation, Article 71, reproduces this amended and consolidated version.[82] Article 71 of the Regulation (and

---

[79] [1990] 1 Q.B. 361 (C.A.).
[80] [1998] A.C. 878.
[81] See Rule 28(8), *supra*.
[82] The differences between the relevant provisions of Art. 71 of the Regulation, Art. 57 of the 1968 Convention (as amended) and Art. 57 of the Lugano Convention are only verbal.

Article 57 of each Convention) deals with conventions on "particular matters" to which Regulation States (and Contracting States to the 1968 and Lugano Conventions) are, or will become, parties; it provides that the operation of such conventions will not be affected by the Regulation (or by the 1968 and Lugano Conventions). Conventions on particular matters are conventions which fall within the general scope of the Regulation (and the 1968 and Lugano Conventions) because they deal with jurisdiction or the enforcements of judgments, but which concern only particular issues (by contrast with the Regulation and the 1968 and Lugano Conventions, which deal with these matters in a general way).[83] Conventions dealing specifically with Admiralty actions *in rem* fall into this category.

S13–027   Article 71(2)(a) of the Regulation (and Article 57(2)(a) of the 1968 Convention and Article 57(2) of the Lugano Convention) makes clear that a court of a Regulation State (or Contracting State) which is a party to a convention on a particular matter may assume jurisdiction in accordance with that convention, even if the defendant is domiciled in another Regulation State (or in a Contracting State to the 1968 or Lugano Convention) and that State is not a party to the convention on a particular matter.[84] Moreover, it is not necessary for the claimant to be domiciled in, or a national of, a Regulation State (or Contracting State), nor is it necessary—unless this is required by the convention on a particular matter—for him to be domiciled in, or a national of, a State party to the convention on a particular matter.[85] A judgment given by an English court in these circumstances must be recognised by all Regulation States (and the Contracting States to the 1968 and Lugano Conventions), even if such State is not a party to the convention on a particular matter.[86]

S13–028   This means that if the United Kingdom is a party to a convention on a particular matter, and if an English court assumes jurisdiction in a claim *in rem* in accordance with the provisions of that convention, the bar imposed by Article 3 of the Regulation and the 1968 and Lugano Conventions is lifted. Where there is conflict between provisions, the jurisdictional provisions of a convention on a particular matter prevail over those contained in the Judgments Regulation, the 1968 Convention or the Lugano Convention (as the case may be); and there is no reason for thinking that the convention on a particular matter should be interpreted narrowly in order that it should impinge as little as possible on the Judgments Regulation, the 1968 Convention or the Lugano Convention.[87] Article 71 of the Regulation (and Article 57 of the 1968 and Lugano Conventions) does not, however, make the convention on a particular matter part of English law, nor does it positively grant jurisdiction to the English court.[88] It is not necessary that

---

[83] For a list, which is not necessarily complete, see Schlosser [1979] O.J. C59/71, para. 238, n. 59.
[84] Art. 26 of the Regulation and Art. 20 of the Conventions must nevertheless be applied. Each provision requires the court in certain cases to declare of its own motion that it has no jurisdiction; it also makes provision for the defendant to be served in sufficient time to enable him to arrange for his defence.
[85] *The Po* [1991] 2 Lloyd's Rep. 206 (C.A.).
[86] Art. 71(2)(b) of the Judgments Regulation; Art. 57(2)(b) of the 1968 Convention. For the Lugano Convention, see Art. 57(3); but see Art. 57(4), which provides that a Contracting State need not enforce such a judgment against a person domiciled in its territory if that state is not a party to the convention on a particular matter. See also Art. 57(5) of the Lugano Convention.
[87] *The Anna H* [1995] 1 Lloyd's Rep. 11 (C.A.).
[88] *The Po* [1991] 2 Lloyd's Rep. 206 (C.A.).

United Kingdom legislation should expressly provide that the convention on a particular matter is to have force of law in England,[89] but, if it does not, the English court must have jurisdiction under some other provision of English law. In other words, the requirements of Rule 33(1) must be satisfied, in addition to those of the convention on a particular matter.

Two conventions on particular matters need to be considered. The first is **S13–029** the Brussels Arrest Convention of 1952.[90] This provides that a ship flying the flag of a Contracting State (to the Arrest Convention) may be arrested for a "maritime claim", but not for any other claim[91]; a ship flying a flag of a non-Contracting State, on the other hand, may be arrested for a maritime claim or for any other claim for which it may be arrested under the law of the Contracting State in which the arrest takes place.[92] The Convention then provides that the courts of the country where the arrest took place will have jurisdiction to hear the claim if they have such jurisdiction under their domestic law.[93] This means that, in the case of a ship flying the flag of a Contracting State, the court has jurisdiction only with regard to a "maritime claim". This is defined in the Convention[94]: the definition covers largely the same ground as section 20 of the Supreme Court Act 1981, but is not identical to it.

The result is that, where the English court has jurisdiction under Rule **S13–030** 33(1), it will normally have jurisdiction under the Arrest Convention. There are, however, two important exceptions. The first results from the fact that the Arrest Convention provides for the arrest only of ships; consequently, it grants jurisdiction *in rem* only against ships. Section 20 of the Supreme Court Act 1981, on the other hand, makes provision for claims *in rem* against certain other kinds of property. One such case is a salvage action against cargo or freight. Article 5(7) of the 1968 Convention (and later the Lugano Convention and the Judgments Regulation) was adopted to allow such a claim.

The second exception is that the Arrest Convention grants jurisdiction **S13–031** only when the ship has been arrested. It is not sufficient that the ship *could have been* arrested, but was not (because security was given).[95] Once the ship has been arrested within the jurisdiction of the English court, the court will not lose its jurisdiction if the ship is then released.[96] It is, therefore, necessary both to serve the process on the ship (to fulfil the requirements of English law) and to arrest it (to fulfil the requirements of the Arrest

---

[89] *ibid.*

[90] The International Convention Relating to the Arrest of Seagoing Ships, signed in Brussels on May 10, 1952. The text is set out in Cmnd. 8954 (1953) and in Singh, *International Maritime Law Conventions* (1983), Vol. 4, pp. 3101–3107. It has been recognised as being a "convention on a particular matter" in terms of Art. 57: Schlosser [1979] O.J. C59/71, para. 238, n. 59; *The Deichland* [1990] 1 Q.B. 361 (C.A.).

[91] Art. 2.

[92] Art. 8(2).

[93] Art. 7(1). For the meaning of domestic law see *The Anna H* [1995] 1 Lloyd's Rep. 11 (C.A.). This also gives additional grounds of jurisdiction, but, since Art. 7(1) as a whole applies only if the ship has been arrested, and the jurisdictional requirements of English law must in any event be satisfied, these additional grounds appear to be of little relevance.

[94] Art. 1(1).

[95] *The Deichland* [1990] 1 Q.B. 361 (C.A.). The court will, however, have jurisdiction *in personam* over the defendant if he voluntarily submits to its jurisdiction, for example by giving bail to prevent the ship's arrest or by acknowledging the issue of the claim form. See *The Prinsengracht* [1993] 1 Lloyd's Rep. 41.

[96] *The Anna H* [1995] 1 Lloyd's Rep. 11 (C.A.).

Convention).[97] Once this has been done, security may be accepted for its release. The court is able to claim jurisdiction under the Arrest Convention even if the defendant has put up security for the claim prior to the arrest and the ship is released immediately afterwards.[98] Although the Arrest Convention defines arrest as "the detention of a ship by judicial process to secure a maritime claim",[99] it has been held that to qualify as an arrest for the purposes of the Convention all that is required is that the legal consequence of judicial detention of the ship is that it becomes security for a maritime claim; there is no requirement that the claimant's motive for the arrest should be to obtain security.[1]

S13–032   The second convention is the Brussels Collision Convention,[2] which concerns claims for collision between seagoing vessels or between seagoing vessels and inland navigation craft.[3] Article 1(1) confers jurisdiction in such claims on (a) the court where the defendant has his habitual residence or a place of business; (b) the court of the place where arrest has been effected of the defendant ship or of any other ship belonging to the defendant which can lawfully be arrested, or where arrest could have been effected and bail or other security has been furnished; or (c) the court of the place of collision when the collision has occurred within the limits of a port or in inland waters.[4] The most important of these grounds is that set out in Article 1(1)(b). To some extent it covers the same ground as the Arrest Convention.[5] However, it goes further in one important respect: it is sufficient if arrest could have been effected and bail or other security was furnished. This means that in collision cases the arrest of the defendant vessel is not essential.[6]

S13–033 **Jurisdictional issues not regulated by conventions on particular matters.** Although it is provided that the operation of conventions on particular matters is not to be affected either by the Judgments Regulation or by the 1968 and Lugano Conventions,[7] this principle was glossed by the European Court in *The Tatry*.[8] The European Court ruled that the

---

[97] If the defendant submits to the jurisdiction of the English court in terms of Art. 23 of the Judgments Regulation or Art. 17 of the 1968 and Lugano Conventions (jurisdiction agreements) or Art. 24 of the Regulation or Art. 18 of the 1968 and Lugano Conventions (defending on the merits) arrest will not of course be necessary.

[98] *The Anna H* [1995] 1 Lloyd's Rep. 11 (C.A.).

[99] Art. 1(2).

[1] *The Anna H, supra.*

[2] International Convention on Certain Rules Concerning Civil Jurisdiction in Matters of Collision, May 10, 1952. The text is set out in Cmnd. 8954 (1953). This has been recognised as a convention on a particular matter: Schlosser [1979] O.J. C59/71, para. 238, n. 59; *The Po* [1991] 2 Lloyd's Rep. 206 (C.A.).

[3] It also concerns certain other actions: see Art. 4.

[4] At first sight, Art. 8 might be thought to limit the application of the Collision Convention to cases where all the vessels concerned fly the flag of a Contracting State, but this view was rejected by the Court of Appeal in *The Po, supra*, where it was held that the action before the court was covered by the Collision Convention, even though the plaintiff's vessels flew the flag of a non-Contracting State. The correct interpretation of Art. 8 may perhaps be that it does no more than preclude additional grounds of jurisdiction where the vessels concerned fly the flag of a Contracting State.

[5] See Art. 1(1)(a) and Art. 7(1) of the Arrest Convention.

[6] *The Po, supra.*

[7] Judgments Regulation, Art. 71(1); Civil Jurisdiction and Judgments Act 1982, Sched. 1, Art. 57(1); Sched. 3C, Art. 57(1).

[8] Case C–406/92 [1994] E.C.R. I–5439; [1999] Q.B. 515.

provisions of a convention on a particular matter prevail over the 1968 Convention only to the extent that there is a conflict; in a case where a specific jurisdictional issue was not covered by a convention on a particular matter the provisions of the 1968 Convention continued to apply. So, even where the court has obtained jurisdiction *in rem* by virtue of an arrest under the Arrest Convention, Articles 27 and 28 of the Judgments Regulation are applicable if there are concurrent proceedings in another Regulation State. This is because the Arrest Convention does not contain provisions dealing with *lis pendens* or related actions.

The European Court's decision in *The Tatry* was distinguished in *The Bergen*,[9] a case in which the defendant challenged the court's jurisdiction *in rem* on the basis that the parties had agreed to the exclusive jurisdiction of the German courts. The defendant argued that, since the Arrest Convention was silent as to the effect of a jurisdiction agreement, the case was governed by Article 17 of the 1968 Convention,[10] according to which the English court had no jurisdiction. Clarke J. distinguished *The Tatry* on the ground that Article 17 (which has the effect of depriving all courts other than those chosen of the jurisdiction which they otherwise would have had) is different from Article 21[11] (which does not deprive courts of jurisdiction but merely requires them not to exercise it); if the court were required to give effect to Article 17 it would have been deprived of jurisdiction under the Arrest Convention, something expressly excluded by Article 57 of the 1968 Convention.[12] **S13–034**

Defendant domiciled in Scotland or Northern Ireland. As was said above, Article 2 of the Regulation (and of the 1968 and Lugano Conventions) confers jurisdiction on the courts of the Regulation State (or Contracting State) in which the defendant is domiciled; consequently, if the defendant is domiciled in the United Kingdom, the courts of the United Kingdom have jurisdiction in terms of the Regulation. It is provided by section 16 of the Civil Jurisdiction and Judgments Act 1982 that, where the defendant is domiciled in the United Kingdom, the provisions of Schedule 4[13] determine whether the courts of any part of the United Kingdom have jurisdiction in any given case. However, paragraph 6(a) of Schedule 5 (read with section 17) provides that Schedule 4 does not apply to proceedings brought in pursuance of a statutory provision which implements a convention on a particular matter or which makes provision with respect to jurisdiction in any field to which the convention relates. Under paragraph 6(b), the same applies to proceedings brought in pursuance of a rule of law which has the effect of implementing such a convention. If one regards the "field" to which the Brussels Arrest Convention relates as being Admiralty claims *in rem*, such claims would seem to be exempt from the requirements of **S13–035**

---

[9] [1997] 1 Lloyd's Rep. 380.
[10] The equivalent of Art. 23 of the Judgments Regulation.
[11] The equivalent of Art. 27 of the Judgments Regulation.
[12] The proceedings were subsequently stayed under the court's inherent jurisdiction: *The Bergen (No. 2)* [1997] 2 Lloyd's Rep. 710.
[13] As substituted by S.I. 2001 No. 3929, Sched. 2.

Schedule 4.[14] It would seem therefore that, as long as the defendant is domiciled in some part of the United Kingdom, compliance with Rule 33(1) is all that is requried.

---

[14] The statutory provision would be s. 20 of the Supreme Court Act 1981 together with such other statutory provisions as may be relevant. Common law rules which have the effect of implementing the Arrest Convention would be covered by para. 6(b). If the "field" to which the Convention relates is regarded as being restricted to claims *in rem* against ships, proceedings in which the *res* is something other than a ship would have to comply with the requirments of Sched. 4. In salvage cases, Rule 3(g) of Sched. 4 would be relevant; in other cases, Rule 3(h)(ii) might possibly be applicable.

CHAPTER 14

FOREIGN JUDGMENTS

NOTE 1. See also Barnett, *Res Judicata, Estoppel, and Foreign Judgments* (2001).

Add at end: With effect from March 1, 2002 the provisions of the 1968 **14–013** Convention will be substantially superseded by Chapter III of Council Regulation (E.C.) 44/2001 ([2001] O.J. L12, January 16, 2001; reproduced in Part I of the appendix to this Supplement) ("the Judgments Regulation" or "the Regulation"), which will become the principal vehicle for the recognition and enforcement of judgments given in civil or commercial matters by courts in the Member States of the European Union. The Judgments Regulation applies to judgments from all Member States except Denmark (judgments from which will continue to take effect under the 1968 Convention). The Member States to which it applies are referred to in this Supplement as "Regulation States". The Lugano Convention will continue to apply to judgments from Iceland, Norway, Poland and Switzerland. The basic structure of Chapter III of the Judgments Regulation is very similar to the corresponding provisions of the 1968 and Lugano Conventions, except that the procedure for obtaining an order for the registration of the judgment has been streamlined, the grounds of objection which may be taken in an appeal against such registration are reduced in number and scope, and the Articles have been re-numbered. For the purposes of explanation, reference to the 1968 Convention, and to the cases decided under it, will be required for some years to come. But as Article 66(2) of the Judgments Regulation provides that Chapter III of the Regulation applies to judgments given by the courts of Member States on or after March 1, 2002, and is not restricted to judgments given in proceedings which were instituted before the courts of a Regulation State after that date (unless the original proceedings were instituted before the entry into force of the 1968 or Lugano Convention in the Regulation State of origin), it will in effect furnish the basis for the enforcement of judgments from other Member States with effect from March 1, 2002.

The third section of this Chapter, as amended in this Supplement, deals **14–017** also with recognition and enforcement under Chapter III of the Judgments Regulation.

2. ENFORCEMENT AND RECOGNITION AT COMMON LAW

A. Enforcement and Recognition

On the finality of default judgments, see also *Schnabel v. Lui* [2002] **14–021** NSWSC 15. The court applied a test derived from *Ainslie v. Ainslie* (1927) 39 C.L.R. 381 and asked whether the default judgment was "entirely floating as a determination, enforceable only as expressly provided and in the course of that enforcement subject to revision" or was "given the effect of finality unless subsequently altered". Deciding that the American judgment in question fell into the latter category, it was to be regarded as final for the purposes of its enforcement in New South Wales. See further *Lewis v. Eliades* [2003] EWHC 368 (QB), [2003] 1 All E.R. (Comm.) 850.

14–025 NOTE 99. Ord. 11, r. 1(1)(*m*) is replaced by CPR, r. 6.20(9).

14–027 If the foreign judgment was given in default of appearance, with the result that it is not possible to tell what was the precise basis upon which the judgment creditor succeeded, no estoppel will arise from the individual allegations made in the pleading: *Masters v. Leaver* [2000] I.L.Pr. 387 (C.A.); see also *Baker v. Ian McCall International Ltd.* [2000] C.L.C. 189.

14–029 NOTE 10. On the identity of parties in relation to Article 21 of the 1968 Convention, and its relationship to the principles of *res judicata*, see Handley (2000) 116 L.Q.R. 191, commenting on Case C–351/96 *Drouot Assurances S.A. v. Consolidated Metallurgical Industries* [1998] E.C.R. I–3075.

There is no reason to suppose that the interpretation of Art. 27 of the Judgments Regulation will be materially different.

14–032 NOTE 22. The current reference to Clerk & Lindsell, *Torts*, is to the 18th ed., 2000, at para. 4–112 (but no authority is cited for the proposition).

14E–044 Add to the provisions listed: (4) Chapter III of Council Regulation (E.C.) 44/2001.

14–045 Text to note 56. There is no reason to suppose that the position is any different when the judgment is one to which Chapter III of the Judgments Regulation applies; and it follows that the fact that a judgment which may be enforced under those provisions serves to preclude the possibility of suing at common law on the original underlying cause of action.

B. Jurisdiction of Foreign Courts at Common Law

14–062 First paragraph. But where the defendant seeks to enter an appearance, but fails to take the necessary procedural steps to do so (with the result that judgment is entered in default of appearance), the attempt to appear will not constitute submission by appearance: *De Santis v. Russo* [2002] 2 Qd. R. 230 (C.A.).

14–063 NOTE 29. The decision in *Henry v. Geoprosco International* [1976] Q.B. 726 (C.A.) was not applied by the High Court of Singapore, with the result that a party who appeared before a foreign court to argue that the proceedings should be stayed for arbitration was not taken to have submitted to the adjudicatory jurisdiction of that court: *WSG Nimbus v. Board of Control for Cricket in Sri Lanka* [2002] 3 Sing. L.R. 603 (H.C.).

14–064 Likewise, if he issues a motion to challenge the jurisdiction of the foreign court, but then fails to have the application heard and determined, he will be taken to have waived his challenge and to have submitted by virtue of appearance: *Starlight International Inc. v. Bruce* [2002] H.C. 374 (Ch), [2002] I.L.Pr. 617.

Order 11, r. 1(1) is replaced by CPR, r. 6.20.   **14–080**

Order 11, r. 1(1) is replaced by CPR, r. 6.20.   **14–081**

Order 11, r. 1(1) is replaced by CPR, r. 6.20.   **14–082**

NOTE 10. Add at end: See also *Old North State Brewing Co. v. Newlands* **14–084** *Services Inc.* [1999] 4 W.W.R. 573 (B.C.C.A.) and *Braintech Inc. v. Kostiuk* (1999) 171 D.L.R. (4th.) 46 (B.C.C.A.), where it was held that American judgments were, in principle, entitled to recognition on the basis of *Morguard*, but (in the latter case) did not meet the standard of a real and substantial connection if the only connection with Texas was the passive posting of material on an internet noticeboard.

Section 32(4) of the 1982 Act is equally inapplicable where the judgment **14–092** falls for recognition and enforcement under the Judgments Regulation: S.I. 2001 No. 3929, Sched. 2, para. 14.

NOTE 40. The question of the exclusion of arbitration arises equally in **14–094** relation to judgments to be recognised under the Judgments Regulation.

Delete the present text and replace with: There is a rule similar to Rule 42 **14–121** under the 1920 Act and the 1933 Act: see 1920 Act, section 9(2)(a) and 1933 Act, section 4(1)(*a*)(ii) and section 8. But where the recognition falls under Chapter III of the Judgments Regulation, the right of the English court to examine the jurisdiction exercised by a court of another Member State is very limited; an identical approach is taken under the 1968 and Lugano Conventions. Under Part II of the 1982 Act the English court has no power to examine the jurisdiction of the Scottish, Northern Irish (or Gibraltar) court: see paras. 14–201 and 14–231.

NOTE 28. Add: *Habib Bank Ltd. v. Ahmed* [2001] EWCA Civ. 1270; [2002] 1 **14R–127** Lloyd's Rep. 444 (C.A.).

NOTES 30 and 31. The proposition that an English judgment may not be set **14–128** aside by an English court on the ground of fraud unless the evidence relied on could not, even had reasonable diligence been exercised, have been adduced at trial, was disapproved by the New South Wales Court of Appeal in *Toubia v. Schwenke* [2002] NSWCA 34, (2002) 54 N.S.W.L.R. 46.

NOTE 38. Add at end: In *Beals v. Saldanha* (2001) 202 D.L.R. (4th) 630 **14–129** (Ont. C.A.) the Ontario Court of Appeal held that the requirement of newly discovered facts were required to impeach a foreign (*in casu*, Florida) judgment for fraud in the same way as would be required in relation to a local judgment. The case contains a detailed analysis of the law on jurisdictional competence, fraud, and breaches of natural justice. An appeal to the Supreme Court of Canada is pending.

14–130 In *Ki Won Yoon v. Young Dung Song* (2000) 158 F.L.R. 295 the Federal Court of Australia considered that *Keele v. Findley* (1991) 21 N.S.W.L.R. 444 was wrongly decided, and applied instead the English approach to judgments alleged to have been obtained by fraud. By contrast, the Singapore Court of Appeal has followed the approach in *Keele v. Findley: Hong Pian Tee v. Les Placements Germain Gauthier Inc.* [2002] 2 Sing. L.R. (C.A.). For a general survey of the fraud defence, see Garnett (2002) 1 J. Int. Comm. L. 1.

NOTE 42. See also *Commercial Innovation Bank Alfa Bank v. Kozeny* [2002] UKPC 66 (P.C.).

14–135 First sentence. Fraud, as defined by the common law, is not a ground to refuse to recognise or enforce a judgment under the Judgments Regulation, any more than it was under the 1968 and Lugano Conventions, because none of these instruments makes provision for a defence of fraud.

14–142 It is likely that this ground of objection to recognition and enforcement will increase in significance in the light of the Human Rights Act 1998. The European Court of Human Rights has considered on two occasions whether a court, called upon to recognise a judgment from the courts of a state not party to the European Convention of Human Rights, is entitled or bound to deny recognition if the proceedings in the adjudicating court fell short of the standards required for proceedings in the courts of a Contracting State to that Convention. In *Drozd & Janousek v. France and Spain* (1992) 14 E.H.R.R. 745, it was held that a court in a Member State was not precluded from recognising a judgment from the courts of a non-contracting state (Andorra) even though the proceedings before the Andorran court were alleged to lack the quality of a fair trial as guaranted by Art. 6 of the European Convention on Human Rights. By contrast, in *Pellegrini v. Italy*, (2002) 35 E.H.R.R. 44, it was held that an Italian court violated Article 6, when it failed to refuse recognition to a judgment from the courts of a non-contracting state (Vatican) which had been obtained in proceedings which fell far short of a fair trial. The earlier case was not referred to in the later one.

It is probably misleading to regard this objection to the recognition of foreign judgments as an example of public policy, for any such obligation to withhold recognition is a statutory one, deriving directly from Human Rights Act 1998. But within the context of judgments sought to be recognised under the Judgments Regulation (see *infra*, Rule 48), the impact of the European Convention has to be accommodated under the rubric of public policy, for there is no separate right for a member state bound by the Regulation to withhold recognition on a ground not expressly mentioned in the Regulation.

14–144 The narrowness of the public policy defence to recognition was reaffirmed by the Ontario Court of Appeal in *Society of Lloyd's v. Meinzer* (2002) 210 D.L.R. (4th) 519 (Ont. C.A.): it was restricted to cases which affected the essential principles of justice or moral interests in the registering court (the decision was one on the 1933 Act).

14–145 The proposition in the first sentence was approved by the High Court of Singapore in *WSG Nimbus Pte. Ltd. v. Board of Control for Cricket in Sri Lanka* [2002] 3 Sing. L.R. 603 (H.C.). But it may require further refinement as a matter of English law if it is considered that the automatic refusal to recognise a judgment in such circumstances is disproportionate to the contempt, and accordingly a violation of Art. 6 of the European Convention on Human Rights. *Cf. Krombach v. France*, February 13, 2001 (E.Ct.H.R.).

NOTE 96. The position under the Judgments Regulation will be the same.

NOTE 98. To this effect also *Old North State Brewing Co. v. Newlands Services Inc.* [1999] 4 W.W.R. 573 (B.C.C.A.).

But in *Kidron v. Green* (2000) 48 O.R. (3d) 775 (Ont.) the court refused to **14–146** grant summary judgment in proceedings to enforce the judgment of a Californian court which had awarded a sum of U.S.$15 million for "emotional distress" on the footing that this arguably raised a question of Canadian public policy (which limits such awards from its own courts to a far smaller sum), and which needed to be resolved by trial of an issue. See also *Schnabel v. Lui* [2002] NSWSC 15 (damages of four times the amount claimed ordered to be paid to claimant in American proceedings held to have been imposed to punish the defendant for his disobedience to court orders regarded as penal, and not recoverable in action on the judgment in New South Wales, even though awarded in favour of claimant personally. The judgment was severed in line with *Raulin v. Fischer* [1911] 2 K.B. 93).

Sixth sentence. The effect of Article 34(1) of the Judgments Regulation is **14–147** that recognition of a judgment from a Regulation State in a civil or commercial matter must be refused if the recognition would be manifestly contrary to public policy in the state addressed: the 1968 and Lugano Conventions contained (Article 27) a similar rule, though without the word "manifestly", which seems to add little.

And see also *Boele v. Norsemeter Holding A/S* [2002] N.S.W.L.R. 363, **14–151** (failure to warn of appeal against judgment).

Text to note 18. It was held in *Masters v. Leaver* [2000] I.L.Pr. 387 (C.A.) that where a judgment set out the procedure for obtaining an assessment of quantum of damages, but then did not follow it, there had been a denial of substantial justice, and one which did not necessarily require to be raised before the foreign court. But in *Minmetals Germany GmbH. v. Fercosteel Ltd.* [1999] C.L.C. 647 (a case on the setting aside of an arbitrators' award) it was held that it was not possible to invoke public policy to point to alleged procedural errors which had already been considered by the supervising court.

Cf. Masters v. Leaver [2000] I.L.Pr. 387 (C.A.). **14–154**

Delete the paragraph in the main work and replace with: The effect of **14–156** Article 34(2) of the Judgments Regulation is that judgments in default of appearance, falling within the scope of the Regulation, will not be entitled to recognition, and may not be enforced, in the United Kingdom if the defendant was not served with the document which instituted the proceedings or with an equivalent document in sufficient time and in such a way as to enable him to arrange for his defence. But if he had the possibility of commencing proceedings to challenge the judgment, yet failed to do so, he will have lost his shield and the judgment will be recognised after all.

Article 34(2) therefore differs in two respects from its predecessor, Article 27(2) of the 1968 and Lugano Conventions. These required that the defendant be "duly" served (it being unclear whether this textual alteration was intended to be of significance), and contained no provision concerning the defendant's failure to take steps to challenge the judgment once he knew about it: see *infra*, para. S14–210. Lack of notice or service, or failure to observe the rules of natural justice, are not grounds for refusal to recognise or enforce Scottish and Northern Irish judgments under Part II of the 1982 Act: main work, para. 14–231.

3. ENFORCEMENT AND RECOGNISITION UNDER STATUTE

14–162 NOTE 62. R.S.C. Ord. 71 is replaced by CPR Part 74; and the corresponding provisions are CPR rr. 74.3 (applications), 4 (evidence in support), and 6 (registration orders); the document which must be served on the judgment debtor is the order granting permission to register the judgment: CPR r. 74.6(1).

14–170 In relation to Austria, Belgium, France, Germany, Italy, Netherlands (Member States of the European Union), the Judgments Regulation provides, in relation to judgments given on or after March 1, 2002, the principal vehicle for recognition and enforcement of judgments. For the precise details of its operation, including the transitional arrangements, see further *infra*, the replacement text for paras. 14R–183 *et seq*.

14–172 NOTE 20. In deciding whether the judgment is that of a recognised court, the English court is entitled to receive expert evidence relating to the foreign court: *Habib Bank Ltd v. Ahmed* [2001] EWCA Civ. 1270; [2002] 1 Lloyd's Rep. 444 (C.A.).

14–173 NOTE 24. See *Habib Bank Ltd v. Ahmed, supra*.

NOTE 26. CPR, Sched. R.S.C. Ord. 71 is superseded by CPR Part 74, which does not deal specifically with this point. See now *Civil Procedure*, 2003, Vol. 1, para. 74.11.9.

14–174 NOTE 28. R.S.C. Ord. 71 is replaced by CPR Part 74; and the corresponding provisions are CPR rr. 74.3 (applications), 4 (evidence in support), and 6 (registration orders); the document which must be served on the judgment debtor is the order granting permission to register the judgment: CPR, r. 74.6(1).

14–177 NOTE 45. R.S.C. Ord. 71 is replaced by CPR Part 74. The provision governing applications to set aside orders for registration is CPR, r. 74.7; the practice is unlikely to have been substantially altered.

14–179 NOTE 54. Appeals are now governed by CPR, r. 74.7, but which does not specifically prescribe the evidence which is required.

14–180 NOTE 55. The same is true under the Judgments Regulation.

14R–183 Delete Rule 48 and Comment and Illustrations in main work and replace with:

(3) Schedule 1 to the Civil Jurisdiction and Judgments Order 2001, and Part 1 of the Civil Jurisdiction and Judgments Act 1982[1]

Rule 48—A judgment given by a court in a State to which Council Regulation (E.C.) 44/2001 applies, or which is a party to the Brussels or Lugano Conventions on jurisdiction and the recognition and enforcement of judgments in civil and commercial matters, and which falls within the scope of the relevant instrument has, on registration in the appropriate court[2] in the United Kingdom, the same force and effect as a judgment of the court in which it is registered, and proceedings for or with respect to its enforcement may be taken, as if the judgment had been originally given by the registering court.[3]   S14R–183

Comment

Introduction. The jurisdictional provisions of Council Regulation (E.C.) 44/2001[4] (the "Judgments Regulation"), and of the 1968 Convention and the Lugano Convention, have been fully discussed in Chapter 11, and Rule 48 states the essence of the judgment enforcement aspects of the Judgments Regulation and the Conventions. These are set out in Chapter III of the Regulation (and Title III of the Conventions), as supplemented by Schedule 1, para. 1 of the Civil Jurisdiction and Judgments Order 2001 (S.I. 2001 No. 3929), and section 4 of the 1982 Act, respectively, and the Civil Procedure Rules.[5] The substantive provisions of the Regulation and the Conventions, dealing with recognition and enforcement of judgments, are broadly similar, but in practice it will be the Regulation, rather than the Conventions, which represents the principal vehicle for the recognition and enforcement of judgments from European states. The Comment to this Rule will therefore deal with the provisions of the Regulation, while noting points of textual divergence between it and the corresponding provisions of the Conventions.   S14–184

Recognition and enforcement under all three instruments is restricted to judgments in civil and commercial matters. The Regulation will apply to the recognition of judgments given on or after March 1, 2002 by courts in the Member States of the European Union, excluding Denmark[6] ("the Regulation States"). But it will also apply to judgments from the courts of a Regulation State which were given before March 1, 2002 if when the   S14–185

---

[1] Collins, pp. 105–125; Hartley, pp. 82–100; Anton, *Civil Jurisdiction*, pp. 128–155; Briggs & Rees, Chap. 7; Kaye, Pt. 8; O'Malley and Layton, Chaps. 26 to 30. For the States to which it applies, see the entry under paras. 11–006—11–007 in this Supplement.
[2] The High Court in England; the Court of Session in Scotland; the High Court in Northern Ireland: Article 39 of, and Annex II to, the Regulation; and Civil Jurisdiction and Judgments Order 2001 (S.I. 2001 No. 3929), Sched. 1, para. 2. (In relation to the Brussels and Lugano Conventions, see 1968 Convention, Art. 32; Lugano Convention, Art. 32, in 1982 Act, Scheds. 1 and 3C), and 1982 Act, s.4(l)).
[3] S.I. 2001 No. 3929, Sched. 1, para. 2(2); in relation to the Conventions, see 1982 Act, s. 4(3). For the recognition of such judgments without the need for registration, see *infra*, para. S14–221.
[4] [2001] O.J. L12, January 16, 2001. The text is reproduced in Part I of the appendix to this Supplement.
[5] CPR, Pt 74.
[6] Art. 1 of the Regulation.

proceedings were instituted, the adjudicating and recognising state were both Contracting States to the 1968 Convention or Lugano Convention. Judgments from the courts of Denmark will continue to be recognised and enforced under the provisions of the 1968 Convention; those from the courts of Iceland, Norway, Poland and Switzerland will be recognised and enforced under the provisions of the Lugano Convention if the judgment falls within the temporal scope of the respective Convention.

S14–186 The most notable features of enforcement under the Judgments Regulation, and in which respect it and the Conventions differ from the regime established by the common law and the 1920 and 1933 Acts, are that enforcement under the Regulation or Conventions is not limited to money judgments, or to final judgments, and that in principle (but subject to certain limitations) the court in which enforcement is sought is not entitled to investigate the jurisdiction of the court which gave the judgment. It is also important to note that the effect of the Regulation or Conventions is that the enforcement procedures apply to all judgments within their scope, whether or not they are against persons domiciled in a Regulation State or Contracting State. Thus an English default judgment against a New York resident in a case where the jurisdiction of the English court was based on the temporary presence of the defendant in England will be enforceable in France; and a French judgment against a New York resident in a case where the jurisdiction of the French court was based on the French nationality of the plaintiff under Article 14 of the Civil Code will be enforceable in England. Article 59 of the 1968 and Lugano Conventions allowed a Contracting State to assume in relation to a non-Contracting State the obligation not to recognise judgments given in other Contracting States against defendants domiciled or habitually resident in the non-Contracting State where the basis of jurisdiction could only be one of the "exorbitant" bases of jurisdiction set out in Article 3(2) of the Conventions[7] (which include the jurisdiction in England based on temporary presence and the jurisdiction in France based on nationality). Such bilateral treaties were negotiated by the United Kingdom with Australia[8] and with Canada.[9] These remain effective where recognition is governed by the Judgments Regulation,[10] but there is no provision for such bilateral treaties to be negotiated in the future.[11]

S14–187 **Judgments.** Article 32 of the Judgments Regulation[12] provides that "judgment" means any judgment given by a court or tribunal of a Regulation State, whatever the judgment may be called, including a decree, order, decision, or writ of execution, as well as the determination of costs by an officer of the court.[13] It does not include judicially approved settlements, but

---

[7] In the Regulation, set out in Annex I.

[8] S.I. 1994 No. 1901.

[9] See para. 14–170, n. 2.

[10] Art. 72 of the Regulation.

[11] Competence in this respect now vests in the European Commission, not in the individual Member States. There were negotiations with the United States, but these were abandoned without success in 1980. Discussions have been underway for some years, under the auspices of the Hague Conference, for a Convention which would be open to signatories worldwide, but this has not yet resulted in the production of even a draft agreement.

[12] Art. 25 of the Conventions is identical.

[13] S.I. 2001 No. 3929, Sched. 1, para. 1(1) provides that "judgment" has the meaning given to it by Article 32 of the Regulation. For maintenance orders see Rule 88.

does include judgments by consent.[14] The expression includes not only judgments ordering the payment of money,[15] orders for costs[16] and for interest,[17] but also non-money judgments and judgments which are not final and which are interlocutory or provisional in nature.[18] This is because there is no requirement that the judgment be "final and conclusive": it may be an interim order providing for periodical payments or a provisional order freezing assets.[19] It may be an order made under Article 31 of the Regulation,[20] made by a court which has no jurisdiction over the substance of the case, provided that it is properly to be seen as a provisional, including protective, measure,[21] and that is not granted *ex parte* and intended to be executed without notice.[22] Thus, for example, the English court may be required to enforce German injunctions. But the mode of enforcement (*e.g.* sequestration or committal) will in principle be a matter for English law,[23] which will determine the procedural requirements (such as the endorsement of a penal notice on the order) and also the extent of the court's discretion to commit or fine.

It is obvious that a judgment must fall within the scope of the Regulation **S14–188** or Convention if it is to fall within Chapter III or Title III, as the case may be, and qualify for recognition and enforcement under this Rule.[24] But these provisions do not extend to "judgments on judgments". Accordingly, a judgment from the courts of State A enforcing a judgment of State B

---

[14] *Landhurst Leasing plc v. Marcq* [1998] I.L.Pr. 822 (C.A.) (a case on the 1968 Convention). On the enforcement of authentic instruments and of settlements approved by courts in the course of proceedings, see Arts. 57 and 58 of the Regulation, *infra*, para. S14–223. For the distinction between court-approved settlements and judgments by consent see Case C–414/92 *Solo Kleinmotoren GmbH v. Boch* [1994] E.C.R. I–2237, 2255, and esp. at p. 2245, *per* Gulmann A.-G.

[15] Including the order to pay under the *"Zahlungsbefehl"* procedure of German law: Case 166/80 *Klomps v. Michel* [1981] E.C.R. 1593, and the order to pay made under the *"decreto ingiuntivo"* procedure of Italian law: Case C–474/93 *Firma Hengst Import BV v. Campese* [1995] E.C.R. I–2113.

[16] S.I. 2001 No. 3929, Sched. 1, para. 5 (1982 Act, s. 7; Scheds. 1 and 3C, Art. 25).

[17] S.I. 2001 No. 3929, Sched. 1, para. 5 (1982 Act, s. 7).

[18] *e.g. The Tjaskemolen (No. 2)* [1997] 2 Lloyd's Rep. 476, 478–479; *Normaco v. Lundman* [1999] I.L.Pr. 381.

[19] *Cf.* Case 143/78 *De Cavel v. De Cavel (No. 1)* [1979] E.C.R. 1055; Case 125/79 *Denilauler v. S.N.C. Couchet Frères* [1980] E.C.R. 1553; *Babanaft International Co. S.A. v. Bassatne* [1990] Ch. 13, 31 (C.A.); *cf.* Case 258/83 *Brennero v. Wendel GmbH* [1984] E.C.R. 3971; *The Atlantic Emperor (No. 2)* [1992] 1 Lloyd's Rep. 624 (C.A.); *Barren International Resorts Ltd. v. Martin*, 1994 S.L.T. 434.

[20] Art. 24 of the Conventions is identical.

[21] Case C–391/95 *Van Uden Maritime B.V. v. Deco-Line* [1998] E.C.R. I–7091; Case C–99/96 *Mietz v. Intership Yachting Sneek B.V.* [1999] E.C.R. I–2277.

[22] Case 125/79 *Denilauler v. S.N.C. Couchet Frères* [1980] E.C.R. 1553; *E.M.I. Records Ltd. v. Modern Music GmbH* [1992] Q.B. 115. But orders for discovery and the taking of evidence are not within its scope: see *CFEM Façades v. Bovis Construction S.A.* [1992] I.L.Pr. 561; see also Schlosser, paras. 184–187; Collins, p. 106.

[23] Schlosser, paras. 212–213; Collins, p. 116. For an illustration of the manner in which a German court enforced an English worldwide *Mareva* injunction (now called a freezing order), by making that German order which appeared to be closest in effect to the English order, see Zuckerman and Grunert, *Zeitschrift für Zivilprozess International*, 1996, 89.

[24] For the approach in cases where the judgment on a matter prima facie within the scope of the Regulation is closely connected to matters which are excluded from the scope of the Regulation, see Case 145/86 *Hoffmann v. Krieg* [1988] E.C.R. 645 (status); Case C–22/95 *Van Den Boogaard v. Laumen* [1997] E.C.R. I–1147 (status); Case C–267/97 *Coursier v. Fortis Bank S.A.* [1999] E.C.R. I–2543 (insolvency). For cases where the judgment was given between parties who had agreed to arbitrate their differences, see *infra*, paras. S14–189 *et seq.*

would not constitute a judgment within Article 32 of the Regulation.[25] A similar result is reached when the courts of Regulation State A enforce the judgment of a non-Regulation State, and the judgment creditor then seeks to enforce the "judgment" of State A under Chapter III of the Regulation in Regulation State B. The European Court held, in *Owens Bank Ltd. v. Bracco*,[26] that in such circumstances the judgment of State A falls outside the scope of the 1968 Convention altogether, presumably because the merits of the dispute will have been adjudicated upon by a judge in a non-Contracting State, and that such a decision falls outside the framework of mutual recognition established by the Convention. The effect of the Regulation will, in this respect, be identical.

S14–189 **Effect of exclusion of arbitration.** Article 1(2)(d) of the Regulation, like Article 1(4) of the Conventions, excludes "arbitration" from its scope. This exclusion has been considered earlier,[27] and in the present context arises in relation to the recognition or enforcement of judgments of Regulation States rendered in connection with disputes which the parties have agreed, or are alleged to have agreed, should be resolved exclusively by arbitration.

S14–190 It is clear from the Jenard Report[28] and the Schlosser Report[29] that the recognition and enforcement of arbitral awards will be outside the scope of the Regulation. It has been held that a French judgment making a French award enforceable was not entitled to enforcement under the 1968 Convention for that reason[30]; the same will certainly apply to the Regulation. There are two more controversial questions.

S14–191 The first is whether a judgment from the courts of a Regulation State, deciding that an alleged arbitration agreement is invalid or non-existent, is entitled to recognition in other Regulation States. The Schlosser Report[31] expressed the view that the effect of what is now Article 1(2)(d) of the Regulation was that a judgment determining whether an arbitration agreement was valid was not covered by the 1968 Convention. One of the questions referred to the European Court in *Marc Rich & Co. A.G. v. Soc. Italiana Impianti P.A.*[32] was whether the exclusion in Article 1(4) of the Convention applied to judgments where the initial existence of an arbitration agreement was in issue. Darmon A.-G.[33] was of the opinion that, where the main issue in a proceeding before a national court related to whether an

---

[25] Droz, para. 437; *cf.* 1982 Act, s. 18(7).

[26] Case C–129/92 [1994] E.C.R. 1–117; [1994] Q.B. 509; *Dubai Bank Ltd v. Abbas* [1998] I.L. Pr. 391.

[27] Main work, paras. 11–233 *et seq.* And see also (2001) 18 J. Arb. L. 13–39.

[28] p. 13, referred to with approval in Case C–190/89 *Marc Rich & Co. A.G. v. Soc. Italiana Impianti P.A.* [1991] E.C.R. I–3855, 3900.

[29] Para. 65(c), referred to with approval in Case C–391/95 *Van Uden Maritime B.V. v. Firma Deco-Line* [1998] E.C.R. I–7091, 7133.

[30] *A.B.C.I. v. Banque Franco-Tunisienne* [1996] 1 Lloyd's Rep. 495; affd. on other aspects [1997] 1 Lloyd's Rep. 531 (C.A.). See Hascher (1996) 12 Arb. Int. 233, who suggests that the decision is supportable on the basis that the French order was not in fact a judgment on the award, but simply an execution order.

[31] Para. 64(b). But the Evrigenis-Kerameus Report on the 1989 Accession Convention suggested (para. 35) that where a court, which is seised of proceedings brought in alleged violation of an arbitration agreement, decides on the validity of the arbitration agreement in the course of proceedings to contest its jurisdiction, the judgment on validity must be considered as falling within the scope of the 1968 Convention.

[32] Case C–190/89 [1991] E.C.R. I–3855.

[33] [1991] E.C.R. I–3855, at 3876, citing the Schlosser Report, and Kaye, p. 150.

arbitration agreement existed between the parties, the dispute did not fall within the 1968 Convention, since a dispute as to the existence of an arbitration agreement fell outside the scope of the Convention. The European Court did not rule expressly on this question: the actual ruling was the narrow one that the exclusion in Article 1(4) extended to litigation pending before a national court concerning the appointment of an arbitrator even if the existence or validity of the arbitration agreement was a preliminary issue in that litigation. But it did expressly reject the argument[34] that the exclusion in respect of arbitration did not apply where the existence or validity of an arbitration agreement was being disputed before different courts, regardless of whether the issue was raised as a main issue or preliminary one.[35]

In *The Heidberg*,[36] however, it was held that a decision of a French court **S14–192** that a bill of lading did not incorporate an arbitration clause was entitled to recognition in England, and that the exclusion for arbitration was irrelevant to the issue before the court. In coming to that conclusion, Judge Diamond Q.C. (sitting as a High Court judge) relied particularly on the opinions given by Professor Schlosser and M. Jenard on behalf of the Italian sellers in the *Marc Rich* case[37] and expressed the view that conflicts would be avoided if the decision of the court which had jurisdiction over the substantive dispute were entitled to recognition. He also relied on section 32(4)(a) of the Civil Jurisdiction and Judgments Act 1982[38]; that subsection provides that nothing in section 32(1) (the basic rule that a foreign judgment in breach of an arbitration agreement is not entitled to recognition or enforcement) "shall affect the recognition or enforcement in the United Kingdom of . . . a judgment which is required to be recognised or enforced" under the Conventions. He appears to have considered that the effect of the subsection was to make judgments rendered in breach of an arbitration agreement enforceable. But it is submitted that it is a wholly neutral provision, the only effect of which is to ensure that there is no conflict between the rule in section 32(1) and any possible contrary rule under the Conventions or the Regulation, without in any way pre-judging whether there is any such contrary rule. Moreover, this aspect of *The Heidberg* has since been judicially doubted in *The Ivan Zagubanski*.[39]

In *Phillip Alexander Securities and Futures Ltd. v. Bamberger*[40] Waller J. **S14–193** accepted the proposition that section 32(4)(a) was neutral and expressed "the strong inclination"[41] that a ruling of a foreign court on the validity of an arbitration agreement should not have to be recognised by the English

---

[34] By the Italian sellers, supported by the Commission.
[35] In *The Atlantic Emperor (No. 2)* [1992] 1 Lloyd's Rep. 624, 628 (C.A.) Neill L.J. said that the decision of the European Court gave no guidance on the question of the applicability of the exclusion where the challenge to the validity of the arbitration agreement constitutes the dispute. But for a contrary view see Hascher (1997) 13 Arb. Int. 33, 39–40. See also Audit (1993) 9 Arb. Int. 1; and (2001) 18 J. Arb. L. 13 (Beraudo) and 27 (van Haersolte-van Hof).
[36] [1994] 2 Lloyd's Rep. 287. See also *Toepfer International GmbH v. Molino Boschi S.r.l.* [1996] 1 Lloyd's Rep. 510.
[37] See para. 14–139. Darmon A.-G. said (at 3872) that Professor Schlosser "puts forward a view which in every aspect contradicts the official report signed by him concerning application of the Convention to disputes relating to arbitration before national courts".
[38] See para. 14–091.
[39] [2002] 1 Lloyd's Rep. 106.
[40] [1997] I.L. Pr. 73; affd. on other grounds *ibid.* 104 (C.A.).
[41] At 100. See also *The Xing Su Hai* [1995] 2 Lloyd's Rep. 15, 21 for the view that *The Heidberg, supra* was a "borderline case".

court. The Court of Appeal would have referred the question to the European Court had it been material, on the basis that the European Court had refrained from answering it when it had the opportunity of doing so in the *Marc Rich* case.

S14–194   It is suggested that, subject to the question of submission mentioned below,[42] a judgment of the court of a Regulation State or of a Contracting State on the existence or validity of an arbitration agreement is covered by the arbitration exception, and is not entitled to recognition in England under the Regulation or the Conventions, and that *The Heidberg* was wrongly decided.

S14–195   The second controversial question is whether the judgment of the court of a Regulation State or a Contracting State, which has given judgment on the substance of the dispute between the parties notwithstanding an arbitration agreement between the parties, is entitled to recognition or enforcement under the Regulation or the Conventions. In the course of the negotiations for the 1978 Accession Convention, the United Kingdom took the position that the court addressed could refuse recognition or enforcement of such a judgment on the basis that it was outside the scope of the 1968 Convention because the exclusion in Article 1(4) of the Convention covered all disputes which the parties had effectively agreed should be settled by arbitration. But the question was not resolved in the negotiations.

S14–196   It is suggested, however, that a judgment from the court of a Regulation State or a Contracting State on the merits of the dispute, notwithstanding that there is an arbitration agreement between the parties, is a judgment which falls within the scope of the Regulation or the Convention, as the case may be.[43] But the view was expressed (correctly, it is submitted) by Waller J. in *Phillip Alexander Securities and Futures Ltd. v. Bamberger*[44] that such a judgment may be refused recognition on the ground of public policy. First, if there were an English injunction restraining the foreign proceedings,[45] recognition of a foreign judgment obtained in breach of the injunction would be manifestly contrary to public policy under what is now Article 34(1) of the Regulation (or, perhaps, debarred from recognition on the basis that it was irreconcilable with the English injunction under Article 34(3)).[46] Secondly, irrespective of whether there was an injunction, it may also be contrary to public policy, though less manifestly[47] so, to enforce a judgment from the courts of a Regulation State obtained in breach of an

---

[42] *infra,* para. S14–194.

[43] This view has been expressed, *obiter,* in *The Heidberg* [1994] 2 Lloyd's Rep. 287, 301 and in *Phillip Alexander Securities and Futures Ltd v. Bamberger* [1997] I.L.Pr. 73, 98; affd. on other grounds *ibid.* 104 (C.A.). See also *Zellner v. Phillip Alexander Securities and Futures Ltd.* [1997] I.L.Pr. 730, 742–743. It also gains some support from the decision in Case C–391/95 *Van Uden Maritime B.V. v. Deco-Line* [1998] E.C.R. I–7091, in which it appears to have been considered that where the parties had agreed to settle their differences by arbitration, any dispute fell within the scope of the Convention, albeit that no court had jurisdiction to adjudicate upon it.

[44] *Supra,* at 101–102. To the same effect (though refusing to allow the arbitration point to be raised as it had not been taken before the adjudicating court) is *Soc. Assurances générales de France v. Goettgens, Rev.crit.* 2001, 172, note Muir-Watt (French *Cour de cassation,* November 14, 2000).

[45] See para. 14–145.

[46] The Court of Appeal agreed: see p. 115.

[47] Art. 34(1) of the Regulation adds this epithet to the wording of the corresponding provision, Art. 27(1), of the Conventions. Its intended effect is clear, but it is difficult to quantify what impact it will have.

arbitration provision, at least where there had been a blatant disregard of the arbitration agreement.[48]

Effect of Submission. If the defendant in the foreign proceedings chal- **S14–197** lenges the jurisdiction of the foreign court (or its exercise), that will not amount to a submission to the jurisdiction of the foreign court: that is expressly provided by section 33 of the 1982 Act, and if (as is submitted above) the decision of the foreign court on the existence or validity of the arbitration agreement is outside the scope of the Regulation or the 1968 and Lugano Conventions, the decision is not entitled to recognition under these instruments. But if the defendant in the foreign proceedings goes on to contest to merits of the dispute, and judgment is given against him, then the judgment of the foreign court will be entitled to recognition and enforcement. This is because he will have submitted to the jurisdiction of the foreign court, or waived the arbitration agreement. In the *Marc Rich* proceedings, prior to the ruling of the European Court, the effect of which was that the provision which now appears as Article 27 of the Regulation[49] did not prevent English proceedings for the appointment of arbitrators, the Italian Corte di Cassazione had decided that the Italian courts had jurisdiction and that there was no binding arbitration agreement. While the ruling of the European Court was pending, the Swiss buyers lodged a pleading on the merits in the Italian proceedings. On their application for an injunction to restrain the Italian proceedings, it was held by the English Court of Appeal that the effect of their pleading in the Italian court was that they had submitted to the jurisdiction of the Italian court to deal with the merits of the claim; that submission covered the whole proceedings, including the prior interlocutory decision by the Italian court that there was a valid arbitration agreement.[50]

Appeals. The pendency of an appeal in the foreign court will not prevent **S14–198** registration of a judgment capable of enforcement,[51] but once it is registered the court may stay enforcement proceedings if an "ordinary" appeal has been lodged against the judgment in the State in which it was given[52]; enforcement may also be stayed if the time for appeal has not yet expired, and an appeal has not been lodged, subject to the power of the English

---

[48] Waller J. thought that the provision in Art. 28(3) of the 1968 Convention (corresponding to Art. 35(3) of the Regulation) that public policy may not be applied to the rules relating to jurisdiction was not a bar to this conclusion; it would not be a ruling on jurisdiction, but a mark of disapproval of breach of agreement: p. 101.
[49] Art. 21 of the 1968 Convention.
[50] *The Atlantic Emperor (No. 2)* [1992] 1 Lloyd's Rep. 624 (C.A.)
[51] Art. 38 of the Regulation, following Art. 31 of the Convention, provides that a judgment may be enforced in a Member State when it is has been declared enforceable in the state of origin; for the meaning of "enforceable" see Case C–267/97 *Coursier v. Fortis Bank S.A.* [1999] E.C.R. I–2843.
[52] Art. 46 of the Regulation confers this power on the first instance court (Art. 43) and also on the court hearing the further appeal under Art. 44. In this respect it is wider than, and an improvement on, Art. 38 of the Conventions, which limited this power to the first instance court: under the Convention there may be no appeal against its refusal to order a stay: Case C–183/90 *Van Dalfsen v. Van Loon* [1991] E.C.R. I–4743; and nor may the court hearing an appeal on a point of law under the second paragraph of Art. 37 of the Conventions (corresponding to Art. 44 of the Regulation) impose such a stay for itself: Case C–432/93 *Société d'Informatique Service Réalisation Organisation v. Ampersand Software B.V.* [1995] E.C.R. I–2269; [1996] Q.B. 127. Art. 37 of the Regulation contains corresponding provisions relating to recognition.

court to specify the time within which the appeal must be lodged.[53] In seeking a stay, the judgment debtor is not entitled to rely on the likelihood of success of his pending appeal in the foreign court, since the enforcing court is not permitted to examine, directly or indirectly, the substance of the case.[54]

S14–199   Article 46(3) of the Regulation provides that the court may also make *enforcement* conditional on the provision of such security as it shall determine.[55] This is primarily designed to ensure that the judgment *debtor* does not find that he is unable to recover the judgment debt from the judgment creditor if the original judgment is overturned. But it has been held that a *stay* of enforcement may be made conditional on the provision of security by the judgment debtor, so that the judgment *creditor* is not prejudiced by the delay.[56]

S14–200   The distinction between ordinary and extraordinary appeals has no counterpart in the United Kingdom, and although the distinction is found in the civil law Member States it is not applied uniformly. The European Court, in *Industrial Diamond Supplies v. Riva*,[57] held that (a) whether an appeal was ordinary or extraordinary depended on an autonomous interpretation rather than on the procedural law of the court of origin; (b) the expression "ordinary appeal" must be understood as meaning any appeal which forms part of the normal course of an action and which, as such, constitutes a procedural development which any party must reasonably expect; (c) any appeal bound by the law to a specific period of time which starts to run by virtue of the actual decision whose enforcement is sought constitutes such a development. Consequently, any appeal which might be dependent on events which were unforeseeable at the date of the original judgment or upon action taken by persons who were extraneous to the judgment would not be an "ordinary appeal". Thus an application for a re-trial after new evidence had come to light or an application for a re-hearing would not be an "ordinary appeal". Article 38(2)[58] of the Regulation provides that where the judgment is given in the United Kingdom or the Republic of Ireland any form of appeal available under their law shall be treated as an ordinary appeal for the purposes of Article 38(1). The special provisions relating to the United Kingdom and Ireland apply only to the enforcement of their judgments in other Regulation States. Therefore the English court may still be required to consider whether an ordinary appeal is pending in another Regulation State in order to decide whether to grant a stay of enforcement proceedings.

---

[53] *Cf.* 1933 Act, s. 5, and para. 14–179.

[54] Case C–183/90 *Van Dalfsen v. Van Loon* [1991] E.C.R. I–4743.

[55] This order may only be made when, or after, the High Court confirms the registration: Case 258/83 *Brennero SAS v. Wendel GmbH* [1984] E.C.R. 3971.

[56] *Petereit v. Babcock International Ltd.* [1990] 1 W.L.R. 350. The inter-relationship of the powers conferred on the court by Arts. 38 and 39 of the Conventions was considered in *William Grant & Sons International Ltd. v. Marie-Brizard Espana S.A.*, 1998 S.C. 536, and various questions referred to the European Court. The reference was subsequently withdrawn; and as the provisions of Article 46 of the Regulation are somewhat different from those of Article 39 of the Convention, this case must now be applied with care. See also *infra*, para. S14–222.

[57] Case 43/77 [1977] E.C.R. 2175, applied in *Interdesco S.A. v. Nullifire Ltd.* [1992] 1 Lloyd's Rep. 180 (*recours en revision* in France not an ordinary appeal; stay refused).

[58] Art. 31 of the Conventions is identical to Art. 38 of the Regulation.

No review of substance. Article 36 of the Regulation[59] provides that "under S14–201
no circumstances may a foreign judgment be reviewed as to its substance".[60]
The grounds for non-recognition or non-enforcement of judgments within
the scope of the Regulation are very limited.[61] The English court has no
right, except within very confined limits, to investigate the jurisdiction of the
court which gave the judgment. There are grounds, such as public policy or
lack of notice, which bear some distant resemblance to the rules at common
law and under the 1920 and 1933 Acts,[62] but these have no effect whatever
on the true construction of the Regulation.

It has not been finally determined whether the court in which recognition S14–202
or enforcement is sought would be precluded from deciding for itself
whether the judgment fell within the scope of the Regulation or the
Conventions (that is, was given in a civil or commercial matter and was not
otherwise excluded from the scope of the relevant instrument), but it is
submitted that it must have this right and duty.[63] Article 36 of the
Regulation does not cover the point, for though it precludes jurisdictional
review for judgments which are within the scope of the Regulation, it does
not apply to the distinct question whether a judgment falls within the
perimeter of the Regulation in the first place: only if it does do the
obligations imposed by Article 36 affect the court addressed. It follows that
the English court must be free to decide this question for itself, not being
bound to accept the view of the adjudicating court upon whether the case
fell within the scope of the Regulation. If the judgment is outside the scope
of the relevant instrument, recognition and enforcement may be sought
under the common law or the 1933 Act.

Jurisdiction of the foreign court. The jurisdiction of the foreign court may S14–203
only be investigated by the English court if the case may fall within Sections
3 (insurance contracts), 4 (certain consumer contracts) or 6 (exclusive
jurisdiction) of Chapter II of the Regulation[64]: if it is found that the
adjudicating court violated these important jurisdictional provisions, recognition must be denied. But even in those cases the English court is bound
by the findings of fact on which the foreign court based its judgment.[65] No
explanation is given for the failure to include Section 5 of Chapter II of the

---

[59] Which is identical to Art. 29 of the Conventions.
[60] But a court must be able to review the substance to the extent necessary to determine whether
Art. 34 of the Regulation requires that the judgment be not recognised: *cf.* Case C–78/95
Hendrickman v. Magenta Druck & Verlag GmbH [1996] E.C.R. I–4943.
[61] They are drawn more tightly than the corresponding provisions of the Conventions.
[62] See paras. 14R–141 *et seq.* and *infra*, paras. S14–206 *et seq.*
[63] *Cf.* Case 29/76 *L.T.U. GmbH v. Eurocontrol* [1976] E.C.R. 1541; Case 133/78 *Gourdain v.
Nadler* [1979] E.C.R. 733; and Case C–172/91 *Sonntag v. Waidmann* [1993] E.C.R. I–1963, where
the court in which recognition was sought apparently undertook this inquiry for itself.
[64] Which correspond (albeit that these are not worded identically) with sections 3, 4, and 5 of
Title II of the Conventions.
[65] Art. 35. For examples see German Federal Supreme Court, 1979, in *Digest* I–28–B3
(insurance); *Tonnoir v. Vanherf S.A.* Ct.App. Douai, 1989 in 1991 *Clunet* 161 (consumer
contract). The court may also investigate the jurisdiction of the foreign court over a defendant
domiciled or habitually resident in a non-Regulation State with which there is a Treaty under
Art. 59 of the Conventions, carried over into the Regulation by Art. 72: see *infra*, para. S14–206;
and it may also do so if the judgment is to be recognised under the transitional provisions of Art.
54 of the Conventions: Case C–163/95 *Van Horn v. Cinnamond* [1997] E.C.R. I–5451; [1998] Q.B.
214. But the transitional provisions of the Regulation make this unlikely to be required in the
context of Article 66 of the Regulation.

Regulation, which deals with contracts of employment,[66] in this list of instances where the jurisdiction of the adjudicating court may be reviewed, but it does not appear possible to argue that Article 35 should read as if such cases were there included. In addition to these cases, if the order of which recognition is sought is one where the court which made it purported to base, or may have based, its jurisdiction on Article 31 of the Regulation, or Article 24 of the Convention, the court asked to recognise or enforce the order is obliged to ascertain for itself whether the order is of the type which is authorised to be made by reason of Article 31 or 24, as the case may be: that is to say, that it was an order which properly fell within the scope of these Articles.[67] This is not, therefore, a review of the jurisdiction of the court which made the order.

S14–204 Because the English court cannot investigate the jurisdiction of the foreign court, it is no objection to enforcement that the foreign court took jurisdiction wrongly, *e.g.* where it is alleged that the parties had agreed to the exclusive jurisdiction of the English court or that the defendant had not voluntarily appeared before the foreign court.[68] These questions must be raised at the outset of proceedings before the foreign court and cannot be raised *de novo*, or re-opened, in England at the point or recognition of the judgment. It is for the court in which the proceedings are begun to rule on whether another court has exclusive jurisdiction by virtue of an agreement under Article 23 of the Regulation or Article 17 of the Conventions.[69] If the foreign court decides that the agreement is invalid or inoperative, or for any other reason that the alleged jurisdiction agreement is inapplicable and that it has jurisdiction, then any resulting judgment will be enforceable in the United Kingdom. This is so notwithstanding the terms of section 32 of the 1982 Act (which would otherwise entitle the United Kingdom court to disregard a foreign judgment given in disregard of a jurisdiction agreement) since that section is expressly subject to the Regulation and the Conventions.[70]

S14–205 Where the defendant has appeared to protest the jurisdiction of the court of another Regulation State, Article 24 of the Regulation[71] provides that the appearance is not a submission. If the foreign court holds that it has jurisdiction under the Regulation (*i.e.* the defendant loses on the question of jurisdiction) and the defendant then contests the proceedings, any resulting judgment against the defendant will be enforceable in England because the foreign court found that it had jurisdiction under the Regulation and the defendant submitted to its jurisdiction; if, however, the defendant takes no further steps in the proceedings and the foreign court enters a judgment in default of defence, it should only do so if it finds that

---

[66] And which has no direct precursor in the Conventions.

[67] *Cf.* Case C–99/96 *Mietz v. Intership Yachting Sneek B.V.* [1999] E.C.R. I–2277.

[68] Or that the foreign court misapplied the *lis alibi pendens* provisions of Art. 21 of the Convention (to which Art. 27 of the Regulation corresponds): *cf. Société Brasserie du Pêcheur v. Kreissparkasse Main-Spessart* [1997] I.L.Pr. 173 (French Cour de Cassation, 1996).

[69] See generally Case C–351/89 *Overseas Union Insurance Ltd. v. New Hampshire Insurance Co.* [1991] E.C.R. I–3317; [1992] Q.B. 434. But if the English court is second seised, and concludes that the court first seised has accepted (or may accept) jurisdiction in breach of a jurisdiction agreement, it may restrain the plaintiff in those foreign proceedings by injunction: see *ante,* Rule 32.

[70] On 1982 Act, s.32 (as amended by S.I. 2001 No. 3929, Sched. 2, para. 14) see *supra,* Rule 37; for further discussion of s.32 in this context, see *supra,* paras. S14–189 *et seq.*

[71] In this respect following Art. 18 of the Conventions.

it has jurisdiction under the Regulation[72] and should not do so merely on the basis of the appearance to contest the jurisdiction; but if it finds it has jurisdiction the resulting judgment will be enforceable in England. There will be no room for refusal to enforce the judgment on the basis of section 33 of the 1982 Act on the theory that the defendant submitted only for the purpose of contesting the jurisdiction.[73]

Grounds for refusal to recognise or enforce. The other grounds for non-recognition and non-enforcement are set out in Articles 34 and 35 of the Regulation, which correspond to, but do not exactly reproduce, Articles 27 and 28 of the Conventions.[74] In addition, the effect of Article 35(1) is that the English court does not have to recognise or enforce a judgment of a Regulation State to the extent that it conflicts with an obligation of the United Kingdom assumed *vis-à-vis* a third state not to recognise "exorbitant" judgments given against domiciliaries or residents of that State.[75] **S14–206**

Public policy. The first ground is that recognition of the foreign judgment would be manifestly contrary to public policy in the State where its recognition or enforcement is sought. The public policy exception is to operate only in exceptional circumstances,[76] a fact which is reinforced by the incorporation of the word "manifestly" into the provision in the Regulation. The European Court, in interpreting the corresponding provision in Article 27(1) of the Convention, has provided a definition of when recognition may be said to be contrary to public policy: whereas the content of English public policy is a matter of English law alone, the role of that public policy within the framework of the Regulation is a matter for the European Court. Before it may find recognition contrary to public policy, the court addressed must conclude that recognition would conflict, to an unacceptable degree, with the legal order in the state of recognition because it would infringe a fundamental principle, or would involve a manifest breach of a rule of law which is regarded as fundamental within that legal order. Accordingly, where the adjudicating court had refused to hear a defendant who had placed himself in contempt of court, the recognising court was entitled to consider this to be a violation of Article 6 of the European Convention on Human Rights, and to refuse to recognise the judgment.[77] By contrast, **S14–207**

---

[72] Art. 26 of the Regulation, which is in this respect identical with Art. 20 of the Conventions.
[73] s. 33 (as amended by S.I. 2001 No. 3929, Sched. 2, para. 15, and on which see para. 14–064) is not intended to affect enforcement under the Regulation or the Conventions: s.33(2).
[74] Other grounds not expressly mentioned include: (a) the judgment has been satisfied; (b) the judgment is not within the scope of the Regulation or the Conventions; (c) the judgment is not enforceable in the State of the original court: see Jenard, p. 50; Schlosser, para. 220.
[75] Under Art. 59 of the Conventions, which is applied to the Regulation by Art. 72. See *supra*, para. S14–186.
[76] Jenard, p. 44; Case 145/86 *Hoffmann v. Krieg* [1988] E.C.R. 645, 668; Case C–78/95 *Hendrickman v. Magenta Druck & Verlag GmbH* [1996] E.C.R. I–4943; *cf. Klopp v. Holder,* Cour de Cassation, France, 1984, in 1985 *Rev. Crit.* 131, note Mezger; *Hupprichs v. Dorthu,* Supreme Court, Netherlands, 1986 in [1990] I.L. Pr. 180. Contrast *Vanclef v. Soc. TTI,* Cour de Cassation, France, in 1979 *Clunet* 380, note Holleaux.
[77] Case C–7/98 *Krombach v. Bamberski* [2000] E.C.R. I–1935. For the proceedings before the European Court of Human Rights which found the French proceedings to have violated the defendent's right to a fair trial, see *Krombach v. France,* February 13, 2001, noted (2001) 12 H.R. Case Digest 76. The failure to notify a defendant that proceedings against him have been revived by a claimant after a delay of several years will also violate the right to a fair trial under Art. 6 E.C.H.R., and recognition of the resultant judgment will conflict with public policy: *Maronier v. Larmer* [2002] EWCA Civ. 774; [2003] Q.B. 620 (C.A.).

where the adjudicating court had misapplied European competition law, the effect could not be regarded as the manifest breach of a fundamental right, serious enough to raise issues of public policy, especially as the adjudicating court had a proper procedure for the correction of errors by appeal or review.[78] It is therefore plain that a mere difference between the substantive law (or the rules of private international law) of the original court and that of the court in which enforcement is sought is not sufficient to justify non-recognition or non-enforcement.[79] Moreover, recourse to public policy is inappropriate when the issue must be resolved on the basis of another provision of Article 34,[80] such as Article 34(2)[81] or Article 34(3).[82] In many countries, including England, a default judgment does not contain reasons, and the mere fact that a foreign judgment does not contain reasons should be insufficient for public policy to be invoked to deny recognition. But it appears that the French courts will not recognise a default judgment from another Regulation State if that judgment does not give reasons.[83] It was on the basis of evidence of a similar practice in other European States that the Commercial Court[84] was prepared, in effect, to conduct a trial (in the absence of the defendant) before giving judgment against a defendant who had not acknowledged service, so as to ensure that the judgment creditor would not be impeded in enforcing the judgment in other Contracting States.[85]

S14–208 In England fraud is a ground for refusal of recognition or enforcement of a foreign judgment, and in this context fraud has a very wide meaning.[86] In civil law countries fraud is not a distinct reason for non-recognition, and neither the Regulation nor the Conventions contain a special provision for fraud. But in civil law countries a judgment procured by fraud may be refused recognition on grounds of public policy, and this is reflected in the bilateral treaties, now superseded, between the United Kingdom and France and Germany. Under the Regulation and the Conventions, though it is theoretically possible that the procurement of a judgment by fraud may be held to offend against the public policy of the court in which enforcement is sought,[87] it will in practice be very difficult. In *Interdesco S.A. v. Nullifire Ltd.*[88] it was held that the English court would not refuse enforcement of a French judgment on the ground of alleged fraud, even if there were newly discovered evidence, if the judgment debtor had a remedy in the French courts. That was because the public policy ground of

---

[78] Case C–38/98 *Régie Nationale des Usines Renault S.A. v. Maxicar S.p.A.* [2000] E.C.R. I–2973.

[79] See also *Re Enforcement of a Guarantee* (Case IX ZB 2/98) (German Fed. Sup. Ct.) [2001] I.L.Pr. 425.

[80] Case C–78/95 *Hendrickman v. Magenta Druck & Verlag GmbH* [1996] E.C.R. I–4943, 4968, citing Jenard, p. 44.

[81] *ibid., infra,* para. S14–210.

[82] Case 145/86 *Hoffmann v. Krieg* [1988] E.C.R. 645, *infra,* para. S14–216.

[83] *Sarl Polypetrol v. Soc. Gen. Routière* [1993] I.L.Pr. 107 (Cour de Cassation, 1991); *Soc Transports Intenationaux Dehbashi v. Ceding* [1996] I.L.Pr. 104 (Cour d'App., Poitiers, 1991); *X Ltd. v. Y SA* (Swiss Federal Sup. Ct., 2001), noted *Int. Lit. News* (International Bar Assn.), October, 2001.

[84] Acting under the inherent jurisdiction.

[85] *Berliner Bank v. Karageorgis* [1996] 1 Lloyd's Rep. 426.

[86] See para. 14–129.

[87] *Cf.* para. 14–135 and *Kendall v. Kendall* [1977] Fam. 208 (foreign divorce obtained by fraud refused recognition on grounds of public policy).

[88] [1992] 1 Lloyd's Rep. 180; *Société d'Informatique Service Réalisation Organisation v. Ampersand Software B.V.* [1994] I.L.Pr. 55 (C.A.).

recognition ought to operate only in exceptional circumstances,[89] and the court in the State in which enforcement was sought should always consider whether the judgment debtor could seek a remedy in the foreign court.[90] On the footing that the legal systems in the Regulation and Contracting States all do allow a party who claims that he has suffered judgment as a result of fraud to bring proceedings to challenge the judgment, albeit that this may be subject to restrictive conditions, it is difficult to see when it will be manifestly contrary to public policy for a judgment obtained from the courts of such a system to be recognised.

Article 35(1) of the Regulation expressly provides that public policy cannot be used to re-open the question of jurisdiction of the original court. This would prevent, for example, an English court from invoking public policy in order to refuse to recognise a French judgment based on Article 14 of the Civil Code, in a case where the party suing was French, the defendant was domiciled in a non-Regulation State, and the case had nothing to do with France,[91] or a German court from refusing to enforce a judgment in favour of a civil party who intervened in criminal proceedings in a French court, and which had been founded on the nationality of the victim of the alleged offence.[92] But if the judgment was obtained by the claimant in defiance of an injunction ordering him not to institute or proceed with the foreign action, it will be contrary to public policy for the judgment to be recognised in England.[93]

S14–209

Right to defend. Article 34(2) of the Judgments Regulation is derived from Article 27(2) of the Conventions, but places additional limits on its scope and effect. According to Article 27(2), a judgment will be denied recognition if the judgment is in default of appearance, and either the defendant was not duly served with the document instituting the proceedings (or an equivalent document), or was duly served, but not in sufficient time to arrange for his defence. Article 34(2) of the Regulation departs from this in two respects: it omits the word "duly" as a quality of the service, and adds a further element: that the defendant is to lose his shield if he failed to commence proceedings to challenge the judgment when it was possible for him to do so. The purpose of this provision, in the Regulation and the Conventions (which is particularly important in relation to default judgments entered following substituted service on a defendant) is to safeguard the interests of the defendant and to ensure that he has sufficient time to defend himself.[94] But the Regulation places the onus on the defendant,

S14–210

---

[89] Jenard, p. 44; *cf.* Case C–78/95 *Hendrickman v. Magenta Druck & Verlag GmbH* [1996] E.C.R. I–4943.

[90] Schlosser, para. 192. In *SA Marie Brizard et Roger International v. William Grant & Sons Ltd.*, 2002 S.L.T. 1365 (O.H.) it was held that where a foreign court's appellate procedure provided a sufficient safeguard against the possibility of bias or incompetence in the lower courts, it would be rare for recognition to be contrary to Scottish public policy.

[91] *Cf.* Case C–7/98 *Krombach v. Bamberski* [2000] E.C.R. I–1935. For a suggestion that a judgment given in breach of an agreement to arbitrate may be denied recognition on grounds of public policy, see *Phillip Alexander Securities & Futures Ltd. v. Bamberger* [1997] I.L.Pr. 73, 100–102; affd. without reference to this point, *ibid.* p. 104 (C.A.), and *supra*, paras. S14–189 *et seq.*

[92] Case C–7/98 *Krombach v. Bamberski* [2000] E.C.R. I–1935 (*cf.* Art. 5(4) for the special jurisdictional basis for such claims).

[93] *Phillip Alexander Securities & Futures Ltd. v. Bamberger* [1997] I.L.Pr. 73; affd. *ibid.* 104 (C.A.); *cf. Fakih Bros. v. A.P. Mailer (Copenhagen) Ltd.* [1994] 1 Lloyd's Rep. 103.

[94] Case 166/80 *Klomps v. Michel* [1981] E.C.R. 1593, 1605; Case 228/81 *Pendy Plastic Products v. Pluspunkt* [1982] E.C.R. 2723.

when he finds out about the entry of judgment, to take such steps as may be open to him to challenge it, in the absence of which the defence is withdrawn.

S14–211　　The defence applies only to judgments given in default of appearance, but this expression has been held to have an autonomous meaning, rather than being defined by reference to the law of the adjudicating court. In *Hendrickman v. Magenta Druck & Verlag GmbH*[95] a German court gave judgment against a defendant in circumstances where a legal representative purported to be authorised to represent the defendant but where, according to the defendant, no such authorisation had been given.[96] As a matter of German law the judgment was not entered in default of appearance, but the European Court accepted that the judgment was to be seen as one in default of appearance, for the defendant had been "quite powerless to defend himself" and was on that account to be regarded as a defendant in default of appearance. It is unlikely that the consequent extension of the scope of Article 34(2) of the Judgments Regulation will be wide, but in some circumstances the argument that a defendant lacked a proper opportunity to be heard may now be accommodated under Article 34(2), whether or not the judgment was technically in default of appearance.[97]

S14–212　　A judgment in default of appearance may retain this character even if the defendant later seeks, unsuccessfully, to set it aside.[98] The opportunity to apply for a legal remedy after the making of the order is not equivalent, but is inferior, to having the right to be heard before the order is made. It is not therefore an adequate substitute; and the judgment will remain as one given in default of appearance.[99]

Article 34(2) applies whether or not the defendant is domiciled or resident in the State of the court of origin.[1]

S14–213　　The court in which enforcement of a default judgment is sought must consider the manner in which service was effected and whether, following service, the defendant had sufficient time to arrange for his defence.[2] So far as concerns the manner of service, Article 27(2) of the Conventions was understood to allow and require an English court to re-open and consider for itself whether service was effected in accordance with the law of the court of origin,[3] provided that the court of origin has not been seised of this

---

[95] Case C–78/95 [1996] E.C.R. I–4943.

[96] This will be a matter for the recognising court to determine for itself: see p. 4967.

[97] This reasoning, however, was not applied to the defendant in Case C–7/98 *Krombach v. Bamberski* [2000] E.C.R. I–1935, even though he had no opportunity to be heard as a direct result of the order of the court.

[98] Case C–123/91 *Minalmet GmbH v. Brandeis Ltd.* [1992] E.C.R. I–5661; Case C–78/95 *Hendrickman v. Magenta Druck & Verlag GmbH* [1996] E.C.R. I–4943.

[99] But under the Judgments Regulation, the defendant may lose the defence if he fails to make the application: see *post*, para. S14–214.

[1] Case 49/84 *Debaecker and Plouvier v. Bouwman* [1985] E.C.R. 1779; *cf.* Case 166/80 *Klomps v. Michel* [1981] E.C.R. at p. 1621, *per* Reischl A.-G.

[2] Case 166/80 *Klomps v. Michel* [1981] E.C.R. 1593, applied in Case 228/81 *Pendy Plastic Products v. Pluspunkt* [1982] E.C.R. 2733. Both conditions must be fulfilled: Case C–305/88 *Isabelle Lancray S.A. v. Peters und Sickert KG* [1990] E.C.R. I–2725; Case C–123/91 *Minalmet GmbH v. Brandeis Ltd.* [1992] E.C.R. I–5661. See also *Artic Fish Sales Co. Ltd. v. Adam (No. 2),* 1996 S.L.T. 970; *Selco Ltd. v. Mercier,* 1996 S.L.T. 1247.

[3] Though a German court has held that even though service may have been made in accordance with the law of the state of origin, this is not due service, as it is an unlawful discrimination on grounds of nationality, proscribed by Art. 12 (ex 6) of the E.C. Treaty. In *Re the Enforcement of a*

question in adversary proceedings.[4] If service was not made in accordance with that law, it could not be said to have been *duly* made, and it was not open to an English court to purport to cure by reference to its own procedural law, or to overlook, the defect in service.[5] Whether this is still so in the context of Article 34(2) of the Regulation is less clear, for the deletion of the word "duly" may be considered to have some significance. On the other hand, the rights of the defendant might be jeopardised if a gross irregularity in service could still give rise to a recognisable judgment. Of course, if the defendant is well aware that there has been purported service, and that judgment has been entered, but has taken no step to challenge the judgment, the effect of Article 34(2) is that the judgment will be recognised, regardless of the quality of service; by contrast, under the Conventions, where service has not been *duly* made, Article 27(2) treats this as sufficient to deny recognition to the judgment (though if the defect in service may be, and has been, cured according to the law of the court of origin, service will be treated as duly made[6]).

The question whether service was effected in sufficient time is a question **S14–214** of fact, which is not to be determined on the basis of the law of the court of origin or of English law as the law of the court in which enforcement is sought. Thus the fact that service was properly effected under the law of the court of origin does not preclude re-examination of whether it was effected in sufficient time.[7] As a general rule the court in which enforcement is sought may confine its examination to ascertaining whether the period reckoned from the date on which service was duly effected allowed the defendant sufficient time to arrange for his defence. Nevertheless the court must consider whether, in the particular case, there are exceptional circumstances which warrant the conclusion that although service was duly effected, it was, however, inadequate for the purpose of enabling the defendant to take steps to arrange for his defence (because it did not in fact come to his notice until some time later) and accordingly could not cause the time stipulated by Article 34(2) of the Judgments Regulation to begin to run. In considering whether it is confronted with such a case, the English court may take account of all the circumstances (including those occurring after service is effected[8]) such as the means employed for effecting service, the relations between the claimant and the defendant or the nature of the steps which had to be taken in order to prevent judgment from being given in default.[9] If, for example, the dispute concerns commercial relations and if

---

French Interlocutory Order [2001] I.L.Pr. 208 (Case 9W 67/97) the court refused to regard as effective service by delivery to the court office (*remise au parquet*) for onward transmission to the defendant, as it was considered to discriminate against non-French defendants on grounds which could not be objectively justified.

[4] See also Case 49/84 *Debaecker and Plouvier v. Bouwman* [1985] E.C.R. 1779. On service under the Hague Convention, see *Noirhomme v. Walklate* [1992] 1 Lloyd's Rep. 427.

[5] Case C–305/89 *Isabelle Lancray S.A. v. Peters & Sickert K.G.* [1990] E.C.R. I–2725. Breaches of the law of the court of origin other than those relating to due service may not be relied on to impugn the quality or effectiveness of service: Case C–474/93 *Hengst Import B.V. v. Campese* [1995] E.C.R. I–2113.

[6] Case C–123/91 *Minalmet GmbH v. Brandeis Ltd.* [1992] E.C.R. I–5661.

[7] Case 49/84 *Debaecker and Plouvier v. Bouwman, supra*.

[8] For a list of possible circumstances see VerLoren van Theemat A.-G. in Case 49/84 *Debaecker and Plouvier v. Bouwman, supra;* see also *Re A Belgian Default Judgment* [1992] I.L.Pr. 528 (German Fed.Sup.Ct. 1991).

[9] See *Jurgens v. TSN Kunststoffrecycling GmbH* [2002] EWCA Civ. 11, [2002] 1 W.L.R. 2459 (C.A.).

the document which instituted the proceedings was served at an address at which the defendant carries on his business activities, the mere fact that the defendant was absent at the time of service should not normally prevent him from arranging his defence, especially if the action necessary to avoid a judgment in default may be taken informally and by a representative. A question which arose in *Klomps v. Michel*,[10] and which has considerable practical importance with regard to certain forms of judgment was whether a *Zahlungsbefehl*, or order to pay, under German law was the document instituting the proceedings for the purposes of enforcement. The European Court ruled that a measure such as the order for payment in German law, service of which on the defendant enables the plaintiff, where no objection to the order is made, to obtain an enforceable decision was to be understood as being covered by the words "the document which instituted the proceedings". The enforcement order, issued following service of an order for payment and which is, in itself, enforceable under the Convention, was not the relevant document.

S14–215   Where recognition of the judgment is to fall under the provisions of the Judgments Regulation, the defendant will lose the protection of Article 34(2) if he failed to commence proceedings to challenge the judgment when it was possible for him to do so. This aims to overcome the sense of disquiet at the behaviour of a defendant who knows perfectly well of the proceedings which have been commenced against him, but who elects to do nothing about them, and who then relies on a shortcoming in the service of process. If it is not possible for him to challenge the judgment, Article 34(2) will not penalise the failure. Moreover, it would accord with principle that the defendant should not be penalised either unless the steps which were open to him to take were not, in effect, steeper and more difficult than would have been the case if he had been properly notified of the institution of proceedings and had had an opportunity to participate.

S14–216   **Incompatibility with a judgment from the courts of the State in which recognition is sought.** Article 34(3) of the Judgments Regulation[11] provides that a judgment[12] irreconcilable with a judgment given[13] in a dispute between the same parties in the State in which recognition is sought shall not be recognised. Its practical importance will be limited by Articles 27 to 30 of the Regulation,[14] which in effect give priority to the court first seised.[15]

---

[10] Case 166/80 [1981] E.C.R. 1593; in Case C–474/93 *Hengst Import B.V. v. Campese* [1995] E.C.R. I–2113 it was held that the Italian *decreto ingiuntivo*, together with the application instituting the proceedings, was "the document which instituted the proceedings".

[11] Art. 27(3) of the Conventions is in identical terms.

[12] The rule applies to judgments, but not to authentic instruments or to settlements approved in the course of judicial proceedings: Case C–414/92 *Solo Kleinmotoren GmbH v. Boch* [1994] E.C.R. I–2237; see also Arts. 57 and 58 of the Regulation. But it does also apply to judgments granting or refusing to grant interim measures where such decisions from the courts of two member states are irreconcilable, it being irrelevant that the irreconcilability arises from divergent perceptions of the need for the orders sought before each court or from other differences of procedural law: Case C–80/00 *Italian Leather S.P.A. v. WECO Polstermoebel GmbH & Co.* [2002] E.C.R. 1–4995.

[13] If there are proceedings pending in England but no judgment which has yet been given, Art. 34(3) of the Regulation has no application: *Landhurst Leasing plc v. Marcq* [1998] I.L.Pr. 822 (C.A.).

[14] Corresponding to Arts. 21–23 of the Conventions, save for the fact that Art. 30 of the Regulation has no precursor in the Conventions.

[15] *supra*, Rule 31(3).

The court which is second to be seised with the same cause of action must give up its jurisdiction or stay its proceedings,[16] and must recognise the judgment of the first court under Article 33. It is not necessary under Article 28 of the Regulation for the same cause of action to be involved. But where (for whatever reason) there are irreconcilable judgments, then the English court may refuse to recognise or enforce the foreign judgment even if it was rendered before the conflicting English judgment, and even if the English judgment is outside the scope of the Regulation or the Conventions.[17]

Judgments are irreconcilable when they entail consequences which are **S14–217** mutually exclusive.[18] A judgment awarding damages for breach of contract would be irreconcilable with one declaring that the contract had been rescinded; and a declaration of non-liability of one party to the other may[19] be irreconcilable with a judgment awarding damages. But a judgment awarding an unpaid seller the price would not be irreconcilable with a judgment awarding damages to the buyer for breach of warranty.

If an English court has granted an injunction ordering the plaintiff in **S14–218** proceedings in the courts of another Regulation State not to continue with the action, but the plaintiff is defiant and obtains judgment, recognition of the judgment may be refused on grounds of public policy.[20] It is not clear whether it would also be permissible to refuse recognition under Article 34(3). As the injunction is formally an order made in proceedings not involving an adjudication on the merits of the underlying claim, there may be no formal irreconcilability between the two judgments. Though a judgment on the merits in Regulation State X, and an order that the plaintiff not obtain that judgment, appear to be mutually irreconcilable in the sense that the one will not be enforced in the face of the other, the reason for the unenforceability will lie in the behaviour of the plaintiff in the foreign proceedings, not in the essence of the matters which have become *res judicata* by the two judgments. It is therefore suggested that Article 34(3) will not apply in such a case. But in the light of Article 34(1), however, the issue is not likely to arise in this context.[21]

Preliminary questions as to status. Article 27(4) of the Conventions **S14–219** provides for the non-recognition of a judgment where the original court, in order to arrive at its judgment, decided a preliminary question concerning the status of legal capacity of natural persons, rights in property arising out of a matrimonial relationship, wills or succession in a way that conflicts with a rule of the private international law of the court in which recognition or enforcement is sought, unless the same result would have been reached by the application of the rules of private international law of the latter. But this provision is not reproduced in the Judgments Regulation and, formally

---

[16] But only until the jurisdiction of the first court is established; when this happens it must dismiss its proceedings.

[17] Case 145/86 *Hoffmann v. Krieg* [1988] E.C.R. 645.

[18] Case 145/86 *Hoffmann v. Krieg* [1988] E.C.R. 645; *Macaulay v. Macaulay* [1991] 1 W.L.R.179.

[19] It will depend on the breadth or basis of the declaration and its compatibility with the basis for the damages award. The question whether an order to constitute a limitation fund is irreconcilable with a judgment made in proceedings to establish liability is now pending before the European Court: Case C–39/02 *Maersk Olie & Gas A/S v. De Haan and De Boer*.

[20] Under Art. 34(1) of the Judgments Regulation, *supra*, para. S14–207.

[21] But it is of importance in relation to Arts. 27 and 28 of the Regulation; see para. 12–039.

at least, this ground of non-recognition is no longer available when the Regulation applies. But the effect of the deletion is much less than this would suggest: as the status or legal capacity of natural persons, rights in property arising out of a matrimonial relationship, wills and succession are excluded from the scope of the Regulation by Article 1(2)(a) in any event, a judgment whose recognition would require the state addressed to give effect to the ruling of a foreign court which contradicted its own view on status, etc., will fall outside the scope of the Regulation. It may therefore be that Article 27(4) of the Conventions was unnecessary, and its disappearance will be without practical significance.

S14–220 **Conflicts with foreign judgments which qualify for recognition.** Article 34(4) of the Regulation[22] provides that a judgment shall not be recognised if it is irreconcilable with an earlier judgment given in a Regulation State or a non-Regulation State[23] involving the same cause of action and between the same parties, provided that this latter judgment fulfils the conditions necessary for its recognition in the State addressed. No further explanation is necessary: as long as the prior judgment qualifies for recognition in the state addressed, whether under the Regulation (if it is a judgment from a Regulation State which falls within the scope of the Regulation) or under the conflict of laws rules of the state addressed (if it is not), this fact precludes recognition of the subsequent Regulation State judgment.

S14–221 **Procedure.** The combined effect of Article 38[24] of the Judgments Regulation and of Schedule 1 to the Civil Jurisdiction and Judgments Order 2001[25] is that enforcement of a judgment under the Regulation, and under the Conventions, is by way of registration. The judgment creditor cannot bring an action on the original cause of action.[26] Nor, it seems, can he proceed by way of enforcement at common law; this follows from the decision in *De Wolf v. Cox*[27] where it was held that it would be incompatible with the enforcement provisions of the 1968 Convention to allow an action on the original cause of action, even though it might be cheaper to obtain summary judgment on the original cause of action than to enforce a foreign judgment. Interest is payable on a registered judgment debt at the rate applicable under the law of the court of origin, not only for the period prior to registration[28] but also until satisfaction of the judgment.[29] It is implicit in the Regulation system that judgments should be registered in their original currency.

---

[22] By contrast, Art. 27(5) of the Conventions applies only to prior judgments from non-contracting states, and neither it nor any other Article makes provision for cases in which two Contracting State judgments are irreconcilable. It is to be supposed that the solution in Art. 34(4) of the Regulation will be applied to fill the gap left by Art. 27(5) of the Conventions; and for the position at common law, see *Showlag v. Mansour* [1995] 1 A.C. 431 (P.C.).

[23] Even though a solution has now been given, it is to be noted that it is the earlier judgment, as distinct from the judgment in the proceedings which were instituted earlier in time, which is given the right to be recognised.

[24] Art. 31 of the Conventions is materially identical.

[25] S.I. 2001 No. 3929, paras. 2 to 6 of which correspond to ss. 4 to 8 of the 1982 Act (which continue to govern in cases to which the Conventions, as opposed to the Regulation, apply).

[26] Case 42/76 *De Wolf v. Cox* [1976] E.C.R. 1759; 1982 Act, s.34.

[27] *Supra.*

[28] As under the 1933 Act.

[29] S.I. 2001 No. 3929, Sched. 1, para. 5 (1982 Act, s.7).

The procedure for registration is regulated by Articles 39 to 52 of the **S14–222** Regulation, as supplemented by the Civil Procedure Rules.[30] Initial registration of the judgment is made by application without notice to the judgment debtor,[31] and the judgment debtor, who has no right to be heard on the initial application, is notified only after registration is effected.[32] By contrast with the position under the Conventions, which permitted the registering court power to refuse registration if it considered that there was a defence to recognition, Article 41 removes any such right from the court when dealing with an application for registration of a judgment under the Regulation: all it may do is ascertain that the formal requirements set out in Article 53[33] have been complied with. If registration is ordered, the judgment debtor may appeal[34] to a judge[35] against registration of the judgment, though the time limits on bringing of the appeal are strict[36]; if registration was refused,[37] the judgment creditor may likewise appeal.[38] According to Article 45(1), the appeal against registration may only be founded on the grounds listed in Articles 34 and 35, but this must be an error on the part of the drafters: an appellant must be entitled to question whether the judgment falls within the scope of the Regulation,[39] or that the provisions of some other law or international treaty preclude its recognition.[40] The decision on the first appeal may be itself appealed by the losing party one further time, but only on a point of law.[41] Before the expiry of the time for appealing against the order for registration has expired, or before such appeal has been determined, the execution of the judgment is not

---

[30] CPR, r. 7. 74.1–11. In relation to Art. 40(2) (which corresponds to Art. 33(2) of the Conventions) see Case 198/85 *Carron v. Germany* [1986] E.C.R. 2437; *Rhatigan v. Textiles Confecciones Europeas S.A.* [1990] I.L.R.M. 825.

[31] But as the Regulation provides for the enforcement of non-money judgments as well, this terminology, though convenient, is not completely accurate.

[32] Art. 42 of the Regulation (which corresponds to Art. 35 of the Conventions, and to which CPR, r. 74.6 applies). For the documents required to make the application, see Art. 53 of the Regulation and Annex V and CPR, r. 74.4(6). For defects in the documents, and the power of the recognising court to cure the defect, see Case C–275/94 *Van der Linden v. B.F.E.* [1996] E.C.R. I–1393, though this authority now needs to be read in the light of the changed formal requirements of the Regulation. For failure to make proper service, see *Barnaby (London) Ltd. v. Mullen* [1997] 2 I.L.R.M. 341 (Sup.Ct.).

[33] That is to say, that there is an authenticated copy of the judgment, and a completed certificate in the form set out in Annex V to the Regulation.

[34] See Art. 43 of and Annex III to the Regulation (Arts. 36 and 37 of the Conventions); CPR r. 74.8. It is the judgment debtor alone who has standing to appeal against the order for registration (and, presumably, the judgment creditor who may appeal against a refusal to order registration): see Case 148/84 *Deutsche Genossenschaftsbank v. Brasserie du Pêcheur S.A.* [1985] E.C.R. 1981; Case C–172/91 *Sonntag v. Waidmann* [1993] E.C.R. I–1963. But the Art. 43 appeal procedure is concerned with appeals against the authorisation of enforcement, and do not permit an appeal from a decision refusing a stay of enforcement under Art. 46 while there is an appeal pending in the state of origin: Case C–183/90 *Van Dalfsen v. Van Loon* [1991] E.C.R. 4743; see also Case 258/83 *Brennero S.A.S. v. Wendel GmbH* [1984] E.C.R. 3971.

[35] The court which will hear the appeal is listed in Annex III to the Regulation.

[36] Art. 43(5) of the Regulation: one month after service of the notice of registration, though if the judgment debtor is domiciled in a Regulation State other than that of enforcement, this is extended to a fixed period of two months. Where he is not domiciled in a Regulation State, the period is two months, but which may, in an appropriate case, be extended: CPR, r. 74.8(3).

[37] Which will be rare, at least if the formal requirements have been met.

[38] Also under Art. 43.

[39] Under Art. 1; also that it does not fall within the temporal scope of the Regulation (Art. 66).

[40] e.g. Arts. 67 and 71(2)(b), second paragraph.

[41] Art. 44, to the court identified in Annex IV to the Regulation. This is the exclusive remedy: Case 145/86 *Hoffmann v. Krieg* [1988] E.C.R. 645

possible,[42] although protective measures may be taken[43]: the policy of the Regulation is that measures should be available to prevent the judgment debtor from being able to frustrate a later enforcement, and there is therefore a strong presumption in favour of their being granted.[44] If the judgment is still subject to appeal in the state of origin, the court hearing the first appeal under Article 43, or the further appeal under Article 44 may stay the proceedings before it to await the outcome in the state of origin, or may grant enforcement conditional upon the giving of security, so as to preserve a proper balance between the parties.[45]

S14–223 **Recognition.** Article 33 of the Judgments Regulation[46] distinguishes between recognition and enforcement and provides that: (a) a judgment given in a Regulation State shall be recognised in the other Regulation States without any special procedure being required.[47] This was designed to abolish special procedures for recognition existing in some countries, such as Italy; (b) any interested party who raises the recognition of a judgment as the principal issue in a dispute may apply for a decision that the judgment be recognised.[48] This is designed to deal with a situation where a person who is not a party to the action in which a judgment was given wishes to raise the judgment as a defence, *e.g.* a bank in Regulation State B presented with a bill of exchange which has already been declared invalid in Regulation State A. In this case the jurisdiction of the court which gave the original judgment does not have to be verified by the court of the Regulation State in which the recognition is sought unless the matter in question falls within the scope of provisions relating to insurance, contracts, consumer contracts, or exclusive jurisdiction; (c) if the outcome of the proceedings in a court of a Member State depends on the determination of an incidental question of recognition that court shall have jurisdiction over the question.

S14–224 The object of Article 33 is to confer on judgments the authority and effectiveness accorded to them in the Regulation State in which they were given,[49] and accordingly a foreign judgment which is to be recognised under Article 33 must in principle have the same effect in the Regulation State in

---

[42] Art. 47 of the Regulation.

[43] Art. 47 of the Regulation. The measures may last only until the expiry of the appeal period: *Citoma Trading Ltd v. Republic of Brazil* [1999] C.L.C. 1847. The nature and availability of these protective measures otherwise depends on national procedural law, See also *Elwyn (Cottons) Ltd. v. Pearle Designs Ltd.* [1989] I.R. 9 (further proceedings: *Elwyn (Cottons) Ltd. v. Master of the High Court* [1989] I.R. 14). See generally Lipstein (1987) 36 I.C.L.Q. 873.

[44] Case 119/84 *Capelloni v. Pelkmans* [1985] E.C.R. 3147 (where it was also held that national law cannot require a separate judicial proceeding for protective measures; or require them to be taken before the appeal procedure under Art. 43 of the Regulation is exhausted; or make an order for protective measures subject to a confirmatory hearing).

[45] Art. 46 of the Regulation, departing from the corresponding provisions in Art. 38 of the Conventions which were held to confer these powers only on the court hearing the first appeal: Case C–432/93 *Société d'Informatique Service Réalisation Organisation v. Ampersand Software B.V.* [1995] E.C.R. I–2269; see also Case 258/83 *Brennero S.A.S. v. Wendel GmbH* (1984) E.C.R. 3971; *Petereit v. Babcock International Ltd.* [1990] 1 W.L.R. 350.

[46] Art. 26 of the Conventions is materially identical.

[47] Recognition involves according to the judgment the same effects in the State in which enforcement is sought as it does in the State in which the judgment was given: Case 145/86 *Hoffmann v. Krieg* [1988] E.C.R. 645. See also *Berkeley Administration Inc. v. McClelland* [1995] I.L.Pr. 201 (C.A.).

[48] See CPR, r. 74.10 for the procedure.

[49] Jenard, p. 43.

which recognition is sought as it does in the Regulation State in which it is given.[50] The grounds for non-recognition are the same as those for refusal to enforce.[51] The effect of Article 33 is that the English court will have to recognise judgments of Regulation States within the scope of the Regulation and will have very limited power to examine the jurisdiction of the foreign court.[52] Neither the Regulation, nor the Conventions or their Official Reports, give an answer to the difficult question of the scope of the estoppel which arises when the foreign judgment dismisses a case on grounds which are regarded in some countries as procedural and in others as substantive.[53]

Authentic instruments and court-approved settlements. Chapter III of the Regulation,[54] deals with the recognition and enforcement of judgments. Though the Title III category is broad enough to include, and does encompass, judgments by consent,[55] it does not extend to certain other procedural measures, found under the law of certain other Regulation States, by which a dispute may be brought to an end. The recognition and enforcement of two such measures is dealt with in Chapter IV. **S14–225**

An authentic instrument is a document which has been formally drawn up or registered as such. It must be drawn up by a public official, usually a civil law notary.[56] Under the law of certain Regulation States, such as Germany, the instrument takes effect as an express, conclusive, and enforceable, statement of a party's indebtedness, but which is obtained without the institution of court proceedings. Authentic instruments may be enforced in another Regulation State in accordance with the procedures in Articles 38 *et seq.* of the Regulation; the application for enforcement may be refused or a declaration of enforceability revoked only if enforcement of the instrument is manifestly contrary to the public policy of the Regulation State in which enforcement is sought. **S14–226**

A settlement which has been approved by a court in the course of proceedings is not regarded as a judgment within the scope of Chapter III, for it derives its authority from the parties' agreement, and not from the adjudication of a court; for this reason it does not enjoy the authority of *res* **S14–227**

---

[50] Case 145/86 *Hoffmann v. Krieg* [1988] E.C.R. 645, 666 (an enforcement case); *Boss Group Ltd. v. Boss France S.A.* [1997] 1 W.L.R. 351 (C.A.) (finding made in provisional proceedings in France not binding).

[51] Art. 34.

[52] See, *e.g. The Atlantic Emperor (No. 2)* [1992] 1 Lloyd's Rep. 624 (C.A.) (judgment of Italian court that contract did not incorporate arbitration clause).

[53] See Schlosser, para. 191. This is not likely to arise frequently in practice since the Foreign Limitation Periods Act 1984: see para. 14–031.

[54] Which corresponds to Title III of the Brussels and Lugano Conventions. For the procedure which governs the enforcement in England of authentic instruments and court settlements from other Regulation States, see S.I. 2001 No. 3928, which makes minor adaptations to the provisions of S.I. 2001 No. 3929.

[55] *Cf.* Case C–414/92 *Solo Kleinmotoren GmbH v. Boch* [1994] E.C.R. I–2237, at 2245, *per* Gulmann A.-G., drawing a distinction between this and a court-approved settlement.

[56] For examples, see German Code of Civil Procedure, Art. 794; *Office de Prevoyance v. Grand,* 1991 *Clunet* 162 (Cour d'App. Paris, 1990); *Tonon v. Office Cantonal de la Jeunesse de Tutlingen* [1995] I.L.Pr. 23 (French Cour de Cassation, 1991). But if the law of the state in question does not require the participation of, and authentication by, a public official, the document drawn up will not be an authentic instrument for the purposes of the Conventions: Case C–260/97 *Unibank A/S v. Christensen* [1999] E.C.R. I–3715: promissory note formally drawn up and enforceable under Danish law not authentic instrument as authentication by public official, even though this was not required by Danish law for the instrument to be enforceable.

judicata.[57] But if it is enforceable in the Regulation State in which it was concluded, it may be enforced under the same conditions as govern the enforcement of authentic instruments.

ILLUSTRATIONS

S14–228   1. A, a Frenchman, obtains a judgment against X, an Englishman, for 500,000 FF in a French court. The judgment is registrable in England under the Judgments Regulation and the Civil Jurisdiction and Judgments Order 2001.[58]

2. A obtains a final order from the French court ordering X to return a chattel to A. X brings the chattel to England. The order is registrable under the Judgments Regulation and the Civil Jurisdiction and Judgments Order 2001.

3. The facts are as in Illustration 2, except that the order is a provisional one pending trial of the merits in France. The provisional order is registrable.

4. A, a Frenchman, sues in France X, who is resident in New York, for 1,000,000 FF for breach of a contract to be performed in New York. X does not appear in the French court, which assumes jurisdiction on the basis of A's French nationality under Article 14 of the Civil Code. A obtains a default judgment. The judgment is registrable in England. The position would be different if the United Kingdom and the United States were to have entered into a treaty requiring non-enforcement of judgments rendered by third states on the basis of exorbitant provisions such as Article 14 of the French Civil Code, or if references to New York and the United States had been to Ontario and Canada, respectively.[59]

S14–229   5. A & Co., a German company, obtains from a German court, without notice to the respondent, X & Co., an English company, an injunction, which restrains X & Co. from various acts in relation to tapes made by a pop music group. The order is not registrable in England.[60]

6. A, a French public authority, obtains a default judgment in France against X, an Englishman who is not present or resident in France, and who has not submitted to the jurisdiction of the French courts. The judgment is registrable under the Judgments Regulation and the 2001 Order if the matter is a "civil or commercial matter" but not otherwise.[61]

7. A, a Frenchman, sues in France X, an Englishman, who is not resident in France, for breach of contract. X does not submit to the French jurisdiction. The French court assumes jurisdiction on the mistaken view that the contract was to be performed in France, and A obtains a default judgment. The judgment is registrable.

8. The facts are as in Illustration 7 except that X appears in the French proceedings to contest the jurisdiction but his objection fails and he takes no further part in the proceedings and judgment is entered in default of appearance. The judgment is registrable, not because of the appearance but because the French court has found that it has jurisdiction.

S14–230   9. The facts are as in Illustration 7, except that service on X under French law is not effected. Without proof of more, the judgment, is not registrable. But if X has since learned of the judgment, but taken no steps before the French court to challenge it, it will be registrable.[62]

10. A, a Frenchman, obtains a judgment in France against X, an Englishman. X appeals the judgment in France. A is entitled to register the judgment, but the English court may stay enforcement pending the appeal.[63]

---

[57] An English judgment by consent, though not an adjudication, has the authority of *res judicata: Landhurst Leasing plc v. Marcq* [1998] I.L.Pr. 822 (C.A.). See *loc. cit., supra,* n. 55, *per* Gulmann A.-G. Contrast the English "Tomlin order", whereby proceedings are stayed except for the purpose of putting into effect the terms of settlement scheduled to the order: that is not a judgment.

[58] S.I. 2001 No. 3929.

[59] Art. 59 of the Conventions, which is carried across into the Regulation by Art. 72.

[60] *E.M.I. Records Ltd. v. Modern Music GmbH* [1992] Q.B. 115.

[61] Case 29/76 *L.T.U. GmbH v. Eurocontrol* [1976] E.C.R. 1851.

[62] Art. 34(2) of the Regulation, making some departures from Art. 27(2) of the Conventions.

[63] Art. 46 of the Regulation.

11. A Frenchman obtains a judgment in France against X, a Frenchman with assets in England, and obtains an order for its registration. X appeals to the judge in chambers against the registration. Pending the appeal, A cannot execute the judgment, but the English court may order X not to remove his assets from the jurisdiction.[64]

12. A & Co., a French company, obtain a judgment in France for damages to be assessed against X & Co., an English company. X & Co.'s appeal fails, and judgment is entered for 7 million FF. A & Co. register the judgment in England. X & Co. institute a special form of procedure before the Court of Appeal in Paris to set aside the judgment on the ground that it was obtained by fraud. X & Co. also seek to set aside the registration in England on the ground that recognition would be manifestly contrary to public policy. Registration is confirmed because X & Co. have a sufficient remedy in the French court, and no stay of enforcement can be ordered because the application to the Court of Appeal in Paris is not an "ordinary appeal" within the meaning of Article 46.[65]

13. A, the receiver of a German company, obtains a judgment in Germany against X & **S14–231** Co., an English company. X & Co. appeal against the judgment. A registers the judgment in England. The court stays execution conditionally on X & Co. providing security pending the outcome of the appeal in Germany.[66]

14. A, a Belgian, brings proceedings in Belgium against X, an Englishman, who has left his residence without leaving a forwarding address. Substituted service pursuant to Belgian law is effected on X at a Belgian police station. Subsequently X informs A's lawyer of his new address, but service is not effected at the new address, and A obtains a judgment in default. In considering whether service was effected on X in sufficient time for him to arrange for his defence, the English court may take into account the fact that A was informed of X's new address, and also the fact that X contributed to the failure of the document originating the proceedings to reach him. But if X has learned of the judgment and has not taken steps before the Belgian court to challenge it, it will be entitled to recognition by reason of his default.[67]

15. The facts are as in Illustration 14, except that the substituted service was not in accordance with Belgian law. Without proof of more, the judgment is not registrable.[68] But if X has learned of the judgment but not taken steps before the Belgian court to challenge it, it will be registrable.[69]

The power to make provision under Section 39 of the 1982 Act extends to **14–235** any colony, and is not limited to Gibraltar and the Sovereign Base Areas: S.I. 1990 No. 2591, Art. 10. The registration in England of judgments from Gibraltar is not effected by the Judgments Regulation. But under the Judgments Regulation, judgments from Gibraltar will have effect in other Regulation States as if they were judgments from the courts of the United Kingdom.

4. PROTECTION OF TRADING INTERESTS ACT 1980

In *Lewis v. Eliades* [2003] EWHC 368 (QB), [2003] 1 All E.R. (Comm.) 850, **14–245** it was held that where an American court has given judgment which includes a sum under RICO (a Federal statute which allows for the trebling of damages in certain cases of fraudulent conduct) which is liable to be

---

[64] Art. 47 of the Regulation.
[65] *Interdesco S.A. v. Nullifire Ltd.* [1992] 1 Lloyd's Rep. 180.
[66] *Petereit v. Babcock International Ltd.* [1990] 1 W.L.R. 350
[67] Case 49/84 *Debaecker and Plouvier v. Bouwman* [1985] E.C.R. 1779 (a case on Art. 27(2) of the 1968 Convention, and which would therefore be reasoned differently under Art. 34(2) of the Regulation). Note also an argument that the service should be held to be ineffective as discriminating against the English defendant on grounds of nationality: *Re the Enforcement of a French Interlocutory Order* [2001] I.L.Pr. 208.
[68] Case C–305/89 *Isabelle Lancray S.A. v. Peters und Sickert K.G.* [1990] E.C.R. 1–2725 (a case on Art. 27(2) of the 1968 Convention).
[69] As a result of the changes brought about by Article 34(2) of the Regulation.

trebled, section 5 of the 1980 Act does not prevent enforcement of the non-RICO element of the judgment. If the sum awarded under RICO is for a compensatory element only, and has not been multiplied, the mere fact that the claimant may apply for its multiplication does not cause section 5 to apply to it either; but if an application to multiply the judgment is successful, the whole of the sum awarded under RICO will then become caught by section 5. A court may impose a condition on the enforcement of a foreign judgment that the claimant not seek to multiply it, or accept an undertaking not to enforce any such award if it be made by the foreign court: *cf. Donohue v. Armco Inc.* [2001] UKHL 64; [2002] 1 Lloyd's Rep. 425 (H.L.).

14–247 NOTE 43. Ord. 11, r. 1(2)(*b*) is replaced by CPR, r. 6.19(2).

14–248 NOTE 45. But the Canadian legislation, which is limited to anti-trust judgments, is not automatically enforceable, and where it is not made applicable by the Federal Attorney-General, a judgment for treble damages may be enforced in Canada: *Old North State Brewing Co. v. Newlands Services Inc.* [1999] 4 W.W.R. 573 (B.C.C.A.).

CHAPTER 15

JURISDICTION AND ENFORCEMENT OF JUDGMENTS UNDER MULTILATERAL CONVENTIONS

First and second sentences. In principle, these jurisdictional rules are **15–003** affected neither by Council Regulation (E.C.) 44/2001 ("the Judgments Regulation", reproduced in Part I of the appendix to this Supplement) nor by the 1968 and Lugano Conventions on jurisdiction and the enforcement of judgments in civil and commercial matters. Article 71 of the Judgments Regulation provides that it is not to affect any conventions to which the Regulation States (as to which see paras. 11–006—11–007, *supra*,) are parties and which, in relation to particular matters, govern jurisdiction or the recognition or enforcement of judgments. Similarly, Article 57 of each Convention provides that they do not affect such conventions to which the Contracting States are or will be parties.

The position under Articles 21 and 22 of the 1968 and Lugano Conventions is replicated (with some amendments) by Articles 27 and 28 of the Judgments Regulation.

NOTE 8. See *Andrea Merzario Ltd. v. Internationale Spedition Leitner Gesellschaft GmbH* [2001] 1 Lloyd's Rep. 490 (C.A.), disapproving *Frans Maas Logistics (U.K.) Ltd.* v. *CDR Trucking B.V.* [1999] 2 Lloyd's Rep. 179.

Text at note 14. Order 11, r. 1(2)(*b*) is replaced by CPR, r. 6.19(2). **15–005**

NOTE 26. Add: *Vertzyas v. Singapore Airlines Ltd.* (2000) 50 N.S.W.L.R. 1. **15–008**

NOTE 30. Add: *Vertzyas v. Singapore Airlines Ltd.* (2000) 50 N.S.W.L.R. 1. **15–009**

NOTE 32. For the parties to Additional Protocol No. 4 see S.I. 2000 No. **15–010** 3061. S. 3(2) of the 1979 Act was brought into force by S.I. 2000 No. 2768.

Text at note 33. See entry at para. 15–005, *supra*. **15–011**

NOTE 35. Order 11, r. 7 is replaced by CPR, r. 6.27.

NOTE 40. See entry at para. 15–005, *supra*. **15–012**

NOTE 64. For the applicability of the Carriage of Goods by Road Act 1965 in cases where the contract involves more than one type of carriage see *Quantum Corp. Inc v. Plane Trucking Ltd* [2002] EWCA Civ. 350; [2002] 1 W.L.R. 2678 (C.A.).

A further Convention for the Unification of Certain Rules for International Carriage by Air was concluded at Montreal in 1999. Provision has been made for the 1999 Convention to come into force in the United Kingdom when the Convention has entered into force internationally: Carriage by Air Acts (Implementation of the Montreal Convention 1999) Order 2002, S.I.

2002 No. 263, Art. 1. The 2002 Order makes various amendments to the Carriage by Air Act 1961 and the Carriage by Air (Supplementary Provisions) Act 1962. When in force, the 1999 Convention will, within its scope of application, supersede the earlier carriage by air conventions.

The jurisdictional provisions of the 1999 Conventio largely mirror those of the earlier Conventions. Under Article 33 of the 1999 Convention (which corresponds to Article 28 of the Warsaw Convention, as amended), an action for damages may be brought in a State Party (i) where the carrier is domiciled or (ii) where the carrier has its principal place of business or (iii) where the carrier has a place of business through which the contract was made or (iv) the place of destination (Art. 33(1)). In relation to damage resulting from the death or injury of a passenger, an additional ground of jurisdiction is provided: an action may also be brought in the State Party in which at the time of the accident the passenger has his principal and permanent residence as long as the carrier (i) operates services for the carriage of passengers by air to or from that place and (ii) conducts its business from premises leased or owned by the carrier or by another carrier with which it has a commercial agreement (Art. 33(2)). For the purposes of this rule, it makes no difference whether the carrier uses its own aircraft or those of another carrier pursuant to a commercial agreement. Article 46 of the 1999 Convention follows Article VIII of the Guadalajara Convention: where the actual carrier is not the contracting carrier, the plaintiff may being proceedings against the actual carrier either in the State Party where the contracting carrier may be sued (under Article 33) or where the actual carrier has its domicile or principal place of business.

15–016 The CMR Convention provides that where, in respect of a claim, an action is pending before a court or tribunal of a contracting country no new action shall be started between the same parties on the same grounds; it is also provided that no new action shall be started where a judgment has been entered by a court or tribunal of a contracting country unless the judgment is not enforceable in the country in which the fresh proceedings are brought.[72a] In *Andrea Merzario Ltd. v. Internationale Spedition Leitner Gesellschaft GmbH* [2001] 1 Lloyd's Rep. 490 (C.A.) it was held that, for the purposes of the CMR Convention, proceedings should not be regarded as pending until they were served. As, on the facts of the case, the claim form in the English action had been issued and served before proceedings had been served in Austria, the English proceedings were not stayed. The majority of the Court of Appeal also held (*obiter*) that the duty to grant a stay arises in a case where the first action is for a declaration of non-liability as well as in cases where the first action is for substantive relief.

15–017 NOTE 73. See entry at para. 15–005, *supra*.

NOTE 75. See entry at para. 15–011, n. 35, *supra*.

15–019 NOTE 85. See entry at para. 15–005, *supra*.

NOTE 87. See entry at para. 15–011, n. 35, *supra*.

15–023 NOTE 99. See entry at para. 15–005, *supra*.

[72a] Carriage of Goods by Road Act 1965, Sched., Art. 31(2).

NOTE 6. See entry at para. 15–005, *supra*.   **15–025**

NOTE 12. See entry at para. 15–005, *supra*.   **15–027**

NOTE 18. Order 71, rr. 40–44 is in Schedule 1 to the Civil Procedure Rules. **15–029**

NOTE 25. See *Algrete Shipping Co. Inc. v. International Oil Pollution* **15–031**
Compensation Fund 1971, The Sea Empress [2002] 2 All E.R. (Comm.) 416.

Third sentence. See entry at para. 15–011, n. 35, *supra*.   **15–032**

The analysis adopted in this paragraph applies (*mutatis mutandis*) to cases **15–043**
governed by the Judgments Regulation, as well as to those governed by the
1968 and Lugano Conventions. The grounds on which judgments are to be
refused recognition and enforcement under the Judgments Regulation are
set out in Articles 34 and 35.

CHAPTER 16

ARBITRATION AND FOREIGN AWARDS

16–008 When required to determine the seat of arbitration for the purposes of section 3 of the Arbitration Act 1996, the court should have regard not to the whole history of the arbitration leading up to the making of the award, but only to the relevant circumstances up to the point at which the relevant arbitration began: *Dubai Islamic Bank PJSC v. Paymentech Merchant Services Inc.* [2001] 1 Lloyd's Rep 65. See Petrochilos [2002] L.M.C.L.Q. 66.

16–010 First sentence. Council Regulation (E.C.) 44/2001 (which substantially replaces the 1968 Convention on jurisdiction and the enforcement of judgments in civil and commercial matters) also excludes arbitration from its scope: Art. 1.

16–014 NOTE 41. See also *XL Insurance Ltd. v. Owens Corning* [2000] 2 Lloyd's Rep. 500 (arbitration agreement governed (at least, in part) by English law; parent contract governed by the law of New York).

16–015 NOTE 46. Add: *Sonatrach Petroleum Corp. v. Ferrell International Ltd.* [2002] 1 All E.R. (Comm.) 627.

NOTE 48. Add: *Sonatrach Petroleum Corp. v. Ferrell International Ltd.* [2002] 1 All E.R. (Comm.) 627.

16–023 On the exercise of the court's discretion to make orders in support of a foreign arbitration (through the exercise of its power under section 44(2)(a) of the 1996 Act to order the taking of the evidence of witnesses) see *Commerce and Industry Insurance Co. of Canada v. Certain Underwriters at Lloyd's of London* [2002] 1 W.L.R. 1323.

NOTE 31. See Petrochilos [2000] L.M.C.L.Q. 99.

16–025 The right to appeal from the arbitral tribunal's decision to the court on a point of law (under section 69 of the 1996 Act) arises only in relation to questions of English law. Where the contract between the parties is governed by Swiss law, there is no possibility of an appeal under section 69: *Egmatra A.G. v. Marco Trading Corporation* [1999] 1 Lloyd's Rep. 862. See also *Sanghi Polyesters Ltd. (India) v. The International Investor (KCFC) (Kuwait)* [2000] 1 Lloyd's Rep. 480, where the arbitration agreement provided that the dispute was to be governed by "the Laws of England except to the extent it may conflict with Islamic Shari'a, which shall prevail"; *Reliance Industries Ltd. v. Enron Oil and Gas India Ltd.* [2002] 1 Lloyd's Rep. 645, where the contract was governed by Indian law, which on the relevant points was identical to English law; *Athletic Union of Constantinople v. National Arbitration Association* [2002] 1 Lloyd's Rep. 305; *Re Independent State of Papua New Guinea (No. 2)* [2001] 2 Qd.R. 162.

Note 84. Add: *Sanghi Polyesters Ltd. (India) v. The International Investor (KCFC) (Kuwait)* [2000] 1 Lloyd's Rep. 480.

Note 91. Order 11, r. 1(1)(*d*) is replaced by CPR, r. 6.20(5).   **16–028**

Note 93. The statement that CPR PD49G, para. 8.1 applies only to applications by and against parties to an arbitration and that it does not allow service out of the jurisdiction on a non-party was approved and applied in *Vale do Rio Doce Navegaçao S.A. v. Shanghai Bao Steel Ocean Shipping Co. Ltd.* [2000] 2 Lloyd's Rep. 1.

Text at note 95. Service out of the jurisdiction is effected under CPR, r. 6.20, which replaces Order 11, r. 1(1).

Note 96. The relevant part of Order 11 is replaced by CPR, r. 6.20.

Note 97. Add Juenger (2000) 60 Louisiana L.R. 1133.   **16–029**

In a case involving an arbitration whose seat is in England, if the parties **16–031** have chosen the law of another country to govern the merits of the dispute, section 46(1)(a) of the 1996 Act does not impose a mandatory requirement on the arbitral tribunal to obtain general evidence and guidance as to that foreign law; if there is no suggestion by the parties that there is an issue on which the chosen law differs from English law, the tribunal is free to decide the matter on the basis of the presumption that the chosen law is the same as English law: *Hussman (Europe) Ltd. v. Al Ameen Development & Trade Co.* [2000] 2 Lloyd's Rep. 83.

Note 14. Add Gaillard (2001) 17 Arb. Int. 59.   **16–032**

2. STAYING OF ENGLISH ACTIONS

It is provided that, "[n]o appeal shall lie to the Court of Appeal . . . except **16–038** as provided by Part I of the Arbitration Act 1996, from any decision of the High Court under that Part" (Supreme Court Act 1981, s. 18(1)(*g*), as amended). In *Inco Europe Ltd. v. First Choice Distribution* [2000] 1 W.L.R. 586 (H.L.) it was argued that, as the 1996 Act makes no provision for appeals against decisions under section 9, there was no mechanism whereby decisions of the High Court (whether to grant a stay under section 9 or to refuse a stay, such as on the basis that the alleged arbitration agreement is null and void) could be reviewed. The House of Lords held that, in view of the legislative history, the amended section 18(1)(*g*) of the Supreme Court Act 1981 should be read as not excluding appeals from decisions of the High Court under section 9 of the 1996 Act.

Note 32. S.I. 1996 No. 3211 is revoked and replaced by S.I. 1999 No. 2167, the effect of which is that, for the purposes of section 91 of the 1996 Act, as long as the other conditions are satisfied, an arbitration agreement is unfair under the Unfair Terms in Consumer Contract Regulations 1999 if it relates to a claim for a pecuniary remedy which does not exceed £5,000.

Note 35. See *Welex AG v. Rosa Maritime Ltd., The Epsilon Rosa (No. 2)* **16–040** [2002] EWHC 2033 Comm); [2002] 2 Lloyd's Rep. 81.

16–041 For the relationship between section 9 of the 1996 Act and section 12 (under which an application for an extension of time in which to commence an arbitration may be brought before the court) see *Grimaldi Compagnia di Navigazione SpA v. Sekihyo Lines Ltd.* [1999] 1 W.L.R. 708. See also *Thyssen Inc. v. Shipping Corp. S.A.* [2001] C.L.C. 805.

NOTE 48. *Patel v. Patel* is now reported at [2000] Q.B. 551.

A party who has initiated an application for a stay pending arbitration has not taken a "step" in the proceedings for the purposes of section 9(3) of the 1996 Act if he, either simultaneously or subsequently, invokes or accepts the court's jurisdiction, provided that he does so only conditionally on his stay application failing: *Capital Trust Investments Ltd. v. Radio Design T.J. A.B.* [2002] 2 All E.R. 159 (C.A.).

16–042 In *Al-Naimi v. Islamic Press Agency Ltd.* [2000] 1 Lloyd's Rep. 522 the Court of Appeal considered a number of procedural aspects of section 9 of the 1996 Act. Before granting a stay under section 9 the court must be satisfied that there is an arbitration clause between the parties and that the subject of the action is within the scope of the clause. Where the court cannot be sure of these matters, the grant of a stay under the court's inherent jurisdiction may nevertheless be the sensible course of action—thereby allowing the arbitral tribunal to determine its jurisdiction under section 30 of the 1996 Act. Although there will be cases in which the court feels unable to resolve the section 9 point without the issue being tried (in which case the court should make an order under CPR PD49G, para. 6.2, which replaced R.S.C. Order 73, r. 6(2)), the court should try to resolve the issue on the affidavit evidence, particularly if the parties agree that they would like the matter resolved on the affidavits.

16–043 In *Downing v. Al Tameer Establishment* [2002] EWCA Civ. 721; [2002] 2 All E.R. (Comm.) 545 the Court of Appeal had to decide when an arbitration clause becomes "inoperative" for the purposes of section 9(4) of the 1996 Act. Following a contractual dispute between the parties, the claimant sought to refer the dispute to arbitrators. When the defendant denied that there was an arbitration agreement between them, the claimant commenced court proceedings and the defendant then applied for stay under section 9 of the 1996 Act. The claimant argued that the arbitation agreement was "inoperative" as a result of its acceptance of the defendant's repudiatory breach of the arbitration agreement. The Court of Appeal accepted that, in view of the previous communications between the parties, the claimant had decided to abandon the remedy of arbitration. In the circumstances, the issue and service of proceedings by the claimant amounted to a clear and unequivocal indication that the claimant had accepted the defendant's repudiatory breach. Accordingly, the arbitration agreement was "inoperative" for the purposes of section 9(4) of the 1996 Act.

NOTE 57. See also *Cangene Corp. v. Octapharma A.G.* [2000] 9 W.W.R. 606 (Man.).

16–044 NOTE 60. See also *Hi-Fert Pty. Ltd. v. Kiukiang Maritime Carriers Inc.* (1996) 150 A.L.R. 54.

NOTE 62. In *Wealands v. CLC Contractors Ltd.* [1999] 2 Lloyd's Rep. 739 the Court of Appeal dismissed the appeal against Tuckey J.'s decision to order a stay under section 9 of the 1996 Act ([1998] C.L.C. 808).

Glencore Grain Ltd. v. Agros Trading Co. [1999] 2 Lloyd's Rep. 410 (noted **16–047** by Berg [2000] L.M.C.L.Q. 153) raised a question relating to the meaning of "dispute" in the context of an application to enforce an award rendered under G.A.F.T.A. arbitration rules. The contract between the parties provided that where an invoice was not settled without delay "a dispute shall be deemed to have arisen" (clause 11) and that neither party shall bring any legal proceedings "in respect of any such dispute until such dispute shall first have been heard and determined by the arbitrator(s) or a Board of Appeal, as the case may be" (clause 29). It was argued on the defendant's behalf that, as the defendant had admitted liability, there was no dispute between the parties. The Court of Appeal held that "dispute" in clauses 11 and 29 should bear the same meaning and that, as clause 11 deemed a dispute to exist in a case of delay in payment, there was a dispute for the purposes of clause 29 (a typical *Scott v. Avery* clause); the fact that the defendant had admitted liability was irrelevant. Although Clarke L.J. left the question open, it is implicit in the Court of Appeal's judgment that, had the case involved an application for a stay under section 9 of the 1996 Act, a stay would have been granted on the basis that the "dispute" deemed by clause 11 was, by virtue of clause 29, a matter which under the agreement was to be referred to arbitration.

NOTE 70. See the entry at para. 16–044, n. 62, *supra*.

NOTE 89. See Petrochilos [2000] L.M.C.L.Q. 99.   **16–053**

NOTE 90. For the position under New Zealand law (which has no equivalent **16–054** to section 11 of the 1996 Act) see *The Irina Zharkikh* [2001] 2 Lloyd's Rep. 319 (N.Z.).

Where legal proceedings are related to current arbitration proceedings, the **16–055** court may, under its inherent jurisdiction, grant a stay of the legal proceedings, pending the outcome of the arbitration. In *Reichhold Norway A.S.A. v. Goldman Sachs International* [2000] 1 W.L.R. 173 (C.A.) disputes arose out of the sale of a subsidiary company. J., a Norwegian company, had engaged the defendants as agent to advise and negotiate the sale on terms that the defendants would indemnify J. against consequent liability. The sale agreement between J. and the plaintiffs, which acquired the share capital, provided for disputes arising under the agreement to be referred to arbitration in Norway. The plaintiffs brought an action against the defendants in England, alleging negligent misstatement, and referred disputes under the sale agreement with J. to arbitration. The defendants were granted a stay of the English proceedings, pending determination of the arbitration in Norway.

NOTE 95. See *Bankers Trust Co. v. P.T. Jakarta International Hotels &* **16–056** *Development* [1999] 1 Lloyd's Rep. 910.

3. ENFORCEMENT OF FOREIGN AWARDS

A. *At Common Law*

NOTE 98. *Uniforêt Pâte Port-Cartier Inc. v. Zerotech Technologies Inc.* [1998] **16R–058** 9 W.W.R. 688 (B.C.) suggests that the test for determining whether an award is final and conclusive is the same as that applicable in the context of the recognition and enforcement of foreign judgments (on which see paras. 14R–018 *et seq.* of the main work). The English authorities involving the enforcement of foreign awards have been concerned with awards requiring the payment of a sum of money and there has been no consideration of the enforcement of other types of award. *Uniforêt Pâte Port-Cartier Inc. v. Zerotech Technologies Inc.* indicates that, in the inter-provincial context in Canada, a judgment which confirms an arbitration award is, in principle, enforceable in other provinces notwithstanding the fact that the judgment is not a monetary judgment.

16–062 NOTE 13. *Westacre Investments Inc. v. Jugoimport-SPDR Holding Co. Ltd.* is reported at [2000] 1 Q.B. 288 (C.A.).

16–064 Order 11, r. 1(1)(*m*) is replaced by CPR, r. 6.20(9).

16–065 *The St. Anna* [1983] 1 W.L.R. 895 was not followed in *The Bumbesti* [2000] Q.B. 559. Aikens J. held that he was bound by *The Beldis* [1936] P. 51 (C.A.) to conclude that the court does not have jurisdiction under section 20(2)(*h*) of the Supreme Court Act 1981 in respect of proceedings to enforce an arbitration award.

16–067 On the question whether, in cases where there is an unsatisfied award in the claimant's favour, the claimant may, in appropriate circumstances, bring proceedings *in rem* on the same cause of action see *The Irina Zharkikh* [2001] 2 Lloyd's Rep. 319 (N.Z.). See also West [2002] L.M.C.L.Q. 259.

16–068 NOTE 31. Add: *Uniforêt Pâte Port-Cartier Inc. v. Zerotech Technologies Inc.* [1998] 9 W.W.R. 688 (B.C.).

16–087 NOTE 84. See entry at para. 16–062, n. 13, *supra*.

C. *Under Part III of the Arbitration Act 1996*

16–106 On the requirement that the claimant should produce the original arbitration agreement or a duly certified copy of it, see *Proctor v. Schellenberg* [2002] 7 W.W.R. 287 (Man. Q.B.).

16–109 A decision of the Islamic Shari'a Council in London is neither a judgment (because the Shari'a Council is not a judicial body established under the law of any State) nor an arbitration award, unless, and to the extent that, the Shari'a Council's decision deals with matters expressly referred to it by the parties to a dispute. Where a dispute between parties entitled under a will is referred to the Shari'a Council by the testator's Trusteeship Council (which is not a party to the dispute), the resulting decision cannot be regarded as an arbitration award: *Al Midani v. Al Midani* [1999] 1 Lloyd's Rep. 923.

NOTE 34. Add: *Cf.* Kojovic (2001) 18 J.Int.Arb. 511.

16–112 Second sentence. See *Corporacion Transnacional de Inversiones S.A. de C.V. v. STET International SpA* (1999) 45 O.R. (3rd) 183, a case concerning an application to set aside an award under Article 34 of the UNCITRAL Model Law, which reproduces the grounds for refusing recognition and enforcement under the New York Convention. The appeal was dismissed: (2000) 49 O.R. (3d) 414 (Ont. C.A.).

NOTE 50. See also *Irvani v. Irvani* [2000] 1 Lloyd's Rep. 412 (C.A.) which **16–114**
suggests that there is a breach of section 103(2)(*c*) if it is established either
that the arbitrator's decision was influenced by pressure brought to bear by
a third party or that the award was based on information which was not
available to one of the parties and, therefore, on which that party was
unable to comment.

In a case where the respondent chooses to take no part in the arbitration, **16–116**
the fact that the hearing takes place in a city other than that designated by
the arbitration agreement (albeit in the same country) is not sufficient to
justify enforcement of the award being refused on the basis of section
103(2)(e): *Tongyuan (U.S.A.) International Trading Group v. Uni-Clan Ltd.*
(2001, unreported).

NOTE 62. See also Freyer (2000) 17(2) J. Int. Arb. 1; Lastenouse (1999) 16 J. **16–118**
Int. Arb. 25; Petrochilos (1999) 48 I.C.L.Q. 856; Wahl (1999) 16 J.Int. Arb.
131. *Cf. Spier v. Calzaturificio Tecnica*, 71 F. Supp. 2d 279 (S.D.N.Y. 1999)
(application for re-argument dismissed: 77 F. Supp. 2d 405 (S.D.N.Y.
1999)) in which enforcement of an arbitration award made by Italian
arbitrators in Italy and annulled by the Italian courts on the basis that the
arbitrators had exceeded their authority was refused. See also Goode (2001)
17 Arb.Int. 73.

It has been held that the English court has power under its inherent **16–121**
jurisdiction to suspend an English award in circumstances where an
application to have the award set aside is pending; the exercise of this
power should be guided by the principles laid down by Staughton L.J. in
Soleh Boneh International Ltd. v. Government of the Republic of Uganda
[1993] 2 Lloyd's Rep. 208: *Apis A.S. v. Fantazia Kereskedelmi K.F.T.* [2001] 1
All E.R. (Comm.) 348. Although the court will normally act under section
103(5) of the 1996 Act on the application of one of the parties, the power to
stay enforcement proceedings under section 103(5) can be exercised by the
court of its own motion: *Dardana Ltd. v. Yukos Oil Co.* [2002] EWCA Civ.
543; [2002] 2 Lloyd's Rep. 326 (C.A.).

NOTE 68. See also *G. v. G.* [2000] 7 W.W.R. 363 (Alta.) in which it was held **16–122**
that a dispute arising out of a prenuptial agreement which purported to
exempt the parties from the provisions of the Matrimonial Property Act
1980 (Alta.) was not incapable of settlement by arbitration. *Cf. Metrocall
Inc. v. Electronic Tracking Systems Pty Ltd* (2000) 52 N.S.W.L.R. 1 (Ind.
Rels Comm.).

Text at notes 71–73. In *Soleimany v. Soleimany* [1999] Q.B. 785 (C.A.) (a
case involving an English award) enforcement of an arbitration award
upholding a contract which involved an illicit enterprise, illegal under the
law of the place of performance, was refused on the ground of public policy.
By contrast, in *Westacre Investments Inc. v. Jugoimport-SPDR Holding Co.
Ltd.* [2000] Q.B. 288 (C.A.), it was held that, if an allegation that the
underlying contract was illegal has been raised before the arbitral tribunal
and rejected, enforcement of an arbitration award upholding the contract
should not be refused on public policy grounds—unless there was fresh
evidence which called into question the arbitral tribunal's conclusion on the
illegality point. The scope of these decisions was considered by Timothy
Walker J. in *Omnium de Traitement et de Valorisation SA v. Hilmarton Ltd.*

[1999] 2 Lloyd's Rep. 222 (noted by Hill [2000] L.M.C.L.Q. 311). OTV had appointed H to act as consultant in connection with a public contract in Algeria. Under the terms of the contract, which was expressly governed by Swiss law and provided for the arbitration of disputes in Switzerland, H was entitled to a commission on the public contract being awarded to OTV. OTV secured the contract, but only half the agreed commission was paid. In the arbitration proceedings, OTV argued that H's claim for the unpaid commission should be dismissed on the ground that it was contrary to a mandatory law of Algeria, the place of performance of the contract. The arbitrator accepted that the appointment of H as a consultant "wittingly" breached Algerian law but, because, as no bribery was involved, the contract was not illegal or contrary to public policy under Swiss law, made an award in H's favour. H sought to enforce the award in England under Part III of the 1996 Act and OTV argued that enforcement would be contrary to public policy. Timothy Walker J. held that enforcement of the award would not be contrary to English public policy: OTV's reliance on the *Soleimany* decision was "misplaced" because in the *Soleimany* case the element of "corruption or illicit practice" was present and "the whole of the judgment of the Court of Appeal has to be read in that context" (at p. 225); the element of corruption or illicit practice was not present in the *OTV* case and, accordingly, there was a parallel with the *Westacre* case, in which the arbitral tribunal had decided that there had been no bribery. However, it should be noted that, whereas performance of the contract in *Westacre* was not contrary to Kuwaiti law, the contract in the *OTV* case involved a breach of Algerian law. Furthermore, the *ratio* of the *Soleimany* case is that, if the English court would not directly enforce the contract because of illegality, it will not enforce an arbitration award based on such a contract; had the dispute in the *OTV* case been litigated in England, the court would have refused to enforce the contract—on the basis of the principle laid down in *Regazzoni v. K.C. Sethia (1944) Ltd.* [1958] A.C. 301 (see Timothy Walker J.'s judgment at p. 224).

For the purposes of Rule 63(5) public policy should be interpreted as including E.C. public policy. In Case C–126/97 *Eco Swiss China Time Ltd. v. Benetton International N.V.* [1999] E.C.R. I–3055 a dispute arising out of a licensing agreement had been referred to arbitration in the Netherlands under Dutch law. The arbitral tribunal ordered the defendant to pay damages to the plaintiff. The defendant applied to the court to have the award set aside on the ground that, because the licensing contract was a nullity under Article 81 E.C. (formerly Article 85), the award was contrary to public policy. During the arbitration proceedings neither the parties nor the arbitrators had raised the point that the licensing contract might be contrary to E.C. law. In response to the questions posed by the Dutch court, the European Court ruled that a national court to which an application is made for annulment of an arbitration award on grounds of public policy must grant that application if it considers that the award in question is in fact contrary to Article 81 E.C. (formerly Article 85). The Court also observed that the provisions of Article 81 E.C. (formerly Article 85) may be regarded as a matter of public policy within the meaning of the New York Convention. Accordingly, in a case where enforcement of an arbitration award is resisted in England on the basis of public policy, if the underlying contract between the parties is contrary to Article 81 E.C. (formerly Article 85) enforcement of the award should be refused.

In a case where the defandant allegies that a New York Convention award has been obtained by fraud and this allegation has been considered (and rejected) by a foreign court, a question arises as to whether the foreign decision should be treated as creating an issue estoppel on the question of fraud. On this point, see the discussion of Judge Chambers Q.C. in *Arab Business Consortium International Finance and Investment Co. v. Banque Franco-Tunisienne* [2002] 1 Lloyd's Rep. 511; 538–541; affd. without reference to this point [2003] EWCA Civ. 205 (C.A.).

NOTE 73. Add: See Enonchong [2000] L.M.C.L.Q. 495.

NOTE 83. See entry at para. 16–062, n. 13, *supra*.   **16–128**

CHAPTER 17

MARRIAGE

1. FORMAL VALIDITY

17R–001 NOTE 10. Foreign Marriages Act 1892, s. 1(2), as inserted by the Foreign Marriages (Amendment) Act 1988, s. 1(2), is amended by the British Overseas Territories Act 2002, s. 2(3); the reference to "a British Dependent Territories citizen" is now to be read as a reference to a British overseas territories citizen.

17–005 A marriage in Hindu form in England, with no attempt being made to comply with the Marriage Acts, was not a valid marriage: *Gandhi v. Patel*, July 31, 2001. For the purposes of section 25(4) of the Inheritance (Provision for Family and Dependants) Act 1975, this was not a "void marriage" but no marriage at all. See also *A-M. v. A-M. (Divorce: Jurisdiction: Validity of Marriage)* [2001] 2 F.L.R. 6 (at entry to para. 17-010, below).

17–010 In *A-M. v. A-M. (Divorce: Jurisdiction: Validity of Marriage)* [2001] 2 F.L.R. 6, the parties had twice gone through ceremonies in England: the first, a marriage in Islamic form, did not comply with English formalities; the second was a ceremony to revoke an earlier *talak* and was equally insufficient to constitute a marriage. It was nonetheless held that there was a marriage which the English court could dissolve, the court referring both to cohabitation and repute (with no discussion of choice of law issues) and to the fact that the parties could have entered into a marriage in an Islamic country without any ceremony (though this does not seem to have been alleged on the facts). *Sed quaere.*

17–014 NOTE 35. Add: Murphy (1996) 47 N.I.L.Q. 35.

17–028 For the view that the exemption from local law enjoyed by belligerent forces of occupation is an emerging rule of customary international law, see Lipstein, *Fetstschrift für Ulrich Drobnig*, 381.

17–031 NOTE 22. In the definition of "United Kingdom national" in s. 1(2) of the 1892 Act, the reference to "a British Dependent Territories citizen" is now to be read as a reference to a British overseas territories citizen: British Overseas Territories Act 2002, s. 2(3).

17–035 NOTE 38. Foreign Marriages Act 1892, s. 1(2), as inserted by the Foreign Marriages (Amendment) Act 1988, s. 1(2), is amended by the British Overseas Territories Act 2002, s. 2(3); the reference to "British Dependent Territories citizen" is now to be read as a reference to a British overseas territories citizen.

17–040 NOTE 47. In the definition of "United Kingdom national" in s. 1(2) of the 1892 Act, the reference to "a British Dependent Territories citizen" is now

to be read as a reference to a British overseas territories citizen: British
Overseas Territories Act 2002, s. 2(3).

2. CAPACITY

See Murphy (2000) 49 I.C.L.Q. 643. For same-sex marriages, see Bates **17–068**
(1999) 21 Liverpool L.R. 49.

4. POLYGAMOUS MARRIAGES

References to British Dependent Territories citizenship in the British **17–186**
Nationality Act 1981 are now to be read as being to British overseas
territories citizenship: British Overseas Territories Act 2002, s. 2(3).

CHAPTER 18

MATRIMONIAL CAUSES

1. DIVORCE, NULLITY AND JUDICIAL SEPARATION

A. *Jurisdiction of the English courts*

18R–001 The 1998 Convention (as to which see para. 18–013) never came into force, and was overtaken by the extension of the competence of the European institutions by the Treaty of Amsterdam's establishment of an "area of freedom, security and justice". The draft Convention was converted, with modifications, into a Regulation, Council Regulation 1347/2000 of May 29, 2000 on jurisdiction and the recognition and enforcement of judgments in matrimonial matters and in matters of parental responsibility for children of both spouses (for text see [2000] O.J. L160) binding on Member States and coming into force on March 1, 2001. Related changes were made in English law by the European Communities (Matrimonial Jurisdiction and Judgments) Regulations 2001 (S.I. 2001 No. 310). The provisions of the Regulation apply only to legal proceedings instituted after March 1, 2001 (Art. 42(1)). See McEleavy (2002) 51 I.C.L.Q. 883. For the present text of the Rule substitute:

English courts have jurisdiction to entertain proceedings for divorce or judicial separation if, but only if,
(a) the spouses are habitually resident in England; or
(b) the spouses were last habitually resident in England, in so far as one of them still resides there; or
(c) the respondent is habitually resident in England; or
(d) in the event of a joint application, either of the spouses is habitually resident in England; or
(e) the applicant is habitually resident in England and resided there for at least a year immediately before the application was made; or
(f) the applicant is habitually resident in England and resided there for at least six months immediately before the application was made and is domiciled in England; or
(g) both spouses are domiciled in England; or
(h) no court of a Member State has jurisdiction under the Council Regulation and either of the parties to the marriage was domiciled in England on the date when the proceedings were begun
Provided that where the respondent spouse (a) is habitually resident in the territory of a Member State of the European Union; or (b) is a national of a Member State other than the United Kingdom or Ireland; or (c) is domiciled in Ireland, the English courts have jurisdiction only under paragraphs (a) to (g) of this Rule.

(Regulation, Arts. 2, 7, 41; Family Law Act 1986, s. 5(2) as amended by European Communities (Matrimonial Jurisdiction and Judgments) Regulations 2001 (S.I. 2001 No. 310), reg. 3(3). Denmark is not a Member State for the purposes of the Regulation: Art. 1(3).).

The Regulation gives jurisdiction to deal with counterclaims (Art. 5) and for a court which has granted a legal separation to have jurisdiction to convert that into a divorce, if the law of that Member State so provides (Art. 6). Article 12 of the Regulation provides that, in urgent cases, the provisions of the Regulation do not prevent the courts of a Member State from taking such provisional, including protective, measures in respect of persons or assets in that State as may be available under the law of that Member State, even if, under the Regulation, the court of another Member State has jurisdiction as to the substance of the matter. The scope of the power to order provisional or protective measures under Brussels II was considered by the Court of Appeal in *Wermuth v. Wermuth* [2003] EWCA Civ. 50, [2003] 1 W.L.R. 942 (C.A.). Emphasising that Art. 12 should be given a strict interpretation to avoid usurping the functions of the court in the other Member State and following the approach taken in respect of claims under Brussels I (see para. 8–024), the court held that maintenance pending suit could not be classed as a provisional or protective measure.

Where the English court is seised of a case over which it has no jurisdiction under the Regulation and over which a court of another Member State has jurisdiction by virtue of the Regulation, it must declare of its own motion that it has no jurisdiction (Art. 9).

Where proceedings are begun in England and the respondent is habitually resident in another Member State and does not enter an appearance, the court must stay the proceedings so long as it is not shown that the respondent has been able to receive the document instituting the proceedings or an equivalent document in sufficient time to enable him to arrange for his defence, or that all necessary steps have been taken to this end (Art. 10(1)); but this provision is replaced by those in Article 19 of Council Regulation 1348/2000 of May 29, 2000 on the service in the Member States of judicial and extrajudicial documents in civil or commercial matters (as to which see para. 8–043) or in Article 15 of the Hague Service Convention of 1965 (as to which see para. 8–040) if the document instituting the proceedings was transmitted abroad under that Regulation or Convention (Art. 10(2)).

For staying of proceedings on other grounds, see para. 18R–227.

Proposals for a new Council Regulation on jurisdiction and the recognition and enforcement of judgments in matrimonial matters and in matters of parental responsibility, which would repeal Regulation 1347/2000 ([2000] O.J. L160/19) and amend Regulation 44/2001 ([2000] O.J. L307/28) in the maintenance context, were presented by the Commission in May 2002: COM (2002) 222 final.

NOTE 5. Add: *I. v. I. (Divorce: Habitual Residence)* [2001] 1 F.L.R. 913 (twelve month qualifying period of habitual residence can be satisfied despite actual residence for part of that period in another country).

In December 2000, the Government finally abandoned any plans to implement Part II of the Family Law Act 1996. **18–012**

Illustration 1. The English court would now have jurisdiction only if W **18–022** became habitually resident in England and either (a) resided there for at least a year; or (b) resided there for at least six months and acquired a domicile in England: Council Regulation 1447/2000, Arts. 2, 7, 41.

Illustration 2. The position is the same under Council Regulation 1447/2000, Arts. 2, 7, 41.

Illustration 3. The position is the same under Council Regulation 1447/2000, Arts. 2, 5, 7, 41; Art. 5 refers to "counterclaims" which would certainly include H's cross-petition; the position is less clear as to W's supplemental petition.

18R–024 The jurisdictional rules in Council Regulation 1347/2000 of May 29, 2000 on jurisdiction and the recognition and enforcement of judgments in matrimonial matters and in matters of parental responsibility for children of both spouses (as to which see para. 18R–001) govern jurisdiction in proceedings for nullity of marriage (Art. 1(1)(a)). Related changes were made in English law by the European Communities (Matrimonial Jurisdiction and Judgments) Regulations 2001 (S.I. 2001 No. 310). The provisions of the Regulation apply only to legal proceedings instituted after March 1, 2001 (Art. 42(1)). For the present text of the Rule substitute:

English courts have jurisdiction to entertain proceedings for divorce or judicial separation if, but only if,
(a) the spouses are habitually resident in England; or
(b) the spouses were last habitually resident in England, in so far as one of them still resides there; or
(c) the respondent is habitually resident in England; or
(d) in the event of a joint application, either of the spouses is habitually resident in England; or
(e) the applicant is habitually resident in England and resided there for at least a year immediately before the application was made; or
(f) the applicant is habitually resident in England and resided there for at least six months immediately before the application was made and is domiciled in England; or
(g) both spouses are domiciled in England; or
(h) no court of a Member State has jurisdiction under the Council Regulation and either of the parties to the marriage
(i) was domiciled in England on the date when the proceedings were begun; or
(ii) died before that date and either was at death domiciled in England or had been habitually resident in England throughout the period of one year ending with the date of death;
Provided that where the respondent spouse (a) is habitually resident in the territory of a Member State of the European Union; or (b) is a national of a Member State other than the United Kingdom or Ireland; or (c) is domiciled in Ireland, the English courts have jurisdiction only under paragraphs (a) to (g) of this Rule.

(Regulation, Arts. 2, 7, 41; Family Law Act 1986, s. 5(3) as amended by European Communities (Matrimonial Jurisdiction and Judgments) Regulations 2001 (S.I. 2001 No. 310), reg. 3(3). Denmark is not a Member State for the purposes of the Regulation: Art. 1(3).).

18–028 Illustration 1. The court now has jurisdiction only after W has become habitually resident in England and has resided there for at least six months: Council Regulation 1447/2000, Arts. 2, 7, 41.

B. *Choice of Law*

When it became unlikely that section 9 of the Family Law Act 1996 would **18–032** be brought into force, other approaches to the problem were explored. In *N. v. N. (Jurisdiction: Antenuptial Agreement)* [1999] 2 F.L.R. 745, the wife sought specific performance of an ante-nuptial agreement that obliged the husband to obtain a ghet after a civil divorce. The court held that it had no jurisdiction to enforce such an agreement, but indicated that in appropriate circumstances the grant of a decree absolute to a husband refusing a ghet could be delayed, he could be denied a hearing on ancillary matters, and his refusal might give rise to "financial or other hardship" for the purposes of sections 5 and 10 of the Matrimonial Causes Act 1973. The court cited M. Freeman, *Law, Religion and the State*, in Lowe and Douglas (eds.), *Families Across Frontiers* (1998). In accordance with the approach in *N. v. N.*, a decree absolute was refused in *O. v. O. (Jurisdiction: Jewish Divorce)* [2000] 2 F.L.R. 147.

Fresh statutory provision was made by the Divorce (Religious Marriages) Act 2002, s. 1, which repeals section 9(3) and (4) of the Family Law Act 1996. This inserts a new section 10A into the Matrimonial Causes Act 1973, applying if a decree of divorce had been granted but not made absolute and the parties to the marriage concerned were married in accordance with the usages of the Jews, or any other religious usages prescribed by an order of the Lord Chancellor, and must co-operate if the marriage is to be dissolved in accordance with those usages (s. 10A(1)). On the application of either party, the court may order that a decree of divorce is not to be made absolute until a declaration made by both parties in a form specified in rules of court that they have taken such steps as are required to dissolve the marriage in accordance with those usages is produced to the court (s. 10A(2)). Any inaccuracy in the declaration does not affect the validity of a decree of divorce made by reference to the declaration (s. 10A(5)). The court may make such an order only if it is satisfied that in all the circumstances of the case it is just and reasonable to do so (s. 10A(3); and an order may be revoked at any time (s. 10A(4).

C. *Recognition of Foreign Decrees*

(1) DECREES GRANTED IN THE BRITISH ISLES

A *talak* pronounced in England is ineffective under Clause (3) of the Rule: **18–055** *Sulaiman v. Juffali* [2002] 1 F.L.R. 479.

(2) DECREES OBTAINED OUTSIDE THE BRITISH ISLES

From March 1, 2001 when Council Regulation 1347/2000 of May 29, 2000 **18R–057** on jurisdiction and the recognition and enforcement of judgments in matrimonial matters and in matters of parental responsibility for children of both spouses (for text see [2000] O.J. L160) comes into force, Rules 79 to 82 apply only in respect of divorces, legal separations or annulments of marriage obtained in countries which are not Member States of the European Union. Denmark is not a Member State for the purposes of the Regulation: Art. 1(3). In relations between Member States, the Regulation takes precedence over the Hague Convention of June 1, 1970 on the

Recognition of Divorces and Legal Separations (Art. 37). Insert new material as follows:

(1A) DECREES OBTAINED IN OTHER MEMBER STATES OF THE EUROPEAN UNION

RULE 78A—**A divorce, legal separation or annulment of marriage pronounced by a court of a Member State will, subject to Rule 82A, be recognised in England** (Council Regulation 1347/2000, Arts. 13(1), 14(1)).

COMMENT

Chapter III of Council Regulation 1347/2000 contains provisions for the recognition and enforcement of judgments pronounced in the courts of other Member States. "Judgment" is defined to include a divorce, legal separation or marriage annulment pronounced by a court of a Member State, whatever the judgment may be called, including a decree, order or decision (Art. 13(1)). Documents which have been formally drawn up or registered as authentic instruments and which are enforceable in a Member State, and settlements which have been approved by a court in the course of proceedings and are enforceable in the Member State in which they were concluded, are subject to the same rules as to recognition and enforcement as judgments (Art. 13(3)). The provisions of the Regulation apply only to legal proceedings instituted, to documents formally drawn up or registered as authentic instruments and to settlements which have been approved by a court in the course of proceedings after March 1, 2001 (Art. 42(1)). With regard to a Member State in which two or more systems of law or sets of rules concerning matters governed by the Regulation apply in different territorial units, (a) any reference to habitual residence in that Member State refers to habitual residence in a territorial unit; (b) any reference to nationality, or in the case of the United Kingdom "domicile", refers to the territorial unit designated by the law of that State; (c) any reference to the authority of a Member State having received an application for divorce or legal separation or for marriage annulment refers to the authority of a territorial unit which has received such an application; and (d) any reference to the rules of the requested Member State refers to the rules of the territorial unit in which jurisdiction, recognition or enforcement is invoked (Art. 41).

No special procedure is required for the recognition of a divorce, legal separation or marriage annulment pronounced by a court of another Member State (Art. 14(1); see also Art. 14(2) on the consequential amendment of records of civil status). Where the recognition of a judgment is raised as an incidental question in a court of a Member State, that court may determine that issue (Art. 14(4)). However, the question of recognition or non-recognition may also be raised by "any interested party" using the procedures prescribed in the Regulation for the enforcement of judgments (Art. 14(3)). Those latter procedures are more appropriately considered below, para. 19–066.

18–062 NOTE 3. Add: For a similar development in Ireland, see *McG. v. D.W. (No. 1)* [2001] 1 I.R.L.M. 107; Hill (2001) 50 I.C.L.Q. 144.

18–068 In *Wicken v. Wicken* [1999] Fam. 224, a divorce in Gambia was held "effective" there. Under Gambian law a particular method of proof would be required, but those evidential requirements were matters for the *lex fori* and had no application in England.

In *Kellman v. Kellman* [2000] 1 F.L.R. 785, it was held in this context but on **18–078** very unusual facts that "effective" connoted a less rigorous standard than "valid". A "mail-order" divorce in Guam, an incorporated territory of the United States, was *prima facie* not entitled to recognition in any other part of the United States. However, in further proceedings in Guam 10 years later, one party attempted to have the decree set aside, but this was refused on estoppel grounds. That judgment was entitled to full faith and credit in other parts of the United States. As a result there was no longer any jurisdiction within the United States in which the validity of the divorce could be challenged, and it was held that in those circumstances, the divorce had to be regarded as "effective".

Illustration 7. Were the divorce granted after March 1, 2001, it, being **18–084** granted in another Member State of the European Union, would now be recognised in England on that basis: Council Regulation 1347/2000, Arts. 13(1), 14(1).

A talak pronounced in Lebanon was recognised under section 46(1) of the **18–094** Family Law Act 1986. The requirement to register the talak after the event in a Sharia court was held sufficient to constitute proceedings. The test was said to be "whether the divorce depends for its validity, at least in part, on what can properly be termed 'proceedings'": the effect of the words "at least in part" is obscure: *El Fadl v. El Fadl* [2000] 1 F.L.R. 175.

A bare talak pronounced by the husband in England was located there, **18–095** despite the fact that the parties were domiciled in and nationals of Saudi Arabia: *Sulaiman v. Juffali* [2002] 1 F.L.R. 479.

Illustrations 1, 2 and 4. The decree, being granted in another Member State **18–109** of the European Union, would now be recognised in England on that basis: Council Regulation 1347/2000, Arts. 13(1), 14(1).

Rule 82 does not apply to divorces, annulments of marriage or judicial **18R–111** separations pronounced in other Member States of the European Union. See Rule 82A. Denmark is not a Member State for the purposes of the Regulation: Art. 1(3).

NOTE 34. See *El Fadl v. El Fadl* [2000] 1 F.L.R. 175 (no need for advance **18–118** notice in case of Lebanese *talak*).

The observation in the text, that it is unclear what policy is served by **18–119** requiring an official document, was referred to with evident approval in *Wicken v. Wicken* [1999] Fam. 224, where a foreign divorce was recognised despite the absence of documentation.

A divorce granted by a court in Northern Cyprus will be recognised in **18–120** England if it was obtained in accordance with the relevant conditions applicable to that part of Cyprus: *Emin v. Yeldag* [2002] 1 F.L.R. 956, not following (after submissions on behalf of the Attorney-General and the Secretary of State for Foreign and Commonwealth Affairs) *B. v. B.*

(*Divorce: Northern Cyprus*) [2000] 2 F.L.R. 707 (where recognition refused on grounds of public policy, the "Turkish Republic of Northern Cyprus" not being recognised by the United Kingdom).

18–121   NOTE 48. Add: *El Fadl v. El Fadl* [2000] 1 F.L.R. 175. *Cf. Wheeler v. Wheeler* [1997] 3 C.I.L.R. 362 (Grand Ct., Cayman Is); Davies (2001) 50 I.C.L.Q. 133.

18–123   Illustrations 1, 2 and 4. Were similar facts to lead to the grant of a divorce after March 1, 2001, the court would now be obliged to refuse recognition: Council Regulation 1347/2000, Art. 15(1); see Rule 82A.

D. Effect in England of foreign decrees

18R–125   Insert new material:

RULE 82A—**A divorce, annulment or legal separation entitled to recognition under Rule 78A must be refused recognition in England**

(a) **if such recognition is manifestly contrary to English public policy; or**

(b) **where it was given in default of appearance, if the respondent was not served with the document which instituted the proceedings or with an equivalent document in sufficient time and in such a way as to enable the respondent to arrange for his or her defence unless it is determined that the respondent has accepted the judgment unequivocally; or**

(c) **if it is irreconcilable with a judgment given in English proceedings between the same parties; or**

(d) **if it is irreconcilable with an earlier judgment given in another Member State or in a non-Member State between the same parties, provided that the earlier judgment fulfils the conditions necessary for its recognition in England (Art. 15(1)).**

COMMENT

The Rule states the effect of Article 15(1) of Council Regulation 1347/2000, which sets out the grounds on which divorces, annulments of marriage or judicial separations pronounced in other Member States must be refused recognition. The provisions of the Regulation apply only to legal proceedings instituted, to documents formally drawn up or registered as authentic instruments and to settlements which have been approved by a court in the course of proceedings after March 1, 2001 (Art. 42(1)). In each case, refusal of recognition is mandatory and is not a matter on which the English court has a discretion. Subject to that, ground (a) corresponds to Family Law Act 1986, s. 51(3)(*c*), as to which see para. 18–120. However, the test of public policy may not be applied to the rules relating to jurisdiction (Art. 17). Ground (b) raises similar issues to those in Family Law Act 1986, s. 51(3)(*a*), as to which see para. 18–115. Grounds (c) and (d) raise similar issues to those addressed in Family Law Act 1986, s.51(1), as to which see para. 18–113.

Article 16 of the Regulation enables a Member State to enter into agreements with non-Member States under which the Member State will not recognise judgments pronounced elsewhere in the European Union where jurisdiction to give that judgment could only have been on grounds of jurisdiction other than those specified in Articles 2 to 7, in other words it was a case of "residual jurisdiction" under Article 8 applying national law. (*Cf.* para. 14–204 for the similar case under the Brussels or Lugano Conventions.)

The jurisdiction of the court of the Member State of origin may not be reviewed (Art. 17). The recognition of a judgment relating to a divorce, legal separation or an annulment of marriage may not be refused because English law would not allow divorce, judicial separation or annulment on the same facts (Art. 18). Under no circumstances may a judgment be reviewed as to its substance (Art. 19). If recognition is sought in England of a judgment given in another Member State the court may stay the proceedings if an ordinary appeal against the judgment has been lodged (Art. 20(1)). If the judgment was given in Ireland, the English court may stay the proceedings if enforcement is suspended in Ireland by reason of an appeal (Art. 20(2)).

The preclusion notion was discussed, without any conclusion being reached, **18–132** in *P.K. v. T.K.* [2002] I.R. 186 (Sup. Ct.).

4. FINANCIAL RELIEF

A. *Jurisdiction of the English courts*

The English court is unlikely to grant leave where the applicant is **18–163** essentially seeking to enforce a foreign order for financial provision and has not exhausted other methods of enforcement: *Jordan v. Jordan* [1999] 2 F.L.R. 1069 (C.A.). The Court of Appeal in that case held that it was not essential that the applicant establish hardship, rejecting a suggestion to that effect in *N.S. v. N. (Foreign Divorce: Financial Relief)* [1997] 1 F.L.R. 900.

NOTE 26. The Maintenance Orders (Facilities for Enforcement) Order 1959, **18–171** S.I. 1959 No. 377, is further amended by S.I. 2002 No. 789.

Maintenance Orders (Facilities for Enforcement) Act 1920, s. 4(5B)(6A) is **18–174** amended by Access to Justice Act 1999, s. 90(1), Sched. 13, para. 7(1), (2) (3)(a), Sched. 15, Pt V, Table (7).

NOTE 47. Additional reciprocating countries are designated by S.I. 2001 No. **18–176** 3501 and S.I. 2002 No. 788. The Magistrates' Courts (Reciprocal Enforcement of Maintenance Orders) Rules 1974, S.I. 1974 No. 668, are further amended by S.I. 2002 No. 1734.

The clerk to the justices is now the justices' chief executive: Maintenance **18–182** Orders (Reciprocal Enforcement) Act 1972, section 26(6), as amended by Access to Justice Act 1999, section 90(1), Sched. 13, paras. 71, 76.

NOTE 89. The Recovery Abroad of Maintenance (Convention Countries) Order 1975, S.I. 1975 No. 423 is further amended by S.I. 2002 No. 2839.

The clerk to the justices is now the justices' chief executive: Maintenance **18–183** Orders (Reciprocal Enforcement) Act 1972, sections 27 and 32, as amended by Access to Justice Act 1999, section 90(1), Sched. 13.

18–185 NOTE 8. The Reciprocal Enforcement of Maintenance Orders (Hague Convention Countries) Orders 1993 is further amended by S.I. 2001 No. 2567 and by S.I. 2002 No. 2838.

C. Enforcement of Foreign Maintenance Orders

18–207 NOTE 64. Add: *Cartwright v. Cartwright* [2002] EWCA Civ. 931, [2002] 2 F.L.R. 610.

18–214 A lump sum order may fall within s. 21 of the Maintenance Orders (Reciprocal Enforcement) Act 1972 as amended if it is intended for maintenance purposes, but not if it represents a division of property: *Cartwright v. Cartwright* [2002] EWCA Civ. 931, [2002] 2 F.L.R. 610.

5. STAYING OF MATRIMONIAL PROCEEDINGS

18R–227 With effect from March 1, 2001, when Council Regulation 1347/2000 (as to which see para. 18R–001) came into force, Rule 89(2) is subject to the following new sub-rule:

(3) Where the jurisdiction of the English court is derived from Council Regulation 1347/2000 and

(i) proceedings involving the same cause of action and between the same parties have been brought in England and in another Member State, or

(ii) proceedings for divorce, legal separation or annulment of marriage not involving the same cause of action and between the same parties are brought in England and in another Member State,

and the courts of the other Member State were seised first, the court must of its own motion stay the English proceedings until such time as the jurisdiction of the court first seised is established; and where the jurisdiction of the court first seised is established, the court must decline jurisdiction (Regulation, Art. 11(1)(2)(3). Denmark is not a Member State for the purposes of the Regulation: Art. 1(3)).

For this purpose, a court is seised (a) at the time when the document instituting the proceedings or an equivalent document is lodged with the court, provided that the applicant has not subsequently failed to take the steps he was required to take to have service effected on the respondent; or (b) if the document has to be served before being lodged with the court, at the time when it is received by the authority responsible for service, provided that the applicant has not subsequently failed to take the steps he was required to take to have the document lodged with the court (*ibid.* Art. 11(4)). The provisions of the Regulation apply only to legal proceedings instituted after March 1, 2001 (Art. 42(1)).

18–231 In *C. v. C. (Divorce: Stay of English Proceedings)* [2001] 1 F.L.R. 624, decisive factors in the decision to stay the English proceedings were the existence of a prenuptial contract and mutual wills, both made under French law, and the fact that, in the circumstances of the case, a French divorce would be recognised in England but an English divorce would probably be refused recognition in France.

Cf. Otobo v. Otobo [2002] EWCA Civ. 949; [2003] 1 F.L.R. 192, where the issue whether an English decree would be recognised in Nigeria was raised at a late stage; a stay of the English proceedings, which had been commenced first, was refused, the Court of Appeal emphasising the test of the balance of fairness.

The habitual residence of a child of the parties is an important factor in considering the appropriate forum for divorce proceedings which would lead to a determination as to who should care for the child: *Cheema v. Cheema* [2001] 3 W.W.R. 629 (B.C.C.A.).

NOTE 43. Add: *Breuning v. Breuning* [2002] EWHC 236 (Fam), [2002] 1 F.L.R. 888.

NOTE 50. Add: *Krenge v. Krenge* [1999] 1 F.L.R. 969 (German forum advantageous to one party, but stay on basis that it is the natural forum).

CHAPTER 19

CHILDREN

2. GUARDIANSHIP AND CUSTODY

A. *Jurisdiction of the English court*

19R–011 The 1998 Convention (as to which see para. 19–034) never came into force, and was overtaken by the extension of the competence of the European institutions by the Treaty of Amsterdam's establishment of an "area of freedom, security and justice". The draft Convention was converted, with modifications, into a Regulation, Council Regulation 1347/2000 of 29 May 2000 on jurisdiction and the recognition and enforcement of judgments in matrimonial matters and in matters of parental responsibility for children of both spouses (for text see [2000] O.J. L160) binding on Member States and coming into force on March 1, 2001. The provisions of the Regulation apply only to legal proceedings instituted after March 1, 2001 (Art. 42(1)). Sub-rule (3) is subject to an additional Proviso:

And provided that where the English court is exercising jurisdiction on an application for divorce, judicial separation or nullity of marriage under Article 2 of Council Regulation 1347/2000, it has jurisdiction in a matter relating to parental responsibility over a child of both spouses if, and only if,

(i) the child is habitually resident in England; or

(ii) the child is not habitually resident in England, but is habitually resident in one of the Member States and (a) at least one of the spouses has parental responsibility in relation to the child; and (b) the jurisdiction of the English courts has been accepted by the spouses and is in the best interests of the child (Regulation, Arts. 3(1)(2), 7, 41; Denmark is not a Member State for the purposes of the Regulation: Art. 1(3)).

The Regulation does not define the concept of "matters relating to parental responsibility". This jurisdiction must be exercised in conformity with the Hague Convention on the Civil Aspects of International Child Abduction, and in particular Articles 3 and 16 thereof (Art. 4) (see *Re L. Abduction: Jurisdiction*) [2002] EWHC 1864 (Fam); [2002] 1 W.L.R. 3208 (so existing case-law on the Hague Convention remains applicable under the Regulation). This prevents decisions on the merits of a custody application being taken where an application under the Hague Convention is pending or imminent (see para. 19–100). Jurisdiction under the Regulation ceases as soon as (a) the judgment allowing or refusing the application for divorce, judicial separation or nullity of marriage has become final; or (b) in those cases where proceedings in relation to parental responsibility are still pending on that date, a judgment in these proceedings has become final; or (c) the proceedings referred to in (a) and (b) have come to an end for another reason (Art. 3(3)).

Insert a new sub-rule (7A):

(7A) Where the jurisdiction of the English court is derived from Council Regulation 1347/2000 and proceedings involving the same cause of action and between the same parties have been brought in England and in another Member State, and the courts of the other Member State were seised first, the court must of its own motion stay the English proceedings until such time as the jurisdiction of the court first seised is established; and where the jurisdiction of the court first seised is established, the court must decline jurisdiction (Regulation, Art. 11(1)(2)(3). Denmark is not a Member State for the purposes of the Regulation: Art. 1(3)).

For this purpose, a court is seised (a) at the time when the document instituting the proceedings or an equivalent document is lodged with the court, provided that the applicant has not subsequently failed to take the steps he was required to take to have service effected on the respondent; or (b) if the document has to be served before being lodged with the court, at the time when it is received by the authority responsible for service, provided that the applicant has not subsequently failed to take the steps he was required to take to have the document lodged with the court (*ibid*. Art. 11(4)).

Proposals for a new Council Regulation on jurisdiction and the recognition and enforcement of judgments in matrimonial matters and in matters of parental responsibility, which would repeal Regulation 1347/2000 ([2000] O.J. L160/19) and amend Regulation 44/2001 ([2000] O.J. L307/28) in the maintenance context, were presented by the Commission in May 2002: COM (2002) 222 final.

When a court in another Member State is seised of a case and has jurisdiction derived from Council Regulation 1347/2000, the English court cannot acquire jurisdiction to deal with issues of parental responsibility on any basis (except for provisional measures in urgent cases (Art. 12)) unless and until the proceedings in the foreign court have become final (Arts 9, 11). Where an appeal is pending in the Member State concerned, the proceedings will not be regarded as final: *A. v. A. (Jurisdiction: Brussels II)* [2002] 1 F.L.R. 1042.

The Adoption and Children Act 2002 (not yet in force) introduces two new forms of order, special guardianship orders which vest parental responsibility in the special guardians to the exclusion of the natural parents (see s. 115 of the 2002 Act), and contact orders under section 26 of the 2002 Act in respect of children placed for adoption (or to be so placed by an adoption agency). These new orders are custody orders for the purposes of Part I of the Family Law Act 1986 (section 1 of which is amended by the 2002 Act, Sched. 3, para. 47), and the jurisdictional rule stated in clause (4) of the Rule applies to them: Family Law Act 1986, s. 2(2A)(2B) as inserted by Adoption and Children Act 2002, Sched. 3, para. 48.

Adoption Act 1976 is largely repealed and replaced by Adoption and **19–012** Children Act 2002 (not yet in force).

In *Al Habtoor v. Fotheringham* [2001] EWCA Civ. 186 (C.A.), Thorpe L.J. **19–016** warned against reliance on British nationality as a basis for assuming jurisdiction: "[T]he courts of this country should be extremely circumspect in assuming any jurisdiction in relation to children physically present in some other jurisdiction founded only on the basis of nationality. *Parens patriae* jurisdiction has a fine resounding history [but] the *parens patriae* concept must seem even more esoteric to other jurisdictions than the concept of domicile".

19–018 "British Dependent Territories citizens" are now British overseas territories citizens: British Overseas Territories Act 2002, s. 2.

NOTE 21. Add: *Cartwright v. Cartwright* [2002] EWCA Civ. 931; [2002] 2 F.L.R. 610.

19–020 NOTE 67. *T. v. R. (Abduction: Forum Conveniens)* [2002] 2 F.L.R. 544 (child present in England; Swedish court could deal with case without the child physically returning there).

19–030 NOTE 93. Children Act 1989, s. 10 is amended by Adoption and Children Act 2002, Sched. 3, para. 56.

19–031 If courts in England and in another part of the United Kingdom are both seised of divorce proceedings and applications for orders relating to a child are made in both sets of proceedings, the English court will resolve the matter by reference to the rules as to staying matrimonial proceedings in Schedule 1 to the Domicile and Matrimonial Proceedings Act 1987, stated in Rule 89: *A. v. A. (Forum Conveniens)* [1999] 1 F.L.R. 1.

19–037 Text and note 19. Proceedings under the Adoption and Children Act 2002 will be "family proceedings" when that Act is in force. Children Act, s. 8 is amended by Adoption and Children Act 2002, Sched. 3, para. 55.

19–038 The jurisdictional rules were given an extended meaning by Singer J. in *Re P. (A Child: Mirror Orders)* [2000] 1 F.L.R. 435. A United States court was prepared to allow a child to travel to England on condition that a "mirror order" was made by the English court to ensure the child's return. The English courts have often adopted a similar practice. The child in the instant case was neither habitually resident nor present in England. Nonetheless an order was made on the basis of "common sense, comity and public policy"; it was expressly limited to the period during which the child was present in England. The convenience of the outcome is clear, but it is not in accordance with the jurisdictional rules in the Family Law Act 1986.

19–043 NOTE 34. Add: *M. v. M.*, 2002 S.C. 103.

19–047 The principles applied in considering applications were restated by the Court of Appeal in *Payne v. Payne* [2001] EWCA Civ. 166; [2002] Fam. 473. The court emphasised the primacy of the welfare principle: although there was no presumption in favour of the applicant parent, reasonable proposals of a parent with a residence order would carry great weight, as would the possibility of future contact.

A court considering the possible removal of a child from the jurisdiction will not generally interfere with what it regards as a reasonable decision by the custodial parent: *Re H. (Application to Remove from Jurisdiction)* [1998] 1 F.L.R. 848 (C.A.); *Re K. (Application to remove Children from Jurisdiction)* [1998] 2 F.L.R. 1006: *Re C. (Leave to Remove from Jurisdiction)* [2000] 2 F.L.R. 457 (C.A.). This practice does not conflict with Article 8 of the European Convention on Human Rights: *Re A. (Permission to Remove Child from Jurisdiction)* [2000] 2 F.L.R. 225 (C.A.).

NOTE 47. The court may require steps to be taken to ensure the return of the child, *e.g.* the taking of oaths on the Koran before a Sharia judge in

Saudi Arabia before the child was taken there for a holiday by its mother, who was separated from the father: *Re A. (Security for Return to Jurisdiction)* [1999] 2 F.L.R. 1; *Re T. (Staying Contact in Non-Convention Country)* [1999] 1 F.L.R. 262n (notarised agreement and mirror order of Cairo court required before child could travel to Egypt); *Re S. (Removal from Jurisdiction)* [1999] 1 F.L.R. 850 (exequatur in foreign court of English order and bond of £135,000 pending such action before child could go to Chile); *Re L. (Removal from Jurisdiction: Holiday)* [2001] 1 F.L.R. 241 (£50,000 bond, sworn undertakings), *Re S. (Leave to Remove from Jurisdiction: Securing Return from Holiday)* [2001] 2 F.L.R. 507 (children made wards, declarations that they were habitually resident in England and British citizens; order on High Commission that only short-term tourist visa be granted). The principles applied are the same, whether the application is under Children Act 1989, s. 13(1) (where a residence order is in force, see para. 19–045) or under 1989 Act, s. 8: *Re M. (Leave to Remove Child from Jurisdiction)* [1999] 2 F.L.R. 334. Because cases of this type may involve a sensitive examination of practice in foreign legal systems, they should be heard by a Family Division judge: *Re K. (Removal from Jurisdiction)* [1999] 2 F.L.R. 1084 (C.A.).

B. *Effect of foreign guardianship and custody orders*

NOTE 56. Add: *Re AGN (Adoption: Foreign Adoption)* [2000] 2 F.L.R. 431. **19–051**

From March 1, 2001, in Rule 94(1) after "1985" insert "and to Council **19R–058** Regulation 1347/2000 of May 29, 2000 on jurisdiction and the recognition and enforcement of judgments in matrimonial matters and in matters of parental responsibility for children of both spouses". See para. 19–066.

Abduction is not always by one parent. See *Re KR (Abduction: Forcible* **19–062** *Removal by Parents)* [1999] 4 All E.R. 954, where a girl, taken by her parents to India against her will with a view to an arranged marriage, was returned after having been made a ward of court in England by her sister.

NOTE 8. Add to first sentence: *Re Z. (A Minor) (Abduction: Non-Convention* **19–064** *Country)* [1999] 1 F.L.R. 1270. In *Osman v. Elisha* [2000] Fam. 62 (C.A.), the return of children to Sudan was ordered: the court was satisfied that the courts there applied a welfare principle, although it would be applied in the context of cultural and religious norms which differed from those prevailing in England. The court rejected the suggestion that *Re M. (Abduction: Peremptory Return Order)* [1996] 1 F.L.R. 478 (C.A.) was decided *per incuriam*: that case had "a legitimate place in the stream of authority". See *Al Habtoor v. Fotheringham* [2001] EWCA Civ. 186 (C.A.) (return to Dubai on similar grounds). It was said of *Osman v. Elisha* that it "perhaps represents the high-water mark in this development of the law": *W. and W. v. H. (Child Abduction: Surrogacy) (No. 2)* [2002] 2 F.L.R. 252.

NOTE 10. The making of orders requiring solicitors to disclose the where- **19–065** abouts of their client or the client's child creates conflicting duties and is a limitation on legal professional privilege. The power will be exercised with sensitivity to this fact: *Re B. (Abduction: Disclosure)* [1995] 2 F.C.R. 601 (C.A.); *Re H. (Whereabouts Order to Solicitors)* [2000] 1 F.L.R. 766.

19–066 **Council Regulation 1347/2000.** The 1998 Convention never came into force, and was overtaken by the extension of the competence of the European institutions by the Treaty of Amsterdam's establishment of an "area of freedom, security and justice". The draft Convention was converted, with modifications, into a Regulation, Council Regulation 1347/2000 of May 29, 2000 on jurisdiction and the recognition and enforcement of judgments in matrimonial matters and in matters of parental responsibility for children of both spouses (for text see [2000] O.J. L160) binding on Member States and coming into force on March 1, 2001. In relations between Member States, the Regulation takes precedence over a number of multilateral Conventions in so far as they concern matters governed by the Regulation (Art. 37). They include the European Convention of May 20, 1980 on Recognition and Enforcement of Decisions concerning Custody of Children and on Restoration of Custody of Children (as to which, see para. 19–067). The provisions of the Regulation apply only to legal proceedings instituted, to documents formally drawn up or registered as authentic instruments and to settlements which have been approved by a court in the course of proceedings after March 1, 2001 (Art. 42(1)).

Chapter III of Council Regulation 1347/2000 contains provisions for the recognition and enforcement of judgments pronounced in the courts of other Member States. Denmark is not a Member State for the purposes of the Regulation: Art. 1(3). "Judgment" is defined to include a judgment relating to the parental responsibility of the spouses given on the occasion of proceedings for divorce, legal separation or annulment of marriage, whatever the judgment may be called, including a decree, order or decision (Art. 13(1). For jurisdiction, see para. 19R–011). Documents which have been formally drawn up or registered as authentic instruments and which are enforceable in a Member State, and settlements which have been approved by a court in the course of proceedings and are enforceable in the Member State in which they were concluded, are subject to the same rules as to recognition and enforcement as judgments (Art. 13(3)).

A judgment relating to the parental responsibility of the spouses given on the occasion of proceedings for divorce, legal separation or annulment of marriage will be recognised in England without any special procedure (Arts. 13(2), 14(1)). Where the recognition of a judgment is raised as an incidental question in a court of a Member State, that court may determine that issue (Art. 14(4)). However, the issue of recognition or non-recognition may also be raised by "any interested party" using the procedures prescribed in the Regulation for the enforcement of judgments (Art. 14(3); see *infra*).

With regard to a Member State in which two or more systems of law or sets of rules concerning matters governed by the Regulation apply in different territorial units, (a) any reference to habitual residence in that Member State refers to habitual residence in a territorial unit; (b) any reference to nationality, or in the case of the United Kingdom "domicile", refers to the territorial unit designated by the law of that State; (c) any reference to the authority of a Member State having received an application for divorce or legal separation or for marriage annulment refers to the authority of a territorial unit which has received such an application; and (d) any reference to the rules of the requested Member State refers to the rules of the territorial unit in which jurisdiction, recognition or enforcement is invoked (Art. 41).

Grounds for non-recognition. However, the English court must not recognise a judgment (a) if such recognition is manifestly contrary to

English public policy; or (b) if it was given, except in case of urgency, without the child having been given an opportunity to be heard, in violation of fundamental principles of English procedure; or (c) where it was given in default of appearance if the person in default was not served with the document which instituted the proceedings or with an equivalent document in sufficient time and in such a way as to enable that person to arrange for his or her defence unless it is determined that such person has accepted the judgment unequivocally; or (d) on the request of any person claiming that the judgment infringes his or her parental responsibility, if it was given without such person having been given an opportunity to be heard; or (e) if it is irreconcilable with a later judgment relating to parental responsibility given in the Member State in which recognition is sought; or (f) if it is irreconcilable with a later judgment relating to parental responsibility given in another Member State or in the non-Member State of the habitual residence of the child provided that the later judgment fulfils the conditions necessary for its recognition in England (Art. 15(2). *Cf.* Rule 82A, setting out the rules for the non-recognition of divorces, legal separations and annulments.)

Article 16 of the Regulation enables a Member State to enter into agreements with non-Member States under which the Member State will not recognise judgments pronounced elsewhere in the European Union where jurisdiction to give that judgment could only have been on grounds of jurisdiction other than those specified in Articles 2 to 7, in other words it was a case of "residual jurisdiction" under Article 8 applying national law. (*Cf.* para. 14–204 for the similar case under the Brussels or Lugano Conventions.)

The jurisdiction of the court of the Member State of origin may not be reviewed (Art. 17). The recognition of a judgment relating to a divorce, legal separation or an annulment of marriage may not be refused because English law would not allow divorce, judicial separation or annulment on the same facts (Art. 18). Under no circumstances may a judgment be reviewed as to its substance (Art. 19). If recognition is sought in England of a judgment given in another Member State the court may stay the proceedings if an ordinary appeal against the judgment has been lodged (Art. 20(1)). If the judgment was given in Ireland, the English court may stay the proceedings if enforcement is suspended in Ireland by reason of an appeal (Art. 20(2)).

Enforcement. A judgment on the exercise of parental responsibility in respect of a child of both parties given in a Member State which is enforceable in that Member State and has been served must be enforced in England when, on the application of any interested party, it has been registered for enforcement in England (Art. 21(1)(2)). An application for a declaration of enforceability must be made to the High Court (Art. 22 and Annex I). The procedure is a matter for the *lex fori* (Art. 23(1); but see Arts. 23(2)(3), 32–35 as to representation and documents, Art. 25 as to notification of the decision, Art. 30 as to legal aid, and Art. 31 as to security for costs). The High Court is required to give its decision without delay. The person against whom enforcement is sought is not at this stage of the proceedings entitled to make any submissions on the application (Art. 24(1)). The application may be refused only for one of the reasons specified in Articles 15, 16 and 17 (Art. 24(2); for Arts. 15, 16, and 17, see above: Art. 17 in fact contains no ground for refusal). Under no circumstances may a judgment be reviewed as to its substance (Art. 24(3)). An applicant may request partial enforcement of a judgment. Where a judgment has been given in respect of several matters and enforcement cannot be authorised for all of them, the court must authorise partial enforcement (Art. 29).

Either party may appeal against the decision to the High Court (see Art. 26 and Annex II; rules of court will determine how the appeal is to be heard). The judgment given on appeal may be contested only by a single further appeal on a point of law (Art. 27 and Annex III. See Art. 28 for suspension pending appeal in the Member State of origin).

19–067 Text to note 15. The inconvenience sometimes resulting from the need to deal with an application under the Hague Convention before an accompanying application under the European Convention was the subject of comment in *Re D. (Abduction: Discretionary Return)* [2000] 1 F.L.R. 24.

19–068 NOTE 19. For parties, see now S.I. 2001 No. 3923.

19–069 In exceptional circumstances, a child may be separately represented in proceedings under the European Convention: *Re T. (Abduction: Appointment of Guardian ad Litem)* [1999] 2 F.L.R. 796. *Cf.* the practice under the Hague Convention: below, para. 19–094.

19–072 NOTE 30. Add: *S.D. v. R.S. (Child Abduction)* [1996] 3 I.R. 524.

NOTE 31. Add: *Re T. (Abduction: Child's Objections to Return)* [2000] 2 F.L.R. 192.

NOTE 38. Add: *T. v. R. (Abduction: Forum Conveniens)* [2002] 2 F.L.R. 544 (where the phrase "effects of the original decision" was interpreted to mean the enforcement of the foreign decision without delay). In *Re L. (Abduction: European Convention: Access)* [1999] 2 F.L.R. 1089, the fact that the foreign court proceeded under a misapprehension as to the country in which the child was then living was treated as a "change of circumstances"; *sed quaere.*

19–076 See Beaumont and McEleavy, *The Hague Convention on International Child Abduction* (1999); Armstrong (2002) 51 I.C.L.Q. 427.

NOTE 52. For parties, see now S.I. 2001 No. 3923.

NOTE 56. Add: *Re H. (Abduction: Child of 16)* [2000] 2 F.L.R. 51 (age at date of hearing decisive).

19–077 See Beaumont and McEleavy, *The Hague Convention on International Child Abduction* (1999), Chap. 7.

NOTE 59. Add: *Re H. (Abduction: Habitual Residence: Consent)* [2000] 2 F.L.R. 294 (where parents held to be habitually resident in different countries); *Re N. (Abduction: Habitual Residence)* [2000] 2 F.L.R. 899 (similar facts); *B. v. H. (Habitual Residence: Wardship)* [2002] 1 F.L.R. 388. *Cf. Re S. (A Child)* [2002] EWCA Civ. 1771 (Family Law Act 1986, s. 41, has no application in Hague Convention cases).

19–078 NOTE 63. Add: *Re V-B. (Abduction: Custody Rights)* [1999] 2 F.L.R. 192 (C.A.) (right under Dutch law to be informed of and consulted as to major decisions affecting child held not to amount to "rights of custody"); *Chief Executive of the Dept for Courts v. Phelps* [2000] 1 N.Z.L.R. 168; *Director-*

General of Families, Youth and Community Care v. Hobbs (2000) F.L.C. 93–007.

NOTE 64. The point discussed in the note was clarified by the House of Lords in *Re H. (Child Abduction: Rights of Custody)* [2000] 2 A.C. 291 (where the rights of custody were held to be vested in a foreign court). Although in one case (*Re S. (Abduction: Separate Representation of Children* [1997] 2 F.C.R. 342) a foreign court had been represented, it was proper, and generally more appropriate, for the application for the return of the child to be made by the parent whose application to the foreign court had given that court rights of custody. In *Re JS (Private International Adoption)* [2000] 2 F.L.R. 638, the rights were vested in an adoption agency in Texas which successfully applied for the return of the child by the prospective adopters in England.

Text to notes 65 to 67. That a court could be an "institution or body" possessing rights of custody for the purposes of the Convention was affirmed by the House of Lords in *Re H. (Child Abduction: Rights of Custody)* [2000] 2 A.C. 291, where the relevant cases are reviewed. In *Re C. (Abduction: Wrongful Removal)* [1999] 2 F.L.R. 859, Hale J. held that a court could have rights of custody for the purposes of the Convention when it was actively seised of an application for a parental responsibility order, and rejected the view of the Child Abduction Unit expressed in the *Practice Note* of 1998. She reached a similar conclusion in *Re J. (Abduction: Rights of Custody)* [1999] 2 F.L.R. 653 (affirmed on grounds unrelated to this point, [2000] 1 F.L.R. 78 (C.A.)), where applications had been made for both a parental responsibility order and a prohibited steps order. These developments were noted by the Court of Appeal in *Re H. (Child Abduction: Rights of Custody)* [2000] 1 F.L.R 201, where Thorpe L.J. offered some further guidance. An application for contact would not vest rights of custody in a court, but one dealing with the physical care of the child or with parental responsibility might do so. It was necessary to scrutinise the nature of the application, its merits, and the commitment of the applicant to its pursuit. The House of Lords, in dismissing a further appeal, merely observed that the application must raise matters of custody within the meaning of the Convention and that required in each case a consideration of the terms of the application. The House also held that the court would be vested with rights of custody in appropriate cases from the time the document initiating the proceedings is served until the proceedings were stayed or disposed of: [2000] 2 A.C. 291. In *Re G. (child abduction) (unmarried father rights of custody)* [2002] EWHC 2219 (Fam), it was held that the issue of proceedings for a residence order, where there had been no service on the other party, did not of itself give the court rights of custody.

NOTE 67. Add: *Brooke v. Director General, Department of Community Services (NSW)* (2002) 29 Fam. L.R. 121 (Full Ct. of Fam. Ct. of Australia) (interim *ne exeat* order).

Rights of custody may be exercised even if the relevant parent is in hospital. **19–079** There is no need for there to be day-to-day exercise of care, section 3 being designed to exclude only those parents with no meaningful role in the child's life: *J.S. v. S.S.* (Court of Session, February 6, 2003). For a similar decision where the parent was in prison, see *M.S.H. v. L.H.* (Irish Supreme Ct., 2000).

NOTE 71. In *Chan v. Chow* (2001) 199 D.L.R. (4th) 478 (B.C.C.A.) it was held that the rights of custody could arise under a judicial or administrative decision made in a country other than that from which the child was abducted (and recognised in that country).

19–080 NOTE 74. Add: *Dellabarca v. Christie* [1999] 2 N.Z.L.R. 548 (N.Z. C.A.). The argument that under the law of Zimbabwe, the country of habitual residence, the separation of the parents gave all custody rights to the mother, so that her removal of the child could not be wrongful in terms of the Convention, was rejected in *Re D. (Abduction: Custody Rights)* [1999] 2 F.L.R. 626. Allowing the domestic law of the country of habitual residence to determine the issue in that way would effectively "negative" the Convention. For criticism of *Re F. (A Minor) (Abduction: Custody Rights Abroad)* [1995] Fam. 224 (C.A.), see Beaumont and McEleavy, *The Hague Convention on International Child Abduction* (1999), pp. 62–63.

NOTE 79. Add: Beaumont and McEleavy, *The Hague Convention on International Child Abduction* (1999), pp. 58–61. In *Re G. (Abduction: Rights of Custody)* [2002] 2 F.L.R. 703, the child was placed with its grandmother, with the consent of the mother. The unmarried father of the child later moved in to help care for the child. Following *Re B. (A. Minor) (Abduction)* [1994] 2 F.L.R. 249 (C.A.) and the "inchoate rights" notion, it was held that he had rights of custody. In such cases, the relevant parent would have had to have spent a "significant time" caring for the child, but in the case of a young child that might be of relatively short duration. However, in *Re G. (child abduction) (unmarried father rights of custody)* [2002] EWHC 2219 (Fam), Munby J. distinguished the earlier cases in which it had been held that an unmarried father had rights of custody: in none of those cases had the mother, who alone had legal custody, been the child's primary carer. He held that an unmarried father sharing the care of the child with the mother did not require rights of custody for the purposes of the Convention. *Re B. (A Minor) (Abduction)* [1994] 2 F.L.R. 249 (C.A.) was not followed by the Irish Supreme Court in *HI. v. MG.* [1999] 2 I.L.R.M. 1: the admitted difficulties in dealing satisfactorily with the claims of unmarried fathers were best dealt with through the machinery of the Hague Conference and not by "innovative judicial responses", producing results which could not have been contemplated by the authors of the Convention.

19–082 NOTE 88. Add: Beaumont and McEleavy, *The Hague Convention on International Child Abduction* (1999), pp. 55–56.

19–083 NOTE 94. Add: *Re L. (children) (Abduction Declaration)* [2001] 2 F.C.R. 1; *Re G. (child abduction) (unmarried father rights of custody)* [2002] EWHC 2219 (Fam).

19–084 Text to note 98. It was held in *Re L. (Abduction: Pending Criminal Proceedings)* [1999] 1 F.L.R. 433 that return does not have to be to the State from which the child was abducted (in that case, re-abducted).

NOTE 98. Add: *Director-General of Families, Youth and Community Care v. Bennett* (2000) F.L.C. 93–011.

19–086 In *Re S. (Child Abduction: Asylum Appeal)* [2002] EWCA Civ. 843, [2002] 2 F.L.R. 465 it was held that section 15 of the Immigration and Asylum Act 1999 (Protection of claimants from removal or deportation) did not preclude the making of an order for the return of the child. A similar decision was reached under Canadian legislation: *Kovacs v. Kovacs* (2002) 212 D.L.R. (4th) 711 (Ont.).

In *Re P. (Abduction: Minor's Views)* [1998] 2 F.L.R. 825 (C.A.), Butler-Sloss **19–087** L.J. said that the courts were "rightly sceptical of attempts by many abducting parents to invoke the provisions of Article 13 to try to stave off the almost inevitable requirement to return the child forthwith to the state of habitual residence. The welfare of the child who has been abducted is generally seen as best served by returning him to the jurisdiction of his habitual residence and leaving the decision of what should happen to him thereafter to the court best equipped to deal with the custodial problems of the family living within its jurisdiction before the child was abducted".

NOTE 8. Oral evidence was taken, but this was regarded as unusual, in *Re M. (Abduction: Leave to Appeal)* [1999] 2 F.L.R. 550 (C.A.). Orders should not be made that one issue be dealt with as a preliminary point of law, as this can lead to delay: the case should be dealt with on one occasion if at all possible: *HI. v. MG.* [1999] 2 I.L.R.M. 1 (Sup. Ct.).

It was suggested by the New Zealand Court of Appeal that the applicant for **19–089** the return of a child has a lesser burden in respect of proving that rights of custody were actually being exercised than that borne by a respondent seeking to rely on Article 13(b): *Chief Executive of the Dept for Courts v. Phelps* [2000] 1 N.Z.L.R. 168, citing paragraph 73 of the Explanatory Report on the Convention.

NOTE 10. Add: *Re M. (Abduction) (Consent: Acquiescence)* [1999] 1 F.L.R. 171.

NOTE 12. In *Re M. (Abduction) (Consent: Acquiescence)* [1999] 1 F.L.R. 171, Wall J. retracted the view he had expressed in *Re W. (Abduction: Procedure)* [1995] 1 F.L.R. 878 that consent would normally be in writing.

Text to note 13. In *T. v. T. (Child Abduction: Consent)* [1999] 2 F.L.R. 912, **19–090** Charles J. held that consent could be vitiated by misunderstanding or non-disclosure. In the instant case, the mother had obtained the apparent consent of the father to her bringing the child to England, but it was held that the consent was vitiated by her failure to disclose to the father her sexual relationship with another man in England. It is submitted that this decision goes considerably further than was required either by earlier authority or sound policy, as opening the door to allegations of incomplete disclosure of the full circumstances.

NOTE 15. Add at end: *Re I. (Abduction: Acquiescence)* [1999] 1 F.L.R. 778.

NOTE 18. Add at end: *Re B. (Abduction: Acquiescence)* [1999] 2 F.L.R. 818.

The grave risk of physical harm need not involve a risk created by the **19–091** family situation. It was held by the Full Court of the Family Court of Australia that as an Australian Government advisory notice warned that Australians should defer all travel to Israel and spoke of a very high risk of terrorists attacks, return to Israel (and on the facts probably to a point very close to the boundary of the Gaza strip) would not be ordered: *Genish-Grant v. Director-General, Department of Community Services* (2002) 29 Fam.L.R. 51. See the reference in *Friedrich v. Friedrich*, 78 F. 3d 1060 (6th Cir., 1996) to "zones of war, famine or disease". However, in *Re S.*

(Abduction: Custody Rights) [2002] EWCA Civ. 908; [2002] 1 W.L.R. 3355 (a case which had been dealt with at first instance primarily on the basis of the mother's psychological problems, which did not preclude return), the Court of Appeal regarded the terrorist threat in Israel as not a grave risk within Art. 13(*b*).

NOTE 26. *Re R. (Minors) (Abduction: Consent)* is now reported *sub nom. Re R. (Abduction: Consent)* [1999] 1 F.L.R. 828.

NOTE 28. Although the reference to a stringent test in *Re F. (A Minor) (Abduction: Custody Rights Abroad)* [1995] Fam. 224 (C.A.) was approved in *Re C. (Abduction: Grave Risk of Psychological Harm)* [1999] 1 F.L.R. 1145 (C.A.), the decision in *Re F.* was there characterised as the high water mark of cases in which return was refused on this ground. Add: *Pollastro v. Pollastro* (1999) 171 D.L.R. (4th) 32 (Ont. C.A.); *Finizio v. Scoppio-Finizio* (2000) 179 D.L.R. (4th) 713 (Alta.); *D.P. v. Commonwealth Central Authority* (2001) 180 A.L.R. 402 (High Ct. of Australia) (where facilities for treating the autistic child were not available in the country of habitual residence).

Text to note 29. This principle was applied in cases involving alleged sexual abuse of the child by the mother's cohabitee: *Re S. (Abduction: Return into Care)* [1999] 1 F.L.R. 843; and the murder by the father (who was shortly to be released from prison) of a man he suspected of having had an affair with the abducting mother: *Re M. (Abduction: Intolerable Situation)* [2000] 1 F.L.R. 930.

NOTE 29. Add: *A.S. v. P.S.* [1998] I.R. 244 (Sup. Ct.); *S. v. S.* [1999] 3 N.Z.L.R. 513; *D.I. (Ptr)* 1999 Fam. L.R. 126; *T.J. and J.B. (Abduction: Grave Risk of Harm)* [2001] 2 F.L.R. 515 (C.A.). Exceptionally, in *P.Q. (Ptr)* (O.H., April 27, 2000), return was refused on the ground that the attitude already shown by the French courts to credible allegations of sexual abuse suggested that the child would not be adequately protected if returned to France.

NOTE 30. In *Re C. (Abduction: Grave Risk of Physical or Psychological Harm)* [1999] 2 F.L.R. 478 (C.A.), the Court of Appeal emphasised that little weight could be given to an abducting parent's self-induced dilemma. To the same effect is *T.J. and J.B. (Abduction: Grave Risk of Harm)* [2001] 2 F.L.R. 515 (C.A.) (abducting parent's depression not a basis for refusing return). Cf. *D.P. v. Commonwealth Central Authority* (2001) 180 A.L.R. 402 (High Ct. of Australia), where the court refused to disturb the trial judge's finding that the mother might commit suicide were return ordered, and that event would cause psychological harm to the child).

19–092 It is not appropriate for an English court to consider allegations that a court in another Hague Convention country will not give the abducting parent a fair hearing: *Re S. (Abduction: Intolerable Situation: Beth Din)* [2000] 1 F.L.R. 454.

NOTE 33. See *Chan v. Chow* (2001) 199 D.L.R. (4th) 478 (B.C.C.A.) where the return of a child to Hong Kong, which for immigration law reasons it would have to leave after a few months, was held to place the child in an intolerable situation. The aim of the Convention was to achieve continuity in the residence of the child.

19–093 In some cases, direct communication between the English court and the judicial or other authorities of the relevant foreign country may be an alternative to, or complement, the taking of undertakings: *Re M. and J. (Abduction: International Judicial Collaboration)* [2000] 1 F.L.R. 803.

Note 34. For the practice in Scotland, see *D.I. (Ptr)*, 1999 Fam. L.R. 126.

Note 44. Add: *Re T. (Abduction: Child's Objections to Return)* [2000] 2 **19–094** F.L.R. 192 (child of 11 had cogent fears concerning his mother's drink problem); *T.J. and J.B. (Abduction: Grave Risk of Harm)* [2001] 2 F.L.R. 515 (C.A.) (objections of child of 14 and a half not decisive); *Re L. (Abduction: Jurisdiction)* [2002] EWHC 1864 (Fam), [2002] 1 W.L.R. 3208 (child aged fourteen; objections respected).

Note 49. Add: *Re T. (Abduction: Child's Objections to Return)* [2000] 2 **19–095** F.L.R. 192.

Text to note 51. The apparent assumption in *Re H. (Abduction: Child of 16)* **19–096** [2000] 2 F.L.R. 51 that the 12 months could be taken to run from the date on which the whereabouts of the abducting parent and child become known to the other parent cannot be reconciled with the words of Article 12.

Note 54. Insofar as *In the Marriage of Graziano and Daniels* [1991] F.L.C. 92–212 adds an unnecessary gloss on the plain meaning of the term "settled", it should not be followed: *Townsend v. Director-General, Department of Families, Youth and Community Care* [1999] F.L.C. 92–842. For an illustration of the approach adopted in cases of claimed settlement, see *P. v. B.* (unreported, Irish Supreme Court, February 26, 1999).

The European Court of Human Rights has held that the treatment of **19–097** married and unmarried fathers under the Hague Convention has an objective and reasonable justification and is not in conflict with Articles 8 and 14 of the European Convention on Human Rights: *B. v. United Kingdom* [2000] 1 F.L.R. 1 (the case dealt with in the English courts as *Re B. (Abduction) (Rights of Custody)* [1997] 2 F.L.R. 594 (C.A.)).

Note 56. The ground for non-return in Article 20 has been said by the Full Court of the Family Court of Australia to be "extremely narrow" (*Director-General of Families, Youth and Community Care v. Bennett*) (2000) 26 Fam. L.R. 71) and that it is difficult to imagine a situation in which that Article could be satisfied as a distinct test from that covered by Article 13(b) (*McCall v. McCall* (1994) 18 Fam. L.R. 307).

Note 57. For the similar practice in Scotland, see *Donofrio v. Burrell*, 2000 **19–098** S.C.L.R. 465.

Note 67. See *Re M. (Abduction: Conflict of Jurisdiction)* [2000] 2 F.L.R. 372, **19–101** illustrating in this context the interplay of the Hague and European Conventions.

Note 68. In *Re L. (Abduction: Pending Criminal Proceedings)* [1999] 1 F.L.R. 433, a Danish court had ordered the return of a child to Florida under the Hague Convention. The abducting parent removed the child to England. The court held that the issue estoppel recognised in *Re O. (Child Abduction: Re-Abduction)* [1997] 2 F.L.R. 712 was applicable, but on facts new issues arose which required consideration.

3. MAINTENANCE AND CONTRIBUTION ORDERS

19R–107 NOTE 85. Children Act 1989, Sched. 1, para. 1 is amended by Adoption and Children Act 2002, Sched. 3, para. 71 (not yet in force).

19–108 NOTE 93. Children Act 1989, Sched. 1, para. 14 is amended by Adoption and Children Act 2002, Sched. 3, para. 71 (not yet in force).

CHAPTER 20

LEGITIMACY, LEGITIMATION AND ADOPTION

1. LEGITIMACY

A. *Jurisdiction of the English Court*

With effect from the coming into force of section 83 of the Child Support, **20R–001**
Pensions and Social Security Act 2000, delete "parentage or". See para. 20–
004, below.

NOTE 2. Family Law Act 1986 is repealed by Child Support, Pensions and
Social Security Act 2000, Sched. 9, Pt. X, but provision to the same effect is
made by Family Law Act 1986, ss. 55, 56 both as amended by Child Support,
Pensions and Social Security Act 2000, Sched. 8, paras 4 and 5.

Text and note 8. Family Law Reform Act 1987, s. 1(3) is amended by **20–003**
Adoption and Children Act 2002, Sched. 3, para. 51 so as to apply the
principle to an adopted person within Chapter 4 of Part I of the 2002 Act.

Sections 56(1)(*a*) and 58(5)(*b*) of the Family Law Act 1986 are repealed by **20–004**
Child Support, Pensions and Social Security Act 2000, Sched. 9, Pt. X. Fresh
provision is made for declarations of parentage by a new section 55A of the
1986 Act, inserted by 2000 Act, section 83. This provides that the High Court,
a county court or a magistrates' court has jurisdiction to make a declaration
as to whether or not a person named in the application is or was the parent
of another person so named if, and only if, either of the persons named in it
(a) is domiciled in England and Wales on the date of the application; or (b)
has been habitually resident in England and Wales throughout the period of
one year ending with that date; or (c) died before that date and (i) was at
death domiciled in England and Wales, or (ii) had been habitually resident in
England and Wales throughout the period of one year ending with the date
of death. The effect of the new provisions is to widen, with certain safeguards
(see s. 55A(3)(5)), the range of persons who may seek declarations of
parentage and to remove the earlier requirement that both parents had to be
respondents. The changes will be of particular use in immigration contexts.

NOTE 36. Section 50(9) of the British Nationality Act 1981 is amended by **20–010**
the Nationality, Immigration and Asylum Act 2002, s. 9 (not yet in force).
See the entry at 20–054, *infra*.

NOTE 38. The relevant provisions of Marriage Act 1949, s. 3 are further
amended by Adoption and Children Act 2002, Sched. 3, paras 1 to 5 (not
yet in force).

C. *Succession by and to Legitimate Persons*

20–036 Text to note 38. The House of Lords' Committee for Privileges has held that the limitation of succession to a peerage to legitimate persons does not offend Article 14 of the European Convention on Human Rights read with Article 1 of the First Protocol: *Re Moynihan* [2000] 1 F.L.R. 113, distinguishing *Inze v. Austria* (1987) 10 E.H.R.R. 394.

2. LEGITIMATION

B. *Recognition of Foreign Legitimations*

(1) AT COMMON LAW

20–054 Section 47 of the British Nationality Act 1981 is repealed by the Nationality, Immigration and Asylum Act 2002 (not yet in force). The 2002 Act (s. 9) amends the British Nationality Act 1981, s. 50(9) by inserting a new subsection (9A) under which, for the purposes of the 1981 Act a child's father is defined as (a) the husband, at the time of the child's birth, of the woman who gives birth to the child, or (b) where a person is treated as the father of the child under section 28 of the Human Fertilisation and Embryology Act 1990, that person, or (c) where neither paragraph (a) nor paragraph (b) applies, any person who satisfies requirements prescribed by regulations of the Secretary of State as to proof of paternity.

20–061 For the repeal of section 47 of the British Nationality Act 1981, see entry at 20–054, *supra*.

20–066 NOTE 35. For the repeal of section 47 of the British Nationality Act 1981, see entry at 20–054, *supra*.

C. *Succession by and to Legitimated Persons*

20–081 NOTE 68. For the repeal of section 47 of the British Nationality Act 1981, see entry at 20–054, above.

3. ADOPTION

A. *Jurisdiction of the English Courts*

20R–091 When section 49 of the Adoption and Children Act 2002 is brought into force, substitute.

**(1) The High Court, a divorce county court or a magistrates' court has jurisdiction to make an adoption order (other than a Convention adoption order) if, and only if, the applicant, or in the case of an application by a couple (a married couple or two persons, of different sexes or the same sex, living as partners in an enduring family relationship (s. 144(4)) one of the couple
(a) is domiciled in a part of the British Islands; or**

(b) has been habitually resident in a part of the British Islands for a period of at least one year ending on the date of the application (s. 49(1)(2)(3)).

NOTES 94 to 96. The relevant provisions of the Adoption Act 1976 are repealed by Adoption and Children Act 2002 (not yet in force). Under the 2002 Act, the child must be under 18 at the date of the application (s. 49(4)) and under 19 at the date of the order (s. 47(9), 49(5)).

The law as to adoption was restated in the Adoption and Children Act **20–093** 2002, most of the provisions of which are not yet in force.

The relevant provisions of the Adoption Act 1976 are repealed by Adoption **20–095** and Children Act 2002 (not yet in force). Under that Act habitual residence in a part of the British Islands for a period of at least one year ending on the date of the application is an alternative to domicile (s. 49(1)(3)).

Adoption (Scotland) Act 1978, s. 56 is amended by Adoption and Children **20–096** Act 2002, Sched. 3, para. 32 (not yet in force).

The relevant provisions of the Adoption Act 1976 are repealed by Adoption **20–098** and Children Act 2002 (not yet in force). Under the 2002 Act, there continue to be requirements that the child must have lived with the adopters for prescribed periods before the application for adoption is made (s. 42). Unless the child is placed for adoption by an adoption agency, notice of intention to adopt has to be given to the appropriate local authority (s. 44). Under the Act habitual residence in a part of the British Islands for a period of at least one year ending on the date of the application is an alternative to domicile (s. 49(1)(3)).

In a number of cases involving inter-country adoptions the issue has arisen **20–100** as to whether a foreign institution in which parental rights have been vested under the relevant foreign law can be recognised as a guardian for the purposes of consent under Adoption Act 1976, s. 16. Although it was held in *Re D. (Adoption: Foreign Guardianship)* [1999] 2 F.L.R. 865 that only an English institution qualified, the better view is that the foreign institution should be recognised, applying the principle stated in Rule 93: *Re AMR (Adoption: Procedure)* [1999] 2 F.L.R. 807; *Re AGN (Adoption: Foreign Adoption)* [2000] 2 F.L.R. 431.

Consent by a natural parent to adoption in the foreign country will not be treated as equivalent to consent to an adoption in England: *Re A. (Adoption of a Russian Child)* [2000] 1 F.L.R. 539 (on this point following, reluctantly, *Re G. (Foreign Adoption: Consent)* [1995] 2 F.L.R. 534, but dispensing with consent). In *Re J. (Adoption: Consent of Foreign Public Authority)* [2002] EWHC 766 (Fam), [2002] 2 F.L.R. 618 it was held that whether the consent of such an authority is required may be tested by analogy with the position of a local authority in England; where the consent of a foreign public authority is required, but it is unable under its own law to give consent, its consent may in appropriate cases to be dispensed with under Adoption Act 1976, s. 16.

The provisions of the Adoption Act 1976 cited in notes 18 and 19 are repealed by Adoption and Children Act 2002 (not yet in force). See sections

47 and 52 of the 2002 Act for provisions as to consent and the power to dispense with consent.

20–101 The relevant provisions of the Adoption Act 1976 are repealed by Adoption and Children Act 2002 (not yet in force). The provisions in the 2002 Act as to Convention adoption orders relate to the Hague Convention on Inter-country Adoption 1993 (s. 144(1)).

20–104 Section 6 of the Adoption Act 1976 is repealed by Adoption and Children Act 2002 (not yet in force). Section 1(2) of the 2002 Act declares that the paramount consideration of a court or adoption agency must be the child's welfare, throughout its life.

20–105 A new section 56A was inserted in the Adoption Act 1976 by the Adoption (Intercountry Aspects) Act 1999, s. 14, making it an offence for a person habitually resident in the British Islands to bring a child into the United Kingdom for the purposes of adoption, save in cases specified in regulations. See the Adoption of Children from Overseas Regulations 2001, S.I. 2001 No. 1251. The relevant provisions of the Adoption Act 1976 are repealed by Adoption and Children Act 2002 (not yet in force), but section 83 of the 2002 Act makes corresponding but strengthened provision.

NOTE 28. *Re C. (Adoption: Legality)* is now reported *sub nom. Re C. (A Minor) (Adoption: Illegality)* [1999] Fam. 128.

Text to note 29. The English courts cannot ignore the benefit to the child of acquiring a right of abode in the United Kingdom: it is an aspect of the welfare of the child to which first consideration must be given under Adoption Act 1976, s. 6. The same principle does not apply if it is a benefit which will be enjoyed when the child is an adult rather than during childhood, and the public policy issues surrounding immigration control may have then have to be given precedence: *Re B. (Adoption Order: Nationality)* [1999] 2 A.C. 136 (where adoption order upheld on facts).

20–106 NOTE 30. *Re R. (A Minor) (Inter-Country Adoptions: Practice)* is now reported *sub nom. Practice Note (Inter-Country Adoptions)* [1999] 1 W.L.R. 1324.

20–107 Text to notes 31 and 32. The relevant provisions of the Adoption Act 1976 are repealed by Adoption and Children Act 2002 (not yet in force). Under the 2002 Act, an adoption order gives parental responsibility for a child to the adopters or adopter (s. 46(1)) and the making of an adoption order operates to extinguish the parental responsibility which any person other than the adopters or adopter had for the adopted child immediately before the making of the order and any order under the Children Act 1989 (s. 46(2)).

Text to note 33. The effect of adoptions after the coming into force of Chapter 4 (sections 66 to 76) of the Adoption and Children Act 2002 is that an adopted person is to be treated in law as if born as the child of the adopters or adopter (s. 67(1)). An adopted person is the legitimate child of the adopters or adopter and, if adopted by a couple or one of a couple, is to be treated as the child of the relationship of the couple in question (s. 67(2)). This applies as does the whole of Chapter 4 of the Act applies to an adoption order made under the Act, a Scottish or Northern Irish adoption order, an adoption by an order made in the Isle of Man or any of the Channel Islands, an adoption effected under the law of a Convention country outside the British Islands, and certified in pursuance of Article 23(1) of the Hague Convention on Intercountry Adoption ("a Convention adoption"), an overseas adoption, and any other adoption recognised by the law of England and Wales and effected under the law of any other country (s. 66).

NOTE 34. British Nationality Act 1981, s. 1(5)(6) is amended by Adoption (Intercountry Aspects) Act 1999, s. 7. "British Dependent Territories citizens" are now British overseas territories citizens: British Overseas Territories Act 2002, s. 2(1) and the references to British Dependent Territories citizenship in the British Nationality Act 1981, s. 15(5) are now to be read as being to British overseas territories citizenship: 2002 Act, s. 2(3).

The relevant provisions of the Adoption Act 1976 are repealed by Adoption **20–108** and Children Act 2002 (not yet in force), but corresponding provisions are made in section 85 of the 2002 Act.

Section 55 applies in this context inter alia section 18 of the Adoption Act **20–109** 1976. The references to adoption orders in that section include an order to be made in a foreign country, and a freeing order can accordingly be made to facilitate such an adoption: *Re S. (Freeing for Adoption)* [2002] EWCA Civ. 798, [2002] 2 F.L.R. 681. Freeing orders are replaced by placement orders in the Adoption and Children Act 2002 (not yet in force). Section 55 of the Adoption Act 1976 is repealed by the 2002 Act, but the corresponding provisions are made in section 84 of that Act.

Illustration 2. When the Adoption and Children Act 2002 is brought into **20–110** force, no English court would have jurisdiction.

Illustration 3. Regulations under Adoption and Children Act 2002, s. 108 (not yet in force) will govern the position where children placed for adoption originate in the Isle of Man.

After Illustration 3, insert as a new Illustration:
3A. H and W are domiciled in the Isle of Man and wish to adopt C, who is in the Isle of Man. The High Court, but no other English court, has jurisdiction (Adoption Act 1976, ss. 14(2), 62(3); *Re J. (Adoption Procedure: Isle of Man)* [2000] 2 F.L.R. 633).

B. *Recognition of Foreign Adoptions*

When the Adoption and Children Act 2002 is brought into force, substitute **20R–111** for clause (2) of the Rule:

(2) An adoption under the law of a country outside the British Islands falling within the definition of "overseas adoption" in the Adoption and Children Act 2002 (s. 87) will be recognised in England (s. 66(1)(d)).

Part IV of the 1976 Act is not repealed by Adoption and Children Act 2002 **20–112** (not yet in force). It will now however apply to adoptions effected after Chapter 4 of the 2002 Act is brought in force. In that Chapter, the same technique is used: see the list of orders in section 66 (entry re para. 20–107, note 33, *supra*).

20–113 The position will be the same when the Adoption and Children Act 2002 is brought into force. See that Act, s. 66(1)(*a*), (*b*).

20–114 When the Adoption and Children Act 2002 is brought into force, similar recognition will be given to "overseas adoptions" in accordance with regulations to be made by the Secretary of State (2002 Act. s. 87).

20–115 For the annulment of adoptions made under the Hague Convention of 1993, see para. 20–149, below.

20–116 Text and note 66. See Adoption and Children Act 2002, s. 66(1)(*e*) (not yet in force), where the same language is used.

20–127 Family Law Act 1986, s. 57(1) is amended by Adoption (Intercountry Aspects) Act 1999, Sched. 2, para. 5 (not yet in force) to enable declarations to be made in respect of the validity of Convention adoption orders made under the Hague Convention of 1993. See Adoption and Children Act 2002, Sched. 3, para. 49 for a similar amendment (not yet in force).

C. *Succession to and by Adopted Persons*

In respect of adoptions effected after Chapter 4 of the Adoption and Children Act 2002 is brought into force, that Chapter (ss. 66–77) makes fresh provision as to the effect of adoption on the devolution of property, substantially similar to that contained in the Adoption Act 1976 and set out in Rule 106 and the Comment thereto.

20–133 NOTE 32. Family Law Reform Act 1987, s. 19(5) is amended by Adoption and Children Act 2002, Sched. 3, para. 52 to preserve the effect of section 69 of the 2002 Act (which is not yet in force).

D. *Adoptions under the Hague Convention of 1965*

20–138– The Adoption (Intercountry Aspects) Act 1999 contained provisions
154 designed to enable the United Kingdom to denounce the Hague Convention of 1965 and become party to the Hague Convention of Intercountry Adoption of 1993. These provisions have not come into force, but provisions to the same effect are contained in the Adoption and Children Act 2002 (also not yet in force). See in particular sections 88 (dealing with adoptions which are not full adoptions), 89 (annulment of Convention adoptions) and 91 (overseas determinations and orders).

20–141 References to British Dependent Territories citizenship in the British Nationality Act 1981 are now to be read as being to British overseas territories citizenship: British Overseas Territories Act 2002, s. 2(3).

Chapter 21

MENTAL DISORDER

A Convention on the International Protection of Adults was agreed under **21–002**
the auspices of the Hague Conference on Private International Law in
October 1999. It applies to the protection in international situations of
adults who, by reason of an impairment or insufficiency of their personal
faculties, are not in a position to protect their interests (Art. 1(1)). It deals
with the questions which State has jurisdiction to take measures directed to
the protection of the person or property of the adult; which law is to be
applied in the exercise of this jurisdiction; which law applies to the
representation of the adult; and it provides for the recognition and
enforcement of such measures of protection in other Contracting States
(Art. 1(2)). The measures covered include "in particular" (a) the determination of incapacity and the institution of a protective regime; (b) the
placing of the adult under the protection of a judicial or administrative
authority; (c) guardianship, curatorship and analogous institutions; (d) the
designation and functions of any person or body having charge of the
adult's person or property, representing or assisting the adult; (e) the
placement of the adult in an establishment or other place where protection
can be provided; (f) the administration, conservation or disposal of the
adult's property; and (g) the authorisation of a specific intervention for the
protection of the person or property of the adult (Art. 3).

The principal rule as to jurisdiction is that it lies with the judicial or
administrative authorities of the Contracting State of the habitual residence
of the adult (Art. 5(1)). The authorities of a Contracting State of which the
adult is a national have jurisdiction if they consider that they are in a better
position to assess the interests of the adult (Art. 7(1)). Other States may be
requested by the authorities of the State seised of the case to deal with
aspects of the adult's protection (Art. 8). The authorities of a Contracting
State where property of the adult is situated have jurisdiction to take
measures of protection concerning that property, to the extent that such
measures are compatible with those taken by the authorities having
jurisdiction under the main provisions of the Convention (Art. 9).

In exercising their jurisdiction under the Convention, the authorities of
the Contracting States are to apply their own law. However, in so far as the
protection of the person or the property of the adult requires, they may
exceptionally apply or take into consideration the law of another State with
which the situation has a substantial connection (Art. 13).

The measures taken by the authorities of a Contracting State are to be
recognised by operation of law in all other Contracting States (Art. 22(1)),
but the Convention sets out a number of grounds on which recognition may
be refused (Art. 22(2)). The Convention also contains detailed provisions as
to practical co-operation between the authorities of the different Contracting States.

The Convention is not yet in force and has not been signed by the United
Kingdom.

CHAPTER 22

NATURE AND SITUS OF PROPERTY

22–026 Text at note 59. Order 11, r. 1 is replaced by CPR, rr. 6.19 and 6.20.

22–046 See entry at para. 22–026, *supra*.

22–061 NOTE 63. Air Navigation (No. 2) Order 1995 (S.I. 1995 No. 1970) was revoked and replaced by provisions of Air Navigation Order 2000 (S.I. 2000 No. 1562).

CHAPTER 23

IMMOVABLES

Delete para. 23R–001 and substitute:

RULE 113—(1) The court has jurisdiction to entertain a claim *in personam* **23R–001**
in a civil or commercial matter falling within the scope of Council
Regulation (E.C.) 44/2001 ("the Judgments Regulation")[1] where the pro-
ceedings have as their object rights *in rem* in, or tenancies of, immovable
property situate in England.[2]
    (2) Where the defendant is domiciled in a State to which the Judgments
Regulation applies ("a Regulation State"), or State party to the 1968
Convention[3] or the Lugano Convention[4] or is domiciled in Scotland or
Northern Ireland, the court has jurisdiction to entertain a claim *in*
***personam* in a civil and commercial matter falling within the scope of the**
Judgments Regulation or the 1968 Convention or the Lugano Convention[5]
where the proceedings relate to a contract and are combined with a claim
against the same defendant relating to rights *in rem* in immovable property
situate in England.[6]
    (3) Subject to the Judgments Regulation, the 1968 Convention and the
Lugano Convention, the court may assume jurisdiction if the whole subject
matter of the claim relates to property located within the jurisdiction.[7]
    (4) In this Rule, "domicile" means domicile as determined by Rule 23.

Delete and substitute: In the past, the general principle underlying Rule 113 **23–004**
found expression, as far as English law was concerned, only in certain
provisions of permission under Order 11 of the Rules of the Supreme
Court. Such provision still exists in CPR 6.20, which allows service of
process outside the jurisdiction (provided permission has been obtained) in
cases involving property located in England, and forms clause (3) of Rule

---

[1] On the scope of the Judgments Regulation see entries paras. 11–011 *et seq*. The Regulation is
at [2001] O.J. L12, January 16, 2001, and is reproduced in Part I of the appendix to this
Supplement.
[2] Judgments Regulation, Art. 22(1)(first sentence) and Civil Jurisdiction and Judgments Act
1982, Sched. 4, Rule 11(a)(i) (as substituted by S.I. 2001 No. 2939). The new 1982 Act, Sched. 4,
is reproduced in Part II of the appendix to this Supplement.
[3] The Brussels Convention on jurisdiction and the enforcement of judgments in civil and
commercial matters of 1968: 1982 Act, Sched. 1.
[4] The Lugano Convention on jurisdiction and the enforcement of judgments in civil and
commercial matters: 1982 Act, Sched. 3C.
[5] The scope of the 1968 and Lugano Conventions is identical to that of the Judgments
Regulation. See Art. 1 of the Regulation and Art. 1 of each Convention.
[6] Judgments Regulation, Art. 6(4); 1968 and Lugano Conventions, Art. 6(4); 1982 Act, Sched. 4,
Rule 5(d).
[7] CPR, r. 6.20(10), which replaced R.S.C. Ord. 11, r. 1(1)(g). Under CPR, r. 6.20 there is no
direct counterpart to R.S.C. Ord. 11, r. 1(1)(h). See, however, CPR, r. 6.20(13), which enables
jurisdiction to be exercised in relation to a claim made in probate proceedings which includes a
claim for the rectification of a will.

113. It has, however, been largely superseded by Article 22(1) of the Judgments Regulation, which is the basis of clause (1) of the Rule.

23–005 First sentence. **Relationship between clauses (1), (2) and (3).** Clause (3) applies only where clauses (1) and (2) are not applicable. Clauses (1) and (2) apply only where the proceedings concern a civil or commercial matter within the scope of the Judgments Regulation as defined by Article 1 or, in the case of clause (2), the identical provisions of Article 1 of the 1968 and Lugano Conventions.

23–006 First sentence. The applicability of clause (1) does not depend on domicile, since Article 22(1) of the Judgments Regulation (which forms the basis of clause (1)) expressly states that it applies "regardless of domicile".

23–008 Final sentence. The relevant part of Order 11 is replaced by CPR, r. 6.20.

23–009 Text at note 17. See entry at para. 23–008, *supra*.

NOTE 14. Order 11, r. 1(2) is replaced by CPR, r. 6.19.

NOTE 15. Order 11, r. 1(1) is replaced by CPR, r. 6.20.

NOTE 16. On the jurisdiction of the European Court to give rulings on the interpretation of Art. 22(1) of the Judgments Regulation see entry at paras. 11–043—11–054.

23–010 For the purposes of Rule 113(1), Article 16(1)(a) of the 1968 Convention is
et seq. replaced by Article 22(1) (first sentence) of the Judgments Regulation. The substance of the two provisions is identical.

23–011 An action for rescission of a contract for the sale of land and for consequential damages does not come within "proceedings which have as their object rights *in rem* in . . . immovable property": Case C–518/99 *Gaillard v. Chekili* [2001] E.C.R. I–2771.

23–012 In *Ashurst v. Pollard* [2001] Ch. 595 (C.A.) (noted by Harris [2001] L.M.C.L.Q. 205) it was held, on the basis of Case C–294/92 *Webb v. Webb* [1994] E.C.R. I–1717, that the effect of Article 16(1) is not to deprive the English court of jurisdiction to make, on the application of the trustee in bankruptcy, an order requiring a bankrupt to sell land situated in Portugal.

23–013 In Case C–8/98 *Dansommer A/S v. Götz* [2000] E.C.R. I–393 a German defendant took a holiday let of a house in Denmark from the plaintiff, a Danish company which acted as agent for the owner. The plaintiff alleged that the defendant had failed to clean the house properly before departure and had caused damage to the property. When the plaintiff started proceedings for damages against the defendant in Germany, a question arose as to whether the court had jurisdiction. In reply to the reference from the German court, the European Court ruled that Article 16(1)(a) is applicable to an action for damages for taking poor care of premises and causing damage to rented accommodation; Article 16(1)(a) applies to any proceedings concerning rights and obligations arising under an agreement for the letting of immovable property, irrespective of whether the action is based on a right *in rem* or a right *in personam*.

First sentence. Clause (2) is based on Article 6(4) of the Judgments **23–016**
Regulation, the 1968 Convention and the Lugano Convention. In substance,
the three provisions are identical.

Final sentence. The provision applies only if the defendant is domiciled
in (i) a Regulation State, (ii) a State party to either the 1968 Convention or
the Lugano Convention or (iii) Scotland or Northern Ireland.

Delete paragraphs 23R–21—23–033 and substitute:

RULE 114—(1) Subject to Clause (2) of this Rule, the court has no **S23R–021**
jurisdiction to entertain proceedings falling within the scope of the
Judgments Regulation, the 1968 Convention or the Lugano Convention
which have as their object rights *in rem* **in, or tenancies of, immovable**
property situated in a Regulation State, in a State party to the 1968
Convention or the Lugano Convention or in Scotland or Northern
Ireland.[58]

(2) The court has jurisdiction to entertain proceedings within the scope
of the Judgments Regulation, the 1968 Convention or the Lugano Conven-
tion which have as their object tenancies of immovable property situated in
another Regulation State, or in another State party to either Convention or
in Scotland or Northern Ireland where the tenancy agreement was con-
cluded for temporary private use for a maximum period of six consecutive
months and the defendant is domiciled in England, provided that

    (a) **where the immovable property is in another Regulation State, the**
        tenant is a natural person and the landlord and the tenant are
        domiciled in the United Kingdom[59]**;**

    (b) **where the immovable property is in Scotland or Northern Ireland,**
        the tenant is a natural person and the landlord and the tenant
        are domiciled in England[60]**;**

    (c) **where the immovable property is in a State party to the 1968**
        Convention (but not a Regulation State),[61] **the landlord and the**
        tenant are natural persons and are domiciled in the United
        Kingdom[62]**;**

    (d) **where the immovable property is in another State party to the**
        Lugano Convention (but not a Regulation State), the tenant is a
        natural person and neither party is domiciled in the State in
        which the property is situated.[63]

(3) Subject to the Judgments Regulation, the 1968 Convention and the
Lugano Convention, the court has no jurisdiction to entertain proceedings
for the determination of the title to, or the right to the possession of,
immovable property situated outside England,[64] **except where**

    (a) **the claim is based on a contract or equity between the parties,**[65] **or**

---

[58] Judgments Regulation, Art. 22(1)(a); 1968 and Lugano Conventions Art. 16(1)(a); Sched. 4,
Rule 11(a)(i). See *Ferguson's Trustee v. Ferguson*, 1990 S.L.T. (Sh.Ct.) 73.

[59] Judgments Regulation, Art. 22(1)(second sentence).

[60] 1982 Act, Sched. 4, Rule 11(a)(ii) (as substituted by S.I. 2001 No. 3929, in force from March 1,
2002).

[61] *i.e.* Denmark.

[62] 1968 Convention, Art. 16(1)(b). See the authorities cited in para. 23R–021, n. 62 of the main
work.

[63] Lugano Convention, Art. 16(1)(b).

[64] 1982 Act, s. 30.

[65] See para. 23R–021, n. 63 of the main work.

    **(b) the question has to be decided for the purpose of the administra-
tion of an estate or trust and the property consists of movables or
immovables in England as well as immovables outside England.**[66]

    (4) In this Rule, "domicile" means domicile as determined by Rule 23.

S23–022 This Rule, which qualifies the general jurisdictional Rules in this book,
gives effect to the negative aspect of the principle that, where the
proceedings concern immovable property, the courts of the country where
the immovable is situate has exclusive jurisdiction. The positive aspect of
this principle formed the basis of Rule 113.

S23–023   Until recently, this Rule was based exclusively on the common law and
was often referred to as the "*Moçambique* rule" after the leading case.[67] It
has, however, been subject to three important changes. First, Article
22(1)(first sentence) of the Judgments Regulation, Article 16(1)(a) of the
two Conventions and Rule 11(a)(i) of Schedule 4 to the Civil Jurisdiction
and Judgments Act 1982 have brought in a similar, though not identical,
rule in proceedings concerning a civil or commercial matter within the
scope of the Regulation and the Conventions; secondly, Article 22(1)(second sentence) of the Regulation, Article 16(1)(b) of the Conventions and
Rule 11(a)(ii) of Schedule 4 have created an exception to that rule in the
case of short tenancies; thirdly, the common law rule has been substantially
restricted by section 30 of the 1982 Act. Clause (1) of the Rule is based on
the first sentence of Article 22(1) of the Regulation, Article 16(1)(a) of the
Conventions and Rule 11(a)(i) of Schedule 4; clause (2) is based on the
second sentence of Article 22(1) of the Regulation, Article 16(1)(b) of the
Conventions and Rule 11(a)(ii) of Schedule 4; what is left of the old
Moçambique rule is formulated in clause (3).

S23–024   The relationship between the clauses is as follows. Clause (2) is an
exception to clause (1). Clauses (1) and (2) apply only where the subject-
matter of the proceedings is within the scope of the Judgments Regulation
and the Conventions, as defined by Article 1. This covers most civil and
commercial matters but expressly excludes certain questions, such as rights
in property arising out of a matrimonial relationship, wills, succession and
bankruptcy.[68] Clause (1) applies only where the land is situated in (i)
another Regulation State, (ii) a Contracting State to either Convention or
(iii) Scotland or Northern Ireland. However, unlike most of the jurisdictional provisions of the Regulation and Conventions, its operation is not
dependent on the domicile of the defendant,[69] nor can jurisdiction be
conferred on the court by submission[70] or by a jurisdiction agreement.[71] Its
operation is, therefore, somewhat limited; but where it applies, clause (3) is
wholly excluded.

S23–025   Clause (3) could come into play where the subject-matter of the
proceedings is outside the scope of the Regulation and the Conventions or

---

[66] See para. 23R–021, n. 64 of the main work.

[67] *British South Africa Co. v. Companhia de Moçambique* [1893] A.C. 602. For a recent discussion
of the rule see *Petrotimor v. Commonwealth of Australia* [2003] FCFCA 3 (Full Court of the
Federal Court of Australia).

[68] See paras. 11–013 *et seq.* of the main work.

[69] Art. 22(1) of the Judgments Regulation; Art. 16(1) of the Conventions; Rule 11(a) of Sched. 4
to the 1982 Act.

[70] Art. 24 of the Judgments Regulation; Art. 18 of the Conventions; Rule 13 of Sched. 4 to the
1982 Act.

[71] Jenard Report [1979] O.J. C59/34.

where the land is not in a Regulation State or a Contracting State. No difficulty arises in the former situation. If, for example, the case concerns succession or matrimonial property rights within the meaning of Article 1 of the Regulation and the Conventions, clause (3) will be applicable. Where, however, the land is situated in neither a Regulation State nor a Contracting State, the position is controversial. As a matter of principle, clause (3) should apply, since both it and clause (1) are based on the same considerations. There is no doubt that it does apply where the main jurisdiction provisions of the Regulation or the Conventions are inapplicable by reason of the fact that the defendant is not domiciled in a Regulation State or Contracting State; but where the defendant is domiciled in a Regulation State or Contracting State, it could be argued that the jurisdiction of the English court is determined solely by the Regulation or either Convention (as the case may be), so that if the Regulation or applicable Convention confers jurisdiction on the court, clause (3) cannot operate so as to deprive it of that jurisdiction.[72]

An example will make the problem clear. Assume that X, who is **S23–026** domiciled in England, is the occupier of a house in New York. A, who is domiciled in France, sues X for a declaration that the house is owned by him. On a strict interpretation of the Judgments Regulation, the English courts would have jurisdiction: the claim is a civil or commercial matter within the scope of the Regulation; the defendant is domiciled in a Regulation State; Article 2 of the Regulation (coupled with Rule 2 of Schedule 4 to the Civil Jurisdiction and Judgments Act 1982) confers jurisdiction on the English courts (because the defendant is domiciled in England), and the exclusionary rule in the first sentence of Article 22(1) (clause (1)) is inapplicable, because the land is not in a Regulation State.

It need hardly be said that this result would be very undesirable. It is the **S23–027** clear policy both of the Regulation and the Conventions and of English law (as well as the law of most other countries) that cases involving title to immovables should be brought only in the courts of the place where the property is situated. It is hard to see what purpose would be served by allowing the Regulation and the Conventions to have the effect of abrogating this principle in those cases where the land is not in a Regulation State or Contracting State. In view of this, it has been suggested that the Regulation and the Conventions should be interpreted so as to permit the application of national rules like that embodied in clause (3) where the land is not in a Regulation State or a Contracting State.[73] In *Re Polly Peck International plc (No. 2)*[74] the Court of Appeal expressed the view,[75] *obiter*, that Article 2 of the 1968 Convention does not prevent the English court from applying the rule that the English court will not adjudicate on title to land in a non-contracting State. The object of the

---

[72] See Collins, p. 80; Hartley, pp. 65–66; Droz, pp. 108–110; A.M., 1987 S.L.T. (News) 53.

[73] Droz, paras. 165–169; Maxwell Report (Scottish Committee on Jurisdiction and Enforcement, 1980), para. 5.159–160; Hartley, p. 66.

[74] [1998] 3 All E.R. 812, 829–830 (C.A.); Briggs (1998) 69 B.Y.I.L. 356.

[75] Applying *Re Harrods (Buenos Aires) Ltd.* Ch. 72 (C.A.). See paras. 12–017 *et seq.* of the main work. Two references to the European Court, which raise the correctness of *Re Harrods (Buenos Aires) Ltd.*, have been made by the Court of Appeal: *Owusu v. Jackson* [2002] EWCA Civ. 877, [2002] I.L.Pr. 813; *American Motorists Insurance Co. v. Cellstar Corp.* [2003] EWCA Civ. 206, [2003] I.L. Pr. 370 (C.A.). In a case on the Lugano Convention, the Court of Appeal has given permission to appeal to the House of Lords on the same point: *Anton Dürbeck GmbH v. Den Norske Bank ASA* [2003] EWCA Civ. 147, [2003] 2 W.L.R. 1296 (C.A.).

Regulation or the Conventions is not impaired by refusing jurisdiction as against the courts of a State which is neither a Regulation State nor a Contracting State. An alternative solution would be to apply clause (1) by analogy in such cases.

S23–028 **Clause (1) of the Rule.** The meaning of this clause was discussed previously when the positive aspect of Article 22(1) of the Regulation (and Article 16(1) of the Conventions) was considered.

S23–029 **Clause (2) of the Rule.** Article 16(1) of the 1968 Convention originally had no provision equivalent to clause (2) of the Rule. In 1985 in *Rösler v. Rottwinkel*[76] the European Court held that Article 16(1) (as it then stood) covered short-term holiday lettings. This result was contrary to what appears to have been the original intention of the authors of the Convention.[77] When the Lugano Convention was drafted, a new provision was inserted, which states that in the case of proceedings which have as their object tenancies of immovable property concluded for temporary private use for a maximum period of six consecutive months, the courts of the Contracting State in which the defendant is domiciled will also have jurisdiction, provided that the tenant is a natural person (*i.e.* not a corporation) and neither party is domiciled in the Contracting State in which the property is situated.[78] Under the 1989 Accession Convention, a similar provision was inserted into the 1968 Convention, where it now forms Article 16(1)(b). A similar provision was also included in Article 22(1) of the Judgments Regulation. Unfortunately, however, the three provisions are not exactly the same: under Article 22(1) of the Regulation, the tenant must be a natural person and both the landlord and tenant must be domiciled in the same Regulation State; under Article 16(1)(b) of the 1968 Convention, both the landlord and the tenant must be natural persons and both must be domiciled in the same Contracting State. For this reason, clause (2) of the Rule has four separate provisos, the first two being based on the Regulation, the third on the 1968 Convention and the fourth on the Lugano Convention. The difference between the provisos could give rise to anomalies. Take, for example, a case where a house in France, owned by an English-domiciled company, is let to private person domiciled in Germany. In these circumstances, the French courts have exclusive jurisdiction. If however, the cottage were situated in Switzerland, the English and Swiss courts would have concurrent jurisdiction in relation to proceedings brought against the landlord.

S23–030 In view of these discrepancies, it is important to know whether the Regulation, the 1968 Convention or the Lugano Convention is applicable in any given case. It is the location of the immovable, rather than the domicile of the defendant, which is the determining factor. This is why, in the example in the previous paragraph, clause (2)(a) of the Rule (the Regulation) applied where the house was in France, but clause (2)(d) (the Lugano Convention) applied when it was in Switzerland. Such a result is entirely logical in view of the fact that clause (2) is in effect (though not in terms) a proviso to clause (1).

---

[76] Case 241/83 [1985] E.C.R. 99; [1986] Q.B. 33.
[77] See the Schlosser Report [1979] O.J. C59/71, para. 164.
[78] Lugano Convention, Art. 16(1)(b).

It should also be mentioned that, under the Lugano Convention, it is **S23–031** possible for a Contracting State to enter a reservation to the effect that, where the property is situated in its territory, it will not recognise a judgment given by the courts of another Contracting State under Article 16(1)(b)—*i.e.* under clause (2) of the Rule.[79] There is no equivalent provision in the Regulation or the 1968 Convention.

Package holidays. Clause (2) may not provide a solution where holiday **S23–032** accommodation is booked through an agent, especially where a travel agent provides a package holiday, including accommodation in a villa or cottage in another Regulation State or Contracting State. If the travel agent is to be regarded as the "landlord" for the purpose of the second sentence of Article 22(1) of the Regulation, that provision applies only if the travel agent is domiciled in the same Regulation State as the tenant. If, on the other hand, the owner is to be regarded as the "landlord," the second sentence of Article 22(1) will be inapplicable if, as is likely to be the case, the owner is domiciled in the Regulation State where the accommodation is situated.

In view of these problems, the decision of the European Court in *Hacker* **S23–033** *v. Euro Relais*[80] is of importance. In that case, a travel agent domiciled in Germany signed in German a contract headed *"Mietvertrag"* (tenancy agreement) with a client also domiciled in Germany. Under the agreement, the travel agent undertook to provide the client with holiday accommodation for a period of several weeks in the Netherlands. The property was not owned by the agent. The travel agent also agreed to make reservations on a shipping service to the resort, though the client had to make separate payment for this to the shipping company. The European Commission argued that Article 16(1) of the 1968 Convention never applies to a contract to provide accommodation where the person providing the accommodation is not the owner of the property. The Court did not go this far; nevertheless, it held that Article 16(1) did not apply to a contract between a travel agent and a client to provide holiday accommodation for a few weeks in another Contracting State if (a) the accommodation is not owned by the travel agent, (b) both the travel agent and the client are domiciled in the Contracting State in which the contract is made and (c) the travel agent also undertakes to make travel reservations. This decision ensures that most package holiday contracts are outside the scope of Article 22(1) of the Regulation and Article 16(1) of the Conventions.

If a testator makes a will, leaving his house in Italy to his son, and then, **23–045** prior to his death, executes (in Ontario) a deed of gift of the same property to his daughters, the Ontario court does not have jurisdiction over the son's application to have the deed of gift set aside. The deed (between the testator and his daughters) does not create any contractual or other legal obligation between the daughters and the son. See *Catania v. Giannattasio* (1999) 174 D.L.R. (4th) 170 (Ont. C.A.).

In *Hlynski v. Hlynski* (1999) 176 D.L.R. (4th) 132 (Sask. C.A.) the question arose as to whether, in the context of an application for a division

---

[79] Lugano Convention, Protocol I, Art. 1b.
[80] Case C–280/90 [1992] E.C.R. I–1111. This case was decided under the 1968 Convention before entry into force of Art. 16(1)(b).

of assets under the Matrimonial Property Act 1997 (Sask.), the courts of Saskatchewan were entitled to take into account the value of land in Manitoba (owned by the husband). The Saskatchewan Court of Appeal held that it did; either this aspect of the application fell outside the scope of the *Moçambique* rule (because the wife's claim to a share of the value of the land in Manitoba was not a claim to any title, right or interest in the Manitoba land itself) or it fell within one of the exceptions to the *Moçambique* rule (because it involved an equity running between the parties which indirectly affected land situated in Manitoba).

23–059 This paragraph was cited and considered in *Birch v. Birch* [2001] 3 N.Z.L.R. 413 (N.Z.C.A.).

CHAPTER 24

PARTICULAR TRANSFERS OF MOVABLES

1. TRANSFER OF TANGIBLE THINGS

NOTE 3. Add: *Glencore International A.G. v. Metro Trading International Inc.* **24R–001**
[2001] 1 Lloyd's Rep. 284.

In *Glencore International A.G. v. Metro Trading International Inc.*, *supra*. it **24–004**
was held that the *lex situs* applied generally to determine whether, and
when, property had passed, and was not displaced by the applicable law of
the transfer even as regards a dispute as to proprietary rights as between
the parties to the transfer.

NOTE 19. Add: *Glencore International A.G. v. Metro Trading International* **24–005**
Inc., *supra*.

In *Glencore International A.G. v. Metro Trading International Inc.*, *supra*, the **24–007**
court examined, but found that it did not need to decide, the question
whether the *lex situs* was to be understood as a reference to the domestic
law, or as including the possibility of *renvoi* to another law.

NOTE 23. S.I. 1994 No. 501 is further amended by S.I. 2001 No. 3972. **24–008**

Final sentence. This sentence was quoted with approval in *Glencore* **24–010**
International A.G. v. Metro Trading International Inc., *supra*, at p. 296

2. ASSIGNMENT OF INTANGIBLE THINGS

In *Raiffeisen Zentralbank Oesterreich A.G. v. Five Star General Trading LLC* **24–048**
[2000] EWCA Civ. 68; [2001] Q.B. 825 (C.A.) (on which, see Briggs (2001)
72 B.Y.B.I.L. 461), the Court of Appeal considered the application of
Article 12 of the Rome Convention to a question of entitlement to the
proceeds of the insurance of a vessel. The mortgagee, to whom the benefit
of the policy of insurance had been assigned, sought as against the owners
of the vessel, the insurers, and the cargo owners (who had obtained an
attachment of the insurance proceeds from a French court) a declaration
that it was absolutely entitled to the proceeds. At first instance ([2001] 1 All
E.R. (Comm.) 897) the judge, who approved passages in para. 24–049 of
the main work, held that the true issue was who, as against the insurer, was
entitled to the insurance, and that Article 12 referred this to English law as
the law governing the insurance. The Court of Appeal upheld the decision
(though varying the orders made). Though it was observed that the issues
might be seen as more complex than appeared from the judgment below,
the Court recognised at para. 48 that "the Rome Convention now views the
relevant issue—that is, what steps, by way of notice or otherwise, require to

be taken in relation to the debtor for the assignment to take effect as between the assignee and the debtor—not as involving any 'property right' but as involving—simply—a contractual issue to be determined by the law governing the obligation assigned". See also Plender *The European Contracts Convention*, 2nd ed. (2001), paras. 11–19 to 11–25.

24–051   NOTE 93. The reasoning of the Dutch and German courts was examined by the Court of Appeal in *Raiffeisen Zentralbank Oesterreich A.G. v. Five Star Trading LLC* [2001] EWCA Civ. 68; [2001] Q.B. 825 (C.A.).

24–056   See also *Raiffeisen Zentralbank Oesterreich A.G. v. Five Star General Trading LLC* [2000] EWCA Civ. 68; [2001] Q.B. 825 (C.A.).

24–062   On the validity of the assignment of English copyright by agreements governed by foreign (Cuban or New York) laws, and on the inability of a Cuban law to affect title to English copyright, which was situated in England, see *Peer International Corp. v. Termidor Music Publishers Ltd.* [2002] EWHC 2675 (Ch); *The Times*, January 2, 2003.

24–064   NOTE 20. The Directive 98/26 ([1998] O.J. L166/45) on Settlement Finality in Payment and Securities Settlement Systems, which deals with indirectly-held securities, was given effect in English law by the Financial Markets and Insolvency (Settlement Finality) Regulations S.I. 1999 No. 2979. A choice of law rule for transactions within the scope of the Directive is contained in Articles 8 and 9 of the Directive and Reg. 23 of the 1999 Regulations. The proposed amendment contained in Financial Markets and Insolvency (Settlement Finality) (Amendment) Regulations 2001, S.I. 2001 No. 997 was repealed on its date of entry into force. Directive 2002/47 on Financial Collateral Arrangements, [2002] O.J. L168/43, came into effect on June 27, 2002, and is required to be implemented in national law by December 27, 2003. It will impose a choice of law rule for transactions in which book entry securities are used as collateral in a cross-border context. In addition, a Convention on the Law Applicable to Certain Rights in Respect of Securities held with an Intermediary is being produced under auspices of the Hague Conference or International Law. For a comprehensive analysis of the law in this area, see Ooi, *Shares and other Securities in the Conflict of Laws* (2003).

24R–071   With effect from March 25, 2002, R.S.C. Ord. 49 is repealed, and replaced by CPR Part 72, which allows an English court to make a "third party debt order". The terminology, and the detail of the procedure, is altered from the rules as they provided for garnishment of a debt, but references in this Chapter to R.S.C. Ord. 49 must now be understood as references to this new procedure.

NOTE 45. Add *Société Eram Shipping Co. Ltd. v. Compagnie Internationale de Navigation* [2001] EWCA Civ. 1317; [2001] 2 All E.R. (Comm.) 721 (C.A.).

NOTE 47. R.S.C. Ord. 49 is repealed from March 25, 2002 and replaced by CPR Part 72.

24–073   See the entry for para. 24R–071, above.

24–075   The issue of double jeopardy, and the circumstances in which a risk that the garnishee will be forced to pay the debt twice over will cause the court to exercise its discretion against making the order, were re-considered in *Société Eram Shipping Co. Ltd. v. Compagnie International de Navigation* [2002] UKHL 30, [2003] 3 W.L.R. 21 (H.L.). The House of Lords noted that the provision of English law (now found in CPR, r. 72.9) was that payment by the garnishee under the order served to discharge the garnishee's debt to the judgment debtor. This statutory rule could only be held to operate if the debt were itself situtated in England; there was no reason to suppose that a foreign court would apply an English statutory rule to a purported attachment of property situated outside the territorial jurisdiction of the English court. The proposition that the garnishee might succeed in establishing his discharge (by reason of payment in accordance with the order in legal proceedings), or advancing a counterclaim for reimbursement, was inconsistent with the automatic nature of the garnishee order. As the debt was situated in Hong Kong, the decision of the Court of Appeal ([2001] EWCA Civ. 1317, [2001] 2 All E.R. (Comm.) 721 (C.A.)) to make the garnishee order absolute was reversed.

In *Kuwait Oil Tanker Co. S.A.K. v. Qabazard* [2003] UKHL 31, [2003] 3 **24–080** W.L.R. 14 (H.L.), the House of Lords held that there was no jurisdiction to make a garnishee order in respect of a debt situated in Switzerland. This followed from its decision in *Société Eram Shipping Co. Ltd. v. Compagnie International de Navigation, supra*, but was reinforced by Article 16(5) of the Lugano Convention.

CHAPTER 25

GOVERNMENTAL ACTS AFFECTING PROPERTY

25R–001 See also *Kuwait Airways Corp. v. Iraqi Airways Co. (Nos. 4 and 5)* [2002] UKHL 19, [2002] 2 A.C. 883, 1108; *Peer International Corp. v. Termidor Music Publishers Ltd.* [2002] EWHC 2675 (Ch); *The Times*, January 2, 2003.

25–004 See also *Kuwait Airways Corp. v. Iraqi Airways Co. (Nos. 4 and 5)* [2002] 2 A.C. 883, 977–983 (C.A.) on the distinction between recognition of states and recognition of governments.

Text at note 21. In *Chen Li Hung v. Ting Lei Miao* [2000] H.K.L.R.D. 252; (2000) 3 H.K.C.F.A.R. 9 the Court of Final Appeal of Hong Kong accepted that where private rights, or acts of everyday occurrence, or perfunctory acts of administration were concerned, the courts might, in the interests of justice and common sense, where no consideration of public policy to the contrary prevailed, give recognition to the acts of an unrecognised government which was in *de facto* control. It was held that the Hong Kong courts will give effect to the orders of courts sitting in countries under the *de jure* sovereignty of the People's Republic of China but presently under the *de facto* (but unlawful) control of a usurper government, where: (i) the rights covered by those orders are private rights; (ii) giving effect to such orders accords with the interests of justice, the dictates of common sense and the needs of law and order; (iii) giving them effect would not be inimical to the interests of the People's Republic of China or otherwise contrary to public policy. Consequently the right of trustees in bankruptcy appointed by order of a Taiwanese court to recover the assets of the bankrupt in Hong Kong would be recognised, notwithstanding that the People's Republic of China regards Taiwan as part of, and under the *de jure* sovereignty of, the People's Republic of China, but as under the *de facto* and unlawful control of a usurper government. The rights were private. The action was not for the benefit of the government in Taiwan, but for the benefit of 100,000 Taiwanese private investors; and to give effect to the order would not involve recognition of the Taiwan regime or its courts.

In *B v. B (Divorce: Northern Cyprus)* [2000] 2 F.L.R. 707 a divorce granted by a court in the Turkish Republic of Northern Cyprus was not recognised, but the decision is not fully reasoned.

25–006 In *Kuwait Airways Corp. v. Iraqi Airways Co. (Nos. 4 and 5), supra*, the Court of Appeal expressed some sympathy with the view (but without actually deciding) that the *lex situs* rule might have no application where the property has been brought unlawfully into the territory of the confiscating state.

25–010 The decision in *Kuwait Airways Corp. v. Iraqi Airways Co. (No. 2)* [1999] C.L.C. 31 has been affirmed: *Kuwait Airways Corp. v. Iraqi Airways Co. (Nos. 4 and 5)* [2002] UKHL 19; [2002] 2 A.C. 883 (C.A. and H.L.), *supra*, paras. 5–038—5–041.

CHAPTER 27

SUCCESSION

3. CHOICE OF LAW

B. *Testamentary succession*

(3) MATERIAL OR ESSENTIAL VALIDITY

According to *Re Barton's Estate, Tod v. Barton*, February 20, 2002, if the **27–045** material validity of a will is established by reference to the law of the domicile of the testator, the validity and effect of a deed of variation executed by the beneficiary legatees in respect of a trust arising under the will is governed by the law which is made applicable to that trust by the Hague Convention on the Recognition of Trusts, and is not referable to the law of the testator's domicile, which is *functus officio*.

(6) REVOCATION

The rule that the law of testator's domicile at the date of marriage **27–086** determines whether that marriage operates to revoke the will was applied in *Allison v. Allison* [1999] 3 W.W.R. 438 (B.C.), with the result that the law of British Columbia (in which province the testator died domiciled) on the essential validity of wills was inapplicable.

NOTE 97. See also *In the Estate of Vickers* [2002] C.L. 378 (Royal Court of **27–092** Jersey).

CHAPTER 28

THE EFFECT OF MARRIAGE ON PROPERTY

See generally Hartley, in *Reform and Development of Private International Law* (Fawcett ed., 2002), p. 215.

CHAPTER 29

TRUSTS

See Harris, in *Reform and Development of Private International Law* **29–002**
(Fawcett ed., 2002), chap. 8.

See *Re Barton's Estate, Tod v. Barton*, February 20, 2002; *Chellaram v.* **29–008—**
Chellaram (No. 2) [2002] EWHC 632 (Ch); [2003] 3 All E.R. 17; *Re* **011**
Carapiet's Trusts, Manoogian (Armenian Patriarch of Jerusalem) v. Sonsino
[2002] EWHC 1304 (Ch).

NOTE 26. Add: *Saliba v. Falzon* (N.S.W. Sup. Ct., 1998, unreported).

CHAPTER 30

CORPORATIONS AND CORPORATE INSOLVENCY

1. DOMICILE AND RESIDENCE

30–002 NOTE 8. In Case C–212/97 *Centros Ltd. v. Erhvervs-og Selskabsstyrelsen* [1999] E.C.R. I–1459, [2000] Ch. 446 the European Court held that it is contrary to what are now Articles 43 and 48 of the EC Treaty for a Member State to refuse to register a branch of a company formed in accordance with the law of another Member State in which it has its registered office but in which it conducts no business, even where the branch is intended to enable the company in question to carry on its entire business in the State in which the branch is to be created, while avoiding the need to form a company there, thus evading the application of the rules governing the formation of companies which, in that State, are more restrictive as regards the paying up of a minimum share capital. The European Court emphasised, however, that this view did not prevent the authorities of the Member State concerned from adopting any appropriate measure for preventing or penalising fraud either in relation to the company itself (if necessary in co-operation with the Member State in which the company was formed) or in relation to its members, where it has been established that they are attempting, by means of the formation of a company, to evade their obligations towards private or public creditors established in the territory of the Member State concerned. See, on this case, Ebke (2000) 48 Am. J. Comp. L. 623; Roth (2003) 52 I.C.L.Q. 177. See also Case C–208/00 *Überseering BV v. Nordic Construction Company Baumanagement GmbH (NCC)* [2002] E.C.R. I–9919; Case C–436/00 *X and Y v. Riksskatterverket* [2002] E.C.R. I–10829.

30–006 NOTE 35. Add: *Cf. Latchin v. General Mediterranean Holdings SA* [2002] C.L.C. 3330.

2. STATUS

30R–009 NOTE 35. Add in line 12: *The Rio Assu* [1999] 1 Lloyd's Rep. 201; *J.H. Rayner (Mincing Lane) Ltd. v. Cafenorte S.A. Importadora* [1999] 2 All E.R. (Comm.) 577 (C.A.); *Eurosteel Ltd. v. Stinnes A.G.* [2000] 1 All E.R. (Comm.) 964; *Astra S.A. Insurance and Reinsurance Co. v. Sphere Drake Insurance Ltd.* [2000] 2 Lloyd's Rep. 550; *Dubai Aluminium Co. Ltd. v. Al Alawi* [2002] EWHC 2051 (Comm).

30–010 NOTE 38. *Cf. Backman v. Canada* [2001] S.C.R. 367 (whether a foreign partnership recognised in Canada for the purposes of tax legislation depends on requirements for existence of a partnership in Canadian law).

30–011 NOTE 44. Add in line 3: *The Rio Assu, supra*; *Astra S.A. Insurance and Reinsurance Co. v. Sphere Drake Insurance Ltd., supra*; *Dubai Aluminium*

Co. Ltd. v. Al Alawi, supra. See *Kuwait Airways Corpn. v. Iraqi Airways Co. (Nos. 4 and 5)* [2002] UKHL 19; [2002] 2 A.C. 883 (C.A. and H.L.), *supra*, entry at paras. 5–038—5–041.

NOTE 46. See also *The Rio Assu, supra*; *Astra S.A. Insurance and Reinsurance Co. v. Sphere Drake Insurance Ltd., supra*.

NOTE 51. Add in line 4: *The Rio Assu, supra*; *J.H. Rayner (Mincing Lane) Ltd. v. Cafenorte S.A. Importadora, supra*; *Eurosteel Ltd. v. Stinnes A.G., supra*; *Astra S.A. Insurance and Reinsurance Co. v. Sphere Drake Insurance Ltd., supra*.

NOTE 55. See also *Eurosteel Ltd. v. Stinnes A.G., supra*.

NOTE 74. Add: *Chen Li Hung v. Ting Lei Miao* [2000] 1 H.K.L.R.D. 252; **30–017** (2000) 3 H.K.C.F.A.R. 9.

3. CAPACITY AND INTERNAL MANAGEMENT

NOTE 76. In line 7 add: *Azov Shipping Co. v. Baltic Shipping Co.* [1999] 2 **30R–020** Lloyd's Rep. 159; *Grupo Torras S.A. v. Al-Sabah* [1999] C.L.C. 1469; rvsd. in part on other grounds [2001] C.L.C. 221 (C.A.).

In penultimate line add: *Marubeni Hong Kong and South China Ltd. v. Mongolian Government* [2002] 2 All E.R. (Comm.) 873.

NOTE 77. In line 10 add: *Azov Shipping Co. v. Baltic Shipping Co., supra*; *Grupo Torras S.A. v. Al-Sabah, supra*; *Base Metal Trading Ltd. v. Shamurin* [2002] C.L.C. 322.

NOTE 85. Some discussion of these provisions can be found in *Azov Shipping* **30–023** *Co. v. Baltic Shipping Co.* [1999] 2 Lloyd's Rep. 159, 170–173.

NOTE 87. It has been said that the expression "authority" in these provisions includes the doctrine of ostensible authority in a situation where the putative contract is governed by English law: see *Azov Shipping Co. v. Baltic Shipping Co., supra*, at p. 172.

NOTE 92 and text thereto. Although the courts of the country of incorpora- **30–024** tion are very likely indeed to be the appropriate forum to give decisions on the control and extent of the powers of the corporation, the development of the doctrine of *forum non conveniens* since the decision in *Pergamon Press Ltd. v. Maxwell* [1970] 1 W.L.R. 1167 means that they will not necessarily be the exclusive forum: *Konamaneni v. Rolls-Royce Industrial Power (India) Ltd.* [2002] 1 W.L.R. 1269.

Add after text to note 94. The law of the country of incorporation should also determine the extent of the duties of the directors of a corporation: *Konamaneni v. Rolls-Royce Industrial Power (India) Ltd., supra*; *Base Metal Trading Ltd. v. Shamurin, supra*. Additionally, it has been stated, *obiter*, that the right of a shareholder to bring a derivative action in respect of wrongs to a corporation is, in a case containing a foreign element, a matter of substance not procedure and is governed, accordingly, by the law of the country of incorporation, notwithstanding the fact that, for purely English domestic purposes, the right has been regarded as a procedural device: *Konamaneni v. Rolls-Royce Industrial Power (India) Ltd., supra*.

NOTE 94. Add: *Azov Shipping Co. v. Baltic Shipping Co.*, *supra*; *Re Macks; Ex p. Saint* (2000) 204 C.L.R. 158, 227–228. See also *Base Metal Trading Ltd. v. Shamurin, supra* (whether director of company can be held account-able to the company in his capacity as director for the way in which he carries out his work is a matter for the law of the place of incorporation).

NOTE 96. Add: *Eurosteel Ltd. v. Stinnes A.G.*, *supra*.

NOTE 97. Add: See also *Society of Lloyd's v. Fraser* [1998] C.L.C. 1630 (C.A.).

30–025 NOTE 2. Add: See *Marubeni Hong Kong and South China Ltd. v. Mongolian Government* [2002] 2 All E.R. (Comm.) 873, 880.

30–029 NOTE 16. See also Art. 22(2) of the Judgments Regulation, *supra*, paras S11R–343—S11–348.

30–030 NOTE 24. Add: See also *Re Joseph Holt plc*, *The Times*, November 14, 2000.

4. WINDING UP PROCEEDINGS NOT FALLING WITHIN COUNCIL REGULATION (E.C.) 1346/2000 ON INSOLVENCY PROCEEDINGS

A. *Jurisdiction of English Courts*

30R–033 Rule 155 and note 33. Rule 155 does not apply to winding up proceedings falling within Council Regulation (E.C.) 1346/2000 of May 29, 2000 on Insolvency Proceedings ([2000] O.J. L160/1), hereinafter "the E.C. Insol-vency Regulation". See *infra*, paras. S30R–137—S30–322. The Regulation replaces the European Union Convention on Insolvency Proceedings referred to in note 33. Insolvency Act 2000, s. 14, in force from November 30, 2000, authorises the Secretary of State to make, by regulations, any provision which he considers necessary or expedient for the purpose of giving effect, with or without modifications, to the model law on cross-border insolvency, *i.e.* the model law contained in Annex I of the report of the 30th session of UNCITRAL: see *infra*, entry at paras. 30–132—30–144.

NOTES 35 and 36 and text thereto. Insolvency Act 1986, s. 117 is amended to make it clear that the High Court and County Court do not have jurisdiction to wind up a company registered in England unless jurisdiction exists to open proceedings under the E.C. Insolvency Regulation: see Insolvency Act 1986. s. 117(7) inserted by Insolvency Act 1986 (Amend-ment) (No. 2) Regulations 2002 (S.I. 2002 No. 1240), Reg. 6. See *post*, paras. S30–159.

NOTE 37. Add: Judgments Regulation, Arts. 1(2)(b), 22(2); S.I. 2001 No. 3928, Sched. 1, para. 10.

NOTES 38 and 39 and text thereto. Insolvency Act 1986, s. 221(4) which provides that no unregistered company shall be voluntarily wound up under the Act has been amended to create an exception in cases falling within the Regulation: see S.I. 2002 No. 1240, Reg. 9. Insolvency Act 1986, s. 225 is amended so as to make the power it confers subject to the E.C. Insolvency Regulation: see Insolvency Act 1986, s. 225(2), inserted by S.I. 2002 No. 1240, Reg. 10. The original version of the section becomes subsection (1): *ibid*. See *infra*, para. S30–159. The limits on the jurisdiction of the court established in the case-law cited in note 39 will not apply where the E.C. Insolvency Regulation applies, since the latter contains its own rules of jurisdiction: see *infra*, paras. S30R–153 *et seq*.

NOTE 39. *Re Richbell Information Services Inc.* is now reported, *sub nom. Atlantic & General Investment Trust Ltd. v. Richbell Information Services Inc.* at [2000] B.C.C. 111. *Re Latreefers Inc.* [1999] 1 B.C.L.C. 271 has been affirmed *sub nom. Stocznia Gdanska S.A. v. Latreefers Inc. (No. 2)* [2001] 2 B.C.L.C. 116 (C.A.).

Add, in line 13: *Banco Nacional de Cuba v. Cosmos Trading Corp.* [2000] 1 B.C.L.C. 813 (C.A.).

Rule 155(2), text after note 39. This part of clause (2) will apply if the company does not have its seat in a Judgments Regulation State: Judgments Regulation, Arts. 1(2)(b), 22(2); S.I. 2001 No. 3929, Sched. 1, para. 10. The English court will lack jurisdiction under the 1968 Convention if the company has its seat in Denmark.

NOTES 40–41. As to the Judgments Regulation see preceding entry.

NOTES 40–42. The E.C. Insolvency Regulation does not apply to the winding up of solvent companies. See *infra*, para. S30–150. This means that "public interest" winding-up petitions are excluded from this Regulation.

NOTE 42. Add: Judgments Regulation, Arts. 29, 30.

NOTE 43. See now Judgments Regulation, Arts. 1(2)(b), 22(2). **30–034**

NOTE 44 and text thereto. This proposition is now subject to the E.C. **30–035** Insolvency Regulation.

NOTE 45 and text thereto. If the company is insolvent this jurisdiction will be subject to the E.C. Insolvency Regulation, *infra*, paras. S30R–153 *et seq*. If the company is solvent, the Judgments Regulation may apply: see Arts. 1(2)(b), 22(2) and S.I. 2001 No. 3929, Sched. 1, para. 10.

NOTE 46 and text thereto. There is no such discretion if the matter falls **30–036** within the scope of the E.C. Insolvency Regulation: see *infra*, paras. S30R–153 *et seq*.

NOTE 46. Order 11, r. 1(1) is replaced by CPR, r. 6.20. The decision in Re Harrods (Buenos Aires) Ltd. [1992] Ch. 72 (Harman J. and C.A.) appears not to have been followed by the High Court of Ireland in *C. (D.) v. O'C. (W.)* [2001] 2 I.R. 1, though in this case the plaintiff and the defendant were domicilied in Ireland and the alternative forum was in Sweden, another Contracting State. The point in issue in *Re Harrods (Buenos Aires) Ltd., supra* was referred to the European Court of Justice in *Owusu v. Jackson* [2002] EWCA Civ. 877; [2002] I.L.Pr. 813 (C.A.), Case C–281/02, pending, and in *American Motorists Insurance Co. v. Cellstar Corp.* [2003] EWCA Civ. 206, [2003] I.L.Pr. 370 (C.A.).

NOTE 47 and text thereto. The position would appear to be the same under the Judgments Regulation if the view in *Re Harrods (Buenos Aires) Ltd., supra* continues to be accepted.

NOTE 48 and text thereto. The position is the same under the Judgments Regulation.

33–037— The principles discussed in these paragraphs will not apply to situations
33–051 falling within the E.C. Insolvency Regulation, *infra*, paras. S30R–153 *et seq.*

33–038 NOTES 53 to 54 and text thereto. The English court will lack jurisdiction to
wind up a solvent company if the company has its seat in another Member
State where the Judgments Regulation is in force; Judgments Regulation,
Arts. 1(2)(b), 22(2); S.I. 2001 No. 3929, Sched. 1, para. 10.

30–041 NOTE 63. In line 2 add: *Banco Nacional de Cuba v. Cosmos Trading Corp.*
[2000] 1 B.C.L.C. 813 (C.A.); *Stocznia Gdanska S.A. v. Latreefers Inc.
(No. 2)* [2001] 2 B.C.L.C. 116 (C.A.).

30–044 NOTE 71. Re *Latreefers Inc.* [1999] 1 B.C.L.C. 271 has been affirmed *sub
nom. Stocznia Gdanska S.A. v. Latreefers Inc. (No. 2)* [2001] 2 B.C.L.C. 116
(C.A.). *Re Richbell Information Services Inc.* is now reported, *sub nom.
Atlantic & General Investment Trust Ltd. v. Richbell Information Services Inc.*
at [2000] B.C.C. 111. Add: *Banco National de Cuba v. Cosmos Trading Corp.*
[2000] 1 B.C.L.C. 813 C.A.) (although a winding-up order, if made, would
enable liquidator to prosecute claims under Insolvency Act 1986, ss. 238
and 423, such claims would be against the Central Bank of Cuba which
would be protected from them by State Immunity Act 1978, ss. 13 (2) and
14 (4): see main work, Chap. 10, para. 10–013: the mere "public relations
benefit" of obtaining a winding-up order is not a benefit for these
purposes). And see *Re Banco Nacional de Cuba* [2001] 1 W.L.R. 2039.

30–046 The approach in *Re Real Estate Development Co.* [1991] B.C.L.C. 210 was
approved by the Court of Appeal in *Stocznia Gdanska S.A. v. Latreefers Inc.
(No. 2)* [2001] 2 B.C.L.C. 116, 130. The relevant principles consisted of
three core requirements, namely (1) there must be a sufficient connection
with England which may, but does not necessarily have to, consist of assets
within the jurisdiction; (2) there must be a reasonable possibility, if a
winding-up order is made, of benefit to those applying for the winding-up
order; (3) one or more persons interested in the distribution of assets of the
company must be persons over whom the court can exercise jurisdiction. In
relation to the first requirement, it was stated in *Banco Nacional de Cuba v.
Cosmos Trading Corp.* [2000] 1 B.C.L.C. 813, 819 (C.A.), that "the courts of
this country should hesitate very long before subjecting foreign companies
with no assets here to the winding-up procedures of this country". It was
also stated (*ibid.*) that the making of an English winding-up order was
generally undesirable where the foreign company continued to trade in its
country of incorporation and elsewhere in the world and that the making of
such an order in such a situation required exceptional circumstances and
exceptional justification.

30–048 NOTE 81. Re *Latreefers Inc.* [1999] 1 B.C.L.C. 271 has been affirmed *sub
nom. Stocznia Gdanska S.A. v. Latreefers Inc. (No. 2)* [2001] 2 B.C.L.C. 116
(C.A.). *Re Richbell Information Services Inc.* is now reported, *sub nom.
Atlantic & General Investment Trust Ltd. v. Richbell Information Services Inc.*
at [2000] B.C.C. 111.

30–050 NOTES 97 to 98. Insolvency Act 1986, s. 225 is amended by S.I. 2002 No.
1240, Reg. 10. S. 225 becomes s. 225(1). A new s. 225(2) states that the
section is subject to the E.C. Insolvency Regualtion.

NOTE 6 and text thereto. The position is the same in cases falling within the **30–052—** Judgments Regulation: see Arts. 1(2)(b), 22(2) and S.I. 2001 No. 3929, **30–053** Sched. 1, para. 10.

NOTES 7 to 12 and text thereto. The same view may be taken under Arts. 35(1) and 29 of the Judgments Regualtion.

NOTE 13 and text thereto. The same view may be taken in relation to cases **30–054** falling within the Judgments Regulation.

NOTES 14 and 15 and text thereto. The position is the same under the **30–055** Judgments Regulation.

NOTE 18 and text thereto. The position is the same under the version of the **30–056** Judgments Regulation which applies in intra-United Kingdom cases: see S.I. 2001 No. 3929, Reg. 4 and Sched. 2, Pt. II, inserting a new Sched. 4 into Civil Jurisdiction and Judgments Act 1982, the relevant provision being para. 4.

Rule 156 is unaffected by the E.C. Insolvency Regulation, the jurisdictional **30R–062** rules of the latter being concerned solely with the international jurisdiction of the English court. Territorial jurisdiction within a Member State is governed by the national law of that State: see E.C. Insolvency Regulation, [2000] O.J. L160/1, Recital 15.

NOTE 43 and text thereto. Insolvency Act 1986, s. 120 is amended to make it **30–063** clear that the international jurisdiction of a Scottish court is subject to the E.C. Insolvency Regulation: see Insolvency Act 1986, s. 120(6), inserted by S.I. 2002 No. 1240, Reg. 7.

NOTES 71 and 72 and text thereto. The position is the same under the **30–068** Judgments Regulation: see Arts. 1(2)(b), 22(2); S.I. 2001 No. 3929, Sched. 1, para. 10, Reg. 4 and Sched. 2, Pt. II, para. 4, inserting a new Sched. 4, para. 4 into Civil Jurisdiction and Judgments Act 1982.

NOTE 74. Insolvency Act 1986, s. 426(10) (*a*), and (*b*) is amended by **30–069** Insolvency Act 2000, Sched. 4, Pt. II, para. 3. The amendments (in force from April 2, 2001) do not affect the point made in the text to note 74.

NOTE 75 and text thereto. The E.C. Insolvency Regulation does not apply in the United Kingdom of Great Britain and Northern Ireland to the extent that it is irreconcilable with the obligations arising in relation to bankruptcy and the winding up of insolvent companies from any arrangements with the Commonwealth existing at the time the Regulation enters into force (May 31, 2002): see Arts. 44(3)(b), 47.

B. *Effect of an English Winding-up Order*

Rule 157 and Comment thereto does not apply to winding-up proceedings **30R–071** falling within the E.C. Insolvency Regulation: see *infra*, paras. S30R–181 *et seq*.

NOTE 86. In *Banco Nacional de Cuba v. Cosmos Trading Corp.* [2000] 1 **30–072** B.C.L.C. 813, 820 (C.A.) it was stated that it is something of a weakness in

English winding-up law that it is not possible to have a winding-up of a foreign company limited to its activities and assets in England. See also *Bank of Credit & Commerce International SA v. Bugshan* [2001] EWCA Civ. 244. *Cf.* the position under the E.C. Insolvency Regulation, *infra*, paras. S30R–153 *et seq.*

NOTE 95. On Insolvency Act 1986, s. 130(2), see *Newcap Reinsurance Corp. v. HIH Casualty and General Insurance Ltd.* [2002] EWCA Civ. 300, [2002] 2 B.C.L.C. 228 (C.A.)

30–073 Text at notes 95–96. In *Cleaver v. Delta American Reinsurance Co.* [2001] 2 A.C. 328 (P.C.), the Privy Council affirmed the general principle that where a company was being wound up in an English liquidation and also in a liquidation in a foreign country, a creditor who had proved and received a dividend in the foreign liquidation could not receive a dividend in the English liquidation unless he brought into hotchpot his foreign dividend. The principle applied only to assets which under English law formed part of the estate in liquidation so that a secured creditor who had obtained his security before the liquidation commenced was entitled to realise his security, apply the proceeds towards the discharge of his debt and prove in the English liquidation for the balance owing to him. He was not required to bring into hotchpot the proceeds of his security because it had not formed part of the liquidation estate.

NOTES 96, 98. Add: *Cleaver v. Delta American Reinsurance Co., supra.*

NOTE 99. Add: *Cf. Raiffeisen Zentralbank Osterreich AG v. Five Star Trading LLC* [2001] EWCA Civ. 68; [2001] Q.B. 825, 848–849 (C.A.).

30–075 NOTE 13. See also *Banco Nacional de Cuba v. Cosmos Trading Corp., supra*, at p. 819.

30–076 NOTE 23. See also Financial Markets and Insolvency (Settlement Finality) Regulations 1999, S.I. 1999 No. 2979, regs. 23 and 24.

30–077 NOTE 24. The Secretary of State may by order provide for a provision of the Insolvency Act 1986 to apply (with or without modification) in relation to a company incorporated outside Great Britain: Enterprise Act 2002, s. 254 (not yet in force).

NOTE 26. Add in line 2. *Jeeves v. Official Receiver* [2002] 2 B.C.L.C 453. *Cf. Re RBG Resources Ltd., Shierson v. Rastogi* [2002] EWCA Civ. 1624; [2003] 1 W.L.R. 586 (C.A.).

30–079 NOTE 31. Add: See also *Jeeves v. Official Receiver, supra; Re RBG Resources Ltd., Shierson v. Rastogi, supra.*

30–081 NOTE 38. See also *Banco Nacional de Cuba v. Cosmos Trading Corp., supra*, at pp. 819–820.

NOTE 39. See previous entry.

30–084 NOTE 46. See also *Banco Nacional de Cuba v. Cosmos Trading Corp., supra*, at pp. 819–820. A claim under the Insolvency Act 1986, s. 423 does not fall within CPR, r. 6.19(2) and, accordingly, permission to serve process out of the jurisdiction is required: *Re Banco National de Cuba* [2001] 1 W.L.R. 2039; *Re Harrods (Buenos Aires) Ltd. (No. 2)* [1992] Ch. 72, 116. Insolvency Rules 1986 do not apply to claims under s. 423 since that section can operate outside insolvency proceedings: *ibid.*

NOTE 51 and text thereto. Company Directors' Disqualification Act 1986 is **30–086** amended by Insolvency Act 2000, ss. 5–8 and Sched. 4, Pt. I. These amendments (in force from April 2, 2001) do not affect the points made in the text.

NOTE 55. See entry at para. 30–068, n. 75. **30–087**

C. *Effect of a Foreign Winding-up Order*

Rule 158 and Comment thereto does not apply to a winding up or other **30R–091** insolvency proceeding falling within the E.C. Insolvency Regulation. See *infra*, paras. S30R–262 *et seq.*

NOTE 74 and text thereto. This passage was cited with approval in *Re* **30–092** *Macks; Ex p. Saint* (2000) 204 C.L.R. 158, 227–228.

NOTE 88. As to the making of an English administration order, see now **30–095** Enterprise Act 2002, ss. 248–249, Sched. 16 and 17 (not yet in force).

NOTE 94. Add: In *Re Singer Sewing Machine Co. of Canada Ltd.* [2000] 5 W.W.R. 598 (Alta.) an American Chapter 11 order in respect of a Canadian company which carried on business only in Canada and which had no assets in Canada was refused recognition in Alberta.

NOTE 6. Regulations made under the Insolvency Act 2000, s. 14, so as to **30–098** implement the model law on cross-border insolvency (*supra*, entry at para. 30R–033, n. 33 and *post*, entry at paras. 30–132—30–136) may amend any provision of s. 426: Insolvency Act 2000, s. 14 (2)(*c*), in force from November 30, 2000. No such regulations have, as yet, been made.

NOTE 11. *England v. Purves* is now reported, *sub nom. Re J.N. Taylor* **30–100** *Finance Pty. Ltd.* at [1999] 2 B.C.L.C. 256. Add: *England v. Smith* [2001] Ch. 419 (C.A.); *Re Duke Group Ltd.* [2001] B.C.C. 144.

NOTES 12, 13. Insolvency Act 1982 s. 426(10)(*a*) is amended by Insolvency Act 2000, Sched. 4, Pt. II (in force from April 2, 2001). The amendments do not affect the point made in the text. The provisions of the Company Directors' Disqualification Act 1986 are amended by Insolvency Act 2000, ss. 5, 8 and Sched. 4, Pt. I (in force from April 2, 2001).

NOTE 13 and text thereto. When applying the insolvency law of a relevant country or territory that corresponds to the insolvency law of England, the court should apply any principles, practices or discretions that the court requesting the assistance would apply in exercising its powers under the foreign law: *England v. Smith* [2001] Ch. 419 (C.A.), disapproving *Re J.N. Taylor Finance Pty. Ltd.* [1999] 2 B.C.L.C. 256. In *England v. Smith, supra*, it was also held that application of the law of the requesting court should not be circumscribed by limitations to be found in the corresponding provisions of the insolvency law of England unless some principle of English public policy would be infringed were the foreign law to be applied according to its terms. Accordingly, the English court was prepared to accede to a request from the Supreme Court of South Australia seeking examination of a person allegedly concerned with the affairs of a company under section 596B of the Australian Corporations Law even though such an order would not have been made under the corresponding (but different) provisions of section 236 of the Insolvency Act 1986 because the order would be regarded as oppressive. To the same effect is *Re Duke Group Ltd.* [2001] B.C.C. 144. Contrast *Re J.N. Taylor Finance Pty. Ltd.*, *supra*, where such an order under the same section of the Australian law was denied because it would not have been granted under section 236 of the 1986 Act.

30–101 NOTE 27. *England v. Purves* is now reported, *sub nom. Re J.N. Taylor Finance Pty. Ltd.* at [1999] 2 B.C.L.C. 256. It was not followed in *England v. Smith*, *supra*. See previous entry.

30–103 NOTE 30. See also Financial Markets and Insolvency (Settlement Finality) Regulations 1999, S.I. 1999 No. 2979, regs. 25 and 26.

30–104 NOTE 31. As to *England v. Purves*, *The Times*, January 29, 1998, see entry at para. 30–101, n. 27. Add: *England v. Smith*, *supra*.

NOTE 32. Add: *England v. Smith*, *supra*; *Re Duke Group Ltd.*, *supra*.

NOTE 33. As to *England v. Purves*, *The Times*, January 29, 1998, see entry at para. 30–101, n. 27. Add: *England v. Smith*, *supra*; *Re Duke Group Ltd.*, *supra*.

NOTE 34. Add: *England v. Smith*, *supra*; *Re Duke Group Ltd.*, *supra*.

NOTE 35. As to *England v. Purves*, *The Times*, January 29, 1998, see entry at para. 30–101, n. 27. A request was granted in *England v. Smith*, *supra*, and in *Re Duke Group Ltd.*, *supra*. See entry at para. 30–100, n. 13 and text thereto.

30–105 NOTE 37. Add: *Re Television Trade Rentals Ltd.* [2002] EWHC 211 (Ch); [2002] B.C.C. 807.

NOTES 38, 39. See also *England v. Smith*, *supra*; *Re Television Trade Rentals Ltd.*, *supra*.

NOTE 41. As to *England v. Purves*, *The Times*, January 29, 1998, see entry at para. 30–101, n. 27. Add: *England v. Smith*, *supra*.

30–106 NOTE 44. In *Re Television Trade Rentals Ltd.*, *supra*, the provisions of the Insolvency Act 1986 relating to company voluntary arrangements were applied to companies incorporated in the Isle of Man even though company voluntary arrangements did not exist under the law of the Isle of Man. The case had strong connections with England since the great majority of creditors were English, the companies carried on business in England and their affairs were inextricably linked with an English company.

NOTE 49. As to *England v. Purves*, *The Times*, January 29, 1998, see entry at para. 30–101, n. 27. This decision was not followed in *England v. Smith* [2001] Ch. 419 (C.A.). See entry at para. 30–100, n. 13 and text thereto.

Note 52. As to *England v. Purves, The Times*, January 29, 1998, see entry at **30–107** para. 30–101, n. 27.

Note 54. Add: *England v. Smith, supra*.

Note 55. As to *England v. Purves, The Times*, January 29, 1998, see entry at para. 30–101, n. 27. Add: *England v. Smith, supra*. See entry at para. 30–100, n. 13 and text thereto.

D. *Receivers*

Rule 159 is not affected by the E.C. Insolvency Regulation since the **30R–110** Regulation does not apply to receiverships: see *infra*, para. S30–150.

Notes 68, 69. The provisions of Companies Act 1989 there referred to will **30–111** not now be brought into force, but a ministerial reference from the Department of Trade and Industry to the Law Commission has led to the production of a Law Commission consultation paper considering reform of the law relating to the registration of company charges: see Law Commission, Consultation Paper No. 164, *Registration of Security Interests: Company Charges and Property Other Than Land* (2002), especially at paras 2.34–2.35, 3.33–3.40, 5.87–5.120. On the application of Companies Act 1985, s. 410 in England, see *Arthur D. Little Ltd. (in administration) v. Ableco Finance LLC* [2002] EWHC 701 (Ch); [2003] Ch. 217.

Notes 71, 72. See previous entry. **30–112**

Notes 87–92 and text thereto. The provisions of the Companies Act 1989 **30–116** discussed in this paragraph will not now be brought into force. See entry at para. 30–111, nn. 68, 69.

Note 94. In line 7 add: *United States v. Levy* (1999) 45 O.R. (3d) 129. **30–118**

Note 95. Add: *United States v. Levy, supra*, at p. 142.

Note 5 and text thereto. In *United States v. Levy, supra*, the Ontario court **30–119** was prepared to recognise a receiver appointed by a United States District Court on the basis of the "real and substantial connection" principle enunciated by the Supreme Court of Canada in *Morguard Investments Ltd. v. De Savoye* [1990] 3 S.C.R. 1077, see main work, para. 14–083. The court appeared to be influenced by reciprocity in the sense that had the claims occurred in Canada, they would have given rise to similar relief, *e.g.* the appointment of a receiver to freeze assets: see (1999) 45 O.R. (3d) 129, 143–144.

Note 14. Companies Act 1989, s. 103 will not now be brought into force: **30–123** see entry at para. 30–111, nn. 68, 69.

Notes 20 to 22 and 24. For limitations on the situations in which an **30–126** administrative receiver can be appointed, see Insolvency Act 1986, ss. 72A– 72H and Sched. 2A, inserted by Enterprise Act 2002, s. 250 and Sched. 18 (not yet in force).

Administration is a proceeding which may fall within the E.C. Insolvency **30–129** Regulation: see *infra*, para. S30–150.

NOTES 35, 37 and 38. See now Insolvency Act 1986, s. 8 and Sched. B1, as substituted by Enterprise Act 2002, s. 248 and Sched. 16 (not yet in force).

30–130 NOTE 43 and text thereto. In *Re BRAC Rent-a-Car International Inc.* [2003] EWHC 128 (Ch), [2003] 1 W.L.R. 1421 it was assumed that an English court could not make an administration order in relation to a foreign company, unless Council Regulation 1346/2000 on Insolvency Proceedings applied: see *infra*, para. S30–150.

NOTES 46 and 49. See previous entry.

30–131 After this paragraph insert new material as follows:

E. *UNCITRAL Model Law on Cross-Border Insolvency*

30–132 The Insolvency Act 2000 provides[57] that the Secretary of State may, by regulations made with the agreement of the Lord Chancellor,[58] make any provision which he considers necessary or expedient for the purpose of implementing "the model law on cross-border insolvency",[59] *i.e.* the model law contained in Annex I of the report of the 30th session of UNCITRAL.[60] Such regulations may, in particular, (a) apply any provision of insolvency law[61] in relation to foreign proceedings,[62] whether begun before or after the regulations enter into force, (b) modify the application of insolvency law, whether in relation to foreign proceedings or otherwise, and (c) amend any provision of section 426 of the Insolvency Act 1986.[63] The relevant provisions of the Act of 2000 entered into force on November 30, 2000.[64] As yet, no relevant regulations have been made. Since the regulations will be critical in determining the effect of the model law on existing United Kingdom law, it is obviously not possible to assess, as yet, the impact of its potential implementation. What follows, therefore, is a brief attempt to identify the principal features of the model law.

30–133 Purpose of model law. The purpose of the model law is to provide effective mechanisms for dealing with cases of cross-border insolvency with a view to promoting the objectives of: co-operation between the courts and other

---

[57] Insolvency Act 2000, s. 14(1).

[58] Insolvency Act 2000, s. 14(6)(*a*).

[59] For the text see Fletcher, *Insolvency in Private International Law* (1999), Appendix IV with commentary, Chap. 8; Lightman and Moss, *The Law of Receivers and Administrators of Companies* (3rd ed., 2000), Appendix 5 with commentary at pp. 551–561.

[60] Insolvency Act 2000, s. 14(4). See Report on the work of the 30th session of UNCITRAL, 12–30 May 1997; Official Records of the General Assembly of the United Nations, 52nd session, Supplement No. 17, Annex I, pp. 68–78.

[61] Insolvency law has the same meaning as in Insolvency Act 1986, s. 426(10)(*a*) and (*b*) (as amended by Insolvency Act 2000, Sched. 4, Pt. II): Insolvency Act 2000, s. 14(4).

[62] "Foreign proceedings" has the same meaning as in the model law on cross-border insolvency: Insolvency Act 2000, s. 14(4). The definition in Art. 2(a) of the model law is as follows: "foreign proceeding means a collective judicial or administrative proceeding in a foreign State, including an interim proceeding, pursuant to a law relating to insolvency in which proceeding the assets and affairs of the debtor are subject to control or supervision by a foreign court, for the purpose of reorganisation or liquidation". This definition would appear to exclude administrative receiverships as defined in English law from the scope of the model law; see *infra*, para. 30–136.

[63] Insolvency Act 2000, s. 14(2).

[64] Insolvency Act 2000, s. 16(2).

competent authorities of the enacting State and foreign States involved in such cases; greater legal certainty for trade and investment; fair and efficient administration of cross-border insolvencies that protects the interests of all creditors and other interested parties, including the debtor; protection and maximization of the value of the debtor's assets; and facilitation of the rescue of financially troubled businesses, thereby protecting investment and preserving employment.[65]

Drafting of the model law. The model law is drafted to enable States which **30–134** enact it to insert into the text of any enacted article specific references which will indicate what terms or procedures of national insolvency legislation are to be brought into the particular article. In the particular context of the United Kingdom, such terms and procedures and likely to be contained in the regulations made pursuant to section 14(1) of the Insolvency Act 2000.[66] It should, however, be emphasized that a State is not required to enact all the provisions of the model law and may therefore enact only such provisions as appear to it to be appropriate.

Scope of the model law. The model law does not purport to provide a **30–135** comprehensive legal regime for the regulation of cross-border insolvency.[67] Thus, for example, the model law contains no rules concerned with the jurisdiction of courts in insolvency matters. Such rules will continue to be found in national law. Similarly, there are no choice of law rules in the model law, so that the relevant choice of law rules to be applied will continue to be found in the national laws of an enacting State. The model law is thus concerned with five principal issues: (i) recognition in the enacting State of foreign insolvency proceedings and the effects of such recognition[68]; (ii) direct rights of access to the courts of the enacting State for foreign representatives[69] and creditors[70]; (iii) the rights of courts and representatives in the enacting State to make requests to courts in foreign jurisdictions for recognition of proceedings commenced in the enacting State and to apply therein for assistance and relief, and for representatives to commence, or participate in, proceedings under the insolvency law of the other State[71]; (iv) co-operation between courts and representatives from different jurisdictions[72]; and (v) co-ordination of concurrent proceedings taking place in two or more jurisdictions.[73] Within these broad headings, more detailed provisions elaborate the particular rules which can be applied, and further elaboration will be contained in any implementing regulations.

---

[65] See Preamble to the model law.

[66] The model law is accompanied by indications, in square brackets, of what it is envisaged should be inserted, as, *e.g.* in Art. 1(2): "This Law does not apply to a proceeding concerning [designate any types of entities, such as banks or insurance companies, that are subject to a special insolvency regime in this State and that this State wishes to exclude from this Law]".

[67] Contrast the E.C. Insolvency Regulation (*infra*, paras. S30–137 *et seq.*) which purports to provide a comprehensive regime.

[68] Arts. 1(1)(a), 15–24.

[69] Defined in Art. 2(d) as "a person or body, including one appointed on an interim basis, authorized in a foreign proceeding to administer the reorganization or the liquidation of the debtor's assets or affairs or to act as a representative of the foreign proceedings".

[70] Arts. 1(1)(b), (d), 9–14.

[71] Arts. 1(1)(b), 5, 25–27.

[72] Arts. 1(1), 25–27.

[73] Arts. 1(1)(c), 28–32.

30–136 **Insolvency procedures covered.** The key definition of the procedures to which the model law is capable of being applied is found in Article 2(a), referred to above.[74] From this definition it would appear to follow that an administrative receivership under English law would not be covered since that institution is, essentially, not of a collective character. On the other hand, administration under the Insolvency Act 1986 would appear to be included since it is a collective procedure involving the court.[75] It is possible that a creditor's voluntary liquidation is included: for although not initiated by a court order, the procedure is collective in nature and matters may be referred to the court at any stage. It is clear that a liquidator is included, as will be a provisional liquidator because of the explicit reference in Article 2 (a) to an "interim proceeding". Cases of individual bankruptcy are capable of falling within the definition though whether the model law will apply to individual bankruptcies in England will probably depend on the implementing regulations.

5. COUNCIL REGULATION (E.C.)1346/2000 OF MAY 29, 2000 ON INSOLVENCY PROCEEDINGS

> **NOTE: DIRECTIVE 2001/17/E.C. OF THE EUROPEAN PARLIAMENT AND OF THE COUNCIL OF MARCH 19, 2001 ON THE REORGANISATION AND WINDING UP OF INSURANCE UNDERTAKINGS WHICH IS REFERRED TO IN THIS ENTRY HAS BEEN IMPLEMENTED IN THE UNITED KINGDOM BY INSURERS (REORGANISATION AND WINDING UP) REGULATIONS 2003, S.I. 2003 NO. 1102, IN FORCE FROM APRIL 20, 2003. TREATMENT OF THESE REGULATIONS MUST AWAIT THE NEXT SUPPLEMENT.**

A. Introduction and Scope

S30R–137 **RULE 159A—(1) Council Regulation (E.C.) 1346/2000 of May 29, 2000 on Insolvency Proceedings shall apply to collective insolvency proceedings which entail the partial or total divestment of a debtor and the appointment of a liquidator,[76] provided that the centre of main interests of the debtor is situated in a Member State.[77]**

(2) The foregoing Regulation shall not apply to insolvency proceedings concerning insurance undertakings, credit institutions, investment undertakings which provide services involving the holding of funds or securities for third parties, or to collective investment undertakings.[78]

---

[74] See *supra*, n. 62.

[75] A Chapter 11 reorganisation under the United States Bankruptcy Code would also probably qualify.

[76] Council Regulation (E.C.) 1346/2000 of May 29, 2000 on Insolvency Proceedings (hereafter the "E.C. Insolvency Regulation" or "the Regulation"), Art. 1(1).

[77] *ibid*. Recital (14) and Art. 3(1), *infra*, para. S30–151. "Member State" means all European Union States with the exception of Denmark: *ibid*. Recital(33), *post*, para. S30–142.

[78] *ibid*., Art. 1(2).

Comment

History. Council Regulation (E.C.) 1346/2000 of May 29, 2000 on Insol- **S30–138**
vency Proceedings[79] (hereafter the "E.C. Insolvency Regulation" or "the
Regulation") entered into force in the United Kingdom and the other
European Union Member States, with the exception of Denmark,[80] on May
31, 2002.[81] The origins of the Regulation began with protracted, if sporadic
negotiations which eventually disgorged, in 1995, the European Union
Convention on Insolvency Proceedings,[82] an instrument signed by all
Member States except the United Kingdom.[83] In the absence of the latter's
signature by the due date (May 23, 1996), the Convention lapsed.[84] The
project was subsequently resurrected in the form of a Regulation,[85] the text
of which when finally adopted, was almost identical to that of the 1995
Convention. The 1995 Convention was the subject of an unofficial Explanatory Report prepared by Professor Miguel Virgos of Spain and M. Etienne
Schmit of Luxembourg. This Report was never approved by the Council nor

---

[79] [2000] O.J. L160/1. A valuable discussion of the Regulation, containing contributions on
particular aspects and an article-by-article commentary can be found in Moss, Fletcher and Isaacs
(eds.), *The E.C. Regulation on Insolvency Proceedings* (2002) (hereafter "Moss *et al.*") where the
text of the Regulation is also printed as Appendix 1.

[80] Denmark, in accordance with Arts. 1 and 2 of the Protocol on the position of Denmark
annexed to the Treaty on European Union and the Treaty establishing the European Community, did not participate in the adoption of the Regulation, and is therefore not bound by it or
subject to its application: Recital (33). In contrast, the United Kingdom and Ireland, in
accordance with Art. 3 of the Protocol on the position of the United Kingdom and Ireland
annexed to the Treaty on European Union and the Treaty establishing the European Community, gave notice of their wish to take part in the adoption and application of the Regulation,
which will thus fully apply in those States: Recital (32).

[81] Art. 47.

[82] For the text of the Convention see *Seventh Report of the House of Lords Select Committee on
the European Communities*, H.L. Paper 59 (1996), p.18; (1996) 35 Int. Legal Mat. 1123; Fletcher,
Insolvency in Private International Law (1999), Appendix II. For the historical development of the
Convention in detail see Fletcher, *ibid.* pp. 247–256; Fletcher in Moss *et al.*, Chap. 1. For
comment on an earlier draft which was withdrawn, see the Report on the Draft by Lemontey in
Bulletin of the European Communities, Supplement 2/82; Nadelmann, *Conflict of Laws: Inter-
national and Interstate* (1972), pp. 340–359; Fletcher, *Conflict of Laws and European Community
Law* (1982), Chap. 6; Lasok and Stone, *Conflict of Laws in the European Community* (1987),
Chap. 10; *Report of the Advisory Committee on the E.E.C. Bankruptcy Convention* (1976) Cmnd.
6602; Muir Hunter (1972) 21 I.C.L.Q. 682; (1976) 25 I.C.L.Q. 310. For discussion of the
Convention in its final form, see Fletcher, *Insolvency in Private International Law* (1999), Chap. 6;
Smart, *Cross-Border Insolvency* (2nd ed., 1998), *passim*; Morse in Borchers and Zekoll (eds.)
International Conflict of Laws for the Third Millenium: Essays in Honor of Friedrich K. Juenger
(2001), pp. 233–260; Fletcher (1997) 23 Brooklyn J. Int. L. 25; Segal, *ibid.* 57; Balz (1996) 70
American Bankruptcy L.J. 485. These references may also be consulted in relation to the
Regulation. The Council of Europe has produced a European Convention on Certain Inter-
national Aspects of Bankruptcy (the Istanbul Convention of June 5, 1990): for the text of the
Convention (which is not in force) see (1991) 30 Int. Legal Mat. 165; Fletcher, *Insolvency in
Private International Law* (1999), Appendix III; Fletcher (ed.), *Cross-Border Insolvency: Compara-
tive Dimensions* (1990), p. 297. As to the UNCITRAL Model Law on Cross-Border Insolvency,
see *supra*, paras. S 30–132—S 30–136.

[83] The United Kingdom did not sign the Convention in part as a reaction to the E.U. ban on
British beef and in part as a result of the controversy regarding sovereignty over Gibraltar: see
Fletcher, *Insolvency in Private International Law* (1999), pp. 298–300.

[84] The legal basis of the Convention lay in Art. 220 of the E.C. Treaty, now Art. 293 of the
Consolidated E.C. Treaty.

[85] The legal basis for the Regulation lies in Arts. 61(c) and 67(1) of the E.C. Treaty: see E.C.
Insolvency Regulation, Preamble, first para.

has it been published officially.[86] The Report (hereafter referred to as "Virgos-Schmit") may, however, have some influence on the interpretation of the Regulation in view of the virtual identical character of the text of each instrument,[87] it being normal practice for E.C Regulations not to be accompanied by explanatory reports of the kind associated with Community Conventions. Unlike the Convention, however, the text of which is preceded only by a short and general preamble, the text of the Regulation is preceded by 33 Recitals, which attempt to indicate, for example, the purpose and policy of the Regulation and which will doubtless be of importance in the interpretation of the text.[88]

S30–139 The E.C. Insolvency Regulation in outline. Essentially, the Regulation is concerned with three broad issues—jurisdiction of Member States to open insolvency proceedings, the law to be applied in those proceedings, and the recognition of judgments concerning insolvency proceedings, handed down in one Member State, in other Member States. Leaving to one side the meaning of "insolvency proceedings" which is discussed below,[89] it can be noted at this stage that the Regulation applies in cases involving the insolvency of natural persons (in English terminology "bankruptcy"). The particular implications of the Regulation in the context of bankruptcy are discussed in Chapter 31. In relation to jurisdiction, the primary focus is on the Member State in which the "centre of a debtor's main interests is situated"[90] and it is that Member State whose courts have jurisdiction to open "main proceedings".[91] There can be only one set of main proceedings which must be recognised in all other Member States.[92] However, the Regulation permits the opening of "secondary proceedings" in Member States, other than that of the main proceedings, in which the debtor has an "establishment."[93] Unlike the case with main proceedings, the effects of secondary proceedings are limited to the assets of the debtor situated in the Member State in which the secondary proceedings are opened.[94] Where secondary proceedings are opened before main proceedings they are described as "territorial proceedings".[95] Territorial proceedings may be either liquidation or rescue measures, but once main proceedings are opened these territorial proceedings automatically become secondary proceedings and if they are rescue measures they may, at the instance of the liquidator[96] in the main proceedings be converted into liquidation proceedings.[97] In relation to choice of law, save as otherwise provided in the

---

[86] The text of the Report, which was never published in the *Official Journal*, can be found in Council Document 6500/1/96 (Annex). The text is reproduced in Moss *et al.*, Appendix 2. An earlier version of the Report can be found in *E.C. Convention on Insolvency Proceedings: A Consultative Document* (1996) produced by the Insolvency Service of the Department of Trade and Industry.

[87] See Isaacs and Brent in Moss *et al.*, p. 28.

[88] *ibid.* p. 27; Fletcher in Moss *et al.*, pp. 13–14 (who points out that a number of Recitals are based on material drawn from Virgos-Schmit).

[89] *infra*, para. S30–150.

[90] Art. 3(1): see *infra*, Rule 159B (1).

[91] *ibid.*

[92] Arts. 16, 17: see *infra*, Rules 159O, 159P.

[93] Art. 3(2): see *infra*, Rule 159B (2).

[94] Arts. 3(2), 27: see *infra*, Rules 159B (2), 159Q.

[95] Art. 3(4): see *infra*, Rule 159B (4).

[96] Which expression is broadly defined: see Art. 2(b), *infra*, para. S30–150.

[97] Art. 34: see *infra*, Rule 159V.

Regulation, the law applicable to insolvency proceedings and their effects shall be the law of the Member State in which the relevant proceedings are opened.[98] A list of issues which "in particular" shall be governed by this law is provided.[99] Special choice of law rules which depart, in varying degrees, from this general applicability of the *lex fori* are supplied for specific issues, such as third party security rights[1] and reservation of title.[2] In relation to recognition and enforcement, a judgment of a court in one Member State opening insolvency proceedings shall be recognised in the other Member States and shall have the same effects in those States as it has in the State where the proceedings are opened.[3] Judgments relating to the conduct and closure of insolvency proceedings which are obtained in one Member State must also be recognised and enforced in other Member States.[4] Enforcement of these judgments as well as other judgments arising from the insolvency proceedings is said to be effected in accordance with Articles 31 to 51 of the 1968 Convention,[5] though it would appear that this provision should now be read as a reference to Articles 38 to 58 of the Judgments Regulation.[6]

The E.C. Insolvency Regulation also provides that the appointment and **S30–140** powers of the liquidator in the main proceedings must be recognised in another Member State as long as no other insolvency proceedings have been opened in that State.[7] The respective liquidators in main proceedings and in secondary proceedings are duty bound to supply each other with information and to co-operate with each other.[8]

Applicability in time. As stated above, the Regulation entered into force **S30–141** on May 31, 2002.[9] Article 43 of the Regulation provides that its provisions shall apply only to insolvency proceedings opened after its entry into force. Where both main and secondary proceedings are opened it would seem that the Regulation applies only if both sets of proceedings are commenced after its entry into force.[10] To reinforce the non-retrospective nature of the Regulation, Article 43 also provides that acts done by a debtor before entry into force shall continue to be governed by the law that was applicable to them at the time they were done.

---

[98] Art. 4 (1): see *infra*, Rule 159C (1).
[99] Art. 4(2): see *infra*, Rule 159C (2).
[1] Art. 5: see *infra*, Rule 159D.
[2] Art. 7: see *infra*, Rule 159F.
[3] Arts 16, 17: see *infra*, Rules 159O, 159P.
[4] Art. 25: see *infra*, Rule 159T.
[5] *ibid.* Art. 34(2) of the 1968 Convention is specifically excluded from the enforcement scheme: *ibid.* See main work, para. 14–219.
[6] Presumably excluding Art. 45(1), the equivalent of Art. 34(2) of the 1968 Convention.
[7] Art. 18 (1): see *infra*, Rule 159R (1).
[8] Art. 31: see *infra*, Rule 159V.
[9] Art. 47.
[10] Moss *et al.*, p. 234. As to the time of opening proceedings, see Art. 2(f), *infra*, para. S30–157. In *Geveran Trading Co. Ltd. v. Skjevesland* [2002] EWHC 2898, [2003] B.C.C. 391 (affirming [2003] B.P.I.R. 73, Mr. Registrar Jaques) it was conceded that bankruptcy proceedings are opened at point in time at which court comes to consider whether it should make a bankruptcy order, not at time when bankruptcy petition is issued or presented to court.

S30–142 Meaning of "Member State". For the purposes of the E.C. Insolvency Regulation, "Member State" means every State which is a member of the European Union with the exception of Denmark which did not participate in the adoption of the Regulation and is not bound by its terms.[11] Cases involving insolvency proceedings with a relevant link to Denmark (as well as non-Member States) will, therefore, be dealt with by rules of English law excluding those established by the Regulation.[12]

S30–143 Applicability in the United Kingdom. The Regulation is "directly applicable" in the United Kingdom.[13] As such, it forms part of United Kingdom law, from May 31, 2002, without the need for domestic legislation to secure its transposition.

S30–144 Effect in English law. Although the Regulation is directly applicable, the United Kingdom has found it necessary to adopt legislation so as to give full effect to the rules that the Regulation establishes.[14] In the context of English law, amendments have been made to the Insolvency Act 1986 and the Insolvency Rules 1986 so as to ensure that the latter instruments comport with the requirements of the Regulation. Reference is made to these amendments, at appropriate points, in what follows.[15]

S30–145 Intra-United Kingdom cases. Since the Regulation only applies if the centre of main interests of the debtor is in a Member State,[16] it follows that the purpose of the measure is the regulation of insolvency proceedings within the European Union,[17] *i.e.* it is concerned with cross-border cases involving different Member States. The Regulation is not, therefore, concerned with the regulation of insolvency proceedings within the United Kingdom. This outcome is reinforced by Recital (15) which states that the "rules of jurisdiction set out in this Regulation establish only international jurisdiction, that is to say, they designate the Member State the courts of which may open insolvency proceedings. Territorial jurisdiction within that Member State must be established by the national law of the Member State concerned".[18] The Regulation applies, of course, in Scotland and Northern Ireland but not only in this class of "international" cases. The Regulation also applies to Gibraltar,[19] but not to the Channel Islands or the Isle of Man.[20]

---

[11] E.C. Insolvency Regulation, Recital (33).

[12] *i.e.* Rules 155, 157–159. As to bankruptcy, see Chap. 31.

[13] By virtue of E.C Treaty, Art. 49.

[14] See Case 94/77 *Zerbone v. Amministrazione delle Finanze* [1978] E.C.R 99.

[15] The principal amendments are to be found in the Insolvency Act 1986 (Amendment No.2) Regulations 2002, S.I. 2002 No. 1240; Insolvency (Amendment) Rules 2002, S.I. 2002 No. 1307. See also Insolvency Act 1986 (Amendment) Regulations 2002, S.I. 2002 No. 1307; Insolvent Partnerships (Amendment) Order 2002, S.I. 2002 No. 1308; Administration of Insolvent Estates of Deceased Persons (Amendment) Order 2002, S.I. 2002 No. 1309. This legislation includes some amendments to the law of Scotland. For Northern Ireland, see Insolvency (Northern Ireland) Order 1989 (Amendment No. 2) Regulations (Northern Ireland) 2002, S.R. 2002 No. 334.

[16] Art. 3(1), Recital (14).

[17] See Recitals (2),(3),(4),(8),(14).

[18] Thus, for example, Rule 156 is unaffected. As to bankruptcy, see Chap. 31.

[19] E.C. Treaty, Art. 299 (4).

[20] E.C. Treaty, Art. 299 (6).

Relationship to Conventions. As from entry into force, the Regulation **S30–146** replaces, in respect of the matters referred to therein, in the relations between Member States, Conventions concluded between two or more Member States,[21] in particular those Conventions listed in Article 44(1)(a). One such Convention involves the United Kingdom, namely the Convention between the United Kingdom and the Kingdom of Belgium providing for the Reciprocal Enforcement of Judgments in Civil and Commercial Matters with Protocol, signed at Brussels on May 2, 1934.[22] Furthermore, the Regulation will not apply in any Member State to the extent that it is irreconcilable with the obligations arising in relation to bankruptcy from a convention concluded by that State with one or more third countries before the entry into force of the Regulation.[23] As far as the United Kingdom is concerned, the Regulation will not apply to the extent that it is irreconcilable with the obligations arising in relation to bankruptcy and the winding-up of insolvent companies from any arrangements with the Commonwealth existing at the time the Regulation enters into force.[24] It is possible that this provision might result, in a particular case, in the Regulation being overridden by a request for assistance under section 426 of the Insolvency Act 1986 from a court in a designated (Commonwealth) country.[25]

References to the European Court of Justice.[26] By Article 68 of the E.C. **S30–147** Treaty, the European Court of Justice is granted jurisdiction to review a measure, such as the E.C. Insolvency Regulation, adopted under Title IV of the Treaty in only one circumstance. This is where a national court or tribunal against whose decision there is no judicial remedy under national law consider that a decision of the European Court is necessary to enable them to give judgment. In this circumstance the national court is required to make a reference to the European Court. Furthermore, under Article 68(3) of the Treaty, the Council, the Commission or a Member State may request the European Court to give a ruling on any question of the interpretation of a measure, such as the Insolvency Regulation, adopted under Title IV. Any ruling given by the European Court in response to such a request shall not apply to judgments of courts or tribunals of the Member States which have become *res judicata.*

Interpretation. Many of the difficulties generated by the Regulation con- **S30–148** cern the correct interpretation to be given to its terminology, and attention is drawn to these difficulties in what follows.[27] In general terms,[28] however, the European Court and national courts will adopt, so far as possible, autonomous, "community" meanings for terms which may have different meanings in the national laws of Member States in much the same way as has been adopted in relation to the 1968 Convention.[29] Furthermore, the

---

[21] E.C. Insolvency Regulation, Art. 44(1).

[22] The conventions listed in Art. 44(1) will continue to have effect with regard to proceedings opened before the Regulation entered into force: Art. 44(2).

[23] Art. 44 (3)(a).

[24] Art. 44(3)(b).

[25] See main work, paras. 30–097—30–108. See Moss *et al.*, pp. 235–236.

[26] See Isaacs and Brent in Moss, *et al.*, pp. 28–33.

[27] Each official language version of the Regulation is equally authentic: see Case 283/81 *CILFIT Srl v. Ministry of Health* [1982] E.C.R. 3415.

[28] See Isaacs and Brent in Moss *et al.*, pp. 23–28.

[29] See main work, paras. 11–041—11–051.

approach to the construction of terminology will be purposive or teleologi-
cal with the principal aim of giving effect to the purpose underlying the
various provisions of the Regulation.[30] As aids to such construction, the
following materials are likely to be relevant: the *travaux preparatoires* (such
as they are), namely the initiative of Germany and Finland,[31] the opinion of
the European Parliament[32] and the opinion of the Economic and Social
Committee[33] all of which are referred to in the Preamble to the Regulation;
more importantly, in practice, the extensive Recitals to the Regulation
which expressly articulate policy objectives at various points[34]; the Virgos-
Schmit Report,[35] although lacking any formal status, and being a Report on
the earlier lapsed Convention on Insolvency Proceedings, may also be
looked at, bearing in mind the common terminology largely existing
between that Convention and the Regulation, although the weight which
will be attached to that Report is not clear[36]; and relevant provisions of the
E.C. Treaty, notably those in Title IV, which are aimed at establishing,
progressively, an area of freedom, security and justice.[37]

S30–149 Some expressions used in the Regulation are defined in Article 2. But not
all these definitions are pellucid.[38] And at least one central feature of the
Regulation, that of the debtor's centre of main interests, is not really
defined at all so that considerable uncertainty surrounds the "connecting
factor" which is the effective trigger to the application of the Regulation.[39]

S30–150 **Meaning of "insolvency proceedings".**[40] In Article 1(1) of the Regulation
(clause (1) of the Rule) it is stipulated that the Regulation shall apply to
"collective insolvency proceedings which entail the partial or total divestment of the debtor and the appointment of a liquidator". Article 2(a)
provides that "'insolvency proceedings' shall mean the collective proceedings referred to in Article 1(1). These proceedings are listed in Annex A".
Annex A sets out a list of proceedings in the Member States which are
deemed to fall within the Regulation. In the United Kingdom the listed
proceedings are: winding up by or subject to the supervision of the court[41];
creditors' voluntary winding up (with confirmation by the court[42]); admin-

---

[30] See, *e.g. Re BRAC Rent-a-Car International Inc.* [2003] EWHC 128 (Ch); [2003] 1 W.L.R. 1421.

[31] [1999] O.J. C221/6.

[32] Of March 2, 2000.

[33] [2000] O.J. C75/1.

[34] See, especially, Recitals (1)–(8). English courts have already referred to the Recitals in
interpreting the Regulation: see *Geveran Trading Co. Ltd. v. Skjevesland* [2003] B.P.I.R. 391 (Mr.
Registrar Jaques); affd. [2002] EWHC 2898; [2003] B.C.C. 391; *Re BRAC Rent-a-Car International Inc, supra.*

[35] *supra*, para. S30–138.

[36] See *Re BRAC Rent-a-Car International Inc., supra.*

[37] See especially, Arts. 61(c), 65. And see Recital (1).

[38] See, *e.g.* the definition of "establishment," *post*, paras. S30–164 *et seq.*

[39] *cf.* Recital (13). See *post*, Rule 159B (1).

[40] See Virgos-Schmit, paras. 48–53; Fletcher in Moss *et al.*, pp. 35–38; Moss and Smith, *ibid.* pp.
156–160.

[41] Winding up subject to the supervision of the court has been abolished, as regards England,
Scotland and Northern Ireland, but still exists in Gibraltar (where the Regulation is applicable).
Winding up by the court includes the winding up of insolvent partnerships: see Insolvency Act
1986, ss. 420 (1A), 436, inserted by S.I. 2002 No. 1307, Reg. 3(5); Insolvent Partnerships Order
1994. No. 2421, as amended by S.1 2002 No. 1308.

[42] In English law a creditors' voluntary winding up does not usually require the participation of
the court. Accordingly a new procedure has been introduced whereby application can be made to
the court for confirmation of a creditors' voluntary winding up for the purposes of the
Regulation: see Insolvency Rules 1986, rr. 7.62, 7.63, inserted by S.I. 2002 No. 1307, r. 9 and
Form 7.20, inserted by *ibid.* r.12.

istration; voluntary arrangements under insolvency legislation; bankruptcy or sequestration.[43] These are the only United Kingdom proceedings which will fall within the Regulation. Despite this, the formula set out in Article 1(1) merits further consideration. First, relevant insolvency proceedings must be "collective". This means that no form of receivership available under English law (or any foreign equivalent) falls within the Regulation, since such procedures are invoked by one creditor for the sole benefit of that creditor alone.[44] Secondly, the proceedings must relate to the "insolvency" of the debtor. "Insolvency" is not defined, as such, in the Regulation itself. According to the Virgos-Schmit Report, the definition of insolvency is to be derived from the national law of the country in which proceedings are opened and only that law provides the necessary criteria.[45] Thus, in England, the Regulation will not apply in the case of a winding-up order made on the grounds of public interest since such an order is not made on the basis of insolvency.[46] Similarly, the Regulation will not apply to a members' voluntary winding up since such a procedure begins on the basis that the company is, or will be able to pay its debts in full.[47] On the other hand, if insolvency ensues and the members' voluntary winding up is converted into a creditor's voluntary liquidation,[48] the Regulation applies.[49] Thirdly, the proceedings must "entail the partial or total divestment of a debtor." Apparently, "divestment" involves transfer to the liquidator "of the powers of administration and of disposal over all or part of [the debtor's] assets, or the limitation of these powers through the intervention and control of [the debtor's] actions. It should be remembered that partial divestment, whether of [the debtor's] assets or his power of administration, is sufficient. The legal nature that such divestment may take, depending on the national legislation applicable, has no bearing on the application of [the Regulation] to the proceedings in question."[50] Fourthly, although there is no definition of a "debtor" in the Regulation, it is obvious that in all insolvency proceedings there must be a debtor. For the purpose of the Regulation a debtor is a legal or natural person[51] whose centre of main interests is in a Member State and who is subject to an insolvency proceeding falling within the Regulation. Fifthly, to fall within the Regu-

---

[43] Unlike the earlier Convention the Regulation makes no explicit mention of the English and Northern Irish procedure for the administration of the insolvent estate of a deceased person or the Scottish equivalent—administration by a judicial factor—but the exclusions are apparently justified on the basis of their inclusion in the respective expressions, bankruptcy and sequestration: see Fletcher in Moss *et al.*, p.13. And see Insolvency Act 1986, s. 421 (1A), inserted by S.I. 2002 No. 1307, Reg. 3(6); S.1 2002 No. 1309.

[44] Fletcher, *ibid.* p. 36; Moss and Smith, *ibid.* p.157.

[45] Virgos-Schmit, para. 49(b).

[46] *Re Marran Brooks CSV Ltd.* [2003] B.C.C. 239; Insolvency Act 1986, s. 124 A. See main work, para. 30–047.

[47] Insolvency Act 1986, ss.89, 90.

[48] Insolvency Act 1986, s.96. See Moss and Smith in Moss *et al.*, p.157.

[49] Note that new statutory forms of application and order require a statement that the Regulation does or does not apply: see Form 2.1 (petition for administration order); Form 2.4 (administration order); Form 4.2 (winding-up petition); Form 4.11 (order for winding up by the court); Form 4.12 (order for winding up by the court following upon discharge of administration order); Form 4.14 (petition by contributory); Form 4.15 (order of appointment of provisional liquidator); Form 7.20 (confirmation by court of creditors' voluntary winding up application and order). The forms are inserted into Insolvency Rules 1986 by S.I 2002 No. 1307, Reg. 13.

[50] Virgos-Schmit, para. 49 (2).

[51] Recital (9).

lation, the proceedings must entail "the appointment of a liquidator". For these purposes, "liquidator" is given a wider meaning than the term bears in English law and means "any person or body whose function it is to administer or liquidate assets of which the debtor has been divested or to supervise the administration of his affairs. Those persons and bodies are listed in Annex C".[52] Annex C lists the relevant persons or bodies of all Member States, but those listed for the United Kingdom are: liquidator; supervisor of a voluntary arrangement; administrator; official Receiver; trustee[53]; judicial factor.[54]

S30–151 **Clause (1) of the Rule: proviso.** This proviso (which is not part of Article 1(1) of the Regulation from which this clause is derived) aims to emphasise the fact that the Regulation is not brought into play unless the centre of main interests of the debtor is located in a Member State.[55] So, for example, a company registered in England which has its centre of main interests in Argentina would not fall within the Regulation. Conversely, it would appear (and it has been held to be the case in England) that a company registered in a non-Member State but which has its centre of main interests in a Member State would be subject to the Regulation.[56]

S30–152 **Clause (2) of the Rule.** Clause (2) reproduces Article 1(2) of the Regulation whereby insolvency proceedings concerning insurance undertakings, credit institutions, investment undertakings which provide services involving the holding of funds or securities for third parties and collective investment undertakings are excluded from the provisions of the Regulation[57]. The reason for exclusion of these entities is that they are already subject to specific Community regulation and that provisions concerned with insolvency proceedings relating to them either are, or will be, contained in separate Community Directives.[58] Directives have so far been concluded on the reorganisation and winding up of insurance undertakings,[59] and credit

---

[52] Art. 2(b). For the procedure for amending the Annexes, see Art. 45. for Annex B, see *infra*, S30–155.

[53] *i.e.* trustee in bankruptcy: see *infra*, S31–092.

[54] A Scottish office-holder.

[55] Recital (14); Art. 3(1).

[56] *Re BRAC Rent-a-Car International Inc.* [2003] EWHC 128 (Ch), [2003] 1 W.L.R. 1421 (company incorporated in Delaware with centre of main interests in England is subject to the Regulation).

[57] Marks in Moss *et al.*, Chap. 7; Virgos-Schmit, paras. 54–60.

[58] Virgos-Schmit, para. 54.

[59] Directive 2001/17/E.C. of the European Parliament and of the Council of March 19, 2001 on the reorganisation and winding up of insurance undertakings ([2001] O.J. L110/28) (hereafter Insurance Undertakings Insolvency Directive) which must be implemented in the Member States by April 20, 2003, but which has not yet been implemented in the United Kingdom. For the purpose of the Directive, "insurance undertaking" means an undertaking which has received official authorisation from the home Member State supervisory authority in accordance with First Council Directive 73/239 of July 24, 1973 on the coordination of laws, regulations and administrative provisions relating to the taking up and pursuit of the business of direct insurance other than life insurance ([1973] O.J. L228/3), Art. 6, or First Council Directive 79/267 of March 5, 1979 on the coordination of laws, regulations and administrative provisions relating to the taking up and pursuit of the business of direct life insurance ([1979] O.J. L63/1), Art. 6: Insurance Undertakings Insolvency Directive, Art. 2(a). It is most unclear what particular insolvency regime is applicable in the case of re-insurance business: see Marks in Moss *et al.*, pp. 146–148; Moss and Smith, *ibid.* pp. 160–161.

institutions.[60] Very broadly, in cross-border cases, each Directive gives jurisdiction in relation to reorganisation measures and winding up to the Member State which is the "home Member State" of the undertaking or institution,[61] provides for recognition of this jurisdiction in other Member States[62] and contains choice of law rules which are reminiscent of those contained in the E.C. Insolvency Regulation.[63] No directives have, as yet, been concluded concerning insolvency proceedings in relation to investment undertakings,[64] or collective investment undertakings.[65]

B. International Jurisdiction

RULE 159B—(1) The courts of the Member State within the territory of which the centre of a debtor's main interests is situated shall have jurisdiction to open insolvency proceedings. In the case of a company or legal person, the place of the registered office shall be presumed to be the centre of its main interests in the absence of proof to the contrary.

(2) Where the centre of a debtor's main interests is situated within the territory of a Member State, the courts of another Member State shall have jurisdiction to open insolvency proceedings against that debtor only if he possesses an establishment within the territory of that other Member State. The effects of these proceedings shall be restricted to the assets of the debtor situated in the territory of that Member State.

(3) Where insolvency proceedings have been opened under clause (1), any proceedings opened subsequently under clause (2) shall be secondary proceedings. These latter proceedings must be winding-up proceedings.

S30R–153

---

[60] Directive 2001/24 of the European Parliament and of the Council of April 4, 2001 on the reorganisation and winding up of credit institutions ([2001] O.J. L125/15) (hereafter Credit Institutions Insolvency Directive) which must be implemented in the Member States by May 5, 2004, but which has not yet been implemented in the United Kingdom. For the purpose of the Directive, a "credit institution" means "an undertaking whose business is to receive deposits or other repayable funds from the public and to grant credits for its own account": Council Directive (E.C.) 2000/12 of March 20, 2000 relating to the taking up and pursuit of the business of credit institutions ([2000] O.J. L126/1); Credit Institutions Insolvency Directive, Art. 1. See also Directive 98/26 of the European Parliament and of the Council on settlement finality in payment and securities settlement systems ([1998] O.J. L166/45), implemented in the United Kingdom by the Financial Markets and Insolvency (Settlement Finality) Regulations 1999, S.I. 1999 No. 2979; Directive 2002/47 of the European Parliament and of the Council of June 6, 2002 on financial collateral arrangements ([2002] O.J. L168/43), which must be implemented in Member States by December 27, 2003, but which has not yet been implemented in the United Kingdom.

[61] As defined in Insurance Undertakings Insolvency Directive, Art. 2(e); Credit Institutions Insolvency Directive, Art. 2. For the rules see Insurance Undertakings Insolvency Directive, Arts. 2, 4(1), 8(1); Credit Institutions Insolvency Directive, Arts. 3(1), 8(1), 9(1), 19(1).

[62] Insurance Undertakings Insolvency Directive, Arts. 4(3), 8(2), 27(2); Credit Institutions Insolvency Directive, Arts. 3(2), 9(1).

[63] Insurance Undertakings Insolvency Directive, Arts. 4(2), 9, 19–26; Credit Institutions Insolvency Directive, Arts. 3(2), 10, 20–27.

[64] An "investment undertaking" is any entity covered by the definition in Council Directive 92/22 of May 10, 1993 on investment services in the securities field ([1993] O.J. L41/27), as amended by Directive 95/28 ([1995] O.J. L 168/7), i.e. any enterprise which carries out a professional activity consisting of supplying third parties with an investment service concerning securities and money-market instruments.

[65] A "collective investment undertaking" is any undertaking covered by the definition set out in Council Directive 85/611 of December 20, 1985 on the coordination of laws, regulations and administrative provisions relating to undertakings for collective investment in transferable securities (UCITS) ([1985] O.J. L375/3) as last amended by Directive 95/26, i.e. any body whose sole aim is the joint investment of securities from capital collected from the public, whose operations are subject to the principles of risk sharing, and the shares of which are, on the bearer's request, bought or paid back, directly or indirectly, from the assets of those bodies.

(4) Territorial insolvency proceedings referred to in clause (2) may be opened prior to the opening of main insolvency proceedings in accordance with clause (1) only:

(a) **where insolvency proceedings under clause (1) cannot be opened because of the conditions laid down by the law of the Member State within the territory of which the centre of the debtor's main interests is situated; or**

(b) **where the opening of territorial proceedings is requested by a creditor who has his domicile, habitual residence or registered office in the Member State within the territory of which the establishment is situated, or whose claim arises from the operation of that establishment.**[66]

COMMENT

S30–154 This Rule reproduces Article 3 of the E.C. Insolvency Regulation which establishes the jurisdictional rules which will be applicable in cases falling within the scope of that instrument. In broad terms, Article 3 envisages three species of jurisdiction. Article 3(1) (clause (1) of the Rule) is concerned with jurisdiction to open "main insolvency proceedings": such jurisdiction is conferred on the courts of the Member State in which the centre of a debtor's[67] main interests is located. Article 3(2) and 3(3) (clauses (2) and (3) of the Rule) concern jurisdiction to open "secondary proceedings", following the opening of main proceedings in the Member State where the centre of a debtor's main interests is located: such jurisdiction is conferred on the courts of any Member State in which the debtor has "an establishment". Whereas the opening of main proceedings affects all assets of a debtor situated in a Member State or States, the effect of secondary proceedings is limited to assets situated within the Member State where the debtor has an establishment. Article 3(4) of the Regulation is concerned with jurisdiction to open "territorial insolvency proceedings", prior to the opening of main proceedings: such jurisdiction is conferred on the courts of the Member State in which the debtor has an establishment if either main proceedings cannot be opened in the Member State where the centre of the debtor's main interests is located because the law of that State forbids the opening of such proceedings or where the opening of such proceedings is requested by a creditor who has his domicile, habitual residence or registered office in the Member State within the territory of which the establishment is situated, or whose claim arises from the operation of that establishment.

S30–155 **Meaning of "insolvency proceedings".** The meaning of this expression was discussed in connection with Rule 159A.[68] In the context of main proceed-

---

[66] E.C. Insolvency Regulation, Art. 3. For discussion, see Fletcher, *Insolvency in Private International Law* (1999), pp. 259–265; Virgos-Schmit, paras. 72–86; Fletcher in Moss *et al.*, pp. 38–44; Moss and Smith, *ibid.* pp. 167–177.
[67] This Comment deals with debtors which are companies or other legal persons. As to bankruptcy of individuals see *infra*, paras. S31–091 *et seq.*
[68] *supra*, para. S30–150.

ings falling within Article 3(1), which are opened in England, the expression means the proceedings referred to in Annex A,[69] namely: winding up by or subject to the supervision of the court; creditors' voluntary winding up (with confirmation by the court); administration; voluntary arrangements under insolvency legislation. Where subsequent secondary proceedings have been opened under Article 3(2), such proceedings must be "winding-up proceedings".[70] These proceedings are defined as proceedings referred to in Article 1(1) (Rule 159A (1)) which involve realising the assets of the debtor including situations where "the proceedings have been closed by a composition or other measure terminating the insolvency, or closed by reason of the insufficiency of the assets. Those proceedings are listed in Annex B".[71] The English proceedings there listed are: winding up by or subject to the supervision of the court; creditors' winding up (with confirmation by the court). It will be noted that this list does not include administration or voluntary arrangements made under insolvency law. As far as "territorial proceedings" (Article 3(4)) are concerned, there is no requirement that the proceedings opened must be winding-up proceedings. Thus, for example, if territorial proceedings were opened in England prior to the opening of main insolvency proceedings such proceedings could be administration proceedings.[72]

Meaning of "court". In terms, Article 3 refers to the jurisdiction of **S30–156** "courts". For these purposes "court" shall mean the judicial body or any other competent body of a Member State empowered to open insolvency proceedings or to take decisions in the course of such proceedings.[73] This definition is intended to broaden the notion of "court", as traditionally understood,[74] since in some Member States bodies other than traditional courts may commence insolvency proceedings or take decisions during the course of such proceedings and such bodies may thus be treated as courts for the purposes of the Regulation.[75] This may be illustrated by reference to the company voluntary arrangement procedure available in English law.[76] Are the meetings of members and creditors summoned to consider and implement any proposed arrangements capable of constituting a "court" for the purpose of the Regulation with the consequence that this "court" must possess international jurisdiction under Article 3? It would seem that this question requires a positive answer,[77] which is suggested by the fact that a supervisor of a voluntary arrangement, where the voluntary arrangement is a main proceeding, comes with the definition of "liquidator", *i.e.* is a person or body listed in Annex C.[78] If the supervisor is to be able to exercise his powers in other Member States,[79] it can only be on the basis that he has

---

[69] Art. 2(a).

[70] Art. 3(3). As to bankruptcy, see *infra*, S31–096.

[71] Art. 2(c).

[72] The liquidator in the main proceedings may request that these territorial proceedings be converted into winding-up proceedings: Art. 37.

[73] Art. 2(d).

[74] Virgos-Schmit, paras. 52, 66.

[75] This interpretation is supported by Art. 2(e) defining "judgment" to "include" (but thus not to be confined to) the "decision of any court".

[76] Insolvency Act 1986, ss. 1–7. Note, particularly, s.1(4), inserted by S.1. 2002 No. 1240, Reg. 4, expressly referring to jurisdiction to make a proposal by virtue of Art. 3 of the Regulation.

[77] Moss and Smith in Moss *et al.*, p. 163.

[78] Art. 2(b).

[79] Art. 18.

been appointed by a court having jurisdiction under Article 3(1). The notion of court, here, must refer to the meeting of creditors which has the relevant powers.[80]

S30–157 Meaning of "opening" of proceedings and "time of opening" of proceedings. Article 3 refers to jurisdiction to "open" the insolvency proceedings which fall within the provision. This raises a definitional question as to the meaning of "open" for these purposes. A closely related issue is the definition of the "time of opening" of proceedings, a concept which is relevant not only in relation to Article 3 but also in relation to other provisions of the Regulation. The "time of the opening" of proceedings is defined in Article 2(f) as "the time at which the judgment opening proceedings becomes effective, whether it is a final judgment or not". This definition suggests, first, that (in England) it will be the making of, *e.g.* a winding-up order or administration order that will constitute the opening of the proceedings and not the presentation of petitions seeking such orders, a view that is supported by the text of Article 3(4)(b) (clause (4)(b) of the Rule) which refers to a request by a creditor to open insolvency proceedings and which indicates an intended distinction between a request to open proceedings and the opening of those proceedings.[81] As regards the "time of opening", therefore, the relevant time will be the making of the order rather than the time at which the petition for the relevant order is presented.[82] Application of this principle is not without difficulty in the context of a creditors' voluntary winding-up in English law. Is the relevant time of opening when the members' meeting passes a resolution for the company to be wound up, at which point the company goes into liquidation as a matter of English law,[83] or the time at which the court subsequently confirms the liquidation, which confirmation is required for the proceeding to fall within Annex A to the Regulation?[84] In support of the latter view is the fact that a creditors' voluntary winding up would not be within the Regulation at all without a confirmation by the court so that this is the crucial step in time.[85] However, reference to the Virgos-Schmit Report supports the first view. The Report states that in relation to the type of proceeding under discussion, there was discussion as to whether the definition of time of opening in Article 2(f) should be applied or whether the date of confirmation by the court and the appointment of a liquidator should be preferred.[86] The discussions concluded that only in order to allow the liquidator to exercise his powers in the territory of another Member State would it be necessary to regard the relevant time as the date of confirmation by the court.[87] For all other matters the rule in Article 2(f) was to apply.[88] Since this is the view expressed by those whose deliberations on

---

[80] Although the chairman of the meeting is required to report the result of the meeting to the court (Insolvency Act 1986, s. 4(6)) the court has no role to play in relation to the approval of the proposed arrangement or in deciding whether the proposed arrangement shall become binding, unless the arrangement is challenged under Insolvency Act 1986, s. 6. As to individual voluntary arrangements, see *post*, paras. S31–092, 097.

[81] Moss and Smith in Moss *et al.*, p. 173.

[82] But see *Geveran Trading Co. Ltd v Skjevesland*, *supra* n. 10.

[83] Insolvency Act 1986, s. 247(2).

[84] Art. 2(a).

[85] Moss and Smith in Moss *et al.*, p. 164.

[86] Para. 68.

[87] Paras. 52, 68.

[88] Para. 68.

the Convention produced the Regulation with identical relevant text, it is tentatively submitted that this view should be preferred.[89]

Clause (1) of the Rule. Clause (1) of the Rule reproduces Article 3(1) of **S30–158** the Regulation which is concerned with jurisdiction to open "main" insolvency proceedings. Such jurisdiction is conferred on the courts of the Member State within the territory of which the centre of the debtor's main interests is situated. The concept of the centre of the debtor's main interests is thus of fundamental importance, not least because the Regulation will not apply at all unless the centre of main interests is located in a Member State.[90] The application of Article 3(1) to the jurisdiction of the English court means that the court will have jurisdiction to open main insolvency proceedings if the centre of the debtor's main interests is situated in England. These proceedings have universal effect in the sense that they encompass all the assets of the debtor which are situated in the Member States.[91] The relevant proceedings are those listed in Annex A.[92]

Unfortunately, the expression "centre of main interests" is not defined in the Regulation itself.[93] According to Recital (13) the "'centre of main interests should correspond to the place where the debtor conducts the administration of his interests on a regular basis and is therefore ascertainable by third parties". This very general guidance is buttressed by a presumption in Article 3(1) to the effect that in "the case of a company or legal person, the place of the registered office shall be presumed to be the centre of its main interests in the absence of proof to the contrary." The justification for this presumption is that the place of the registered office "normally corresponds to the debtor's head office."[94] This suggests that for the purposes of rebutting the presumption, it will be necessary to show (the burden of proof lying on the party who makes the assertion) that the "head office" functions of a company or legal person are carried out in a Member State other than the State (whether a Member State or non-Member State) in which the registered office is situated[95]: it will be in the former State that the company or legal person is likely to conduct the administration of its interests on a regular basis.[96] Also relevant to the inquiry is the notion that the centre of main interests makes the appropriate jurisdiction to open main insolvency proceedings "ascertainable by third parties".[97] In an appropriate case, a court might be prepared to conclude that the impression given by a debtor in the conduct of its activities is such that third parties could reasonably conclude that the centre of main interests is located in a Member State other than that in which the registered office is situated.[98]

---

[89] This view is also preferred by Fletcher in Moss *et al.*, p. 195.

[90] Recital (14).

[91] Any potential extension of the effects of proceedings, commenced under Art. 3(1), on assets situated outside the Member States would appear to depend on national law: see main work, Rule 157(1).

[92] See *supra*, para. S30–150.

[93] For discussion, see Fletcher in Moss *et al.*, pp. 39–41; Moss and Smith, *ibid.* pp. 168–174. As to bankruptcy, see *infra*, para. S31–095.

[94] Virgos-Schmit, para. 75.

[95] *Re BRAC Rent-a-Car International Inc.* [2003] EWHC 12 & (Ch), [2003] 1 W.L.R. 1421. As to evidential questions, see Insolvency Proceedings-Practice Note 1/2002.

[96] *ibid*; Recital (13).

[97] Recital (13).

[98] See Fletcher, *supra*, n.93, at p. 40; Virgos-Schmit, para. 75.

More generally, the court will have to scrutinise the whole range of activities[99] of the company or legal person so as to ascertain where the true administration of its interests on a regular basis really lies.[1]

S30–159 **Amendment of English law**. Since the E.C. Insolvency Regulation is directly applicable in England, it takes effect without any amendment to existing English law. Nonetheless, however, certain amendments have been made to particular rules concerned with jurisdiction with a view to indicating that their application is subject to the Regulation. First, section 1(4) of the Insolvency Act 1986[2] provides that a reference to a company in the provisions concerned with company voluntary arrangements includes a company in respect of to which a proposal for a voluntary arrangement may be made by virtue of Article 3 of the Regulation.[3] Secondly, section 8(7) of the 1986 Act[4] provides that in respect of the power of the court to make an administration order, a reference to a company includes a reference to a company in relation to which an administration order may be made by virtue of Article 3 of the Regulation.[5] Thirdly, an amendment contained in a new section 117(7) of the Insolvency Act 1986[6] makes it clear that the jurisdiction of the High Court to wind up any company registered in England is subject to Article 3 of the Regulation.[7] Fourthly, section 124(1) of the 1986 Act is amended so as to permit a liquidator within the meaning of Article 2(b) of the Regulation, appointed in proceedings by virtue of Article 3(1) of the Regulation, or a temporary administrator within the meaning of Article 38 of the Regulation, to apply to the court for a winding-up order.[8] Fifthly, section 221(4) of the Insolvency Act 1986 which prevented an unregistered company from being wound up voluntarily is amended to make it clear that such a company can be so wound up in accordance with the Regulation.[9] Sixthly, section 225 of the Insolvency Act 1986 which provides for the winding up of a company incorporated outside Great Britain even though it has been dissolved under the law of its place of incorporation[10] is amended to make it clear that the exercise of this jurisdiction is subject to the Regulation.[11] Seventhly, a new section 436A of the 1986 Act supplies a modified definition of "property" for the purposes of proceedings under the Regulation.[12] Where the 1986 Act applies to proceedings by virtue of Article 3 of the Regulation, a reference to property is a reference to property which may be dealt with in the proceedings.[13] In

---

[99] *Re BRAC Rent-a-Car International Inc., supra; Telia v. Hillcourt* [2002] EWHC 2377 (Ch).

[1] *ibid*; Recital (13).

[2] Inserted by S.1. 2002 No. 1240, Reg. 4.

[3] *cf. Re Television Trade Rentals Ltd*. [2002] EWHC 211 (Ch), [2002] B.C.C 807.

[4] Inserted by S.1. 2002 No. 1240, Reg. 5.

[5] This suggests that such an order could not be made in cases not falling within the Regulation: see *Re BRAC Rent-a-Car International Inc., supra. Cf.* main work, paras. 30–129—30–130.

[6] Inserted by S.1. 2002 No. 1240, Reg. 6. For Scotland see S.1. 2002 No. 1240, Reg. 7 inserting a new s. 120(6) into the 1986 Act. For partnerships, see S.I. 2002 No. 1308, Reg. 5.

[7] The general jurisdiction to wind up unregistered companies under section 221(5) of the 1986 Act is circumscribed by case law (see main work, Rule 155(2)) which must now be read subject to the Regulation.

[8] Inserted by S.1. 2002 No. 1240, Reg. 8. As to partnerships, see S.1. 2002 No 1308, Regs. 3 and 4.

[9] Inserted by S.1. 2002 No. 1240, Reg. 9.

[10] See main work, para. 30–050.

[11] Inserted by S.1. 2002 No. 1240, Reg. 10.

[12] Inserted by S.1. 2002 No. 1240, Reg. 18.

[13] *ibid*. For changes in the relevant statutory forms, see *supra*, para. S30–150. As to bankruptcy, see *infra*, entry at para. 31–090.

relation to secondary proceedings, the reference is to property situated in the Member State in which such proceedings are opened.

Conflicts of jurisdiction. It is implicit in the Regulation that a debtor can **S30–160** have only one centre of main interests in which proceedings may be opened.[14] However, the fact that the expression is not defined in the Regulation and is also an expression of considerable imprecision which is capable of being applied differently by courts in different Member States to the same set of facts could lead to claims to open main insolvency proceedings against the same debtor in different Member States.[15] As the Virgos-Schmit Report points out, the Regulation does not provide any express rule to resolve cases where the courts of two Member States concurrently claim jurisdiction in accordance with Article 3(1), though the Report expresses the view that such conflicts of jurisdiction must be an exception given the necessary uniform nature of the criteria of jurisdiction used.[16] Where such disputes do arise, continues the Report,[17] then to resolve them courts will be able to take account of: (1) the system established by the Regulation whereby each court is required to verify its own international jurisdiction under the Regulation[18]; (2) the principle of Community trust according to which once the first court of a Member State has adopted a decision, the other Member States are required to recognise it[19]; (3) the possibility of referring a question of interpretation to the European Court of Justice; and (4) the general principles of procedural law which are valid in all Member States (including those derived from the 1968 Convention and the Judgments Regulation). It is suggested that if this problem of conflicting jurisdictions were to arise, then the first two considerations identified above will be particularly important, so that save in the most exceptional cases, the decision in the first Member State in which main proceedings are opened will be respected in all the other Member States.

Extent of jurisdiction. Although Article 3(1) of the Regulation supplies a **S30–161** jurisdictional rule for the opening of "insolvency proceedings", a question may arise as to whether a particular issue (*e.g.* an ancillary action) falls to be judged as an "insolvency" issue subject to the jurisdictional rule of Article 3(1) or whether such an issue—if it does not relate to "insolvency"—is governed by a different jurisdictional regime, say that contained in the Judgments Regulation or, as the case may be, national law. As far as the Judgments Regulation is concerned, Article 1 (2)(b) provides that that Regulation does not apply to "bankruptcy, proceedings relating to the winding up of insolvent companies or other legal persons, judicial arrangements, compositions and analogous proceedings."[20] In elaborating the meaning of this provision, the European Court (in relation to the identical

---

[14] See *Re BRAC Rent-a-Car International Inc, supra* n. 99.
[15] Note Recital (4) stressing that it "is necessary for the proper functioning of the internal market to avoid incentives for the parties to transfer assets or judicial proceedings from one Member State to another, seeking to obtain a more favourable legal position (forum shopping)".
[16] Virgos-Schmit, para. 79.
[17] *ibid.*
[18] Virgos-Schmit, paras. 202, 215, 220; Fletcher in Moss *et al.*, p. 41.
[19] Virgos-Schmit, paras. 202, 220. See also Recital (22).
[20] See main work, para. 11–021; Virgos-Schmit, paras. 77, 191–197; Recital (7).

terminology of the 1968 Convention) held that for proceedings to be excluded under its terms they must be derived directly from the bankruptcy or winding up and be closely connected with those proceedings.[21] Thus a claim by a liquidator to recover debts due to an insolvent company would fall within the Judgments Regulation and not within the E.C. Insolvency Regulation since such a claim does not relate to bankruptcy.[22] A claim for breach of duty against directors would be treated in the same way even if the company is subject to insolvency proceedings in another Member State.[23] Conversely, a claim by a liquidator against directors in respect of wrongful trading would fall within the E.C. Insolvency Regulation and not within the Judgments Regulation.[24]

S30–162 **Preservation measures**. A court having jurisdiction under Article 3(1) of the E.C. Insolvency Regulation has the power to order preservation measures (provisional and protective measures) from the time of the request to open main proceedings.[25] Such measures may also be granted after the main proceedings have been opened.[26] The purpose of granting such preservation measures is to guarantee the effectiveness of the insolvency proceedings. Such measures may be ordered by the jurisdictionally competent court irrespective of the Member State where the assets or persons concerned are located. Available measures will depend on the national law of the court which orders them, *e.g.* the appointment of a temporary administrator[27] (provisional liquidator in English law) or measures freezing or attaching assets.[28] It is envisaged that such preservation measures shall be recognised and enforced in other Member States under Article 25 of the Regulation.[29] Additionally, it has been suggested that Article 3(1) does not prevent, *e.g.* a liquidator from going to a Member State (say the State in which assets are located) for the purpose of seeking from the courts of such a State whatever measures are available under that State's national law.[30] The jurisdiction of that State to grant such measures will depend on national law rather than on the Regulation.[31] Article 38 is also concerned with preservation measures. It provides that where "the court of a Member State which has jurisdiction pursuant to Article 3(1) appoints a temporary administrator in order to ensure the preservation of the debtor's assets, that temporary administrator shall be empowered to request any measures to secure and preserve any of the debtor's assets situated in another Member State, provided for under the law of that State, for the period between the request

---

[21] Case 133/78 *Gourdain v. Nadler* [1979] E.C.R. 733; *UBS A.G. v. Omni Holding A.G.* [2000] 1 W.L.R. 910. See also Case C-267/97 *Coursier v. Fortis Bank* [1999] E.C.R. 1–2543.

[22] *Re Hayward* [1997] Ch. 45.

[23] *Grupo Torras S.A. v. Sheik Fahad Mohammed Al-Sabah* [1995] 1 Lloyd's Rep 374; affd. on other grounds [1996] 1 Lloyd's Rep. 7 (C.A.).

[24] Case 133/78 *Gourdain v. Nadler, supra*; Virgos-Schmit, para. 196. See also E.C. Insolvency Regulation, Art. 25. Examples of proceedings under English law which would fall within the latter Regulation are claims under Insolvency Act 1986, s. 238 (transactions at an undervalue) and *ibid.* s. 239 (preferences). See *UBS A.G. v Omni Holding A.G., supra.*

[25] Virgos-Schmit, para. 78.

[26] *ibid.*

[27] *ibid.*

[28] *ibid.*

[29] See Art. 25(1), third sub-paragraph, *infra*, Rule 159T.

[30] Virgos-Schmit, para. 78.

[31] *ibid.*

for the opening of insolvency proceedings and the judgment opening the proceedings."[32] This Article appears in Chapter III of the Regulation which is concerned with the treatment of secondary proceedings (see clause (2) of the Rule). It can therefore be argued that the temporary administrator is only entitled to request relevant measures in Member State in which the debtor has an establishment which State would therefore be capable of opening secondary proceedings,[33] but that the temporary administrator would not have power to seek relevant measures in Member States where no such establishment is situated.[34] Since there is no such limitation in the actual text of Article 38, this argument has been rejected.[35] It may be, however, that Article 38 is concerned with preservation measures in Member States where, potentially, secondary proceedings can be opened. To secure the legal position in that Member State, pending opening of proceedings, the temporary administrator is given (perhaps by way of clarification) power to seek measures there.[36] In Member States where there is no establishment, but say the presence of assets, preservation measures granted by the court having jurisdiction pursuant to Article 3(1) will be automatically recognised under Articles 16 and 25 of the Regulation.[37]

Clauses (2) and (3) of the Rule. These clauses reproduce Article 3(2) and (3) of the E.C. Insolvency Regulation. Article 3(2) and (3) limit the effect of the universal scope of main proceedings opened under Article 3(1) of the Regulation by allowing separate proceedings (secondary proceedings) with limited scope to be opened in a Member State other than that in which the centre of the debtor's main interests is located in certain circumstances. Article 3(2) (clause (2) of the Rule) provides that where the centre of a debtor's main interests is situated in the territory of a Member State, the courts of another Member State shall have jurisdiction to open insolvency proceedings against that debtor only if he possesses an establishment in that State. The effects of those proceedings shall be restricted to the assets of the debtor situated in the territory of the latter Member State. Article 3(3) (clause (3) of the Rule) goes on to provide that where insolvency proceedings have been opened under Article 3(1) (clause (1) of the Rule), any proceedings opened subsequently under Article 3(2) shall be secondary proceedings. These latter proceedings must be winding-up proceedings. In what follows the expression "secondary proceedings" will be used, in the sense of Article 3(3), to mean proceedings opened in a Member State subsequent to the opening of main proceedings in the Member State where the centre of the debtor's main interests is located.[38] The following issues call for comment.

S30–163

---

[32] Examples of a "temporary administrator" in English law include a provisional liquidator in a winding-up petition or an interim manager in an administration petition: Moss and Bayfield in Moss *et al.*, p. 88.

[33] See Recital (16); Virgos-Schmit, paras. 78, 268. The observations in these references are not unambiguous.

[34] See Moss and Smith in Moss *et al.*, p. 229.

[35] *ibid.*

[36] See Balz (1996) 70 American Bankruptcy L.J. 485. Art. 29 authorises the liquidator in the main proceedings but not a temporary administrator to request the opening of insolvency proceedings. According to Virgos-Schmit, para. 263 a "temporary administrator, whose task is more limited, does not correspond exactly with the definition in Article 2(b) of a liquidator in insolvency proceedings and is not necessarily listed in Annex C."

[37] See Virgos-Schmit, para.78.

[38] Where such proceedings are opened before main proceedings, see Art. 3(4) (clause (4) of the Rule).

S30–164 **Meaning of "establishment"**.[39] Since secondary proceedings may only be opened in a Member State in which the debtor has an establishment, it is crucial to identify the meaning of this term. Article 2(h) provides that "establishment" shall mean any place of operations where the debtor carries out a non-transitory economic activity with human means and goods. This "very open definition"[40] was adopted as a way of achieving consensus on the abandonment of the mere presence of assets in a Member State as a basis of jurisdiction.[41] In more particularity, "place of operations" means a place from which economic activities are exercised on the market (*i.e.* externally) whether the relevant activities are commercial, industrial or professional.[42] That the economic activity must be "non-transitory" is designed to indicate that an occasional or temporary place of operations cannot qualify as an establishment without specifically stipulating a minimum requirement of time.[43] The relevant economic activity must be carried out using "human means" and "goods" which appear to be cumulative, rather than alternative requirements. The reference to human means would appear to connote operations conducted through personnel, including employees and some forms of agent, in circumstances which in effect give the debtor a degree of stability in the Member State concerned.[44] The reference to "goods" is more problematic. In the literal English sense goods means chattels or tangible movables, but in the broader sense of, *e.g.* the French text of the Regulation, *"biens"* means property or assets of whatever kind.[45] Similarly, goods is not apt to include "services",[46] though in so far as services are provided by human means, they would be capable of being included in the latter concept. It is likely, overall, that the reference to human means and goods is intended to indicate that to be an establishment, a place of operations must have a minimum level of organisation so as to appear to be materially equipped to do business with third parties.[47] Where, however, a parent company, with its centre of main interests in one Member State has a separately incorporated subsidiary in another Member State, that subsidiary does not constitute an "establishment" of the parent company.[48]

---

[39] See Virgos-Schmit, paras 70–71; Fletcher in Moss *et al.*, pp. 43–44; Moss and Smith, *ibid.* pp. 165–166.

[40] Virgos-Schmit, para. 70.

[41] *ibid.*

[42] *ibid.*, para. 71.

[43] *ibid.*

[44] *ibid.*

[45] Moss and Smith, *supra*, n. 39, at p.175.

[46] *cf.* UNCITRAL Model Law, Art. 2(f) (goods *or* services, emphasis added).

[47] *cf.* Case 33/78 *Somafer S.A. v. Saar-Ferngas A.G.* [1978] E.C.R. 2183 (a case on Art. 5(5) of the 1968 Convention); Case 218/86 SAR *Schotte GmbH v. Parfums Rothschild SARL* [1987] E.C.R. 4905 (also on Art. 5(5) of the 1968 Convention); see main work, para 11–272. Virgos-Schmit, para. 71 stresses the importance of the stable appearance of the activity externally. Whether elements of the analysis in cases involving Art. 5(5) will be adopted in construing the meaning of "establishment" is unclear. According to Virgos-Schmit, para. 70 importing a concept from the 1968 Convention might place a restrictive interpretation on the concept in the Regulation which is the opposite of what was intended.

[48] See Virgos-Schmit, para. 76; Moss and Smith in Moss *et al.*, pp. 173–174. If parent and subsidiary both have their respective main centres of interests in Member States, main proceedings will have to be opened in respect of each entity. *Cf.* Case 218/86 *SAR Schotte & GmbH v. Parfums Rothschild SARL, supra*, where it was held, in the context of Art. 5(5) of the 1968 Convention, that a parent could be an establishment of a subsidiary, a more liberal interpretation than is suggested for the E.C. Insolvency Regulation.

It would appear from a literal interpretation of Article 3(2) that the debtor **S30–165**
must have an establishment in the relevant Member State at the time
secondary proceedings are opened since the text stipulates that jurisdiction
exists if the debtor "possesses" an establishment in that Member State.
However, it is conceivable that the debtor may move the establishment or
close it down altogether, realising impending insolvency, before a request to
open proceedings is made and/or before proceedings are opened,[49] with a
view to avoiding secondary proceedings. In such circumstances it has
reasonably been suggested that "the courts can and should prevent the
evasion of Article 3(2) jurisdiction by means of a purposive, non-literal
form of interpretation of the Regulation".[50]

Proceedings may be opened under Article 3(2) in as many Member States **S30–166**
in which the debtor possesses an establishment.

Situation of assets. The effects of proceedings opened under Article 3(2) **S30–167**
extend only to assets of the debtor situated in the Member State where such
proceedings are opened.[51] This raises the question of how it is to be
determined whether assets of the debtor are located in the relevant
Member State. According to Article 2(g) of the Regulation,

"'the Member State' in which assets are situated shall mean in the case of:

- tangible property, the Member State within the territory of which
  the property is situated,

- property and rights ownership of or entitlement to which must be
  entered in a public register, the Member State under the authority
  of which the register is kept,

- claims, the Member State within the territory of which the third
  party required to meet them has the centre of his main interests,
  as determined in Article 3(1)."

This provision, it has been said, "does no more than stress traditional **S30–168**
solutions of private international law which are well known in all the"[52]
Member States. The following particular points may, nonetheless, be made.
First, the second indent is applicable, for example, in the case of ship and
aircraft registers, and also extends to intangible property such as patents or
securities.[53] The State under whose authority the register is kept is not
necessarily the State in which the register is physically located (*e.g.* it may be
a consular register or centralised international register).[54] Secondly, public
register does not mean a register kept by a public authority, but rather a
register for public access an entry in which produces effects as against third

---

[49] The same problem could arise in relation to the debtor's centre of main interests: see Moss *et al.*, pp. 170–171.
[50] *ibid.* p. 175. See Recital (4) stressing the need to avoid forum shopping.
[51] It is not part of the jurisdictional criteria that there must be assets in that State, but only an establishment. It is hard, however, to conceive of proceedings being opened in a Member State where the debtor has an establishment but no assets.
[52] Virgos-Schmit, para. 69.
[53] *ibid.*
[54] *ibid.*

parties. Apparently, it also includes private registers with the foregoing characteristics recognised by the national legal system concerned.[55] Thirdly, in the case of community patents, trademarks and other similar rights of community origin, Article 12 of the Regulation provides that these can only be included in main proceedings bases on Article 3(1) of the Regulation: they cannot be included in secondary proceedings opened under Article 3(2) or in territorial proceedings opened under Article 3(4).[56]

S30–169 **Winding-up proceedings**. Article 3(3) of the Regulation (clause (3) of the Rule) requires that proceedings opened under Article 3(2) must be winding up proceedings, *i.e.* proceedings listed in Annex B.[57] In the English context, these proceedings are compulsory winding up by the court,[58] creditors' voluntary winding up (with confirmation by the court) and bankruptcy. This means that reorganisation proceedings such as English administration proceedings cannot be opened, as secondary proceedings, after the opening of main proceedings under Article 3(1) in another Member State.[59]

S30–170 **Clause (4) of the Rule.** This clause reproduces Article 3(4) of the E.C. Insolvency Regulation. It concerns the right to open proceedings in a Member State where the debtor has an establishment, the effects of which are limited to assets situated in that State, before main proceedings have been opened, under Article 3(1), in the Member State where the centre of the debtor's main interests is situated. Such proceedings are hereafter referred to as "territorial proceedings". Territorial proceedings may be opened prior to the opening of main insolvency proceedings under Article 3(1) in only two circumstances: (a) where insolvency proceedings under Article 3(1) cannot be opened because of the conditions laid down by the law of the Member State within the territory of which the centre of the debtor's main interests is located[60]; or (b) where the opening of territorial insolvency proceedings is requested by a creditor who has his domicile, habitual residence or registered office in the Member State within the territory of which the establishment is situated or whose claim arises from the operation of that establishment.[61] As to condition (a), an example would be the case in which the law of the Member State in which the debtor has his centre of main interests does not permit the opening of insolvency proceedings because the debtor is not a trader, as required by that State's law or a case in which the debtor is a public company with its centre of main interests in a Member State whose law does not permit insolvency proceedings to be opened against such a company.[62] In this type of case, it is likely that main proceedings will never be capable of being opened so that territorial proceedings can be brought in every Member State where the debtor has an establishment. Condition (b) may only be invoked by a

---

[55] *ibid.*

[56] *ibid.* and para 133. See Fletcher in Moss *et al.*, p.63; Moss and Smith, *ibid.* p.190. See *post*, Rule 159K.

[57] Art. 2(c). As to bankruptcy, see *infra*, para. S31–096.

[58] In Gibraltar they will include winding up subject to the supervision of the court.

[59] See also Art. 27, *infra*, Rule 159Q. For criticism, see Moss and Smith in Moss *et al.*, p.176. For justification, see Virgos-Schmit, para. 221. *Cf.* the position under Art. 3(4) (clause (4) of the Rule).

[60] Art. 3(4)(a).

[61] Art. 3(4)(b).

[62] Virgos-Schmit, para. 85.1.

creditor who has his domicile, habitual residence or registered office in the relevant Member State. The meaning of registered office is self explanatory. "Domicile" is not defined in the Regulation.[63] In so far as the term appears in a European instrument which should be interpreted uniformly by reference to autonomous definitions, it might be thought unlikely that "domicile" is used in the sense which is attributed to it in English common law.[64] On the other hand, since domicile in the continental sense equates approximately, to habitual residence, it is difficult to see what other meaning than the English meaning can be attributed to it, unless it means the professional domicile of an individual trader (as opposed to a legal person). The meaning of habitual residence is discussed elsewhere in this work.[65] A creditor bearing any of the above characteristics may, as such, request the opening of territorial insolvency proceedings prior to the opening of main proceedings.[66] Additionally such a creditor may also make such a request if the creditor's claim arises from the operation of the establishment. Examples of the latter situation might include an employee working for the establishment or the tax or social security authorities of the Member State.[67] Where condition (b) applies, it is likely that main proceedings will be subsequently opened in the Member State in which the centre of the debtor's main interests is situated. If such be the case, it is thought that the territorial proceedings become "secondary proceedings".[68] The ramifications of the provisions of the Regulation in such a situation are considered below.[69]

It should be noted that territorial proceedings opened prior to main proceedings do not have to be winding-up proceedings. Accordingly, reorganisation measures may be sought in such territorial proceedings.[70]

Insolvency Rules 1986. The new English insolvency forms introduced in consequence of the Regulation coming into effect require the petitioner to state whether it is sought to open main proceedings, secondary proceedings or territorial proceedings.[71] Similarly the court order opening the proceedings will also state whether the proceedings so opened are main, secondary or territorial in nature.[72] The Rules also indicate that "centre of main interests" and "establishment" are to have the same meaning as those expressions bear in the Regulation[73] and that "main", "secondary" and

S30–171

---

[63] Or in the Virgos-Schmit Report.

[64] As to the meaning of domicile, see main work, Chap. 6.

[65] Main work, paras. 6–123—6–126.

[66] Note that the right is a right to *request* the opening of proceedings. After the proceedings have been opened under condition (b), there seems to be no reason why other creditors, not bearing the required characteristics to request an opening, should not be able to participate by filing claims: see Bogdan in Moss *et al.*, p.177.

[67] Virgos-Schmit, para. 85.2.

[68] See Recital (17); Virgos-Schmit, para. 86. This is not explicitly stated in Art. 3(4).

[69] See *post*, Rule 159P.

[70] Territorial proceedings may be any measures referred to in Annex A or Annex B: Virgos-Schmit, para. 86.

[71] See Form 2.1 (petition for administration order); Form 4.2 (winding-up petition); Form 4.14 (petition by contributory).

[72] See Form 2.4 (administration order); Form 4.11 (order for winding up by the court); Form 4.12 (order for winding up by the court following upon discharge of an administration order); Form 4.15 (order of appointment of provisional liquidator); Form 7.20 (confirmation by court of creditors' voluntary winding up application and order).

[73] Rules 13(8) and 13(9), inserted by S.1. 2002 No. 1307, Reg. 10.

"territorial" proceedings are to mean proceedings opened, respectively, in accordance with Article 3(1), 3(2) and 3(3), or 3(4) and which are defined in Article 2(a) or 2(c) and listed in Annex A or B.[74]

S30–172 **Insurance undertakings.** As already indicated, the Regulation does not apply to insolvency proceedings involving insurance undertakings.[75] The relevant rules applicable in relation to such institutions are to found in Directive 2001/17 of the European Parliament and of the Council of March 19, 2001 on the reorganisation and winding up of insurance undertakings.[76] The Directive must be implemented before April 20, 2003.[77] Until the relevant United Kingdom regulations are produced it is not possible to give a detailed account of the application of this measure. Nonetheless, the following remarks, based upon the terms of the Directive will provide a general overview.[78]

S30–173 By Article 4(1) of the Directive, it is provided that only the competent authorities[79] of the "home Member State" shall be entitled to decide on reorganisation measures with regard to an insurance undertaking, including its branches in other Member States. For these purposes, "home Member State" means the Member State in which an insurance undertaking has been authorised in accordance with Article 6 of Directive 73/239 of July 24, 1973 on the coordination of laws, regulations and administrative provisions relating to the taking up and pursuit of the business of direct insurance other than life insurance, or Article 6 of Directive 79/267 of March 5, 1979 on the coordination of laws, regulations and administrative provisions relating to the taking up and pursuit of the business of direct life insurance.[80] "Reorganisation measures" mean measures involving any intervention by administrative bodies or judicial authorities which are intended to preserve or restore the financial position of an insurance undertaking and which affect pre-existing rights of parties rather than the insurance undertaking itself, including, but not limited to measures involving the possibility of a suspension of payments, suspension of enforcement measures or reduction of claims.[81] The general effect of these provisions is to subject the opening of reorganisation measures to the jurisdiction of the home Member State, which will also supply the applicable law except where the Directive otherwise provides.[82] Reorganisation measures shall be fully effective throughout the Community, in accordance with the legislation of the home Member State without any further formalities, including against third parties in other Member States, even if the legislation of those Member States does not provide for such reorganisation measures or alternatively makes their implementation subject to conditions which are

---

[74] Rule 13(10), (12) and (14) inserted by S.I. 2002 No. 1307, Reg. 10.
[75] E.C. Insolvency Regulation, Art. 1(2). For the definition of "insurance undertaking" see *ante*, para. S30–152.
[76] [2001] O.J. L110/28.
[77] Art. 31(1). The Directive has not yet been implemented in the United Kingdom.
[78] For discussion, see Marks in Moss *et al.*, pp. 140–148.
[79] Defined in Art. 2(g) as the administrative or judicial authorities of the Member States which are competent for the purpose of the reorganisation measures or the winding-up proceedings.
[80] For the text of these Directives see, respectively, [1973] O.J. L228/3 and [1979] O.J. L63/1.
[81] Art. 2(c). In England, the provisions for administration contained in Insolvency Act 1986, Pt. II have been extended to insurance companies by S.I 2002 No. 1242.
[82] Art. 4(2). The exceptions to the general rule are contained in Arts. 19–26.

not fulfilled.[83] Reorganisation measures become effective throughout the Community once they become effective in the Member State where they have been taken.[84]

Control by the home Member State also applies to winding-up proceedings.[85] These are defined as collective proceedings involving the realisation of assets of an insurance undertaking and distributing the proceeds among the creditors, shareholders or members as appropriate, which necessarily involve any intervention by the administrative or the judicial authorities of a Member State, including where the collective proceedings are terminated by a composition or other analogous measure, whether or not they are founded on insolvency or are voluntary or compulsory.[86] Only the competent authorities[87] of the home Member State are entitled to take a decision concerning the opening of winding-up proceedings with regard to an insurance undertaking, including its branches in other Member States.[88] The law of that Member State will supply the applicable law except as otherwise provided in the Directive.[89] A decision adopted according to the home Member State's legislation concerning the opening of winding-up proceedings, including its branches in other Member States, shall be recognised without further formality within the territory of all other Member States and shall be effective in these Member States as soon as the decision is effective in the Member State in which the proceedings are opened.[90]

S30–174

Credit institutions. It was also pointed out above that the E.C. Insolvency Regulation does not apply to insolvency proceedings concerning credit institutions.[91] Insolvency proceedings concerning such institutions will be subject to Directive 2001/24 of the European Parliament and of the Council of April 4, 2001 on the reorganisation and winding up of credit institutions.[92] This Directive must be implemented in the Member States on May 5, 2004.[93] The following discussion provides a general overview of the main features of this Directive.[94]

S30–175

As regards credit institutions having their head office within the Community,[95] Article 3(1) of the Directive provides that the administrative or judicial authorities of the home Member State shall alone be empowered to decide on the implementation of one or more reorganisation measures in relation to a credit institution, including branches established in Member

S30–176

---

[83] Art. 4(3).

[84] Art. 4(4).

[85] Art. 8.

[86] Art. 2(d).

[87] See *supra*, n. 79.

[88] Art. 8(1).

[89] Art. 9. The exceptions to the general rule are contained in Arts. 19–26.

[90] Art. 8(2). As to the position in relation to reorganisation measures and winding-up proceedings concerning a branch situated in a Member State of an insurance undertaking whose head office is located outside the Community, see Art. 30.

[91] E.C. Insolvency Regulation, Art. 1(2). For the definition of "credit institution", see *supra*, para. S30–152.

[92] [2001] O.J. L125/15.

[93] Art. 34(1).

[94] For discussion, see Marks in Moss *et al.*, pp. 134–140.

[95] As to reorganisation measures in relation to a credit institution having its head office outside the Community, see Art. 8.

States. For these purposes "home Member State" means the Member State in which a credit union has been authorised in accordance with Articles 4 to 11 of Directive 2000/12 of the European Parliament and of the Council of March 20, 2000 relating to the taking up and pursuit of the business of credit institutions.[96] "Reorganisation measures" shall mean measures which are intended to preserve or restore the financial situation of a credit institution and which could affect third parties' pre-existing rights, including measures involving the possibility of a suspension of payments, suspension of enforcement measures or reduction of claims.[97] The effect of these provisions is to submit the opening of reorganisation measures to the jurisdiction of the home Member State, which State's law will also be the applicable law except as otherwise provided in the Directive.[98] Such reorganisation measures shall be fully effective in accordance with the legislation of the home Member State throughout the Community including as against third parties, even where the rules of the host Member State[99] applicable to them do not provide for such measures or make their implementation subject to conditions which are not fulfilled.[1] The reorganisation measures should be effective throughout the Community once they become effective in the Member State where they have been taken.[2]

S30–177 Control by the home Member State also applies to winding-up proceedings[3] involving credit institutions having their head offices within the Community,[4] and the relevant administrative or judicial authorities of that Member State are solely responsible for the opening of such proceedings in respect of credit institutions including branches established in other Member States.[5] The law applicable to such proceedings shall be the law of the home Member State except in so far as the Directive otherwise provides.[6] A decision to open winding-up proceedings taken by the administrative or judicial authorities of the home Member State shall be recognised, without further formality, within the territory of all other Member States and shall be effective there when the decision is effective in the Member State in which the proceedings are opened.[7]

ILLUSTRATIONS

CLAUSE (1) OF THE RULE

S30–178 1. X is company registered in England under the Companies Act. It carries on business in France and Germany, as well as in England. Its directors reside in England, its head office

---

[96] Art. 2, referring to Art. 1(6) of the Directive of March 20, 2000, [2000] O.J. L126/1.

[97] Art. 2.

[98] Art. 3(2). The exceptions are to be found in Arts. 20–32.

[99] Defined as the Member State in which a credit institution has a branch or in which it provides services: Art. 2, referring to Art. 1(7) of the Directive of March 20, 2000, *supra*, n. 96.

[1] Art. 3(2).

[2] *ibid*.

[3] Defined as collective proceedings opened and monitored by the administrative or judicial authorities of a Member State with the aim of realising assets under the supervision of those authorities, including where the proceedings are terminated by a composition or other similar measure: Art. 2.

[4] As to winding-up proceedings in relation to credit institutions the head office of which is outside the Community, see Art. 19.

[5] Art. 3(2).

[6] Art. 10. The exceptions are to be found in Arts. 20–32.

[7] Art. 3(2).

is situated in England, and most business decisions are taken in England. The English court has jurisdiction to open main insolvency proceedings[8] in respect of X.[9]

2. X is a company incorporated in Germany, where its registered office is situated. X does business in England through an English agent but its principal business activities are conducted in France and Germany. The English court has no jurisdiction to open main insolvency proceedings[10] in respect of X.[11]

3. X is a company incorporated in Delaware, and has its registered office in the United States. X does not trade from that office and has never traded in the United States. It trades from an address in England, conducts its operations almost entirely in the United Kingdom, it has no employees in the United States and all its employees work in England under contracts of employment governed by English law. The English court has jurisdiction to make an administration order in respect of X.[12]

4. X is a company incorporated in Delaware where its registered office is situated. It has a branch in England, but all relevant business decisions concerning its English operations are taken in Delaware which is where the directors of the company reside and where its head office is situated. The English court has no jurisdiction to open main insolvency proceedings[13] in respect of X under the E.C. Insolvency Regulation since X's centre of main interests is not situated within the territory of a Member State.[14]

5. X is a company incorporated in Sweden where its registered office is situated. X is the parent company of Y, a wholly owned subsidiary, incorporated, and with its registered office, in England. The English court has no jurisdiction to open main insolvency proceedings[15] in respect of X.[16]

Clauses (2) and (3) of the Rule

6. X is a company, incorporated in the Netherlands, where its registered office is situated and all of its business is conducted. It has assets situated in England, in the form of a bank account in credit at an English bank. Insolvency proceedings (main proceedings) in respect of X are opened in the Netherlands. A, an English creditor of X, seeks to bring winding-up proceedings (secondary proceedings) in respect of X in England. The English court does not have jurisdiction to open such proceedings, since X does not have an establishment in England.[17]

S30–179

7. The facts are the same as in Illustration 6, except that the company has a branch in England, which conducts a substantial amount of X's business, and where X employs a branch manager and several employees. The English court has jurisdiction to open winding-up proceedings (secondary proceedings), the effects of which are limited to assets situated in England.[18]

8. X is a company, incorporated in Sweden, where its registered office is situated. Y is a company, incorporated in England, where its registered office is situated. Y is a wholly owned subsidiary of X. Insolvency proceedings in respect of X are opened in Sweden. A, an English creditor of X, seeks a winding-up order against X from the English court. The

---

[8] E.C. Insolvency Regulation, Art. 2(a), Annex A.

[9] *ibid*. Art. 3(1); and see Insolvency Act 1986, s. 117(7).

[10] E.C. Insolvency Regulation, Art. 2(a), Annex A.

[11] *ibid*. Art 3(1); and see Insolvency Act 1986, ss. 1(4), 8(7), 221(4).

[12] E.C. Insolvency Regulation, Art. 3(1); Insolvency Act 1986, s.8(7); *Re BRAC Rent-a-Car International Inc.* [2003] EWHC 128 (Ch); [2003] 1 W.L.R. 1421.

[13] E.C. Insolvency Regulation, Art. 2(a), Annex A.

[14] *ibid*. Art. 3(1); and see Insolvency Act 1986, ss. 1(4), 8(7), 221(4); *Re BRAC Rent-a-Car International Inc., supra*.

[15] E.C. Insolvency Regulation, Art. 2(a), Annex A.

[16] *ibid.* Art. 3(1); and see Insolvency Act 1986, ss. 1(4), 8(7), 221(4); *Telia v. Harcourt* [2002] EWHC 2377 (Ch).

[17] E.C. Insolvency Regulation, Art. 3(2), (3); Art. 2 (c), Annex B.

[18] E.C. Insolvency Regulation, Art. 3(2), (3); Art. 2(c), Annex B; Insolvency Act 1986, s. 436A.

court has no jurisdiction to open such proceedings since X's centre of main interests is in Sweden and Y does not constitute an establishment of X which is situated in England.[19]

CLAUSE (4) OF THE RULE

S30–180   9. X is a company incorporated in Italy, where its registered office is situated and where it does business. X has a branch in England, which conducts X's business, has a branch manager and several employees. No insolvency proceedings have been opened in Italy in respect of X. A, a company incorporated in England, where its registered office is situated is a creditor of X, having supplied goods to X's head office in Italy, for which A has not been paid. X has assets in a bank account in London. A seeks to open winding-up proceedings[20] (territorial proceedings) in respect of X in London. The English court has jurisdiction to open such proceedings since X has an establishment in England and A has its registered office in England.

10. The facts are the same as in Illustration 9, except that A seeks to open proceedings for an administration order. The English court has jurisdiction to open such proceedings.[21]

11. The facts are the same as in Illustration 9 except that the debt owed by X to A has been incurred as a result of non-payment for goods supplied to X's English branch. The English court has jurisdiction to open winding-up proceedings or proceedings for an administration order (territorial proceedings) in respect of X since X has an establishment in England and A's claim arises from the operation of that establishment.[22]

C. Choice of Law[23]

S30R–181   RULE 159C—(1) **Subject to Rules 159D – to 159N, the law applicable to insolvency proceedings and their effects shall be that of the Member State within the territory of which such proceedings are opened, hereafter referred to as the "State of the opening of proceedings".**

(2) **The law of the State of the opening of proceedings shall determine the conditions for the opening of those proceedings, their conduct and their closure. It shall determine in particular:**

(a) **against which debtors insolvency proceedings may be brought on account of their capacity;**

(b) **the assets which form part of the estate and the treatment of assets acquired by or devolving on the debtor after the opening of the insolvency proceedings;**

(c) **the respective powers of the debtor and the liquidator;**

(d) **the conditions under which set-offs may be invoked;**

(e) **the effects of insolvency proceedings on current contracts to which the debtor is a party;**

---

[19] *ibid; Telia v. Harcourt, supra.*

[20] E.C. Insolvency Regulation, Art 3(4)(b); Art. 1(1), 2(a), Annex A.

[21] *ibid.*

[22] *ibid.*

[23] See Virgos-Schmit, paras. 87–142, 225; Fletcher, *Insolvency in Private International Law* (1999), pp. 265–282; Morse in Borchers and Zekoll (eds.), *International Conflict of Laws for the Third Millenium: Essays in Honor of Friedrich K. Juenger* (2001), pp. 245–256; Fletcher in Moss *et al.*, Chap. 4; Isaacs, Toube, Segal and Marshall, *ibid.* Chap. 6; Moss and Smith, *ibid.* pp.177–193; Balz (1996) 70 American Bankruptcy L.J. 485, 506–514; Segal (1997) 23 Brooklyn J.Int. L. 57.

(f) the effects of insolvency proceedings on proceedings brought by individual creditors, with the exception of lawsuits pending;

(g) the claims which are to be lodged against the debtor's estate and the treatment of claims arising after the opening of insolvency proceedings;

(h) the rules governing the lodging, verification and admission of claims;

(i) the rules governing the distribution of proceeds from the realisation of assets, the ranking of claims and the rights of creditors who have obtained partial satisfaction after the opening of insolvency proceedings by virtue of a right *in rem* or through a set-off;

(j) the conditions for and the effects of closure of insolvency proceedings, in particular by composition;

(k) creditors' rights after the closure of insolvency proceedings;

(l) who is to bear the costs and expenses incurred in the insolvency proceedings;

(m) the rules relating to voidness, voidability or unenforceability of legal acts detrimental to all the creditors.[24]

(3) Subject to Rules 159D to 159N, the law applicable to secondary proceedings shall be that of the Member State within the territory of which the secondary proceedings are opened.[25]

COMMENT

Clauses (1) and (2) of this Rule are derived from Article 4 of the E.C. **S30–182** Regulation on Insolvency Proceedings. Clause (3) of the Rule is derived from Article 28 of the Regulation. The latter provision is contained in Chapter III of the Regulation, entitled "Secondary Insolvency Proceedings", unlike Article 4 which is contained in Chapter 1 entitled "General Provisions." Nonetheless, since each provision is concerned with applicable law and since each provision applies the same general choice of law principle, it is convenient to treat the provisions together.

Clause (1) of the Rule. Article 4(1) of the Regulation, as reproduced in this **S30–183** clause, states the general choice of law rule applicable in cases falling within the Regulation. According to that general rule the law applicable to insolvency proceedings and their effects is that of the Member State within the territory of which such proceedings are opened—the law of the "State of the opening of proceedings." This general rule applies in main, secondary and territorial proceedings.

---

[24] E.C. Insolvency Regulation, Art. 4. See the similar provision contained in Insurance Undertakings Insolvency Directive, Art. 9; Credit Institutions Insolvency Directive, Art. 9.

[25] *ibid.* Art. 28. As regards "territorial insolvency proceedings", the rules on choice of law are probably those which apply to main proceedings contained in Art. 4 (clause (1) and (2) of the Rule) rather than that of Art. 28 (clause (3) of the Rule) which applies to secondary proceedings: see Virgos-Schmit, para. 89. But this will make little difference in practice since Art. 28 "reiterates" the solution contained in Art. 4 for secondary proceedings.

S30–184 For the purposes of Article 4 (and other choice of law provisions contained in the Regulation) the reference to "law" denotes a reference to the domestic law of the relevant Member State: the doctrine of *renvoi* (although not formally excluded by the text of the Regulation) is inapplicable.[26] The relevant domestic law which is applicable includes both the substantive and procedural law of the Member State whose courts have jurisdiction.[27] Accordingly, where an English court has jurisdiction to open main, secondary or territorial proceedings, it will, as a general rule apply English insolvency law as contained in the Insolvency Act 1986[28] and any relevant provisions to be found in the Insolvency Rules 1986.

S30–185 Article 4(1) states a general rule which is subject to exceptions set out in Articles 5 to 15 (Rules 159D to 159N). Where one of the exceptions applies, the applicable law will not necessarily be the law of the Member State in which the proceedings are opened. The exceptions relate to the following issues: third parties' rights *in rem* (Article 5, Rule 159D); set-off (Article 6, Rule 159E); reservation of title (Article 7, Rule 159F); contracts relating to immovable property (Article 8, Rule 159G); payment systems and financial markets (Article 9, Rule 159H); contracts of employment (Article 10, Rule 159I); effect on rights subject to registration (Article 11, Rule 159J); community patents and trade marks (Article 12, Rule 159K); detrimental acts (Article 13, Rule 159L); protection of third-party purchasers (Article 14, Rule 159M); and the effects of insolvency proceedings on lawsuits pending (Article 15, Rule 159N).

S30–186 **Clause (2) of the Rule.** This clause reproduces Article 4(2) of the Regulation. It is designed to facilitate the interpretation of Article 4.[29] The law of the State of opening will determine the "conditions for the opening of proceedings", their "conduct" and their "closure". These generalised issues are rendered more specific in Articles 4(2)(a) to 4(2)(m), which issues will "in particular" be governed by the applicable law. Use of "in particular" in Article 4(2) indicates clearly that the list which it contains is not intended to be exhaustive[30]: courts may include other issues within the scope of the Article[31] provided those issues are not dealt with by reference to other provisions of the Regulation and provided the relevant issue relates to insolvency proceedings (as opposed to proceedings which do not so relate[32]).

Article 4(2)(a). The law of the State of opening will determine against which debtors insolvency proceedings may be brought on account of their capacity. The applicable law will determine, therefore, whether insolvency proceedings may be brought, *e.g.* against a non-trader or a "public law company".[33] Thus, a foreign entity which could not be subject to insolvency proceedings under the law of the Member State which created it may be subject to main insolvency proceedings in England if its centre of main

---

[26] Virgos-Schmit, para. 87.
[27] *ibid.* para. 90.
[28] *cf.* Rule 157(2).
[29] Virgos-Schmit, para. 91.
[30] *ibid.*
[31] Moss and Smith in Moss *et al.*, p.179.
[32] See *supra*, para. S30–161.
[33] Virgos-Schmit, para. 91(a).

interests is located in England. If the entity's centre of main interests is located in the Member State under whose law it is created, but it has an establishment in England the English court has jurisdiction to open secondary or territorial proceedings in respect of the entity.[34] It is, of course, possible that the courts of the Member State in which the debtor's centre of main interests is located and those of the Member State in which the debtor has an establishment will reach different conclusions on this issue, in relation to the same debtor, because of the different rules on capacity existing in each Member State.[35]

Article 4(2)(b). This provision submits the question of what assets form part of the estate and the treatment of assets acquired by or devolving on the debtor after the opening of the insolvency proceedings to the control of the law of the State of opening. Thus it would seem that the law of the State of opening would determine whether assets subject to a security right (*e.g.* in England, a fixed charge) are excluded from the estate,[36] what is eventually comprised in the estate for distribution, and the appropriate treatment to be accorded to after-acquired property.   **S30–187**

Article 4(2)(c). The law of the State of opening will also determine the respective powers of the debtor and the liquidator, save in so far as these are subject to the control of other provisions of the Regulation.[37]

Article 4(2)(d). This provision is concerned with the difficult question of set-off.[38] It appears to establish, as a general rule, that the law of the State of opening will determine the conditions under which set-offs may be invoked in insolvency proceedings falling within the Regulation.[39] On this basis the rights of any creditor who is also a debtor to the insolvent estate primarily depend on the set-off rules of the law of the State of opening. Accordingly, if an English court has jurisdiction to open main, secondary or territorial insolvency proceedings, then the English rule on insolvency set-off will be applied.[40] Conversely, if the court has no such jurisdiction, but the debtor is subject to insolvency proceedings in another Member State which is the debtor's centre of main interests, then the English court will be required to recognise any judgment given by a court of that State, including any aspect of that judgment which relates to set-off and which gives effect to a more limited right to set-off than is available in English insolvency law.[41] It is submitted that it would not be open to the court to deny regulation to the   **S30–188**

---

[34] E.C. Insolvency Regulation, Art. 3(4)(a), *supra*, Rule 159B.

[35] Virgos-Schmit, para. 91(a).

[36] Subject to Art. 5 (Rule 159D). See Isaacs, Toube, Segal and Marshall in Moss *et al.*, p. 96.

[37] *e.g.* in relation to the debtor, Art. 14 (*infra*, Rule 159M) (protection of third-party purchasers) and, in relation to the liquidator, Art. 18 (*infra*, Rule 159R) (powers of liquidator). See Virgos-Schmit, paras. 141, 159, 164. "Liquidator" would seem to bear the meaning given to that term in Art. 2(b): see Virgos-Schmit, para. 158.

[38] See Fletcher in Moss *et al.*, pp. 55–58; Isaacs, Toube, Segal and Marshall, *ibid.* pp. 96–97, 129–130; Moss and Smith, *ibid.* pp. 184–186; Segal (1997) 23 Brooklyn J. Int. L. 57, 65.

[39] The laws of the Member States differ considerably in their attitude to set-off: see *e.g.*, *Re Bank of Credit and Commerce S.A. (No. 10)* [1997] Ch. 213.

[40] Insolvency Rules 1986, r. 4.90. See *Re Bank of Credit and Commerce S.A. (No. 10)* [1997] Ch. 213. See main work, para. 30–075.

[41] Art. 17.

judgment on public policy grounds.[42] To comprehend fully the position in relation to set-off under the Regulation, it is necessary, at this stage, to refer to Article 6.[43] Whereas Article 4(2)(d) expresses the general rule, Article 6 introduces an exception. According to Article 6(1) the "opening of insolvency proceedings shall not affect the rights of creditors to demand the set-off of their claims against the claims of the debtor, where such a set-off is permitted by the law applicable to the insolvent debtor's claim". The effect of this rule is that where the law of the state of opening does not permit set-off, then a creditor may nonetheless rely on set-off if set-off is permitted by the law which governs the insolvent debtor's claim against the creditor. The law which governs the relevant claim will be determined, if the claim is contractual, by reference to choice of law rules for contracts.[44] Presumably, if the set-off emanates from a claim in tort, the relevant choice of law rules will be those applicable to tort.[45] It will be noted that Article 6 does not require that the law applicable to the insolvent debtor's claim be the law of a Member State. It is possible that such a requirement is implied,[46] but in view, for example, of the fact that the choice of law rules for contract as stated in the Rome Convention on the Law Applicable to Contractual Obligations do not limit the applicable law to that of a Member State,[47] it is suggested that a creditor may rely on any set-off permitted by the law of a non-Member State if that law is the applicable law of the contract.[48]

Article 6(2) makes it clear, however, that Article 6(1) does not preclude actions for voidness, voidability or unenforceability under the law of the State of opening, as contemplated by Article 4(2)(m).[49]

S30–189 **Article 4(2)(e).** This provision establishes the general principle that the law of the State of opening determines the effects of insolvency proceedings on current contracts to which the debtor is a party. Specific exceptions to this general principle are provided in Article 8, concerned with contracts relating to immovable property[50] and Article 10, concerned with contracts of employment.[51]

S30–190 **Article 4(2)(f).** According to Article 4(2)(f), the law of the State of opening governs the effects of the insolvency proceedings on proceedings brought by individual creditors, with the exception of lawsuits pending. This exception

---

[42] Although Insolvency Rules 1986, r. 4.90 may express, in some contexts, an overriding rule of public policy or, possibly, constitutes a mandatory rule of the law of the forum (see Fletcher [1997] J.B.L. 471, 473; Smart, pp. 319–321; *Stein v. Blake* [1996] A.C. 243, 251) it should not be so regarded for the purposes of Art. 26 of the Regulation. The Regulation contains no reservation in favour of the application of the mandatory rules of the law of the forum. And see Fletcher, in Fawcett (ed.), *Reform and Development of Private International Law* (2002), pp. 182–184.
[43] Rule 159E, *infra*.
[44] Main work, Rules 172 *et seq.*
[45] Main work, Rules 201 *et seq.*
[46] See Virgos-Schmit, para. 93; Bogdan in Moss *et al.*, p.184. The passage in Virgos-Schmit is notably ambiguous.
[47] See main work, para. 30–027.
[48] See Fletcher in Moss *et al.*, p.57.
[49] See *infra*, para. In relation to set-off regarding a payment or settlement system or a financial market, Art. 9 of the Regulation seems to require that the availability of such set-off is governed solely by the law of the Member State applicable to the relevant system or market: see *infra*, para. S30–325.
[50] See *infra*, Rule 159G.
[51] See *infra*, Rule 159I.

is the subject of separate treatment in Article 15 of the Regulation.[52] Article 4(2)(f) would seem to be concerned with questions such as whether there will be a stay on enforcement, commencement or continuation of legal proceedings after insolvency proceedings have been opened.[53] In this regard, however, it is not clear whether proceedings brought by creditors must be judicial proceedings to be caught by Article 4 (2)(f)[54] or whether it would be possible to include within the provision a statutory moratorium on proceedings,[55] or the appointment of a receiver without the assistance of a court.[56]

Article 4(2)(g). The law of the State of the opening will determine the claims which are to be lodged against the debtor's estate and the treatment of claims which arise after the opening of the insolvency proceedings. The provision will include the question of what debts are provable.

Article 4(2)(h). The law of the State of opening also governs the rules concerned with the lodging, verification and admission of claims. In principle, this provision includes all matters concerned with proof of debt procedure.[57]   S30–191

Chapter IV of the Regulation, entitled "Provision of Information for Creditors and Lodgement of their Claims,[58] "establishes certain uniform substantive rules which derogate from the application of national law as envisaged by Article 4(2)(h) and it is appropriate to consider these rules at this point.   S30–192

Normally, it will be for the national law of the State of opening to determine whether a creditor situated in that State has the right to lodge a claim.[59] Similarly, it would seem that that law will determine whether a creditor from outside the Member States has the right to lodge a claim.[60] Article 39 specifically provides, however, that any creditor who has his habitual residence, domicile or registered office in a Member State other than the State of the opening of proceedings, including the tax authorities and social security authorities of Member States, shall have the right to lodge claims in the insolvency proceedings in writing.[61] The most significant aspect of this provision is that it excludes the normal rule that the forum will not enforce foreign tax claims[62] from cases falling within the Regulation.[63]   S30–193

---

[52] See *post*, Rule 159N.
[53] Virgos-Schmit, para. 91(f).
[54] For discussion, see Isaacs, Toube, Segal and Marshall in Moss *et al.*, pp. 97–98, 107–114.
[55] Insolvency Act 1986, s.11(3)(*b*), (*c*) and (*d*).
[56] See main work, Rule 159.
[57] Including the time limit for lodging claims, the effect of a late lodgement, the admissibility and well-foundedness of the lodgement (Virgos-Schmit, para. 267) and "the costs, to the charge of a creditor, attached to the claim and to the verification of the debts" (*ibid.* para. 208).
[58] See Virgos-Schmit, paras. 264–277; Moss and Smith in Moss *et al.*, pp. 229–233.
[59] Virgos-Schmit, para. 269.
[60] *ibid.*
[61] Apparently, Art. 39 although giving creditors the right to lodge claims in writing does not prevent national law from permitting claims to be lodged in any other more favourable form for creditors: *ibid.* para. 270.
[62] See main work, Rule 3.
[63] Art. 39 does not affect the priority which a tax claim might enjoy. Priorities will be governed by the law of the State of opening. The claims of taxation authorities are often accorded a considerable preference in proceedings in their own States. For the abolition of Crown preference in England, see Enterprise Act 2002, s. 251 (not yet in force).

S30–194   Article 40 of the Regulation requires that as soon as insolvency proceedings are opened, the court of the State having jurisdiction or the liquidator appointed by it must immediately inform known creditors who have their habitual residences, domiciles or registered offices in the other Member States.[64] That information, provided by individual notice, must, in particular, include time limits, the penalties laid down in relation to time limits, the body or authority empowered to accept the lodgement of claims and the other measures laid down: the notice must also indicate whether creditors whose claims are preferential or secured *in rem* need lodge their claims.[65] The information referred to above must be provided in the official language or one of the official languages of the State of the opening proceedings.[66] A creditor is required to send copies of supporting documents, if any, and must indicate the nature of the claim, the date on which it arose and the amount, as well as whether he alleges preference,[67] security *in rem*[68] or a reservation of title in respect of the claim and what assets are covered by the guarantee[69] he is invoking.[70] Any creditor who has his habitual residence, domicile or registered office in a Member State other than the State of the opening of proceedings may lodge his claim in the official language or one of the official languages of that other State.[71]

S30–195   **Article 4(2)(i).** Importantly, the rules governing the distribution of proceeds from the realisation of assets, the ranking of claims[72] and the rights of creditors who have obtained partial satisfaction after the opening of insolvency proceedings by virtue of a right *in rem* or through a set-off[73] are also matters to be governed by the law of the State of opening. While the general purport of Article 4(2)(i) is clear, difficulties may arise in determining whether a particular rule of national law falls within its purview. For example, in an English liquidation certain categories of preferential debt rank ahead of the holder of a floating charge.[74] It has been suggested that it is arguable that although these rules are contained in English insolvency legislation they relate to the priority of security since they regulate the relationship between secured creditors and preferential creditors and are

---

[64] Art. 40(1).

[65] Art. 40(2).

[66] Art. 42(1). This provision also requires that a form shall be used bearing the heading "Invitation to lodge a claim. Time limits to be observed" in all the official languages of the institutions of the European Union.

[67] Which probably means "claims preferential ranking": see Moss and Smith in Moss *et al.*, p. 232.

[68] *cf.* Insolvency Act 1986, s. 248(*b*)(i). See Moss and Smith, *ibid*. The precise meaning of "security *in rem*" is most unclear: *ibid*.

[69] This term seems to be intended to be generally descriptive of "preference" "security *in rem*" and "reservation of title".

[70] Art. 41.

[71] Art. 42(2). The lodgement of claim must bear the heading "Lodgement of claim" in the official language or one of the official languages of the State of opening of proceedings. Additionally, the creditor may be required to provide a translation into the official language or one of the official languages of the State of opening of proceedings: *ibid*.

[72] See *supra*, n. 63. The same claim may rank differently in main and secondary proceedings: see Virgos-Schmit, para. 91(i).

[73] *i.e.* whether a creditor who has obtained partial satisfaction in this way can claim in the insolvency proceedings for the balance of the claim.

[74] Insolvency Act 1986, s. 175(2)(*b*). This is not the case where the company creates a fixed charge over its assets: *Re Lewis Merthyr Consolidated Collieries* [1929] 1 Ch. 498; Lightman & Moss, *The Law of Receivers and Administrators of Companies* (3rd ed., 2000), pp. 402–403.

not, therefore, an effect of the insolvency procedure.[75] It is suggested, however, that such rules should, adopting a purposive interpretation of Article 4(2)(i), be treated as falling within that provision, since they are rules that may fall to be applied in winding up in an appropriate case.

Article 4(2)(j). According to this provision, the law of the State of opening governs the conditions for and effects of closure of insolvency proceedings, in particular by composition. Thus, for example, the question of whether main proceedings bring about a variation or discharge of the claims of a creditor because the main proceedings are closed by a company voluntary arrangement will be determined by the law of the State of the opening.[76] Indeed, it would also appear that where main proceedings in another Member State have been closed by a composition and that has the effect of discharging the obligations of the debtor, then an English court will have to recognize this effect even if there is no discharge of the liability according to the law applicable to the contract if the claim arises out of a contract.[77] This is contrary to the position adopted by English common law,[78] where a discharge from any debt or liability under the insolvency law of a foreign country outside the United Kingdom is regarded as a discharge therefrom in England if, and only if, it is a discharge under the law applicable to the contract.[79]

Article 4(2)(k). The law of the State of opening will govern creditors' rights after the closure of insolvency proceedings. There would appear to be an overlap between this provision and Article 4(2)(j): according to the Virgos-Schmit Report it is this provision (rather than the provision previously discussed) which governs discharge of the debtor.[80] Since both provisions apply the law of the State of opening, this difference produces no practical effect.[81] S30–196

Article 4(2)(l). This provides quite simply that the law of the State of opening will determine who is to bear the costs and expenses incurred in the insolvency proceedings. S30–197

Article 4(2)(m). This Article is of considerable importance and provides that the law of the State of opening will govern the rules relating to the voidness, voidability or unenforceability of legal acts detrimental to all the creditors.[82] Thus the extent to which and the method by which the debtor's pre-insolvency transactions can be struck down will be determined by the law of the State of opening, which State's law will also determine the extent S30–198

---

[75] See Isaacs, Toube, Segal and Marshall in Moss *et al.*, pp. 99–100, 112–113.

[76] For English law, see Insolvency Act 1986, s. 5(2), as amended by Insolvency Act 2000, Sched. 2.

[77] Art. 17.

[78] See Fletcher, in Fawcett (ed.), *Reform and Development of Private International Law* (2002), pp. 184–186; Isaacs, Toube, Segal and Marshall in Moss *et al.*, pp. 100, 123.

[79] *Gibbs v. Société Industrielle des Métaux* (1890) 25 Q.B.D. 399 (C.A.), approved by the House of Lords in *National Bank of Greece and Athens S.A. v. Metliss* [1958] A.C. 509. See main work, Rule 170.

[80] Virgos-Schmit, para. 91(k).

[81] Indeed the issue of discharge of a contractual obligation (other than in respect of a contract relating to immovable property or a contract of employment) could also be fitted into Art. 4(2)(e), *supra*, para. S30–189.

[82] It appears that "all the creditors" is not to be interpreted as "each and every creditor" but rather as the "general body of creditors": see Moss and Smith in Moss *et al.*, p.180.

to which and the methods by which acts and proprietary transactions effected by the debtor after the opening of proceedings can be impeached. In this regard, the law of the State of opening displaces the law normally applicable to the act or transaction in question.[83] Consequently only one system of law will normally be applicable to the matters falling within Article 4(2)(m).

S30–199 According to the Virgos-Schmit Report, in the case of secondary proceedings the local rules of the State of opening of such proceedings which are concerned with invalidation of a detrimental act will be applicable only in so far as damage has been caused to the debtor's assets which are situated in that State, as for example, where an asset sold is located in that State at the relevant time.[84]

S30–200 It is appropriate at this point to refer to Article 13[85] which places a limit on the operation of Article 4(2)(m). Article 13 provides that Article 4(2)(m) will not apply where the person who benefited from an act detrimental to all the creditors[86] provides proof that the said act is subject to the law of a Member State other than that of the State of the opening of proceedings, *and* that law does not allow any means of challenging that act in the relevant case.

S30–201 The purpose of Article 13 is to permit a "defence" to the application of the law of the State of opening which acts as a "veto" against the invalidity of the act "decreed by"[87] the latter State's law. For the provision to operate it must first be established by the person who benefited from the relevant act that the relevant act is "subject to" the law of a Member State other than the State of the opening. The expression "subject to" appears to equate to "governed by" and might involve a choice of law question, presumably to be determined by the relevant choice of law rules of the law of the forum.[88] Secondly, the person who benefited must prove that the law applicable to the relevant act does not permit the act to be challenged by "any means" in the "relevant case". The former expression is intended to convey the notion that the act cannot be challenged either under the rules of insolvency law or under the general law of the particular Member State which is applicable to the act in question.[89] The latter expression is intended to indicate that the act must not be capable of being challenged in the particular circumstances of the case in hand. It is not enough to show that the act can not be challenged "in the abstract".[90]

S30–202 The purpose of Article 13 is the protection of the expectations of creditors and third parties who will have acted under the belief (if such proves to be

---

[83] Virgos-Schmit, para. 91(m). Examples in English insolvency law include Insolvency Act 1986, ss. 238, 239: see main work, paras. 30–081—30–085.

[84] Virgos-Schmit, para. 91, last sub-paragraph.

[85] *infra*, Rule 159L.

[86] The same point as that made in n. 82, *supra*, applies here as well.

[87] Virgos-Schmit, para. 136.

[88] *e.g.* if the act is a contract, the law applicable to the contract determined according to Rules 172 *et seq.*

[89] Virgos-Schmit, para. 137.

[90] *ibid.*

the case) that the relevant act is legally effective under the national law applicable to it.[91] The potentially retroactive nature of a subsequently opened insolvency proceeding should not be allowed to defeat those expectations.[92] It follows from this that Article 13 does not apply to save acts which occur after the opening of insolvency proceedings.[93] The powers to attack those acts depend upon Article 4(2)(m).

Clause (3) of the Rule. This clause reproduces Article 28 of the Regulation. **S30–203** Except as otherwise indicated, the law applicable to secondary proceedings will be the law of the Member State in which those proceedings are opened. Article 28 "reiterates"[94] the principles of Article 4 (clauses (1) and (2) of the Rule) in the context of secondary proceedings. It will be recalled, however, that the opening of secondary proceedings can only affect assets situated in the Member State where those proceedings are opened.[95] Similarly, the law of the State in which those proceedings are opened will only have effect in relation to those assets.[96] Consequently, the identical claims made in main and secondary proceedings may well be adjudicated by reference to different laws.[97]

ILLUSTRATIONS

1. X is a company with its centre of main interests in England. Winding-up proceedings **S30–204** (main proceedings) are opened in England in respect of X. A, an English bank, holds a fixed charge over certain assets belonging to X. English law will determine whether those assets form part of X's estate.[98]

2. X is a company with its centre of main interests in Luxembourg. X is insolvent and liquidation proceedings (main proceedings) are opened in Luxembourg. X has no establishment in England. X is indebted to A, a Luxembourg bank, in respect of an unpaid loan. X has two bank accounts at the English branch of the bank which are in credit. These accounts are expressed to be governed by the law of Luxembourg. The Luxembourg liquidator claims these sums.[99] A cannot claim set-off since although set-off is permitted by English law[1], it is not permitted by Luxembourg law.[2]

3. The facts are the same as in Illustration 2, except that X has an establishment in England and A opens secondary proceedings (winding-up proceedings) in England. A can rely on any set off permitted by English law.[3]

4. X is a company with its centre of main interests in England and assets consisting of two bank accounts in credit at the A bank in Luxembourg. Main proceedings (winding-up proceedings) are opened, in respect of X, in England. Whether A can set-off the sums in the bank accounts against X's total indebtedness to A is governed by English law.[4]

5. X is a company with its centre of main interests in France. X is insolvent, and main proceedings (*liquidation judiciaire*) are opened against X in France. X has two accounts

---

[91] *ibid.* para. 138.

[92] *ibid.*

[93] *ibid.* Art. 13 will apply in both main and secondary proceedings (*ibid.* para. 139) and, presumably, also in territorial proceedings.

[94] Virgos-Schmit, para. 225.

[95] Art. 3(2).

[96] Virgos-Schmit, para. 91, final sub-paragraph.

[97] *e.g., ibid.* para. 91(a).

[98] E.C. Insolvency Regulation, Art. 4(1), 4(2)(b).

[99] *ibid.* Arts. 17,18.

[1] Insolvency Rules 1986, r. 4.90.

[2] E.C. Insolvency Regulation, Art. 4(1), 4(2)(d). *Cf. Re Bank of Credit and Commerce International S.A. (No. 10)* [1997] Ch. 213.

[3] *ibid.*

[4] *ibid.*

with A bank, an English bank, in London, which are expressed to be governed by English law. By English law though not by French law, A has a right to set off these amounts against X's total indebtedness to A. A may claim the right to set-off in English law in the French insolvency proceedings.[5]

6. X is a company with its centre of main interests in England. X is indebted to the taxation authorities of the Netherlands in respect of unpaid taxes. Main proceedings (winding-up proceedings) are opened against X in England. The Netherlands taxation authorities may prove for the unpaid taxes in the English proceedings.[6]

7. X is a company with its centre of main interests in Luxembourg and an establishment in England. X is insolvent. Main proceedings are opened in respect of X in Luxembourg. A, a creditor of X, lodges its claim in the Luxembourg proceedings. Secondary proceedings in relation to X are opened in England. A lodges a claim in these proceedings. The ranking of A's claim in the Luxembourg proceedings will be determined by the law of Luxembourg.[7] The ranking of A's claim in the English proceedings will be governed by English law.[8]

8. X is a company with its centre of main interests in France. By a contract governed by English law, A, who carries on business in England, agrees to sell copper to X. X refuses to accept, and to pay for, the copper tendered by A. Subsequently, main proceedings (*liquidation judiciaire*) are opened against X in France. As a result, X's liability is, by French law, deemed to be discharged. A claims damages from X in England. The claim does not succeed for although X's liability is not discharged under English law, the law applicable to the contract, the English court must recognise the discharge under French law.[9]

9. X is a company with its centre of main interests in England. X is insolvent. Main proceedings (winding-up proceedings) are opened, in respect of X, in England. Prior to the opening of these proceedings X had entered into a transaction with A, governed by English law by which X transferred a Rolls Royce, owned by the company, to A, as a gift. Whether the English court will, at the instance of the liquidator, set aside this transaction will be determined by the Insolvency Act 1986, s. 238.[10]

10. X is a company with its centre of main interests in England. X is insolvent. Main proceedings (winding-up proceedings) are opened, in respect of X, in England. Prior to the opening of proceedings, X has sold property belonging to the company in France to A S.A, a French company. It appears that, by English law, the transaction would constitute a transaction at an undervalue, contrary to Insolvency Act 1986, s. 238. A S.A. establishes that its transaction with X is subject to French law. A S.A. also establishes that French law does not allow any means of challenging the transaction in the particular circumstances of the case. The English court will not, at the instance of the liquidator, make an order under Insolvency Act 1986, s. 238 against A S.A.[11]

S30R–205 **RULE 159D—(1) The opening of insolvency proceedings shall not affect the rights *in rem* of creditors or third parties in respect of tangible or intangible, moveable or immoveable assets – both specific assets and collections of indefinite assets as a whole which change from time to time – belonging to the debtor which are situated within the territory of another Member State at the time of the opening of proceedings.**

(2) The rights referred to in clause (1) shall in particular mean:

(a) the right to dispose of assets or have them disposed of and to obtain satisfaction from the proceeds of or income from those assets, in particular by virtue of a lien or a mortgage;

(b) the exclusive right to have a claim met, in particular a right guaranteed by a lien in respect of the claim or by assignment of the claim by way of a guarantee;

---

[5] E.C. Insolvency Regulation, Art. 6.

[6] *ibid.* Arts. 4(1), 4(2)(h), 39.

[7] *ibid.* Art. 4(1), 4(2)(i).

[8] *ibid.*

[9] *ibid*. Arts. 4(1), 4(2)(j), (k) and 17. *Cf. Gibbs v. Société Industrielle des Métaux* (1890) 25 Q.B.D. 399 (C.A.).

[10] E.C. Insolvency Regulation, Art. 4(1), 4(2)(m).

[11] *ibid*. Art. 13.

(c) **the right to demand the assets from, and/or to require restitution by anyone having possession or use of them contrary to the wishes of the party so entitled;**

(d) **a right *in rem* to the beneficial use of assets.**

(3) The right, recorded in a public register and enforceable against third parties, under which a right *in rem* within the meaning of clause (1) may be obtained, shall be considered a right *in rem*.

(4) Clause (1) shall not preclude actions for voidness, voidability or unenforceability as referred to in Article 4(2)(m) (Rule 159C (2)(m)).[12]

COMMENT

This Rule reproduces Article 5 of the E.C. Insolvency Regulation which is headed "Third Parties' rights in rem". The provisions of Article 5 constitute an exception, of some practical importance, to the general choice of law rule, stated in Article 4(1) of the Regulation (Rule 159C (1)), to the effect that the law applicable to insolvency proceedings and their effects shall be the law of the Member State within the territory of which such proceedings are opened. Article 5 also constitutes an exception to the general principle that main insolvency proceedings have universal effect in relation to all the assets of the debtor which are situated in the Member States.[13] Very broadly, as stated in Article 5(1), the provision aims at protecting rights *in rem* of creditors and third parties over assets of the debtor situated in a Member State other than the Member State in which the proceedings are opened from being affected by the opening of the insolvency proceedings. The justification of the provision is the pursuit of the "fundamental policy. . . to protect the trade in the State where the assets are situated and legal certainty of the rights over them. Rights *in rem* have a very important function with regard to credit and the mobilization of wealth. They insulate their holders against the risk of insolvency of the debtor and the interference of third parties. They allow credit to be obtained under conditions that would not be possible without this type of guarantee."[14] The following questions of interpretation call for discussion. **S30–206**

Situation of assets. Article 5 only applies if the relevant asset is situated in Member States other than that of the opening of proceedings: where assets are situated in a non-Member State, the provision has no application[15] and the applicable law will, instead, be determined by Article 4 (where the law of the State of opening may make reference to the law of that non-Member State as the *lex situs* of the relevant asset).[16] It follows that, for the purposes **S30–207**

---

[12] E.C. Insolvency Regulation, Art. 5. See Virgos-Schmit, paras. 94–106; Fletcher, *Insolvency in Private International Law* (1999), pp. 269–273; Morse, in Borchers and Zekoll (eds.), *International Conflict of Laws for the Third Millenium: Essays in Honor of Friedrich K. Juenger* p. 233, at pp. 248–250; Fletcher in Moss *et al.*, pp. 50–55; Isaacs, Toube, Segal and Marshall, *ibid*. Chap. 6; Moss and Smith, *ibid*. pp. 181–184; Balz (1996) 70 American Bankruptcy L.J. 485, 508–511; Segal (1997) 23 Brooklyn J. Int. L. 57, 62–65. See also Insurance Undertakings Insolvency Directive, Art. 20; Credit Institutions Insolvency Directive, Art. 21.
[13] Virgos-Schmit, para. 95.
[14] *ibid.* para. 97. See, in particular, Recitals (24) and (25).
[15] Virgos-Schmit, para. 94.
[16] See Fletcher in Moss *et al.*, p. 53. And see main work, para. 30–123.

of Article 5, it may be necessary to determine where an asset is situated. Some guidance on this issue is to be found in Article 2(g) of the Regulation.[17] where it is stipulated that the Member State in which assets are situated shall mean in the case of (a) tangible property, the Member State in which the property is situated; (b) property and rights ownership of or entitlement to which must be entered in a public register, the Member State under the authority, of which the register is kept; and (c) claims, the Member State in which the third party required to meet them has its centre of main interests, as determined in Article 3(1).[18] The last part of this definition may, in some cases, lead to curious outcomes. Thus, if the debtor has a bank account in England with the English branch of a Luxembourg bank, the definition suggests that the bank account (the relevant claim or asset) is situated in Luxembourg rather than England.[19]

S30–208 The relevant time for identifying the *situs* of the asset is the time of opening of proceedings.[20] This might create difficulties (usually with regard to tangible moveable assets) for a creditor or third party holding a right *in rem* in such as asset which is enforceable under the law of the *situs* of the asset at the time of the creation of the right *in rem* if by the time of the opening of proceedings the asset has been moved to another Member State which does not recognise the right *in rem*. Equally, prior to the opening such an asset might be moved from the Member State in which proceedings are subsequently opened to another Member State and a right *in rem* created over that asset, as permitted by that Member State, which right *in rem* would not be recognised in the State of the opening of proceedings. In the latter situation, Aritcle 5(4) (clause 4 of the Rule) enables Article 4(2)(m) to be invoked in the State of opening, in an appropriate case, to set aside the transaction.[21]

S30–209 **Meaning of "assets".** Article 5(1) includes within its scope a wide range of assets: these may be tangible or intangible (including claims[22]), movable and immovable assets including specific assets and collections of indefinite assets as a whole which change from time to time. The reference to "specific assets and collections of indefinite assets" etc. did not appear in the earlier proposed Convention but was inserted into Article 5(1) of the Regulation to remove any uncertainty as to whether Article 5 applies to floating charges, as understood in the United Kingdom (and the Republic of Ireland).[23]

S30–210 **Meaning of "right *in rem*".** According to the Virgos-Schmit Report, Article 5 of the proposed Convention referred to rights *in rem* without defining what such rights were.[24] The characterisation of a right as a right *in rem* had

---

[17] See *supra*, paras. S30–167 *et seq.*
[18] See *supra*, para. S30–158.
[19] See Isaacs, Toube, Segal and Marshall in Moss *et al.*, p. 105. *Cf.* main work, Rule 112.
[20] Art. 5(1).
[21] *ante*, Rule 159C (2)(m). See Virgos-Schmit, paras 105–106.
[22] Art. 2(g). See also main work, Rule 112.
[23] See Fletcher in Moss *et al.*, pp. 54–55. A passage in the Virgos-Schmit Report envisaged that "security rights such as the floating charge recognised in the United Kingdom and Irish law" were to be characterised as rights *in rem* under the proposed earlier Convention: see para. 104.
[24] Virgos-Schmit, para. 100.

to be "sought" in the national law which, according to the normal pre-insolvency conflict of laws rules, governs rights *in rem* (in general, the *lex rei sitae* at the relevant time).[25] The only departure from this view was to be found in what is now Article 5(3) of the Regulation (clause (3) of the Rule).[26] This makes specific specific provision to the effect that a right, recorded in a public register and enforceable against third parties, under which a right *in rem* is obtained within the meaning of Article 5(1) is to be considered a right *in rem*. Nonetheless, the Virgos-Schmit Report countenanced against "an unreasonably wide interpretation of the national concept of a right *in rem* so as to include, for example, rights simply reinforced by a right to claim preferential payment".[27] Accordingly, what is now Article 5(2) of the Regulation provides a non-exhaustive list of the rights which are covered by Article 5(1), a list which is at least a partial definition of such rights and which consists of rights which "are normally considered by national laws as rights *in rem*".[28]

The guidance provided by Article 5(2) is somewhat general and its application will depend on the extent to which alleged rights *in rem* existing under national law correspond with the characteristics identified in the provision (which is in any event not exhaustive). Characteristics will include (a) the right to dispose of assets or have them disposed of and to obtain satisfaction from the proceeds or income from those assets, in particular by virtue of a lien or a mortgage[29]; (b) the exclusive right to have a claim met, in particular a right guaranteed by a lien in respect of the claim or by assignment of the claim by way of a guarantee[30]; (c) the right to demand the assets from, and/or to require restitution by, anyone having possession or use of them contrary to the wishes of the party so entitled[31]; and (d) a right *in rem* to the beneficial use of assets.[32] **S30–211**

The list set out above was inspired by two considerations which may be helpful in the elucidation of whether, in any given case, the relevant right is a right *in rem*.[33] The first consideration is that a right which exists or arises only *after* insolvency proceedings have been opened is not a right *in rem* for the purposes of Article 5.[34] It is of the essence that the right be created or otherwise arise *before* insolvency proceedings are opened.[35] The second consideration is that a right *in rem* basically has two characteristics. The first is that the right has a direct and immediate relationship with the asset it covers, "which remains linked to its satisfaction without depending on the asset belonging to a person's estate or on the relationship between the holder of the right *in rem* and another person".[36] The second is the absolute **S30–212**

---

[25] *ibid*: see Recital (25).
[26] *ibid.* para. 101.
[27] *ibid.* para. 102.
[28] *ibid.* para. 103.
[29] Art. 5(2)(a).
[30] Art. 5(2)(b). "Guaranteed" would seem to mean "secured" and "guarantee" would seem to mean "security".
[31] Art. 5(2)(c).
[32] Art. 5(2)(d).
[33] Virgos-Schmit, para. 103.
[34] *ibid*. The nature of any rights allegedly created after the opening of insolvency proceedings will be governed by Art. 4.
[35] *ibid*.
[36] *ibid*.

nature of the allocation of the right to the holder. A person who holds a right *in rem* can enforce it against anyone who breaches or harms his right, and can enforce such right against third parties even in collective insolvency proceedings, where the right-holder may exercise the right to separate the right from the estate and, as necessary, realise the asset individually to satisfy his claim.[37]

S30–213   As mentioned above, Article 5 appears to cover floating charges as understood in the law of the United Kingdom and the Republic of Ireland.[38] It is also apt to cover fixed charges, *e.g.* over receivables and book debts,[39] though the laws of other Member States may not classify such rights as rights *in rem*. Article 5 covers liens and mortgages[40] as well as the classical security by way of pledge.[41]

S30–214   **Main proceedings and secondary proceedings**. Where main proceedings are opened in the Member State where the debtor's centre of main interests is situated, then Article 5 protects the right of a creditor or third party who holds a right *in rem* over an asset situated in another Member State. Such creditor or third party may therefore enforce his right in that other Member State by realising the asset, though it would appear that any surplus after the realisation may be claimed by the liquidator in the main proceedings.[42] If there is no such surplus so that, say, the creditor claims in the main proceedings for the balance due to him, as secured by the right *in rem*, then that creditor would have to bring the fruits of his earlier execution into hotchpot.[43] Where the debtor has an establishment[44] in the Member State in which the asset is situated then the liquidator may open secondary proceedings in that State. In such proceedings the liquidator may rely on any relevant rules of the national law of that Member State which might regard the opening of secondary proceedings as affecting the right *in rem* in some way.[45] Where the right *in rem* is not so affected any surplus after realisation of the asset may be claimed by the liquidator since Article 5 stipulates that the proceedings shall not affect a right *in rem*: it does not stipulate that the proceedings do not affect the assets subject to that right.[46]

S30–215   **Clause (4) of the Rule.**Article 5(4) makes it clear that the exception to the general rule applicable by way of Article 4 which is contained in Article 5(1) does not operate so as to preclude actions in relation to voidness, voidability or unenforceability of legal acts detrimental to the interests of all the creditors. Such issues will be subject to the law of the State of opening in accordance with Article 4(2)(m).[47]

---

[37] *ibid.*
[38] *supra*, para. S30–209.
[39] Fletcher in Moss *et al.*, pp. 54–55.
[40] Art. 5(2)(a) and (b).
[41] See main work, Rule 183.
[42] Recital (25); Virgos-Schmit, para. 99.
[43] Art. 20.
[44] *supra*, para. S30–164.
[45] Recital (25); Virgos-Schmit, para. 99.
[46] Virgos-Schmit, *ibid.*
[47] *Supra*, para. S30–198. See also Art. 13.

ILLUSTRATIONS

1. X is a company with its centre of main interests in France. X has no establishment in **S30–216**
England, but it owns a large quantity of whisky which is situated in a warehouse in
England, operated by B. X borrows a sum of money from A Bank, an English bank, which
takes a fixed charge over the whisky to secure the loan. Insolvency proceedings (main
proceedings) are subsequently opened in respect of X in France. A Bank may realise its
security in England by disposing of the whisky, but must turn over any surplus to the
liquidator of X.[48]

2. X is a company with its centre of main interests in France. X has an establishment in
London. X creates a floating charge over its English assets in favour of A Bank, an English
bank, as security for a loan. Insolvency proceedings are subsequently opened in respect of
X in France. A Bank may realise its security in England by enforcing its charge.[49] The
liquidator of X may open secondary proceedings in England, in which he can rely on, *e.g.*
the provisions of the Insolvency Act 1986[50] concerned with extortionate credit transactions,
if relevant, to attack the charge.[51] Alternatively, it there are no such grounds he may claim
any surplus after the realisation of the assets from A Bank.[52]

3. X is a company with its centre of main interests in England. X creates a floating
charge in English form, over its assets in France, in favour of A Bank, an English bank. X
has no establishment in France. Insolvency proceedings (main proceedings) are opened, in
respect of X, in England. As a matter of English law (law of the State of opening), the
charge extends to X's French assets.[53] But whether A Bank can enforce its charge in
France will depend on French law.[54]

RULE 159E—(1) The opening of insolvency proceedings shall not affect the S30R–217
rights of creditors to demand the set-off of their claims against the claims
of the debtor, where such a set-off is permitted by the law applicable to the
insolvent debtor's claim.

(2) Clause (1) shall not preclude actions for voidness, voidability or
unenforceability as referred to in Article 4(2)(m) (Rule 159C (2)(m)).[55]

COMMENT

This Rule reproduces Article 6 of the E.C. Insolvency Regulation (headed **S30–218**
"Set-off"). It has already been discussed in the context of Article 4(2)(d)
(Rule 159C (1)(d)).[56]

RULE 159F—(1) The opening of insolvency proceedings against the pur- S30R–219
chaser of an asset shall not affect the seller's rights based on a reservation
of title where at the time of the opening of proceedings the asset is situated
within the territory of a Member State other than the State of opening of
proceedings.

(2) The opening of insolvency proceedings against the seller of an asset,
after delivery of the asset, shall not constitute grounds for rescinding or

---

[48] E.C. Insolvency Regulation, Art. 5.
[49] *ibid*.
[50] Insolvency Act 1986, s. 244.
[51] E.C. Insolvency Regulation, Arts. 4(2)(m), 5(4) and 28.
[52] *ibid*; Recital (25); Virgos-Schmit, para. 99.
[53] *Re Anchor Line (Henderson Brothers) Ltd*. [1937] Ch. 483 (C.A.).
[54] E.C. Insolvency Regulation, Art. 5. For a discussion of the position in French law, see
Kessedjian, in *Cross-Border Security and Insolvency* (Bridge and Stevens, eds. 2001), p. 159, at pp.
173–177.
[55] E.C. Insolvency Regulation, Art. 6. See also Insurance Undertakings Insolvency Directive, Art.
22; Credit Institutions Insolvency Directive, Art. 23.
[56] *supra*, para. S30–188.

terminating the sale and shall not prevent the purchaser from acquiring title where at the time of the opening of proceedings the asset is situated within the territory of a Member State other than the State of the opening of proceedings.

(3) Clauses (1) and (2) shall not preclude actions for voidness, voidability or unenforceability as referred to in Article 4(2)(m) (Rule 159C (2)(m)).[57]

COMMENT

S30–220 Rule 159F reproduces Article 7 of the E.C. Insolvency Regulation (headed "Reservation of title"). It constitutes a further exception to the general principle of Article 4 that the applicable law in that of the law of the State of the opening of proceedings. The approach of the national laws of the Member States to clauses in a contract of sale reserving title in the seller so as to protect the seller (should he be unpaid) in the event of the buyers' insolvency is by no means uniform[58] and therefore a special rule was necessary to achieve more certainty and to protect trade.[59]

S30–221 **Clause (1) of the Rule.** Article 7(1), as reproduced in this clause, deals with the situation in which insolvency proceedings are opened against the purchaser of an asset for which the price has not been paid in full. In such a situation the seller's rights based on a reservation of title are not affected by the opening of proceedings if the relevant asset is situated, at the time of the opening, in a Member State other than the State of the opening.[60] Accordingly, any provision of the law of the State of opening which might render the reservation of title clause void or otherwise ineffective against the liquidator in the insolvency proceedings will not affect the seller's right to claim the asset if the seller has the right to claim the asset under the law of the Member State where it is situated. It also seems that it is irrelevant to the application of Article 7(1) that the asset is moved to a Member State different to the other Member State in which it was originally located after the opening of the insolvency proceedings.[61]

S30–222 Article 7(1) is of relatively straight forward application in a case of "simple" reservation of title where the seller merely reserves title in goods (tangible movables) until the price is paid in full. But often reservation of title clauses

---

[57] E.C. Insolvency Regulation, Art. 7. See Virgos-Schmit, paras 112–115; Fletcher, *Insolvency in Private International Law* (1999), pp. 275–277; Morse in Borchers and Zekoll (eds.), *International Conflict of Laws for the Third Millenium: Essays in Honor of Friedrich K. Juenger* (2001), p. 233, at pp. 251–252; Fletcher in Moss *et al.*, pp. 58–59; Moss and Smith, *ibid.* pp.186–187. For a discussion of reservation of title in English private international law, see main work, paras 33–111 *et seq; Benjamin's Sale of Goods* (6th ed., 2002), paras 25–134 *et seq.* For comparative studies, see Voskuil and Wade (eds), *Hague-Zagreb Essays on the Law of International Trade*, Vol. 5 (1985), pp. 54 *et seq*; Schilling (1985) 34 I.C.L.Q. 87; Kreuzer, 1995 Rev. Crit. 465. For discussion of German conflict of laws rules, see Drobnig, in Bridge and Stevens (eds.), *Cross-Border Security and Insolvency* (2001), Chap. 8. For discussion of French conflict of laws rules, see Kessedjian, *ibid.* Chap. 9. See also Insurance Undertakings Insolvency Directive, Art. 21; Credit Institutions Insolvency Directive, Art. 22.
[58] See Pennington (1978) 27 I.C.L.Q. 277.
[59] Virgos-Schmit, para. 112.
[60] As to where an asset may be situated, see *supra*, paras. S30–167 *et seq.*, S30–207 *et seq.*
[61] Virgos-Schmit, para. 113.

in a contract of sale contain much more sophisticated provisions.[62] For example, a reservation of title clause may give the seller a right to the proceeds of sale of an asset[63] and it is not clear how such a provision fits in (if at all) to Article 7(1). Further, if the purchaser has sold the original asset but is holding the proceeds of sale on behalf of the seller, as required by the reservation of title clause, do the proceeds of sale become the relevant asset[64]? It is not even stated in Article 7(1) that the *lex situs* is the applicable law which will determine whether the reservation of title is effective, though it would seem that such an outcome is to be inferred.[65] Clearly, in the interests of consistency and uniformity in the application of this provision, it would be desirable if it were interpreted in as autonomous and uniform fashion in the various Member States.

Article 7(1) will not apply at all if, at the time of the opening of **S30–223** proceedings, the asset is situated in a non-Member State. In such a case the law of the State of opening (including its rules on private international law, which may make reference to the *situs* of the asset) will determine the applicable law pursuant to the general rule in Article 4.

Clause (2) of the Rule. Article 7(2), as reproduced in this clause, is **S30–224** concerned with the situation where insolvency proceedings are opened against the seller of an asset after delivery of that asset. In such a situation, the opening of insolvency proceedings shall not constitute grounds for rescinding or terminating the sale and shall not prevent the purchaser from acquiring title where, at the time of the opening of the proceedings the asset sold is situated in a Member State other than the State of the opening of proceedings. This rule is not a choice of law rule but a uniform rule of substantive law.[66] Its effect is that where, pursuant to a reservation of title clause, the seller retains ownership of the asset even after delivery so that the asset might be part of the debtor's estate which can be claimed by the liquidator, the purchaser, nonetheless, may acquire title since the sale will remain valid.[67]

Article 7(2) has no application if the asset is located in a non-Member **S30–225** State. In such a case the law of the State of opening (including its rules of private international law, which may make reference to the *lex situs*) will determine the applicable law.

Clause (3) of the Rule. This clause (Article 7(3) of the Regulation) **S30–226** preserves the applicability of Article 4(2)(m) enabling actions for voidness, voidability or unenforceability to be taken where relevant.[68]

---

[62] See main work, paras 33–111 *et seq.* and references in n. 57, *supra*.

[63] *ibid.*

[64] If the purchaser holds the proceeds of sale in trust for the seller (*cf. Kruppstahl A.G. v. Quittmann Products Ltd.* [1982] I.L.R.M. 551 and main work, para. 33–113), does this give the seller "a right *in rem* to the beneficial use of assets" so that Art. 5 of the Regulation becomes relevant?

[65] The reservation of title clause will be contained in a contract of sale so that the law applicable to that contract may become relevant to some issues: see Fletcher in Moss *et al.*, p. 59.

[66] Virgos-Schmit, para. 112.

[67] The purchaser will acquire title at the end of the payment period set out in the contract if he continues to make the required payments: *ibid.* para.114.

[68] See *supra*, paras. S30–198 *et seq.*

ILLUSTRATIONS

S30–227 1. X is a company with its centre of main interests in England. It purchases goods from A, a French company, the contract of sale containing a reservation of title clause in favour of A until X pays the price in full. While the goods are still in France, winding-up proceedings are opened, in respect of X, in England. A can enforce its reservation of title in respect of the goods even if the reservation of title clause is ineffective by English law.[69]

2. X is a company with its centre of main interests in England. X sells goods to A, a French company, the contract of sale containing a reservation of title clause in favour of X until A pays the price. After the goods have been delivered to A in France, winding-up proceedings are opened, in respect of X, in England. The opening of such proceedings shall not constitute grounds for rescinding or terminating the sale and shall not prevent the purchaser, A, from acquiring title to the goods.[70]

S30R–228 RULE 159G—**The effects of insolvency proceedings on a contract conferring the right to acquire or make use of immoveable property shall be governed solely by the law of the Member State within the territory of which the immoveable property is situated.**[71]

COMMENT

S30–229 This Rule sets out the terms of Article 8 of the E.C. Insolvency Regulation (headed "Contracts relating to immoveable property"). It constitutes an exception to the general choice of law rule that the law of the Member State of the opening of proceedings governs those proceedings,[72] including the effects of insolvency proceedings or current contracts to which the debtor is a party.[73] The justification of the exception, which involves making reference to the *lex situs* of the immovable, is that such contracts are, in the national law of Member States, subject to special rules for the choice of law and for international jurisdiction.[74] Further, it is necessary to make reference to the *lex situs* so as to properly take account of the interests of the parties to the contract and the general interests protected by the Member State in which the immovable property is situated.[75]

S30–230 The effect of Article 8 is that the effects of the opening of insolvency proceedings on contracts conferring the right to acquire or make use of immovable property are governed solely by the law of the Member State in which the immovable property is situated. No other State's law can ever be relevant to this issue since Article 8 constitutes an exclusive rule.[76] For the purpose of the rule the reference to the law of the Member State in which the immovable is situated includes a reference to the insolvency law of that State.[77] It must be emphasised that the rule in Article 8 is limited to

---

[69] E.C Insolvency Regulation, Art. 7(1).

[70] *ibid.* Art. 7(2).

[71] E.C. Insolvency Regulation, Art. 8. See Virgos-Schmit, paras. 116–119; Fletcher in Moss *et al.*, pp. 59–60; Moss and Smith, *ibid.* p. 187. See also Insurance Undertakings Insolvency Directive, Art. 19(b); Credit Institutions Insolvency Directive, Art. 20(b).

[72] E.C. Insolvency Regulation, Art. 4(1).

[73] *ibid.* Art. 4(2)(e).

[74] Virgos-Schmit, para. 118.

[75] *ibid.*

[76] This is indicated by the presence of the word "solely" in the provision. The law applicable to the contract (see main work, Rule 188) is irrelevant: Virgos-Schmit, para. 117.

[77] *ibid.* para. 118.

contracts "to acquire" or "make use of" immovable property. Specific examples given are, in relation to the former expression, contracts for the sale of immovable property and, in relation to the latter expression, contracts to rent or to lease immovable property.[78]

Article 8 only applies in cases where the immovable property is situated in a Member State. If such property is situated in a non-Member State the effect of the insolvency proceedings on such property will be determined by the law of the State of opening,[79] including its conflict of laws rules which might, in a particular case, make reference to the *lex situs*.[80]

S30–231

ILLUSTRATION

X is a company with its centre of main interests in England. X enters into a contract with A, a German company, whereby it agrees to sell land situated in Germany to A. Subsequently, winding-up proceedings are opened in respect of X in England. The effects of such proceedings on the contract between X and A are governed exclusively by German law.[81]

S30–232

RULE 159H—(1) Without prejudice to Article 5 (Rule 159D), the effects of insolvency proceedings on the rights and obligations of the parties to a payment or settlement system or to a financial market shall be governed solely by the law of the Member State applicable to that system or market.

(2) Clause (1) shall not preclude any action for voidness, voidability or unenforceability which may be taken to set aside payments or transactions under the law applicable to the relevant payment system or financial market.[82]

S30R–233

COMMENT

This Rule reproduces Article 9 of the E.C. Insolvency Regulation (headed "Payment systems and financial markets"). Article 9 constitutes a further exception to the general choice of law rule contained in Article 4 of the Regulation in cases where what is in issue is the effects of insolvency proceedings on the rights and obligations of the parties to a "payment or settlement system" or to a "financial market". In such cases, subject only to Article 5, the effects of insolvency proceedings are to be determined solely by reference to the law of the Member State applicable to that system or market. The justification for Article 9 is the need to provide special rules to guarantee the smooth operation of payment systems and financial markets

S30–234

---

[78] *ibid.* para. 119.

[79] E.C. Insolvency Regulation, Art. 4(1), 4(2) (e).

[80] Insolvency Act 1986, s.144 (1) provides that where a winding-up order has been made, or where a provisional liquidator has been appointed, the liquidator or the provisional liquidator (as the case may be) shall take into his custody or under his control all the property and things in action to which the company is or appears to be entitled. In theory this provision could extend to immovable property situated in a non-Member State, but even if it does it is highly unlikely that the liquidator or provisional liquidator could discharge the obligation without an order of the courts of the *situs*.

[81] E.C. Insolvency Regulation, Art. 8.

[82] E.C. Insolvency Regulation, Art. 9. See also Insurance Undertakings Insolvency Directive, Art. 23; Credit Institutions Insolvency Directive, Arts. 25–27.

307

on which large scale transactions may be engaged in, with a view to protecting general confidence in the mechanisms adopted in the particular system or market to which the parties have agreed by participation therein.[83]

S30–235 The distinction between "payment or settlement system" and "financial markets" is not a clear one since trading on financial markets is commonly done through standard forms providing the system of payment or settlement.[84] Since the relevant instruments will almost inevitably be governed by the law of the Member State applicable to the relevant trading market, the distinction is unlikely to make a practical difference.[85] More particularly, in determining the law applicable to payment and settlement systems account should be taken of the work of the European Community in this area.[86] In relation to financial markets (which like payment and settlement systems are not defined in the Regulation[87]) the Virgos-Schmit Report states that they are to be understood as markets in a member State where financial instruments, other financial assets or commodity futures and options are traded.[88] Such markets are characterised by regular trading and conditions of operation and access and are subject to the law of the relevant Member State, including appropriate supervision by the regulatory authorities of that Member State.[89] Such characteristics are easily matched in the case of the English financial markets[90] in which transactions (including payment and settlement) will inevitably be governed by English law as a result of an express choice of law.[91] The effects of insolvency proceedings in another Member State on such transactions will, therefore, be governed exclusively by English law. The only limitation on the exclusive scope of Article 9(1) is the proviso that its operation is subject to Article 5 which submits the effect of insolvency proceedings on rights *in rem* over the assets of the debtor to the law of the Member State in which the relevant asset is situated.[92]

S30–236 Article 9(2) (clause (2) of the Rule) reinforces the control of the law of the Member State which is applicable to the payment or settlement system or

---

[83] Recital (27); Virgos-Schmit, para. 120. Relevant mechanisms include closing out contracts and netting and the realisation of securities: *ibid*.

[84] See, *e.g.* London International Financial Futures and Options Exchange, (LIFFE), Exchange Contract No. 27 (German Government Bond ("Bund") Contract) (Denominated in Euro), issued December 16, 1999; LIFFE, Contract No. 29 (FTSE 100 Index Contract), issued December 5, 1999; LIFFE, Exchange Contract No. 501 (Options on Commodity Contracts), dated March 20, 2002.

[85] The contracts referred to in the previous note are all governed by English law as a result of an express choice.

[86] Virgos-Schmit, para. 123. See Directive of the European Parliament and of the Council of May 19, 1998 on settlement finality in payment and securities settlement systems, [1998] O.J. L166/45, implemented in the United Kingdom by the Financial Markets and Insolvency (Settlement Finality) Regulations 1999, S.I 1999 No. 2979. See also Directive of the European Parliament and of the Council of June 6, 2002 on financial collateral arrangements, [2002] O.J. L168/43, which must be implemented by December 23, 2003. For relevant English law, see Companies Act 1989, Part VII.

[87] The Settlement Finality Directive mentioned in the preceding note is referred to in Recital (27) of the Regulation and contains a definition of "system" in Art. 2(a). See also S.I. 1999 No. 2979, Art. 2(3) which appears to adopt this definition.

[88] Virgos-Schmit, para. 120.

[89] *ibid*.

[90] *e.g.* LIFFE *(supra, n. 84)*.

[91] See the instruments referred to in n. 84, *supra*.

[92] *supra*, Rule 159D.

financial market by stipulating that any actions for voidness, voidability or unenforceability which may be taken to set aside payments or transactions shall be governed by the law of the relevant system or financial market. Article 4(2)(m) will, therefore, be inapplicable to such matters.[93]

Article 9 will not apply if the law applicable to the payment or settlement system or financial market is not that of a Member State.

RULE 159I—The effects of insolvency proceedings on employment contracts and relationships shall be governed solely by the law of the Member State applicable to the contract of employment.[94]   S30R–237

COMMENT

This Rule reproduces Article 10 of the E.C. Insolvency Regulation (headed "Contracts of employment") and constitutes yet another exception to the general choice of law rule contained in Article 4 of the Regulation and particularly Article 4(2)(e), to the effect that the effects of insolvency proceedings on current contracts to which the debtor is a party are regulated by the law of the Member State in which the proceedings are opened.   S30–238

Article 10 establishes that the effect of insolvency proceedings on employment contracts or relationships[95] shall be governed solely by the law of the Member State applicable to the contract of employment. The purpose of this rule is to protect employees and labour relations from the application of a foreign law different to that which governs the contractual relations between employer and employee.[96]   S30–239

To determine the law applicable to the contract it will be necessary to apply the provisions of the Rome Convention on the Law Applicable to Contractual Obligations, particularly Articles 3, 6 and 7 of that Convention.[97] If application of those provisions leads to the conclusion that the contract of employment is governed by the law of a Member State, then Article 10 will apply. If, on the other hand, the applicable law is found to be that of a non-Member State, then Article 10 will not apply and the effect of the insolvency proceedings on the contract will be governed by the law of the State of the opening, including, where relevant, any of its rules of the conflict of laws.   S30–240

Article 10 is an exclusive provision: the law of the Member State applicable to the employment contract "solely" governs the effect of the insolvency proceedings.[98] The provision is, nonetheless, of rather narrow compass,   S30–241

---

[93] *supra*, Rule 159C (2)(m).
[94] E.C. Insolvency Regulation, Art. 10. See also Insurance Undertakings Insolvency Directive, Art. 19(a); Credit Institutions Insolvency Directive, Art. 20(a).
[95] Difficulties might arise as to whether a particular contract is a contract of employment and no definition is provided in the Regulation: see main work, paras. 33–052—33–055. It is not clear whether the inclusion of the word "relationship" in Art. 10 is intended to expand the meaning of "contract of employment".
[96] Virgos-Schmit, para. 125.
[97] See main work, Rule 182; Virgos-Schmit, para. 126.
[98] Virgos-Schmit, para. 127.

since it is confined to the effect of the insolvency proceedings on the contract, so as to be applicable to the effect of the proceedings on the continuation or termination of the employment contract and on the rights and obligations of the parties to the employment contract.[99] Article 10 does not apply to issues such as the ranking of employees' claims for unpaid wages, which will be governed by the law of the State of opening pursuant to Article 4(2)(i),[1] or to matters such as the lodging, verification and admission of claims which will fall within Article 4(2)(h)[2] and thus be subject to the law of the State of opening.

S30–242 If an issue falls within Article 10 it would seem that the law of the Member State applicable to the contract of employment will apply even if application of that law would have less beneficial consequences for the employee than would result from application of the law of the State of the opening.[3] This would seem to follow from the use of the word "solely" in the provision which is designed to indicate its exclusivity.

S30–243 Where a Member State has a national scheme under which employees are entitled to claim guaranteed payments out of a national fund, in the event of the insolvency of the employer,[4] the right of an employee to claim such a payment will depend on the national law of the Member State which creates the scheme.[5]

ILLUSTRATION

530–244 X is a company with its centre of main interests in France. Insolvency proceedings (main proceedings) are opened in respect of X in France. A is an employee of X who works in England under a contract governed by English law. The effect of the French insolvency proceedings on A's contract of employment (*e.g.* whether the contract is terminated) is governed by English law.[6] The ranking of A's claim for unpaid wages in the French proceedings is governed by French law as the law of the State of the opening.[7] If X has an establishment in England and secondary insolvency proceedings (winding-up proceedings) are opened in England, the effect of those proceedings on A's contract of employment (*e.g.* whether the contract is terminated) is governed by English law.[8] The ranking of A's claim for unpaid wages in the English secondary proceedings is also governed by English law as the law of the State of the opening.[9]

S30R–245 **RULE 159J—The effects of insolvency proceedings on the rights of the debtor in immoveable property, a ship or an aircraft subject to registration in a public register shall be determined by the law of the Member State under the authority of which the register is kept.[10]**

---

[99] *ibid.* para. 125.

[1] *ibid.* para. 128.

[2] *ibid.*

[3] *supra*, para. S30–189.

[4] See in England, Employment Rights Act 1996, ss. 182–190.

[5] Virgos-Schmit, para. 128.

[6] E.C. Insolvency Regulation, Art. 10. See also Insurance Undertakings Insolvency Directive, Art. 19(c); Credit Institutions Insolvency Directive, Art. 20(c).

[7] *ibid.* Art. 4(2)(i).

[8] *ibid.* Arts. 10, 28.

[9] *ibid.* Arts. 4(2)(i), 28.

[10] E.C. Insolvency Regulation, Art. 11. See Virgos-Schmit, paras. 129–132; Fletcher in Moss *et al.*, pp. 62–63; Moss and Smith, *ibid.* pp. 189–190.

COMMENT

As a further exception to Article 4, Article 11 of the Regulation (headed **S30–246**
"Effects on rights subject to registration"), reproduced in this Rule provides
that the "effects of insolvency proceedings on the rights of the debtor in
immovable property, a ship or an aircraft subject to registration in a public
register shall be determined by the law of the Member State under the
authority of which the register is kept". Systems of registration of property
play an important role in promoting legal certainty and protecting trade.[11]
Accordingly, an exception to the general application of the law of the State
of opening is justified in such cases.

First, it will be noted that Article 11 applies to rights, and to rights of the **S30–247**
debtor[12] in the relevant assets and not to the assets themselves, since it is
the rights in the relevant assets which will be entered on the register.[13]
Secondly, the register must be a public register[14] kept under the authority of
a Member State. Thirdly, the rights that fall within the Article are limited to
rights in immovable property, a ship or an aircraft, thereby excluding rights
in other species of property which may be subject to a requirement of
registration. Fourthly, such rights are subject to the law of the Member
State under whose authority the register is kept and thus it might appear
that the law of the State of opening is excluded. Fifthly, however, the
position is rather more complicated. Article 11 does not say that the law of
the Member State under whose authority the register is kept "solely"
determines the issues that fall within the provision.[15] The omission of
"solely" from the provision was deliberate.[16] According to the Virgos-
Schmit Report this "means that the general applicability of the law of the
State of opening in accordance with Article 4 is not displaced. Hence, a sort
of cumulative application of both laws is necessary".[17] This appears to mean
that the law of the Member State of registration will govern the "modifications which, required by the law of the State of opening, may be prompted
by the insolvency proceedings and affect the rights of the debtor. . ., the
requisite entries in the register and the consequences thereof."[18] The law of
the State of registration thus decides which effects of the insolvency
proceedings are admissible and affect the rights of the debtor which are
subject to registration in that State.[19]

Article 11 has no application to rights of the debtor in immovable property, **S30–248**
a ship or an aircraft which are subject to registration in a public register in a
non-Member State. The effect of insolvency proceedings on such rights will
presumably be governed by the law of the State of opening including its

---

[11] Virgos-Schmit, para. 130.
[12] For rights *in rem*, whether registered or not, of creditors and third parties, see *supra*, Rule
159D (Art. 5 of the Regulation).
[13] Virgos-Schmit, para. 13.
[14] For the meaning of "public register", see *supra*, para. S30–168.
[15] Contrast Arts. 8, 9,10.
[16] Virgos-Schmit, para. 130.
[17] *ibid.* This may require cooperation between the liquidator and the person responsible for
keeping the register: see Fletcher in Moss *et al.*, p. 62.
[18] *ibid.*
[19] *ibid.*

conflict of laws rules (which may make a reference to the law of the State of registration).

S30R–249 **RULE 159K—For the purposes of the E.C. Insolvency Regulation, a Community patent, a Community trade mark or any other similar right established by Community law may be included only in the proceedings referred to in Article 3(1) (Rule 159B(1)).**[20]

COMMENT

S30–250 Patents, trademarks and similar rights are already subject to elaborate regulation under European Community law.[21] The relevant instruments essentially provide that in cases relating to those who own or have more limited interests in such rights who become insolvent, such rights may only be included in the first proceedings that are opened in a Member State.[22]

S30–251 Rule 159K reproduces Article 12 of the E.C. Insolvency Regulation (headed "Community patents and trade marks"). The Regulation sometimes may produce the result that the first insolvency proceedings to be opened are territorial proceedings under Article 3(2) or (4) rather than main proceedings under Article 3(1).[23] Accordingly, Article 12 provides a special rule whereby a Community patent, trade mark or similar right established under Community law may only be included in main insolvency proceedings which are opened under Article 3(1) of the Regulation. Article 12 can only apply where the debtor's centre of main interests is situated in a Member State since this is required by Article 3(1).[24] Where the debtor's centre of main interests is situated in a non-Member State the rules contained in the relevant instruments apply without the qualification contained in Article 12. These rules generally indicate that the right in issue is included in the insolvent estate of the first proceedings opened in a Member State.[25]

S30R–252 **RULE 159L—Article 4(2)(m) (Rule 159C(2)(m)) shall not apply where the person who benefited from an act detrimental to all the creditors provides proof that:**

> **(1) the said act is subject to the law of a Member State other than that of the State of the opening of proceedings, and**

---

[20] E.C. Insolvency Regulation, Art. 12. See Fletcher in Moss *et al.*, p.63; Moss and Smith, *ibid.* p. 190.
[21] Community Patent Convention of December 15, 1975, [1975] O.J. L17/1, as amended by Luxembourg Agreement of December 30, 1989, [1989] O.J. L140/10; First Council Directive 89/104 of December 21, 1988, L40/1, to approximate the laws of the Member States relating to trade marks, [1989] O.J. L 40/1, implemented in the United Kingdom in Trade Marks Act 1994; Council Regulation (E.C.) No. 40/94 of December 20, 1993 on the Community trade mark, [1994] O.J. L11/1; Council Regulation (E.C.) No. 2100/94 of July 27, 1994 on Community plant variety rights, [1994] O.J. L227/1.
[22] Luxembourg Agreement, Art. 41; Council Regulation on the Community trade mark, Art. 21; Council Regulation on Community plant variety rights, Art. 25.
[23] *supra*, para. S30–170.
[24] See Virgos-Schmit, para. 134.
[25] See n. 22, *supra*; Virgos-Schmit, *ibid.*

(2) that law does not allow any means of challenging that act in the relevant case.[26]

COMMENT

This rule reproduces Article 13 of the E.C. Insolvency Regulation (headed "Detrimental acts"). It has already been discussed in connection with Article 4(2)(m) (Rule 159C(2)(m)).[27] S30–253

RULE 159M—Where, by an act concluded after the opening of insolvency proceedings, the debtor disposes, for consideration of: S30R–254

(1) an immoveable asset, or

(2) a ship or aircraft subject to registration in a public register, or

(3) securities whose existence presupposes registration in a register laid down by law,

the validity of that act shall be governed by the law of the State within the territory of which the immoveable asset is situated or under the authority of which the register is kept.[28]

COMMENT

Normally, the law of the State of opening of proceedings will, once the proceedings are opened, prohibit the debtor from disposing of his property (unless, perhaps, the court orders otherwise).[29] Applying the general rule in Article 4 any such disposal by the debtor would be ineffective in relation to a third party. Article 14 (headed "Protection of third-party purchasers") reproduced in Rule 159M creates an exception to that general rule so as to protect (in relatively limited circumstances) a third-party purchaser. Where, by an act concluded after the opening of insolvency proceedings, the debtor disposes, for consideration, of an immovable asset or a ship or aircraft subject to registration in a public register, or securities whose existence presupposes registration in a register laid down by law, the validity of that act shall be governed by the law of the State within the territory of which the immovable asset is situated or under the authority of which the register is kept. S30–255

Although Article 14 does not explicitly say this, it would seem clear that the immovable or relevant register must be situated in a State other than the State of the opening, since otherwise application of the law of the State of opening or the *lex situs* of the immovable or relevant register would lead to S30–256

---

[26] E.C. Insolvency Regulation, Art. 13. See also Insurance Undertakings Insolvency Directive, Art. 24; Credit Institutions Insolvency Directive, Art. 30.

[27] *supra* paras. S30–200 *et seq.*

[28] E.C. Insolvency Regulation, Art. 14. See Virgos-Schmit, paras 140–141; Fletcher in Moss *et al.*, pp. 63–64; Moss and Smith, *ibid.* p. 192. See also Insurance Undertakings Insolvency Directive, Art. 25; Credit Institutions Insolvency Directive, Art. 31.

[29] In England, see Insolvency Act 1986, s.127.

the same result. But it will be noticed that Article 14 does not stipulate that this "State" must be a Member State. In commenting on the earlier Convention on Insolvency Proceedings the Virgos-Schmit Report consistently referred to State as "Contracting State"[30] so that it is likely that State should be construed as "Member State".[31] Secondly, Article 14 presupposes (after the opening of insolvency proceedings), an act[32] of disposal for consideration: a gratuitous act of disposal will not qualify. Thirdly, the provision is limited to disposal of immovable property, a ship or an aircraft subject to registration in a public register or securities whose existence presupposes registration in a register laid down by law.[33] Fourthly, the validity of the act of disposal will, in the case of an immovable, depend on the *lex situs*,[34] or, in the case of ships, aircraft or relevant securities, on the law of the State in which the register is kept.

ILLUSTRATION

S30–257   X is a company with its centre of main interests in England. Winding-up proceedings are opened in respect of X in England. After the opening, X disposes of immovable property in France to A, a French company, and the company jet aircraft, which is subject to registration in a public register in the Netherlands, to B, a Dutch company. Each disposal is for valuable consideration. Each disposal is void by English law.[35] The validity of the disposals to A and B will be governed, respectively, by French and Dutch law.[36]

S30R–258   **RULE 159N—The effects of insolvency proceedings on a lawsuit pending concerning an asset or a right of which the debtor has been divested shall be governed solely by the law of the Member State in which that lawsuit is pending.**[37]

COMMENT

S30–259   This Rule reproduces Article 15 of the Regulation (headed "Effects of insolvency proceedings on lawsuits pending"). It is normal practice for a legal system to provide for a stay of individual actions which have been begun against the debtor once insolvency proceedings have been commenced against that debtor.[38] By way of exception to the general rule contained in Article 4, Article 15 of the Regulation provides that the effects

---

[30] Virgos-Schmit, para. 141.

[31] Although, apparently, the Dutch text refers to "Member State", the French, German, Spanish, Portugese and Italian texts refer to "State": see Moss and Smith in Moss *et al.*, p. 192, n. 108. *Cf.* Arts. 5 and 11.

[32] According to Virgos-Schmit, para. 141, an "act of disposal must be understood to include not only transfers of ownership but also the constitution of a right *in rem* relating to such property".

[33] It is not clear whether a register "laid down by law" is different from a "public" register. Since the rationale of Art. 14 is to protect a purchaser who acquires an asset after the insolvency proceedings have been opened but before the insolvency proceedings have been recorded on the register, it would seem that both types of register must be open to public access: and see Art. 2(g); Virgos-Schmit, para. 69.

[34] Which is likely to require some form of registration.

[35] Insolvency Act 1986, s. 127.

[36] E.C. Insolvency Regulation, Art. 14.

[37] E.C. Insolvency Regulation, Art. 15. See also Insurance Undertakings Insolvency Directive, Art. 26; Credit Institutions Insolvency Directive, Art. 32.

[38] See, *e.g.* in relation to winding up in England, Insolvency Act 1986, s. 130 (2). *Cf.* main work, para. 30–073.

of insolvency proceedings on a lawsuit pending concerning an asset or a right of which the debtor has been divested shall be governed solely by the law of the Member State in which that lawsuit is pending.

It must first be emphasised that it is intended that the Article distinguishes **S30–260** between the effects of insolvency proceedings on individual enforcement proceedings and the effects of insolvency proceedings on lawsuits pending. The former category of proceedings is governed by the law of the State of opening pursuant to Article 4(2)(f). Accordingly, the law of the State of opening will determine whether insolvency proceedings will stay or prevent any individual enforcement action brought by creditors against the debtor's assets.[39] Other types of legal proceedings concerning assets or rights of the debtor's estate fall within Article 15. Thus the law of the Member State in which the lawsuit is pending will decide whether those proceedings are to be suspended, how they are to be continued and "whether any procedural modifications are needed in order to reflect the loss or restriction of the powers of disposal and administration of the debtor and the intervention of the liquidator in his place".[40] Secondly, Article 15 only has effect in relation to litigation concerning an asset or right of which the debtor has been divested by the insolvency proceedings. If a particular asset or right is excluded from the scope of the insolvency proceedings by the law of the State of opening, then Article 15 does not apply to litigation concerning it.[41] Thirdly, Article 15 is an exclusive rule—the law of the Member State in which the lawsuit is pending "solely" determines the effect of insolvency proceedings on that lawsuit. Fourthly, the particular lawsuit must be pending in a Member State. Article 15 does not apply to litigation which is pending in non-Member States.

ILLUSTRATION

X is a company with its centre of main interests in Italy. A Bank, an English bank, has **S30–261** commenced proceedings in England against X to recover sums due under a loan agreement on which X has defaulted. These proceedings are pending in the High Court. Subsequently, insolvency proceedings are opened in respect of X in Italy. The effect of these insolvency proceedings on the action brought by A Bank against X will be determined exclusively by English law.[42]

D. Recognition of Insolvency Proceedings[43]

RULE 159O—(1) Any judgment opening insolvency proceedings handed **S30R–262** down by a court of a Member State which has jurisdiction pursuant to Article 3 (Rule 159B) shall be recognised in all the other Member States from the time that it becomes effective in the State of the opening of proceedings. This clause shall also apply where, on account of his capacity, insolvency proceedings cannot be brought against the debtor in other Member States.

---

[39] Virgos-Schmit, para. 142.

[40] *ibid*.

[41] This is most likely to happen in cases of individual bankruptcy where certain assets are excluded from the debtor's estate: see, *e.g.* in England, Insolvency Act 1986, s. 283(2).

[42] E.C. Insolvency Regulation, Art. 15.

[43] Virgos-Schmit, paras. 143–263; Fletcher, *Insolvency in Private International Law* (1999), pp. 283–294; Moss and Bayfield in Moss *et al.*, Chap. 5; Moss and Smith, *ibid.* pp. 196–229.

(2) Recognition of the proceedings referred to in Article 3(1) (Rule 159B (1)) shall not preclude the opening of the proceedings referred to in Article 3(2) (Rule 159B(2)) by a court in another Member State. The latter proceedings shall be secondary insolvency proceedings within the meaning of Chapter III of the E.C. Insolvency Regulation.[44]

COMMENT

S30–263   The rules concerned with recognition of insolvency proceedings (Articles 17 to 26) are to be found in Chapter II of the Regulation. Chapter III (Articles 27 to 38) is concerned with rules relating to secondary proceedings (including recognition) and with the inter-relationship between main and secondary, including territorial, proceedings.

S30–264   Rule 1590 reproduces Article 16 of the Regulation (headed "Principle"). It establishes the general principle that a judgment[45] opening insolvency proceedings which is handed down by a court[46] of a Member State which has jurisdiction according to Article 3(Rule 159B) shall be recognised in all the other Member States from the time it becomes effective in the State of the opening of proceedings. Accordingly, recognition is automatic,[47] subject only to the possibility of non-recognition on the grounds of public policy.[48] The principle of automatic recognition extends to main, secondary and territorial insolvency proceedings amongst all Member States. The principal effect of automatic recognition is, however, in relation to main proceedings. Such proceedings are to have universal effect over all of the debtor's assets situated in the Member States, except in so far as the Regulation otherwise provides. The principle of automatic recognition is less important in relation to secondary and territorial proceedings since those proceedings are limited to assets situated in the territory in which they are opened.[49] Such is the strength of the principle of automatic recognition that it requires recognition of insolvency proceedings in another Member State even if insolvency proceedings could not have been opened in respect of that debtor in that State.[50]

S30–265   Article 16(2) provides that recognition of main proceedings shall not preclude the opening of secondary proceedings by a court in another Member State. The opening of such proceedings may only occur if the debtor has an establishment in that Member State[51] and the effects of such proceedings are, of course, limited to the assets of the debtor situated in that Member State.[52]

---

[44] E.C. Insolvency Regulation, Art. 16.
[45] As defined in Art. 2(e). See *supra*, para. S30–156.
[46] As defined in Art. 2(d). See *supra*, para. S30–156.
[47] Recital (22).
[48] Art. 26. See *infra*, Rule 159U.
[49] Art. 18(2) (*infra*, Rule 159R (2)) enables a liquidator appointed by a court having jurisdiction pursuant to Art. 3(2) to claim in any other Member State, through the courts or out of court, that movable property was removed from the territory of the State of opening of proceedings to the territory of that other Member State after the opening of proceedings. Such a liquidator may also bring any action to set aside which is in the interests of the creditors.
[50] *e.g.* due to the debtor's "professional capacity or to his public or private nature, as in the case of non-traders in certain States". Virgos-Schmit, para. 148.
[51] Art. 3(2).
[52] *ibid*. See Insolvency Act 1986, s. 436 A, inserted by S.I 2002 No. 1240, Reg. 18, *supra*, para. S30–159.

**RULE 159P—(1) The judgment opening proceedings referred to in Article S30R–266
3(1) (Rule 159B (1)) shall, with no further formalities, produce the same
effects in any other Member State as under the[53] law of the State of the
opening of proceedings unless the Regulation provides otherwise and as
long as no proceedings referred to in Article 3(2) (Rule 159B (2)) are
opened in that other Member State.**

**(2) The effects of the proceedings referred to in Article 3(2) (Rule 159B
(2)) may not be challenged in other Member States. Any restriction of the
creditors' rights, in particular a stay or discharge, shall produce effects vis-
à-vis assets situated within the territory of another Member State only in
the case of those creditors who have given their consent.[54]**

COMMENT

Article 17 of the E.C. Insolvency Regulation, as stated in this Rule, is S30–267
concerned with the effects of recognition (and is so headed). The provision
distinguishes between the effects of recognition of main, secondary and
territorial proceedings.[55]

Main proceedings. Article 17(1) provides that the judgment opening main S30–268
proceedings under Article 3(1) shall, with no further formalities, produce
the same effects in any other Member State as under the law of the State of
opening unless the Regulation provides otherwise as long as no secondary
proceedings are opened in another Member State under Article 3(2). That
no further formalities may be required indicates that no proceedings need
to be brought in another Member State to create the effects of recognition.
"Effects" are not defined but presumably will be determined by the law of
the State of opening. These effects may be both substantive and procedural,[56] and are likely to include, in particular, the following: the
divestment of the debtor; the appointment of the liquidator; the prohibition
on individual executions; the inclusion of the debtor's assets in the estate
regardless of the Member State in which they are situated; the obligation to
return what has been obtained by individual creditors after the opening.[57]

Secondary and territorial proceedings. Recognition of main proceedings S30–269
opened under Article 3(1) is limited by the opening of secondary proceedings under Article 3(2). If follows that the main proceedings cannot affect
assets subject to secondary proceedings.[58] Article 17(2) provides for the
recognition of secondary proceedings. Because, however, such proceedings
are limited to assets situated in the State of the opening it is not necessary
that the effects of such proceedings be recognised in respect of assets
situated in other Member States. However, it is nonetheless necessary that

---

[53] "This" in Art. 17 is clearly a misprint for "the".
[54] E.C. Insolvency Regulation, Art. 17.
[55] The new forms of order require a statement as to whether proceedings are main, secondary or
territorial proceedings. See *supra*, para. S30–171.
[56] Virgos-Schmit, para. 153.
[57] *ibid.* para. 154. In the English context effects would include the mandatory statutory stay on
execution by judgment creditors when main proceedings for an administration order are opened:
see Insolvency Act 1986, s. 11.
[58] A duty to co-operate is imposed on the liquidators in the main and secondary proceedings: Art.
31, *infra*, Rule 159V.

the effects of secondary and territorial proceedings (opened before main proceedings) which concern assets located in the State of opening to be recognised in other Member States, and, accordingly, Article 17(2) provides that the effects of proceedings opened under Article 3(2) cannot be challenged in other Member States.

S30–270 The second sentence of Article 17(2) provides that any restriction of the creditors' rights, in particular a stay or discharge, shall produce effects vis-à-vis assets situated in another Member State only in the case of those creditors who give their consent. Thus, for example, if proceedings opened under Article 3(2) have the effect of staying creditors' remedies, the stay will not have any effect in other Member States unless the relevant creditors have consented. Further, where proceedings under Article 3(2) are closed as a result of creditors agreeing to discharge the debtor, *e.g.* by way of compromise, Article 17(2) means that, without specific consent from a creditor, the effect of the discharge is limited to assets of the debtor which are situated in the Member State in which secondary (or territorial) proceedings were opened. The creditor may then pursue any claim for the balance which may be due to him in other Member States.

S30–271 As to the requirement of consent, it would appear that individual creditors must consent personally and that it is insufficient that consent is obtained by a majority vote.[59]

ILLUSTRATIONS

S30–272 1. X is a company with its centre of main interests in England and assets in France and Germany. Winding-up proceedings (main proceedings) are opened in England in respect of X. The judgment opening the proceedings produces the same effects in France and Germany as it produces in English law.[60]

2. The facts are the same as in Illustration 1, except that secondary proceedings are also opened in France where X has an establishment. The effects of such secondary proceedings cannot be challenged in England.[61]

3. The facts are the same as in Illustration 2, except that the secondary proceedings in France are closed by a compromise. In the absence of consent from each creditor, the effect of the compromise is limited to assets in France.[62]

S30R–273 RULE 159Q—**The opening of the proceedings referred to in Article 3(1) (Rule 159B(1)) by a court of a Member State and which is recognised in another Member State (main proceedings) shall permit the opening in that other Member State, a court of which has jurisdiction pursuant to Article 3(2) (Rule 159B(2)) of secondary insolvency proceedings without the debtor's insolvency being examined in that other State. These latter proceedings must be among the proceedings listed in Annex B of the E.C. Insolvency Regulation. Their effects shall be restricted to the assets of the debtor situated within the territory of that other Member State.[63]**

---

[59] See Virgos-Schmit, para. 157. See also Art. 34(2), *infra*, para. S30–318 *Cf.* Moss and Smith in Moss *et al.*, p. 198.

[60] E.C. Insolvency Regulation, Art. 17(1).

[61] *ibid.* Art. 17(2).

[62] *ibid.*

[63] E.C. Insolvency Regulation, Art. 27.

COMMENT

This Rule reflects the terms of Article 27 of the E.C. Insolvency Regulation. **S30–274**
Article 27 (headed "Opening of proceedings") appears in Chapter III of the
Regulation which contains provisions concerned with secondary proceed-
ings and with the relationship between main and secondary proceedings. If
main proceedings have been opened by a court of a Member State pursuant
to Article 3(1) and these proceedings are entitled to recognition in another
Member State, then secondary proceedings may be opened in that other
Member State if the courts of that State have jurisdiction under Article
3(2). These latter proceedings must be among the proceedings listed in
Annex B of the Regulation: the listed English proceedings are winding-up
by the court, creditors' voluntary winding up (with confirmation by the
court) and bankruptcy.[64] The provision repeats what has already been stated
in Article 3(2) namely that the effects of secondary proceedings are limited
to the assets of the debtor situated in the Member State where such
secondary proceedings are opened. The new principle introduced by Article
27 is that if the main insolvency proceedings are recognised in the Member
State in which it is sought to open secondary proceedings, then the
secondary proceedings may be opened without the debtor's insolvency being
examined by the court whose jurisdiction is invoked. This means that
whether the debtor is insolvent is, for the court opening secondary
proceedings, not a matter for the law of the State of opening according to
the general choice of law rule contained in Article 4 of the Regulation.

Although it will, presumably, be open to the court in which secondary
proceedings are opened to determine whether the proceedings opened in
another Member State are main proceedings, it should not be open to that
court to review the jurisdictional competence of the court in which main
proceedings are opened: if the latter court has ruled that the debtor's centre
of main interests is in that Member State, the principle of automatic
recognition should ensure that that finding is accepted.[65]

In permitting the opening of secondary proceedings without the need to **S30–275**
examine the debtor's insolvency, Article 27 appears to presume that such
insolvency will have been established in the main proceedings. This may not
necessarily be the case. Thus, for example, in England an administration
order may be made if a company "is likely to become unable to pay its
debts".[66] If English adminstration proceedings are the main proceedings
and an order is made on the ground just mentioned, then any secondary
proceedings must be winding-up proceedings, as defined in Annex B, but
there will be no finding that the debtor is insolvent. It is unclear how the
interplay between main and secondary proceedings operates in this context.

If the principle of automatic recognition does not ensure recognition of the **S30–276**
opening of main proceedings on public policy grounds,[67] then, presumably,
Article 27 will not operate and the court opening secondary proceedings

---

[64] For bankruptcy, see Chap. 31.
[65] Recital (22); Virgos-Schmit, paras 215, 216. Note the public policy exception in Art. 26, *infra*,
Rule 159U.
[66] Insolvency Act 1986, s. 8(1)(*a*).
[67] Art. 26, *infra*, Rule 159U.

will have to determine whether the debtor is insolvent according to its own law, pursuant to Article 4 of the Regulation.

S30–277 **Right to request opening of secondary proceedings.** Article 29(a) provides that the liquidator[68] in the main proceedings has the right to request the opening of secondary proceedings. This will be so even if the liquidator does not have the right to request the opening under the law of the State of opening. Article 29(b) permits a request to open secondary proceedings to be made by any other person or authority empowered to request the opening of insolvency proceedings under the law of the Member State within the territory of which the opening of secondary proceedings is requested.

S30–278 **Advance payment of costs and expenses.** Apparently, the law of some Member States prohibits commencement of insolvency proceedings against a debtor unless the debtor has sufficient assets to cover the costs and expenses of the proceedings.[69] Article 30 takes account of this fact by providing that where the law of a Member State in which the opening of secondary proceedings is requested requires that the debtor's assets be sufficient to cover in whole or part the costs and expenses of the proceedings, the court may, when it receives such a request, require the applicant to make an advance payment of costs or to provide appropriate security.[70]

ILLUSTRATION

S30–279 1. X is a company with its centre of main interests in France. X has assets and an establishment in England. Winding-up proceedings (*liquidation judiciaire*) are opened in respect of X in France. These proceedings (main proceedings) must be recognised in England. The liquidator of X requests the opening of secondary proceedings (winding-up proceedings) in England.[71] The English court has jurisdiction to open such proceedings, pursuant to Article 3(2) of the Regulation, and will grant the request, without examining X's insolvency.[72] The effects of the English proceedings are limited to X's assets situated in England.[73]

S30R–280 **RULE 159R—(1) The liquidator appointed by a court which has jurisdiction pursuant to Article 3(1) (Rule 159B(1)) may exercise all the powers conferred on him by the law of the State of the opening of proceedings in another Member State as long as no other insolvency proceedings have been opened there nor any preservation measure to the contrary has been taken there further to a request for the opening of insolvency proceedings in that State. He may in particular remove the debtor's assets from the territory of the Member State in which they are situated, subject to Articles 5 and 7 (Rules 159D and 159F).**

---

[68] As defined in Art 2(b), *supra*, para. S30–150. Annex C lists for England a liquidator, a supervisor of a voluntary arrangement, an administrator, the Official Receiver and a trustee in bankruptcy. As to proof of the liquidator's appointment, see Art. 19, *infra*, para. S30–286.
[69] Virgos-Schmit, para. 228.
[70] Art. 30 is to be "understood to mean that where national law does not require sufficient assets in order to open insolvency proceedings it cannot introduce such a requirement for secondary proceedings only": *ibid*.
[71] E.C. Insolvency Regulation, Art. 29 (a).
[72] *ibid*. Art. 28.
[73] *ibid*.

(2) The liquidator appointed by a court which has jurisdiction pursuant to Article 3(2) (Rule 159B(2)) may in any other Member State claim through the courts or out of court that immovable property was removed from the territory of the State of the opening of proceedings to the territory of that other Member State after the opening of the insolvency proceedings. He may also bring any action to set aside which is in the interests of the creditors.

(3) In exercising his powers, the liquidator shall comply with the law of the Member State within the territory of which he intends to take action, in particular with regard to procedures for the realisation of assets. These powers may not include coercive measures or the right to rule on legal proceedings or disputes.[74]

COMMENT

This Rule reproduces Article 18 of the E.C. Insolvency Regulation (headed "Powers of the liquidator"). **S30–281**

Clause (1) of the Rule. Article 18(1) initially provides that the liquidator[75] **S30–282** appointed by a court which has jurisdiction pursuant to Article 3(1) may exercise all the powers conferred on him by the law of the State of the opening of proceedings, in another Member State. This principle is the logical consequence of the principle of the automatic recognition of main proceedings in other Member-States.[76] One aspect of the liquidator's powers is specifically mentioned: the liquidator may "in particular" remove the debtor's assets from the territory of the Member State in which they are situated, though this power is subject to Articles 5 and 7 of the Regulation.[77]

The liquidator may only exercise his powers in another Member State if no **S30–283** other insolvency proceedings have been opened there or any preservation measure to the contrary has been taken there further to a request for the opening of insolvency proceedings in that State. If insolvency proceedings are opened in another Member State subsequent to main proceedings, the former proceedings will of necessity be secondary proceedings which have effect over assets situated in the Member State in which those secondary proceedings are opened. It follows from this that the powers of the liquidator cannot be exercised in relation to those assets. Equally, a request to open secondary proceedings[78] may be made in another Member State and a preservation measure may have been put in place in that State pending the opening of proceedings. If such a preservation measure is inconsistent with recognition of the powers of the liquidator in the main proceedings, then recognition of those powers will be similarly denied.

---

[74] *ibid*. Art. 18. See Virgos-Schmit, paras. 158–166; Moss and Bayfield in Moss *et al.*, pp. 78–83; Moss and Smith, *ibid*. pp. 198–202.
[75] Defined in Art. 2(b), *supra*, para. S30–150. In English law it is a criminal offence to act as an insolvency practitioner without proper authorisation: Insolvency Act 1986, s. 389. This rule is inapplicable in respect of acts in the United Kingdom or elsewhere in relation to insolvency proceedings within the Regulation taking place in another Member State: Insolvency Act 1986, s. 388(6), inserted by S.I. 2002 No. 1240, Reg. 17.
[76] Recital (22); Virgos-Schmit, paras 158–159.
[77] *supra*, Rules 159D, 159F.
[78] Art. 29, *supra*, para. S30–277.

S30–284 Clause (2) of the Rule. Article 18(2) deals with the powers of the liquidator appointed in relation to secondary proceedings. Such a liquidator may clearly exercise his powers in relation to assets situated in the Member State in which secondary proceedings are opened. However, Article 18(2), firstly, gives such a liquidator the power to claim in another Member State, through that State's courts or out of court, that movable property was removed from the territory of the State of the opening of secondary proceedings to the territory of that Member State after the opening of proceedings. Secondly, the liquidator may bring in any Member State any action to set aside which is in the interests of the creditors.[79]

S30–285 Clause (3) of the Rule. Article 18(3) requires that in exercising his powers, the liquidator must comply with the law of the Member State in which he intends to take action, in particular with regard to procedures for realisation of assets. The requirement would seem to mean that while the content and extent of the liquidator's powers will depend on the law of the State of opening, the manner in which these powers are to be exercised will be governed by the law of the Member State in which the liquidator intends to act (and the latter in particular includes observance of procedures in that Member State for realisation of assets).[80] More specifically, the powers of the liquidator do not include "coercive measures" or the "right to rule on legal proceedings or disputes". Consequently, it would appear that if a liquidator needs to take coercive measures in another Member State, "with regard to assets or persons"[81] located there, "the liquidator must apply to the authorities of the State where the assets or persons are located to have them adopted or implemented".[82] As regards the second limitation it is, apparently, the case that in some Member States a liquidator may also act as a judge, and rule on disputes.[83] Such a power may not be exercised by a liquidator under the Regulation.

S30–286 Proof of liquidator's appointment. Article 19 provides that the liquidator's appointment shall be evidenced by a certified copy of the original decision appointing him or by any other certificate issued by the court which has jurisdiction.[84] A translation into the official language or one of the official languages of the Member State within the territory of which the liquidator intends to act may be required. No legalisation or other similar formality shall be required. The Regulation contains no rules regarding the means of proving the scope of the powers of the liquidator.[85] According to the Virgos-Schmit Report, these powers must be established by the person who invokes them.[86] The Report goes on to say that proof "may be by means of a certificate issued by the Court appointing the liquidator, which shall define his powers, or by any other means of evidence admitted by the law of the State where the liquidator intends to exercise his powers".[87]

---

[79] See Arts. 4(2)(m) and 13, *supra*, paras. S30–198 *et seq.*

[80] See Virgos-Schmit, para. 164(c).

[81] *ibid.* para. 164(a).

[82] *ibid.*

[83] Moss and Smith in Moss *et al.*, p. 201.

[84] For England see Form 7.20 (confirmation by court of creditors' voluntary winding up); Form 2.4 (administration order); Form 4.11 (order for winding up by the court); Form 4.12 (order for winding up by the court following upon discharge of adminstration order).

[85] Virgos-Schmit, para. 170.

[86] *ibid.*

[87] *ibid.* For the position in English law, see main work, Chap. 9.

Publication. Although publication is not necessary for recognition of S30–287 insolvency proceedings, or for the recognition of the powers of a liquidator, in other Member States, Article 21 makes provision for such publication.[88] Thus the liquidator may request that notice of the judgment opening insolvency proceedings and, where appropriate, the decision appointing him, be published in any other Member State in accordance with the publication procedures provided for in that State. Such publication shall also specify the liquidator appointed and whether the jurisdiction rule applied is based on Article 3(1) or 3(2) of the Regulation.[89] Article 21(2) provides that any Member State in which the debtor has an establishment may require mandatory publication. In such cases, the liquidator or any authority empowered to that effect in the Member State where main proceedings have been opened shall take all necessary measures to ensure that such publication takes place. Such a mandatory requirement of publication cannot, however, constitute a pre-condition for recognition.[90]

Registration in a public register. Further, the liquidator may request that S30–288 the judgment opening the proceedings under Article 3(1) be registered in the land register, the trade register or any other public register kept in the Member States.[91] Additionally, a Member State may require mandatory registration and in such cases the liquidator or any authority empowered to that effect in the Member State where proceedings under Article 3(1) have been opened shall take all necessary measures to ensure such registration takes place.[92] It will be noted that this provision (Article 22) only applies to main proceedings whereas the rule on publication in Article 21 applies to both main and secondary proceedings. Registration in a public register (whether mandatory or not) cannot be a pre-condition of recognition of the insolvency proceedings.[93] And it is only the judgment opening the main proceedings (and not the appointment of the liquidator) which may be registered.[94]

Costs. The costs of publication and registration provided for in Articles 21 S30–289 and 22 shall be regarded as costs and expenses incurred in the proceedings.[95] Presumably, this means that such costs are borne by the liquidator.

Honouring of an obligation to a debtor. The judgment opening insolvency S30–290 proceedings and the appointment of the liquidator are entitled to automatic recognition in other Member States, and, in principle, affect any assets of the debtor situated in Member States. Normally, the law of the Member State in which main proceedings are opened will regard the honouring of an obligation for the benefit of the debtor which should have been honoured for the benefit of the liquidator as not discharging that obligation. To avoid potential injustice which could arise in cases where the person honouring the obligation of the debtor was unaware of the opening of the insolvency

---

[88] See Virgos-Schmit, paras. 177–181.
[89] Art. 21(1).
[90] Virgos-Schmit, para. 180.
[91] Art. 22(1).
[92] Art. 22(2).
[93] Virgos-Schmit, paras. 182, 185.
[94] *cf.* Art. 21.
[95] Art. 23.

proceedings, Article 24(1) provides that the person honouring the obligation in *another* Member State shall be deemed to have discharged the obligation if he was unaware of the opening of proceedings. Where such an obligation is honoured *before* the publication provided for in Article 21, the person honouring the obligation shall be presumed, in the absence of proof to the contrary, to have been unaware of the opening of insolvency proceedings.[96] Where the obligation is honoured *after* such publication has been effected, the person honouring the obligation shall be presumed, in the absence of proof to the contrary, to have been aware of the opening of proceedings.[97]

ILLUSTRATIONS

S30–291   1. X in a company with its centre of main interests in England. Assets belonging to X are situated in France. Winding-up proceedings (main proceedings) are opened in respect of X in England and A is appointed liquidator of X. A may exercise any of the powers conferred on him by English law, in France.[98] A may remove X's French assets from France and bring them to England unless these assets are subject to a right *in rem* held by a third party[99] or to a reservation of title.[1]

2. X is a company with its centre of main interests in England. X has an establishment and assets situated in France. Winding-up proceedings (main proceedings) are opened in respect of X in England and A is appointed liquidator of X. Subsequently B, a creditor of X, opens secondary proceedings (*liquidation judiciaire*) in respect of X in France and C is appointed liquidator in those proceedings. A may not exercise his powers in France,[2] though A and C may be under a mutual duty to cooperate with each other in the administration of X's estate.[3]

3. X is a company with its centre of main interests in Germany. X has an establishment and assets in England. Insolvency proceedings (main proceedings) are opened in respect of X in Germany, and A is appointed liquidator. B, an English creditor of X requests the opening of secondary (winding-up) proceedings in respect of X in England.[4] Pursuant to a winding-up petition seeking the making of a winding-up order, C is appointed provisional liquidator of X.[5] A cannot exercise his powers in England to the extent that they conflict with the powers of C.[6]

4. X is a company with its centre of main interests in Italy. X has an establishment and assets in England. Insolvency proceedings (main proceedings) in respect of X are opened in Italy and A is appointed liquidator. B, a creditor of X, opens secondary proceedings (winding-up proceedings) in respect of X in England and C is appointed liquidator. After the opening of these proceedings Y, a director of X, takes a valuable painting belonging to X and removes it to France. C may claim the return of the painting in the French courts.[7]

5. X is a company with its centre of main interests in England. Winding-up proceedings (main proceedings) in respect of X are opened in England. After the opening of proceedings but before notice of the judgment opening the proceedings and the appointment of A as liquidator is published in France, B pays a debt due from X to C in France. This payment discharges the debt if B was unaware of the opening of proceedings.[8] B is deemed to be unaware of the opening of proceedings in the absence of proof to the contrary.[9]

---

[96] Art. 24(2).
[97] *ibid.*
[98] Subject to Art. 18(3).
[99] Arts. 5 and 18(1).
[1] Arts. 7 and 18(1).
[2] Art. 18(1).
[3] Art. 31.
[4] Art. 29(b).
[5] Insolvency Act 1986, s. 135. This would be a preservation measure for the purposes of Art. 18(1). See also Art. 38.
[6] Art. 18(1).
[7] Art. 18(2).
[8] Art. 24(1).
[9] Art. 24(2).

RULE 159S—(1)A creditor who, after the opening of the proceedings **S30R–292** referred to in Article 3(1) (Rule 159B(1)) obtains by any means, in particular through enforcement, total or partial satisfaction of his claim on the assets belonging to the debtor situated within the territory of another Member State, shall return what he has obtained to the liquidator, subject to Articles 5 and 7 (Rules 159D and 159F).

(2) In order to ensure equal treatment of creditors a creditor who has, in the course of insolvency proceedings, obtained a dividend on his claim shall share in distributions made in other proceedings only where creditors of the same ranking or category have, in those other proceedings, obtained an equivalent dividend.[10]

COMMENT

A principal aim of the Regulation is to ensure equal treatment of unsecured **S30–293** creditors throughout the Member States.[11] To this end, Article 20(1) of the Regulation, as reproduced in clause (1) of this Rule (and headed "Return and imputation") provides that a creditor who, after the opening of main proceedings obtains by any means, but in particular through enforcement, total or partial satisfaction of his claim on the assets of the debtor situated within the territory of another Member State shall return what he has obtained to the liquidator. This rule is the consequence of the universality of the main proceedings which affect all the debtor's assets situated in Member States and affect all the creditors.[12] A creditor who attempts to "steal a march" on other creditors in this way breaches the "principle of collective satisfaction on which the insolvency proceedings are based",[13] and thus comes under an obligation to return what he has so obtained. The liquidator may demand either the return of the assets or the equivalent in money.[14] Presumably this obligation may be enforced in the main proceedings or in the Member State where the assets are situated by virtue of the obligation on the latter Member State to recognise main proceedings opened under Article 3(1). It will be noted that assets subject to rights *in rem* held by third parties (Article 5) and assets subject to a reservation of title (Article 7) are excluded from the operation of this principle.

Clause (2) of the Rule reproduces Article 20(2) of the Regulation. Article **S30–294** 20(2) continues the principle of equal treatment of creditors by providing that in order to ensure such equal treatment, a creditor who, in the course of insolvency proceedings has obtained a dividend on his claim will share in distributions made in other proceedings only where creditors of the same ranking or category have, in those other proceedings, obtained an equivalent dividend.[15]

---

[10] E.C. Insolvency Regulation, Art. 20. See Virgos-Schmit, paras. 171–176; Moss and Bayfield in Moss *et al.*, pp. 83–84; Moss and Smith, *ibid.* pp. 203–204.

[11] Recital (21); Virgos-Schmit, para. 171.

[12] Virgos-Schmit, para. 172. *Cf.* the position in English law: main work, paras. 30–073—30–074, 31–035—31–037.

[13] Virgos-Schmit, *ibid.*

[14] *ibid.*

[15] As to the "rules" concerning the method of calculation, see Virgos-Schmit, para. 174.

ILLUSTRATION

S30–295   X is a company with its centre of main interests in England. Winding-up proceedings (main proceedings) are opened against X in England and A is appointed liquidator. B, a creditor of X, subsequently levies execution against X's assets in France in satisfaction of his claim. B is required to return the assets or the value of the assets in money to A.[16]

S30R–296   RULE 159T—(1) Judgments handed down by a court whose judgment concerning the opening of proceedings is recognised in accordance with Article 16 (Rule 159O) and which concern the course and closure of insolvency proceedings, and compositions approved by that court shall also be recognised with no further formalities. Such judgments shall be enforced in accordance with Articles 38 to 58, with the exception of Article 45(1), of Council Regulation (E.C.) 44/2001 on jurisdiction and the recognition and enforcement of judgments in civil and commercial matters.[17] This clause also applies:

(a) to judgments deriving directly from the insolvency proceedings and which are closely linked with them, even if they were handed down by another court; and

(b) to judgments relating to preservation measures taken after the request for the opening of insolvency proceedings.

(2) The recognition and enforcement of judgments other than those referred to in clause (1) shall be governed by the Regulation referred to in clause (1), provided that that Regulation[18] is applicable.

(3) The Member States shall not be obliged to recognise or enforce a judgment referred to in clause (1) which might result in a limitation of personal freedom or postal secrecy.[19]

COMMENT

S30–297   Rule 159T reproduces Article 25 of the E.C. Insolvency Regulation (headed "Recognition and enforceability of other judgments").

S30–298   **Clause (1) of the Rule.** Article 16 of the Regulation provides for automatic recognition of the judgment opening insolvency proceedings, Article 17 for the automatic recognition of the effects of insolvency proceedings and Article 18 for the automatic recognition of the powers of the liquidator. The first sentence of Rule 159T (1) (Article 25(1) of the Regulation) provides that once a court judgment concerning the opening of proceedings is recognised under Article 16, judgments handed down by the court which

---

[16] Art. 20(1).

[17] The text of Art. 25(1) that appears in the Official Journal refers to Arts 31 to 51, excluding Art. 34(2) of the Brussels Convention on Jurisdiction and the Enforcement of Judgments in Civil and Commercial Matters, as amended by the conventions of Accession to that Convention. Reference to that Convention should now be read as a reference to Council Regulation (E.C.) 44/2001 on jurisdiction and the recognition and enforcement of judgments in civil and commercial matters, Arts 38 to 58, excluding Art. 45(1). See *infra*, para. S30–299.

[18] The original text referred to "Conventions": see preceding note.

[19] E.C. Insolvency Regulation, Art. 25. See Virgos-Schmit, paras. 189–201.

concern the course and closure of insolvency proceedings and compositions approved by that court shall also be recognised with no further formalities. This principle of automatic recognition is extended, by clause (1)(a), to judgments deriving directly from the insolvency proceedings and which are closely linked with them, even if they were handed down by another court,[20] and, by clause (1)(b) to judgments relating to preservation measures taken after the request for the opening of insolvency proceedings. The recognition of a judgment falling within clause (1) is subject to public policy.[21]

The second sentence of clause (1) is concerned with enforcement of **S30–299** judgments which fall within Article 25(1). The text of Article 25(1), as printed in the Official Journal, stipulates that enforcement of the judgment shall be in accordance with Articles 31 to 51, with the exception of Article 34(2) of the Brussels Convention on Jurisdiction and the Enforcement of Judgments in Civil and Commercial Matters, as amended by the Conventions of Accession to this Convention. It would appear, however, that reference to the Brussels Convention should now be read as a reference to Council Regulation (E.C.) 44/2001 on jurisdiction and the recognition and enforcement of judgments in civil and commercial matters (the "Judgments Regulation"), the relevant Articles of which are Articles 38 to 58, with the exception of Article 45(1).[22] The enforcement procedure under the Judgments Regulation is discussed elsewhere in this work.[23] However, it may be mentioned that the exclusion of Article 45(1) of the Judgments Regulation[24] from the enforcement regime applicable under the E.C. Insolvency Regulation means that enforcement of a judgment under the latter Regulation can only be resisted on public policy grounds, as permitted by Article 26 of the latter Regulation,[25] or by reference to Article 25(3) (clause 3 of the Rule).[26]

Clause (2) of the Rule. Article 25(2), reproduced in this clause, states that **S30–300** the recognition and enforcement of judgments other than those referred to in clause (1) will be governed by the Judgments Regulation if that Regulation is applicable. The purpose of Article 25(2) is to avoid "gaps" between the E.C. Insolvency Regulation and the Judgments Regulation.[27]

Clause (3) of the Rule. This provides specific grounds for refusing to **S30–301** recognise or enforce a judgment falling within clause (1) if such recognition or enforcement might result in a limitation of personal freedom[28] or postal secrecy.[29] This would seem to be a specific instance of the public policy principle referred to in Article 26[30] but will enable recognition and

---

[20] See Case 133/78 *Gourdain v. Nadler* [1978] E.C.R. 733. See *supra*, para. S30–161.

[21] Art. 26. *infra* Rule 159U.

[22] Civil Jurisdiction and Judgments Act 1982, s. 1(4), inserted by S.1. 2001 No. 3929, Art. 4 and Sched. 2, Pt. 1, para. 1; Judgments Regulation, Art. 68(2).

[23] See *supra*, paras. S14–221—S14–222.

[24] This provides that enforcement can be challenged on the grounds specified in Arts. 34 and 35: see *ante* paras. S14–206 *et seq.*

[25] *infra*, Rule 159U.

[26] *infra*, para. S30–301.

[27] Virgos-Schmit, para. 197.

[28] *cf.* European Convention on Human Rights, Art. 5.

[29] *ibid.* Art. 8(1).

[30] *infra*, Rule 159U.

enforcement to be denied without reference to that principle in the circumstances envisaged in the clause.[31] Judgments falling within the Judgments Regulation (clause (2)) may be challenged as to recognition and enforcement on any ground permitted by that Regulation.

S30–302 A judgment falling within the E.C. Insolvency Regulation cannot be reviewed as to its substance in a court of a Member State in which recognition of enforcement is sought. Matters of substance must be taken before the courts of the Member State in which proceedings are opened.[32] Further, the court of the Member State in which recognition or enforcement is sought may not review the jurisdiction of the court of the Member State in which proceedings are opened.[33] It is for the court of the latter State to verify its own jurisdiction, any challenge to which must be taken by way of appeal in that State[34] (or ultimately to the European Court of Justice).[35]

ILLUSTRATIONS

S30–303 1. X is a company with its centre of main interests in England. An administration order is made which results in the English court sanctioning a compromise between X and its creditors under section 425 of the Companies Act 1985.[36] The compromise will be recognised in France where X has assets but no establishment.[37]

2. X is a company with its centre of main interests in England. A winding-up petition is presented in respect of X in England and A is appointed provisional liquidator of X. The judgment appointing A will be recognised in France where X has assets but no establishment.[38]

S30R–304 **RULE 159U—Any Member State may refuse to recognise insolvency proceedings opened in another Member State or to enforce a judgment handed down in the context of such proceedings where the effects of such recognition or enforcement would be manifestly contrary to that State's public policy, in particular its fundamental principles or the constitutional rights and liberties of the individual.[39]**

COMMENT

S30–305 Article 26 of the E.C. Insolvency Regulation (headed "Public policy"), reproduced in this Rule, provides that a Member State may refuse to recognise insolvency proceedings opened in another Member State or to enforce a judgment handed down in the context of such proceedings where the effects of such recognition or enforcement would be "manifestly contrary to that State's public policy, in particular its fundamental principles or the constitutional rights and liberties of the individual".[40] Public policy

---

[31] Virgos-Schmit, para. 208.
[32] Virgos-Schmit, para. 202(1).
[33] *ibid.* para. 202(2).
[34] *ibid.*
[35] See *supra*, para. S30–147.
[36] See Insolvency Act 1986, s. 8(3)(c).
[37] E.C. Insolvency Regulation, Art. 25(1) (first sentence).
[38] *ibid.* third sub-paragraph (clause (1)(b) of Rule 159T).
[39] E.C. Insolvency Regulation, Art. 26. See Virgos-Schmit, paras. 202–210.
[40] *cf.* Art. 25(3), *supra*, Rule 159T (3).

constitutes a traditional reservation to the recognition and enforcement of a foreign judgment.[41]

The use of the word "manifestly" is intended to indicate that the public S30–306 policy principle should operate only in exceptional cases.[42] Its exceptional nature may be emphasised in the particular reference to a contravention of the recognising State's fundamental principles or of the constitutional rights and liberties of the individual. Within the latter concept may be included principles of European Community public policy.[43] It is the result of recognition or enforcement of the judgment which must offend public policy rather than the rule or principle applied by the foreign court in the abstract.[44] The principle of public policy includes both fundamental principles of substance and fundamental principles of procedure.[45]

Application of the doctrine can only be assessed in the context of a S30–307 particular case. However, the following are some examples of the broad contours which might surround the principle: adequate opportunity to be heard in insolvency proceedings[46]; the right to participate fully in the proceedings, *e.g.* as a creditor[47]; the principle of non-discrimination against a particular creditor or class of creditors on illegitimate grounds[48]; appropriate guarantees of due process in the grant of preservation measures.[49]

It would also seem that public policy may be used to strike down part of a S30–308 judgment but will not necessarily result in the whole judgment being denied recognition or enforcement.[50] Furthermore, some of the substantive rules of the Regulation build public policy considerations into their terms.[51]

E. Cooperation and Coordination[52]

RULE 159V—(1) Subject to the rules restricting the communication of S30R–309 information, the liquidator in the main proceedings and the liquidators in the secondary proceedings shall be duty bound to communicate information to each other. They shall immediately communicate any information which may be relevant to the other proceedings, in particular the progress made in lodging and verifying claims and all measures aimed at terminating the proceedings.

(2) Subject to the rules applicable to each of the proceedings, the liquidator in the main proceedings and the liquidators in the secondary proceedings shall be duty bound to cooperate with each other.

---

[41] See main work, Rule 2, Rule 44 (see also Rule 45), paras 14–163, 14–177, 14–205—14–213.
[42] Virgos-Schmit, paras. 204–205.
[43] *ibid.* para. 205. *Cf.* Case C-7/98 *Krombach v. Bamberski* [2000] E.C.R. 1–1935; [2001] Q.B. 709; Case C-38/98 *Régie Nationale Usines Renault S.A. v. Maxicar SpA* [2000] E.C.R. 1–2973.
[44] Virgos-Schmit, para. 204.
[45] *ibid.* para. 206.
[46] *ibid.*
[47] *ibid.*
[48] *ibid.*
[49] *ibid.* para. 207.
[50] *ibid.* para. 209.
[51] See, *e.g.* Art. 16(1) (second subparagraph), *supra*, Rule 159O(1); Art. 25(3), *supra*, Rule 159T(3).
[52] Virgos-Schmit, paras. 229–261; Moss and Bayfield in Moss *et al.*, pp. 84–89; Moss and Smith, *ibid.* pp. 217–228.

(3) The liquidator in the secondary proceedings shall give the liquidator in the main proceedings an early opportunity of submitting proposals on the liquidation or use of the assets in the secondary proceedings.[53]

COMMENT

S30–310   Articles 31 to 37 of the E.C. Insolvency Regulation appear in Chapter III of the Regulation which is headed "Secondary Proceedings". In reality, however, Articles 31 to 35 are concerned with the duty on liquidators in the main and secondary proceedings to cooperate with each other, whereas Articles 36 and 37 are concerned with the relationship between territorial proceedings opened prior to main proceedings and the main proceedings which are subsequently opened. Rule 159V sets out the text of Article 31 of the Regulation (headed "Duty to cooperate and communicate information"). Articles 32 to 37 will be discussed in the Comment to this Rule.[54] Main proceedings and secondary proceedings are interdependent and may concern a debtor organised in, and with assets in, several Member States. Accordingly, creditors and liquidators may find it appropriate to participate in several proceedings in different Member States. In such circumstances cooperation and exchange of information between the liquidators is necessary so as to "ensure the smooth course of operations in the various proceedings".[55]

S30–311   **Clause (1) of the Rule.** Article 31(1) provides, subject to any rules restricting the communication of information,[56] that the liquidator in the main proceedings and the liquidators in the secondary proceedings shall be duty bound to communicate information to each other. They must immediately communicate information which may be relevant to the other proceedings. In particular such information will include the progress made in lodging and verifying claims and all measures aimed at termination of the proceedings. The Virgos-Schmit Report specifies in greater detail the nature of the information to be provided under this general rubric as information concerning: the assets; the actions planned or under way in order to recover assets; actions to obtain payment or actions to set aside; the possibilities for liquidating assets; the claims lodged; the verification of claims and disputes concerning them; the ranking of creditors; any planned reorganisation measures; any proposed compositions; any plans for the allocation of dividends; the progress of operations in the proceedings.[57]

S30–312   **Clause (2) of the Rule.** Article 31(2) imposes an important duty on liquidators in the main and secondary proceedings to cooperate with each other. Such cooperation is not voluntary in nature but compulsory and thus, presumably, could be enforced by the court administering the main or

---

[53] E.C. Insolvency Regulation, Art. 31.
[54] Art. 38 relates to preservation measures. This provision is discussed *supra*, para. S30–162. Chapter IV of the Regulation, concerned with the provision of information for creditors and lodgement of their claims is discussed *supra*, paras. S30–193 *et seq*.
[55] Virgos-Schmit, para. 229.
[56] Such rules might be contained in legislation relating to the protection of computerised personal data: *ibid.* para. 231.
[57] *ibid.* para. 230.

330

secondary proceedings, as the case may be.[58] It is incumbent on the liquidators to "act in concert with a view to the development of the proceedings and their coordination, and to facilitate their respective work."[59]

Clause (3) of the Rule. Article 31(3) imposes a specific obligation on the liquidator in the secondary proceedings to give the liquidator in the main proceedings an early opportunity of submitting proposals on the liquidation of or use of assets in the secondary proceedings. This obligation refers to important assets or decisions (*e.g.* the continuation or cessation of the activities of the establishment).[60] The liquidator in the main proceedings should not use the obligation in such a way as to "paralyse the work of the liquidator in the secondary proceedings."[61]

S30–313

Exercise of creditor's rights. Article 32(1) establishes the general principle that any creditor may lodge his claim in the main proceedings and in any secondary proceedings.[62] This takes account of the fact that the assets in the relevant Member States will be different and the rules, *e.g.* as to ranking of claims in those Member States may also be different.[63] Article 32(2) provides assistance[64] to creditors by permitting the liquidators in the main and secondary proceedings to lodge, in other proceedings, claims which have already been lodged in the proceedings for which they were appointed, provided the interests of creditors in the latter proceedings are thereby served. This permission is subject to the right of a creditor to oppose the lodgement on his behalf or to withdraw the lodgement of the claim where the applicable law so allows.[65] Equally, the liquidator in the main or secondary proceedings is empowered to participate in other proceedings on the same basis as a creditor, in particular by attending creditors' meetings.[66]

S30–314

Stay of liquidation. Reflecting the primacy given by the Regulation to main proceedings, Article 33(1) provides that the court which opened the secondary proceedings shall stay the process of liquidation, in whole or in part, on receipt of a request from the liquidator in the main proceedings. In granting a stay, the court may require the liquidator in the main proceedings to take any suitable measure to guarantee the interests of creditors (or individual classes of creditors) in the secondary proceedings. The court may only reject an application for a stay if a stay is manifestly of no interest to the creditors in the main proceedings.[67] A stay may be ordered for up to three months and may be continued or renewed for similar periods.[68]

S30–315

---

[58] *cf.* Insolvency Act 1986, s. 168(5). See Virgos-Schmit, para. 234.

[59] Virgos-Schmit, para. 232.

[60] *ibid.* para. 233.

[61] *ibid.*

[62] According to Art. 39 (*supra*, para. S30–193), creditors entitled to lodge claims in both proceedings are those creditors who have their habitual residence, domicile or registered office in a Member State. But the national law applicable to the relevant proceedings may allow other creditors not so circumstanced to lodge claims.

[63] See Moss and Smith in Moss *et al.*, p. 219.

[64] Virgos-Schmit, para. 236.

[65] See *ibid.* paras. 237–239.

[66] Art. 31(3). Apparently, the right to attend meetings on behalf of creditors does not include the right to vote on behalf of those creditors: see *ibid.* para. 240.

[67] See Virgos-Schmit, paras. 243–244.

[68] The number of successive extensions is not, apparently, limited: *ibid.* para. 245.

S30–316 Should a stay have been granted, the relevant court must terminate the stay on the process of liquidation at the request of the liquidator in the main proceedings, or at the request of a creditor, or at the request of the liquidator in the secondary proceedings, if the stay no longer appears justified, in particular having regard to the interests of the creditors in the main proceedings and the interests of the creditors in the secondary proceedings.[69]

S30–317 **Measures ending secondary proceedings**. Article 34 of the Regulation is concerned with the measures which may be resorted to to end secondary proceedings. Where the law applicable to secondary proceedings allows such proceedings to be closed without liquidation by a rescue plan, a composition or a comparable measure, the liquidator in the main proceedings is given the power to propose such a measure himself,[70] even if he would not possess that power under the national law applicable to the secondary proceedings.[71] Further reflecting the primacy of main proceedings, where such a measure is proposed by a person other than the liquidator in the main proceedings, closure of the secondary proceedings by that measure shall not become final without the consent of the liquidator in the main proceedings.[72] Should the liquidator in the main proceedings oppose the relevant measure, closure of the proceedings pursuant to the measure may become final if the "financial interests of the creditors in the main proceedings are not affected by the measures proposed".[73] For these purposes, "financial interests" are estimated by evaluating the effects which the measure will have on the dividend to be paid to the creditors in the main proceedings—if those creditors could not reasonably have expected to receive more, in the absence of the measure, their financial interests are not affected by it.[74]

S30–318 A rescue plan, composition or other measure which allows secondary proceedings to be closed only affects assets situated in the Member State in which such proceedings are opened.[75] Article 34(2) specifically provides that any restriction on creditors' rights arising out of such a measure does not have effect in respect of the debtor's assets which are not covered by the secondary proceedings "without the consent of all the creditors having an interest". It is thought that consent of the creditors has to be unanimous[76] and that the expression "having an interest" means "interested" (as opposed, *e.g.* to having a "proprietary interest").[77]

S30–319 During a stay of the process of liquidation as a result of an order made under Article 33 of the Regulation,[78] only the liquidator in the main

---

[69] Art. 33(2).

[70] Art. 34(1) (first subparagraph). It is thought that the measures referred to include in England a company voluntary arrangement and an individual voluntary arrangement even though these do not qualify as proceedings which may be opened as secondary proceedings under Annex B: See Moss and Smith in Moss *et al.*, p. 225.

[71] Virgos-Schmit, para. 248.

[72] Art. 34(1) (second subparagraph).

[73] *ibid.*

[74] Virgos-Schmit, para. 249.

[75] Art. 3(2).

[76] Virgos-Schmit, para. 250. A majority vote is permitted in relation to assets subject to the secondary proceedings if it is effective under the law of the Member State in which those proceedings are opened: Art. 4. *Cf.* Art. 17(2), *supra*, para. S30–271.

[77] Moss and Smith in Moss *et al.*, p. 224. See also Virgos-Schmit, para. 250.

[78] *supra*, para. S30–316.

proceedings or the debtor, with the consent of the liquidator in the main proceedings, may propose a rescue plan, composition or other comparable measure, within the meaning of Article 34(1), in the secondary proceedings: no other proposal for such a measure will be put to the vote or approved.[79] This gives the liquidator in the main proceedings a measure of control over the secondary proceedings and also enables the interests of creditors who may have obtained the stay to be taken into account.[80]

Assets remaining in secondary proceedings. According to Article 35, if by the liquidation of assets in the secondary proceedings it is possible to meet all claims submitted in those proceedings, the liquidator appointed in those proceedings shall immediately transfer any assets remaining to the liquidator in the main proceedings. Accordingly, any surplus in the secondary proceedings will be so transferred to pay claims which are admitted in the main proceedings: the surplus will not go to the debtor. This rule reflects the primacy of the main proceedings.[81] It will be noted that there is no provision for any surplus in the main proceedings to be made available to creditors in secondary proceedings whose claims cannot be wholly satisfied in those proceedings. This omission could work unfairly in relation to a creditor with a claim which is only admissible in the secondary proceedings, for whom the opportunity to prove in main proceedings is not available. In such cases the surplus will go the debtor.   S30–320

Subsequent opening of main proceedings. Article 36 of the Regulation is concerned with situations in which territorial proceedings are opened in a Member State, pursuant to Article 3(2), prior to the opening of main proceedings in a different Member State, pursuant to Article 3(1). The provision stipulates that Articles 31 to 35 of the Regulation, discussed above, shall apply to the proceedings opened first, in so far as the progress of these proceedings permits. How far the progress of territorial proceedings permits application of the cooperation and coordination measures contained in Articles 31 to 35 will depend on the circumstances of the particular case. The potentially incomplete application of Articles 31 to 35 to territorial proceedings will generally make the opening of secondary proceedings subsequent to the opening of main proceedings a more attractive option if it is available, as might be the case if the opening of territorial proceedings were to be based on Article 3(4)(b) (Rule 159B (4)(b)).   S30–321

Conversion of earlier proceedings. Where main proceedings are opened subsequent to territorial proceedings, there will be an obvious need to coordinate both sets of proceedings and a particular question arises as to the character to be assumed by the territorial proceedings. Article 37 provides that the liquidator in the main proceedings may request that proceedings listed in Annex A previously opened in another Member State be converted into winding-up proceedings if this proves to be in the interests of the creditors in the main proceedings. The liquidator thus has power to make such an application even if he would not otherwise have that   S30–322

---

[79] Art. 34(3).
[80] Virgos-Schmit, para. 251.
[81] *ibid.* para. 252.

power under the law of the Member State in which the territorial proceedings were opened.[82] On such an application, the provision stipulates that the court with jurisdiction under Article 3(2) "shall" order conversion into one of the proceedings listed in Annex B of the Regulation. That list sets out the proceedings in the Member States which are to be treated as winding-up proceedings for the purposes of the Regulation. Despite the mandatory nature of the language used ("shall" order conversion) it appears that there is a discretion as to whether to order conversion or not.[83] Once the court exercises its discretion in favour of making an order, conversion must be into one of the sets of proceedings listed in Annex B.[84]

---

[82] The English Insolvency Rules 1986 make express provision for such applications. See rr. 1.31–1.33 (company voluntary arrangement to winding up); see also rr. 5.31–5.33 (individual voluntary arrangement to bankruptcy), *infra*, para. S31–104. These rules were inserted by S.1. 2002 No. 1307.

[83] This is clear in relation to the English Insolvency Rules 1986: see rr. 1.33, 2.61, 5.33.

[84] See Moss and Smith in Moss *et al.*, pp. 228–229. Note the special declaration in respect of Art. 37 made by Portugal, [2000] O.J. C183/1. "Article 37 of Council Regulation (E.C.) No. 1346/2000 of May 29, 2000 on insolvency proceedings, which mentions the possibility of converting territorial proceedings opened prior to the main proceedings into winding-up proceedings, should be interpreted as meaning that such conversion does not exclude judicial appreciation of the state of the local proceedings (as is the case in Article 36) or of the application of the interests of public policy as provided for in Article 26". For consequential amendments to the Insolvency Act 1986, see ss. 240(3)(*aa*), 247(3), 387(3) (*aa*), (*ab*), inserted by S.I. 2002 No. 1240, Regs. 11, 12 and 16.

CHAPTER 31

BANKRUPTCY

1. ENGLISH BANKRUPTCIES NOT FALLING WITHIN COUNCIL REGULATION (E.C.) 1346/2000 ON INSOLVENCY PROCEEDINGS

A. *Jurisdiction of the English Court*

Rule 160 is, as from May 31, 2002, subject to the operation of Council **31R–001** Regulation (E.C.) 1346/2000 on Insolvency Proceedings, hereafter "the E.C. Insolvency Regulation" or "the Regulation" which applies to bankruptcy: see Insolvency Act 1986, s. 265(3), inserted by S.I. 2002 No. 1240, Reg. 14. The Regulation is discussed in detail in Chapter 30 (*supra*, paras. S30R–137 *et seq.*). Attention is drawn to particular issues arising in cases of bankruptcy which fall within the Regulation, *infra*, entry at para. 31–090. Essentially, the jurisdiction of the English court to open bankruptcy proceedings as main proceedings will exist if the debtor's centre of main interests is situated in England: E.C. Regulation Art. 3(1), *supra* Rule 159B (1). The English court will have jurisdiction to open bankruptcy proceedings as secondary or territorial proceedings if the debtor has an establishment in England: *ibid*. Art. 3(2), (3) and (4), *supra*, Rule 159B (2), (3) and (4). In cases covered by the Regulation it will be these provisions and not Rule 160 which will determine whether the English court has jurisdiction.

NOTE 2. The European Council Regulation on Insolvency Proceedings has replaced the European Union Convention on Insolvency Proceedings. See previous entry. The UNCITRAL model law on cross-border insolvency (*supra*, entry at paras. 30–140—144) can apply to bankruptcy but whether it will be so applied will depend on the implementing regulations made pursuant to Insolvency Act 2000, s. 14. Council Regulation (E.C.) 44/2001 ([2000] O.J. L307/28) on jurisdiction and the recognition and enforcement of judgments in civil and commercial matters ("the Judgments Regulation") does not apply to bankruptcy: see Art. 1(2)(b), and *supra*, para. S30–161.

NOTE 8. Part VIII of Insolvency Act 1986 is amended by Insolvency Act **31–003** 2000, s. 3 and Sched. 3 but the amendments do not affect the propositions in the text.

NOTE 17. Add: See also *Geveran Trading Co. Ltd. v. Skjevesland* [2003] **31–007** B.P.I.R. 73 (Mr. Registrar Jaques), affd. [2002] EWHC 2898, [2003] B.C.C. 391.

NOTE 36. The provisions of Order 11 are now in CPR, Part 6: see, **31–012** especially, rr. 6.20–6.30. *Practice Direction* [1988] 1 W.L.R. 461 is replaced by *Practice Direction—Insolvency Proceedings*, para. 10.

31R–016 Rule 161 is subject to the effect of the E.C. Insolvency Regulation. The English court will not have jurisdiction to adjudge a debtor bankrupt if the debtor has his centre of main interests in another Member State (Art. 3(1), *supra*, Rule 159B (1)), unless the debtor has an establishment in England (Art. 3(2), *supra*, Rule 159B (2)), in which case the court's jurisdiction to adjudge the debtor bankrupt is limited in effect to the assets of the debtor which are situated in England (*ibid*. and Insolvency Act 1986, s. 436A, inserted by S.I. 2002 No. 1240, Reg. 18. See *infra*, entry at para. 31–090.

B. *Effect of an English bankruptcy as an assignment of property*

31R–021 Rule 162 must be read in the light of the E.C. Insolvency Regulation. If the centre of the debtor's main interests is situated in England, the opening of main proceedings in England must be given effect in other Member States, except as the Regulation otherwise provides (Arts. 3(1), 16 and 17, *ante*, Rules 159B (1), 159O and 159P). The opening of main proceedings means, thus, that English law as the law of the State of opening (Art. 4, *ante*, Rule 159C) is capable of affecting property situated in other Member States and such property may be dealt with in the English proceedings unless the Regulation otherwise provides (Insolvency Act 1986, s. 436A, inserted by S.I. 2002 No. 1240, Reg. 18). If, however, secondary or territorial proceedings are opened in another Member State because the debtor has an establishment in that Member State, then the law of the State of opening of the secondary proceedings will apply to the debtor's property situated in that Member State, to the exclusion of English law (Arts. 3(2), 4 and 27, *supra*, Rules 159B (2) and 159C). If the debtor has his centre of main interests in another Member State, the English court will have jurisdiction to open secondary or territorial proceedings if the debtor has an establishment in England (Art. 3(2), *supra*, Rule 159B (2)). The effects of these proceedings are limited to property situated in England (*ibid*.; Insolvency Act 1986, s. 436A, inserted by S.I. 2002 No. 1204, Reg. 18). As regards immovable property, Article 8 of the Regulation (*supra*, Rule 159G) provides that the effects of insolvency proceedings on a contract conferring a right to acquire or make use of immovable property shall be governed solely by the law of the Member State within the territory of which the immovable property is situated. The Regulation, in this way, is of more limited scope than Rule 162(1). As regards movables, where English law is the law of the State of opening, its effect may be limited by Articles 5 and 7 (*supra*, Rules 159D and 159F). In this respect also the scope of the Regulation is more limited than Rules 162.

Rule 162 will continue to apply in intra-United Kingdom cases since the Regulation does not apply in such cases: see *supra*, para. S30–145.

31–028 Note 87. Insolvency Act 1986, s. 426 (10) is amended by Insolvency Act 2000, Sched. 4, Pt. II, para. 16(3).

31–029 Note 90. Add: *England v. Smith* [2001] Ch. 419 (C.A.).

31–030 Note 94. In line 3 add: *England v. Smith, supra*.

31–035 Note 9. Add: *Cleaver v. Delta American Reinsurance Co.* [2001] 2 A.C. 328 (P.C.).

31–036 Note 11. Add in line 3: *Cleaver v. Delta American Reinsurance Co., supra*. See *supra*, entry at para. 30–073, text at nn. 95–96.

C. *Choice of law*

Rule 163 must be read subject to the E.C. Insolvency Regulation. If the **31R–039**
English court has jurisdiction to open main, secondary or territorial
proceedings, then although English law (including the Insolvency Act 1986),
as the law of the State of the opening will be the applicable law as a general
rule (Art. 4, *supra*, Rule 159C), there may be situations where, by way of
exception, an issue may be governed by the law of another Member State
(see Arts. 5 to 15, *supra*, Rules 159D to 159N).

D. *Effect of English bankruptcy as a dischage of debts*

The position under the E.C. Insolvency Regulation is the same as under **31R–047**
Rule 164: see Art. 4(2)(j) and (k), *supra*, Rule 159C (2)(j) and (k). See
infra, entry at para. 31–090.

2. FOREIGN BANKRUPTCIES NOT WITHIN COUNCIL REGULATION (E.C.) 1346/2000 ON INSOLVENCY PROCEEDINGS

A. *Jurisdiction of foreign courts*

Rule 165(1) is unaffected by the E.C. Insolvency Regulation since the **31R–052**
Regulation does not apply to intra-United Kingdom bankruptcies. See
supra, para. S30–145.

Rule 165(2) is inapplicable in cases falling within the E.C. Insolvency
Regulation. Under the Regulation the English court will recognise that the
courts of another Member State have jurisdiction to open main proceedings
in respect of the debtor if the debtor has his centre of main interests in that
Member State (Arts. 3(1) and 16, *supra*, Rules 159B (1) and 159O).
Equally, the English court will recognise that the courts of another Member
State have jurisdiction to open secondary or territorial proceedings in
respect of the debtor if the debtor has an establishment in that Member
State (Arts. 3(2), (3), (4) and 16, *supra*, Rules 159B (2), (3), (4) and 159O).

B. *Effect in England of foreign bankruptcy as an assignment of property*

(1) BANKRUPTCY IN SCOTLAND OR NORTHERN IRELAND

Rule 166 is unaffected by the E.C. Insolvency Regulation in relation to **31R–058**
Scottish and Northern Irish bankruptcies, since intra-United Kingdom
bankruptcies do not fall within the Regulation. The Regulation applies in
Scotland and Northern Ireland. Consequently, when the Regulation is
applicable, the extent to which a Scottish or Northern Irish bankruptcy
operates as an assignment to the bankrupt's representative of the immovables or movables of the bankrupt will depend on the Regulation and not
on Rule 166.

(2) BANKRUPTCY IN ANY OTHER FOREIGN COUNTRY

31R–063   Rule 167 does not apply to cases falling within the E.C. Insolvency Regulation.

31–066   The first sentence of this paragraph was cited with approval in *Holt Cargo Systems Inc. v. ABC Containerline N.V.* [2001] 3 S.C.R. 907 (Sup. Ct. Can.).

31–068   This passage was cited with approval in *Chen Li Hung v Ting Lei Miao* [2000] 1 H.K.L.R.D. 252, 258, (2000) 3 H.K.C.F.A.R. 9, 16.

31R–071   Rule 168 does not apply in cases falling within the E.C. Insolvency Regulation.

(3) SUCCESSIVE BANKRUPTCIES IN DIFFERENT COUNTRIES

31R–075   Rule 169 does not apply in cases falling within the E.C. Insolvency Regulation.

C. *Effect in England of foreign bankruptcy as a discharge of debts*

31R–080   Rule 170 does not apply in cases falling within the E.C. Insolvency Regulation.

31R–087   Rule 171 is unaffected by the E.C. Insolvency Regulation.

31–090   After this paragraph insert the following material.

3. BANKRUPTCIES FALLING WITHIN COUNCIL REGULATION (E.C.) 1346/2000 ON INSOLVENCY PROCEEDINGS

Council Regulation (E.C.) 1346/2000 on insolvency proceedings (hereafter "the E.C. Insolvency Regulation" or "the Regulation" is capable of applying to the insolvency of both legal and natural persons.[38] The rules which apply to individual debtors are the same as those which apply to debtors who are legal persons. The Regulation is subject to detailed examination in Chapter 30, primarily in the context of debtors who are legal persons.[39] The present commentary is designed to draw attention to issues which may arise in applying the Regulation in the particular context of the insolvency of natural persons (in English legal terminology, cases of bankruptcy).

A. *Introduction and Scope*

Most of what is said in the Comment to Rule 159A[40] applies to cases of bankruptcy. Thus the Regulation will only apply to collective insolvency

---

[38] E.C. Insolvency Regulation, Recital (9).
[39] *supra*, paras. S30R–137 *et seq*.
[40] Reproducing Art. 1 of the E.C. Insolvency Regulation.

proceedings which entail the partial or total divestment of a debtor and the appointment of a liquidator, provided that the centre of main interests of the debtor is situated in a Member State.[41] For the purposes: "insolvency proceedings" include, in England, individual voluntary arrangements and bankruptcy[42]; "liquidator" includes, in England, the Official Receiver and a trustee in bankruptcy[43]; and "Member State" means any State which is a member of the European Union except Denmark.[44] The Regulation does not apply to intra-United Kingdom cases of bankruptcy.[45]

B. *International Jurisdiction*

Jurisdictional rules applicable in bankruptcy are those stated in Rule 159B which reproduces Article 3 of the Regulation.

Main proceedings; Article 3(1). Jurisdiction to open main proceedings is conferred on the courts of the Member State in which the debtor's centre of main interests is situated.[46] Thus an English court only has jurisdiction to open main insolvency proceedings in respect of an individual debtor if that debtor has his centre of main interests in England and it will have no jurisdiction if that debtor's centre of main interests is situated in another Member State. In the latter situation jurisdiction to open main proceedings is conferred on the courts of that Member State. Where it is concluded that the centre of the debtor's main interests is situated in a non-Member State the Regulation will not apply at all.[47] In such a situation, the jurisdiction of the English court will depend on section 265(1) and (2) of the Insolvency Act 1986[48], and the jurisdiction of courts in other Member States will depend on the relevant national law (excluding, of course, the provisions of the Regulation). Identification of the debtor's centre of main interests is, therefore, critical.

"Centre of main interests". The drafting of Article 3(1) employs the present tense ("centre of a debtor's main interests is situated") suggesting that the relevant time to locate the centre of the debtor's main interests is the time when proceedings are opened.[49] But the expression "centre of main interests" is not defined.[50] Recital (13) states, rather generally, that

---

[41] E.C. Insolvency Regulation, Art. 1(1).

[42] *ibid.* Art. 2(a) and Annex A.

[43] *ibid.* Art. 2(b) and Annex C.

[44] *ibid.* Recital (33).

[45] *ibid.* Recital (15). *supra*, paras. S30–145.

[46] *ibid.* Art. 3(1). In England "court" will normally means the High Court or county court: Insolvency Act 1986, s. 373(1). But note the more expansive definition of "court" in Art. 2(d) of the Regulation (see *supra*, para. S30–156). In the context of individual voluntary arrangements under English law, on the basis of Art. 2(d), "court" may be construed to mean the relevant creditors' meeting: see Moss in *The E.C. Regulation on Insolvency Proceedings* (Moss, Fletcher and Isaacs (eds.) 2002), p. 163 (hereafter referred to as Moss *et al.*).

[47] Recital (14); see *Geveran Trading Co. Ltd. v. Skjevesland*, *supra*, entry at para. 31–007.

[48] Main work, Rule 160.

[49] Fletcher in *Reform and Development of Private International Law* (Fawcett ed., 2002), p. 167, at p. 178. See *Geveran Trading Co. Ltd. v. Skjevesland, supra.*

[50] There is no presumption as to where the centre of main interests of an individual is located as there is with a company or legal person. For discussion of the issue, see Moss *et al.*, pp. 169–170; Fletcher, *supra*, n. 49, pp. 178–180.

the expression "should correspond to the place where the debtor conducts the administration of his interests on a regular basis and is therefore ascertainable by third parties." According to the Virgos-Schmit Report,[51] reference to the term "interests" was intended "to encompass not only commercial industrial or professional activities, but also general economic activities, so as to include the activities of private individuals (*e.g.* consumers). The expression 'main' serves as a criterion for the cases where these interests include activities of different types which are run from different centres. In principle the centre of main interests will in the case of professionals be the place of their professional domicile and for natural persons in general, the place of their habitual residence."[52] Applying these principles involves a wide ranging inquiry requiring consideration, *e.g.* of where the debtor's home is, where he conducts his business (if any), where he can be contacted, where his emotional ties are and the amount of time the debtor spends or has spent in various places.[53] In the case of the non-professional individual debtor, the centre of main interests will normally be the country in which he had his habitual residence. But in the case of the professional debtor engaged in business, the centre of main interests will normally be the country from which, or in which, he conducts his principal business activities and this palace may well be different from that in which he has his habitual residence.[54] Since Article 3(1) contemplates main proceedings which, in general, have universal effect, it follows that an individual debtor may have only one centre of main interests.[55]

Secondary proceedings: Article 3(2). Article 3(2) (Rule 159B (2)) provides that where the centre of a debtor's main interests is situated within the territory of a Member State, the courts of another Member State have jurisdiction to open insolvency proceedings against that debtor only if that debtor has an "establishment" in that Member State. The opening of such proceedings only affects assets of the individual debtor which are situated in that Member State.[56] These secondary proceedings must be "winding-up proceedings", as defined in Article 2(c) of, and listed in Annex B to, the Regulation.[57] In relation to England, the proceeding listed is bankruptcy. Accordingly, if the English court has jurisdiction to open secondary proceedings they must be bankruptcy proceedings.[58] The definition of "establishment" in Article 2(h) seems suited, mainly, to an individual carrying on a busines activity since establishment means "any place of operations where the debtor carries out a non-transitory economic activity

---

[51] This was the Report which commented on the text of the earlier Convention which was replaced by the Regulation: see *supra*, para. S30–135.

[52] Para. 75.

[53] See *Geveran Trading Co. Ltd. v. Skjevesland, supra.*

[54] See Moss and Smith in Moss *et al.* pp. 169–170, discussing a Dutch decision (Court of Assen, June 5, 2002). See also Moss (2003) 16 *Insolvency Intelligence* 113.

[55] Though because of the imprecision of the expression, courts in different Member States may conclude that the centre of main interests of the same debtor is situated in difference Member States.

[56] See Insolvency Act 1986, s. 436A, inserted by S.I. 2002 No. 1240, Reg. 18.

[57] Art. 3(3).

[58] Note the amendments to Insolvency Act 1986, s. 264(1) which permit a bankruptcy petition to be presented by a temporary administrator within the meaning of Art. 38 of the Regulation and by a liquidator within the meaning of Art. 2(b) of the Regulation appointed in proceedings by virtue of Art. 3(1) of the Regulation: Insolvency Act 1986, s. 264(1)(*ba*) and (*bb*), inserted by S.I. 2002 No. 1240, Reg. 13.

with human means and goods."[59] In the case of a non-professional, there will normally, one suspects, be no such establishment, though it is possible that such an individual might be held to have an establishment in a Member State if he had a holiday home there at which he spends a reasonable amount of time and engages in, say, private share transactions on that Member State's stock market. But it may well be that the opening of secondary proceedings against a non-professional individual debtor will be unusual.

Territorial proceedings: Article 3(4). Territorial proceedings may be opened in a Member State in respect of a debtor who is a natural person prior to the opening of main proceedings in a different Member State, provided the debtor has an establishment in the former Member State, in two situations. The first is where main proceedings cannot be opened in the Member State in which the centre of the debtor's main interests is located.[60] Such a situation could well come about in the context of the European Community since, in some Member States it is not possible to open insolvency proceedings against a person who is not a trader.[61] Secondly, the opening of such territorial proceedings may be requested by a creditor who has his domicile, habitual residence or registered office in the Member State in which the debtor's establishment is situated, or whose claim arises from the operation of that establishment.[62] In view of the fact that each of these conditions requires the debtor to have an establishment in the Member State where territorial proceedings are to be opened, the jurisdiction is likely to assume more prominence in relation to professional individual debtors than it will in the case of non-professionals.[63] The categories of proceedings that can be opened as territorial proceedings prior to the opening of main proceedings are broader than the winding-up proceedings available as secondary proceedings. In the present context, in England, such proceedings will include an individual voluntary arrangement as well as bankruptcy.[64] As with secondary proceedings, however, the effect of these territorial proceedings will be confined to assets of the debtor situated in the Member State in which the territorial proceedings are opened.

Relationship with English law. An English court will only have jurisdiction to open main bankruptcy proceedings if the debtor's centre of main interests is situated in England. The English court will only have jurisdiction to open secondary proceedings if the debtor has an establishment in England whereas territorial proceedings may be opened in England prior to the opening of main proceedings in another Member State if the debtor has an establishment in England and if one of the conditions set forth in Article 3(4)(Rule 159B (4) is satisfied.[65] It follows from this that section 265(1) and

---

[59] See *supra*, para. S30–164.
[60] Art. 3(4)(a) (Rule 159B (4)(a)).
[61] See Fletcher in Moss *et al.*, p. 43.
[62] Art. 3(4)(b) (Rule 159B (4)(b)).
[63] And it is more than likely that Art. 3(4)(b) will assume greater prominence than Art. 3(4)(a) since a non-professional debtor is less likely to have an establishment than a professional.
[64] Virgos-Schmit, para. 86. See Annex A. As to conversion of territorial proceedings once main proceedings have been opened, see Art. 37.
[65] New court forms require a statement as to whether proceedings are main, secondary or territorial: see Form 6.25 (Bankruptcy Order on Creditor's Petition); Form 6.30 (Bankruptcy Order on Debtor's Petition); Form 6.32 (Order of Appointment of Interim Receiver).

(2) of the Insolvency Act 1986 (Rule 160) will not ground jurisdiction in the English court when the Regulation applies.[66] This is so even if the debtor personally seeks to petition for his own bankruptcy.[67]

C. *Choice of Law*

Rules 159C to 159N (Articles 4 to 16 of the Regulation) apply in much the same way in cases of individual bankruptcy as they do in the case of the insolvency of legal persons.[68] Thus the general rule is that the law applicable to individual insolvency proceedings and their effects is that of the Member State within the territory of which the proceedings are opened.[69] This rule applies in main[70] and in secondary (including territorial) proceedings.[71] Two aspects of the general rule deserve specific mention.

Capacity of the debtor. Generally, the law of the State of opening determines the conditions for the opening of the proceedings, their conduct and their closure.[72] In particular, though, that law will determine against which debtors proceedings may be brought on account of their capacity.[73] Several Member States do not permit insolvency proceedings to be brought against non-traders.[74] Thus, for example, if the individual debtor has his centre of main interests in France, it may not be possible to open main proceedings in respect of that debtor in France.[75] If such a debtor has an establishment in England, it will, nonetheless, be possible to open territorial proceedings in respect of that debtor in England. Alternatively, if a non-trading French debtor has his centre of main interests in England, it will be possible to open main proceedings in respect of that debtor in England. If that debtor has an establishment in France, it may not be possible to open secondary proceedings in respect of that debtor in France if French law does not enable insolvency proceedings to be opened in respect of a non-trading debtor.

Discharge. It is a well established principle of English law that a discharge from any debt or liability under the bankruptcy law of a foreign country outside the United Kingdom is a discharge therefrom in England if, and only if, it is a discharge under the law applicable to the contract.[76]

---

[66] Fletcher in *Reform and Development of Private International Law* (Fawcett ed., 2002), p. 167, at pp. 178–179. As to the possible operation of the rule in *Theophile v. Solicitor General* [1905] A.C. 186 (main work, para. 31–008) in the context of the Regulation, see Fletcher, *ibid*. pp. 179–180; Fletcher in Moss *etal.*, p. 171.

[67] Fletcher in *Reform and Development of Private International Law* (Fawcett ed., 2002), p. 167 at p. 178.

[68] *supra*, paras. S30R–181 *et seq.*

[69] E.C. Insolvency Regulation, Art. 4(1) (Rule 159C (1)).

[70] *ibid.*

[71] Art. 28 (Rule 159C (3)). It is not entirely clear whether the choice of law rule for territorial proceedings depends on Art. 4 or Art. 28 but the distinction is of no practical importance since each provision leads to the application of the law of the State of opening.

[72] Art. 4(2) (Rule 159C (2)).

[73] Art. 4(2)(a) (Rule 159C (2)(a)).

[74] Fletcher in *Reform and Development of Private International Law* (Fawcett ed., 2002), p. 167, at p.180.

[75] In France, apparently, insolvency proceedings cannot be taken in respect of persons who are not traders: see Fletcher, *ibid*.; Fletcher in Moss *et al.*, p. 48.

[76] Main work, Rule 170.

Accordingly to Article 4(2)(j) of the Regulation (Rule 159C (2)(j)), the law of the State of the opening determines the conditions for and effects of closure of insolvency proceedings. This means that where main proceedings in another Member State are closed and the closure has, under the law of that Member State, the effect of discharging the debtor, that discharge must be recognised in England even if it is not an effective discharge under the law applicable to the contract.[77]

Exceptions. The exceptions to the general rule in Article 4 (Rule 159C) contained in Articles 5 to 15 (Rules 159D to 159N) would seem to apply in cases of individual insolvency in the same way as they apply to the insolvency of a legal person.[78]

D. *Recogniton of Insolvency Proceedings*

The rules relating to recognition of insolvency proceedings contained in Chapter II of the Regulation and Articles 27 to 30, contained in Chapter III of the Regulation apply to individual insolvency in the same way as they apply to the insolvency of a legal person.[79] Especially important is the principle of automatic recognition of the judgment opening the proceedings under Article 3 in other Member States[80] and the rule that that judgment shall produce the same effects in other Member States as it has in the State of opening without further formalities.[81] The powers of the trustee (or equivalent) as conferred by the law of the State of opening may be exercised in other Member States in accordance with Article 18 (Rule 159R). Further judgments handed down by a court whose judgment concerning the opening of proceedings is recognised under Article 16 (Rule 159O) and which concern the course and closure of insolvency proceedings are also to be recognised with no further formalities.[82] The only defence to recognition is public policy,[83] a concept which, in the context of the Regulation, is to be narrowly circumscribed.[84]

E. *Cooperation and Coordination*

Articles 31[85] to 35 of the Regulation concerned with the duties on liquidators[86] in main and secondary proceedings to cooperate with each

---

[77] See also Art. 4(2)(k) (Rule 159C(2)(k)).

[78] See *supra*, paras. S30R–205 *et seq.*

[79] *supra*, Rules 159O to 159T.

[80] E.C. Insolvency Regulation, Art. 16 (Rule 159O). The judgment must be recognised even where on account of his capacity insolvency proceedings cannot be brought against the debtor in other Member States.

[81] Art. 17 (Rule 159P). Neither Art. 16 nor Art. 17 preclude the opening of secondary proceedings in a Member State in which an individual debtor has an establishment.

[82] Art. 25 (Rule 159T).

[83] Art. 26 (Rule 159U).

[84] *supra*, para. S30–306. The rules contained in Chapter IV of the Regulation (Arts. 39 to 42) concerned with provision of information for creditors and lodgement of their claims and the transitional and final provisions contained in Chapter V (Arts 43 to 47) also apply to individual bankruptcy.

[85] Rule 159V.

[86] Which include an English trustee in bankruptcy and the other Member States' equivalents thereto: see Art. 2(b) and Annex C.

other and Articles 36 and 37 concerned with the relationship between territorial proceedings opened prior to main proceedings and the main proceedings which are subsequently opened apply equally in individual insolvency proceedings as they apply in respect of proceedings in respect of legal persons.[87] Article 38, dealing with preservation measures, may be invoked in both types of insolvency.[88] Two points relevant to these provisions in England may be mentioned.

Surplus in secondary proceedings. Article 35 stipulates that if by the liquidation of assets in the secondary proceedings it is possible to meet all claims submitted in those proceedings, the liquidator appointed in those proceedings shall immediately transfer any assets remaining to the liquidator in the main proceedings.[89] According to section 330(5) of the Insolvency Act 1986, if a surplus remains after payment in full and with interest of all the bankrupt's creditors and the payment of the expenses of the bankruptcy, the bankrupt is entitled to the surplus. An amendment to section 330 of the 1986 Act now makes it clear that section 330(5) is subject to Article 35 of the Regulation.[90]

Measures ending secondary proceedings. Article 34(1) provides that where the law applicable to secondary proceedings allows for such proceedings to be closed without liquidation by a rescue plan, a composition or comparable measure, the liquidator in the main proceedings shall be allowed to propose such a measure himself.[91] It his thought that the measures referred to include an individual voluntary arrangement, as available in England, even though such an arrangement does not qualify as a proceeding which may be opened as a secondary proceeding under Annex B to the Regulation.[92]

---

[87] *supra* paras. S30–321, *et seq*. These provisions appear in Chapter III of the Regulation.
[88] *supra* para. S30–162.
[89] *supra* para. S30–320.
[90] Insolvency ACt 1986, s. 330(6), inserted by S.I. 2002 No. 1204, Reg. 15.
[91] *supra*, para. S30–319.
[92] See Moss and Smith in Moss *et al.*, p. 255.

CHAPTER 32

CONTRACTS. GENERAL RULES

1. THE LAW GOVERNING A CONTRACT

The Rome Convention. The Rome Convention is being reviewed by the **32–008**
European Commission, and its replacement by a Council Regulation is
under consideration.

NOTE 30. The 1996 Accession Convention is now in force: S.I. 2000 No. **32–102**
1825.

Order 11, r. 1(1)(*d*)(iii) is replaced by CPR, r. 6.20(5)(c). **32–026**

See now Contracts (Applicable Law) Act 1990, s. 2(1A), as substituted by **32–041**
S.I. 2001 No. 3649, Art. 320, and *infra*, para. S33–125.

Text to notes 21 and 22. This passage was approved in *Centrax Ltd. v.* **32–049**
Citibank NA [1999] 1 All E.R. (Comm.) 557, 562 (C.A.).

2. DETERMINATION OF THE APPLICABLE LAW

It was also approved in *Samcrete Egypt Engineers and Contractors SAE v.* **32–078**
Land Rover Exports Ltd. [2002] EWCA Civ. 2019; [2002] C.L.C. 533, 540
(C.A.).

Cf. American Motorists Insurance Co. v. Cellstar Corp. [2003] EWCA Civ. **32–089**
206, [2003] I.L.Pr. 370 (C.A.) (a case on insurance contracts).

It has been held consistently that reinsurance contracts broked in the **32–090**
London market are impliedly governed by English law: *Gan Insurance Co.*
Ltd. v. Tai Ping Insurance Co. Ltd. [1999] I.L.Pr. 729 (C.A.); *Tiernan v.*
Magen Insurance Co. Ltd. [2000] I.L.Pr. 517; *Ace Insurance S.A.-N.V. v.*
Zurich Insurance Co. [2000] 2 Lloyd's Rep. 423; affd. [2001] EWCA Civ.
173; [2001] 1 Lloyd's Rep. 618 (C.A.).

NOTE 25. See also *Aeolian Shipping SA v. ISS Machinery Services Ltd.* [2001] **32–091**
EWCA Civ. 1162; [2001] 2 Lloyd's Rep. 641 (C.A.).

See also *Marubeni Hong Kong and South China Ltd. v. Mongolian Govern-* **32–095**
ment [2002] 2 All E.R. (Comm.) 873.

See on conflicting standard terms of contract *Ferguson Shipbuilders Ltd. v.* **32–101**
Voith Hydro GmbH, 2000 S.L.T. 229; Danneman, in *Lex Mercatoria: Essays*
in Honour of Francis Reynolds (ed. Rose, 2000), p. 199.

32–111 NOTE 73. See also *Print Concept GmbH v. GEW (EC) Ltd.* [2002] C.L.C. 382 (C.A.); *Definitely Maybe (Touring) Ltd. v. Lieberberg GmbH* [2001] 1 W.L.R. 1745; *Kenburn Waste Management Ltd. v. Bergmann* [2002] EWCA Civ. 98; [2002] F.S.R. 711 (C.A.); *Caledonia Subsea Ltd. v. Microperi Srl*, 2001 S.C. 76.

32–117 On the meaning of "under the contract" see *Ennstone Building Products Ltd. v. Stanger Ltd.* [2002] EWCA Civ. 916; [2002] 1 W.L.R. 3059, 3068 (C.A.) (the words connote that "the contract terms specify that performance is to be effected through some other place of business.")

32–123 Text at note 2. The approach suggested here has been adopted by the English courts. In *Samcrete Egypt Engineers and Contractors SAE v. Land Rover Exports Ltd.* [2002] EWCA Civ. 2019; [2002] C.L.C. 533, 545 (C.A.) it was said that the presumption "should only be disregarded in circumstances which clearly demonstrate the existence of connecting factors justifying the disregarding of the presumption in Article 4(2)". That decision has been applied in *Ennstone Building Products Ltd. v. Stanger Ltd.* [2002] EWCA Civ. 916, [2002] 1 W.L.R. 3059, 3070 (C.A.) and in *Iran Continental Shelf Oil Co. v. IRI International Corp* [2002] EWCA Civ. 1024 (C.A.). For a similar view see *Caledonia Subsea v. Micoperi SRL, The Times*; 2002 S.L.T. 1022 (Inner House); *Definitely Maybe (Touring) Ltd v. Lieberberg GmbH* [2001] 1 W.L.R. 1745, 1747–8. See also Briggs (2001) 72 B.Y.I.L. 465.

32–124 NOTE 3. But see *Caledonia Subsea v. Micoperi SRL*, 2002 S.L.T. 1022 (Inner House).

3. MANDATORY RULES

32–142 NOTE 40. See also *Society of Lloyd's v. Fraser* [1998] C.L.C. 1630, 1652 (C.A.); *Fox v. Henderson Investment Fund Ltd.* [1999] 2 Lloyd's Rep. 303.

4. MATERIAL VALIDITY

32–156 See entry at para. 32–026.

32–159 See *Welex AG v. Rosa Maritima Ltd. (The Epsilon Rosa) (No. 2)* [2002] EWHC 2033 (Comm); [2002] 2 Lloyd's Rep. 81.

8. PUBLIC POLICY

32–230 NOTE 35. *Cf.* also *Re COLT Telecom Group plc* [2002] EWHC 2815 (Ch); [2003] B.P.I.R. 324.

32–235 NOTE 55. See also *Westacre Investments Inc. v. Jugoimport-SPDR Ltd.* [2000] Q.B. 288, 304 (C.A.).

32–236 The carrying out of prohibited acts within the territory of the foreign country is an essential and necessary element of the principle in *Foster v. Driscoll* [1929] 1 K.B. 470 (C.A.): *Ispahani v. Bank Melli Iran* [1998] Lloyd's Rep. Bank. 133.

CHAPTER 33

PARTICULAR CONTRACTS

1 CERTAIN CONSUMER CONTRACTS

See Commission of the European Communities, *Green Paper on the* **33R–001** *conversion of the Rome Convention of 1980 on the law applicable to contractual obligations into a Community instrument and its modernisation* COM (2002) 654 final, paras 3.2.7.1–3.2.7.3.

NOTE 12. Add: Case C–96/00 *Gabriel v. Schlank & Schick GmbH* [2002] **33–004** E.C.R. I–6367 [2002] I.L.Pr. 642.

NOTE 27. *Cf. Standard Bank London Ltd. v. Dimitrios Apostolakis* [2002] **33–009** C.L.C. 939; *Rayner v. Davies* [2002] EWCA Civ. 1880; [2003] I.L.Pr. 258 (C.A.); Case C–96/00 *Gabriel v. Schlank & Schick GmbH, supra.*

NOTE 29. European Parliament and Council Directive of May 20, 1997 on **33–011** the protection of consumers in respect of "distance contracts" [1997] O.J. L144/19, is implemented in the United Kingdom in the Consumer Protection (Distance Selling) Regulations 2000, S.I. 2000 No. 2334.

NOTE 31. Add: European Parliament and Council Directive of June 8, 2000 on certain legal aspects of information society services, in particular electronic commerce ("Directive on electronic commerce") ([2000] O.J. L178/1), implemented in the United Kingdom in the Electronic Commerce (E.C. Directive) Regulations 2002, S.I. 2002 No. 2013 (Reg. 16 in force from October 23, 2002, remainder in force from August 21, 2002) is generally thought to support a "country of origin" principle for regulating electronic commerce, a principle which might be thought to support application of the supplier's law rather than the law of the consumer's habitual residence. However, it is submitted that the Directive has no bearing on the issue discussed in the Main Work. This is because (a) Art. 1(4) and Recital 23 of the Directive (not reproduced in the Regulations) state that the Directive does not establish additional rules on private international law though see *post*, entry at para. 35R–119; (b) the Directive and the Regulations are explicitly expressed not to apply to the freedom of the parties to choose the law applicable to their contract and to consumer contracts (Directive, Art. 3(3) and Annex, Regulations, reg. 4(4) and Schedule); (c) Recital 55 of the Directive (not reproduced in the Regulations) states that "this Directive cannot have the result of depriving the consumer of the protection afforded to him by the mandatory rules relating to contractual obligations of the law of the Member State in which he has his habitual residence".

NOTES 81–83. The Sale and Supply of Goods to Consumers Regulations **33–028** 2002, S.I. 2002 No. 3045, which entered into force on March 31, 2003, implement in the United Kingdom the Directive of the European Parliament and Council of May 25, 1999 on certain aspects of the sale of consumer goods and associated guarantees ([1999] O.J. L171/12) and amends Sale of Goods Act 1979, s. 14 and Supply of Goods (Implied Terms) Act 1973, s. 10: Regs. 3 and 14. The applicability of these amended provisions will thus depend on Unfair Contract Terms Act 1977, s. 27(2). The definition of "deals as consumer" in Unfair Contract Terms Act 1977, s. 12 is amended by Reg. 14 so that the use of that expression in s. 27(2)(b) of the 1977 Act has to be understood to include this amendment. The provisions of the Regulations (Reg. 16) which deal with "consumer guarantees", as defined in Reg. 2 are not made subject to any explicit anti-avoidance provision in the Regulations. Art. 7(2) of the Directive requires that "Member States shall take the necessary measures to ensure that consumers are not deprived of the protection afforded by this Directive as a result of opting for the law of a non-member State as the law applicable to the contract where the contract has a close connection with the territory of the Member States" and it would seem likely the a court would not countenance avoidance of Reg. 16 in contravention of Art. 7(2).

33–031 NOTE 93. The European Parliament and the Council has made a proposal for a Directive on the laws, regulations and administrative provisions of the Member States concerning credit for consumers: see COM (2002) 443 final. Art. 30(5) of the proposed Directive provides that Member States shall take the necessary measures to ensure that the consumer does "not lose the protection granted by this directive by virtue of the choice of the law of a non-member country as the law applicable to the agreement, if the agreement has a close link with the territory of one or more Member States."

33–038 NOTE 13. S.I. 1999 No. 2083 is amended by S.I. 2001 No. 1186.

NOTE 14. See now Directive of the European Parliament and Council of May 25, 1999 on certain aspects of the sale of consumer goods and associated guarantees ([1999] O.J. L171/12), implemented in the United Kingdom by Sale and Supply of Goods to Consumers Regulations 2002, *ante*, entry at para. 33–028, nn. 81–83.

NOTE 22. A jurisdiction clause may be an unfair term for the purposes of the Directive and the Regulations: see Joined Cases C–240/98—C–244/98 *Oceano Grupo Editorial SA v. Rocio Murciano Quintero* [2000] E.C.R. I–4941; *Standard Bank London Ltd. v. Dimitrios Apostolakis* [2002] C.L.C. 939.

33–039 NOTE 25. The same formula is adopted in the Consumer Protection (Distance Selling) Regulations 2000, Reg. 25(5) (S.I. 2000 No. 2334). These Regulations implement Directive 97/7 of the European Parliament and Council of May 20, 1997 on the protection of consumers in respect of distance contracts, [1997] O.J. L144/19. See also Directive of the European Parliament and Council of September 23, 2002 concerning the distance marketing of consumer financial services ([2002] O.J. L271.16), Art. 12(2), which adopts an identical formula. Art. 3 (3)(f) of this Directive requires that prior to the conclusion of the distance contract the consumer be given information as to "any contractual clause on law applicable to the distance contract and/or on competent court". Art. 3 (4) provides that information "on contractual obligations, to be communicated to the consumer during the pre-contractual phase, shall be in conformity with the contractual obligations which would result from the law presumed to be applicable to the distance contract if the latter were concluded". This Directive must be implemented not later than October 9, 2004. As to the Directive of the European Parliament and Council of May 25, 1999, implemented in the United Kingdom in the Sale and Supply of Goods to Consumers Regulations 2002, S.I. 2002 No. 3045, see *supra*, entry at para. 33–028, nn. 81–83.

2 CONTRACTS OF EMPLOYMENT

See Commission of the European Communities, *Green Paper on the conversion of the Rome Convention of 1980 on the law applicable to contractual obligations into a Community instrument and its modernisation*, COM (2002) 654 final, paras. 3.2.9.1–3.2.11. **33R–047**

NOTE 77 and text thereto. See *Base Metal Trading Ltd. v. Shamurin* [2002] C.L.C. 322; *Swithenbank Foods Ltd. v. Bowers* [2002] 2 All E.R. (Comm.) 974. **33–055**

NOTE 84 and text thereto. Employment Rights Act 1996, s. 196 is repealed by Employment Relations Act 1999, s. 32(3). Accordingly, whether rights conferred by the 1996 Act or the 1999 Act extend to employees working outside Great Britain will now depend on the true construction of the relevant legislation. The legislation has been said to apply to employees temporarily working in Great Britain and to employees working outside Great Britain when the employment has a "proper connection with the U.K.". See H.C. Deb. 1998–1999, Vol. 336, col. 31. See also, *infra*, entry at para. 30–072, nn. 26, 27, 28. **33–059**

NOTE 85. See previous entry.

See entry at para. 33–059, n. 84 and text thereto. The principles referred to in this paragraph (and those in para. 33–065) could still be relevant to the determination of the question of where an employee "habitually" works for the purposes of Art. 6(2)(a) (clause (2)(a) of the Rule) of the Rome Convention. **33–064**

NOTE 97. Add: Case C–37/00 *Weber v. Universal Ogden Services Ltd.* [2002] E.C.R. I–2013; [2002] Q.B. 1189. **33–065**

NOTE 13. Add: See also *Base Metal Trading Ltd. v. Shamurin* [2002] C.L.C. 322. **33–068**

NOTE 25. Employment Rights Act 1996, s. 196(5) is repealed by Employment Relations Act 1999, s. 32(3). As to employees employed on board a ship, see Employment Relations Act 1999, s. 32(4). Add at end: Case C–37/00 *Weber v. Universal Ogden Services Ltd., supra*. **33–071**

NOTE 26, 27, 28. Although the "Posted Workers" Directive ([1997] O.J. L18/1) has not been formally implemented in the United Kingdom by regulations, it has been said that the repeal of Employment Rights Act 1996, s. 196 has facilitated the implementation of the Directive by extending **33–072** rights which are derived from European Union legislation (and also, presumably, English employment law) to workers who are "temporarily" working in Great Britain: H.C. Deb. 1998–1999, Vol. 336, col. 1. Repeal of section 196 also "means that people who may have worked for some years in the U.K., but who are nevertheless excluded from claiming under the Employment Rights Act 1996 will be able to rely upon the protection of U.K. legislation": *ibid*.

NOTE 35 and text thereto. Employment Rights Act 1996, s. 196(3) is repealed by Employment Relations Act 1999, s. 32(3). The rights conferred by the Working Time Regulations 1998 may be invoked by employees who are temporarily working in Great Britain.

33–073 NOTE 37 and text thereto. Order 11, r. 1(1)(*d*) is replaced by CPR, r. 6.20(5).

NOTES 40, 41, 42. Add: See *Base Metal Trading Ltd. v. Shamurin, supra.*

33–077 NOTE 62 and text thereto. Employment Rights Act 1996, s. 196(1) is repealed by Employment Relations Act 1999, s. 32(3). The right to a statement of particulars of employment and minimum periods of notice will apply to employment during any period when the employee is engaged to work wholly or mainly outside Great Britain even if the employee does not ordinarily work in Great Britain and the work outside Great Britain is not for the same employer and even if the law which governs the employee's contract of employment is not the law of England or Scotland.

NOTE 63. Employment Rights Act 1996, s. 196(2),(3), is repealed by Employment Relations Act 1999, s. 32(3).

NOTE 65. Employment Rights Act 1996, s. 196(4) is repealed by Employment Relations Act 1999, s. 32(3). See also Employment Relations Act 1999, ss. 7–9 (leave for family and domestic reasons).

NOTE 66. Employment Rights Act 1996, s. 196(7) is repealed by Employment Relations Act 1999, s. 32(3).

NOTE 67. Employment Rights Act 1996, s. 196(6) is repealed by Employment Relations Act 1999, s. 32(3).

33–081 NOTE 76. Add: Trade Union and Labour Relations (Consolidation) Act 1992 is also amended by Employment Relations Act 1999.

NOTE 77. As a consequence of Employment Relations Act 1999, s. 32(1), Trade Union and Labour Relations (Consolidation) Act 1992, s. 285(1) is amended so that the duty to consult employee representatives prior to redundancy dismissals (see 1992 Act, s. 188) is no longer excluded in respect of employees working outside Great Britain.

33–083 NOTE 88. Employment Rights Act 1996, s. 196(3)(*f*) and (3A) are repealed by Employment Relations Act 1999, s. 32(3).

33–084 NOTE 89. See Council Regulation 44/2001 (E.C.) of December 22, 2000, Art. 21 ([2001] O.J. L12/1) which entered into force on March 1, 2002. See *supra*, entry at para. S11–339.

NOTE 93. As to the Posted Workers Directive, see *supra*, entry at para. 33–072, nn. 26, 27, 28.

Employment Rights Act 1996, s. 196(3) is repealed by Employment **33–086**
Relations Act 1999, s. 32(3). It would seem, however, that there is a
"proper connection with the U.K." sufficient to justify the same result as
that reached in Illustration No. 6. See entry at para. 33–059, n. 84.

NOTE 10. Add at end: *Base Metal Trading Ltd. v. Shamurin, supra.*

3 CONTRACTS FOR THE SALE, PLEDGE AND HIRE OF MOVABLES

NOTE 25. On the effect on choice of law clauses where standard terms **33–091**
conflict, see Dannemann in *Lex Mercatoria: Essays in Honour of Francis
Reynolds* (ed. Rose, 2000), p. 199, at pp. 206–210.

NOTE 35. See *Print Concept GmbH v. GEW (EC) Ltd.* [2002] C.L.C. 382 **33–094**
(C.A.); *ISS Machinery Services Ltd. v. Aeolian Shipping S.A.* [2001] 2 Lloyd's
Rep. 641 (C.A.); *Iran Continental Shelf Oil Co. v. IRI International Oil Corp.*
[2002] EWCA Civ. 1024. And see *Definitely Maybe (Touring) Ltd. v. Marek
Lieberberg Konzertagentur GmbH* [2001] 1 W.L.R. 1745 (in contract to
supply services of a pop group to concert organisers, characteristic performance is that of the supplier); *Ennstone Building Products Ltd. v. Stanger
Ltd.* [2002] EWCA Civ. 916; [2002] 1 W.L.R. 3059 (C.A.) (in contract to
supply advisory services, characteristic performance is that of the advisor);
Caledonia Subsea Ltd. v. Microperi SRL, 2002 S.L.T. 1022 (in contract to
supply diving services, characteristic performance is that of the supplier).

NOTE 36. Add: *Iran Continental Shelf Oil Co. v. IRI International Corp.*
[2002] EWCA Civ. 1024 (C.A.).

NOTE 49. Add at end: *Definitely Maybe (Touring) Ltd. v. Marek Lieberberg* **33–098**
Konzertagentur GmbH, supra; *Samcrete Egypt Engineers and Contractors
S.A.E. v. Land Rover Exports Ltd.* [2001] EWCA Civ. 2019; [2002] C.L.C.
533 (C.A.); *Kenburn Waste Management Ltd. v. Bergmann* [2002] EWCA
Civ. 98; [2002] F.S.R. 711 (C.A.); *Ennstone Building Products Ltd. v. Stanger
Ltd.* [2002] EWCA Civ. 916; [2002] 1 W.L.R. 3059 (C.A.); *Iran Continental
Shelf Oil Co. v. IRI International Corp.* [2002] EWCA Civ. 1024 (C.A.);
Ferguson Shipbuilders Ltd. v. Voith Hydro GmbH, 2000 S.L.T. 229. Contrast
Caledonia Subsea Ltd. v. Microperi SRL, supra.

NOTE 72. Finland is a party to the Hague Convention of the Law Applicable **33–102**
to the International Sale of Goods 1955. Belgium has denounced this
Convention.

NOTE 85. As to Unfair Contract Terms Act 1977, s. 26, see *Ocean Chemical* **33–106**
Transport Inc. v. Exnor Craggs Ltd. [2000] 1 All E.R. (Comm.) 519 (C.A.);
Amiri Flight Authority v. BAE Systems plc [2002] EWHC 2481 (Comm);
[2003] 1 All E.R. (Comm.) 1 (a single contract for the sale of goods and the
supply of services is excluded by s. 26).

NOTE 94. Add: *Glencore International A.G. v. Metro Trading International* **33–109**
Inc. [2001] 1 Lloyd's Rep. 284, 293.

NOTE 97. Add: For further discussion, see *Glencore International A.G. v.* **33–111**
Metro Trading International Inc., supra, at pp. 291–296. For discussion of the
special rule relating to retention of title contained in Council Regulation of

May 29, 2000 on insolvency proceedings ([2000] O.J. L160/1), Art. 7(1), see *supra*, entry at paras. S30R–219 *et seq.*. The Directive of the European Parliament and Council of June 29, 2000 on combating late payment in commercial transactions ([2000] O.J. L200/35), Art. 4(1) requires that "Member States shall provide in conformity with the applicable national provisions designated by private international law that the seller retains title to goods until they are fully paid for if a retention of title clause has been expressly agreed between the buyer and the seller before the delivery of the goods". The legislation which implements this Directive in the United Kingdom (S.I. 2002 No. 1674, see *infra*, entry at para. 33–376) does not specifically implement this requirement. For discussion of Art. (71), see *Benjamin's Sale of Goods* (6th ed., 2002), para. 25–146.

Note 99. Add: *Glencore International A.G. v. Metro Trading International Inc., supra*, at p. 293.

4 CONTRACTS OF INSURANCE AND RE-INSURANCE

S33R–116 **Rule 184—(1) This Rule applies to determine the law applicable to a contract of insurance covering risks situated outside the territories of the European Economic Community[1] unless the contract of insurance is a consumer contract within the meaning of Rule 181, concluded in circumstances in which that Rule applies,[2] or the contract of insurance is subject to Rule 185 or 186.[3]**

(2) To the extent that the law applicable to such contract has not been chosen in accordance with Rule 173,[4] the contract is, in general, governed by the law of the country with which it is most closely connected.[5]

(3) It will be presumed that the contract is most closely connected with the country in which (*semble*) the insurer's principal place of business is situated, or where, under the terms of the contract, the insurer's performance is to be effected through a place of business other than the principal place of business, the country in which that other place of business is situated.[6]

(4) The presumption in clause (3) will be disregarded if it appears from the circumstances as a whole that the contract is more closely connected with another country.[7]

COMMENT

S33–117 **Introduction.** This Rule is intended to state the effect of the Rome Convention as implemented in the United Kingdom by the Contracts (Applicable Law) Act 1990 in so far as that Convention applies to contracts

---

[1] Rome Convention (Contracts (Applicable Law) Act 1990, Sched. 1), Art. 1(3). See Commission of the European Communities, *Green Paper on the conversion of the Rome Convention of 1980 on the law applicable to contractual obligations into a Community instrument and its modernisation*, COM (2002) 654 final, paras. 3.2.2.1–3.2.2.3.

[2] Main work, paras. 33R–001 *et seq.*; *infra*, paras. S33–127, S33–133.

[3] *infra*, paras. S33R–138 *et seq.*

[4] Main work, paras. 32R–059 *et seq.*

5 Rome Convention, Art. 4(1).

[6] *ibid*. Art. 4(2) The characteristic performance of an insurance contract is probably that of the insurer: see *infra*, para. S33–130. Since that performance will always be effected in the course of the insurer's trade or profession, the habitual residence or central administration of the insurer will not be relevant (unless the place of the latter is the principal place of business of the insurer): see *infra*, para. S33–131.

[7] Rome Convention, Art. 4(5).

of insurance. The sources of choice of law rules concerning insurance contracts are, however, a matter of some complexity and it is therefore necessary to identify these sources at this point. First, this Rule will apply, subject to what is said below, to determine the law applicable to a contract of insurance which covers a risk situated outside the territories of the Member States of the European Communities. This is because Article 1(3) of the Rome Convention provides that the rules of the Convention "do not apply to contracts of insurance which cover risks situated in the territories of the Member States of the European Economic Community." Article 1(3) goes on to provide that in "order to determine whether a risk is situated in these territories the court shall apply its internal law." The meaning and effect of this is discussed in the Comment to clause (1) of this Rule.[8] Further, it should be noted that this Rule applies both to life and to non-life insurance but it does not apply to contracts of re-insurance. Contracts of re-insurance, however, are within the scope of the Convention since Article 1(4) provides that the exclusion in Article 1(3) does not apply to such contracts. Contracts of re-insurance are dealt with separately in Rule 187.[9]

There are a number of European Community Directives relating to insurance which seek to further the policy of establishing freedom to provide services within the Community by enabling an insurer in one Member State to provide insurance in another Member State with minimum interference from the latter State's regulatory authorities.[10] As part of this programme it was regarded as desirable to establish rules for determining the law applicable to contracts of insurance which covered risks situated in a Member State. Three Directives contain such choice of law rules. The Second Non-Life Directive of June 1988[11] contains choice of law rules for, broadly speaking, all types of non-life policy where the policy covers a risk situated in a Member State.[12] The Third Non-Life Directive of June 18, 1992,[13] amends the choice of law rules established in the Second Non-Life Directive. These Directives were originally implemented in the United Kingdom by Regulations which inserted new provisions into the Insurance Companies Act 1982.[14] The current position is now, however, to be found in Regulations made under the Financial Services and Markets Act 2000,[15] namely Part II of the Financial Services and Markets Act 2000 (Law Applicable to Contracts of Insurance) Regulations 2001[16] which apply to contracts of general insurance.[17] These Regulations use slightly different

S33–118

---

[8] See *infra*, paras. S33–124 *et seq.*

[9] See main work, paras. 33R–198 *et seq.* and *infra*, entries at paras. S33–199 *et seq.*

[10] See, generally, Merkin, *Insurance Contract Law*, Chap. D. 5.1; Macneill (1995) 44 I.C.I.Q. 19.

[11] Second Council Directive of June 22, 1988 on the co-ordination of laws, regulations and administrative provisions relating to direct insurance other than life assurance and laying down provisions to facilitate the effective exercise of freedom to provide services: [1988] O.J. L172/1, amending the First Council Directive of July 24, 1973, [1973] O.J. L228/3.

[12] The choice of law rules are contained in Art. 7 of the Second Directive.

[13] Third Council Directive of June 18, 1992 on the co-ordination of laws, regulations and administrative provisions relating to direct insurance other than life insurance: [1992] O.J. L228/1.

[14] See main work, para. 33–118.

[15] The Regulations under this Act are made by the Treasury: see ss. 417(1), 424(3), 428(3). An Order made under the Act repeals Insurance Companies Act 1982 (S.1. 2001 No. 3649, art. 3(1) (c)) and revokes the Insurance Companies (Third Insurance Directives) Regulations 1994, referred to in the main work, para. 33–118 (S.1. 2001 No. 3649, art. 3(2) (b)).

[16] S.1. 2001 No. 2653, as amended by S.1. 2001 No. 3542, which entered into force on December 1, 2001.

[17] See *infra*, para. S33–141.

language from their predecessors but they also contain the important extension of the Directives to contracts of insurance covering risks situated in an EEA State as opposed to a Member State of the European Union.[18] These provisions form the substance of Rule 185.[19] The third relevant Directive is the Second Life Directive of November 1990,[20] which contains choice of law rules to be applied to life policies covering risks situated in a Member State.[21] This Directive and the Third Life Directive of November 10, 1992[22] (which amended the Second Life Directive in a relatively minor respect from the perspective of the conflict of laws) were originally implemented in the United Kingdom in the same manner as the Non-Life Directive,[23] but the relevant provisions are now to be found in Part III of the Financial Services and Markets Act 2000 (Law Applicable to Contracts of Insurance) Regulations 2001.[24] These provisions, which apply to contracts of long-term insurance, extend to risks situated in an EEA State, as opposed to a Member State of the European Union[25] and also entered into force on December 1, 2001. These provisions form the substance of Rule 186.[26]

S33–119   The Friendly Societies Act 1992 contained choice of law rules applicable in cases where the insurer was a friendly society and the contract covered risks situated in the United Kingdom or another Member State.[27] Such contracts are now subject, with relatively minor modifications, to the new Regulations referred to above.

S33–120   The choice of law rules in the Rome Convention and those contained in the Directives, as implemented in the United Kingdom, apply in cases involving conflicts between the laws of the different parts of the United Kingdom.[28]

S33–121   Common law background. Essentially the common law rules will now apply only to contracts of insurance entered into on or before April 1, 1991, the date on which the Rome Convention entered into force and such cases are now likely to arise infrequently, if at all.[29]

---

[18] "EEA State" means a State which is a contracting party to the agreement on the European Economic Area signed at Oporto on May 2, 1992 as it has effect for the time being: Financial Services and Markets Act 2000, Sched. 3, Pt. 1, para. 8.

[19] *infra*, paras. S33R–138 *et seq.*

[20] Second Council Directive of November 8, 1990 on the co-ordination of laws, regulations and administrative provisions relating to direct life assurance, laying down provisions to facilitate the effective exercise of freedom to provide services: [1990] O.J. L330/50, amending the First Council Directive of March 5, 1979, [1979] O.J. L63/1.

[21] The choice of law rules are contained in Art. 4.

[22] Third Council Directive of November 10, 1992 on the co-ordination of laws, regulations and administrative provisions relating to direct life assurance: [1992] O.J. L360/1.

[23] See main work, para. 33–118.

[24] *supra*, nn. 15–18.

[25] *supra*, n. 18.

[26] *infra*, paras. S33R–177 *et seq.*

[27] See main work, paras. 33–119, 33–167—33–173, 33–194—33–196.

[28] Contracts (Applicable Law) Act 1990, s.2(3); Financial Services and Markets Act 2000 (Law Applicable to Contracts of Insurance) Regulations 2001, reg. 2(4).

[29] There are some complications arising from the date of implementation of the various Insurance Directives: see main work, para. 33–121.

At common law, a contract of insurance was governed by its proper law, **S33–122** that law being determined by applying general principles to the particular context of insurance.[30] Thus the parties were permitted (within the general constraints[31]) to choose the law to govern the contract.[32] In the absence of a choice, the contract was governed by the system of law with which it had the closest and most real connection. In the case of life insurance, there was an observable tendency in the case law to regard, as the most closely connected law, the law of the country in which the insurer carried on business[33] or, where the insurer carried on business in more than one country (as is commonly the case), the law of the country in which the insurer's head office was situated.[34] There were good reasons for such an approach. It is in the interests of the insurer to have all policies governed by the same system of law, particularly since the contract is normally effected on a standard form which should receive uniform interpretation, irrespective of the policy-holder's residence or the place of performance of the contracts. Further, the approach is consistent with insurance practice since the head office normally reserves to itself the ultimate decision on the acceptance or rejection of each proposal and the local branches or agents are left with little discretion except in matters such as temporary cover.[35] This centralisation of the decision-making process offers a powerful argument for saying that the contract is most closely connected with the legal system prevailing in the country of the head office.[36]

---

[30] Main work, paras. 32–003 *et seq.* See generally 11th ed. of this work, pp. 1289–1296; Wolff, s.147; Westlake, ss.210–221; Rabel, Vol. 3. pp. 319–352; Unger (1964) 13 I.C.L.Q. 482; Carnahan, *Conflict of Laws and Life Insurance Contracts* (2nd ed. 1958); Restatement, s.192; Lenhoff (1956) 21 Law and Contemporary Problems 549; Merkin in Rose (ed.), *New Foundations for Insurance Law* (1987), pp. 61–79; Clarke, *The Law of Insurance Contracts* (3rd ed. 1997), pp. 15–39.

[31] See *DR Insurance Co. v. Central National Insurance Co.* [1996] 1 Lloyd's Rep. 74; *Akai Pty. Ltd. v. People's Insurance Co. Ltd.* (1996) 188 C.L.R. 418; *cf. Akai Pty. Ltd. v. People's Insurance Co. Ltd.* [1998] 1 Lloyd's Rep. 90. Main work, paras. 32–062 *et seq.*

[32] *Anderson v. Equitable Life Assurance Society of the United States* (1926) 134 L.T. 557 (C.A.); *Buerger v. New York Life Assurance Co.* (1927) 96 L.J.K.B. 930 (C.A.); *Perry v. Equitable Life Assurance Society* (1929) 45 T.L.R. 468; *Royal Boskalis Westminster N.V. v. Mountain* [1999] Q.B. 674 (C.A.); *Akai Pty. Ltd. v. People's Insurance Co. Ltd.* [1998] 1 Lloyd's Rep. 90 (express choice of law); *Spurrier v. La Cloche* [1902] A.C. 446 (P.C.) (implied choice of law). *Cf. Akai Pty. Ltd. v. People's Insurance Co. Ltd.* (1996) 188 C.L.R. 418. See also *Society of Lloyd's v. Fraser* [1998] C.L.C. 1630 (C.A.) (contract of membership between Canadian "names" and Lloyd's governed by English law as a result of an express choice).

[33] *Greer v. Poole* (1880) 5 Q.B.D. 272.

[34] *Pick v. Manufacturers' Life Insurance Co.* [1958] 2 Lloyd's Rep. 93; *Rossano v. Manufacturers' Life Insurance Co.* [1963] Q.B. 352; *Imperial Life Assurance Co. v. Colmenares* (1967) 62 D.L.R. (2d) 138 (Sup.Ct.Can.); *Serpa v. Confederation Life Association* (1974) 43 D.L.R. (3d) 324 (Ont.). *Cf. Ex p. Dever* (1887) 18 Q.B.D. 660 (C.A.); *Crosland v. Wrigley* (1895) 73 L.T. 60, 327 (C.A.); *Rowett Leakey & Co. v. Scottish Provident Institution* [1927] 1 Ch. 55 (C.A.).

[35] Contrast the position in relation to the organisation of banking where managers of bank branches usually have authority to open accounts and the law in force at the place of the branch is likely to be the law governing the contract between banker and customer: see *infra*, Rule 191.

[36] Though *cf.* the last three cases cited in n. 34 *supra.* on which see Unger, *supra*, pp. 485–486. In the United States the case is often made out for applying the law of the policyholder's place of business or residence with a view to protecting him against the superior bargaining power of foreign insurance companies: see Restatement, s.192; Carnahan, *supra*, pp. 204, 269, 701 *et seq.*; Clarke, *supra*, pp. 34–35. Insurance is very much interstate business in the United States, and the conflicts problems to which it gives rise may differ both in their legal and in their social setting from those likely to arise in international cases. The philosophy of protecting the insured does, however, have a role to play in the European Community Directives: see *infra*, Rules 185, 186.

S33–123   There was also a tendency to focus on the head office of the insurer in cases concerned with indemnity insurance.[37] However, the emphasis in more recent decisions was on the market by reference to which the insurance contract was made.[38] In any event the use of standard forms, particularly in marine insurance,[39] could permit an inference as to an implied choice of law by the parties[40] or could be regarded as a factor pointing to a particular insurance market thus linking the contract most closely with the legal system of that market.[41]

S33–124   **Clause (1) of the Rule.** Critical to the elucidation of the choice of the law rules applicable to insurance contracts is the determination whether a risk covered by the policy is or is not situated within the territories of a Member State of the European Communities, or, since the entry into force of the Financial Services and Markets Act 2000 (Law Applicable to Contracts of Insurance) Regulations 2001 (hereinafter referred to as "the Regulations"), on December 1, 2001, an EEA State.[42] If it is not so situated, the relevant choice of law régime is to be found in clauses (2)–(4) of this Rule. If it is so situated the relevant régime will be found in Rule 185[43] or Rule 186,[44] as the case may be.

S33–125   According to Article 1(3) of the Rome Convention, in "order to determine whether a risk is situated" in the territories of a Member State, the court is to apply its "internal law." The latter expression means the "rules in force in the judge's country, to the exclusion of the rules of private international law."[45] Traditionally, however, the *situs* of a risk had played no role in insurance law in the United Kingdom, so that in the absence of any legislative indication of how to determine the *situs* of a risk, considerable difficulties could have arisen. These difficulties were originally resolved, however, by the existence of rules for this purpose in the Second Non-Life Directive[46] which were incorporated into United Kingdom law in the legislation implementing that Directive[47] and into the legislation imple-

---

[37] *Greer v. Poole* (1880) 5 Q.B.D. 572; *Atlantic Underwriting Agencies Ltd. v. Compagnia di Assicurazione di Milano SpA* [1979] 2 Lloyd's Rep. 240, 245. See also *Armadora Occidental S.A. v. Horace Mann Insurance Co.* [1977] 1 W.L.R. 520, 1098 (C.A.).

[38] *Cantieri Navali Riuniti SpA v. N.V. Omne Justitia* [1985] 2 Lloyd's Rep. 428; *E.I. du Pont de Nemours v. Agnew* [1987] 2 Lloyd's Rep. 585 (C.A.).

[39] Note the special rule for average adjustment. In the absence of a special marine agreement to the contrary, the parties to a contract of marine insurance are bound by an average adjustment duly taken according to the law of the place of adjustment: *Walpole v. Ewer* (1789) 2 Park.Mar.Ins. 8th ed., 898; *Newman v. Cazalet, ibid.* 900; in *Power v. Whitmore* (1815) 4 M. & S. 141 there was no proper allegation of fact as to the law and usage at the port of destination, see *Dent v. Smith* (1869) L.R. 4 Q.B. 414, 450 *et seq.*; *Harris v. Scaramanga* (1872) L.R. 7 C.P. 481; *Hendricks v. Australian Insurance Co.* (1874) L.R. 9 C.P. 460; *Mavro v. Ocean Marine Insurance Co.* (1875) L.R. 10 C.P. 414 (Ex.Ch.); *The Mary Thomas* [1894] P. 108 (C.A.); *De Hart v. Compania Anonima de Seguros "Aurora"* [1903] 2 K.B. 503 (C.A.). It is unlikely that this rule is affected by the implementation of the Rome Convention, and average adjustment is normally governed by the generally accepted York-Antwerp Rules rather than by rules of the conflict of laws.

[40] See *Amin Rasheed Shipping Corp. v. Kuwait Insurance Co.* [1984] A.C. 50.

[41] *ibid. per* Lord Wilberforce at 71. See also the cases cited in n. 38 *supra*.

[42] See *supra*, para. S33–118.

[43] *infra*, paras. S33R–138 *et seq.*

[44] *infra*, paras. S33R–177 *et seq.*

[45] Giuliano-Lagarde, p. 13.

[46] Art. 2(d).

[47] S.I. 1990 No. 1333, reg. 2, inserting a new s.96A into the Insurance Companies Act 1982. The relevant provisions were contained in s.96A(3).

menting the Second Life Directive,[48] and by an amendment to the Contracts
(Applicable Law) Act 1990 which provided that these rules constitute the
relevant internal law in Article 1(3).[49] The position, as from December 1,
2001 is to be found in the new Regulations for determining the law
applicable to insurance contracts and in a new amendment to the Contracts
(Applicable Law) Act 1990. According to the latter amendment, the
relevant internal law, for the purposes of Article 1 (3) of the Rome
Convention, is the provisions of regulations for the time being in force
under section 424(3) of the Financial Services and Markets Act 2000,[50] so
that it is necessary to look to the Regulations. There is, however, an
apparent conflict within this amendment since the provisions of Article 1(3)
of the Rome Convention speak to a risk which is situated in the territories
of the Member States of the European Communities, whereas the Regulations apply when the risk is situated in a broader category of States,
namely EEA States.[51] The change is presumably justified by the extension of
the internal market brought about by the EEA agreement,[52] so that in what
follows, reference will be made to "EEA state", rather than "Member
State", bearing in mind that this appears to be the position after December
1, 2001. According to the relevant provisions of the Regulations, where the
contract of insurance relates to buildings or their contents (in so far as the
contents are covered by the same policy) the risk covered by the contract is
situated in the EEA State in which the property is situated.[53] If the contract
relates to vehicles of any type, the relevant EEA State is that of the
registration of the vehicle.[54] Where the contract covers travel or holiday
risks and has a duration of four months or less, the relevant EEA State is
that in which the policyholder entered into the contract.[55] In any other case,
if the policyholder is an individual, the EEA State where the risk covered by
the contract is situated is that in which the policyholder resides on the date
the contract is entered into,[56] and the State in which an individual resides,
for these purposes, is to be treated as being the country in which he has his
habitual residence,[57] whereas if the policyholder is not an individual the
relevant EEA State is that in which the establishment[58] of the policyholder
to which the contract relates is situated on the date the contract is entered
into.[59] The scope of the choice of law rules for life assurance is defined by
reference to these last two grounds. If the policyholder is an individual,
these choice of law rules will apply if that individual is habitually resident in
an EEA State.[60] If the policyholder is, *e.g.* a company insuring the lives of

---

[48] S.I. 1993 No. 174. The Second Life Directive does not expressly refer to the *situs* of a risk. The
implementing legislation contained explicit indication, however, as to when the provisions
applied. See Insurance Companies Act 1982, s.94B(1A), inserted by S.I. 1993 No. 174. See Rule
186(1), main work, paras. 33–179 *et seq.*

[49] Contracts (Applicable Law) Act 1990, s.2(1A)(*a*), inserted by S.I. 1993 No. 2519; for Friendly
Societies, see *ibid.* s.2(1A)(*b*) inserted by the same Regulations.

[50] Contracts (Applicable Law) Act 1990, s.2 (1A), as substituted by S.1. 2001 No. 3649, art. 320.

[51] Regulations, regs. 4(1), 8(1).

[52] European Economic Area Act 1993; EEA Agreement, Art. 36 and Annex IX.

[53] Regulations, reg. 2(2)(a).

[54] *ibid.* reg. 2(2)(b).

[55] *ibid.* reg. 2(2)(c).

[56] *ibid.* reg. 2(2)(d)(i).

[57] *ibid.* reg. 2(3)(a).

[58] "Establishment" is defined, *ibid.* reg. 2(1). See *infra*, para. S33–186.

[59] *infra.* reg. 2(2)(d)(ii).

[60] *Post*, para. S33–186.

an employee or employees, these choice of law rules will apply if the establishment at which the employee is, or employees are, employed is situated in an EEA State.[61]

S33–126   One question which is not explicitly resolved in the Directives or in the implementing legislation is as to the applicable legal régime in a situation where a risk is situated both within and outside an EEA State.[62] Further, a contract may cover two or more risks, one of which may be situated in an EEA State, whereas the other or others of which, is, or are, situated in a different (non-EEA) State.[63] There is no obvious answer to this question. For reasons of convenience, it is obviously desirable to have one legal régime to determine the law applicable to the insurance contract: this might point to the conclusion that the risk should be regarded as situated in an EEA State if it is principally or predominantly situated there and not otherwise.[64] But this solution assumes that it will be possible to determine whether the risk is principally or predominantly located in an EEA State, which may be difficult to do, and yields no answer where a policy covers two or more risks which are situated, respectively, in an EEA State and outside such a State. Another solution would be to regard the contract as "severable"[65] in such situations, so that the applicable law would be determined by reference to the Rome Convention in so far as the risk is situated outside an EEA State but according to whichever other régime is relevant to the extent that the risk is situated within an EEA State. This approach is, however, somewhat artificial. Further, application of it may lead to inconsistent results as between (if such be the case) the different laws which may be found to govern the contract under the different régimes. And it may yield no result, for example, in a case of a policy which insures the life of an individual habitually resident in both Belgium and New York, the policy being void according to the law applicable to the contract under the Second Life Directive but valid according to the law applicable to it under the Rome Convention. Perhaps, therefore, the most likely solution to this problem is that if the risk is "indivisible" (*e.g.* in the case of a policy on the life of an individual habitually resident in an EEA

---

[61] *infra*, paras. S33–186—S33–187.

[62] *e.g.* in the case of a policy insuring the life of an individual habitually resident in England and New York.

[63] *e.g.* in the case of buildings insurance, a policy insuring buildings in England and New York. For a case where this issue was considered in the context of the applicability of Art. 4 of the Rome Convention and the now repealed Insurance Companies Act 1982, Sched. 3A, Pt. I (main work, para. 33–118, see *American Motorists Insurance Co. v. Cellstar Corp.* [2002] EWHC 421 (Comm.); [2002] 2 Lloyd's Rep. 216; affd. [2003] EWCA Civ. 206; [2003] I.L.Pr. 370 (C.A.) (where no firm conclusion was reached).

[64] This solution was adopted in *American Motorists Insurance Co. v. Cellstar Corp., supra*, by David Steel J. in relation to a global policy of transportation insurance on the grounds that (a) it was obviously more convenient that the contract should be governed by one legal regime (b) the separation of the contract into a large number of different contracts was in complete contradiction to the concept of a global contract and (c) because such separation gave rise to the potential for startling inconsistencies in the way the contract would be interpreted depending on the particular applicable law of the different contracts. *Cf.* [2003] EWCA Civ. 206; [2003] I.L.Pr. 370 (C.A.). *Cf.* Case 158/87 *Scherrens v. Maenhout* [1988] E.C.R. 3791; Case 266/85 *Shenavai v. Kreischer* [1987] E.C.R. 239. Neither of these cases is a particularly strong analogy in this context: see main work, paras. 11–249, 23–015.

[65] *Cf.* Rome Convention, Arts. 3(1), 4(1), main work, paras. 32–046 *et seq.*; Financial Services and Markets Act 2000 (Law Applicable to Contracts of Insurance) Regulations 2001, reg. 4(8). See also *CGU International Insurance plc v. Szabo* [2002] 1 All E.R. (Comm.) 83.

State and a non-EEA State) then the régime in the Directive will apply.[66] If the risk is "divisible" (*e.g.* a policy covering buildings, situated in an EEA State and a non-EEA State), then the contract may be severed so that the law applicable to the parts of the contract insuring each risk will be determined separately according to the régime which is relevant for each of them.[67] This conclusion is at best, however, speculative.

Clause (1) of this Rule is also designed to draw attention to the fact that an insurance contract may be a consumer contract for the purposes of Article 5 of the Rome Convention, elaborated in Rule 181.[68] This is because Article 5 applies to a contract for the supply of services,[69] an example of which is insurance services.[70] In the particular context of insurance, the application of Article 5 could be attracted if, prior to the conclusion of the contract, the policyholder received in the country of his habitual residence a specific invitation addressed to him by the insurer or responded to an advertisement in that country by the insurer,[71] or if the insurer or his agent[72] received the policyholder's application in the country where the policy holder was habitually resident.

S33–127

Clause (2) of the Rule. It is very common for an insurance contract (whether life or non-life) to contain a choice of law clause.[73] Such clauses will be respected according to Article 3(1) of the Rome Convention.[74] Equally, it is not uncommon for insurance contracts to contain a jurisdiction clause[75] or an arbitration clause[76] each of which, in appropriate circumstances, might demonstrate a choice of law with reasonable certainty for the purposes of Article 3(1).[77] A similar conclusion may be reached[78] if the insurance contract is drawn in a form which links it intimately or ineluctably

S33–128

---

[66] *Cf. The Deichland* [1990] 1 Q.B. 361 (C.A.) (company domiciled in a Contracting State to the 1968 Convention subject to the jurisdictional rules of that Convention notwithstanding the fact that it is also domiciled in a non-Contracting State).

[67] See the discussion of this passage in *American Motorists Insurance Co. v. Cellstar Corp., supra.* And see [2003] EWCA Civ. 206; [2003] I.L.Pr. 370 (C.A.) where the Court of Appeal rejected the notion of "severance". *Cf.* Case 158/87 *Scherrens v. Maenhout* [1988] E.C.R. 3791.

[68] Main work, paras. 33R–001 *et seq.*

[69] Art. 5(1), main work, paras. 33–004 *et seq.*

[70] Giuliano-Lagarde, p. 23.

[71] Art. 5(2), main work, paras. 33–008 *et seq.*

[72] Where a broker is involved, it is generally the rule that the broker is the agent of the policyholder so that it is arguable that this aspect of Art. 5(2) is not satisfied if the agent is a broker. However, it is more likely that "agent" will be interpreted in a non-technical sense and will be held to include a broker: see Giuliano-Lagarde, p. 24; Merkin, *Insurance Contract Law*, Chap. D. 4.2.38.

[73] *Anderson v. Equitable Life Assurance Society of the United States* (1926) 134 L.T. 557 (C.A.); *Buerger v. New York Life Assurance Co.* (1927) 96 L.J.K.B. 930 (C.A.); *Perry v. Equitable Life Assurance Society* (1929) 45 T.L.R. 468; *Youell v. Kara Mara Shipping Co. Ltd.* [2000] 2 Lloyd's Rep. 102. See also *Burrows v. Jamaica Private Power Co. Ltd.* [2002] 1 All E.R. (Comm.) 374.

[74] Rule 173.

[75] See *Royal Exchange Assurance Corp. v. Vega* [1902] 2 K.B. 384 (C.A.) (re-insurance contract). *Cf. Armadora Occidental S.A. v. Horace Mann Insurance Co.* [1977] 1 W.L.R. 520; affd. *ibid.* 1095 (C.A.).

[76] See *Spurrier v. La Cloche* [1902] A.C. 446 (P.C.). *Cf. XL Insurance Ltd. v. Owens Corning* [2000] 2 Lloyd's Rep. 500 where it was held that although the policy of insurance was governed by New York law as a result of an express choice, the arbitration clause contained in the policy was governed by English law since the parties had stipulated for arbitration in London under the provisions of the Arbitration Act 1996.

[77] Giuliano-Lagarde, p. 17. Main work, paras. 32–092 *et seq.*

[78] *ibid.*

with a particular country's law[79] or uses terminology which associates it with the law of a particular country.[80] If it is concluded that the insurance contract contains a choice of law for the purposes of Article 3(1), then the choice of law will be subject to the general limitations placed upon the effect to be given to the choice, notably in Article 3(3)[81] and Article 7(2)[82] of the Convention. Further, by their choice the parties may select the law applicable to a part only of the contract and it may be open to a court to conclude that a severable part of the contract is governed by a different system of law.[83]

S33–129   To the extent that the law applicable to the insurance contract has not been chosen by the parties, the contract will be governed by the law of the country with which it is most closely connected. This law, presumptively, is to be identified by reference to clause (3) of the Rule.

S33–130   **Clause (3) of the Rule.** The Rome Convention supplies no special presumption to determine the law of the country with which an insurance contract is most closely connected. Accordingly, it will be necessary to have recourse to the general presumption contained in Article 4(2) of the Convention.[84] First, it is necessary to determine the party who is to effect the performance which is characteristic of the contract. The Giuliano-Lagarde Report suggests that the characteristic performance of an insurance contract is the provision of insurance cover.[85] If this is correct, then the characteristic performance will be that of the insurer even though, in the event of the occurrence of a risk covered by the policy, the insurer's performance will be the payment of money, something which the Report

---

[79] Cf. *Amin Rasheed Shipping Corp. v. Kuwait Insurance Co.* [1984] A.C. 50, though here an additional factor was the absence, at the time of the conclusion of the contract, of any indigenous code of marine insurance law in Kuwait.

[80] In *American Motorists Insurance Co. v. Cellstar Corp.* [2002] EWHC 421 (Comm.); [2002] 2 Lloyd's Rep. 216, David Steel J. was prepared to conclude that a choice of Texas law had been demonstrated with reasonable certainty by the circumstances that Texas was the State in which the policy was negotiated and issued, as between an assured who employed a Texas broker, and an insurer situated in Texas and by a term in the policy which imposed a one-year period within which suit had to be brought unless such a limit was invalid by the law of the State in which the policy was issued in which case the action had to be commenced within the shortest limit of time permitted under the law of the latter State. This view was upheld by the Court of Appeal: [2003] EWCA Civ. 206; [2003] I.L.Pr. 370 (C.A.) Cf. *Armadora Occidental S.A. v. Horace Mann Insurance Co., supra* ("follow London" clause). See also *Cantieri Navali Riuniti SpA v. N.V. Omne Justitia* [1985] 2 Lloyd's Rep. 428 (C.A.); *E.I. du Pont de Nemours v. Agnew* [1987] 2 Lloyd's Rep. 585 (C.A.). See also *Chase v. Ram Technical Services Ltd.* [2000] 2 Lloyd's Rep. 418. If a lead policy contains a choice of law it is also possible that following policies which contain no choice of law will be held to be governed by the law which applies to the lead policy: see Giuliano-Lagarde, p. 17. Cf. *E.I. du Pont de Nemours v. Agnew, supra*.

[81] Rule 175(1).

[82] Rule 175(2). *Quaere*, whether there are any English rules of insurance law which are mandatory in the sense of Art. 7(2). There are such rules in Canada; see North (1990) *Recueil des Cours*, 1, 9, 165. The controls on exemption clauses in Unfair Contract Terms Act 1977 (main work, paras. 33–028 *et seq.*, 33–106 *et seq.*) do not apply to insurance contracts. The provisions of the Unfair Terms in Consumer Contracts Regulations 1999 (main work, paras. 33–038 *et seq.*) are capable of applying to an insurance contract where the insured is a "consumer" as defined in the Regulations.

[83] This technique might help to solve the problem posed at common law in *Forsikringsaktieselskapet Vesta v. Butcher* [1989] A.C. 852, *infra*, Rule 187. And see *XL Insurance Ltd. v. Owens Corning* [2000] 2 Lloyd's Rep. 500.

[84] Rule 174.

[85] p. 20.

says cannot be characteristic performance.[86] Since the view expressed in the Giuliano-Lagarde Report has not gone unchallenged[87] (it having been suggested that it might be concluded that it is not possible to determine the characteristic performance of an insurance contract[88]) this aspect of clause (3) has been expressed in tentative form. Nonetheless it is submitted that the characteristic performance is that of the insurer, a view that has been approved, *obiter*, in the Court of Appeal.[89]

Since an insurance contract will of necessity be entered into in the course **S33–131** of the insurer's business, the second sentence of Article 4(2) will apply so that the most closely connected law will initially be presumed to be the law of the country in which the principal place of business[90] of the insurer is situated. This is reminiscent of the leaning in the common law, particularly in cases of life insurance, towards the system of law of the country in which the insurer's head office is situated.[91] A difficulty arises, however, with the application in practice of the alternative provision in the sentence "or where under the terms of the contract performance is to be effected through a place of business other than the principal place of business," the applicable law is to be presumed to be the country in which the other place of business is situated. First, it is unclear how this rule applies if the policy is issued by a branch of an insurance company located in one country but the insurer's principal place of business is located in another country and (as is often the case) ultimate authorisation of the policy is required from the principal place of business, as the head office of the insurer.[92] Since the "performance" referred to is the provision of cover, it would seem, though the matter is by no means certain, that the applicable law will be that of the insurer's principal place of business since it is through that place that the provision of cover is effected.[93] Secondly, if the policy is effected through a broker, it appears that the provisions of the Rome Convention do not apply at all if the question which arises is whether the broker had authority to bind the insurer or policyholder, since this question is expressly excluded from the rules contained in the Convention.[94] However, if the issue in the case is a different one (*e.g.* whether the policy is void for non-disclosure), then the rules of the Convention will apply and it then becomes unclear whether the relevant place of business (principal place of business or other place of business, as the case may be) is that of the broker or that of the insurer. The likely answer to this question, it is submitted, depends on whether final authorisation is required from the insurer. If it is, then it is at

---

[86] *ibid.*

[87] Merkin, *Insurance Contract Law*; Chap. D. 4.2.24.

[88] *ibid.* See also Clarke, *The Law of Insurance Contracts* (3rd ed. 1997), pp. 42–43.

[89] *Crédit Lyonnais v. New Hampshire Insurance Co.* [1997] 2 Lloyd's Rep. 1.6 (C.A.). The same view was expressed in *American Motorists Insurance Co. v. Cellstar Corp.* [2002] EWHC 421 (Comm.); [2002] 2 Lloyd's Rep. 216; [2003] EWCA Civ. 206, [2003] I.L.Pr. 370 (C.A.).

[90] Main work, paras. 11–100 *et seq.*, 32–118. As to the possibility of severance, see *CGU International Insurance plc v. Szabo* [2002] 1 All E.R. (Comm.) 83.

[91] See cases cited at para. S33–122, n. 34, *supra*.

[92] See, *e.g. Pick v. Manufacturers' Life Insurance Co.* [1958] 2 Lloyd's Rep. 93.

[93] But *cf. American Motorists Insurance Co. v. Cellstar Corp.*, *supra*, where this point is not explicitly considered. This would not seem to be affected by the fact that the proceeds of the policy are payable elsewhere: *cf. Pick v. Manufacturers' Life Insurance Co.*, *supra; Rossano v. Manufacturers' Life Insurance Co.* [1963] 2 Q.B. 352.

[94] Art. 1(2)(f). Main work, para. 32–038; Rule 198. The characteristic performance of a contract *between* an insurance broker and an insurance company is that of the broker: *HIB Ltd. v. Guardian Insurance Co. Ltd.* [1997] 1 Lloyd's Rep. 412.

the insurer's principal place of business or other place of business, as the case may be, through which the insurer's performance (*i.e.* the provision of cover) is effected. If, however, no such authorisation is required then the insurer's performance would appear to be effected through the principal place of business, or other place of business, as the case may be, of the broker,[95] so that the law of whichever of those places is relevant on the facts will supply the governing law.

S33–132   In both of these situations, it may be possible to disregard the law found to be applicable according to the presumption in Article 4(2) on the ground that it appears from the circumstances as a whole that the contract is more closely connected with another country. Thus, in appropriate circumstances, the law of the insurer's principal place of business may be displaced in favour of the law of the branch which issued the policy.[96] Similarly, in appropriate circumstances, the law of the relevant place of business of the insurer may prevail even though, presumptively, the applicable law is that of the relevant place of business of the broker, or the law of the relevant place of business of the broker may prevail even though, presumptively, the applicable law is that of the relevant place of business of the insurer.

S33–133   As already indicated in the Comment to clause (1) of this Rule,[97] this Rule will not apply if the insurance contract is a consumer contract within the meaning of Article 5 of the Convention which is concluded in circumstances which attract the application of that provision.[98] If Article 5 applies then, in the absence of a choice of law in the contract,[99] the contract will be governed by the law of the country in which the insured is habitually resident.[1] The potential application of this law is not open to displacement even if the contract is more closely connected with another country.

S33–134 **Clause (4) of the Rule.** Article 4(5) of the Rome Convention provides that the law indicated by application of Article 4(2) may be disregarded if it appears from the circumstances as a whole that the contract is more closely connected with another country. How this provision operates depends, ultimately, on the strength which is accorded to the presumption and on the degree of ease with which courts allow it to be rebutted.[2] In the context of insurance, it has been said, *obiter*, that "formally" the presumption in Article 4(2) is "very weak",[3] but this statement cannot be accepted at face value and further elucidation is necessary. Thus it is possible that the ease with which the presumption may be rebutted may well be found to depend on the particular type of insurance in issue. In cases of life insurance, the common law tendency to favour the law of the head office of the insurer[4]

---

[95] See Merkin, *Insurance Contract Law*, Chap. D. 4.2.24. *Cf. American Motorists Insurance Co. v. Cellstar Corp., supra.*

[96] See *American Motorists Insurance Co. v. Cellstar Corp.* [2002] EWHC 421 (Comm.); [2002] 2 Lloyd's Rep. 216, affd. [2003] EWCA Civ. 206; [2003] I.L.Pr. 370 (C.A.). *Cf. Buerger v. New York Life Assurance Co.* (1927) 96 L.J.K.B. 930 (C.A.).

[97] *supra*, para. S33–127.

[98] *supra*, Rule 181.

[99] The effect of which may be restricted: see Rule 181.

[1] See main work, para. 33–019.

[2] Main work, paras. 32–123 *et seq.*

[3] *Crédit Lyonnais v. New Hampshire Insurance Co.* [1997] 2 Lloyd's Rep. 1, 5 (C.A.). This case was concerned with the application of the now repealed Insurance Companies Act 1982, Sched. 3A, Pt. 1. See *infra*, Rule 185.

[4] *supra*, para. S33–123.

might suggest that the presumption in Article 4(2), application of which produces much the same result, will be difficult to rebut. The philosophy of the Community Directive on life insurance is, however, to favour the insured who is often in a weaker bargaining position *vis-à-vis* the insurer,[5] and, accordingly, it might be unwise to draw too ready an analogy with the common law approach even in the application of the Rome Convention.[6] This consideration may lead to a tendency to favour application of the law of the insured's place of habitual residence, even in a case not falling within Article 5, despite the fact that one is dealing with application of the Rome Convention rather than with the application of the Community Directive.[7] This tendency may be strengthened by the fact that in cases of individual life insurance the risk will generally be situated in the country where the insured habitually resided[8]: it may well be the case that even under the Rome Convention the *situs* of the risk will be treated as a much more important factor identifying the law of the country with which the contract is most closely connected than it was at common law.[9] And the tendency may further be strengthened if the insured concludes the contract with a branch office or agent operating in the country where the insured habitually resides,[10] though such circumstances, it must be conceded, are almost certain to involve the application of Article 5,[11] rather than this Rule.

In cases of indemnity insurance, particularly marine insurance, the **S33–135** common law, in some cases, favoured the law of the insurance market by reference to which the contract was made, rather than the law of the insurer's head office.[12] It is unclear whether this will be a factor relevant to rebutting the presumption in Article 4(2) according to Article 4(5). It seems likely that, where an insurance contract is made with reference to a particular market, that reference will emerge from the terms of the contract[13] or the circumstances of the case and that in such a case the court is likely to conclude that the parties have demonstrated a choice of law with reasonable certainty according to Article 3(1) of the Rome Convention.[14] But were a court to conclude that despite such circumstances no choice of law had been made in the contract itself, the presence of factors pointing to a market in a country other than that indicated by virtue of the presumption could be treated as rebutting the presumption.[15]

---

[5] *Cf. Crédit Lyonnais v. New Hampshire Insurance Co., supra.* See *infra*, Rule 186.

[6] *Cf. Crédit Lyonnais v. New Hampshire Insurance Co., supra.*

[7] This tendency seems to have existed in French practice prior to the implementation of the Convention: see Lando, *Contracts*, in Lipstein (ed.). *International Encyclopedia of Comparative Law*, Vol. III. Chap. 24, pp. 147–148.

[8] *supra*. para. S33–125 and *infra*, Rule 186.

[9] Rabel, Vol. III, pp. 341–342; Lando, pp. 148–152. See *supra*, para. S33–125 and *infra*, Rule 185.

[10] Lando, pp. 147–148.

[11] Main work, Rule 181.

[12] See *Cantieri Navali Riuniti SpA v. N.V. Omne Justitia* [1985] 2 Lloyd's Rep. 428; *E.I. du Pont de Nemours v. Agnew* [1987] 2 Lloyd's Rep. 585 (C.A.); *cf. Amin Rasheed Shipping Corp. v. Kuwait Insurance Co.* [1984] A.C. 50; *Armadora Occidental S.A. v. Horace Mann Insurance Co.* [1977] 1 W.L.R. 520, 1098 (C.A.).

[13] *Cf. Amin Rasheed Shipping Corp. v. Kuwait Insurance Co., supra; Armadora Occidental S.A. v. Horace Mann Insurance Co. supra* (implied choice of law).

[14] Rule 174. See also *Burrows v. Jamaica Private Power Co. Ltd.* [2002] 1 All E.R. (Comm.) 374.

[15] *Cf. Amin Rasheed Shipping Corp. v. Kuwait Insurance Co., supra*, at 71 *et seq.* where Lord Wilberforce could, in disagreement with Lords Diplock, Roskill, Brandon and Brightman, find no ground for inferring an intention to choose English law from the use of a Lloyd's standard form of marine insurance policy and the absence of any indigenous code of marine insurance in Kuwait, the other possible applicable law.

ILLUSTRATIONS

S33–136 1. English underwriters execute in England a policy of marine insurance on a ship registered in Liberia. An express term of the policy is that it shall be construed and applied in accordance with New York law. The law applicable to the contract is the law of New York.[16]

2. A, habitually resident in New York, insures his life with X & Co., an American corporation, at its English branch office. The policy provides that all disputes shall be settled under English law by English courts. The law applicable to the contract is English law.[17]

3. A, a resident of New Jersey, insures his stamp collection, which is situated there, with X & Co., an English company. The policy, which is made in New York through the New York agent of X & Co., provides that disputes shall be settled by arbitration in England before English arbitrators. The law applicable to the contract is English law since (*semble*) the clause providing for arbitration in England demonstrates with reasonable certainty an intention to choose English law as the applicable law.[18]

4. The facts are the same as in Illustration 3, except that the clause in the policy provides that all disputes shall be referred to the English courts. This clause (*semble*) demonstrates with reasonable certainty an intention to choose English law as the applicable law. The law applicable to the contract is English law.[19]

S33–137 5. X & Co., an insurance company incorporated and resident in Florida, issues in California an insurance policy by which it provides partial cover for a ship registered in Panama and owned by A & Co., a Panamanian company. Premiums and claims are payable in California. The rest of the cover is provided by other American, by English and by other insurers. All policies incorporate the English Institute Time Clauses relating to Hulls and a "follow London" clause by which all insurers undertake to follow British insurers in regard to all matters pertaining to the insurance including, *inter alia*, the settlement of claims. By this clause X & Co. bound itself to follow the actions of the London market whose decisions would be based on English law and practice and in these circumstances it must have been an overriding consideration in the minds of all of the parties that all of the policies should be governed by one system of law, *viz.* English law, the law of the London policies. Accordingly, (*semble*) it would appear from the terms of the contract or the circumstances of the case that the parties have demonstrated with reasonable certainty an intention to choose English law as the applicable law. The law applicable to the contract is English law.[20]

6. X & Co., a Kuwait insurance company with no office or representation in England, issues a policy insuring a small cargo vessel owned by A & Co., a Liberian corporation carrying on business in Dubai, against war and marine risks. The policy is in the English language and is based on Lloyd's S.G. Policy scheduled to the Marine Insurance Act 1906. The policy is negotiated by brokers in London, premiums are paid to those brokers and claims are settled through them. The use of the English standard form and the absence of any developed law of marine insurance in Kuwait at the time of the conclusion of the contract (*semble*) demonstrates with reasonable certainty by the terms of the contract or the circumstances of the case, an intention to choose English law as the applicable law. The law applicable to the contract is English law.[21]

7. X & Co., a Canadian life assurance company with branches in many countries including Egypt, and with its head office in Toronto, issues three endowment policies to A, an Egyptian national, habitually resident in Egypt. The policies are executed in the form normally used by X & Co. for their foreign business and are handed to A in Egypt, A's

---

[16] Rome Convention, Arts. 1(3) and 3(1). *Cf. Greer v. Poole* (1880) 5 Q.B.D. 272, 274.

[17] Rome Convention, Arts. 1(3) and 3(1). *Cf. Perry v. Equitable Life Assurance Society* (1929) 45 T.L.R. 468.

[18] Rome Convention, Arts. 1(3) and 3(1): Giuliano-Lagarde, p. 17. *Cf. Spurrier v. La Cloche* [1902] A.C. 446 (P.C.).

[19] Rome Convention, Arts. 1(3) and 3(1): Giuliano-Lagarde, p. 17. See also *Chase v. Ram Technical Services Ltd.* [2000] 2 Lloyd's Rep. 418.

[20] Rome Convention, Arts. 1(3) and 3(1): Giuliano-Lagarde, p. 17. *Cf. Armadora Occidental S.A. v. Horace Mann Insurance Co.* [1977] 1 W.L.R. 520; affd. *ibid.* 1098 (C.A.).

[21] Rome Convention, Arts. 1(3) and 3(1); Giuliano-Lagarde, p. 17. *Cf. Amin Rasheed Shipping Corp. v. Kuwait Insurance Co.* [1984] A.C. 50.

application form having been received by X & Co. in Toronto.[22] They are payable after two years. Two are expressed in pounds sterling and payable in London, one is expressed in United States dollars and payable in New York. A pays the premiums in advance, those on the sterling policies to the Egyptian branch, and that on the dollar policy to the head office of X & Co. The law applicable to the policies is (*semble*) the law of Ontario.[23]

8. A. habitually resident in Egypt, insures his life with X & Co., a Canadian insurance company, whose head office is in Toronto in response to an advertisement by X & Co. in an Egyptian journal. A takes out the policy for a purpose which can be regarded as being outside his profession.[24] There is no express choice of law in the policy nor is a choice of law demonstrated with reasonable certainty by the terms of the contract or the circumstance of the case.[25] Since A is habitually resident in Egypt, the law applicable to the policy is the law of Egypt.[26]

RULE 185[27]—(1) This Rule applies to determine the law applicable to a contract of general insurance which covers risks situated in an EEA State.[28] S33R–138

(2) If the risk covered by the contract is a large risk the parties to the contract may choose any law as the applicable law.[29]

(3) Subject to clause (2) of this Rule:

(a) If the policyholder resides in the EEA State in which the risk is situated, the applicable law is the law of that EEA State unless, if such a choice is permitted under the law of that EEA State, the parties to the contract choose the law of another country.[30]

(b) If the policyholder does not reside in the EEA State where the risk is situated, the parties to the contract may choose as the applicable law either—

(i) the law of the EEA State in which the risk is situated; or

(ii) the law of the country in which the policyholder resides.[31]

---

[22] Assuming that the making of the contract was not proceeded by a specific invitation addressed to A, in Egypt, by X & Co., or by advertising in Egypt by X & Co., and A's order (if applicable) was not received by X & Co. or its agent in Egypt, Art. 5 (main work, Rule 181) cannot apply. *Cf.* Illustration 8.

[23] Rome Convention, Arts. 1(3), 4(1) and (2). *Cf. Rossano v. Manufacturers' Life Insurance Co.* [1963] 2 Q.B. 352: see also *Pick v. Manufacturers' Life Insurance Co.* [1958] 2 Lloyd's Rep. 93.

[24] Rome Convention, Art. 5(1).

[25] *ibid.* Art. 3(1).

[26] *ibid.* Art. 5(3). *Cf. Pick v. Manufacturers' Life Insurance Co.* [1958] 2 Lloyd's Rep. 93.

[27] See Merkin, *Insurance Contract Law* (1988), Chap. D. 4.2.39–D. 4.2.55; Clarke, *The Law of Insurance Contracts* (3rd ed. 1997). pp. 45–49; Philip, in *Festkrift Till Kurt Grönfors* (1991), pp. 347–356. For discussion of Rule 185 see *American Motorists Insurance Co. v. Cellstar Corp.* [2003] EWCA Civ. 206; [2003] I.L.Pr. 370 (C.A.). And see Commission of the European Communities, *Green Paper on the conversion of the Rome Convention of 1980 on the law applicable to contractual obligations into a Community instrument and its modernisation*, COM (2002) 654 final, paras. 3.2.2.1–3.2.2.3.

[28] Financial Services and Markets Act 2000 (Law Applicable to Contracts of Insurance) Regulations 2001 (S.I. 2001 No. 2635, as amended by S.I. 2001 No. 3542), reg. 4(1), made under Financial Services and Markets Act 2000, s.424(3), in force from December 1, 2001. For ease of exposition, the shorthand expression, "Regulations" will be used in what follows. As to contracts made prior to December 1, 2001, see Rule 185 in the main work, and Comment thereto.

[29] Regulations, reg. 4(7). "Large risk" is as defined in Art. 5(d) of the first non-life insurance directive, [1973] O.J. L228/3: Regulations, reg. 2(1). See *infra*, para. S33–146. "Applicable law" in relation to this Rule means the law that is applicable to the contract of insurance: Regulations, reg. 2(1).

[30] Regulations, reg. 4(2). "Residence" in relation to an individual means the country in which the individual has his habitual residence: *ibid.* reg. 2(3)(a). "Residence" in any other case means the country in which a person has his central administration: *ibid.* reg. 2(3)(b).

[31] *ibid.* reg. 4(3).

    (c) **If the policyholder carries on a business (including a trade or profession) and the contract covers two or more risks relating to that business which are situated in different EEA States, the freedom of the parties to choose the applicable law extends to the law of any of those EEA States and of the country in which the policyholder resides.**[32]

    (d) **If any of the EEA States referred to in clause 3(b) and 3(c) of this Rule grant greater freedom of choice of the applicable law, the parties to the contract may take advantage of that freedom.**[33]

    (e) **Notwithstanding clause 3(a) to 3(c) of this Rule, if the risks covered by the contract are limited to events occurring in one EEA State other than the EEA State in which the risk is situated, the parties may choose the law of the former EEA State as the applicable law.**[34]

(4) Any choice made by the parties under clauses (2) to 3(e) of this Rule must be expressed or demonstrated with reasonable certainty by the terms of the contract or the circumstances of the case.[35]

(5) Where clause (3) (a) to 3(d) of this Rule allows the parties to choose the applicable law and if no choice has been made, or no choice has been made which satisfies clause (4) of this Rule, the applicable law is the law of the country from amongst those considered in clause 3(a) to 3(d) ("the relevant countries") which is most closely connected to the contract.[36]

(6) However, where a severable part of the contract has a closer connection with another relevant country, the law applicable to that part is, by way of exception, the law of that relevant country.[37]

(7) For the purposes of clause (5) of this Rule, the contract is rebuttably presumed to be most closely connected with the EEA State in which the risk is situated.[38]

COMMENT

S33–139–
140
    Introduction. The origins of this Rule lie in the choice of law provisions contained in the European Community's Second[39] and Third[40] Directives on Non-Life Insurance, which are now implemented in the United Kingdom by

---

[32] *ibid.* reg. 4(4).

[33] *ibid.* reg. 4(5).

[34] *ibid.* reg. 4(6).

[35] *ibid.* reg. 6(1). Where the parties to the contract may choose the applicable law under this Rule, and where the risk to which the contract relates is covered by Community co-insurance (within the meaning of Council Directive 78/473 on the co-ordination of laws, regulations and administrative provisions relating to community co-insurance, [1978] O.J.L151/25) co-insurers other than the leading insurer (within the meaning of that Directive) are not to be treated as parties to the contract: Regulations, reg. 6(2).

[36] Regulations, reg. 4(8).

[37] *ibid.*

[38] *ibid.* reg. 4(9). See *Crédit Lyonnais v. New Hampshire Insurance Co.* [1997] 2 Lloyd's Rep. 1 (C.A.).

[39] Second Council Directive of June 22, 1988 on the co-ordination of laws, regulations and administrative provisions relating to direct insurance other than life insurance and laying down provisions to facilitate the effective exercise of freedom to provide services: [1988] O.J. L172/1, amending the First Council Directive of July 24, 1973, [1973] O.J. L228/3.

[40] Third Council Directive of November 10, 1992 on the co-ordination of laws, regulations and administrative provisions relating to direct insurance other than life insurance: [1992] O.J. L228/1.

the Financial Services and Markets Act 2000 (Law Applicable to Contracts of Insurance) Regulations 2001,[41] with an important modification brought about by those Regulations which is described below.[42]

Scope of the Rule. The scope of this Rule is specifically delimited in two ways. First, it only applies to "contracts of general insurance", as defined in the 2001 Regulations[43] and the Financial Services and Markets Act 2000 (Regulated Activities) Order 2001.[44] Thus the Rule will apply where the contract relates to accident or sickness insurance; the insurance of land vehicles, railway rolling stock, aircraft, ships or goods in transit; insurance against loss or damage arising out of fire and natural forces, damage to property, use of motor vehicles, aircraft and ships; general third party liability insurance; credit insurance and suretyship; miscellaneous financial loss insurance; legal expenses insurance and contracts of insurance providing for assistance to travellers.[45] Secondly, while the Directives and the earlier implementing legislation only applied if the risk covered by the policy was situated in a State which was a member of the European Community,[46] the new provisions set out in Rule 185 apply where the risk covered by the contract is situated in an EEA State. The rules for determining the EEA State in which the risk is situated are to be found in the 2001 Regulations,[47] an amendment to the Contracts (Applicable Law) Act 1990 making it clear that these are the relevant rules for this purpose.[48] Thus, where the contract relates to buildings or to buildings and their contents (in so far as the contents are covered by the same policy), the risk is situated in the EEA State in which the property is situated[49]; where the contract relates to vehicles of any type, the risk is situated in the EEA State in which the vehicle is registered[50]; if the contract covers travel or holiday risks and has a duration of four months or less, the risk is situated in the EEA State in which the policyholder entered into the contract[51]; in any other case, if the policyholder is an individual, the risk is situated in the EEA State in which the policyholder resides on the date the contract is entered into,[52] the reference to the country in which a person resides being taken to mean the country in which he has his habitual residence,[53] whereas if the policyholder is not an individual, the risk is situated in the EEA State in which the establishment of the policyholder to which the contract relates

---

[41] S.I. 2001 No. 2635, in force from December 1, 2001. For the choice of law rules applicable to contracts entered into before this date, see main work, Rule 185 and Comment thereto.

[42] See *infra*, para. S33–141.

[43] Regulations, reg. 2(1).

[44] S.I. 2001 No. 544.

[45] *ibid.* art. 3(1) and Sched. 1, Pt. 1. This would seem to include compulsory insurance. Although Art. 8 of the Second Non-Life Directive permits a Member State, by way of derogation from Art. 7 (the provision which contains the choice of law rules which are the subject matter of this Rule), to establish that the law applicable to a compulsory insurance contract is the law of the State which imposes the obligation to take out insurance, the United Kingdom has not taken advantage of this permission.

[46] See main work, para. 33–141.

[47] Reg. 2(2).

[48] Contracts (Applicable Law) Act 1990, s.2 (1A), as substituted by S.I. 2001 No. 3649, art. 320.

[49] Regulations, reg. 2(2)(a).

[50] *ibid.* reg. 2(2)(b).

[51] *ibid.* reg. 2(2)(c).

[52] *ibid.* reg. 2(2)(d)(i).

[53] *ibid.* reg. 2(3)(a).

is situated on that date.[54] For the purposes of the latter provision, "establishment" may mean a head office, any agency of the policyholder, any of the policyholder's branches or any permanent presence of the policyholder in an EEA State, which need not take the form of a branch or agency and which may consist of an office managed by the policyholder's staff or by a person who is independent of the policyholder but has permanent authority to act for the policyholder as if the were an agency.[55] It has already been pointed out that these provisions yield no obvious answer where one risk is situated in more than one EEA State (a difficulty which persists despite clause (3)(c) of the Rule),[56] or where the policy covers one risk which is partially situated in an EEA State and partially situated outside such a State, or where the policy covers two or more risks situated, respectively, in an EEA State and outside an EEA State.[57]

S33–142   The choice of law rules in Rule 185 apply to conflicts between the laws of the different parts of the United Kingdom.[58] Further, where an EEA State includes several territorial units, each of which has its own rules of law concerning contractual obligations, each unit shall be considered as a separate State for the purposes of identifying the applicable law.[59]

S33–143   **Relationship with Rome Convention.** The Second Non-Life Directive, as implemented in the United Kingdom in the 2001 Regulations does not provide a complete code of private international law rules, as does the Rome Convention, to deal with all questions of choice of law which can arise. Furthermore, the Regulations envisage that specific reference will have to be made to English choice of law rules: *e.g.* according to Regulation 4(2) (clause 3(a) of the Rule) in a case where a risk is situated in England, if English law permits, the parties may choose the law of another country. It is necessary to identify, for the purposes of applying this provision, what are the relevant English choice of law rules by reference to which the power to choose may be ascertained.[60] Regulation 7(1) provides that, subject to the preceding provisions of the Regulations (*i.e.* Rule 185) the Contracts (Applicable Law) Act 1990 is to be treated as applying to the contract for the purposes of determining the applicable law,[61] and further, that Act is to be treated as applying to the contract for the purposes of determining what freedom of choice of the applicable law the parties have under the law of a part of the United Kingdom.[62]

S33–144   **Principles underlying Second Non-Life Directive.** The harmonised choice of law rules contained in the Directive are seen as part of the general policy of extending freedom to provide insurance services across the European Community and now across the EEA.[63] Despite this, the implementing legislation does not, as far as choice of law rules are concerned, limit itself

---

[54] *ibid.* reg. 2(2)(d)(ii).
[55] *ibid.* reg. 2(1).
[56] See *supra*, para. S33–126; *infra*, para. S33–157.
[57] *supra*, paras. S33–125 *et seq.*
[58] Regulations, reg. 2(4).
[59] *ibid.*
[60] A similar problem arises in relation to clause (3)(d) of the Rule: see *infra*, para. S33–158.
[61] Regulations, reg. 7(1).
[62] *ibid.* reg. 7(3). As to: reg. 7(2), see *infra*, para. S33–149.
[63] See Second Non-Life Directive, Art. 1 (b).

to an insurer with an establishment in an EEA State. The Rule may thus apply to a contract concluded, say, with an American insurer with no establishment in an EEA State which covers a risk situated in an EEA State. At the same time, account has to be taken of the need to protect policyholders who are assumed to be in a weaker bargaining position *vis-à-vis* the insurer.[64] This philosophy explains the rather strict approach taken to freedom to choose the applicable law, despite the limited extension of that freedom brought about by adoption of the Third Non-Life Directive (clause (2) of the Rule). Thus while there is virtually unlimited freedom to choose the applicable law in a contract covering so called "large risks" (see clause (2) of the Rule[65]) freedom of choice, in relation to "mass risks",[66] is rather more circumscribed.[67] In the former situation the policyholder is likely to be a commercial concern which will not suffer from any inequality of bargaining power as against the insurer. In the latter situation such a consideration may well not be present. The result of the implementation of these policies in the 2001 Regulations is, however, an extremely complex web of choice of law rules.

Structure of the Rule. The 2001 Regulations distinguish between the power of the parties to choose the law applicable to the insurance contract and the rules which will be applied if no choice of law is made in the contract itself. Clauses (2) to (4) of the Rule deal with the former question. Clauses (5) to (7) deal with the latter question. Clause (1) of the Rule delimits its scope and has been the subject of comment above.[68] **S33–145**

Clause (2) of the Rule. Regulation 4(7) of the 2001 Regulations provides that if the risk covered by the contract is a "large risk", the parties may choose any law as the applicable law, providing that the risk is situated in an EEA State.[69] Large risks are those so defined in Article 5(d) of the First Non-Life Insurance Directive,[70] as follows: railway rolling stock; aircraft; ships; goods in transit; liability for ships; credit and suretyship insurance which relates to a business carried on by the policyholder; and in relation to policyholders who carry on a business satisfying detailed conditions specified in the Directive, insurance of land vehicles, insurance against fire and natural forces, insurance against damage to property, motor vehicle liability insurance, general liability insurance and insurance against miscellaneous financial loss. **S33–146—147**

In cases falling within this clause, the parties to the contract may choose the law of a country whether or not the particular country is an EEA State. The freedom to choose the applicable law is, in this context, subject to two limitations. First, nothing in Regulation 4 of the Regulations restricts the application of the mandatory rules[71] of any part of the United Kingdom **S33–148**

---

[64] See the preamble to the Second Non-Life Directive.
[65] *infra*, text at n. 70.
[66] Large risks are defined in Art. 5(d) of the First Council Directive of July 24, 1973 on the co-ordination of laws, regulations and administrative provisions relating to the taking up and pursuit of the business of direct insurance other than life insurance, [1973] O.J. L228/3: Regulations, reg. 2(1). The term "mass risks" is used to refer to all non-life risks other than "large risks."
[67] See *infra*, paras. S33–146 *et seq.*
[68] *supra*, para. S33–141.
[69] Reg. 4(1).
[70] Reg. 2(1); First Non-Life Insurance Directive, *supra*, n. 66, Art. 5(d).
[71] "Mandatory rules" means the rules from which the law allows no derogation by way of contract: Regulations, reg. 2(1).

irrespective of the applicable law of the contract.[72] This provision is a replica of Article 7(2) of the Rome Convention which is discussed in Chapter 32 of the main work.[73] Secondly, it is provided that if the parties to the contract choose the applicable law under Regulation 4 "and if all the other elements relevant to the situation at the time when the parties make their choice are connected with one EEA State only, the application of the mandatory rules[74] of that EEA State is not prejudiced".[75] This provision bears a strong resemblance to, but is not identical with, Article 3(3) of the Rome Convention.[76] It is narrower than the latter provision in that before it can operate all the elements relevant to the situation other than the choice of law must be connected with one EEA State (as opposed to one country, as is the case in the Rome Convention) only. Thus, the only mandatory rules that can be applied, despite the choice of law, are mandatory rules of EEA States. Further, there is a difference in formulation between the two provisions. Article 3(3) secures the potential application of the mandatory rules of the only connected country where there is a choice of "a *foreign law, whether or not accompanied by the choice of a foreign tribunal.*" The italicised words in this formulation do not appear in the formulation in Regulation 5(2) of the 2001 Regulations. It is likely that the first difference will be of no significance since it is probable that the parties have chosen a foreign law even if they have chosen the law of the forum in a case falling within Article 3(3), if all the other elements relevant to the situation are connected with one country only which is not the country of the forum.[77] If this is correct, the position is the same as it is under Regulation 5(2), which merely refers to choosing "a law," presumably English or foreign law.[78] The second difference may, however, be of greater significance. Assume a contract of insurance where the situation is entirely connected with France apart from an English choice of law clause and an English jurisdiction clause. If there were no jurisdiction clause in the contract, Regulation 5(2) would seem to envisage application of any French mandatory rules if proceedings occur in England. But does the presence of the jurisdiction clause mean that the English courts can ignore those mandatory rules? Such a result is clearly possible since the presence of the English jurisdiction clause is an element relevant to the situation which points to a conclusion that all the elements relevant to the situation are not connected with France only, with the consequence that Regulation 5(2) of the Regulations does not apply. Such a result may also be likely: if the only link with England is a choice of English law, it is unlikely that the English court would ever have jurisdiction under the 1968 Convention as amended[79] or under Council Regulation (E.C.) 44/2001 ("the Judgments Regulation") but, in the case of a policy covering risks presently being discussed, a clause which conferred

---

[72] *ibid.* reg. 5(1).

[73] Rule 175(2).

[74] *supra*, n. 71.

[75] Regulations, reg. 5(2).

[76] See main work, paras. 32–130 *et seq.* And see *Crédit Lyonnais v. New Hampshire Insurance Co.* [1997] 2 Lloyd's Rep. 1 (C.A.).

[77] Main work, para. 32–131.

[78] This seems clear from reg. 7(2) which says that in determining whether the mandatory rules of another EEA State should be applied in accordance with reg. 5(2) where the parties have chosen the law of a part of the United Kingdom as the applicable law, the 1990 Act (*i.e.* the Rome Convention) is to be treated as applying to the contract.

[79] Main work, paras. 11–162 *et seq.*; 11–170 *et seq*; *supra*, paras. S11–317—S11–318.

jurisdiction on the English courts may well be effective under the 1968 Convention or under the Judgments Regulation.[80] However, it is likely that the absence of any reference to a jurisdiction clause in Regulation 5(2) of the 2001 Regulations and from its equivalent in the Second Non-Life Directive was not intended to have the substantial effect outlined above.

The general characteristics (as opposed to the actual content) of those **S33–149** rules which will be regarded as mandatory for the purposes of the provision would appear to be the same as those discussed in relation to Article 3(3) of the Rome Convention in Chapter 32.[81] Thus it appears to be clear from the wording of Regulation 5(2) that the law of the EEA State concerned will determine whether its rules can be derogated from by contract.[82] Further, mandatory rules in the provision may include rules, it would seem, other than rules of insurance contract law. It is unlikely however that many rules of English insurance law will be treated as mandatory in this context,[83] though of course an English court may well have to apply mandatory rules of another EEA State which is the only connected EEA State if that State regards such rules as mandatory in the situation envisaged.[84] Confusingly, however, Regulation 7(2) of the 2001 Regulations stipulates that "in determining whether the mandatory rules of another EEA State should be applied in accordance with regulation 5(2) where the parties have chosen the law of a part of the United Kingdom as the applicable law, the 1990 Act", (*i.e.* the Contracts (Applicable Law) Act 1990[85]), "is to be treated as applying to the contract". In an English court this would be English law. It is most unclear what this provision is intended to convey, since Regulation 7(1) makes the application of the 1990 Act subject to the preceding provisions of the Regulations, one provision of which is Regulation 5(2). At first sight it would seem that Regulation 5(2) is intended to provide a self-contained rule limiting party autonomy: but Regulation 5(2), combined with Regulation 7(2), suggests that the principles of the 1990 Act must be looked to in order to determine, when the law otherwise applicable (presumably because it is chosen) is English law, whether the mandatory rules of the otherwise only connected country should apply. The latter provision thus seems to contradict Regulation 5(2). One possible solution is that Regulation 5(2) is only a self-contained rule where foreign law is chosen, but that when, say, English law is chosen, all that Regulation 5(2) does is define the meaning of mandatory rule, it being, pursuant to Regulation 7(2), for relevant provisions of the 1990 Act to determine when the mandatory rules of the other EEA State are applicable. But such an argument resolves little of the difficulty. First, it does not square with the wording of Regulation 5(2): that wording refers to a choice of "law," rather than to choice of a foreign law. Secondly, the only relevant provision of the 1990 Act which is germane to the question being considered is Article 3(3) which, subject to the differences outlined above, which are not material in this context, is framed in terms almost identical to Regulation 5(2).

---

[80] Rule 32.

[81] Rule 175(1).

[82] For the definition of "mandatory rules" see reg. 2(1), *supra*, para. S33–148, n.71.

[83] *i.e.* in the context of the particular risks to which reg. 4(7) (clause (2) of the Rule) applies. It is, further, highly unlikely that reg. 5(2) will arise at all in such situations since there will, invariably, be a foreign element additional to the choice of law. See *infra*, paras. S33–150—S33–151.

[84] *supra*, para. S33–148.

[85] Regulations, reg. 2(1).

S33–150— Whatever the impact of Regulation 7(2) on Regulation 5(2) may be, the
151 latter paragraph is not likely to have much practical effect on insurance of
risks which are the subject of this clause since insurance thereof will almost
inevitably involve foreign elements additional to the choice of a law: one
would have to envisage, for example, an insurance contract covering goods
in transit which was purely domestic and which contained a choice of the
law of a country other than that where the transit was being carried out.
Such a case would be very unlikely.

S33–152 **Clause (3)(a) of the Rule.** Clause (3)(a) to (3)(e) of the Rule applies a
rather different and more limited notion of party autonomy to insurance
contracts covering risks other than those which are the subject of clause (2).
Essentially, the risks which are the subject of clause (3)(a) to (3)(e) consist
of the following classes: accident insurance; sickness insurance; legal
expenses insurance; insurance for assistance; credit and suretyship insurance
where the risks do *not* relate to a business carried on by the policyholder;
and, where the policyholder does *not* carry on a business which satisfies
certain detailed requirements of the First Non-Life Directive,[86] land vehicle
insurance, fire insurance, damage to property, motor vehicle liability,
general liability (other than aircraft liability and liability for ships), and
insurance against miscellaneous financial loss.[87]

S33–153 According to clause (3)(a), which reproduces Regulation 4(2), if the
policyholder resides in the EEA State in which the risk is situated, the
applicable law is the law of that EEA State. For these purposes, reference
to the law of the country in which a person resides are, in the case of an
individual, the country in which he has his habitual residence and, in any
other case, the country in which a person has his central administration.[88]
This rule is not, in terms, a rule permitting choice of law by the parties. The
provisions for identifying the *situs* of the risk were discussed above and the
rules for determining the habitual residence of an individual and the central
administration of a legal entity are discussed in the main work.[89]

S33–154 The provision goes on to say, however, that where the law of that EEA
State (*i.e.* the State in which the risk is situated and in which the
policyholder resides, as defined above) permits, the parties to the contract
may choose the law of another country as the applicable law. Accordingly, if
the contract purports to choose as its governing law the law of a country (it
need not be an EEA State) which is a country other than the EEA State in
which both the risk is situated and the policyholder has his habitual
residence or central administration, the validity of that choice of law will be
tested by reference to the law of the latter EEA State. "Law" for these
purposes means the choice of law rules of the particular EEA State
concerned.[90] Thus, for example, if an insurance contract insures a building
in France, the policyholder being habitually resident in France, and the
contract contains a choice of English law, the validity of that choice of law
will be determined according to the rules of French private international

---

[86] First Non-Life Directive, Art. 5(d)(iii); Regulations, reg. 2(1); S.I. 2001 No. 544, Sched. 1,
Pt. 1.
[87] *ibid.*
[88] Regulations, reg. 3(3).
[89] Main work, paras. 6–123 *et seq.*, 30–005 *et seq.*, 32–118.
[90] The draftsmen of the Directive appear to have overlooked, or to be unconcerned by, the
general principle that renvoi has no place in the law of contract: main work, para. 32–042.

law. Similarly if a building in England is insured under a contract governed by the law of New York, the policyholder being habitually resident in England, the validity of the choice of New York law will be determined according to the rules of English private international law. This much is made clear by Regulation 7(3) which provides that in determining what freedom of choice the parties have under the law of a part of the United Kingdom, the Contracts (Applicable Law) Act 1990 is to be treated as applying to the contract.[91] Freedom of choice is also subject to Regulation 5, discussed above.[92] In practice, where the risk is situated in England and the policyholder is habitually resident there, there is a wide freedom to choose the applicable law because of the generosity, in this regard, of the provisions of the Rome Convention, as implemented in the 1990 Act, unless the contract is a consumer contract falling within Article 5 of the Convention.[93]

Clause (3)(b) of the Rule. Freedom to choose the governing law is more S33–155
limited in cases where the policyholder does not have his habitual residence or central administration in the EEA State where the risk is situated. In these circumstances, Regulation 4(3), reproduced in this clause, permits the parties to choose as the applicable law *either* the law of the EEA State where the risk is situated *or* the law of the country (which need not be an EEA State) in which the policyholder resides, *i.e.* the State in which he is habitually resident or has his central administration, as the case may be. As a result, however, of clause 3(d) of the Rule, which states the terms of Regulation 4(5), if the law of the EEA State in which the risk is situated grants greater freedom of choice of the applicable law, the parties to the contract may take advantage of that freedom. Where the *situs* of the risk is a part of the United Kingdom, the extent to which the parties are free to choose the law of another country as the applicable law will be determined by the rules of the Rome Convention, as implemented in the 1990 Act.[94] Where the *situs* of the risk is an EEA State other than the United Kingdom, the extent of the parties' freedom to choose the governing law will be determined by the law of that EEA State. The combined effect of these provisions may be illustrated as follows. If the policyholder is habitually resident in New York and the policy covers a building situated in London, the parties may choose New York law or English law as the applicable law. A choice of any other law will also be effective if such a choice is valid according to the Rome Convention. But it is important to note that a choice of another law which is valid according to the private international law of New York though invalid according to the Rome Convention will not be effective because Regulation 4(5) only permits the parties to take advantage of greater freedom of choice available in the law of an EEA State referred to in Regulation 4(3) and the only such EEA State is that in which the risk is situated. If, in the above example, the policyholder was habitually resident in France and French law permitted greater freedom of choice than did English law (which is highly unlikely since the Rome Convention is in force in both countries), the parties would not be able to take advantage of that freedom.

---

[91] Main work, para. 32–042.
[92] *supra*, para. S33–148.
[93] Main work, Rule 181.
[94] Regulations, reg. 7(3).

S33–156   The power to choose the laws indicated in Regulation 4 (3) and any other freedom of choice available under the law of the EEA State where the risk is situated is subject to the limits imposed in Regulation 5, discussed above.[95]

S33–157 **Clause (3)(c) of the Rule.** Regulation 4(4), reproduced in this clause, stipulates that if the policyholder carries on a business (which includes a trade or profession) and the contract covers two or more risks relating to that business which are situated in different EEA States, the freedom of the parties to choose the law applicable to the contract extends to the laws of those EEA States and to the law of the country in which the policyholder resides, *i.e.* in which he has his habitual residence or central administration, as the case may be.[96] The provision is further supplemented by Regulation 4(5) (clause (3)(d) of the Rule) so that if the "EEA States referred to" grant greater freedom of choice, the parties may take advantage of that freedom. They cannot, however, take advantage of any greater freedom available under the law of the place of the policyholder's habitual residence or central administration because the only EEA States referred to are those in which the risks are situated. Since Regulation 4(5) states that "if any of the EEA States referred to in paragraph 3 or 4" (of Regulation 4) grant greater freedom of choice of law, the parties may take advantage of it, then it is possible that in Regulation 4(4) the law of each EEA State in which the risk is situated must regard the choice of law as valid: on this basis it would not be enough that the choice of law was regarded as effective under the law of one such EEA State. If, therefore, a policyholder with his central administration in New York insures risks situated in England, France and Belgium under a contract governed by New York law, the choice of which is effective by English law but ineffective by the law of France or Belgium, the choice of New York law will be invalid if this argument is accepted. Conversely, if it is necessary that only one EEA State regards the choice as valid then it will be upheld. Since the purpose of the choice of law rules applicable to contracts of general insurance contained in the 2001 Regulations is, in part, to limit the power to choose the governing law, there is something to be said for the view that the choice of law must be regarded as valid under the laws of each EEA State involved. On the other hand, since Regulation 4(4) is limited to cases where the policyholder carries on business, there is much to be said for expanding the power to choose the governing law. On this basis it should be enough that the choice is effective under the law of one EEA State in which a risk is situated. On balance, it is submitted that this latter view should be preferred both as a matter of principle and because it is more consistent with the wording of Regulation 4(5) which speaks of "*any* of the EEA States" referred to in Regulation 4(3) and 4(4).[97]

S33–158 **Clause (3)(d) of the Rule.** Regulation 4(5), which is the subject of this clause, extends the freedom of choice permitted in Regulation 4(3) and 4(4) and has been discussed in relation to clause (3)(b) and (3)(c) of this Rule.

---

[95] *supra*, para. S33–148.

[96] Regulations, reg. 2(3).

[97] Emphasis added. Reg. 5(2) could not, it is thought, limit the effect of a choice of law since because the risks are situated in more than one EEA State, the situation cannot, in the nature of things be connected with one EEA State only. Reg. 5(1) could, of course, apply in appropriate circumstances.

Clause (3)(e) of the Rule. This states the effect of Regulation 5(6) of the S33–159
2001 Regulations. Notwithstanding Regulation 4(2), 4(3) and 4(4), where
the risks covered by the contract are limited to events occurring in an EEA
State other than the EEA State in which the risk is situated, the parties may
choose the law of the former State as the applicable law. By this provision
the parties are given another law which they may choose in addition to
those otherwise available under Regulation 4(2), 4(3) and 4(4), but its
operation is not entirely free from difficulty. Presumably it would permit a
liability policy covering a lawyer qualified to practise in England and France
to contain an effective choice of French law in relation to any indemnity for
liability for negligence in respect of advice on French law given in France
(the policy being so limited) if the lawyer was habitually resident in England
(where the risk would thus be situated[98]). But it may not always be easy to
determine whether the events insured against have occurred in one
Member State. Thus, if a lawyer gave negligent advice in France in relation
to litigation which he was qualified to conduct in France and England, it
would seem that the events insured against have occurred in France and
England with the consequence that the choice of French law is not
effective.[99]

It should be noted that the fact that the choice of law rules of the EEA S33–160
State where the events occur might give greater freedom of choice of law is
irrelevant since Regulation 4(6) is not supplemented by Regulation 4(5).

Clause (4) of the Rule. Regulation 6(1) deals with the form of a choice of S33–161
law necessary to satisfy the foregoing provisions which permit a choice of
law by the parties. The choice must be "expressed or demonstrated with
reasonable certainty by the terms of the contract or the circumstances of the
case". This formula is almost identical to that contained in Article 3(1) of
the Rome Convention.[1] The formula is discussed generally in the Comment
to Rule 173[2] and with particular reference to insurance contracts in the
Comment to Rule 184.[3]

If the parties have sought to take advantage of any greater freedom of S33–162
choice of law available under Regulation 4(5) (clause (3)(d) of the Rule)
then, it seems, the choice of law must be in the form required by whichever
EEA State's law is invoked to validate the choice of law.

Clauses (5)–(7) of the Rule. These clauses reproduce Regulations 4(8) and S33–163
4(9) of the 2001 Regulations, and provide the rules for determining the
applicable law where no choice of law has been made or no choice of law
has been expressed or demonstrated with reasonable certainty by the terms
of the contract or the circumstances of the case.[4] The clauses are discussed
together for ease of exposition. The general rule (clause (5) of the Rule) is
that "the applicable law is the law of the country, from among those
considered in the relevant paragraph ('the relevant countries') which is
most closely connected with the contract".[5] The phrase in parenthesis

---

[98] Regulations, reg. 2(2)(d)(i) and 2(3)(a).
[99] See Merkin, *Insurance Contract Law.* Chap. D. 4.2.52.
[1] Rule 173.
[2] Main work, paras. 32–089 *et seq.*
[3] *supra,* paras. S33–128 *et seq.*
[4] Regulations, reg. 4(8).
[5] *ibid.*

refs, it seems, to the countries to which reference is made in Regulation 4(2)–(6), *viz.* the EEA State or States where the risk or risks, is, or are situated[6]; the EEA State or country where the habitual residence or central administration of the policyholder is situated[7]; and the EEA State where the events occur when the risks covered by the contract are limited to events occurring in an EEA State other than the EEA State where the risk is situated.[8] The factors by reference to which the most closely connected law may be determined are thus strictly limited, in contrast to the greater generality of the enquiry in cases falling within Article 4 of the Rome Convention.[9] In particular, regard may not, apparently, be had to the law of the place of incorporation, central administration, principal place of business or place of business of the insurer, to the currency in which premiums are to be paid,[10] to provisions of foreign law which may be incorporated into the contract,[11] or to what the parties might have contemplated as the governing law by way of an inferred choice.[12]

S33–164   Furthermore, Regulation 4(9) (clause (7) of the Rule), provides that the contract is "rebuttably presumed to be most closely connected with the EEA State in which the risk is situated". Thus, if the insurance relates to buildings or to buildings and their contents (in so far as the contents are covered by the same policy) the contract will be presumed to be governed by the law of the EEA State in which the building is situated[13]; if the insurance relates to vehicles of any type the contract will be presumed to be governed by the law of the EEA State in which the vehicle is registered[14]; if the contract covers travel or holiday risks and has a duration of four months or less, the contract will be presumed to be governed by the law of the EEA State in which the policyholder entered into the contract[15]; in any other case, (i) if the policyholder is an individual, the contract will be presumed to be governed by the law of the EEA State in which the individual is habitually resident[16] on the date the contract is entered into and (ii) otherwise, the contract will be presumed to be governed by the law of the EEA State in which the establishment of the policyholder to which the contract relates is situated on that date.[17] These presumptions which point towards the law of the country in which the relevant risk is situated may be rebutted: but the factors by reference to which such rebuttal can be accomplished are limited indeed, because, as pointed out previously, the most closely connected law can itself only be identified according to a limited range of relevant factors.[18] In effect the presumptively applicable law can only be displaced in favour of (a) the law of the habitual residence of the policyholder if the *situs* of the risk covered by the policy is not in that

---

[6] Regulations, regs. 2(3), 4(2), (3), (4) and (5).

[7] *ibid.* regs. 2(3), 4(2), (3)(a).

[8] *ibid.* reg. 4(6).

[9] Rule 174.

[10] *Crédit Lyonnais v. New Hampshire Insurance Co.* [1997] 2 Lloyd's Rep. 1 (C.A.).

[11] *ibid.*

[12] *ibid.*

[13] Regulations, reg. 2(2) (a).

[14] *ibid.* reg. 2(2)(b).

[15] *ibid.* reg. 2(2) (c).

[16] *ibid.* reg. 2(2)(d) (i), (3)

[17] *ibid.* reg. 2(2) (d) (ii). As to the meaning of "establishment", see *ibid.* reg. 2(1), *supra*, para S33–141.

[18] *Crédit Lyonnais v. New Hampshire Insurance Co. supra.*

EEA State; (b) the law of the place of central administration of the policyholder if this is not in the EEA State where the risk is situated; and (c) when the risks covered by the contract are limited to events occurring in an EEA State other than the EEA State in which the risk is situated, in favour of the law of the country in which those events occur.

The foregoing suggests that the presumption in favour of the law of the **S33–165** country where the risk is situated will be difficult to rebut.[19] However, it could be regarded as being rebutted if the contract covers two or more risks situated in different EEA States, if, for example, the policyholder entered into the contract at his place of habitual residence or central administration.[20] It might also be regarded as being rebutted in a case where, say, a policyholder insures the building and contents of his holiday home in Italy by entering into a contract at the place where he habitually resides, say England, so that English law is the governing law. The presumption may be easier to rebut in some types of insurance than in others.

Clause (6) of the Rule reproduces a part of Regulation 4(8) which **S33–166** provides that where a severable part of the contract has a closer connection with another "relevant country",[21] the law applicable to that part is, by way of exception, the law of that relevant country. This provision is closely analogous to the second sentence of Article 4(1) of the Rome Convention,[22] with the important difference that the factors which can be relied upon to indicate that a severable part of the contract is more closely connected with the law of another country are limited to those factors referred to in Regulation 4(2)–(6) identified above. It seems likely that the presence of the words "by way of exception" is designed to indicate that severance is to be indulged in as rarely as possible.[23]

Friendly Societies. The Regulations reproduced in Rule 185 apply to a **S33–167—** contract of insurance entered into by a friendly society which qualifies as a **172** Non-Life Directive Society.[24] Unless the contract of insurance falls within Rule 186,[25] Rule 185 will also apply to any other contract of insurance entered into by a friendly society which is not a Non-Life Directive Society and which covers a risk situated in an EEA State, subject to three modifications. First, Regulation 4(1) does not apply[26] since that provision is limited to "contracts of general insurance". The broader expression "contract of insurance" is apt to include both contracts of general insurance and long-term insurance.[27] And as is pointed out in connection with Rule 186,

---

[19] *ibid.*

[20] *Cf. Crédit Lyonnais v. New Hampshire Insurance Co., supra.*

[21] *supra,* para. S33–163.

[22] Rule 174.

[23] *Cf.* Giuliano-Lagarde, p. 23.

[24] Regulations, reg. 3(2)(a). A Non-Life Directive Society is defined in the Friendly Societies Act 1992, s.37(3). Broadly such a society is one which carries on general insurance contract business, and one that the rules of which do not contain provision for calling up additional contributions or benefits or one that the annual income of which from general insurance contract business in any previous year, excluding years ended before January 1, 1993, exceeded 1,000,000 ECU: *ibid.* The choice of law rules applicable to contracts of general insurance entered into by Non-Life Directive Societies were formerly contained in the Friendly Societies Act 1992, s.101 (1), (3) and Sched. 20, Pt.1: see main work, paras. 33–167 *et seq.* These provisions have been repealed, in relation to contracts entered into after December 1, 2001 by S.1. 2001 No. 3649, art. 202, made under Financial Services and Markets Act 2000, ss. 426, 427.

[25] See *infra,* paras. S33R–177 *et seq.*

[26] Regulations, reg. 3(2)(c)(i).

[27] See Financial Services and Markets Act 2000 (Regulated Activities) Order 2001 (S.1. 2001 No. 544), art. 3(1).

Rule 185 can apply to certain types of long-term insurance contracts entered into by friendly societies.[28] Secondly, Regulation 4, which contains the principal choice of law rules set out in Rule 185 only applies if the policyholder is an individual.[29] Where the policyholder is not an individual, Regulations 5 and 6(1)[30] will apply to the contract, but, and this is the third modification, Regulation 7 is applied in an amended form. According to the amendment, first, Regulation 7 (1) applies as if for the words "the 1990 Act is to be treated as applying" there were substituted "a court in a part of the United Kingdom must apply the general rules of private international law of that part of the United Kingdom concerning contractual obligations."[31] Secondly, it is provided that Regulation 7(2) and 7(3) apply as if for the words "the 1990 Act is to be treated as applying" in each case, there were substituted the words "the general rules of private international law of that part of the United Kingdom apply".[32]

S33–173 It is unclear whether, by this change in language, it is intended to substitute common law choice of law rules[33] for contracts for those contained in the 1990 Act.[34] Such a result would be curious indeed, since those common law rules would not apply to any other contract entered into after April 1, 1991,[35] and it is difficult to see what policy consideration justifies subjecting contracts of insurance made by friendly societies which are not Non-Life Directive Societies to (a) a legal regime for general choice of law questions concerning contractual obligations which is different from that applicable to Non-Life Directive Societies and (b) a legal regime which would not apply to any other insurance contract entered into after April 1, 1991. Accordingly, it is submitted that the expression "general rules of private international law . . . concerning contractual obligations"[36] should be construed as including the provisions of the Contracts (Applicable Law) Act 1990.

ILLUSTRATIONS

S33–174 1. X & Co., a French insurance company, enters into a contract of insurance with A & Co., a Dutch company, to insure a ship belonging to A & Co. which is registered in the Netherlands. The insurance contract is expressed to be governed by English law. The law applicable to the contract is English law.[37]

2. X & Co., an English insurance company, enters into a contract of insurance with A & Co., a German company, to insure an aircraft belonging to A & Co. which is registered in Germany. A term of the contract provides that all disputes shall be referred to the English courts. The law applicable to the contract is English law.[38]

3. The facts are the same as in Illustration 2 except that instead of the jurisdiction clause the contract contains a clause requiring that all disputes shall be referred to arbitration before English arbitrators in London. The law applicable to the contract is English law.[39]

---

[28] *infra*, paras. S33–194 *et seq*.
[29] Regulations, reg. 3(2)(c)(ii).
[30] *supra*, paras. S33–145—149, S33–161.
[31] Regulations, reg. 3(2)(c)(iii), as amended by S.1. 2001 No. 3542.
[32] *ibid.*
[33] Main work, paras. 32–003 *et seq.*
[34] See main work, Rules 173 and 174.
[35] *i.e.* the date on which the Act entered into force.
[36] Regulations, reg. 3(2)(c)(iii) as amended by S.I. 2001 No. 3542.
[37] Contracts (Applicable Law) Act 1990, s.2 (1A), as substituted by S.I. 2001 No. 3649, art. 320; Regulations, regs. 2(1), 4(7), 6(1).
[38] *ibid.*
[39] *ibid.*

4. X & Co., a New York insurance company, enters into a contract of insurance with A & Co., a company with its central administration in England, whereby X & Co. insure a building in London belonging to A & Co. The contract is governed by English law.[40]

5. The facts are the same as in Illustration 4 except that the contract is expressed to be governed by the law of New York. The law applicable to the contract is New York law.[41]

6. X & Co., a German insurance company, enters into a contract of insurance with A, **S33–175** habitually resident in New York, whereby it agrees to insure A's holiday home in London. The contract is expressed to be governed by English law. The law applicable to contract is English law.[42]

7. The facts are the same as in Illustration 6 except that the contract of insurance is expressed to be governed by the law of New York. The law applicable to the contract is New York law.[43]

8. The facts are the same as in Illustration 6 except that the contract is expressed to be governed by the law of Germany. The law applicable to the contract is German law.[44]

9. X & Co., an English insurance company, enters into a contract of insurance with A & Co., a Delaware company, whereby it agrees to insure A & Co.'s business premises in England and the Netherlands. A & Co.'s central administration is in New York. The contract is expressed to be governed by English law. The law applicable to the contract is English law.[45]

10. The facts are the same as in Illustration 9 except that the contract is expressed to be governed by the law of the Netherlands. The law applicable to the contract is Dutch law.[46]

11. The facts are the same as in Illustration 9 except that the contract is expressed to be governed by the law of New York. The law applicable to the contract is New York law.[47]

12. The facts are the same as in Illustration 9 except that the contract is expressed to be governed by the law of Delaware. The law applicable to the contract is the law of Delaware.[48]

13. A, a lawyer habitually resident in England, is entitled to practise in France. He takes **S33–176** out an insurance policy with X & Co., an English insurance company, covering him in respect of professional negligence relating to advice on French law given in France to French clients. The policy is expressed to be governed by French law. The law applicable to the contract is, *semble*, the law of France.[49]

14. X & Co., an English insurance company, enters into a contract of insurance with A & Co., a German company, whereby it agrees to insure a ship, registered in the Netherlands, which belongs to A & Co. There is no choice of law in the contract. The contract is governed by Dutch law.[50]

15. X & Co., an insurance company incorporated in the United States with its head office in New York but registered in England as an overseas company under Companies Act 1985, enters into a contract with A Bank, a French bank with an establishment in England, whereby it agrees to insure A Bank in relation to frauds perpetrated on the bank by third parties arising out of its English business. There is no choice of law in the contract. The law applicable to the contract is English law.[51]

---

[40] Contracts (Applicable Law) Act 1990, s. 2(1A), as substituted by S.I. 2001 No. 3649, art. 320; Regulations, regs. 2(1), 2(3)(b), 4(2).
[41] Contracts (Applicable Law) Act 1990 s.2(1A), as substituted by S.I. 2001 No. 3649, art. 320; Regulations, regs. 2(1), 2(3)(b), 4(2), 6(1); Rome Convention, Art. 3(1).
[42] Contracts (Applicable Law) Act 1990, s.2(1A), as substituted by S.I. 2001 No. 3649, art. 320; Regulations, regs. 2(1), 2(3)(a), 4(3)(b), 6(1).
[43] *ibid*.
[44] Contracts (Applicable Law) Act 1990, s.2(1A), as substituted by S.I. 2001 No. 3649, art. 320; Regulations, regs. 2(1), 2(3)(a), 4(3)(b), 4(5), 6(1); Rome Convention, Art. 3(1).
[45] Contracts (Applicable Law) Act 1990, s.2(1A), as substituted by S.I. 2001 No. 3649, art. 320; Regulations, regs. 2(1), 4(4).
[46] *ibid*.
[47] *ibid*.
[48] *ibid*. and reg. 4(5); Rome Convention, Art. 3(1).
[49] Contracts (Applicable Law) Act 1990 s.2(1A), as substituted by S.I. 2001 No. 3649, art. 320; Regulations, regs. 2(1), 4(6).
[50] Contracts (Applicable Law) Act 1990, s.2(1A), as substituted by S.I. 2001 No. 3649, art. 320; Regulations, regs. 2(1), 4(8), 4(9).
[51] *ibid*. See *Crédit Lyonnais v. New Hampshire Insurance Co.* [1997] 2 Lloyd's Rep. 1 (C.A.).

16. X & Co., a German insurance company, enters into a contract of insurance with A, habitually resident in New York, whereby it agrees to insure A's holiday home in London. There is no choice of law in the contract. The law applicable to the contract is English law.[52]

17. X & Co., an English insurance company, enters into a contract of insurance with A, habitually resident in England, whereby it agrees to insure the building and contents of A's holiday villa in Tuscany. There is no choice of law in the contract. Although the risk is situated in Italy, it appears that the contract is more closely connected with England. The law applicable to the contract is, *semble*, English law.[53]

S33R–177 RULE 186—(1) This Rule applies to determine the law applicable to a contract of long-term insurance[54] if

   (a) where the policyholder is an individual, he resides in an EEA State[55]; or

   (b) otherwise, the establishment of the policyholder to which the contract relates is situated in an EEA State.[56]

(2) The law applicable to such contract is, subject to clauses (3) and (4) of the Rule, the law of the EEA State of the commitment, which means, in relation to a contract of long-term insurance entered into on a date,

   (a) if the policyholder is an individual, the EEA State in which he resides on that date[57]; or

   (b) otherwise, the EEA State in which the establishment of the policyholder to which the contract relates is situated on that date.[58]

(3) If the law of the EEA State of the commitment (as defined in clause (2)) so permits, the parties may choose the law of another country as the applicable law.[59]

(4) If the policyholder is an individual and resides in one EEA State but is a national or citizen of another, the parties to the contract may choose the law of the EEA State of which he is a national or citizen as the applicable law.[60]

---

[52] Contracts (Applicable Law) Act 1990, s.2 (1A), as substituted by S.I. 2001 No. 3649, art. 320; Regulations, regs. 2(1), 4(8), 4(9).

[53] *ibid.*

[54] This rule reproduces Regulation 8 of Financial Services and Markets Act 2000 (Law Applicable to Contracts of Insurance) Regulations 2001, S.I. 2001 No. 2635, as amended by S.I. 2001 No. 3542, made under Financial Services and Markets Act 2000, ss. 417(1), 424(3) and 428(3). In what follows these Regulations are referred to as "Regulations". "Contract of long-term insurance" bears the meaning given to the expression in Financial Services and Markets Act 2000 (Regulated Activities) Order 2001 (S.I. 2001 No. 544), art. 3(1) and Sched. 1, Pt. II. The Rule applies to contracts of long-term insurance entered into after December 1, 2001. Such contracts which are entered into before that date are governed by Rule 186 as set out in the main work, paras. 33R–177 *et seq*. See Commission of the European Communities, *Green Paper on the conversion of the Rome Convention of 1980 into a Community instrument and its modernisation*, COM (2002) 654 final, paras 3.2.2.1–3.2.2.3.

[55] Regulations, reg. 8(1)(a).

[56] *ibid.* reg. 8(1)(b).

[57] *ibid.* regs. 2(1), 8(2). For these purposes an individual resides in the EEA State in which he is habitually resident: *ibid.* reg. 2(3)(a).

[58] *ibid.* regs. 2(1), 8(2). "Establishment" is defined, *ibid.* reg. 2(1): see *infra*, para. S33–186.

[59] *ibid.* reg. 8(2).

[60] *ibid.* reg. 8(3).

COMMENT

Introduction. This Rule states the effect of the choice of law provisions **S33–178**
contained in the European Community's Second Directive on Life
Assurance,[61] now implemented in the United Kingdom in the Financial
Services and Markets Act 2000 (Law Applicable to Contracts of Insurance)
Regulations 2001,[62] Part III. These choice of law rules will apply to
contracts of long-term insurance entered into after December 1, 2001.[63] The
law applicable to contracts of long-term insurance entered into before that
date will be determined by reference to the choice of law rules discussed in
the Main Work.[64]

This Rule is slightly modified where a contract of long-term insurance is **S33–179**
entered into by a friendly society, and the relevant modifications are
discussed below.[65]

Scope of the Rule. The scope of the Rule is, first, limited to a "contract of **S33–180**
long-term insurance", as defined in the Financial Services and Markets Act
2000 (Regulated Activities) Order 2001.[66] Thus the Rule will apply to
contracts of life insurance and contracts to pay annuities on human life;
contracts of insurance relating to marriage and birth; linked long term
insurance; and permanent health insurance; tontines; capital redemption
contracts; pension fund management; certain contracts involving collective
insurance and certain contracts involving social insurance.[67] Secondly, the
Rule only applies, where the policyholder is an individual, if he resides in
an EEA State,[68] "resides", for these purposes, being defined as habitually
resident,[69] or where the policyholder is not an individual, if the establishment of the policyholder to which the contract relates is situated in an EEA
State.[70] In effect these provisions determine when the risk to be covered by
the policy is to be regarded as being situated, in an EEA State. In
consequence, in such cases, the choice of law rules contained in the Rome
Convention, as implemented in the Contracts (Applicable Law) Act 1990,
are excluded,[71] and, in relation to contracts entered into after December 1,
2001, are replaced (subject to what is said below) by the provisions of this

---

[61] Council Directive of November 8, 1990 on the co-ordination of laws, regulations and
administrative provisions relating to direct life assurance, laying down provisions to facilitate the
effective exercise of freedom to provide services, [1990] O.J. L330/50, amending First Council
Directive of March 5, 1979 on the co-ordination of laws, regulations and administrative
provisions relating to the taking up and pursuit of the business of direct life assurance, [1979] O.J.
L63/1. The Third Council Directive of November 10, 1992 on the co-ordination of laws,
regulations and administrative provisions relating to direct life assurance, [1992] O.J. L360/1, has
only a marginal effect on the applicable conflict of laws rules: see *infra*, para. S33–186, n. 95.
[62] S.I. 2001 No. 2635, as amended by S.I. 2001 No. 3542, in force from December 1, 2001.
[63] For the rules applicable to contracts entered into before that date and for the history of the
legislation, see main work, paras. 33R–177, *et seq.* The original choice of law rules were contained
in Art. 4 of the Second Life Directive, *supra*.
[64] Main work, paras. 33R–177 *et seq.*
[65] *post*, paras. S33–194 *et seq.*
[66] S.I. 2001 No. 544; Regulations, reg. 2(1).
[67] S.I. 2001 No. 544, art. 3(1) and Sched. 1.
[68] Regulations, reg. 8(1)(a).
[69] *ibid.* reg. 2(3)(a).
[70] *ibid.* reg. 2(3)(b). "Establishment" is defined in reg. 2(1): see *infra*, para. S33–186.
[71] Rome Convention, Art. 1(3); Contracts (Applicable Law) Act 1990, s.2(1A), as substituted by
S.I. 2001 No. 3649, art. 320.

Rule. Contracts entered into between May 20, 1993 and December 1, 2001 which fall within Rule 186, as set out in the main work, will be governed by the provisions of that Rule.[72] Where, however, the conditions set out in clause (1) of this Rule are not present, the relevant rules for determining the law applicable to the contract of insurance are those contained in the Rome Convention, as set out in Rule 184, unless the contract of insurance is entered into on or before April 1, 1991, in which case the applicable law will be identified by reference to the common law rules discussed in outline in the Comment to Rule 184.[73]

It should also be emphasised that the choice of law rules in Rule 186 apply, in terms, where the risk covered by the contract is situated in an EEA State in contrast to the version of this Rule contained in the main work which only applied if the risk was situated in a Member State. This must also mean that where the risk is situated in an EEA State which is not a Member State of the European Union, the law applicable to the contract will be determined by this Rule (assuming clause (1) of the Rule is satisfied) and not by the Rome Convention, despite the fact that the Rome Convention only excludes application of its provisions to insurance contracts covering risks situated in the territories of a Member State of the European Community.[74]

S33–181 The choice of law rules contained in this Rule will apply to conflicts between the laws of the different parts of the United Kingdom.[75] Further, where any other Member State includes several territorial units, each of which has its own rules of law concerning contractual obligations, each unit is to be considered as a country for the purposes of identifying the applicable law.[76]

S33–182 **Relationship with Rome Convention.** It can be seen that the provisions of the 2001 Regulations, as reproduced in this Rule, do not provide a code of choice of law rules in any complete form. Further, one of the provisions contained in those Regulations (clause (3) of the Rule) requires reference to be made to some of the choice of law rules of the EEA State of the commitment to determine whether that State permits the parties to choose another law as the applicable law of the contract.[77] As to the first point, Regulation 10(1) of the 2001 Regulations generally provides that subject to the specific choice of law rules applicable to contracts of long-term insurance contained in the Regulations, the provisions of the Contracts (Applicable Law) Act 1990 shall be treated as applying to the contract for the purpose of determining the applicable law.[78] As to the second point, where the EEA State of the commitment is the United Kingdom, and it is necessary to determine what freedom of choice of law the parties have under the law of a part of the United Kingdom, the 1990 Act is also to be treated as applying to the contract.[79] In the English context, therefore, the provisions of the Rome Convention, as implemented in the 1990 Act, will

---

[72] Main work, paras. 33R–177 *et seq.*

[73] *supra*, paras. 33–121 *et seq.*

[74] See *supra*, para. S33–125.

[75] Regulations, reg. 2(4).

[76] *ibid.*

[77] Regulations, reg. 8(2).

[78] *ibid.* regs. 2(1), 10(1).

[79] *ibid.* regs. 2(1), 10(2).

apply to any issues not explicitly covered by the 2001 Regulations, as set out in this Rule.[80]

Principles underlying Second Life Directive. One of the purposes which underlies the Second Life Directive is the extension of freedom to provide insurance services throughout the Community with a view to the creation of an internal market in insurance services,[81] a principle now extended more broadly into the European Economic Area.[82] But the provisions of the implementing legislation do not confine the choice of law rules to contracts concluded with insurers with an establishment in any EEA State. Accordingly, the Rule may apply to contracts of insurance concluded, say, with an American insurer where the State of the commitment is an EEA State. However, the principle of the protection of the "consumer" of insurance services is also prominent in its provisions[83]: indeed this principle seems to be the main driving force behind the choice of law rules in the Directive which are now implemented in Part II of the 2001 Regulations.[84] As will be seen in what follows, the scope of freedom to choose the applicable law is strictly limited, so that the freedom of the insurer to insert a choice of law clause in favour of the law of its home State is consequently curtailed.[85] Furthermore, where there is no choice of law in the contract the governing law will always be the law of the EEA State of the commitment, which, in relation to a contract of long-term insurance entered into on a date, means, in the case of a policyholder who is an individual, the EEA State in which that individual resides[86] on that date,[87] and otherwise the EEA State in which the establishment[88] of the policyholder to which the contract relates is situated on that date.[89] The consumer protection principle is thus expressed much more strongly in relation to a contract of long-term insurance than it is in relation to a contract of general insurance covered by the Second Non-Life Directive.[90] **S33–183**

Clause (1) of the Rule. This is discussed in relation to the scope of Rule 186 above.[91] **S33–184**

Clause (2) of the Rule. This clause, which reproduces, in part, Regulation 8(2) of the 2001 Regulations as amplified in definitions applicable by virtue of Regulation 2(1), sets out the basic choice of law rule in cases falling within this Rule. The law applicable to the insurance contract will be the law of the EEA State of the commitment except to the extent that the parties to the contract are free to choose another law according to clauses (3) or (4). Accordingly, the contract will be governed by the law of the EEA State of the commitment if the parties purport to choose, as the governing **S33–185**

---

[80] As to friendly societies, see *infra*, paras. S33–194 *et seq.*
[81] See Preamble to the Second Life Directive, paras. 5, 8.
[82] European Economic Area Act 1993; EEA Agreement, Art. 36 and Annex IX.
[83] *ibid.* paras. 9, 11, 13, 15, 19.
[84] *ibid.* para. 11.
[85] Clauses (3) and (4) of the Rule.
[86] Defined as the State in which the individual is habitually resident: Regulations, reg. 2(3)(a).
[87] Regulations, reg. 2(1).
[88] *ibid.*, for the definition. See *infra*, para. S33–186.
[89] *ibid.*
[90] *supra*, Rule 185.
[91] *supra*, para. S33–180.

law, the law of another EEA State or country which they cannot validly choose according to clauses (3) or (4). Furthermore, where the contract contains no choice of law, the law applicable to it will be the law of the EEA State of the commitment.

S33–186   If the policyholder is an individual the EEA State of the commitment is the EEA State in which the individual resides on the date on which the contract is entered into,[92] the State in which an individual resides being defined, for these purposes, as being that in which he has his habitual residence.[93] The meaning of habitual residence is discussed in the main work.[94] In any other case, the EEA State of the commitment is the EEA State in which the establishment of the policyholder to which the contract relates is situated on the date the contract is entered into.[95] For these purposes "establishment" in relation to the policyholder means: the policyholder's head office; any of the policyholder's agencies; any of the policyholder's branches; or any permanent presence of the policyholder in an EEA State which need not take the form of a branch or agency and which may consist of an office managed by the policyholder's staff or by a person who is independent of the policyholder but has permanent authority to act for the policyholder as if he were an agency.[96]

S33–187   The provisions concerning policyholders who are not individuals are likely to be of particular importance in cases where employers provide cover under a contract of long-term insurance[97] for their employees. For example, an employer with its head office in EEA State A may provide cover for its employees at its branch in EEA State B. Here the establishment to which the contract relates would seem to be the branch in EEA State B so that when clause (2) applies the applicable law will be the law of EEA State B. Where, therefore, in a case falling within the clause, the employer has branches in different EEA States and the same contract of insurance covers all the employees, the law applicable to the contract will differ according to whichever branch at which the employee or employees, is, or are, employed.[98]

S33–188   **Clause (3) of the Rule.** This clause is obviously linked to clause (2) and is derived from the same Regulation as clause (2).[99] If the law of the EEA State of the commitment so permits, the parties may choose the law of another country.[1] It is clear, if implicit, that reference to the law of the EEA State of the commitment, in this context, is a reference to the rules of private international law which exist in the relevant EEA State.[2] Accordingly, where the parties have chosen in the contract the law which is to apply to it and the chosen law is the law of a country other than the law of the EEA State of the commitment, the validity of that choice of law must be determined according to the private international law rules of the EEA

---

[92] Regulations, reg. 2(1).
[93] *ibid.* reg. 2(2)(a).
[94] paras. 6–123 *et seq.*
[95] Regulations, reg. 2(1).
[96] *ibid.*
[97] *supra*, para. S33–180.
[98] This result could be avoided by an effective choice of law under clause (3).
[99] Regulations, reg. 8(2).
[1] *ibid.*
[2] That the general principle is to exclude *renvoi* appears to have been overlooked or thought to have been of no significance: main work, para. 32–042.

State of the commitment. As far as the United Kingdom is concerned, it is explicitly provided in the Regulations that in determining what freedom of choice the parties have under the law of a part of the United Kingdom, the Contracts (Applicable Law) Act 1990 is to be treated as applying to the contract.[3] Accordingly, if England is the State of the commitment,[4] the validity of a choice of foreign law (it is important to note that this need not be the law of an EEA State) will be tested by reference to the provisions of the Rome Convention, as implemented in the 1990 Act.[5] Hence, if the policyholder is an individual habitually resident in England, the validity of the choice of another country's law will be determined by reference to the Rome Convention, as also will be the case where the policyholder is, for example, a legal person whose establishment to which the contract relates is in England.

Clause (4) of the Rule. If the policyholder is an individual and resides[6] in one EEA State but is a national or citizen of another, the parties to the contract may choose the law of the EEA State of which he is a national or citizen as the applicable law.[7] First, it would seem that "national" or "citizen" are meant to be synonymous terms. This is because (a) that is generally the case, (b) there is no textual indication (*e.g.* either . . . or) that the terms are alternatives, (c) the provision of the Second Life Directive which corresponds to the provision which implements it merely uses the term "national"[8] and (d) the provision of that Directive, as originally implemented in the United Kingdom, similarly merely used the term "national"[9] and there is no indication in the new provision that there is an intention to change this policy. Rather, it is thought, the use of the expression "national or citizen" is designed to cater for countries, such as the United Kingdom, which generally ascribe nationality to a person through citizenship.[10] Secondly it is clear that the provision is only capable of operating where the individual is a national or citizen of an EEA State and can thus only lead to the application of an EEA State's law. But it would also seem that this choice of law is open to the parties even if the rules of private international law of the law of the EEA State in which the individual is habitually resident would not, in its capacity as EEA State of the commitment, regard the choice as effective under a provision equivalent to clause (3) of the Rule. The provision can also operate (it seems) if the individual has more than one habitual residence, provided at least one of these is in an EEA State. If the individual is a national or citizen of an EEA State in which he is habitually resident this clause cannot apply, but the

S33–189

---

[3] Regulations, regs. 2(1), 10(2).

[4] "Where an EEA State (including the United Kingdom) includes several territorial units each of which has its own laws concerning contractual obligations, each unit is to be considered as a separate state for the purposes of identifying the applicable law" under the Regulations: *ibid.* reg. 2(4).

[5] As to friendly societies, see *infra*, paras. S33–194 *et seq.*

[6] Defined, for these purposes, as the EEA State in which the individual has his habitual residence: Regulations, reg. 2(3)(a).

[7] *ibid.* reg. 8(3).

[8] Second Life Directive (*supra*, para. S33–183), Art. 4(2).

[9] Insurance Companies Act 1982, Sched. 3A, Pt. II, para. 7, repealed by S.I. 2001 No. 3649, art. 3(1)(c) made under Financial Services and Markets Act 2000.

[10] See, *e.g.* British Nationality Act 1981; State Immunity Act 1978, s.4(2)(*b*) and (5) as amended by British Nationality Act 1981, Sched. 7.

applicable law in such circumstances will in any event be the law of that State, as the law of the EEA State of the commitment, pursuant to clause (2) of the Rule unless, pursuant to clause (3), the parties have validly chosen the law of another country as the governing law according to the rules of private international law prevailing in the EEA State of the commitment.

S33–190   Adoption of the concept of the law of nationality or citizenship in this context does, however, give rise to several difficulties.[11] In the specific context of the United Kingdom, the problem which arises is as to what is the national law of a British citizen. The strict answer is that there is no such law, at least in the field of contract, but only English law, Scottish law and Northern Irish law, and there is no British or United Kingdom contract law that can be chosen, say, by a British citizen who is habitually resident in Belgium. This difficulty is only partially ameliorated by the Regulations, which provide, in pertinent part, that "where an EEA State (including the United Kingdom) includes several territorial units each of which has its own laws concerning contractual obligations, each unit is to be considered as a separate state for the purposes of identifying the applicable law . . ."[12] For while this provision means that the law of England or the law of Scotland, etc., can be treated as the law of a country it does not identify the national law of a British citizen since it does not establish what link has to exist between the individual and one of those territorial units for these purposes. Any solution to the problem thus has to be found in general principles.[13] Establishment of the requisite link on the basis of the unit (if any) in which the individual is domiciled has very little to be said for it. It is clear that a person may be a British citizen without being domiciled in any part of the United Kingdom, and equally clear that a person may be domiciled in a part of the United Kingdom without being a British citizen. Alternatively, the relevant law may be that unit with which the individual is most closely connected at the time the contract is entered into. A rule of this kind is found in the Wills Act 1963 in relation to the formal validity of wills.[14] But it may be very difficult to determine what the relevant unit is because, *ex hypothesi*, the individual will be habitually resident in another country. Another difficulty would be that it would mean that a choice of English law in a contract between a Scotsman, habitually resident in Belgium, who has had no connection with England, and an English insurance company would be ineffective, a result which might be thought to be at variance with common sense. Consequently, an English court should, it is suggested, regard clause (4) of the Rule as permitting, in the case of United Kingdom citizens habitually resident in another EEA State, the parties to choose the law of any part of the United Kingdom.

S33–191   The next difficulty is where the individual has dual nationality or citizenship. If one of those nationalities or citizenships is that of an EEA

---

[11] As is well known, nationality plays little or no role in the common law rules of the conflict of laws affecting contractual obligations.

[12] Regulations, reg. 2(4).

[13] There are no specific conflict of laws rules within the United Kingdom according to which such a decision may be made.

[14] s.6(2)(*b*). Section 6(2)(*a*) enables the applicable law to be identified according to a choice of law rule laid down for this purpose in the relevant country but there are no such choice of law rules in the United Kingdom. See Rule 135 in the main work.

State, the other being of a State outside the European Economic Area, the view could be taken that clause (4) permits a choice of the law of the EEA State as an appropriate national law, assuming that the individual is habitually resident in yet another EEA State which is, perhaps, an unlikely case. Where the individual is a national or citizen of more than one EEA State the question which arises is, first, assuming that he is habitually resident in neither of those States but in a different EEA State (an unlikely case), can the law of either nationality or citizenship be chosen or is the choice limited to one of them and, secondly if he is a national or citizen of, and habitually resident in, one EEA State can the law of the other nationality or citizenship be chosen? To promote freedom of choice of law, the view could be taken that the parties in the first case may choose either law but this might be inconsistent with one of the purposes of the Second Directive,[15] which is to limit the freedom of the parties to make a choice of law.[16] If the view is taken, on the other hand, that only one such law can validly be chosen, which law is that to be? One solution might be to prefer the law of the most recently acquired nationality or citizenship: another solution would be to prefer the law of the nationality or citizenship with which the individual is most closely connected at the time the contract is entered into,[17] so that only the choice of that law will be acceptable.

It is submitted that, on balance, the better view is that in the first case the **S33–192** choice of either law should be regarded as effective and in the second case a choice of the law of the nationality or citizenship of the EEA State in which the individual is not habitually resident should similarly be regarded as effective. Cases in which an individual is a national or citizen of more than one EEA State but who is habitually resident in yet a different EEA State are likely to be rare. And, perhaps, even as regards the second case, situations will be uncommon in which an individual will be a national or citizen of more than one EEA State. Accordingly this extension of the power to choose the law applicable to the insurance contract is likely to be of marginal relevance.

Mandatory rules. Regulation 9 of the 2001 Regulations provides that **S33–193** nothing in Regulation 8 affects the application of the mandatory rules of any part of the United Kingdom, irrespective of the applicable law of the contract.[18] There is no provision in the Regulations concerned with the law applicable to contracts of long-term insurance equivalent to that of Regulation 5(2) concerned with contracts of general insurance.[19]

---

[15] See *supra*, para. S33–183.

[16] The Wills Act 1963 contains no provision which indicates the solution to be adopted in cases of dual nationality. It has been argued that since the purpose of the Wills Act is to promote the formal validity of wills, a will should be formally valid if it complies with either national law: see F.A. Mann (1986) 35 I.C.I.Q. 423. First, however, the Wills Act does not permit choice of law by the testator but rather allows reference to the national law of the testator as a connecting factor. Secondly, the policy of promoting the validity of wills cannot be equated with a policy of promoting the validity of contracts in the context of a legal régime in which part of the policy is to protect consumers.

[17] *Cf.* Hague Convention on the Conflict of Nationality Laws 1950: see Cheshire and North, pp. 988–989.

[18] "Mandatory rules" are defined as "rules from which the law allows no derogation by way of contract": Regulations, reg. 2(1).

[19] See *supra*, paras. S33–146 *et seq.*

S33–194 **Friendly societies.** Rule 186 applies to a contract of insurance entered into by a friendly society which is a "Life Directive Society[20]" for the purposes of the Friendly Societies Act 1992.[21]

S33–195— If the contract of insurance is entered into with a friendly society which is
196 *not* a Life Directive Society within the meaning of the 1992 Act, then the relevant legal regime is to be found in Rule 185, with the amendments which are applicable to contracts entered into with societies which are *not* Non-Life Directive Societies.[22]

ILLUSTRATIONS

S33–197 1. A, a Belgian citizen, habitually resident in Belgium, insures his life with X & Co., an English insurance company. There is no choice of law in the contract. The contract is governed by the law of Belgium.[23]

2. A & Co., an English company, insures the lives of its employees who are employed at its branch in the Netherlands with X & Co., an English insurance company. There is no choice of law in the contract. The contract is governed by the law of the Netherlands.[24]

3. A, habitually resident in England, insures his life with X & Co., a German insurance company. The insurance contract is expressed to be governed by German law. The law applicable to the contract is German law.[25]

4. A & Co., a German company, insures the lives of its employees who are employed at its branch in London with X & Co., a New York insurance company. The insurance contract is expressed to be governed by New York law. The law applicable to the contract is the law of New York.[26]

5. A, a citizen of the Republic of Ireland, is habitually resident in England. He insures his life with X & Co., an Irish insurance company. The insurance contract is expressed to be governed by the law of the Republic of Ireland. The law applicable to the contract is the law of the Republic of Ireland.[27]

33–199 NOTE 56. *Cf.* Case C-412/98 *Universal General Insurance Co. (UGIC) v. Group Josi Reinsurance Co. S.A.* [2000] E.C.R. I–5925; [2001] Q.B. 68 (re-insurance does not fall within rules applicable to insurance contained in Arts 7–12A of the 1968 Convention (main work, Rule 28(13), *ante*, entry at para. 11–302) since neither re-insured nor re-insurer could be presumed to be in a weak position compared with the other); *Agnew v. Länsförsäkringsbolagens A.B.* [2001] 1 A.C. 223.

NOTE 57. Rules 184, 185 and 186, set out *ante*, paras. S33R–116 *et seq.*, do not apply to contracts of re-insurance: see Financial Services and Markets

---

[20] As defined in Friendly Societies Act 1992, s.37(2). Broadly, such a society is a society which carries on long term business and one the rules of which do not contain provision for calling up additional contributions, for reducing benefits or for claiming assistance from other persons who have undertaken to provide it, or one the annual contribution income of which from long term business exceeded 500,000 ECU for three consecutive years, excluding years ended before January 1, 1995.

[21] Regulations, reg. 3(2)(b). For the rules applicable to contracts entered into before December 1, 2001, see main work, para. 33–194.

[22] Regulations, reg. 3(2)(c). For discussion of these provisions, see *supra*, paras. S33–167 *et seq.* For the rules applicable to such contracts entered into before December 1, 2001, see main work, paras. 33–167 *et seq.*, 33–195 *et seq.*

[23] Regulations, regs. 2(1), 8(1), 8(2).

[24] *ibid.*

[25] *ibid.*

[26] *ibid.*

[27] Regulations, regs. 2(1), 8(1), 8(3).

Act 2000 (Law Applicable to Contracts of Insurance) Regulations 2001 (S.I. 2001 No. 2635), reg. 3(1).

Text after note 57. Delete "Member" and substitute "EEA" in relation to contracts entered into after December 1, 2001 and also delete, in relation to such contracts, "of the European Community". See *supra*, entry at para. S33–125.

NOTE 63. Add: *Gan Insurance Co. Ltd. v. Tai Ping Insurance Co. Ltd.* [1999] **33–201** I.L.Pr. 729 (C.A.); *Groupama Navigation et Transports v. Catatumbo C.A. Seguros* [2000] 2 Lloyd's Rep. 350 (C.A.).

NOTE 64. Add: *Gan Insurance Co. Ltd. v. Tai Ping Insurance Co. Ltd., supra;* **33–202** *Groupama Navigation et Transports v. Catatumbo C.A. Seguros, supra*.

NOTE 65 and text thereto. See now, in relation to this material, Rules 185 and 186 *supra*, entry at paras. S33R–138 *et seq*.

NOTE 74 and text thereto. In *Tiernan v. Magen Insurance Co. Ltd.* [2000] I.L. **33–203** Pr. 517 it was held that where a re-insurance contract was placed on the Lloyd's market in the usual way, the contract was on a Lloyd's form and contained London market clauses, such factors were sufficient to demonstrate with reasonable certainty a choice of English law for the purposes of Article 3(1) of the Rome Convention. In *Gan Insurance Co. Ltd. v. Tai Ping Insurance Co. Ltd., supra*, it was held that although the insurance policy was governed by the law of Taiwan, the re-insurance policy was governed by English law since the contract was made in London between London underwriters and brokers in the conventional way and contained London market clauses, thereby demonstrating with reasonable certainty a choice of English law for the purposes of Article 3(1) of the Rome Convention. See also *Ace Insurance S.A.-N.V. v. Zurich Insurance Co. of Europe* [2000] 2 Lloyd's Rep. 423, affd. [2001] EWCA Civ. 173; [2001] 1 Lloyd's Rep. 618 (C.A.); *Assicurazioni Generali SpA v. Ege Sigorta* [2002] Lloyd's Rep. I.R. 480.

NOTE 77. Add *Tiernan v. Magen Insurance Co. Ltd., supra; Gan Insurance Co. Ltd. v. Tai Ping Insurance Co. Ltd., supra; Groupama Navigation et Transports v. Catatumbo C.A. Seguros, supra; Ace Insurance S.A.-N.V. v. Zurich Insurance Co. of Europe, supra*.

NOTE 78. The position has been held to be the same under Art. 3 (1) of the Rome Convention: see entry at para. 33–203, n. 74 and text thereto.

NOTE 79. Add: *Gan Insurance Co. Ltd. v. Tai Ping Insurance Co. Ltd., supra*. **33–204**

NOTE 81. That such a conclusion can be drawn is supported by *Gan Insurance Co. Ltd. v. Tai Ping Insurance Co. Ltd., supra*, although it was not drawn in this particular case: see entry at para. 33–203, n. 74 and text thereto. And see *Groupama Navigation et Transports v. Catatumbo C.A. Seguros, supra; Assicurazioni Generali SpA v. Ege Sigorta, supra*.

NOTE 82. As was the case in *Gan Insurance Co. Ltd. v. Tai Ping Insurance Co. Ltd., supra*.

NOTE 85. Add: And see *Group Navigation et Transports v. Catatumbo C.A. Seguros, supra; Assicurazioni Generali SpA v. Ege Sigorta, supra*.

33–206 NOTES 88 and 89 and text thereto. In *Tiernan v. Magen Insurance Co. Ltd.* [2000] I.L.Pr. 517, 523, it was said that the characteristic performance of a re-insurance contract was that of the re-insurer. The same view is expressed in *Lincoln National Life Insurance Co. v. Employers Re-Insurance Corp.* [2002] EWHC 28 (Comm); [2002] Lloyd's Rep. I.R. 853.

33–209 NOTE 95. Add: See *Lincoln National Life Insurance Co. v. Employers Re-Insurance Corp., supra.*

NOTE 96. *Cf. Tiernan v. Magen Insurance Co. Ltd., supra.*

NOTE 97. Add: See *Lincoln National Life Insurance Co. v. Employers Re-Insurance Corp., supra.*

NOTE 98. Also relevant may be the fact that the particular form of insurance is a specialised one developed in a particular market and/or that the slips incorporate by reference particular market clauses: *Lincoln National Life Insurance Co. v. Employers Re-Insurance Corp., supra.*

33–211 NOTE 9. See *Gan Insurance Co. Ltd. v. Tai Ping Insurance Co. Ltd., supra.* See also *Groupama Navigation et Transports v. Catatumbo C.A. Seguros, supra.*

5. CONTRACTS WITH REGARD TO IMMOVABLES

33R–212 See Commission of the European Communities, *Green Paper on the Conversion of the Rome Convention of 1980 on the law applicable to contractual obligations into a Community instrument and its modernisation*, COM (2002) 654 final, paras. 3.2.6.1–3.2.6.3.

33–220 NOTE 52. Add: *Ashurst v. Pollard* [2001] Ch. 595 (C.A.); Case C–8/98 *Dansommer A/S v. Götz* [2000] E.C.R. 1–393; [2001] 1 W.L.R. 1069.

33–223 NOTE 2. The Consumer Protection (Distance Selling) Regulations 2000, regs 7–20 do not apply to a contract which is a "timeshare agreement" within the meaning of Timeshare Act 1992 and to which that Act applies: Consumer Protection (Distance Selling) Regulations 2000, reg. 6(1).

6. CONTRACTS FOR THE CARRIAGE OF PERSONS OR GOODS GENERALLY

33–243 The provisions of Montreal Additional Protocol No. 4, which modernises the rules on the carriage of cargo by air, were given effect in English law by the Carriage by Air Acts (Implementation of Protocol No. 4 of Montreal, 1975) Order 1999, S.I. 1999 No. 1312. See for parties, S.I. 2000 No. 3061. A new version of the Warsaw Convention, known as the Montreal Convention 1999 was agreed in May 1999; it is not yet in force.

The Carriage by Air Acts (Implementation of Protocol No. 4 of Montreal, 1975) Order 1999, S.I. 1999 No. 1312 gives effect to the Protocol, which further amends the Convention as amended at The Hague, in English law by adding a new Schedule 1A to the Carriage by Air Act 1961. For parties, see S.I. 2000 No. 3061. The Carriage by Air Acts (Implementation of the

Montreal Convention 1999) Order 2002, S.I. 2002 No. 263 gives effect to the Convention in English law by adding a new Schedule 1B to the Carriage by Air Act 1961; it is not yet in force.

NOTE 51. The relevant passage in Shawcross and Beaumont, *Air Law*, is now para. VII [124].

NOTE 52. Carriage by Air Act 1961 (Application of Provisions) Order 1967 is further amended by S.I. 1999 Nos 1312 and 1737.

NOTE 57. Add: *Herd v. Clyde Helicopters Ltd.* [1997] A.C. 534; *King v. Bristow Helicopters Ltd.* [2002] UKHL 7; [2002] 2 W.L.R.578 (H.L.).

NOTE 59. The relevant passage in Shawcross and Beaumont, *Air Law*, is now para. VII [414].

An amending European Parliament and Council Regulation 889/2002 **33–248** makes radical amendments to Regulation 2027/97 and seeks to apply the principles of the Montreal Convention 1999 to all cases of involving liability for passengers and baggage, even those cases in which a Member State is bound by a treaty obligation to apply some version of the Warsaw Convention. It has not yet come into effect.

7. CONTRACTS OF AFFREIGHTMENT

NOTE 30. R.S.C. Ord. 11, r. 1(d)(iii) is replaced by C.P.R., r. 6.20(5)(c).   **33–260**

NOTE 70. Add: *East West Corp. v. DKBS 1912 A/S* [2003] EWCA Civ. 83; **33–271** [2003] 2 All E.R. 700 (C.A.); *Import Export Metro Ltd. v. Compania Sud Americana De Vapores S.A.* [2003] EWHC 11 (Comm); [2003] 1 All E.R. (Comm.) 703.

NOTE 71. Add: *East West Corp. v. DKBS 1912 A/S, supra*.

NOTE 74. Add: See also *East West Corp. v. DKBS 1912 A/S, supra; Import Export Metro Ltd. v. Compania Sud Americana De Vapores S.A., supra*.

NOTE 75. See also *The Ikariada* [1999] 2 Lloyd's Rep. 365.   **33–271**

NOTE 99. See also on the applicability of the Hague-Visby Rules, *The Happy* **33–278** *Ranger* [2002] EWCA Civ. 694; [2002] 2 Lloyd's Rep. 357 (C.A.).

NOTE 10. *Cf. The Ikariada, supra; East West Corp. v. DKBS 1912 A/S, supra*.   **33–282**

8. CONTRACTS BETWEEN BANKER AND CUSTOMER

NOTE 35. Add in line 1: *Centrax Ltd. v. Citibank N.A.* [1999] 1 All E.R. **33R–289** (Comm.) 557 (C.A.). *Cf. Raiffeisen Zentralbank Osterreich AG v. National Bank of Greece S.A.* [1999] 1 Lloyd's Rep. 408, 412.

NOTE 37. Add: *Raiffeisen Zentralbank Osterreich AG v. National Bank of Greece S.A., supra*.

33–292 NOTE 51 and text thereto. A banking transaction may be effected under a standard form containing an express choice of law: see *Credit Suisse First Boston (Europe) Ltd. v. M.L.C. (Bermuda) Ltd.* [1999] 1 Lloyd's Rep. 77 (Global Master Repurchase Agreement containing an express choice of English law). See also *Credit Suisse First Boston (Europe) Ltd. v. Seagate Trading Co. Ltd.* [1999] 1 Lloyd's Rep. 784. In penultimate line add: *Centrax Ltd. v. Citibank N.A., supra.*

33–294 NOTE 60: See also *Marubeni Hong Kong and South China Ltd. v. Mongolian Government* [2002] 2 All E.R. (Comm.) 873.

NOTE 64. Add: *Centrax Ltd. v. Citibank N.A., supra. Cf. Raiffeissen Zentralbank Osterreich AG v. National Bank of Greece S.A., supra,* at p. 412.

33–296 NOTE 83. Add: See also *Barclays Bank plc v. Inc. Inc.* [2001] 6 W.W.R. 511 (Alta.).

33–299 NOTE 99. *Raiffeissen Zentralbank Osterreich AG v. National Bank of Greece S.A., supra* (in a "bank to bank" contract under which one bank undertakes to make payment due under a separate loan agreement to another bank and to warrant that there has been no default under the loan agreement, the characteristic performance is that of the bank which makes the payment and provides the warranty).

33–312 NOTE 63. See *Centrax Ltd. v. Citibank N.A.* [1999] 1 All E.R. (Comm.) 557 (C.A.).

NOTE 64 and text thereto. The Financial Services Act 1986 and the Banking Act 1987 have both been repealed by Financial Services and Markets Act 2000, ss. 426, 427 and Financial Services and Markets Act 2000 (Consequential Amendments and Repeals) Order 2001, S.I. 2001 No. 3649, arts. 1 and 3 (1)(c) and (d), with effect from December 1, 2001.

11. INTEREST

33R–371 NOTE 58. Add: Guest in *Lex Mercatoria: Essays in Honour of Francis Reynolds* (ed. Rose, 2000), p. 271.

NOTES 60–63. Rule 196 in the main work was cited with approval in *Lesotho Highlands Development Authority v. Impregilo SpA* [2002] EWHC 2435 (Comm); [2003] 1 All E.R. (Comm.) 22.

NOTE 60. In line 8 add: *Lesotho Highlands Development Authority v. Impregilo SpA, supra.*

NOTE 61. As to *Kuwait Oil Tanker Co. SAK v. Al Bader* see [2000] 2 All E.R. (Comm.) 271, 339–344 (C.A.) allowing the appeal in part, but without expressing a concluded view on this point. In *Lesotho Highlands Development Authority v. Impregilo SpA, supra,* Morison J. preferred the view expressed in the main work (Rule 196(2)) to that adopted by Hobhouse J. in *Midland International Trade Services v. Sudairy, Financial Times,* May 2, 1990. And see *post,* entry at para. 33–385, nn. 8–11 and text thereto.

NOTE 62. In line 1 add: *Lesotho Highlands Development Authority v. Impregilo SpA, supra.*

NOTE 63. Add: *Lesotho Highlands Development Authority v. Impregilo SpA, supra.*

NOTES 69–72. Add: *Lesotho Highlands Development Authority v. Impregilo SpA, supra.*   **33–374**

NOTE 76. See also S.I. 1999 No. 1816; S.I. 2000 No. 2225; S.I. 2000 No.   **33–376**
2740; S.I. 2002 No. 1673. The substantive provisions of the Late Payment of
Commercial Debts (Interest) Act 1998 have been amended by the Late
Payment of Commercial Debts Regulations 2002, S.I. 2002 No. 1674. These
Regulations implement in England and Northern Ireland the Directive of
the European Parliament and Council of June 29, 2000 on combating late
payment in commercial transactions ([2000] O.J. L200/35).

NOTE 83. See now S.I. 2002 No. 1675.

NOTES 8–11 and text thereto, In *Kuwait Oil Tanker Co. SAK v. Al Bader*   **33–385**
[2000] 2 All E.R. (Comm.) 271, 339–344, the Court of Appeal, in allowing
the appeal in part, did not find it necessary to form a concluded view as to
whether section 35A of the Supreme Court Act 1981 was procedural (as
held by Hobhouse J. in *Midland International Trade Services v. Sudairy,
Financial Times*, May 2, 1990 and by Moore-Bick J. in the court below, *The
Independent*, January 11, 1999) or substantive as submitted in the main
work, para. 33–385. While the Court of Appeal acknowledged (at p. 343)
"the force of Hobhouse J.'s reasoning as an analysis of the nature and
origins of the English court's general power to award interest", it went on
to say (*ibid.*) that "it is also right to observe that the creation of that power
creates a right in a claimant to claim interest, which right is recognized and
consistently given effect on the basis that it represents compensation to the
claimant for having been kept out of money to which he has been held
entitled." Additionally, the Court of Appeal expressed no view on the
question of whether the right to claim interest by way of damages belonged
to the "consequences of breach" for the purposes of Article 10(1)(c) of the
Rome Convention since no argument had been heard on this point. In
Lesotho Highlands Development Authority v. Impregilo SpA [2002] EWHC
2435 (Comm); [2003] 1 All E.R. (Comm) 22 it was held that the right to
claim interest as damages for breach of contract was a matter for the law
applicable to the contract. Morison J. preferred the view put forward in
Miliangos v. George Frank (Textiles) Ltd. (No. 2) [1997] Q.B. 489 and in the
main work, para. 33–385 to that expressed in *Midland International Trade
Services v. Sudairy, supra.*

NOTES 14, 15 and text thereto. See previous entry. In *Kuwait Oil Tanker Co.*   **33–386**
SAK v. Al Bader, supra, the Court of Appeal also found it unnecessary to
express a view on the question of whether jurisdiction to make an award of
compound interest depended on the *lex fori* or on the "double actionability"
choice of law rule which was applicable to the tort in that case since, at first
instance (*The Independent*, January 11, 1999) Moore-Bick J. had also
considered the position under the "double actionability" rule in case he was
wrong in his preference for the *lex fori* and had found that a right to
compound interest was available on both analyses.

NOTE 19 and text thereto. In *Lesotho Highlands Development Authority v.
Impregilo SpA, supra*, Morison J. stated that the right to claim interest as

damages in a claim in tort was to be characterised as a substantive issue in tort which fell within the choice of law rules contained in the Private International law (Miscellaneous Provisions) Act 1995. See also *Somers v. Fournier* (2002) 214 D.L.R. (4th) 611 (Ont. C.A.) (right to claim pre-judgment interest in a tort claim is a matter of substance not procedure).

33–387 NOTES 29–28 and text thereto. In *Lesotho Highlands Development Authority v. Impregilo SpA, supra*, the question of the applicable rate of interest was said to be a procedural issue, governed by the applicable procedural law.

33–393 NOTE 48. See entry at para. 33–385, nn. 8–11 and text thereto.

12. CONTRACTS THROUGH AGENTS

A. Contracts of Agency

33–401 NOTE 76. See *Print Concept GmbH v. GEW (EC) Ltd.* [2001] EWCA Civ. 352; [2001] E.C.C. 36 (C.A.) (characteristic performance of a distributorship agreement intended to be fulfilled by individual contracts of sale and purchase is that of the vendor).

33–405 NOTE 97. On the use of French law in interpreting the compensation provisions of the Regulations see *Moore v. Piretta Ltd.* [1999] 1 All E.R. 174; see also *Duffen v. Firabo SpA* [2000] 1 Lloyd's Rep 180; *King v. T. Tunnock Ltd.*, 2000 S.L.T. 744.

33–407 NOTE 3. On *Ingmar G.B. Ltd. v. Eaton Leonard Technologies Inc.* [1998] C.L.Y. 115, see now Case C-381/98 *Ingmar G.B. Ltd. v. Eaton Leonard Technologies Inc.* [2000] E.C.R. I–9305.

33–409–412 In Case C-381/98 *Ingmar G.B. Ltd. v. Eaton Leonard Technologies Inc., supra*, the European Court held that Articles 17 and 18 of the Council Directive on the co-ordination of the laws of Member States relating to self-employed commercial agents ([1986]) O.J. L382/17) implemented in England and Scotland by Commercial Agents (Council Directive) Regulations 1993, regs. 17 and 18, which guarantee certain rights to commercial agents after the termination of an agency contract, must be applied where the commercial agent carries on his activity in a Member State even though the principal is established in a non-Member State and a clause in the contract stipulates that the contract is to be governed by the law of that country. It follows from this ruling that where a commercial agent carries on activities in England on behalf of a principal established in California under an agency contract governed by Californian law, the 1993 Regulations will apply. The same result should ensue where the agency contract is governed by the law of any non-Member State providing the agent carries on activities in England and the principal is established in any non-Member State. See Verhagen (2002) 51 I.C.L.Q. 135.

33–415 Add new Illustration:

8. P, a Californian company, appoints A, an English company, to act as its agent in England. The contract contains a choice of Californian law. Commercial Agents (Council Directive) Regulations 1993, regs. 17 and 18 will govern A's rights after the termination of the contract, irrespective of the choice of Californian law and irrespective of the fact that P

is established in a non-Member State: Case C–381/98 *Ingmar G.B. Ltd. v. Eaton Leonard Technologies Inc.* [2000] E.C.R. I–9305.

B. Relation of Principal and Third Party

NOTE 34. Add in penultimate line: *Azov Shipping Co. v. Baltic Shipping Co.* **33R–416**
[1999] 2 Lloyd's Rep. 159, 172; *Grupo Torras S.A. v. Al-Sabah* [1999] C.L.C. 1469, 1505–1506; rvsd. in part on other grounds, [2001] C.L.C. 221; *Marubeni Hong Kong and South China Ltd. v. Mongolian Government* [2002] 2 All E.R. (Comm.) 873.

NOTE 47. Add: *Azov Shipping Co. v. Baltic Shipping Co., supra*; *Marubeni* **33–421**
Hong Kong and South China Ltd. v. Mongolian Government, supra.

NOTE 48. Add: *Grupo Torras S.A. v. Al-Sabah, supra*; *Marubeni Hong Kong and South China Ltd. v. Mongolian Government, supra*.

NOTE 49. Add: *Marubeni Hong Kong and South China Ltd. v. Mongolian Government, supra*.

NOTE 53 and text thereto. In *Marubeni Hong Kong and South China Ltd v.* **33–422**
Mongolian Government, supra, it seems to have been accepted that the question of whether an agent has actual authority is governed by Rule 197 whereas the question of whether the agent has ostensible authority is governed by Rule 198.

NOTE 54. Whether *e.g.*, a director of a company is authorised to confer actual authority on an agent will depend on Rule 154(2): see *Grupo Torras S.A. v. Al-Sabah, supra*; *Marubeni Hong Kong and South China Ltd. v. Mongolian Government, supra*.

NOTE 55. See *Marubeni Hong Kong and South China Ltd v. Mongolian Government, supra*.

NOTE 58. Add: *Azov Shipping Co. v. Baltic Shipping Co., supra*. **33–424**

NOTES 62 and 63. The distinction between actual and ostensible authority was explicitly drawn in *Marubeni Hong and South China Ltd. v. Mongolian Government, supra*.

CHAPTER 34

RESTITUTION

34R–001 NOTE 1. Add Panagopoulos, *Restitution in Private International Law* (2000).

34–004 See also *Kuwait Oil Tanker S.A.K. v. Al Bader* [2000] 2 All E.R. (Comm.) 271 (C.A.), and *Grupo Torras S.A. v. Al Sabah* [2001] C.L.C. 221 (C.A.), discussed in more detail under para. 34–032, *infra*.

34–010 See also *Kuwait Oil Tanker S.A.K. v. Al Bader*, *supra*, and *Grupo Torras S.A. v. Al Sabah*, *supra*, which suggest that this category is too wide, and needs to be confined to liability based on receipt, while liability based on wrongful breach of an obligation is treated separately.

34–011 NOTE 26. But see *Grupo Torras S.A. v. Al Sabah*, *supra*, in which it was considered more correct to speak of a claim for contribution (which is restitutionary) in respect of (equitable) wrongdoing.

34–013 Insert after sixth sentence: But if the claim is not one for the vindication of proprietary rights, it will be restitutionary if based on wrongful receipt, though not (and based on a choice of law for wrongdoing) if based on fault: *Kuwait Oil Tanker S.A.K. v. Al Bader*, *supra*, and *Grupo Torras S.A. v. Al Sabah*, *supra*, discussed in more detail under para. 34–032, *infra*.

34–019 The effect of sub-rule 2(a) was applied in *Barclays Bank plc v. Inc. Inc.* [2000] 6 W.W.R. 511 (Alta.).

34–029 According to *Christopher v. Zimmerman* (2001) 192 D.L.R. (4th) 476 (B.C. C.A.), a claim for a declaration that a cohabitee holds certain property on a constructive trust, on the basis of unjust enrichment, raises a claim in equity which was therefore governed by the law of the place of enrichment. In reaching this conclusion, the court approved and applied sub-rule 2(c) from the 12th edition of this Work.

34–030 First sentence. Clause (2)(c) was approved in *Kuwait Oil Tanker S.A.K. v. Al Bader*, *supra*.

34–032 See generally on choice of law for equitable wrongs Yeo (1999) 115 L.Q.R. 571.

In *A–G for England and Wales v. R.*, [2002] 2 N.Z.L.R. 91 (C.A.) it was said *obiter* that where a claim was founded on an equitable obligation which arose from or in connection with a contract between the parties, the equitable claim was governed by the proper law of the contract (*in casu*, English law), and not by the *lex fori*. To that extent the court declined to apply the reasoning in *Paramasivam v. Flynn* (1998–99) 160 A.L.R. 203.

The choice of law rule or rules to be applied to cases in which the defendant is alleged to have acted in a manner which, in English law, would be regarded as a breach of fiduciary duty or equitable wrong has been considered by the Court of Appeal in two cases, and this paragraph must now be read in the light of these decisions.

In *Kuwait Oil Tanker S.A.K. v. Al Bader* [2000] 2 All E.R. (Comm.) 271 (C.A.), the claim against the defendant was primarily formulated in tort, alleging an unlawful conspiracy. But liability was also asserted on the basis that the wrongful acts of the defendant were independently actionable as breaches of the duties of good faith and honesty which had resulted in the unjust enrichment of the defendant. The Court of Appeal held that in such a case, the correct approach was to enquire (1) what was the proper law of the relationship between the defendant and the person for whose benefit the powers and duties are created; (2) what, under that law, are those duties; (3) whether these duties, thus defined, have the general characteristics of being fiduciary according to English standards; and if so, (4) whether it is unconscionable for the defendant to retain the assets. As to the first point, the court applied the law of Kuwait, appearing to do so by reference to Rule 200(2)(c) as being that of the place where the enrichment occurred.

By contrast, a differently constituted court in *Grupo Torras S.A. v. Al Sabah* [2001] C.L.C. 221 (C.A.), agreed that where it was claimed against a defendant that he was liable for his dishonest assistance of another's breach of trust, neither the choice of law rules for restitutionary claims, nor the common law choice of law rules for tort claims (the facts which gave rise to the claim pre-dated the coming into force of the Private International Law (Miscellaneous Provisions) Act 1995, and the court did not say whether the 1995 Act would have applied had the material dates been different) were applicable. It rejected the view that it was appropriate to apply a restitutionary choice of law rule to a claim which was for equitable compensation based on fault; and that there was a single choice of law rule for all claims in which the defendant was alleged to be liable as a constructive trustee. In the result the court, having freed itself from other constraints, applied Spanish law, *semble* as the law where the defendant had carried out those acts from which his liability was alleged to flow, to ascertain that his conduct gave rise to liability; and upon its being shown that it did, the liability which his conduct gave rise to under English law was confirmed and established.

The conclusion to be drawn from these two cases is that a claim which is founded on an allegation of unlawful or knowing receipt or unjust enrichment will fall within the scope of the present Rule. But a claim which is founded on an allegation of wrongdoing for which compensation is due does not do so, even if English domestic law would regard the liability as equitable, and even though an English court would impose the status of constructive trusteeship on the defendant.

On the restitutionary claim which arises against a judgment debtor when a **34–035** garnishee is ordered to pay the judgment creditor, it was said in *Société Eram Shipping Co. Ltd v. Compagnie Internationale de Navigation* [2001] EWCA Civ. 1317; [2001] 2 All E.R. (Comm.) 721 (C.A.), and which is considered above under the entry for para. 24–075, that this was governed by English law (as the law of the place where a benefit was conferred on the judgment debtor by the discharge of its liability) or by the law of Hong Kong (as the law of the place where the judgment debtor resided). The Court was prepared to accept the second as correct, though without analysis. In the context of the issue of whether a garnishee is exposed to a risk of double jeopardy, it may be appropriate to look to both laws, but the narrow question would be better regarded as falling under the general principle of sub-rule (c).

34–041 NOTE 24. *Kuwait Oil Tanker S.A.K. v. Al Bader* was affirmed [2000] 2 All E.R. (Comm.) 271 (C.A.); see also *Grupo Torras S.A. v. Al Sabah* [2001] C.L.C. 221 (C.A.), both discussed in more detail under para. 34–032, *supra*.

CHAPTER 35

TORTS

1. THE LAW APPLICABLE TO ISSUES IN TORT

NOTE 1. The European Commission has presented a proposal for a Regu- **35R–001**
lation of the European Parliament and the Council on the Law Applicable to
Non-Contractual Obligations (Rome II): see COM (2003) 427 final.

NOTE 25. Add: Symeonides (1999) 47 Am. J. Comp. L. 322; (2000) 48 Am. **35–004**
J. Comp. L. 143; (2001) 49 Am. J. Comp. L. 1; (2002) 50 Am. J. Comp. L. 1.

NOTE 33. *Pearce v. Ove Arup Partnership Ltd.* is now reported at [2000] Ch. **35–005**
403 (C.A.). *Kuwait Oil Tanker Co. SAK v. Al Bader* is now reported at
[2000] 2 All E.R. (Comm.) 271 (C.A.) affirming in part and reversing in
part on other grounds the decision of Moore-Bick J., *The Independent*,
January 11, 1999.

Add at end: *Ennstone Building Products Ltd. v. Stanger Ltd.* [2002] EWCA
Civ. 916; [2002] 1 W.L.R. 3059 (C.A.); *Kuwait Airways Corp. v. Iraqi Airways
Co. (Nos. 4 and 5)* [2002] UKHL 19, [2002] 2 A.C. 883.

NOTE 34. See now *Lubbe v. Cape plc* [2000] 1 W.L.R. 1545 (H.L.) affirming,
without reference to the point, [1999] I.L.Pr. 113 (C.A.), and reversing the
second Court of Appeal decision in this case reported at [2000] 1 Lloyd's
Rep. 139, 155. As to *Kuwait Oil Tanker Co. SAK v. Al Bader*, see previous
entry.

Add at end: *Ennstone Building Products Ltd. v. Stanger Ltd., supra; Kuwait
Airways Corp. v. Iraqi Airways Co. (Nos. 4 and 5), supra.*

NOTE 37. In line 6 add: *George v. Gubernowicz* (1999) 44 O.R. (3d) 247;
Buchan v. Non-Marine Underwriters, Members of Lloyd's of London, England
(1999) 44 O.R. (3d) 685; *Wong v. Wei* [1999] 10 W.W.R. 296 (B.C.);
Barclays Bank plc v. Inc. Inc. [2000] 6 W.W.R. 511 (Alta.); *Gill v. Gill,* 2000
B.C.S.C. 870; *Harrington v. Dow Corning Corp.* [2000] 11 W.W.R. 201
(B.C.C.A.); *Lebert v. Skinner Estate* (2001) 53 O.R. (3d) 559; *Lau v. Li*
(2001) 53 O.R. (3d) 727; *Schultz v. Panorama Transportation Inc.,* 2001
CarswellOnt 2334; *Landry v. Roy* (2001) 55 O.R. (3d) 605; *Gill v. Canamex
Trucking System Inc.,* 2001 CarswellOnt 4329; *Integral Energy & Environ-
mental Engineering Ltd. v. Schenker of Canada Ltd.* (2001) 206 D.L.R. (4th)
265 (Alta. C.A.); *Wong v. Lee* (2002) 211 D.L.R. (4th) 69 (Ont. C.A.);
Somers v. Fournier (2002) 214 D.L.R. (4th) 611 (Ont. C.A.); *Teja v. Rai*
(2002) 209 D.L.R. (4th) 148 (B.C.C.A.); *Day v. Guarantee Co. of North
America* (2002) 200 N.S.R. (2d) 331; *Chomos v. Economical Mutual
Insurance Co.* (2002) 61 O.R. (3d) 28 (Ont. C.A.); *Castillo v. Castillo* (2002)
3 Alta. L.A. (4th) 84; *Britton v. O'Callaghan* (2002) 219 D.L.R. (4th) 300
(Ont. C.A.); *Brown v. Kerr-McDonald* [2002] A.B.Q.B. 955 (Alta.).

Add at end: Walker (2000) 38 Osgoode Hall L.J. 331.

NOTE 38 and text thereto. In *John Pfeiffer Pty. Ltd. v. Rogerson* (2000) 203 C.L.R. 503 the High Court of Australia discarded the rule of double actionability in respect of torts committed in Australia which possessed an interstate element. It was held that the common law of Australia should now be developed (Gleeson C.J., Gaudron, McHugh, Gummow and Hayne JJ.) or re-expressed (Kirby J.) so that the *lex loci delicti* is the governing law. Application of this law by courts exercising federal jurisdiction and non-federal jurisdiction reflected the fact that the tort is committed within a federation and, more particularly, recognised and gave effect to the statutes of the legislatures of the States and Territories, as required by section 118 (the "full faith and credit clause") of the Australian Constitution. The High Court expressly refused to follow *Phillips v. Eyre* (1870) L.R. 6 Q.B.1; *Koop v. Bebb* (1951) 84 C.L.R. 629, *Anderson v. Eric Anderson Radio & TV Pty. Ltd.* (1965) 114 C.L.R. 20, *McKain v. R.W. Miller & Co. (South Australia) Pty. Ltd.* (1991) 104 A.L.R. 257 and *Stevens v. Head* (1993) 176 C.L.R. 463 and regarded *Breavington v. Godleman* (1988) 169 C.L.R. 41 as inconclusive since the constitutional dimension of the problem was not considered in that case. It was further held that, in an interstate context, there was no room for an exception to the application of the *lex loci delicti*. The court expressed no considered view on the relevant choice of law rules to be applied in cases where the foreign element in the case was supplied by a connection with a foreign (*i.e.* non-Australian) jurisdiction (see Gleeson C.J., at p. 647, Kirby J. at p. 655). However, in *Régie Nationale des Usines Renault SA v. Zhang* (2002) 187 A.L.R. 1 the High Court of Australia held that the new choice of law rule should be applied in respect of torts committed in a foreign country, with application of the doctrine of public policy to exclude application of the *lex loci delicti* where necessary. For further comment on these cases, see *post*, entries at paras. 35–049, 35–053—35–055. See also *Dow Jones & Co. Inc. v. Gutnick* [2002] HCA 56, (2002) 194 A.L.R. 433, *infra*, entry at para. 35–137. For discussion of the *Pfeiffer* case, see Davis (2000) 24 Melbourne Univ. L.Rev. 982; James (2001) 23 Sydney L.Rev. 145. For discussion of the *Zhang* case, see Briggs, 2002 *Oxford University Commonwealth Law Journal* 133; Smart (2002) 118 L.Q.R. 512; Olbourne [2002] 61 C.L.J. 537.

35–006   NOTE 41. *Pearce v. Ove Arup Partnership Ltd.* is now reported at [2000] Ch. 403 (C.A.). For *Lubbe v. Cape plc* [2000] 1 W.L.R. 1545 (H.L.) see entry at para. 35–005, n. 33. Add: *Kuwait Oil Tanker Co. SAK v. Al Bader* [2000] 2 All E.R. (Comm.) 271 (C.A.); *Ennstone Building Products Ltd. v. Stanger Ltd.* [2002] EWCA Civ. 916; [2002] 1 W.L.R. 3059 (C.A.); *Kuwait Airways Corp. v. Iraqi Airways Co. (Nos. 4 and 5)* [2002] UKHL 19; [2002] 2 A.C. 883, 1112–1114, 1121–1122.

35–008   NOTE 53. Add: See also *Ennstone Building Products Ltd. v. Stanger Ltd.*, *supra*.

NOTE 54. As to *Lubbe v. Cape plc*, see previous entry.

35–010   NOTE 58. *Pearce v. Ove Arup Partnership Ltd.* is now reported at [2000] Ch. 403 (C.A.).

35–013   NOTE 78. See entry at para. 35–010, n. 58.

35–014   NOTE 82. See *Kuwait Oil Tanker Co. SAK v. Al Bader* [2000] 2 All E.R. (Comm.) 271, 330 (C.A.); *Ennstone Building Products Ltd. v. Stanger Ltd.*, *supra*.

NOTE 89. Add in line 2: *Ennstone Building Products Ltd. v. Stanger Ltd.,* **35–019**
supra.

NOTE 92. In *Roerig v. Valiant Trawlers Ltd.* [2002] EWCA Civ. 21; [2002] 2 **35–019**
W.L.R. 2304 (C.A.) it was assumed without argument that Part III of the
Private International Law (Miscellaneous Provisions) Act 1995 applied to
torts committed in England.

Private International Law (Miscellaneous Provisions) Act 1995, s. 9(5) was **35–020**
applied in *Anton Durbeck GmbH v. Den Norske Bank ASA* [2002] EWHC
1173 (Comm), rvsd., but not on this point, [2002] EWCA Civ. 147; [2003] 2
W.L.R. 1296 (C.A.).

NOTE 1. See *Edmunds v. Simmonds* [2001] 1 W.L.R. 1003; *Hulse v.* **35–021**
Chambers [2001] 1 W.L.R. 2386. And see *post*, entry at para. 35–093.

NOTE 6. See entry at para. 35–010, n. 58. *Cf.* Case C–334/00 *Fonderie* **35–022**
Officine Meccaniche Tacconi SpA v. Heinrich Wagner Sinto Maschinefabrik
GmbH (HWS) [2002] E.C.R. I–7357 (action founded on the pre-contractual
liability of the defendant is a matter relating to tort, delict or quasi-delict
within the meaning of Art. 5(3) of the 1968 Convention). See also Withers
[2002] J.B.L. 250; Thunken (2002) 51 I.C.L.Q. 909.

Text after note 6 (para. 35–022). See *Douglas v. Hello! Ltd.* [2003] EWCA **35–023**
Civ. 139; *The Independent*, February 19, 2003 (C.A.).

NOTE 8. See *The Amur 2528* [2001] 1 Lloyd's Rep. 421. **35–025**

NOTE 10. See *Glencore International A.G. v. Metro Trading International Inc.* **35–026**
[2001] 1 Lloyd's Rep. 284.

NOTE 12. Add: Lipstein (2002) 61 C.L.J. 295. **35–027**

NOTE 16. See entry at para. 35–010, n. 58. Add in line 2: *Peer International* **35–028**
Corp. v. Termidor Music Publishers Ltd [2002] EWHC 2675 (Ch); *The*
Times, January 2, 2003.

NOTE 26. See entry at para. 35–010, n. 58. **35–029**

NOTES 31, 32, 35. See entry at para. 35–010, n. 58. **35–030**

NOTE 39. Add: See also *John Pfeiffer Pty. Ltd. v. Rogerson* (2000) 203 C.L.R. **35–032**
503, 541.

NOTE 43. See also *John Pfeiffer Pty. Ltd. v. Rogerson, supra*, at pp. 664–666.

NOTE 45. Add: *Buchan v. Non-Marine Underwriters, Members of Lloyd's of*
London, England (1999) 44 O.R. (3d) 247.

35–033 NOTE 47. *Koop v. Bebb* was not followed by the High Court of Australia in *John Pfeiffer Pty. Ltd. v. Rogerson* (2000) 203 C.L.R. 503: see *supra*, entry at para. 35–006, n. 38.

35–034 NOTE 49. See also *Buchan v. Non-Marine Underwriters, Members of Lloyd's of London, England* (1999) 44 O.R. (3d) 685. As to *Koop v. Bebb*, see previous entry.

35–042 NOTE 95 and text thereto. The European Communities (Rights against Insurers) Regulations 2002, S.I. 2002 No. 3061, in force from January 19, 2003, implement in the United Kingdom Art. 3 of the Directive of the European Parliament and Council of May 16, 2000 on the approximation of the laws of the Member States relating to insurance against civil liability in respect of the use of motor vehicles and amending Council Directives 73/239 and 88/357 (Fourth Motor Insurance Directive) ([2000] O.J. L181/65. The Regulations (Reg. 3) provide that where an entitled party has a cause of action against an insured person in tort or (as the case may be) delict, and that cause of action arises out of an accident, the entitled party may, without prejudice to his right to issue proceedings against the insured person, issue proceedings against the insurer which issued the policy of insurance relating to the insured vehicle, and that insurer shall be directly liable to the entitled party to the extent that he is liable to the insured person. For the purposes of the Regulations, "accident" means an accident on a road or other public place in the United Kingdom, caused by, or arising out of, the use of any insured vehicle and "entitled party" means a resident of a Member State or EEA State (Reg. 2(1)). "Vehicle" means, in general, any motor vehicle intended for travel on land which is normally based in the United Kingdom and a vehicle will, in general, be so normally based if it bears a United Kingdom registration plate (Reg. 2(1) and (2)(a)).

NOTE 95. Add: And see *Kingsway General Insurance Co. v. Canada Life Insurance Co.* (2001) 149 O.A.C. 303 (Ont.C.A.) (right of insurer to subrogate to the position of its insured depends not on tort law but on the contract of insurance); *Matt (Guardian of) v. Barber* (2002) 216 D.L.R. (4th) 574 (Ont. C.A.) (right of subrogation in a statute depends on the statute and not on the law applicable to the tort).

NOTES 96, 98. *Cf. Hulse v. Chambers* [2001] 1 W.L.R. 2386 where it may have been assumed that the existence of the direct action against the insurer was governed by the Greek law applicable to the tort, but since the Greek insurer admitted liability and the point was not argued, a firm conclusion cannot be drawn from the case. The point did not arise in *John Pfeiffer Pty. Ltd. v. Rogerson, supra*, and was expressly reserved by Kirby J., at pp. 560–561.

35–047 NOTE 18. The point did not arise in *John Pfeiffer Pty. Ltd. v. Rogerson, supra*, and was expressly reserved by Kirby J., at p. 560.

35–049 NOTE 24 and text thereto. In *Edmunds v. Simmonds* [2001] 1 W.L.R. 1003, it was stated that Part III of the Private International Law (Miscellaneous Provisions) Act 1995 had not abrogated the distinction between substance and procedure, and that section 14(3)(*b*) of the Act expressly reserved questions of procedure for determination in accordance with the law of the forum. See, to the same effect, *Hulse v. Chambers* [2001] 1 W.L.R. 2386; *Roerig v. Valiant Trawlers Ltd.* [2002] EWCA Civ. 21; [2002] 1 W.L.R. 2304 (C.A.), *post*, entry at para. 35–053, nn. 35, 36 and text thereto. See also *Komarek v. Ramco Energy plc* (November 21, 2002) (rule deriving from inviolability of diplomatic documents whereby court would decline to investigate contents of certain embassy documents where they were alleged to give rise to a claim in libel is a procedural rule).

NOTE 27. In *John Pfeiffer Pty. Ltd. v. Rogerson, supra*, it was stated (in the context of interstate cases arising within Australia) that only the rules regulating the mode or conduct of court proceedings were procedural. In *Régie National des Usines Renault SA v. Zhang* (2002) 187 A.L.R. 1 the High Court of Australia reserved for further consideration whether the latter proposition was applicable to a tort committed in a foreign country.

NOTE 28. *Cf. John Pfeiffer Pty. Ltd. v. Rogerson, supra.*   **35–051**

This paragraph was cited with approval in *Hulse v. Chambers, supra.*   **35–052**

NOTES 35, 36 and text thereto. In *Roerig v. Valiant Trawlers Ltd.* [2002]   **35–053**
EWCA Civ. 21; [2002] 1 W.L.R. 2304 (C.A.) it was confirmed that the question whether or not deductions should be made for benefits in assessing damages for loss of dependency was a matter for the *lex fori*. The question whether deductions should be made for benefits was not a question going to liability, but one going to assessment. In *Edmunds v. Simmonds, supra*, it was stated, *obiter*, that questions relating to the quantification or assessment of damages were matters of procedure to be determined by the law of the forum, and that the 1995 Act did not affect this position. In *Hulse v. Chambers, supra*, it was held that a question relating to the quantification of damages continued to be procedural, despite the 1995 Act, principally because such a question remains a "jury question" for the judge and is, thus, essentially of a procedural character. Paragraph 35–053 of the main work was cited with approval in this case. *Cf. John Pfeiffer Pty. Ltd. v. Rogerson* (2000) 203 C.L.R. 503 where it was held (in the context of torts committed within Australia) that all matters affecting the existence, extent or enforceability of the rights and duties of the parties to an action, including all questions of the type or amount or damages recoverable were matters of substance governed (in the view of Australian law) by the law of the place of the tort. In *Régie National des Usines Renault SA v. Zhang* (2002) 187 A.L.R. 1 the High Court of Australia expressly reserved its position as to whether the same conclusion would follow in relation to a tort committed in a foreign country. In *Wong v. Wei* [1999] 10 W.W.R. 296 (B.C.) it was held that the issue of quantification of damages was procedural, though the court appears to have contemplated that if it was not, then the application of the higher measure of damages under the *lex loci delicti*, the law of California, would be denied since both parties were Canadian citizens, ordinarily resident in British Columbia. Contrast *Wong v. Lee* (2002) 211 D.L.R. (4th) 69 (Ont. C.A.) where the court applied the law of New York, the *lex loci delicti*, under which a higher measure of damages was available than that which obtained under the *lex fori*.

NOTE 37. Add: *Hulse v. Chambers, supra.*

NOTE 38. Add: *Hulse v. Chambers, supra.*

35–055 NOTES 43, 44. Add: *Edmunds v. Simmonds, supra; Hulse v. Chambers, supra; Wong v. Wei, supra; Lau v. Li* (2001) 53 O.R. (3d) 727; *John Pfeiffer Pty. Ltd. v. Rogerson, supra* (heads of damage a matter of substance to be determined by the law applicable to the tort). *Cf. Régie National des Usines Renault SA v. Zhang, supra.*

NOTE 48. *Stevens v. Head* (1993) 176 C.L.R. 433 was not followed by the High Court of Australia in *John Pfeiffer Pty. Ltd. v. Rogerson, supra*. In the latter case it was stated that the existence and extent of financial ceilings on recoverable damages were questions of substantive law. *Cf. Régie National des Usines Renault SA v. Zhang, supra*. See also *Wong v. Wei* (1999) 10 W.W.R. 296 (B.C.); *Lebert v. Skinner Estate* (2001) 53 O.R. (3d) 559; *Wong v. Lee* (2002) 211 D.L.R. (4th) 69 (Ont. C.A.); *Somers v. Fournier* (2002) 214 D.L.R. (4th) 611 (Ont. C.A.).

35–056 NOTE 51 and text thereto. The point was not adverted to in *John Pfeiffer Pty. Ltd. v. Rogerson, supra*, and was expressly reserved by Kirby J., at p. 560.

Add: See Takahashi, *Claims for Contribution and Reimbursement in an International Context* (2000), Chap. 3.

NOTE 54. Add: *The Baltic Flame* [2001] 2 Lloyd's Rep. 203 (C.A.) (Civil Liability (Contribution) Act 1978 unequivocal in its application to all proceedings brought in England and there is nothing in the Act, or in particular s. 1(6), to limit the right to contribution to liabilities incurred in England).

35–060 NOTE 63. See also *Kuwait Oil Tanker Co. SAK v. A1 Bader* [2000] 2 All E.R. (Comm.) 271, 335–336 (C.A.).

33–063 NOTE 70. Add: *Base Metal Trading Ltd. v. Shamurin* [2002] C.L.C. 322. See also *Neilson v. Overseas Projects Corp. of Victoria Ltd.* [2002] W.A.S.C. 231 (October 2, 2002).

35–064 NOTES 77, 78. See also *Grupo Torras S.A. v. Al-Sabah* [2001] C.L.C. 221 (C.A.); *Kuwait Oil Tanker Co. SAK v. Al Bader, supra*; entry at para. 34–032, *supra*.

35–068 NOTES 95. Add: See also *Commonwealth of Australia v. Stankowski* [2002] N.S.W.C.A. 348 (October 8, 2002); *Burk v. The Commonwealth* [2002] V.S.C. 453 (October 21, 2002).

35–073 NOTES 27–33 and text thereto. *Cf. Union Shipping New Zealand Ltd. v. Morgan* (2002) 54 N.S.W.L.R. 690.

2. DETERMINATION OF THE APPLICABLE LAW

A. *The General Rule*

35–079 NOTES 53–55. See also *Protea Leasing Ltd. v. Royal Air Cambodge Co. Ltd* [2002] EWHC 2731 (Comm); *The Times*, January 13, 2003.

35–080 NOTE 61 and text thereto. In *Edmunds v. Simmonds* [2001] 1 W.L.R. 1003, a case arising out of a motor accident in Spain, the *lex loci delicti*, Spanish law, was displaced in favour of English law, pursuant to section 12 of the

1995 Act (Rule 203). Contrast *Hulse v. Chambers* [2001] 1 W.L.R. 2386 where, on markedly similar facts, Greek law was applied to the substantive aspects of the tort, pursuant to section 11(1) of the 1995 Act and no argument was advanced to displace it in favour of English law by virtue of section 12. In *Glencore International A.G. v. Metro Trading International Inc.* [2001] 1 Lloyd's Rep. 284, 298 it was held that all the relevant events occurred in Fujairah the law of which was therefore applicable under section 11(1) and that there were no factors present which justified displacement of that law by reference to section 12. See too *Roerig v. Valiant Trawlers Ltd.* [2002] EWCA Civ. 21; [2002] 1 W.L.R. 2304 (C.A.); *Anton Durbeck GmbH v. Den Norske Bank ASA* [2002] EWHC 1173 (Comm); rvsd., but not on this point, [2003] EWCA Civ. 137; [2003] 2 W.L.R. 1296 (C.A.). See *infra*, entries at paras. 35R–091, 35–093.

NOTE 66. For *Lubbe v. Cape plc* [2000] 1 W.L.R. 1545 (H.L.) see entry at **35–082** para. 35–005, n. 33.

NOTE 75. For examples of the application of section 11(2)(c) of the 1995 **35–085** Act see *The Amur 2528* [2001] 1 Lloyd's Rep. 421 (alleged inducement of breach, or interference with, contract committed in Denmark since acts of inducement or interference, the most significant element or elements of the tort, took place there and were designed to bring about a breach there, even though claimant was a Russian corporation which would suffer economic loss in Russia); *Protea Leasing Ltd. v. Royal Air Cambodge Co. Ltd., supra* (most significant elements in the events occurred in Cambodia even though some damage arising from the tort (in substance that of inducing breach of contract) was felt elsewhere).

NOTE 76. In *Protea Leasing Ltd. v. Royal Air Cambodge Co. Ltd., supra*, Moore-Bick J. expressed caution about too readily turning to earlier common law authorities in applying Private International Law (Miscellaneous Provisions) Act 1995, s. 11(2)(c). In his view the 1995 Act establishes a new set of principles which make it unnecessary for the court to identify a single country in which the tort was in substance committed. S. 11(2)(c) only requires the court to identify the country in which the most significant element of the events constituting the tort occurred, a much more flexible principle which might yield different answers in different cases even in relation to the same kind of tort.

NOTE 80. Add: *Grupo Torras S.A. v. Al-Sabah* [1999] C.L.C. 1469, 1653–1657, rvsd. in part on other grounds [2001] C.L.C. 221, (C.A.); *Kuwait Oil Tanker Co. SAK v. Al Bader* [2000] 2 All E.R. (Comm.) 271, 332–333 (C.A.). (conspiracy); *Barclays Bank plc v. Inc. Inc.* [2000] 6 W.W.R. 511 (Alta.). Cf. *The Amur 2528, supra* (inducement of breach of, and interference with, contract); *Protea Leasing Ltd. v. Royal Air Cambodge Co. Ltd.* [2002] EWHC 2731 (Comm); *The Times*, January 13, 2002 (inducing breach of contract); *Hyundai Auto Canada v. Bordeleau* (2002) 60 O.R. (3rd) 641 (fraud).

NOTE 82. Add in line 2: *Henderson v. Jaouen* [2002] EWCA Civ. 75; [2002] 1 W.L.R. 2971 (C.A.).

NOTE 85. *Pearce v. Ove Arup Partnership Ltd.* is now reported at [2000] Ch. **35–088** 403 (C.A.).

B. *Rule of Displacement*

35R–091   In *Roerig v. Valiant Trawlers Ltd.* [2002] EWCA Civ. 21; [2002] 1 W.L.R. 2304 (C.A.) the claimant was Dutch. She was the widow of a Dutchman killed on a trawler registered in England and owned by an English company. The English company was the subsidiary of a Dutch company by which the deceased was employed, and the accident happened when the trawler was on a fishing expedition from the Netherlands. The action was brought by the widow on her own behalf and on behalf of her children as dependants under the Fatal Accidents Act 1976. Under the 1976 Act benefits obtained as a result of death are disregarded, but the evidence was that under Dutch law all social security benefits would be taken into account and deducted from the compensation. It was held that there was no basis for the application of Dutch law through the rule of displacement. Although it might be said to be appropriate for damages to be assessed under the law of the country where the injured party or his dependants were likely to feel their loss, it was not intended that the general rule should be dislodged so easily. The key word was "substantially" and where the defendant was English and the tort took place in England it could not be said that it was substantially more appropriate for damages to be assessed by Dutch law simply because the claimant or the deceased was Dutch. As an alternative ground, it was held that in any event the question of deduction of benefits was a matter of assessment of damages for the *lex fori* (see entry at para. 35–053).

NOTE 97. Add: *Edmunds v. Simmonds* [2001] 1 W.L.R. 1003.

NOTE 98. Add: *Edmunds v. Simmonds, supra.*

35–092   NOTE 1. *Pearce v. Ove Arup Partnership Ltd.* is now reported at [2000] Ch. 403 (C.A.). For *Lubbe v. Cape plc.* [2000] 1 W.L.R. 1545 (H.L.) see entry at para. 35–005, n. 33.

Add: *Grupo Torras S.A. v. Al-Sabah* [2001] C.L.C. 221 (C.A.); *Kuwait Oil Tanker Co. SAK v. A1 Bader* [2000] 2 All E.R. (Comm.) 271 (C.A.).

NOTE 2. In line 8 add. See also *Wong v. Wei* [1999] 10 W.W.R. 296 (B.C.) (*lex fori* applied, to tort committed in California); *Lebert v. Skinner Estate* (2001) 53 O.R. (3d) 559 (*lex fori* applied to tort committed in Utah); *Lau v. Li* (2001) 53 O.R. (3d) 727 (*lex fori* applied to tort committed in Quebec). In *Wong v. Lee* (2002) 211 D.L.R. (4th) 69 (Ont. C.A.) it was emphasised that *Tolofsen v. Jensen* [1994] S.C.R. 1022 (Sup. Ct. Can.) envisaged application of an exception to the law of the place of the wrong only in international cases and even in such cases the exception would only be available where application of the law of the place of the wrong would lead to injustice. The court applied New York law to a motor accident occurring in New York, reversing the court below (2000) 50 O.R. (3d) 419. The court also disapproved *Lau v. Li, supra,* where the exception had been applied in an inter-provincial case.

Add at end: *George v. Gubernowicz* (1999) 44 O.R. (3d) 685. In *John Pfeiffer Pty. Ltd. v. Rogerson* (2000) 203 C.L.R. 503 where the High Court of Australia discarded the rule of double actionability in favour of a choice of law rule requiring reference to the *lex loci delicti* (*ante,* entry at para. 35–006, n. 38), it was stated that no exception should exist to the application of this law in the context of torts committed within Australia. In *Régie National des Usines Renault SA v. Zhang* (2002) 187 A.L.R. 1 the High

Court of Australia stated that, in the context of torts committed in foreign countries, public policy could be used to exclude application of the *lex loci delicti* in an appropriate case: see *supra*, entry at para. 35–006, n. 38. *Cf. Nelson v. Overseas Projects Corp. of Victoria Ltd.* [2002] WASC 231.

NOTE 3 and text thereto. In *Edmunds v. Simmonds* [2001] 1 W.L.R. 1003, **35–093** the claimant suffered personal injuries while travelling as a passenger in a hire-car driven by the defendant in Spain. The car had been hired in Spain by the parties who were on holiday in that country. The accident was caused by the defendant negligently losing control of the car which, in consequence, collided with a Spanish lorry. The car was insured by a Spanish insurer. It appeared that although there was no relevant difference between Spanish law and English law on the issue of liability, the method of assessing the quantum of damages in each system was wholly different and likely to result in a much lower award to the claimant if Spanish law were applied on this issue. Garland J. held that the quantification of damages was to be determined by reference to English law. This conclusion could be reached pursuant to section 14(3)(*b*) of the 1995 Act since that sub-section expressly referred questions of procedure to the *lex fori* and the question of quantification of damages was to be classified as procedural: see main work, paras. 35–052—055; *supra*, entry at para. 35–053, nn. 35, 36 and text thereto). However, Garland J. also considered that if Spanish law was applicable to the substantive issue of heads of damage, pursuant to section 11(1) of the 1995 Act, there was an overwhelming case for the displacement of that law, in favour of English law, pursuant to section 12 of the 1995 Act. Since the accident had arisen out of the defendant's loss of control of the car, the involvement of the Spanish lorry was irrelevant and, in consequence, the only Spanish element present in the case was the involvement of the Spanish insurer. But this factor was not of overwhelming weight, as insurers of hire-cars in tourist areas or those who provide fly-drive services must contemplate that the majority of hirers would be foreign and accidents involving them might result in damages being quantified according to a different system of law. In making the comparison required by section 12, the factors connecting the tort to England were overwhelming and it was substantially more appropriate that damages were assessed according to English law. This was because (*cf. Boys v. Chaplin* [1971] A.C. 356) heads of damage were strongly linked to the country where the claimant normally resided, a link rendered stronger when the defendant resided in the same country and no policy or interest of Spain was infringed by one English resident being required to compensate another English resident according to the heads of damage available in English law. Contrast *Hulse v. Chambers* [2001] 1 W.L.R. 2386, where, despite markedly similar facts, no argument was advanced for displacing the Greek law, applicable pursuant to section 11(1), by reference to section 12. In this case, the court applied English law to matters of quantification of damages, having concluded such matters were procedural: see *supra*. In *Glencore International A.G. v. Metro Trading International Inc.* [2001] 1 Lloyd's Rep. 284, 298 it was held that there were no factors present which justified displacement of the general rule in section 11(1) by reference to section 12. See too *Roerig v. Valiant Trawlers Ltd.* [2002] EWCA Civ. 21; [2002] 1 W.L.R. 2304 (C.A.), *supra*, entry at para. 35R–091; *Anton Durbeck GmbH v. Den Norske Bank ASA* [2002] EWHC 1173 (Comm), rvsd., but not on this point, [2003] EWCA Civ. 147; [2003] 2 W.L.R. 1296 (C.A.).

35–095 NOTES 5–7 and text thereto. In *Edmunds v. Simmonds, supra*, while Spanish law seems to have been regarded as determinative of liability, the issue of heads of damage was held to be governed by English law: see previous entry.

NOTE 8. For *Lubbe v. Cape plc* [2000] 1 W.L.R. 1545 (H.L.) see entry at para. 35–005, n. 33. *Pearce v. Ove Arup Partnership Ltd.* is now reported at [2000] Ch. 403 (C.A.).

35–099 NOTES 16–22 and text thereto. See the discussion in *Edmunds v. Simmonds* [2001] 1 W.L.R. 1003, *supra*, entry at para. 35–093, n. 3 and text thereto.

NOTE 20. *Cf. Glencore International A.G. v. Metro Trading International Inc., supra*. See also *Base Metal Trading Ltd. v. Shamurin* [2002] C.L.C. 322.

35–100 NOTE 25. See previous entry.

35–101 NOTE 26 and text thereto. See the discussion *in Edmunds v. Simmonds, supra*, entry at para. 35–093, n. 3 and text thereto.

NOTE 28. As to *Lubbe v. Cape plc*, see entry at para. 35–005, n. 33.

35–102 NOTES 29–31. See the discussion in *Edmunds v. Simmonds, supra*, entry at para. 35–093, n. 3 and text thereto.

35–103 NOTES 32, 33. The correctness of these submissions appears to be supported by *Edmunds v. Simmonds, supra*, entry at para. 35–093, n. 3 and text thereto, where the text in the main work at nn. 32–33 was cited with approval.

35–104 NOTES 34, 35. See previous entry.

35–105 NOTE 40. See *Codd v. Thomson Tour Operations Ltd., The Times*, October 20, 2000 (C.A.) (although English law applied in respect of the establishment of negligence, Spanish rather than English safety standards were the appropriate standards to apply in respect of a hotel in Majorca).

35–107 Add new Illustration:

7. A, an English resident, is injured in a motor accident in Spain caused by the negligence of X, also an English resident, who lost control of the car in which A was a passenger and collided with a Spanish lorry. A and X had hired the car in Spain where they were on holiday. The car was insured by Spanish insurers. There is no difference between Spanish law and English law on the issue of the defendant's liability but, under Spanish law, A would be likely to receive an award of damages substantially less than would be available under English law. Spanish law determines the question of liability.[58a] Since the question of quantification of damages is procedural, English law applies to this question.[58b] With

---

[58a] Private International Law (Miscellaneous Provisions) Act 1995, s. 11(1); *Edmunds v. Simmonds* [2001] 1 W.L.R. 1003. *Cf. Hulse v. Chambers* [2001] 1 W.L.R. 2386.
[58b] 1995 Act, s. 14(3)(*b*); *Edmunds v. Simmonds, supra*.

regard to heads of damages, a question of substance, although Spanish law applies as a general rule,[58c] in the light of a comparison between the significance of the factors which connect the tort with Spain and those that connect the tort with England,[58d] it is substantially more appropriate for this issue to be determined by English law.[58e]

3. PUBLIC POLICY AND RELATED QUESTIONS

NOTE 63. The Human Rights Act 1998 entered into force on October 2, **35–112** 2000.

NOTE 64. The European Court of Justice has referred to decisions of the European Convention on Human Rights in the context of public policy as contained in Article 27(1) of the 1968 Convention: see Case C–7/98 *Krombach v. Bamberski* [2000] E.C.R. I–1935; [2001] Q.B. 709; Case C–38/98 *Régie Nationale Usines Renault S.A. v. Maxicar SpA* [2000] E.C.R. I–2973; *Maronier v. Larmer* [2002] EWCA Civ. 774, [2003] Q.B. 620 (C.A.). On the relationship between international law and public policy, see *Kuwait Airways Corpn. v. Iraqi Airways Co. (Nos. 4 and 5)* [2002] UKHL 19; [2002] 2 A.C. 883. And see Lord Hope of Craighead, *ibid.*, at p. 1116 (principle of English public policy which is purely domestic or parochial in character does not provide clear and satisfying grounds for disapplying primary rule which favours *lex loci delicti*).

NOTE 68. See also *Wong v. Wei* (1999) 10 W.W.R. 296 (B.C.); *Wong v. Lee* **35–113** (2002) 58 O.R. (3rd) 398 (Ont. C.A.).

NOTE 72. Add: *Cf.* Withers [2002] J.B.L. 250, 268–270. **35–115**

4. LAW APPLICABLE TO DEFAMATION AND RELATED CLAIMS

For discussion of some of the issues of jurisdiction and applicable law in **35R–119** relation to defamation and the internet, see Law Commission, *Defamation and the Internet, A Preliminary Investigation, Scoping Study No. 2* (December 2002). This study addresses, amongst other things, the very difficult question of the effect of the implementation in the United Kingdom of the Directive of the European Parliament and Council of June 8, 2000 on certain legal aspects of information society services, in particular electronic commerce, in the Internal Market ("Directive on electronic commerce") ([2000] O.J. L178/1) in the Electronic Commerce (EC Directive) Regulations 2002 (S.I. 2002 No. 2013) in relation to the law applicable to defamation through the internet: see paras. 4.37–4.49. At first sight, the Regulations do not supersede the rules of private international law in this area. This is because Recital 23 to the Directive begins by stating that the "Directive neither aims to establish additional rules on private international law relating to conflicts of law nor does it deal with the jurisdiction of Courts" but it then goes on to say that "provisions of the applicable law designated by rules of private international law must not restrict the

---

[58c] 1995 Act, s. 11(1).
[58d] 1995 Act, s. 12.
[58e] 1995 Act, s. 12.

freedom to provide information society services as established in" the Directive. The Directive (Recital 22) and the Regulations (Reg. 4) provide for country of origin regulation whereby an "information society service provider" (Reg. 2(1)) is governed by the rules of the Member State (which includes an EEA State, Reg. 2(1)) in which it is established (Regs. 2(1), 4(1), 4(3)). The Law Commission argue (para. 4.39) that "it is difficult to understand how one could introduce country of origin regulation" and prevent the restrictions referred to in Recital 23, "without making at least some changes to rules about applicable law". A similar view appears to have been accepted in the Government's Response to a Public Consultation on draft legislation to implement the Directive of July 31, 2002. The draft legislation explicity stated that it neither established additional rules of private international law nor dealt with the jurisdiction of courts, but this provision was removed from the Regulations in response to consultees who argued strongly that preserving private international law was inconsistent with the intent of the Directive to establish country of origin regulation of information society services. If, therefore, the Directive and the Regulations have an impact on private international law, the next question is whether there is any specific impact on the law relating to defamation in that context. The answer to this question depends on whether the law relating to defamation is a requirement which falls within the "coordinated field", which means (Reg. 2(1)) a requirement applicable to information society service providers or information society services, regardles of whether they are of a general nature or specifically designed for them, and covers a requirement with which the service provider has to comply in respect of (a) the taking up of the activity of an information society service, such as a requirement concerning qualifications, authorisation or notification, and (b) the pursuit of an information society service, such as a requirement concerning the behaviour of the service provider, a requirement regarding the quality or content of the service including those applicable to advertising and contracts, or a requirement concerning the liability of the service provider. Clearly the law relating to defamation could be regarded as a requirement regarding the "content of the service" as well as a requirement concerning "the liability of the service provider". And while the relevant provisions of the Directive (Art. 3(3) and Annex) and the Regulations (Reg. 4(4) and Schedule) are said not to apply to certain issues, the law relating to defamation is not one of those issues. If the foregoing arguments are accepted then, pursuant to Reg. 4(1), the English law of defamation will be applied to a service provider established in England irrespective of whether their service is provided in the United Kingdom or in another Member State, with the consequence that where a defamatory statement is published throught the internet in another Member State, Rule 205 will not apply. Conversely, Reg. 4(3) stipulates that a requirement falling within the "coordinated field" shall not be applied to a service provider established in another Member State if its "application would restrict the freedom to provide information society services to a person in the United Kingdom from that Member State". If the law relating to defamation falls within the "coordinated field", then it would appear that any aspect of English defamation law which restricts freedom to provide information society services which exists under the law of the Member State in which the service provider is established cannot be applied as against that provider The court may, however, have a power to derogate from Reg. 4(3) in certain cases, see Reg. 5, in particular, on public policy grounds (Reg. 5(1)).

with the consequence that it could apply a requirement which would otherwise be inapplicable. In the context of defamation, the only public policy grounds are measures to protect violations of human dignity concerning individual persons (*ibid.*), which violation must also prejudice a person's dignity or present a grave and serious risk of prejudice (Reg. 5(3)). Application of the measure must be necessary and proportionate to achieve the above objective (Reg. 5(1) and (2)). These criteria are likely to be satisfied, in relation to defamation, in only the most serious of cases.

Whether the above argument is correct depends ultimately on whether it was intended to include defamation within the "coordinated field" a matter which is not clear from the Directive or the Regulations. If, however, it is correct the scope of application of Rule 205 in relation to defamatory statements published on the internet will be restricted.

NOTE 11. See Kyu Ho Hum (2000) 49 I.C.L.Q. 131. **35–124**

NOTE 15. Add in line 1: *Ennstone Building Products Ltd. v. Stanger Ltd.* **35–125** [2002] EWCA Civ. 916, [2002] 1 W.L.R. 3059 (C.A.).

NOTE 19. *Pearce v. Ove Arup Partnership Ltd.* is now reported at [2000] Ch. 403 (C.A.). *Kuwait Oil Tanker Co. SAK v. Al Bader* [2000] 2 All E.R. (Comm.) 271 (C.A.) affirmed in part and reversed in part on other grounds the decision of Moore-Bick J., *The Independent*, January 11, 1999. For *Lubbe v. Cape plc* [2000] 1 W.L.R. 1545 (H.L.) see entry at para. 35–005, n. 33.

Add at end: *Kuwait Airways Corp. v. Iraqi Airways Co. (Nos. 4 and 5)* [2002] UKHL 19; [2002] 2 A.C. 883.

NOTE 20. Add: *Loutchansky v. Times Newspapers Ltd. (Nos. 2–5)* [2001] **35–126** EWCA Civ. 1805; [2002] Q.B. 783, 819–821 (C.A.); *Komarek v. Ramco Energy plc* (November 21, 2002).

NOTE 21 and text thereto. Order 11, r. 1(1)(*f*) is replaced by CPR, r. 6.20 (8).

NOTE 24. See also *Berezovsky v. Michaels* [2000] 1 W.L.R. 1004 (H.L.) (claims limited to damage sustained in England as a result of publication in England, even though more substantial publication of alleged defamatory material had occurred in the United States). *Cf. Loutchansky v. Times Newspapers Ltd. (Nos. 2–5), supra.*

NOTE 29. Add: See *Komarek v. Ramco Energy plc, supra.* See also **35–129** *Loutchansky v. Times Newspapers Ltd. (Nos. 2–5), supra.*

NOTE 35. As to *Lubbe v. Cape plc*, see *ante*, entry at para. 35–005, n. 33. **35–129** Add at end: See also *Kuwait Oil Tanker Co. SAK v. Al Bader* [2000] 2 All E.R. (Comm.) 271 (C.A.).

NOTE 41. Add: *Ennstone Building Products Ltd. v. Stanger Ltd.* [2002] **35–130** EWCA Civ. 916; [2002] 1 W.L.R. 3059 (C.A.); *Kuwait Airways Corp. v. Iraqi Airways Co. (Nos. 4 and 5)* [2002] UKHL 19; [2002] 2 A.C. 883, 1112–1116.

NOTE 43. As to *Pearce v. Ove Arup Partnership Ltd.* and *Lubbe v.Cape plc*, **35–131** see entry at para. 35–125, n. 19. Add at end: *Grupo Torras S.A. v. Al-Sabah* [2001] C.L.C. 221 (C.A.); *Ennstone Building Products Ltd. v. Stanger Ltd., supra; Kuwait Airways Corp. v. Iraqi Airways Co. (Nos. 4 and 5), supra.*

35–132 NOTE 48. See previous entry.

35–136 NOTE 64. Add: *Loutchansky v. Times Newspapers Ltd. (Nos. 2–5)* [2001] EWCA Civ. 1805; [2002] Q.B. 783 (C.A.).

NOTE 65. Add: *Berezovsky v. Michaels* [2000] 1 W.L.R. 1004 (H.L.).

35–137 NOTES 66–71 and text thereto. In *Dow Jones & Co. Inc. v. Gutnick* [2002] H.C.A. 56; (2002) 194 A.L.R. 433) the High Court of Australia held that normally defamation is to be located at the place where the damage to reputation occurs. Ordinarily that will be where the material which is alleged to be defamatory is avilable in comprehensive form, assuming that the person defamed has a reputation in that place which is thereby damaged. It is only when the material is in comprehensible form that damage to reputation is done and it is damage to reputation which is the principal focus of defamation, not any quality of the defendant's conduct. In the case of material on the internet, it is not available in comprehensible form until downloaded by a person who has accessed the defendant's web server. Consequently, it is where that person downloads the material that the damage to reputation may be done and ordinarily, therefore, that will be the place where the tort of defamation is committed. In this case the defendant's server was located in New Jersey, U.S.A. whereas the material was downloaded in Victoria where the plaintiff was resident and had a substantial reputation.

Focus on the place where a claimant/plaintiff has a reputation will operate, in many cases to limit the foreign laws to which a defendant will be exposed to in practice. The doctrine of *forum non conveniens* may also assist in this regard, assuming the defendant is subject to the jurisdiction of the forum. See also the view expressed in *Bonnier Media Ltd. v. Greg Lloyd Smith*, 2002 S.C.L.R. 977; *The Times*, July 10, 2002 where, in the context of jurisdiction over trademark infringement and passing off under Art. 5(3) of the 1968 Convention, the Outer House of the Court of Session stated that although a person who sets up a website can be regarded as committing a delict in any country where the website can be seen, it does not follow that he actually commits a delict in every country in the world. This is because the overwhelming majority of websites will be of no interest whatsoever in more than a single country or group of counties. In the view of the court a website should not be regarded as having delictual consequences in any country where it is unlikely to be of significant interest, a result which could readily be achieved by a vigorous application of the maxim *de minimis non curat praetor*. Cf. *Euromarket Designs Inc. v. Peters* [2001] F.S.R. 20; *R. v. 800–Flowers Trade Mark* [2001] EWCA Civ. 21, [2002] F.S.R. 12 (C.A.); *Menashe Business Mercantile Ltd. v. William Hill Organisation Ltd.* [2002] EWCA Civ. 1702, [2003] 1 W.L.R. 1762 (C.A.).

Text following note 71. In *Dow Jones & Co. Inc. v. Gutnick, supra,* Callinan J. expressly disagreed with this proposition.

35–139 NOTES 74–77 and text thereto. The views expressed in the main work were discussed in *Kuwait Oil Tanker Co. SAK v. Al Bader* [2000] 2 All E.R. (Comm.) 271, 335–336 (C.A.) and it was said that whether or not the claimant incorporates in his pleading an averment that the matters relied or are civilly actionable under the *lex loci delicti*, the burden in practice lies upon the defendant to plead and prove that his conduct was not actionable under the *lex loci delicti*. The debate between the two views referred to in the main work was thus a "somewhat arid one" (at p. 336) which was likely to give rise to controversy only at the interlocutory stages of an action where the court is concerned to consider and give directions in relation to any issue of foreign law arising on the face of the pleadings and as to the form and extent of any expert evidence sought to be adduced by the parties. The court expressed the view that questions of where the burden lies and its practical consequences for the progress of the action were best dealt with on a case by case basis than by the application of an inflexible rule.

NOTE 86. As to *McKain v. R.W. Miller & Co. (South Australia.) Pty. Ltd.* **35–146** (1991) 104 A.L.R. 257, see now *John Pfeiffer Pty. Ltd. v. Rogerson* (2000) 203 C.L.R. 503, *supra*, entry at para. 35–006, n. 38 and text thereto.

NOTE 90. Add; See *Loutchansky v. Times Newspapers Ltd. (Nos. 2–5)* [2002] **35–147** EWCA Civ. 1805; [2002] Q.B. 783, 819–821 (C.A.) (evidentiary standard of proof of "moral damage" under Russian law a matter of procedure not substance); *Komarek v. Ramco Energy plc* (November 21, 2002) (possible rule of Czech law as to inviolability of diplomatic documents in a claim for libel a rule of procedure not substance).

NOTE 91. Add: *Loutchansky v. Times Newspapers Ltd. (Nos. 2–5), supra.* **34–148**

CHAPTER 36

FOREIGN CURRENCY OBLIGATIONS

36–008 NOTES 26 and 27. As from January 1, 2001 the euro is the currency of Greece. See Council Decision (E.C.) 427/00, which abrogates the derogation in favour of Greece laid down in recital 4 of Council Decision (E.C.) No. 317/98. Council Regulation (E.C.) No. 974/98 was amended by Council Regulation (E.C.) No. 2586/2000 ([2000] O.J. L300/2).

36–010 NOTE 38. For the technical specification and issue of euro banknotes see Decision (E.C.B.) No. 7/2001 ([2001] O.J. L233/55) and Decision (E.C.B. No. 15/2001 ([2001] O.J. L337/52).

36–064 NOTE 65. The range of contracts to which the 1998 Act applies has been extended by S.I. 1999 No. 1816, S.I. 2000 No. 2225 and S.I. 2000 No. 2740. For further implementation of the Act see S.I. 2002 No. 1673. The Act has also been amended to implement Council Directive 2000/35 ([2000] O.J. L200/35): S.I. 2002 No. 1674.

NOTE 68. For the current rate of interest see S.I. 2002 No. 1675.

Appendix

Part I

COUNCIL REGULATION (EC) No 44/2001

**of 22 December 2000
on jurisdiction and the recognition and enforcement of
judgments in civil and commercial matters**

([2001] O.J. L 12/1, January 16, 2001)

The Council of the European Union.
Having regard to the Treaty establishing the European Community, and in particular Article 61(c) and Article 67(1) thereof,
Having regard to the proposal from the Commission,[1]
Having regard to the opinion of the European Parliament,[2]
Having regard to the opinion of the Economic and Social Committee,[3]
Whereas:

(1) The Community has set itself the objective of maintaining and developing an area of freedom, security and justice, in which the free movement of persons is ensured. In order to establish progressively such an area, the Community should adopt, amongst other things, the measures relating to judicial cooperation in civil matters which are necessary for the sound operation of the internal market.

(2) Certain differences between national rules governing jurisdiction and recognition of judgments hamper the sound operation of the internal market. Provisions to unify the rules of conflict of jurisdiction in civil and commercial matters and to simplify the formalities with a view to rapid and simple recognition and enforcement of judgments from Member States bound by this Regulation are essential.

(3) This area is within the field of judicial cooperation in civil matters within the meaning of Article 65 of the Treaty.

(4) In accordance with the principles of subsidiarity and proportionality as set out in Article 5 of the Treaty, the objectives of this Regulation cannot be sufficiently achieved by the Member States

---

[1] OJ C 376, 28.12.1999, p. 1.
[2] Opinion delivered on 21 September 2000 (not yet published in the Official Journal). [The opinion and the report of the Committee on Legal Affairs and the Internal Market (Rapporteur: Diana Wallis) are on the website of the European Parliament: www.europarl.eu.int]
[3] OJ C 117, 26.4.2000, p. 6.

and can therefore be better achieved by the Community. This Regulation confines itself to the minimum required in order to achieve those objectives and does not go beyond what is necessary for that purpose.

(5) On 27 September 1968 the Member States, acting under Article 293, fourth indent, of the Treaty, concluded the Brussels Convention on Jurisdiction and the Enforcement of Judgments in Civil and Commercial Matters, as amended by Conventions on the Accession of the New Member States to that Convention (hereinafter referred to as the "Brussels Convention").[4] On 16 September 1988 Member States and EFTA States concluded the Lugano Convention on Jurisdiction and the Enforcement of Judgments in Civil and Commercial Matters, which is a parallel Convention to the 1968 Brussels Convention. Work has been undertaken for the revision of those Conventions, and the Council has approved the content of the revised texts. Continuity in the results achieved in that revision should be ensured.

(6) In order to attain the objective of free movement of judgments in civil and commercial matters, it is necessary and appropriate that the rules governing jurisdiction and the recognition and enforcement of judgments be governed by a Community legal instrument which is binding and directly applicable.

(7) The scope of this Regulation must cover all the main civil and commercial matters apart from certain well-defined matters.

(8) There must be a link between proceedings to which this Regulation applies and the territory of the Member States bound by this Regulation. Accordingly common rules on jurisdiction should, in principle, apply when the defendant is domiciled in one of those Member States.

(9) A defendant not domiciled in a Member State is in general subject to national rules of jurisdiction applicable in the territory of the Member State of the court seised, and a defendant domiciled in a Member State not bound by this Regulation must remain subject to the Brussels Convention.

(10) For the purposes of the free movement of judgments, judgments given in a Member State bound by this Regulation should be recognised and enforced in another Member State bound by this Regulation, even if the judgment debtor is domiciled in a third State.

(11) The rules of jurisdiction must be highly predictable and founded on the principle that jurisdiction is generally based on the defendant's domicile and jurisdiction must always be available on this ground save in a few well-defined situations in which the subject-matter of the litigation or the autonomy of the parties warrants a different linking factor. The domicile of a legal person

---

[4] OJ L 299, 31.12.1972, p. 32. OJ L 304, 30.10.1978, p. 1. OJ L 388, 31.12.1982, p. 1. OJ L 285, 3.10.1989, p. 1. OJ C 15, 15.1.1997, p. 1. For a consolidated text, see OJ C 27, 26.1.1998, p. 1.

must be defined autonomously so as to make the common rules more transparent and avoid conflicts of jurisdiction.

(12) In addition to the defendant's domicile, there should be alternative grounds of jurisdiction based on a close link between the court and the action or in order to facilitate the sound administration of justice.

(13) In relation to insurance, consumer contracts and employment, the weaker party should be protected by rules of jurisdiction more favourable to his interests than the general rules provide for.

(14) The autonomy of the parties to a contract, other than an insurance, consumer or employment contract, where only limited autonomy to determine the courts having jurisdiction is allowed, must be respected subject to the exclusive grounds of jurisdiction laid down in this Regulation.

(15) In the interests of the harmonious administration of justice it is necessary to minimise the possibility of concurrent proceedings and to ensure that irreconcilable judgments will not be given in two Member States. There must be a clear and effective mechanism for resolving cases of *lis pendens* and related actions and for obviating problems flowing from national differences as to the determination of the time when a case is regarded as pending. For the purpose of this Regulation that time should be defined autonomously.

(16) Mutual trust in the administration of justice in the Community justifies judgments given in a Member State being recognised automatically without the need for any procedure except in cases of dispute.

(17) By virtue of the same principle of mutual trust, the procedure for making enforceable in one Member State a judgment given in another must be efficient and rapid. To that end, the declaration that a judgment is enforceable should be issued virtually automatically after purely formal checks of the documents supplied, without there being any possibility for the court to raise of its own motion any of the grounds for non-enforcement provided for by this Regulation.

(18) However, respect for the rights of the defence means that the defendant should be able to appeal in an adversarial procedure, against the declaration of enforceability, if he considers one of the grounds for non-enforcement to be present. Redress procedures should also be available to the claimant where his application for a declaration of enforceability has been rejected.

(19) Continuity between the Brussels Convention and this Regulation should be ensured, and transitional provisions should be laid down to that end. The same need for continuity applies as regards the interpretation of the Brussels Convention by the Court of Justice of the European Communities and the 1971 Protocol[5] should

---

[5] OJ L 204, 2.8.1975, p. 28. OJ L 304, 30.10.1978, p. 1. OJ L 388, 31.12.1982, p. 1. OJ L 285, 3.10.1989, p. 1. OJ C 15, 15.1.1997, p. 1. For a consolidated text see OJ C 27, 26.1.1998, p. 28.

remain applicable also to cases already pending when this Regulation enters into force.

(20) The United Kingdom and Ireland, in accordance with Article 3 of the Protocol on the position of the United Kingdom and Ireland annexed to the Treaty on European Union and to the Treaty establishing the European Community, have given notice of their wish to take part in the adoption and application of this Regulation.

(21) Denmark, in accordance with Articles 1 and 2 of the Protocol on the position of Denmark annexed to the Treaty on European Union and to the Treaty establishing the European Community, is not participating in the adoption of this Regulation, and is therefore not bound by it nor subject to its application.

(22) Since the Brussels Convention remains in force in relations between Denmark and the Member States that are bound by this Regulation, both the Convention and the 1971 Protocol continue to apply between Denmark and the Member States bound by this Regulation.

(23) The Brussels Convention also continues to apply to the territories of the Member States which fall within the territorial scope of that Convention and which are excluded from this Regulation pursuant to Article 299 of the Treaty.

(24) Likewise for the sake of consistency, this Regulation should not affect rules governing jurisdiction and the recognition of judgments contained in specific Community instruments.

(25) Respect for international commitments entered into by the Member States means that this Regulation should not affect conventions relating to specific matters to which the Member States are parties.

(26) The necessary flexibility should be provided for in the basic rules of this Regulation in order to take account of the specific procedural rules of certain Member States. Certain provisions of the Protocol annexed to the Brussels Convention should accordingly be incorporated in this Regulation.

(27) In order to allow a harmonious transition in certain areas which were the subject of special provisions in the Protocol annexed to the Brussels Convention, this Regulation lays down, for a transitional period, provisions taking into consideration the specific situation in certain Member States.

(28) No later than five years after entry into force of this Regulation the Commission will present a report on its application and, if need be, submit proposals for adaptations.

(29) The Commission will have to adjust Annexes I to IV on the rules of national jurisdiction, the courts or competent authorities and redress procedures available on the basis of the amendments forwarded by the Member State concerned; amendments made to Annexes V and VI should be adopted in accordance with Council

Decision 1999/468/EC of 28 June 1999 laying down the procedures for the exercise of implementing powers conferred on the Commission,[6]

HAS ADOPTED THIS REGULATION:

CHAPTER I

SCOPE

Article 1

1. This Regulation shall apply in civil and commercial matters whatever the nature of the court or tribunal. It shall not extend, in particular, to revenue, customs or administrative matters.

2. The Regulation shall not apply to:

(a) the status or legal capacity of natural persons, rights in property arising out of a matrimonial relationship, wills and succession;

(b) bankruptcy, proceedings relating to the winding-up of insolvent companies or other legal persons, judicial arrangements, compositions and analogous proceedings;

(c) social security;

(d) arbitration.

3. In this Regulation, the term "Member State" shall mean Member States with the exception of Denmark.

CHAPTER II

JURISDICTION

Section 1

General provisions

Article 2

1. Subject to this Regulation, persons domiciled in a Member State shall, whatever their nationality, be sued in the courts of that Member State.

2. Persons who are not nationals of the Member State in which they are domiciled shall be governed by the rules of jurisdiction applicable to nationals of that State.

Article 3

1. Persons domiciled in a Member State may be sued in the courts of

---

[5] OJ L 184, 17.7.1999, p. 23.

another Member State only by virtue of the rules set out in Sections 2 to 7 of this Chapter.

2. In particular the rules of national jurisdiction set out in Annex I shall not be applicable as against them.

Article 4

1. If the defendant is not domiciled in a Member State, the jurisdiction of the courts of each Member State shall, subject to Articles 22 and 23, be determined by the law of that Member State.

2. As against such a defendant, any person domiciled in a Member State may, whatever his nationality, avail himself in that State of the rules of jurisdiction there in force, and in particular those specified in Annex I, in the same way as the nationals of that State.

Section 2

Special Jurisdiction

Article 5

A person domiciled in a Member State may, in another Member State, be sued:

1. (a) in matters relating to a contract, in the courts for the place of performance of the obligation in question;

   (b) for the purpose of this provision and unless otherwise agreed, the place of performance of the obligation in question shall be:

   — in the case of the sale of goods, the place in a Member State where, under the contract, the goods were delivered or should have been delivered,
   — in the case of the provision of services, the place in a Member State where, under the contract, the services were provided or should have been provided,

   (c) if subparagraph (b) does not apply then subparagraph (a) applies;

2. in matters relating to maintenance, in the courts for the place where the maintenance creditor is domiciled or habitually resident or, if the matter is ancillary to proceedings concerning the status of a person, in the court which, according to its own law, has jurisdiction to entertain those proceedings, unless that jurisdiction is based solely on the nationality of one of the parties;

3. in matters relating to tort, *delict* or *quasi-delict*, in the courts for the place where the harmful event occurred or may occur;

4. as regards a civil claim for damages or restitution which is based on an act giving rise to criminal proceedings, in the court seised of those proceedings, to the extent that that court has jurisdiction under its own law to entertain civil proceedings;

5. as regards a dispute arising out of the operations of a branch, agency or other establishment, in the courts for the place in which the branch, agency or other establishment is situated;

6. as settlor, trustee or beneficiary of a trust created by the operation of a statute, or by a written instrument, or created orally and evidenced in writing, in the courts of the Member State in which the trust is domiciled;

7. as regards a dispute concerning the payment of remuneration claimed in respect of the salvage of a cargo or freight, in the court under the authority of which the cargo or freight in question:

(a) has been arrested to secure such payment, or

(b) could have been so arrested, but bail or other security has been given;

provided that this provision shall apply only if it is claimed that the defendant has an interest in the cargo or freight or had such an interest at the time of salvage.

Article 6

A person domiciled in a Member State may also be sued:

1. where he is one of a number of defendants, in the courts for the place where any one of them is domiciled, provided the claims are so closely connected that it is expedient to hear and determine them together to avoid the risk of irreconcilable judgments resulting from separate proceedings;

2. as a third party in an action on a warranty or guarantee or in any other third party proceedings, in the court seised of the original proceedings, unless these were instituted solely with the object of removing him from the jurisdiction of the court which would be competent in his case;

3. on a counter-claim arising from the same contract or facts on which the original claim was based, in the court in which the original claim is pending;

4. in matters relating to a contract, if the action may be combined with an action against the same defendant in matters relating to rights *in rem* in immovable property, in the court of the Member State in which the property is situated.

Article 7

Where by virtue of this Regulation a court of a Member State has jurisdiction in actions relating to liability from the use or operation of a ship, that court, or any other court substituted for this purpose by the internal law of that Member State, shall also have jurisdiction over claims for limitation of such liability.

Section 3

Jurisdiction in matters relating to insurance

Article 8

In matters relating to insurance, jurisdiction shall be determined by this Section, without prejudice to Article 4 and point 5 of Article 5.

Article 9

1. An insurer domiciled in a Member State may be sued:

   (a) in the courts of the Member State where he is domiciled, or

   (b) in another Member State, in the case of actions brought by the policyholder, the insured or a beneficiary, in the courts for the place where the plaintiff is domiciled,

   (c) if he is a co-insurer, in the courts of a Member State in which proceedings are brought against the leading insurer.

2. An insurer who is not domiciled in a Member State but has a branch, agency or other establishment in one of the Member States shall, in disputes arising out of the operations of the branch, agency or establishment, be deemed to be domiciled in that Member State.

Article 10

In respect of liability insurance or insurance of immovable property, the insurer may in addition be sued in the courts for the place where the harmful event occurred. The same applies if movable and immovable property are covered by the same insurance policy and both are adversely affected by the same contingency.

Article 11

1. In respect of liability insurance, the insurer may also, if the law of the court permits it, be joined in proceedings which the injured party has brought against the insured.
2. Articles 8, 9 and 10 shall apply to actions brought by the injured party directly against the insurer, where such direct actions are permitted.
3. If the law governing such direct actions provides that the policyholder or the insured may be joined as a party to the action, the same court shall have jurisdiction over them.

Article 12

1. Without prejudice to Article 11(3), an insurer may bring proceedings only in the courts of the Member State in which the defendant is domiciled, irrespective of whether he is the policyholder, the insured or a beneficiary.
2. The provisions of this Section shall not affect the right to bring a counter-claim in the court in which, in accordance with this Section, the original claim is pending.

Article 13

The provisions of this Section may be departed from only by an agreement:
1. which is entered into after the dispute has arisen, or
2. which allows the policyholder, the insured or a beneficiary to bring proceedings in courts other than those indicated in this Section, or

3. which is concluded between a policyholder and an insurer, both of whom are at the time of conclusion of the contract domiciled or habitually resident in the same Member State, and which has the effect of conferring jurisdiction on the courts of that State even if the harmful event were to occur abroad, provided that such an agreement is not contrary to the law of that State, or

4. which is concluded with a policyholder who is not domiciled in a Member State, except in so far as the insurance is compulsory or relates to immovable property in a Member State, or

5. which relates to a contract of insurance in so far as it covers one or more of the risks set out in Article 14.

Article 14

The following are the risks referred to in Article 13(5):
1. any loss of or damage to:

    (a) seagoing ships, installations situated offshore or on the high seas, or aircraft, arising from perils which relate to their use for commercial purposes;

    (b) goods in transit other than passengers' baggage where the transit consists of or includes carriage by such ships or aircraft;

2. any liability, other than for bodily injury to passengers or loss of or damage to their baggage:

    (a) arising out of the use or operation of ships, installations or aircraft as referred to in point 1(a) in so far as, in respect of the latter, the law of the Member State in which such aircraft are registered does not prohibit agreements on jurisdiction regarding insurance of such risks;

    (b) for loss or damage caused by goods in transit as described in point 1(b);

3. any financial loss connected with the use or operation of ships, installations or aircraft as referred to in point 1(a), in particular loss of freight or charter-hire;

4. any risk or interest connected with any of those referred to in points 1 to 3;

5. notwithstanding points 1 to 4, all "large risks" as defined in Council Directive 73/239/EEC,[7] as amended by Council Directives 88/357/EEC[8] and 90/618/EEC,[9] as they may be amended.

---

[7] OJ L 228, 16.8.1973, p. 3. Directive as last amended by Directive 2000/26/EC of the European Parliament and of the Council (OJ L 181, 20.7.2000, p. 65).
[8] OJ L 172, 4.7.1988, p. 1. Directive as last amended by Directive 2000/26/EC.
[9] OJ L 330, 29.11.1990, p. 44.

Section 4

Jurisdiction over consumer contracts

Article 15

1. In matters relating to a contract concluded by a person, the consumer, for a purpose which can be regarded as being outside his trade or profession, jurisdiction shall be determined by this Section, without prejudice to Article 4 and point 5 of Article 5, if:

(a) it is a contract for the sale of goods on instalment credit terms; or

(b) it is a contract for a loan repayable by instalments, or for any other form of credit, made to finance the sale of goods; or

(c) in all other cases, the contract has been concluded with a person who pursues commercial or professional activities in the Member State of the consumer's domicile or, by any means, directs such activities to that Member State or to several States including that Member State, and the contract falls within the scope of such activities.

2. Where a consumer enters into a contract with a party who is not domiciled in the Member State but has a branch, agency or other establishment in one of the Member States, that party shall, in disputes arising out of the operations of the branch, agency or establishment, be deemed to be domiciled in that State.

3. This Section shall not apply to a contract of transport other than a contract which, for an inclusive price, provides for a combination of travel and accommodation.

Article 16

1. A consumer may bring proceedings against the other party to a contract either in the courts of the Member State in which that party is domiciled or in the courts for the place where the consumer is domiciled.

2. Proceedings may be brought against a consumer by the other party to the contract only in the courts of the Member State in which the consumer is domiciled.

3. This Article shall not affect the right to bring a counter-claim in the court in which, in accordance with this Section, the original claim is pending.

Article 17

The provisions of this Section may be departed from only by an agreement:

1. which is entered into after the dispute has arisen; or

2. which allows the consumer to bring proceedings in courts other than those indicated in this Section; or

3. which is entered into by the consumer and the other party to the contract, both of whom are at the time of conclusion of the contract domiciled or habitually resident in the same Member State, and which confers jurisdiction on the courts of that Member State, provided that such an agreement is not contrary to the law of that Member State.

Section 5

Jurisdiction over individual contracts of employment

Article 18

1. In matters relating to individual contracts of employment, jurisdiction shall be determined by this Section, without prejudice to Article 4 and point 5 of Article 5.

2. Where an employee enters into an individual contract of employment with an employer who is not domiciled in a Member State but has a branch, agency or other establishment in one of the Member States, the employer shall, in disputes arising out of the operations of the branch, agency or establishment, be deemed to be domiciled in that Member State.

Article 19

An employer domiciled in a Member State may be sued:
1. in the courts of the Member State where he is domiciled; or
2. in another Member State:

    (a) in the courts for the place where the employee habitually carries out his work or in the courts for the last place where he did so, or

    (b) if the employee does not or did not habitually carry out his work in any one country, in the courts for the place where the business which engaged the employee is or was situated.

Article 20

1. An employer may bring proceedings only in the courts of the Member State in which the employee is domiciled.

2. The provisions of this Section shall not affect the right to bring a counter-claim in the court in which, in accordance with this Section, the original claim is pending.

Article 21

The provisions of this Section may be departed from only by an agreement on jurisdiction:
1. which is entered into after the dispute has arisen; or
2. which allows the employee to bring proceedings in courts other than those indicated in this Section.

Section 6

Exclusive jurisdiction

Article 22

The following courts shall have exclusive jurisdiction, regardless of domicile:

1. in proceedings which have as their object rights *in rem* in immovable property or tenancies of immovable property, the courts of the Member State in which the property is situated.

However, in proceedings which have as their object tenancies of immovable property concluded for temporary private use for a maximum period of six consecutive months, the courts of the Member State in which the defendant is domiciled shall also have jurisdiction, provided that the tenant is a natural person and that the landlord and the tenant are domiciled in the same Member State;

2. in proceedings which have as their object the validity of the constitution, the nullity or the dissolution of companies or other legal persons or associations of natural or legal persons, or of the validity of the decisions of their organs, the courts of the Member State in which the company, legal person or association has its seat. In order to determine that seat, the court shall apply its rules of private international law;

3. in proceedings which have as their object the validity of entries in public registers, the courts of the Member State in which the register is kept;

4. in proceedings concerned with the registration or validity of patents, trade marks, designs, or other similar rights required to be deposited or registered, the courts of the Member State in which the deposit or registration has been applied for, has taken place or is under the terms of a Community instrument or an international convention deemed to have taken place.

Without prejudice to the jurisdiction of the European Patent Office under the Convention on the Grant of European Patents, signed at Munich on 5 October 1973, the courts of each Member State shall have exclusive jurisdiction, regardless of domicile, in proceedings concerned with the registration or validity of any European patent granted for that State;

5. in proceedings concerned with the enforcement of judgments, the courts of the Member State in which the judgment has been or is to be enforced.

Section 7

Prorogation of jurisdiction

Article 23

1. If the parties, one or more of whom is domiciled in a Member State, have agreed that a court or the courts of a Member State are to have jurisdiction to settle any disputes which have arisen or which may arise in connection with a particular legal relationship, that court or those courts shall have jurisdiction. Such jurisdiction shall be exclusive unless the parties have agreed otherwise. Such an agreement conferring jurisdiction shall be either:

(a) in writing or evidenced in writing; or

(b) in a form which accords with practices which the parties have established between themselves; or

(c) in international trade or commerce, in a form which accords with a usage of which the parties are or ought to have been aware and which in such trade or commerce is widely known to, and regularly observed by, parties to contracts of the type involved in the particular trade or commerce concerned.

2. Any communication by electronic means which provides a durable record of the agreement shall be equivalent to "writing".

3. Where such an agreement is concluded by parties, none of whom is domiciled in a Member State, the courts of other Member States shall have no jurisdiction over their disputes unless the court or courts chosen have declined jurisdiction.

4. The court or courts of a Member State on which a trust instrument has conferred jurisdiction shall have exclusive jurisdiction in any proceedings brought against a settlor, trustee or beneficiary, if relations between these persons or their rights or obligations under the trust are involved.

5. Agreements or provisions of a trust instrument conferring jurisdiction shall have no legal force if they are contrary to Articles 13, 17 or 21, or if the courts whose jurisdiction they purport to exclude have exclusive jurisdiction by virtue of Article 22.

Article 24

Apart from jurisdiction derived from other provisions of this Regulation, a court of a Member State before which a defendant enters an appearance shall have jurisdiction. This rule shall not apply where appearance was entered to contest the jurisdiction, or where another court has exclusive jurisdiction by virtue of Article 22.

Section 8

Examination as to jurisdiction and admissibility

Article 25

Where a court of a Member State is seised of a claim which is principally concerned with a matter over which the courts of another Member State have exclusive jurisdiction by virtue of Article 22, it shall declare of its own motion that it has no jurisdiction.

Article 26

1. Where a defendant domiciled in one Member State is sued in a court of another Member State and does not enter an appearance, the court shall declare of its own motion that it has no jurisdiction unless its jurisdiction is derived from the provisions of this Regulation.

2. The court shall stay the proceedings so long as it is not shown that the defendant has been able to receive the document instituting the proceedings or an equivalent document in sufficient time to enable him to arrange for his defence, or that all necessary steps have been taken to this end.

427

3. Article 19 of Council Regulation (EC) No 1348/2000 of 29 May 2000 on the service in the Member States of judicial and extrajudicial documents in civil or commercial matters[10] shall apply instead of the provisions of paragraph 2 if the document instituting the proceedings or an equivalent document had to be transmitted from one Member State to another pursuant to this Regulation.

4. Where the provisions of Regulation (EC) No 1348/2000 are not applicable, Article 15 of the Hague Convention of 15 November 1965 on the Service Abroad of Judicial and Extrajudicial Documents in Civil or Commercial Matters shall apply if the document instituting the proceedings or an equivalent document had to be transmitted pursuant to that Convention.

Section 9

Lis pendens—related actions

Article 27

1. Where proceedings involving the same cause of action and between the same parties are brought in the courts of different Member States, any court other than the court first seised shall of its own motion stay its proceedings until such time as the jurisdiction of the court first seised is established.

2. Where the jurisdiction of the court first seised is established, any court other than the court first seised shall decline jurisdiction in favour of that court.

Article 28

1. Where related actions are pending in the courts of different Member States, any court other than the court first seised may stay its proceedings.

2. Where these actions are pending at first instance, any court other than the court first seised may also, on the application of one of the parties, decline jurisdiction if the court first seised has jurisdiction over the actions in question and its law permits the consolidation thereof.

3. For the purposes of this Article, actions are deemed to be related where they are so closely connected that it is expedient to hear and determine them together to avoid the risk of irreconcilable judgments resulting from separate proceedings.

Article 29

Where actions come within the exclusive jurisdiction of several courts, any court other than the court first seised shall decline jurisdiction in favour of that court.

Article 30

For the purposes of this Section, a court shall be deemed to be seised:

---

[10] OJ L 160, 30.6.2000, p. 37.

1. at the time when the document instituting the proceedings or an equivalent document is lodged with the court, provided that the plaintiff has not subsequently failed to take the steps he was required to take to have service effected on the defendant, or

2. if the document has to be served before being lodged with the court, at the time when it is received by the authority responsible for service, provided that the plaintiff has not subsequently failed to take the steps he was required to take to have the document lodged with the court.

Section 10

Provisional, including protective, measures

Article 31

Application may be made to the courts of a Member State for such provisional, including protective, measures as may be available under the law of that State, even if, under this Regulation, the courts of another Member State have jurisdiction as to the substance of the matter.

CHAPTER III

RECOGNITION AND ENFORCEMENT

Article 32

For the purposes of this Regulation, "judgment" means any judgment given by a court or tribunal of a Member State, whatever the judgment may be called, including a decree, order, decision or writ of execution, as well as the determination of costs or expenses by an officer of the court.

Section 1

Recognition

Article 33

1. A judgment given in a Member State shall be recognised in the other Member States without any special procedure being required.

2. Any interested party who raises the recognition of a judgment as the principal issue in a dispute may, in accordance with the procedures provided for in Sections 2 and 3 of this Chapter, apply for a decision that the judgment be recognised.

3. If the outcome of proceedings in a court of a Member State depends on the determination of an incidental question of recognition that court shall have jurisdiction over that question.

Article 34

A judgment shall not be recognised:

1. if such recognition is manifestly contrary to public policy in the Member State in which recognition is sought;

2. where it was given in default of appearance, if the defendant was not served with the document which instituted the proceedings or with an equivalent document in sufficient time and in such a way as to enable him to arrange for his defence, unless the defendant failed to commence proceedings to challenge the judgment when it was possible for him to do so;

3. if it is irreconcilable with a judgment given in a dispute between the same parties in the Member State in which recognition is sought;

4. if it is irreconcilable with an earlier judgment given in another Member State or in a third State involving the same cause of action and between the same parties, provided that the earlier judgment fulfils the conditions necessary for its recognition in the Member State addressed.

Article 35

1. Moreover, a judgment shall not be recognised if it conflicts with Sections 3, 4 or 6 of Chapter II, or in a case provided for in Article 72.

2. In its examination of the grounds of jurisdiction referred to in the foregoing paragraph, the court or authority applied to shall be bound by the findings of fact on which the court of the Member State of origin based its jurisdiction.

3. Subject to the paragraph 1, the jurisdiction of the court of the Member State of origin may not be reviewed. The test of public policy referred to in point 1 of Article 34 may not be applied to the rules relating to jurisdiction.

Article 36

Under no circumstances may a foreign judgment be reviewed as to its substance.

Article 37

1. A court of a Member State in which recognition is sought of a judgment given in another Member State may stay the proceedings if an ordinary appeal against the judgment has been lodged.

2. A court of a Member State in which recognition is sought of a judgment given in Ireland or the United Kingdom may stay the proceedings if enforcement is suspended in the State of origin, by reason of an appeal.

Section 2

Enforcement

Article 38

1. A judgment given in a Member State and enforceable in that State shall be enforced in another Member State when, on the application of any interested party, it has been declared enforceable there.

2. However, in the United Kingdom, such a judgment shall be enforced in England and Wales, in Scotland, or in Northern Ireland when, on the application of any interested party, it has been registered for enforcement in that part of the United Kingdom.

Article 39

1. The application shall be submitted to the court or competent authority indicated in the list in Annex II.

2. The local jurisdiction shall be determined by reference to the place of domicile of the party against whom enforcement is sought, or to the place of enforcement.

Article 40

1. The procedure for making the application shall be governed by the law of the Member State in which enforcement is sought.

2. The applicant must give an address for service of process within the area of jurisdiction of the court applied to. However, if the law of the Member State in which enforcement is sought does not provide for the furnishing of such an address, the applicant shall appoint a representative *ad litem*.

3. The documents referred to in Article 53 shall be attached to the application.

Article 41

The judgment shall be declared enforceable immediately on completion of the formalities in Article 53 without any review under Articles 34 and 35. The party against whom enforcement is sought shall not at this stage of the proceedings be entitled to make any submissions on the application.

Article 42

1. The decision on the application for a declaration of enforceability shall forthwith be brought to the notice of the applicant in accordance with the procedure laid down by the law of the Member State in which enforcement is sought.

2. The declaration of enforceability shall be served on the party against whom enforcement is sought, accompanied by the judgment, if not already served on that party.

Article 43

1. The decision on the application for a declaration of enforceability may be appealed against by either party.

2. The appeal is to be lodged with the court indicated in the list in Annex III.

3. The appeal shall be dealt with in accordance with the rules governing procedure in contradictory matters.

4. If the party against whom enforcement is sought fails to appear before the appellate court in proceedings concerning an appeal brought by the applicant, Article 26(2) to (4) shall apply even where the party against whom enforcement is sought is not domiciled in any of the Member States.

5. An appeal against the declaration of enforceability is to be lodged within one month of service thereof. If the party against whom enforcement is sought is domiciled in a Member State other than that in which the declaration of enforceability was given, the time for appealing shall be two

months and shall run from the date of service, either on him in person or at his residence. No extension of time may be granted on account of distance.

Article 44

The judgment given on the appeal may be contested only by the appeal referred to in Annex IV.

Article 45

1. The court with which an appeal is lodged under Article 43 or Article 44 shall refuse or revoke a declaration of enforceability only on one of the grounds specified in Articles 34 and 35. It shall give its decision without delay.

2. Under no circumstances may the foreign judgment be reviewed as to its substance.

Article 46

1. The court with which an appeal is lodged under Article 43 or Article 44 may, on the application of the party against whom enforcement is sought, stay the proceedings if an ordinary appeal has been lodged against the judgment in the Member State of origin or if the time for such an appeal has not yet expired; in the latter case, the court may specify the time within which such an appeal is to be lodged.

2. Where the judgment was given in Ireland or the United Kingdom, any form of appeal available in the Member State of origin shall be treated as an ordinary appeal for the purposes of paragraph 1.

3. The court may also make enforcement conditional on the provision of such security as it shall determine.

Article 47

1. When a judgment must be recognised in accordance with this Regulation, nothing shall prevent the applicant from availing himself of provisional, including protective, measures in accordance with the law of the Member State requested without a declaration of enforceability under Article 41 being required.

2. The declaration of enforceability shall carry with it the power to proceed to any protective measures.

3. During the time specified for an appeal pursuant to Article 43(5) against the declaration of enforceability and until any such appeal has been determined, no measures of enforcement may be taken other than protective measures against the property of the party against whom enforcement is sought.

Article 48

1. Where a foreign judgment has been given in respect of several matters and the declaration of enforceability cannot be given for all of them, the court or competent authority shall give it for one or more of them.

2. An applicant may request a declaration of enforceability limited to parts of a judgment.

Article 49

A foreign judgment which orders a periodic payment by way of a penalty shall be enforceable in the Member State in which enforcement is sought only if the amount of the payment has been finally determined by the courts of the Member State of origin.

Article 50

An applicant who, in the Member State of origin has benefited from complete or partial legal aid or exemption from costs or expenses, shall be entitled, in the procedure provided for in this Section, to benefit from the most favourable legal aid or the most extensive exemption from costs or expenses provided for by the law of the Member State addressed.

Article 51

No security, bond or deposit, however described, shall be required of a party who in one Member State applies for enforcement of a judgment given in another Member State on the ground that he is a foreign national or that he is not domiciled or resident in the State in which enforcement is sought.

Article 52

In proceedings for the issue of a declaration of enforceability, no charge, duty or fee calculated by reference to the value of the matter at issue may be levied in the Member State in which enforcement is sought.

Section 3

Common provisions

Article 53

1. A party seeking recognition or applying for a declaration of enforceability shall produce a copy of the judgment which satisfies the conditions necessary to establish its authenticity.

2. A party applying for a declaration of enforceability shall also produce the certificate referred to in Article 54, without prejudice to Article 55.

Article 54

The court or competent authority of a Member State where a judgment was given shall issue, at the request of any interested party, a certificate using the standard form in Annex V to this Regulation.

Article 55

1. If the certificate referred to in Article 54 is not produced, the court or competent authority may specify a time for its production or accept an equivalent document or, if it considers that it has sufficient information before it, dispense with its production.

2. If the court or competent authority so requires, a translation of the documents shall be produced. The translation shall be certified by a person qualified to do so in one of the Member States.

Article 56

No legalisation or other similar formality shall be required in respect of the documents referred to in Article 53 or Article 55(2), or in respect of a document appointing a representative *ad litem*.

CHAPTER IV

AUTHENTIC INSTRUMENTS AND COURT SETTLEMENTS

Article 57

1. A document which has been formally drawn up or registered as an authentic instrument and is enforceable in one Member State shall, in another Member State, be declared enforceable there, on application made in accordance with the procedures provided for in Articles 38, et seq. The court with which an appeal is lodged under Article 43 or Article 44 shall refuse or revoke a declaration of enforceability only if enforcement of the instrument is manifestly contrary to public policy in the Member State addressed.

2. Arrangements relating to maintenance obligations concluded with administrative authorities or authenticated by them shall also be regarded as authentic instruments within the meaning of paragraph 1.

3. The instrument produced must satisfy the conditions necessary to establish its authenticity in the Member State of origin.

4. Section 3 of Chapter III shall apply as appropriate. The competent authority of a Member State where an authentic instrument was drawn up or registered shall issue, at the request of any interested party, a certificate using the standard form in Annex VI to this Regulation.

Article 58

A settlement which has been approved by a court in the course of proceedings and is enforceable in the Member State in which it was concluded shall be enforceable in the State addressed under the same conditions as authentic instruments. The court or competent authority of a Member State where a court settlement was approved shall issue, at the request of any interested party, a certificate using the standard form in Annex V to this Regulation.

CHAPTER V

GENERAL PROVISIONS

Article 59

1. In order to determine whether a party is domiciled in the Member State whose courts are seised of a matter, the court shall apply its internal law.

2. If a party is not domiciled in the Member State whose courts are seised of the matter then, in order to determine whether the party is domiciled in another Member State, the court shall apply the law of that Member State.

Article 60

1. For the purposes of this Regulation, a company or other legal person or association of natural or legal persons is domiciled at the place where it has its:

  (a) statutory seat, or

  (b) central administration, or

  (c) principal place of business.

2. For the purposes of the United Kingdom and Ireland "statutory seat" means the registered office or, where there is no such office anywhere, the place of incorporation or, where there is no such place anywhere, the place under the law of which the formation took place.
3. In order to determine whether a trust is domiciled in the Member State whose courts are seised of the matter, the court shall apply its rules of private international law.

Article 61

Without prejudice to any more favourable provisions of national laws, persons domiciled in a Member State who are being prosecuted in the criminal courts of another Member State of which they are not nationals for an offence which was not intentionally committed may be defended by persons qualified to do so, even if they do not appear in person. However, the court seised of the matter may order appearance in person; in the case of failure to appear, a judgment given in the civil action without the person concerned having had the opportunity to arrange for his defence need not be recognised or enforced in the other Member States.

Article 62

In Sweden, in summary proceedings concerning orders to pay (*betalningsföreläggande*) and assistance (*handräckning*), the expression "court" includes the "Swedish enforcement service" (*kronofogdemyndighet*).

Article 63

1. A person domiciled in the territory of the Grand Duchy of Luxembourg and sued in the court of another Member State pursuant to Article 5(1) may refuse to submit to the jurisdiction of that court if the final place of delivery of the goods or provision of the services is in Luxembourg.
2. Where, under paragraph 1, the final place of delivery of the goods or provision of the services is in Luxembourg, any agreement conferring jurisdiction must, in order to be valid, be accepted in writing or evidenced in writing within the meaning of Article 23(1)(a).
3. The provisions of this Article shall not apply to contracts for the provision of financial services.

4. The provisions of this Article shall apply for a period of six years from entry into force of this Regulation.

Article 64

1. In proceedings involving a dispute between the master and a member of the crew of a seagoing ship registered in Greece or in Portugal, concerning remuneration or other conditions of service, a court in a Member State shall establish whether the diplomatic or consular officer responsible for the ship has been notified of the dispute. It may act as soon as that officer has been notified.

2. The provisions of this Article shall apply for a period of six years from entry into force of this Regulation.

Article 65

1. The jurisdiction specified in Article 6(2), and Article 11 in actions on a warranty of guarantee or in any other third party proceedings may not be resorted to in Germany and Austria. Any person domiciled in another Member State may be sued in the courts:

(a) of Germany, pursuant to Articles 68 and 72 to 74 of the Code of Civil Procedure (*Zivilprozessordnung*) concerning third-party notices,

(b) of Austria, pursuant to Article 21 of the Code of Civil Procedure (*Zivilprozessordnung*) concerning third-party notices.

2. Judgments given in other Member States by virtue of Article 6(2), or Article 11 shall be recognised and enforced in Germany and Austria in accordance with Chapter III. Any effects which judgments given in these States may have on third parties by application of the provisions in paragraph 1 shall also be recognised in the other Member States.

CHAPTER VI

TRANSITIONAL PROVISIONS

Article 66

1. This Regulation shall apply only to legal proceedings instituted and to documents formally drawn up or registered as authentic instruments after the entry into force thereof.

2. However, if the proceedings in the Member State of origin were instituted before the entry into force of this Regulation, judgments given after that date shall be recognised and enforced in accordance with Chapter III,

(a) if the proceedings in the Member State of origin were instituted after the entry into force of the Brussels or the Lugano Convention both in the Member State or origin and in the Member State addressed;

(b) in all other cases, if jurisdiction was founded upon rules which accorded with those provided for either in Chapter II or in a convention concluded between the Member State of origin and the Member State addressed which was in force when the proceedings were instituted.

CHAPTER VII

RELATIONS WITH OTHER INSTRUMENTS

Article 67

This Regulation shall not prejudice the application of provisions governing jurisdiction and the recognition and enforcement of judgments in specific matters which are contained in Community instruments or in national legislation harmonised pursuant to such instruments.

Article 68

1. This Regulation shall, as between the Member States, supersede the Brussels Convention, except as regards the territories of the Member States which fall within the territorial scope of that Convention and which are excluded from this Regulation pursuant to Article 299 of the Treaty.

2. In so far as this Regulation replaces the provisions of the Brussels Convention between Member States, any reference to the Convention shall be understood as a reference to this Regulation.

Article 69

Subject to Article 66(2) and Article 70, this Regulation shall, as between Member States, supersede the following conventions and treaty concluded between two or more of them:

— the Convention between Belgium and France on Jurisdiction and the Validity and Enforcement of Judgments, Arbitration Awards and Authentic Instruments, signed at Paris on 8 July 1899,

— the Convention between Belgium and the Netherlands on jurisdiction, Bankruptcy, and the Validity and Enforcement of Judgments, Arbitration Awards and Authentic Instruments, signed at Brussels on 28 March 1925,

— the Convention between France and Italy on the Enforcement of Judgments in Civil and Commercial Matters, signed at Rome on 3 June 1930,

— the Convention between Germany and Italy on the Recognition and Enforcement of Judgments in Civil and Commercial Matters, signed at Rome on 9 March 1936,

— the Convention between Belgium and Austria on the Reciprocal Recognition and Enforcement of Judgments and Authentic Instruments relating to Maintenance Obligations, signed at Vienna on 25 October 1957,

- the Convention between Germany and Belgium on the Mutual Recognition and Enforcement of Judgments, Arbitration Awards and Authentic Instruments in Civil and Commercial Matters, signed at Bonn on 30 June 1958,
- the Convention between the Netherlands and Italy on the Recognition and Enforcement of Judgments in Civil and Commercial Matters, signed at Rome on 17 April 1959,
- the Convention between Germany and Austria on the Reciprocal Recognition and Enforcement of Judgments, Settlements and Authentic Instruments in Civil and Commercial Matters, signed at Vienna on 6 June 1959,
- the Convention between Belgium and Austria on the Reciprocal Recognition and Enforcement of Judgments, Arbitral Awards and Authentic Instruments in Civil and Commercial Matters, signed at Vienna on 16 June 1959,
- the Convention between Greece and Germany for the Reciprocal Recognition and Enforcement of Judgments, Settlements and Authentic Instruments in Civil and Commercial Matters, signed in Athens on 4 November 1961,
- the Convention between Belgium and Italy on the Recognition and Enforcement of Judgments and other Enforceable Instruments in Civil and Commercial Matters, signed at Rome on 6 April 1962,
- the Convention between the Netherlands and Germany on the Mutual Recognition and Enforcement of Judgments and Other Enforceable Instruments in Civil and Commercial Matters, signed at The Hague on 30 August 1962,
- the Convention between the Netherlands and Austria on the Reciprocal Recognition and Enforcement of Judgments and Authentic Instruments in Civil and Commercial Matters, signed at The Hague on 6 February 1963,
- the Convention between France and Austria on the Recognition and Enforcement of Judgments and Authentic Instruments in Civil and Commercial Matters, signed at Vienna on 15 July 1966,
- the Convention between Spain and France on the Recognition and Enforcement of Judgments and Arbitration Awards in Civil and Commercial Matters, signed at Paris on 28 May 1969,
- the Convention between Luxembourg and Austria on the Recognition and Enforcement of Judgments and Authentic Instruments in Civil and Commercial Matters, signed at Luxembourg on 29 July 1971,
- the Convention between Italy and Austria on the Recognition and Enforcement of Judgments in Civil and Commercial Matters, of Judicial Settlements and of Authentic Instruments, signed at Rome on 16 November 1971,
- the Convention between Spain and Italy regarding Legal Aid and the Recognition and Enforcement of Judgments in Civil and Commercial Matters, signed at Madrid on 22 May 1973,

— the Convention between Finland, Iceland, Norway, Sweden and Denmark on the Recognition and Enforcement of Judgments in Civil Matters, signed at Copenhagen on 11 October 1977,

— the Convention between Austria and Sweden on the Recognition and Enforcement of Judgments in Civil Matters, signed at Stockholm on 16 September 1982,

— the Convention between Spain and the Federal Republic of Germany on the Recognition and Enforcement of Judgments, Settlements and Enforceable Authentic Instruments in Civil and Commercial Matters, signed at Bonn on 14 November 1983,

— the Convention between Austria and Spain on the Recognition and Enforcement of Judgments, Settlements and Enforceable Authentic Instruments in Civil and Commercial Matters, signed at Vienna on 17 February 1984,

— the Convention between Finland and Austria on the Recognition and Enforcement of Judgments in Civil Matters, signed at Vienna on 17 November 1986, and

— the Treaty between Belgium, the Netherlands and Luxembourg in Jurisdiction, Bankruptcy, and the Validity and Enforcement of Judgments, Arbitration Awards and Authentic Instruments, signed at Brussels on 24 November 1961, in so far as it is in force.

Article 70

1. The Treaty and the Conventions referred to in Article 69 shall continue to have effect in relation to matters to which this Regulation does not apply.

2. They shall continue to have effect in respect of judgments given and documents formally drawn up or registered as authentic instruments before the entry into force of this Regulation.

Article 71

1. This Regulation shall not affect any conventions to which the Member States are parties and which in relation to particular matters, govern jurisdiction or the recognition or enforcement of judgments.

2. With a view to its uniform interpretation, paragraph 1 shall be applied in the following manner:

(a) this Regulation shall not prevent a court of a Member State, which is a party to a convention on a particular matter, from assuming jurisdiction in accordance with that convention, even where the defendant is domiciled in another Member State which is not a party to that convention. The court hearing the action shall, in any event, apply Article 26 of this Regulation;

(b) judgments given in a Member State by a court in the exercise of jurisdiction provided for in a convention on a particular matter shall be recognised and enforced in the other Member States in accordance with this Regulation.

Where a convention on a particular matter to which both the Member State of origin and the Member State addressed are parties lays down conditions for the recognition or enforcement of judgments, those conditions shall apply. In any event, the provisions of this Regulation which concern the procedure for recognition and enforcement of judgments may be applied.

Article 72

This Regulation shall not affect agreements by which Member States undertook, prior to the entry into force of this Regulation pursuant to Article 59 of the Brussels Convention, not to recognise judgments given, in particular in other Contracting States to that Convention, against defendants domiciled or habitually resident in a third country where, in cases provided for in Article 4 of that Convention, the judgment could only be founded on a ground of jurisdiction specified in the second paragraph of Article 3 of that Convention.

CHAPTER VIII

FINAL PROVISIONS

Article 73

No later than five years after the entry into force of this Regulation, the Commission shall present to the European Parliament, the Council and the Economic and Social Committee a report on the application of this Regulation. The report shall be accompanied, if need be, by proposals for adaptations to this Regulation.

Article 74

1. The Member States shall notify the Commission of the texts amending the lists set out in Annexes 1 to IV. The Commission shall adapt the Annexes concerned accordingly.

2. The updating or technical adjustment of the forms, specimens of which appear in Annexes V and VI, shall be adopted in accordance with the advisory procedure referred to in Article 75(2).

Article 75

1. The Commission shall be assisted by a committee.

2. Where reference is made to this paragraph, Articles 3 and 7 of Decision 1999/468/EC shall apply.

3. The Committee shall adopt its rules of procedure.

Article 76

This Regulation shall enter into force on 1 March 2002.

This Regulation is binding in its entirety and directly applicable in the Member States in accordance with the Treaty establishing the European Community.

Done at Brussels, 22 December 2000.

ANNEX I

Rules of jurisdiction referred to in Article 3(2) and Article 4(2)

The rules of jurisdiction referred to in Article 3(2) and Article 4(2) are the following:
— in Belgium: Article 15 of the Civil Code (*Code civil/Burgerlijk Wetboek*) and Article 638 of the Judicial Code (*Code judiciaire/ Gerechtelijk Wetboek*):
— in Germany: Article 23 of the Code of Civil Procedure (*Zivilprozessordnung*),
— in Greece, Article 40 of the Code of Civil Procedure (Κώδικας Πολιτικῆς Δικονομίας)
— in France: Articles 14 and 15 of the Civil Code (*Code civil*).
— in Ireland: the rules which enable jurisdiction to be founded on the document instituting the proceedings having been served on the defendant during his temporary presence in Ireland,
— in Italy: Articles 3 and 4 of Act 218 of 31 May 1995,
— in Luxembourg: Articles 14 and 15 of the Civil Code (*Code civil*),
— in the Netherlands: Articles 126(3) and 127 of the Code of Civil Procedure (*Wetboek van Burgerlijke Rechtsvordering*),
— in Austria: Article 99 of the Court Jurisdiction Act (*Jurisdiktionsnorm*),
— in Portugal: Articles 65 and 65A of the Code of Civil Procedure (*Código de Processo Civil*) and Article 11 of the Code of Labour Procedure (*Código de Processo de Trabalho*),
— in Finland: the second, third and fourth sentences of the first paragraph of Section 1 of Chapter 10 of the Code of Judicial Procedure (*oikeudenkäymiskaari/rättegångsbalken*),
— in Sweden: the first sentence of the first paragraph of Section 3 of Chapter 10 of the Code of Judicial Procedure (*rättegångsbalken*),
— in the United Kingdom: rules which enable jurisdiction to be founded on:
  (a) the document instituting the proceedings having been served on the defendant during his temporary presence in the United Kingdom; or
  (b) the presence within the United Kingdom of property belonging to the defendant; or
  (c) the seizure by the plaintiff of property situated in the United Kingdom.

ANNEX II

The courts or competent authorities to which the application referred to in Article 39 may be submitted are the following:

— in Belgium, the *"tribunal de première instance"* or *"rechtbank van eerste aanleg"* or *"erstinstanzliches Gericht"*,
— in Germany, the presiding judge of a chamber of the *"Landgericht"*,
— in Greece, the *"Μονομελές Πρωτοδικείο"*,
— in Spain, the *"Juzgado de Primera Instancia"*,
— in France, the presiding judge of the *"tribunal de grande instance"*,
— in Ireland, the High Court,
— in Italy, the *"Corte d'appello"*,
— in Luxembourg, the presiding judge of the *"tribunal d'arrondissement"*,
— in the Netherlands, the presiding judge of the *"arrondissementsrechtbank"*:
— in Austria, the *"Bezirksgericht"*,
— in Portugal, the *Tribunal de Comarca"*,
— in Finland, the *"käräjäoikeus/tingsrätt"*,
— in Sweden, the *"Svea hovrätt"*,
— in the United Kingdom:
  (a) in England and Wales, the High Court of Justice, or in the case of a maintenance judgment, the Magistrates' Court on transmission by the Secretary of State;
  (b) in Scotland, the Court of Session, or in the case of a maintenance judgment, the Sheriff Court on transmission by the Secretary of State;
  (c) in Northern Ireland, the High Court of Justice, or in the case of a maintenance judgment, the Magistrates' Court on transmission by the Secretary of State;
  (d) in Gibraltar, the Supreme Court of Gibraltar, or in the case of a maintenance judgment, the Magistrates' Court on transmission by the Attorney General of Gibraltar.

ANNEX III

The courts with which appeals referred to in Article 43(2) may be lodged are the following:
- in Belgium,
  - (a) as regards appeal by the defendant: the *"tribunal de première instance"* or *"rechtbank van eerste aanleg"* or *"erstinstanzliches Gericht"*,
  - (b) as regards appeal by the applicant: the *"Cour d'appel"* or *"hof van beroep"*,
- in the Federal Republic of Germany, the *"Oberlandesgericht"*,
- in Greece, the *"Εφετείο"*,
- in Spain, the *"Audiencia Provincial"*,
- in France, the *"cour d'appel"*,
- in Ireland, the High Court,
- in Italy, the *"corte d'appello"*,
- in Luxembourg, the *"Cour supérieure de Justice"* sitting as a court of civil appeal,
- in the Netherlands;
  - (a) for the defendant: the *"arrondissementsrechtbank"*,
  - (b) for the applicant: the *"gerechtshof"*,
- in Austria, the *"Bezirksgericht"*,
- in Portugal, the *"Tribunal de Relação"*,
- in Finland, the *"hovioikeus/hovrätt"*,
- in Sweden, the *"Svea hovrätt"*,
- in the United Kingdom:
  - (a) in England and Wales, the High Court of Justice, or in the case of a maintenance judgment, the Magistrates' Court;
  - (b) in Scotland, the Court of Session, or in the case of a maintenance judgment, the Sheriff Court;
  - (c) in Northern Ireland, the High Court of Justice, or in the case of a maintenance judgment, the Magistrates' Court;
  - (d) in Gibraltar, the Supreme Court of Gibraltar, or in the case of a maintenance judgment, the Magistrates' Court.

ANNEX IV

The appeals which may be lodged pursuant to Article 44 are the following
- in Belgium, Greece, Spain, France, Italy, Luxembourg and the Netherlands, an appeal in cassation,
- in Germany, a *"Rechtsbeschwerde"*,
- in Ireland, an appeal on a point of law to the Supreme Court,
- in Austria, a *"Revisionsrekurs"*,
- in Portugal, an appeal on a point of law,
- in Finland, an appeal to the *"korkein oikeusjhögsta domstolen"*,
- in Sweden, an appeal to the *"Högsta domstolen"*,
- in the United Kingdom, a single further appeal on a point of law.

ANNEX V

Certificate referred to in Articles 54 and 58 of the Regulation on judgments and court settlements

(English, inglés, anglais, inglese, . . .)

1. Member State of origin
2. Court or competent authority issuing the certificate
   2.1. Name
   2.2. Address
   2.3. Tel./fax/e-mail
3. Court which delivered the judgment/approved the court settlement(*)
   3.1. Type of court
   3.2. Place of court
4. Judgment/court settlement(*)
   4.1. Date
   4.2. Reference number
   4.3. The parties to the judgment/court settlement(*)
      4.3.1. Name(s) of plaintiff(s)
      4.3.2. Name(s) of defendant(s)
      4.3.3. Name(s) of other party(ies), if any
   4.4. Date of service of the document instituting the proceedings where judgment was given in default of appearance
   4.5. Text of the judgment/court settlement(*) as annexed to this certificate
5. Names of parties to whom legal aid has been granted

The judgment/court settlement(*) is enforceable in the Member State of origin (Articles 38 and 58 of the Regulation) against:

Name:

Done at . . . ., date . . . .

Signature and/or stamp . . . .

(*) Delete as appropriate.

Certificate referred to in Article 57(4) of the Regulation on authentic instruments

(English, inglés, anglais, inglese . . .)

1. Member State of origin
2. Competent authority issuing the certificate
   2.1. Name
   2.2. Address
   2.3. Tel./fax/e-mail
3. Authority which has given authenticity to the instrument
   3.1. Authority involved in the drawing up of the authentic instrument (if applicable)
      3.1.1. Name and designation of authority
      3.1.2. Place of authority
   3.2. Authority which has registered the authentic instrument (if applicable)
      3.2.1. Type of authority
      3.2.2. Place of authority
4. Authentic instrument
   4.1. Description of the instrument
   4.2. Date
      4.2.1. on which the instrument was drawn up
      4.2.2. if different: on which the instrument was registered
   4.3. Reference number
   4.4. Parties to the instrument
      4.4.1. Name of the creditor
      4.4.2. Name of the debtor
5. Text of the enforceable obligation as annexed to this certificate

The authentic instrument is enforceable against the debtor in the Member State of origin (Article 57(1) of the Regulation)

Done at . . . ., date . . . .

Signature and/or stamp . . . .

PART II

CHAPTER II OF THE REGULATION AS MODIFIED: RULES FOR ALLOCATION OF JURISDICTION WITHIN UK

[Civil Jurisdiction and Judgments Act 1982, Schedule 4, as Subsituted by S.I. 2001 No. 3929, Sched. 2, para. 4]

General

1. Subject to the rules of this Schedule, persons domiciled in a part of the United Kingdom shall be sued in the courts of that part.

2. Persons domiciled in a part of the United Kingdom may be sued in the courts of another part of the United Kingdom only by virtue of rules 3 to 13 of this Schedule.

Special jurisdiction

3. A person domiciled in a part of the United Kingdom may, in another part of the United Kingdom, be sued—

   (a) in matters relating to a contract, in the courts for the place of performance of the obligation in question;

   (b) in matters relating to maintenance, in the courts for the place where the maintenance creditor is domiciled or habitually resident or, if the matter is ancillary to proceedings concerning the status of a person, in the court which, according to its own law, has jurisdiction to entertain those proceedings, unless that jurisdiction is based solely on the nationality of one of the parties;

   (c) in matters relating to tort, delict or quasi-delict, in the courts for the place where the harmful event occurred or may occur;

   (d) as regards a civil claim for damages or restitution which is based on an act giving rise to criminal proceedings, in the court seised of those proceedings, to the extent that that court has jurisdiction under its own law to entertain civil proceedings;

   (e) as regards a dispute arising out of the operations of a branch, agency or other establishment, in the courts for the place in which the branch, agency or other establishment is situated;

   (f) as settlor, trustee or beneficiary of a trust created by the operation of a statute, or by a written instrument, or created orally and evidenced in writing, in the courts of the part of the United Kingdom in which the trust is domiciled;

   (g) as regards a dispute concerning the payment of remuneration claimed in respect of the salvage of a cargo or freight, in the court under the authority of which the cargo or freight in question—

(i) has been arrested to secure such payment; or

(ii) could have been so arrested, but bail or other security has been given;

provided that this provision shall apply only if it is claimed that the defendant has an interest in the cargo or freight or had such an interest at the time of salvage;

(h) in proceedings—

(i) concerning a debt secured on immovable property; or
(ii) which are brought to assert, declare or determine proprietary or possessory rights, or rights of security, in or over movable property, or to obtain authority to dispose of movable property,

in the courts of the part of the United Kingdom in which the property is situated.

4. Proceedings which have as their object a decision of an organ of a company or other legal person or of an association of natural or legal persons may, without prejudice to the other provisions of this Schedule, be brought in the courts of the part of the United Kingdom in which that company, legal person or association has its seat.

5. A person domiciled in a part of the United Kingdom may, in another part of the United Kingdom, also be sued—

(a) where he is one of a number of defendants, in the courts for the place where any one of them is domiciled, provided the claims are so closely connected that it is expedient to hear and determine them together to avoid the risk of irreconcilable judgments resulting from separate proceedings;

(b) as a third party in an action on a warranty or guarantee or in any other third party proceedings, in the court seised of the original proceedings, unless these were instituted solely with the object of removing him from the jurisdiction of the court which would be competent in his case;

(c) on a counter-claim arising from the same contract or facts on which the original claim was based, in the court in which the original claim is pending;

(d) in matters relating to a contract, if the action may be combined with an action against the same defendant in matters relating to rights in rem in immovable property, in the court of the part of the United Kingdom in which the property is situated.

6. Where by virtue of this Schedule a court of a part of the United Kingdom has jurisdiction in actions relating to liability arising from the use or operation of a ship, that court, or any other court substituted for this purpose by the internal law of that part, shall also have jurisdiction over claims for limitation of such liability.

Jurisdiction over consumer contracts

7.—(1) In matters relating to a contract concluded by a person, the consumer, for a purpose which can be regarded as being outside his trade or profession, jurisdiction shall be determined by this rule and rules 8 and 9, without prejudice to rule 3(e) and (h)(ii), if—

    (a) it is a contract for the sale of goods on instalment credit terms; or

    (b) it is a contract for a loan repayable by instalments, or for any other form of credit, made to finance the sale of goods; or

    (c) in all other cases, the contract has been concluded with a person who pursues commercial or professional activities in the part of the United Kingdom in which the consumer is domiciled or, by any means, directs such activities to that part or to other parts of the United Kingdom including that part, and the contract falls within the scope of such activities.

(2) This rule shall not apply to a contract of transport other than a contract which, for an inclusive price, provides for a combination of travel and accommodation, or to a contract of insurance.

8.—(1) A consumer may bring proceedings against the other party to a contract either in the courts of the part of the United Kingdom in which that party is domiciled or in the courts of the part of the United Kingdom in which the consumer is domiciled.

(2) Proceedings may be brought against a consumer by the other party to the contract only in the courts of the part of the United Kingdom in which the consumer is domiciled.

(3) The provisions of this rule shall not affect the right to bring a counter-claim in the court in which, in accordance with this rule and rules 7 and 9, the original claim is pending.

9. The provisions of rules 7 and 8 may be departed from only by an agreement—

    (a) which is entered into after the dispute has arisen; or

    (b) which allows the consumer to bring proceedings in courts other than those indicated in those rules; or

    (c) which is entered into by the consumer and the other party to the contract, both of whom are at the time of conclusion of the contract domiciled or habitually resident in the same part of the United Kingdom, and which confers jurisdiction on the courts of that part, provided that such an agreement is not contrary to the law of that part.

Jurisdiction over individual contracts of employment

10.—(1) In matters relating to individual contracts of employment, jurisdiction shall be determined by this rule, without prejudice to rule 3(e).

(2) An employer may be sued—

    (a) in the courts of the part of the United Kingdom in which he is domiciled; or

(b) in the courts of the part of the United Kingdom where the employee habitually carries out his work or in the courts of that part where he last did so; or

(c) if the employee does not or did not habitually carry out his work in any one place, in the courts of the part of the United Kingdom where the business which engaged the employee is or was situated.

(3) An employer may bring proceedings only in the courts of the part of the United Kingdom in which the employee is domiciled.

(4) The provisions of this rule shall not affect the right to bring a counter-claim in the court in which, in accordance with this rule, the original claim is pending.

(5) The provisions of this rule may be departed from only by an agreement on jurisdiction—

(a) which is entered into after the dispute has arisen; or

(b) which allows the employee to bring proceedings in courts other than those indicated in this rule.

Exclusive jurisdiction

11. The following courts shall have exclusive jurisdiction, regardless of domicile:—

(a)

(i) in proceedings which have as their object rights in rem in immovable property or tenancies of immovable property, the courts of the part of the United Kingdom in which the property is situated;

(ii) however, in proceedings which have as their object tenancies of immovable property concluded for temporary private use for a maximum period of six consecutive months, the courts of the part of the United Kingdom in which the defendant is domiciled shall also have jurisdiction, provided that the tenant is a natural person and that the landlord and the tenant are domiciled in the same part of the United Kingdom;

(b) in proceedings which have as their object the validity of the constitution, the nullity or the dissolution of companies or other legal persons or associations of natural or legal persons, the courts of the part of the United Kingdom in which the company, legal person or association has its seat;

(c) in proceedings which have as their object the validity of entries in public registers, the courts of the part of the United Kingdom in which the register is kept;

(d) in proceedings concerned with the enforcement of judgments, the courts of the part of the United Kingdom in which the judgment has been or is to be enforced.

Prorogation of jurisdiction

12.—(1) If the parties have agreed that a court or the courts of a part of the United Kingdom are to have jurisdiction to settle any disputes which have arisen or which may arise in connection with a particular legal relationship, and, apart from this Schedule, the agreement would be effective to confer jurisdiction under the law of that part, that court or those courts shall have jurisdiction.

(2) The court or courts of a part of the United Kingdom on which a trust instrument has conferred jurisdiction shall have jurisdiction in any proceedings brought against a settlor, trustee or beneficiary, if relations between these persons or their rights or obligations under the trust are involved.

(3) Agreements or provisions of a trust instrument conferring jurisdiction shall have no legal force if they are contrary to the provisions of rule 9, or if the courts whose jurisdiction they purport to exclude have exclusive jurisdiction by virtue of rule 11.

13.—(1) Apart from jurisdiction derived from other provisions of this Schedule, a court of a part of the United Kingdom before which a defendant enters an appearance shall have jurisdiction.

(2) This rule shall not apply where appearance was entered to contest the jurisdiction, or where another court has exclusive jurisdiction by virtue of rule 11.

Examination as to jurisdiction and admissibility

14. Where a court of a part of the United Kingdom is seised of a claim which is principally concerned with a matter over which the courts of another part of the United Kingdom have exclusive jurisdiction by virtue of rule 11, it shall declare of its own motion that it has no jurisdiction.

15.—(1) Where a defendant domiciled in one part of the United Kingdom is sued in a court of another part of the United Kingdom and does not enter an appearance, the court shall declare of its own motion that it has no jurisdiction unless its jurisdiction is derived from the provisions of this Schedule.

(2) The court shall stay the proceedings so long as it is not shown that the defendant has been able to receive the document instituting the proceedings or an equivalent document in sufficient time to enable him to arrange for his defence, or that all necessary steps have been taken to this end.

Provisional, including protective, measures

16. Application may be made to the courts of a part of the United Kingdom for such provisional, including protective, measures as may be available under the law of that part, even if, under this Schedule, the courts of another part of the United Kingdom have jurisdiction as to the substance of the matter.